THE FIRST RUSSIAN VOYAGE AROUND THE WORLD: THE JOURNAL OF HERMANN LUDWIG VON LÖWENSTERN (1803–1806)

For information, contact:
University of Alaska Press
P.O. Box 756240
Fairbanks, AK 99775-6240
907-474-5831
fypress@uaf.edu
www.uaf.edu/uapress

LIBRARY OF CONGRESS CATALOGING-IN-PUBLICATION DATA

Löwenstern, Hermann Ludwig von, 1771–1836.
The first Russian voyage around the world : the journal of Hermann Ludwig von Löwenstern, 1803–1806 / translated by Victoria Joan Moessner.
p. cm.
Includes bibliographical references and index.
ISBN 1-889963-45-3 (alk. paper)
1. Löwenstern, Hermann Ludwig von, 1771–1836—Diaries.
2. Löwenstern, Hermann Ludwig von, 1771–1836—Journeys.
3. Voyages around the world. 4. *Nadezhda* (Ship)
I. Moessner, Victoria Joan. II. Title.
G420.L858 L68 2003
914.704'72—dc21
2003002140

Cover design: Mike Kirk
Text design: Rachel Fudge
Printed in China

The First Russian Voyage Around the World

The Journal of Hermann Ludwig von Löwenstern (1803–1806)

TRANSLATED BY

Victoria Joan Moessner

University of Alaska Press
Fairbanks

This book is dedicated to my daughters, Petra and Susan.

Contents

List of Illustrations

Color plates

Translator's Introduction

The name citizen of the world only sounds good. It isolates a human being too much, because a citizen of the world is not at home anywhere . . . (6/18 February, 1803) A curious life. From the age of fifteen I have been roaming the world and, it seems, will roam for the rest of my life. As much as I am for a life at sea, it is indeed a restless, transient, half-relished life. (7/19 February, 1803)

—Hermann Ludwig von Löwenstern

Diaries, unlike memoirs, autobiographies and biographies can put an unedited human personality into the thoughts, actions and reactions, prejudices and political events of another time. The Age of Enlightenment, the Age of Discovery and the turmoil of the Napoleonic wars still influence all aspects of present-day life, as the continuing appearance of fiction and nonfiction books, magazine articles, and films attests.

The diary kept by Hermann Ludwig von Löwenstern (Levenshtern) (1777–1836) gives the modern reader unfiltered access to the world as seen by a thoughtful, well-read and much-traveled naval officer at the beginning of the nineteenth century, by a man who reflects many of the positive aspects of the Age of Enlightenment that are often lost in the search for the roots of western colonialism and theories of white and western supremacy over the globe. In our age of cross-cultural and multicultural studies, Löwenstern's diary offers an account of one man's emotions, personal values, reactions to big and small events, and people around him that are valid today or offer insights into an earlier age that is often characterized as bigoted and prejudiced, especially toward non-European cultures. He recorded the irritations, hardships, and tragedies typical of long, arduous voyages as well as the pleasures and even the jokes that seamen played on each other.

Löwenstern was the fourth officer and cartographer under Captain Adam Johann von Krusenstern (Kruzenshtern) (1770–1846) of the *Nadezhda* during the first Russian expedition around the world from 1803–1806. Prior to the expedition, Krusenstern had served in the British Navy. He had visited Canton and other Asian ports in the 1790s with the British Navy. He had seen with his own eyes the extent and importance of trade conducted by Russia's rivals and hoped for Russia to take a more active role in international trade, especially in the Far East, where Russian America and Kamchatka might be better supplied by sea than overland from European Russia.

Krusenstern was fulfilling plans promoted by the Russian Admiralty and formulated by one of his earlier commanders, one of Russia's most distinguished naval officers, Grigorii Ivanovich Mulovskii. At Mulovskii's urging in 1787, Catherine the Great had authorized a naval expedition of four ships to sail to the North Pacific to assert Russia's claim to being a power in the Pacific. From the Hawaiian Islands, two ships were to sail to Kamchatka and then to explore the Kuril Islands, while the other two ships were to sail to the Pacific coast of North America and to claim for Russia, based on Chirikov's logs from 1741, lands between the southern point of Prince of Wales Island to Nootka Sound on Vancouver Island, to counter English or Spanish establishments in the area. However, the expedition was cancelled on the eve of its departure when war broke out with Turkey and was imminent with Sweden. The ships and their crews were needed at home. In the war with Sweden, Mulovskii was killed in 1789 during the battle of the Aland Islands.

Not until Alexander I succeeded Paul I to the throne in 1801 did Krusenstern find renewed support for an expedition. The new Minister of Commerce, Count Rumianzoff (Rumiantsov) and the new Minister of the Navy Admiral Mordvinov recommended the project to the emperor. Krusenstern was appointed commander of the expedition and set about signing on crew members (he wanted Löwenstern for his cartographic expertise), ordering supplies, and arranging for the purchase of ships through his co-commander on the second ship Captain I. F. Lisianski, who had served with him in the British fleet.

Krusenstern and many of the other participants rewrote their diaries and published accounts of the expedition upon their return to St. Petersburg. Many of these accounts were then translated into other European languages and have become a major source of early information about the Russian's ports of call upon the voyage. These diaries, however, had had to be revised and submitted to censorship, since the Russian emperor required the deletion of disclosures about the altercation between his ambassador to Japan, Nikolai Petrovich Resanoff (Rezanov), and Captain Krusenstern over the leadership of the expedition and the control of the ship. The emperor forbade the disclosure of the imbroglio between Ambassador Resanoff and Captain Krusenstern, for it would have damaged Russia's reputation in Europe.[1]

Prior to the voyage, Resanoff had been a court chamberlain and high official in the American Company. He had never been to sea. Unknown to Krusenstern, he had obtained documents signed by the emperor naming him the titular head of the expedition. In this diary, Löwenstern documents Resanoff's revelation of the fact long after the expedition had set sail from Kronstadt, Resanoff's repeated attempts to assert himself, and their devastating results for all concerned. Löwenstern also chronicles Resanoff's many plans for his future as well as the future of the American Company and the Russian Empire.

In the second half of the eighteenth and the beginning of the nineteenth centuries, diaries were popular.[2] Indeed, many of them were published. Löwenstern's diary, however, was intended for his own private use. Only his family and close friends would read it. He never intended it for publication and therefore never submitted it to government censorship. In his published version of his diary, Krusenstern writes of his attitude towards his sailors:

> I allowed the men a cask of fresh water to wash their linen. I mention this otherwise insignificant circumstance to show the great economy necessary with fresh water on shipboard. Every man suffered a drop to drink as much as he pleased, but I never suffered a drop taken for any other purpose without my express permission.[3]

In contrast, Löwenstern's diary is valuable because it abounds in such "insignificant circumstances" about life onboard ship and at ports of call. Since he had no one onboard with whom he could talk openly, he used his diary as a friend who listened to his personal feelings, animosities, dislikes, frustrations, and even catty observations about his fellow officers, the natural scientists, artists, and the Russian ambassador and his suite.

> Well, my dear ones, you who in the future will leaf through my diary, have to be kind to its writer. I have written for me. My passionate character has led me to conclusions that I have written down only as they occurred to me. You know me too well to need a diary of my life in order to get to know me and will therefore soon distinguish between what has been said in passion and what has been composed calmly. (December 31/19, 1803)

As ship's cartographer and as an officer standing watch, even on occasion doing a sailor's work, Löwenstern could write only in his free moments and thus usually "off the top of his head." When he does have more leisure time, as in Japan, the entries become detailed and more thoughtful and include cartoons and drawings. Fortunately, unlike his letters and the second half of his brother Eduard's memoirs, his diary and its pictures have been preserved almost intact. Here and there, as indicated in this translation, short passages have been deleted or cut out. Löwenstern also added some comments later.

A comparison of this diary with the published versions of the expedition gives one a quite different view of the imbroglio on the *Nadezhda*. It underscores the need for a revised assessment of the often glowing appraisal of the Russian ambassador's character and statesmanship and his expansive vision for his and Russia's future. Resanoff seemed to lack those qualities that were second nature to Löwenstern and Krusenstern: pride but not arrogance, respect for others' knowledge, introspection, decorum derived from social class, good breeding, common sense, and experience. Löwenstern, however, did not generalize Resanoff's faults to his being Russian and not Baltic German.

Like other Baltic or Estonian Germans, Löwenstern was proud to serve in the Russian Navy, although, as his diaries before and after the expedition indicate, he was also highly critical of its leadership, or rather lack of it, and quite often would have preferred to retire from it. It was a matter of course for the sons of the German nobility in Estonia to enter military service, the branch and country being a personal choice. Most entered the Russian service.[4]

There are no overt references to the history of Germans in Estonia in his diaries. Like Krusenstern, Löwenstern's character and multilingual abilities derived from his having been a member of the small, close-knit, German-speaking, landed elite with roots dating back to the Middle Ages, when crusaders conquered and christianized the area.[5] At that period, the area was under Danish hegemony. In 1346, after a widespread revolt of the Estonian peasants, the Danes came to consider the area too remote and costly. Except for the island of Ösel (Saaremaa), they sold their possessions in northern Estonia including Reval (Tallinn—*taani linn* or "Danish castle") to the Germans.[6] The formal sale took place on August 29, 1346, for 1,900 marks pure silver Cologne weight.[7]

In 1523, the Reformation began, making Lutheranism the dominant religious confession. Wars continually plagued the area as neighboring states sought to dominate it, until 1629, with the Peace of Altmark, when Sweden took control of Estonia except for the island of Ösel, which the Danes turned over to them in 1645. The Swedes undertook extensive social and educational reforms including the founding of Dorpat (Tartu) University in 1632.

At the end of the century, Peter the Great ascended the Russian throne and began a westward expansion of Russian territory to protect St. Petersburg and her naval installations. By 1710, he had conquered Estonia, including Reval. The Great Northern War ended officially at the Peace of Nystad (Uuskaupunki) in 1721. Peter ensured himself the support of the Baltic Germans by recognizing their previous rights and not interfering with their political and religious domination of the area. He respected German administrative and military skills as well as the fact that they were multilingual and well-educated, and he correctly saw them as useful to Russia's future.[8] Thus began the most extended period of peace for the area since the Middle Ages. The following century saw the recovery from the devastation of wars, starvation, and plagues which had depopulated both the cities and countryside.[9]

The German-speaking landed nobility together with the town merchants, craftsmen, and clergy continued to form the ruling elite. In 1774, there were 515 private *Rittergüter* (landed estates) and by 1818, 546. Many were relatively small and contained moorland. Toward the end of the eighteenth century and into the nineteenth century, members of the landed nobility traveled more and more to St. Petersburg and to Western Europe, resulting in a desire for more gracious homes and manner of living. At the same time, the pressure was mounting to free the peasants or serfs. They officially received their freedom in 1812.[10] There were no German peasants. Estonians were the peasants, the serfs, the corvee workers on estates, and the lowest class.

The Löwenstern family traced its name to two brothers Dietrich and Christoph Rigeman (Rigemann or Riman) in Riga. In 1650, they were elevated to the Swedish nobility under the name of Rigeman(n) von Leijonstjerna. The name lost the Rigeman(n) and became the germanized form von Löwenstern.

In 1743, Löwenstern's grandfather (1716–1781) married Barbara Sophia von Brevern (1725–1750), whose dowry consisted of the estates of Rasick, Campen, and Allafer (Rausikii, Kambi, and Alavere) in the parish of St. Johann (Harju Jaani) in Estonia. He sold his estates in Livonia and moved to Estonia. Löwenstern's father, also Hermann Ludwig (1747–1815), acquired these estates as well as the estates of Wallküll and Jendel through marriage to Hedwig Margarethe Staël von Holstein auf Hannijöggi (1756–1799). Löwenstern's father was politically active his entire life. He was *Kreismarschall* (County Marshal) in 1787, *Governmentsadelsmarschall* (government noble marshal) in Estonia from 1789 to 1792, and later *Landrat* (councilor) and *Präses Consistorii* (secular bishop in the Lutheran Church from 1803–1815).[11]

Löwenstern was the fourth child of ten. He had two older brothers and a sister and three younger brothers and three younger sisters. Of some little, of others much information has survived. In many ways, the family was typical of the period and its class in Estonia.

1. Carl Johann Ernst (1774–1805) had been a major in Russian Armenia before retiring to his estates of Forell, Muddis, and Tamsel. He was married to Elisabeth von Friesel. They had several children who died young.

2. Margarethe Sophie Helene (1775–1795) married Magnus von Reutern (?–1808?).[12]

3. Woldemar Hermann (1776–1858) became the most eminent of the brothers. At the age of 14 on May 14, 1790, filled with excitement, he watched a Russian ship blow up a Swedish ship near Reval. He longed to experience such excitement again. At the age of 17 (1793), he entered the Russian military service with the rank of sergeant. He advanced quickly through the ranks while serving with distinction under Field Marshal A.V. Suvorov in the campaigns against Napoleon in Poland, Italy, and Switzerland.

In 1800, Woldemar returned home and because of poor health resigned from the army. In 1804, he married Countess Natalie von Tiesenhausen (?–1809). In 1808, seeking a cure for his health problems, he and his wife left Reval. In 1809, they were in Vienna, where they found themselves subjected to Napoleon's siege of the city. His wife died there on June 10, 1809.

In 1812, Woldemar once again entered the military service and served with distinction as an adjunct to General Michael Andreas Barclay de Tolly (1761–1818) (Russian: Mikhail, Prince Bogdanovich, the descendant of a Scottish family that had settled in Riga in the seventeenth century) and then Mikhail Illarionovich Kutuzov (1745–1813) and once again, after Kutuzov's death, in Poland under Barclay de Tolly.

Woldemar received the order of St. Vladimir for saving 60 cannon at the battle of Smolensk on August 5/17, 1812. For his daring and bold attack at Borodino on August 26/September 7, 1812, he was promoted to *Oberstleutnant* (lieutenant colonel). In addition, near Sonnenwalde, he captured a company of French-Saxon troops and 700,000 francs, which he immediately distributed among his men. He occupied Bernburg, for which the Russian emperor granted him the Swedish Order of the Sword, and then Göttingen, for which he received the Order of St. Ann second class with diamonds. He concluded a treaty of neutrality with the city of Altona, which included 100,000 thaler retribution. Finally in 1814, he was ordered to France, where he participated in the victory over Napoleon and was advanced to *General Leutnant*.

After the Peace of Paris, Woldemar went to Karlsbad (Czech: Karlovy Vary) to restore his health. There and in St. Petersburg, he discovered that others enjoyed hearing his stories so he began to write his memoirs when time allowed. Thus, he passed his time until 1828, when during the Russo-Turkish war he served as Governor of Wallachia.

In 1833, Woldemar returned to his homeland spending summers on his estate Rasik and winters in St. Petersburg until his death in 1858.

> He was a beloved guest in the first houses of the capital and eminent personages visited him in his modest apartment where one always met ministers and generals, diplomats, artists, scholars and even educated ladies.[13]

Woldemar's apartment may have been "modest," but for a modern reader the two versions of his undoubtedly embroidered memoirs are those of a self-confident, charming, witty, adventure-loving man who was at times addicted to gambling and womanizing and loved the field of battle.

P.Th. Falck maintains that the French and German versions of his memoirs differ. His two volume memoir *Denkwürdigkeiten eines Livländers aus den Jahren 1790–1815* (Leipzig: Winter, 1854) is the version given his friend, the historian Friedrich von Smitt (Fedor Ivanovich). *Mémoires du général Major Baron de Löwenstern, publiés original et annotés par M.H.Weil* (Paris 1903, 2 v.) is the version Löwenstern gave the archives of the Ministry of war; thus it is an official not private one.

4. Hermann Ludwig (1777–1836).

5. Hedwig Henriette Elisabeth "Jettchen" (1779–November 23, 1806) married Count Johann (Ivan) Stenbock of Sellie (1774–1838) in 1796.[14]

6. Juliane Wilhelmine Karoline (1781–1797)

7. Amalie Christina (1785–1877?) married in 1800 Baron Carl Gustav Andreas von Tiesenhausen (1779–18?) of Neuenhoff (Uumosa) in the parish of Kosch (Kose), a member of the most powerful family in the province. After eighteen years of marriage and eight children, she secretly left him and the children to join Dr. Ferdinand Johann Jencken (1786–1864), a commoner and *Stadsphysicus* (city physician) in Reval. Jencken had studied medicine in Dorpat, Göttingen, Bamberg, and Vienna. In 1809, he had married Anna Müller of Würzburg. They too had children.[15]

Amalie's brother Woldemar described Tiesenhausen as "a rejuvenated image of a knight of old,"[16] that is, probably not well-traveled or educated, provincial, and conceited. By contrast, Jencken was educated, well-traveled, and handsome. As a medical doctor, he must have had empathy for others. Amalie must have felt stifled, trapped as a wife of an aristocratic estate owner with all its petty social and housewifely obligations. She had to know that her actions would be considered scandalous, that she would be castigated and called a *Rabenmutter.*[17]

Amalie knew that the extended families would look after her children well, as is attested to, for example, by the concern Krusenstern shows for his nephews, Moritz and Otto von Kotzebue, on the expedition around the world. She had undoubtedly heard the colorful stories her brothers told of life in Germany, France, England, Italy, and America, indeed of life around the globe. Unlike her brother Woldemar, who once considered an unconventional marriage a misalliance, she risked her future for passion and potential travel and excitement.

At a ball, Woldemar had wandered

> into a secondary circle whose middle point was also a beautiful star, even though of secondary size. She was a young Israelite with a dowry of two million, the daughter of an

> overly rich banker. This charming Shulamite[18] with glowing dark looks, a small arched nose, beautiful lips and teeth, small hands and feet and especially with the intoxicating smell of the oil of roses from two million guilders was indeed able to awaken thoughts of conquest in a young corsair's heart; and I admit such thoughts flew through my heart and kidneys [pockets], but H[einrich] Heine had not yet sung his captivating and winning songs. [Ludwig] Börne had not yet written his destructive books. Still an Israelite, even if baptized, was called a Jewish girl. I thought with horror of the *zeter mordio* (cry of murder) of my female relatives in Estonia and desisted from that beautiful Shulamite, whose grace would have been worthy of a wise King Solomon, as good as that earlier one whose charms he describes.[19]

Eduard's *Memoirs* contain loving references to Amalie and the atmosphere of her home. In 1808, Eduard arrived home unexpectedly on leave.

> Heavenly Amalie was beside herself with joy; and as usual had a thousand tales to tell, questions to ask and answers to give. I was happy to see her, to cuddle her, pretty, charming, vivacious as usual—I found my adorable sister totally unchanged (65)

In retrospect, he wrote of a month's stay in 1814:

> There is no dearer spot for me than Neuenhoff—as a small school child Neuenhoff was my vacation playground. I only knew happiness in Neuenhoff. Never did anything unpleasant spoil my experiences in that home—seeing Amalie surrounded by her lovely family was the most divine sight I can imagine. Ah, unfortunately, I was never able to enjoy that happiness again. It was too great for a mortal in this world. Thank goodness, my sister, my only dear sister, shared my intimacies with her complete heart; no secret separated us at that time. (265)

Amalie and Eduard shared each other's cares and worries, but one evening after dinner, however, Amalie's husband and the Löwenstern brothers Woldemar, Hermann, and Georges got into a heated argument. Unfortunately, someone, probably Eduard's editor, deleted the reasons.

Even though Amalie's brothers, except for Eduard, and sisters, all married within the close-knit aristocratic class in Estonia, there had been other divorces and liaisons in their circle of friends, for example, in the Krusenstern family. August von Kotzebue, the father of Otto and Moritz von Kotzebue, caused perhaps the best-documented one. It was easier to obtain a divorce from the clerical court of the Lutheran Church than the Anglican or Catholic churches.[20] In his introduction to Eduard's *Memoirs*, Georges Wrangell maintains it is clear from Eduard's *Memoirs* that Amalie's "disloyal" acts pained him so much that he avoided Estonia and her memories the rest of his life.[21]

Amalie and Jencken went to Germany, where he worked until 1851, then they moved on to London, then to Bonn and Eisenach and in 1854 to Mainz. After that they were on the Isle of Jersey and finally in Kingston, Ireland.[22] Family documents indicate that Jencken's wife continued to be included in Löwenstern family gatherings after his elopement.[23]

8. Georges Heinrich (1786–1856), like his brothers, entered the Russian military service and rose to Lieutenant Colonel. He participated in the campaigns against Napoleon from 1812–1814. He later became a Danish General Marshal and served as ambassador to Rio de Janeiro and Vienna. In 1815, he married Countess Adelaide Juliane Ernestine Friederike von Schimmelmann (1796–1876). They lived on estates near Kiel. On June 8, 1827, he was granted the right to use the title of baron by the Danish king.[24]

9. Theodor Moritz (1789–1808) was a cornet in the Smusch Hussar Regiment and took part in the campaign against Napoleon in 1806–1807.[25]

10. Johann (Ivan) Peter Eduard (1790–1837) was perhaps the most colorful and wayward of the brothers. He was a soldier with body and soul (*Memoir*, 119). He rose through the ranks to become a general major and died in Astrakhan as a Cossack hetman. In 1826, he married Ekaterina Gavrilovna Gamalei (1808–1887), heir to Gamalejevska in the *gubernia* of Kursk. He took part in the suppression of the Decembrist revolt and, on January 3, 1826, captured the main instigator in the south Sergei Muravjev Apostol (Sergei Murawjew-Apostel).[26] In 1814, he began writing his memoirs. Georges von Wrangell edited and published them in 1910, but he deleted passages out of consideration for prominent names, since Eduard described "the manifold adventures and experiences of his hectic and eventful life as an officer most often very bluntly and with surprising openness." Unfortunately, only the first half of the memoirs survived because a servant used the stout paper of the second half for wrapping up pork for mailing in the 1890s. His granddaughter recognized his handwriting and rescued some pages, but the others were lost.[27] He, like his brother Woldemar, enjoyed the life of balls, women, duels, gambling, theater (he saw Goethe at the theater in Weimar and sat next to Schiller's widow), and war. In 1815, for example, he, Woldemar, and Georges were at home in Estonia on leave when they heard of Napoleon's landing in Cannes. All left immediately to join their units in Germany and to become part of the occupation troops in France. It is from the memoirs of Eduard and Woldemar that we can infer the most about Hermann Ludwig's upbringing and early family life. Herman Ludwig mentions his family in his diaries, indeed at times, he "talks" with them but he gives few details about his upbringing and education. His diaries also reveal that his *Weltanschauung* was quite different from his brothers' as revealed in their memoirs.

A contemporary Baron Eugenus von Rosen said of his father's home:

> For years his was the most beloved and sought after in the area. Only after the death of his wife [1799] did it become desolate, for he had lost his friend, his companion, inclined toward and created for social ability, and an active, skilled but nevertheless thrifty hostess.[28]

In his *Memoirs*, Woldemar described their father as

> one of the most respected leaders of [Estonia's] inner administration, a wealthy estate owner and hospitable neighbor, praised especially as a mild master of his Estonian hold-

> ings. Next to him was the dear image of my mother, a Stael von Holstein, whose loving care and tenderness I have to thank for the untroubled happy years of childhood. My education was directed attentively. I must be grateful to my earliest tutors in my father's house, to whose encouragement and intellectual care I am indebted that my thoughts were not totally of swords and horses, hunting, dueling, and manifold tumults of life which dissipate, but also to growing in strength in more noble directions. The learning of French and proper behavior in society was seen to by a light-minded, nimble-footed Frenchman Pourpier, who accompanied me as a kind guide to St. Petersburg and in the end found a position in Dorpat. I received my formal education at the *Ritterakademie* [academy for the children of the landed nobility]. (4)

The Löwenstern brothers attended the school while it was still under the influence of reforms introduced by Johann Bernhard Heinrich Göbel, who came to Reval in 1766 at the request of the *Ritterschaft* (noble trustees) to reform the school away from the rigidity of the church curriculum. He left Reval in 1881. In his *Grundzüge der Erziehung* [The Bases of an Education] (Reval: 1774), he states that schooling has as its goal the education of happy, useful members of society, of men thoughtful and noble in their actions.[29]

In his *Memoirs*, Woldemar describes his experience at the *Ritterakademie*.

> There we studied Latin and antiquities, world history, geography, geometry, physics, philosophy, and a lot of other things along with riding and fencing lessons. My father, one of the twelve noble *Kuratoren* [trustees] of the institution, spared nothing. From the curriculum, I selected those subjects I considered necessary for the military and preferred what are called the *schöne Wissenschaften* [belle lettres]. I imagined a future which was totally the opposite of what is called a homebody. (5) . . . Everyone thought about my preparations for military service, which according to the typical practice at that time could not begin soon enough. In 1793, I was sent to St. Petersburg. (17)

At the time, it was customary for the sons of the landed nobility to enter military service, usually, but not always, in Russia. They were welcomed into the social life of the highest circles and valued for their multilingual abilities. Besides, the estates in Estonia tended to be small, not large enough to support all of the sons in the manner they would wish. Eduard states the case bluntly in his memoirs.

> "I was just 14 [actually 16]. As a poor Estonian nobleman, I had no other future but to seek my fortune in the military."

The family had a sense of humor. Woldemar relates a very good example of it in his *Memoirs*.

> Brother Hermann, who had decided on the Naval service at 14 [actually 16] and had been on a Russian warship as midshipman during many voyages in the Baltic and North

> Seas, had found an opportunity to volunteer for the English Navy and visited ports on distant seas on English ships. He had learned to speak English 'quite perfectly', and acquired the habit of having a crooked English corner to his mouth, looked approximately like an admirer of plum pudding and a drinker of soda water. To obtain this goal, he had been away from home for six years [actually five according to his diary], and I had therefore not seen him in so long. (56)

Hermann had arrived when Woldemar was not at home. The family decided to tell him that Hermann was an English naval officer just arrived in Reval, who wanted to become acquainted with the joys of life on an Estonian country estate. Thus, Hermann was to appear a military looking gentleman who spoke English with those who could and a mixture of German and Low German with others. Woldemar did not recognize his weather-tanned brother. Hermann deliberately made inappropriate remarks about the Battle of Zürich on September 14–15/ 25–26, 1799, when the French forced the Russians to retreat to Winterthur. Woldemar would have taken the remarks from a brother, but not from a foreign guest breaking the rules of etiquette. Woldemar challenged him to a duel on the Ziegelskoppel in Reval. The family with a good laugh at Woldemar's expense revealed the truth, and the two brothers renewed their friendship.

In *The Rebel on the Bridge: A Life of the Decembrist Baron Andrey Rozen* (Rosen) (1800–1884)[30] Glynn Barratt writes of the Rosens:

> We see from several Barons Rozen of the 17th and 16th centuries, all of them soldiers, landowners and members of the ruling class, that the more apparent vices of such castes—pride, narrowness of vision—were well developed in them. (9)

After reading the memoirs of Woldemar and Eduard, one could say this of them, but not, however, of Hermann Ludwig von Löwenstern and Adam Johann von Krusenstern. By the time the *Nadezhda* set sail around the world, they, though subject to the prejudices and mores of the time, had acquired a humane set of values, derived from observations, experiences, and reflections during their naval service in the Russian and English navies.

Löwenstern's diaries begin with short summaries of the years 1793, 1794, 1795, and 1796. Only after April 17, 1797 (New Style), with his descriptions of the revolt of English sailors, did he begin to keep regular, dated entries in his diary. Winston Churchill summed up the Royal Navy at that time with the words "rum, buggery, and the lash!"[31] As Löwenstern notes, all that the sailors wanted was better pay and more freedom to go on land, since they had often been prevented from doing so for five or six years at a time for fear that they would desert.

Löwenstern's diaries show the growing maturity of a sensitive, insightful, well-read man as he observes foreign cultures and lands, of a man who would revise his judgments of people and countries; for example, upon seeing the Japanese for the first time on the *Nadezhda*, he called them ugly hedgehogs. Later, he leaves Japan full of admiration for Japanese achievements and culture, though not for the system of government.

As a schoolboy in 1793, Löwenstern volunteered to go to sea during the dog days of summer.

> As a result, I took such pleasure in the Naval Service that my fate was determined. I understood not a word of Russian. I had lessons in navigation from a Russian pilot and tried to learn. I went to a lot of trouble with it but did not get very far.

In 1794, he again volunteered and crisscrossed the Baltic Sea.

> Every merchant ship was interrogated. The *Venus* sailed exceedingly well. It was a true pleasure to take up the chase. We wintered in Reval. At that time Captain Bodisco was building a house and garden in the suburbs. If we were at the roadstead in Reval, then often there was only the guard onboard because the rest of the crew was working on the estate.

In 1795, Löwenstern was still a volunteer, even though he had passed his examination, when the ship was ordered to England by way of Copenhagen. In Deal, the ship weathered a furious storm, which wrought havoc with the Russian fleet. Continual storms scattered the Russian fleet and drove the ship to the Dutch coast and Cuxhaven, where she was superficially repaired before returning to England and the docks in Chatham.

In 1796, Löwenstern applied for permission to enter the British East India Service. He learned English and navigation for a pleasant five months, dreaming of the East Indies and China when he was advanced to midshipman and then ordered to reenter the Russian service and to return to Kronstadt. His stay in England had given him time to visit English cities and to experience the embarrassment of serving under a "coarse and thoughtless lout of a captain whom the English let feel their displeasure from time to time."

The excitement Löwenstern had experienced as a schoolboy had been destroyed: "Wrangling, strife, envy, hate, deceit, cheating, egoism, uncharitableness, lies and laziness: those are the driving forces that belong to the order of the day on our ship."

He applied repeatedly for leave and received none. Because he did not want to incur debts and had not been paid, he had a uniform made from soldier's cloth ("during [Emperor] Paul's time that was nothing unusual.") because he knew how unpleasant debts were for his father, since his older brothers had contracted them and his father had had to pay them. Löwenstern did, however, in the end obtain permission from his father to petition to leave the service.

> A few weeks later, I received my petition back with the remark that I had not yet served five years. That was the law for naval men who had been trained at the Crown's expense.

Löwenstern desperately wanted to leave the service because he looked around Kronstadt and became depressed with the loneliness and uselessness of his life.

> I abhorred the thought of vegetating for 8 or 9 years as a midshipman. . . . On the old *Rinok* [market] in Kronstadt were decaying Russian booths, the abode of thieves and robbers. Every evening between eight and eight-thirty, you had to go past through the filth.

He knew that Emperor Paul had ordered any officer who was ill for more than six weeks be released from service. Löwenstern reported ill. The doctors in St. Petersburg refused to say he was incapable of serving and should be mustered out. In January 1798, Admiral Wilhelm Petrovich Fandesen told him he should report back as healthy. Löwenstern replied that he would if he were given 28 days of leave. This he was granted, but he was given no money with which to travel to his father's estate. He hired a Russian peasant and his horse by promising to pay upon arrival and headed through the icy cold night for Reval and his family.

> The fourteen days I spent in Reval were like a dream. When my leave was up, I returned to Kronstadt with the post coach and began completing service that was now doubly unpleasant for me.

In April, however, it became possible for him to return to England, where he "went to great trouble to fulfill my duty and succeeded." His official military record for his entire career in the Navy contains nothing but praise for his nobility of bearing, intelligence, and knowledge of naval life and duties.

For the next few years, Löwenstern served on ships crisscrossing the waters from the Baltic to the Mediterranean and Black seas, participating in the scrimmages of the Napoleonic wars, observing and judging the life and events around him, visiting balls, theaters, concerts, religious ceremonies, festivals, churches, and archeological sites whenever he could. He met kings and nobles, Lord Nelson and Lady Hamilton and admirals and high officials, as well as ordinary merchants, ordinary citizens, and prostitutes and port rabble. He visited the ships and officers of other nations anchored in the ports of call.

In August 1799, Löwenstern was in Palermo when a race riot broke out over prostitutes plying their trade with Turkish sailors (who had money), even though the king had ordered that every prostitute found with a Turk be beaten.

> The Sicilians could not suppress their religious hate. Envy and the king's interdiction made the people feel that they could insult the Turks they found with girls.

The Russians helped to rescue the Turks by collecting them in their midst "like a hen with her chicks" and escorting them to their ships.

In his diaries, Löwenstern complains of the drunkenness, debauchery, and gambling of officers and crew. He himself seldom gambled, and then only for small sums, because "I was always unlucky," and he did not want unnecessary debts. He strongly disapproved of the behavior of the captain of his ship, who brought prostitutes onboard and permitted other members of the crew to do the same. Löwenstern felt that the captain was unworthy of his post.

> Neledinskoi has turned our ship into a bordello. He always has a girl at his side who cheats him out of his money. Our officers follow his example. Volchonski's officers are in the main common soldiers who have been promoted. They are characterized by quarrelsomeness and debauchery.

Löwenstern spent time in Constantinople, where the Divan had ordered Russians be treated courteously. He had to deal with suppliers for the ship and with the Russian Minister Tamara, who filled his own coffers at the Navy's expense. Löwenstern complains that he, and others, did not receive their pay. He spent his time taking walks, viewing the gardens and the surroundings of the city, and frequenting a Turkish bath. Here, too, he tells of a sailor who had deserted and then returned because he did not want to be circumcised. He knew a number of men who had converted to the Mohammedan faith and were in Turkish service. They had been provided with houses and women and were totally satisfied with their lot. Denying the Christian faith seemed too great a sin for him.

> Uschakoff ordered the deserter to be punished without mercy by the cat [-o'-nine-tails]. We were all of the opinion that he had earned a milder punishment because he himself had returned out of love for Christianity. The devil knows what overcame Alviniotti, who hastened its execution and had the poor fellow mercilessly whipped. I was very angry about this misplaced severity.

In the fall of 1801, Löwenstern left the service and returned home to a house filled with sadness since the death of his mother in 1799.

> Being the fifth wheel on the wagon is an oppressive feeling. I have to go away from here. There is nothing for me in my fatherland where I am superfluous. Away from here, all the same how and where to? Normally, I am interested in everything and now in nothing. It is as if my life force had ceased.

In 1802, he requested permission of the emperor to enter the French service since he could not tolerate Reval. His father generously offered his help. On June 17, 1802, Löwenstern set out for France by way of Lübeck, Bremen, Amsterdam, Leiden, The Hague, Antwerp, and Lille, sightseeing and exploring at each stop. He arrived in Paris on August 16, 1802, and found himself lodgings in a rooming house owned by an attractive "widow" from Zweibrücken with a troubled past who became his lover.

While in Paris, Löwenstern went to the opera and to the theater. He visited an institute for the deaf and dumb to witness a demonstration of sign language. He explored churches, museums, especially the Louvre, parks, factories, and towns of historical interest near Paris. He visited Versailles.

> The palace was desolate. All of the rooms had been stripped of their decorations. All were bare. (An uncanny, sinister feeling overtook me.) The natural history collection, the opera and the library were preserved the best. The park was nice, but the fountains no longer worked. The munitions factory is the main thing in Versailles now.

On September 25, 1802, he garnered a comfortable spot from which he could watch Napoleon inspecting his troops from the back of his "colossal white horse" given to him by the King of Spain.

> Very simply clothed with a simple three-cornered hat, he rode up and down the line. His figure was not at all imposing. He had a pale yellow face and was quite haggard. As he rode, he was handed a great many petitions and papers, which he received very condescendingly and for the most part, handed over to his attendants. After he had inspected all of the troops, he and his magnificently clothed attendants took up positions in the middle of the square and every regiment, one after another, paraded past him and gave him the honors, in all around 10,000 men. . . . The view was inimitable.

From there, Löwenstern went to the square where all the street girls gathered to spend the evening.

As much as Löwenstern was enjoying his stay in Paris, he was not achieving his goal of entering French service. Thus, on November 19, 1802, he set out on his return trip to Reval, this time overland by way of Strasbourg, Karlsruhe, Nuremberg, Weimar, Leipzig, and Berlin, where he learned abut the coming voyage around the world.

> Krusenstern's voyage around the world has me totally enthused. I would like to go along, for even though the Russian Naval Service is worth so little, I am still a passionate seaman.

Upon a firm offer for him to join the expedition, Löwenstern left Berlin immediately and hurried back to St. Petersburg to get his naval papers in order and to meet with Krusenstern and then go onboard ship in Kronstadt. The translation of his diary begins and ends in Kronstadt.

Language

Translating Löwenstern's diary of his voyage around the world into English has been an adventure. A transcription of the diary from 1799 to 1806, first handwritten and then typed, was made after World War II. Transcribing it was politically safe.[32] The transcribers of Löwenstern's handwriting deserve the highest respect; but, in order to produce a more accurate translation, I have compared the transcription with the original and added passages and words that were not transcribed or were incorrectly transcribed before translating the diary into English. Löwenstern wrote German as spoken at that time in Estonia or among German speakers serving in the Russian Navy, but with an admixture of the other languages he knew or were spoken where he happened to be. Thus, his uses of grammar as well as orthography and punctuation often do not correspond to practices of published works of the period and certainly not to modern standard usages.

Löwenstern undoubtedly spoke Russian most of the time on the *Nadezhda* with the sailors and with most of the officers, including Captain Krusenstern, who also were Baltic Germans, and Ambassador to Japan Resanoff. He used German with the natural scientists, most of whom did not know Russian. When need be, he spoke English and French. Thus, the diary is a mixture of languages and levels of language usage. The reader has the impression that he, at times, no longer noticed which words belonged to which language. As a man who spoke and read extensively in several languages, he was aware of the fact that he was not writing "the standard" language. Originally, judging by the most intimate details of his life in Paris, one has the impression that he undoubtedly considered his diary private, not for the eyes of others. This changed with the voyage around the world when he knew that others would be eagerly awaiting his reminisces. Thus, on December 31, 1803, he defensively wrote:

> As far as spelling and legibility are concerned, you may criticize as much as you like. If you understand what I want to say, then I don't care if I hurriedly write an x for u or not.

The version of the diary used for this translation is most likely a later copy, perhaps done after his retirement from the Navy. There is no evidence that any corrections were made to the original document so that the language conformed to the printed standards of the day. It is not surprising that Löwenstern wrote very colloquially, since he went to sea at fifteen and learned some of his languages orally. His spellings sometimes reflect his pronunciation of words or the way in which he thought he heard them pronounced. I had to turn to nineteenth century dictionaries and occasionally go from Russian to German before finding an English translation for a word, e.g. *Schkala*—Шкала—Verstärkungshölzer des Mastbaums— wooden blocks for supporting the masts.[32] I leave his English indicated by italics and [sic], and provide some examples of his other languages, so that the reader has an indication of the multilingual freshness of the original text and the ways in which a multilingual person comes to use his languages. At the first occurrence of one of these examples written in the Latin alphabet, I give a translation. For words written in the Cyrillic alphabet, I give a translation each time.

Sometimes Löwenstern wrote German and English words in the Cyrillic alphabet or Russian in the Latin alphabet, particularly sailing terms. During the reign of Peter the Great, many sailing terms came into Russian from Dutch, English, and German. Löwenstern often used the Russian term with German endings. He possibly did not know the actual German terms since he served only in the Russian and English navies and most of the Russian terms originated from Germanic languages. Very often these are sailing terms, which do not appear in the multi-language dictionaries from the last two centuries I consulted or they are abbreviations. If he wrote Russian, he usually gave a German translation, since he was also keeping the diary for his family in Estonia, most of whom did not know Russian. Löwenstern left untranslated many Russian crudities of the kind men used among themselves but not in polite society, of the kind he probably would not have used so readily in his mother tongue where he would have felt the depth of their crudity. They would have shocked his women readers. Indeed, this is no doubt the explanation for a few deletions in the text describing inappropriate behavior or rows.

As the *Nadezhda* sailed around the world, Löwenstern incorporated words and expressions current at ports of call. This was particularly true of Japan, where the expedition spent six months communicating with the Japanese by means of Dutch, and in China, where he found the pidgin English fascinating. He often first spelled names and terms as he heard them and then changed his spellings later when he learned the correct ones. The reader will find examples of Löwenstern's unselfconscious mixture of languages. The Russian I give in modern orthography and, where only written in the Cyrillic alphabet, a translation. Where Löwenstern gives a translation of Russian, I give a translation of his German. This is the explanation for some deviations from a more literal translation of the Russian. If he only wrote a person's name in Russian, I provide the transliteration. His French, Estonian, Latin, and Dutch I leave as he spelled them and give translations. The brackets [ ] are mine. An additional way of giving the flavor of the original is to retain his most consistent German spellings of personal names rather than using the modern transliteration from Russian, i.e., Löwenstern instead of Levenshtern, Krusenstern instead of Kruzenshtern, Bellingshausen instead of Bellingsgauzen, Resanoff instead of Rezanov. These spelling variations are found in the secondary literature. Alternate spellings are given in the index. Because of the possible mispronunciation of the ships' names *Nadegda* or *Nadeschda* and *Newa,* I use the contemporary transliteration from the Russian *Nadezhda* and *Neva.* Since the German w is pronounced like the English v, I substitute v for w.

Illustrations

Löwenstern uses symbols for the days of the week, beginning with Sunday:

These have been converted to abbreviations. The illustrations are a selection of color and black-and-white photographs of the mostly unsigned drawings, maps, and cartoons in Hermann Ludwig von Löwenstern's diary, which is preserved in the Estonian Historical Archives in Tartu, Estonia (Eesti Ajalooarhiiv F1414 N3 S3 and S4). I have provided translations of Löwenstern's captions under the illustrations and provide captions where he has none. Members of the expedition shared drawings with each other because certain of the drawings and watercolors are similar to ones published in the Krusenstern *Atlas* and other works of the period about the voyage. The drawing of a horse and rider on Tenerife was signed by Wilhelm Gottlieb Tilesius and sent after the voyage. As this watercolor indicates, members of the expedition did share and exchange their drawings from the voyage, just as we do today with photographs. Löwenstern helped draw at least some of the maps of harbors, roadsteads, and towns, if they were not obtained from other sources. He was a highly skilled cartographer and draughtsman, as the sketches of ships, tools, Japanese flags, and mons indicate. He had a sharp wit as his cartoons indicate.

The question arises, however, as to who made most of the watercolors, especially the striking ones from Japan, and drawings in the diary. For, when one compares the range in the quality and style of the drawings and watercolors in the diary, one has to ask which ones can be attributed to Löwenstern or someone else, namely Tilesius. For example, there are two drawings of tattooed men on Nukahiva. The one is naive and cartoonlike, the other strikingly alive and vibrant. The brightly colored watercolors of interpreters and Japanese housewares resemble works attributed to Tilesius. If, however, one compares the drawing technique of these works with works attributed to Tilesius in the Lenin State Library in Moscow (F 178, d.M.1093 [a], M 10693 [b]), one sees that Tilesius provided more details in the faces, sketched outlines less sharply and clearly, drew hands in detail, whereas the watercolors in Löwenstern's diary display a sharpness of outline, a cartoonlike physiognomy but poorly drawn hands. A comparison of all of the available original illustrations from the voyage might clarify which unsigned illustrations in this diary should be attributed to Löwenstern and which to Tilesius or Langsdorff or some other member of the expedition.

Löwenstern's sketches of Japanese flags and mons are very accurate, as are the maps included in his diary. It, however, is worth noting, as Dr. Günther Sterba (*Freshwater Fishes of the World,* N.Y.: Viking 1963) made clear to me in a conversation in June 1998, that many of the pictures associated with the voyage are not useful for scientific purposes. Many of them were probably completed after the voyage. As striking as some drawings are, they are not scientifically accurate even for the time. Details important for scientific purposes are missing, for example, accurately drawn fish scales or tattoos (the expedition had a very short, busy stay at Nukuhiva). Nevertheless, the illustrations preserved in this diary give additional insights into the voyage and Löwenstern's perception of his fellow voyagers and of the landscapes, people, and cultures the *Nadezhda* visited when sailing around the globe.

Acknowledgements

A translation of this magnitude and difficulty cannot be done alone. Therefore, I wish to acknowledge and thank all of those individuals, libraries, and archives around the world who have helped me and given me advice. I begin with the transcribers in Estonia after World War II and Sirje Annist of the Estonian Historical Museum in Tallinn and Tiiu Oja and Urmas Märtin of the Estonian Historical Archives in Tartu, also Helje

Kannik of Tallinn, Inge Kangor and her family, and Tiiu Müürsepp in Tartu, and Malle Burggraf for translating Löwenstern's Estonian. Lydia Black kindly translated the longer passages from Russian. Alla Grikurova and Trina Manoon helped me with individual Russian words and phrases, Tity Devries with Dutch, and Frieder Sondermann of Tohoku Gakuin University in Sendai, Japan with the Japanese view of the Russians. I am grateful for the day spent at the Kustodie of the Universität Leipzig when I was permitted to inspect the Tilesius' drawings from the voyage preserved there. Gerd von Pistohlkors of the Seminar für Mittlere und Neuere Geschichte of the Universität Göttingen also provided helpful advice as did the librarians at the University of Alaska Fairbanks, the Universität Göttingen, and the University of Michigan in my search for dictionaries and reference materials. I wish to thank Renate von Rappard of Hanover, Germany for helping with untranscribed sections of the diary and her husband Achim and his brother for their help with "den letzten Schlag."

I dare not forget my editors, Professor Richard Pierce (who was instrumental in awakening my interest in the period) and Pamela Odom, who edited the translation as well as the introduction and epilogue. Laura Lee Potrikus was invaluable in leading me through the intricacies of the modern computer world. Carrie Carnes generously copy-edited and corrected my outdated punctuation. Next, I wish to thank Valerest Yencken of Kojonup, Western Australia, and Heinz Baron v. Löwenstern of Oberalm, Austria, for permission to use the paintings of Hermann Ludwig v. Löwenstern in their possession, as well as all of the people around the world whom I have met and with whom I have talked about the diary. And finally, I wish to thank the University of Alaska Fairbanks for supporting this project and making this book possible.

—*Victoria Joan Moessner*

The Crew of the Nadezhda

If Löwenstern mentions a crewmember in his diary, his spellings are followed by contemporary transliterations from Russian; otherwise, only contemporary transliterations are given.

Captain Lieutenant:	Adam Johann von Krusenstern / Ivan Fedorovich Kruzenshtern
Eldest Lieutenant:	Makar Ivanowitsch Ratmanoff / Ratmanov
Lieutenants:	Fedor Romberg / Romberkh
	Peter Golovatscheff / Piotr Golovachev
	Hermann Ludwig von Löwenstern / Ermolai Levenshtern
	Fabian von Bellingshausen / Faddei Bellingsgausen
Mate:	Filip Kamentschikoff / Kamenshchikov
Second Mate:	Vasilii Spolochoff / Spolokhov
Doctor of Medicine:	Karl Espenberg / Espenberkh
His Assistant:	John Sydham/ Sidham/ Ivan Sidgam
Astronomer:	Johann Caspar Horner / Ivan Gorner
Natural Scientists:	Wilhelm Gottlieb Tilesius
	Georg Heinrich von Langsdorff
Artillery Sergeant:	Aleksei Raefski / Raevskii
Cadets:	Otto von Kotzebue / Kotsebu
	Moritz von Kotzebue / Kotsebu
Clerk:	Tschugaeff / Grigorii Chugaev
Sail Maker:	Pavel Semenoff / Semenov
Head Carpenter:	Taras Gledianoff /Gledianov
Carpenter:	Kiril Tschschekin / Shchekin
Head Caulker:	Pautoff / Evsevii Pautov
Caulker:	Ivan Verschinin / Vershinin
Cooper:	Peter Jakovleff / Piotr Iakovlev
Bombardiers:	Nikita Schegalin / Zhegalin
	Karpoff / Artemii Karpov
Locksmith:	Mikhail Svägin / Zviagin
Mate:	Vasilii Zadorin
Quartermasters:	Ivan Kurganoff / Kurganov
	Efdokim Michailoff / Evdokim Mikhailov
	Mikhail Ivanoff / Ivanov
	Aleksei Fedotoff / Fedotov
Boatswain:	Karp Petroff / Petrov

Cook:	Neumann (died in the Pacific) Charitonoff / Filipp Kharitonov
Sailors:	Tschernoi
	Ivan Elizarov
	Fedosei Leont'ev
	Iakovleff / Ivan Iakovlev 1st
	Egor Martiukov
	Vasilii Fokin
	Filin Bichenkov
	Feodor Filippov
	Matvei Pigulin
	Ivanoff / Perfilii Ivanov
	Kuprian Semenoff / Kyprian Semenov
	Ivan Mikhailov 1st
	Daniil Filippov
	Nikolai Stepanov
	Istrekoff / Nefed Istrekov
	Martimian Martimianov
	Ivan Mikhailov 2nd
	Aleksei Krasil'nikov
	Kovedeeff / Gregorii Koved'ev
	Spiridon Larionov
	Golkeeff / Emmanuil Golkeev
	Reseb Boyasitoff / Rezep Baiazitov
	Sergei Ivanov
	Dmitrii Ivanov
	Klim Grigorieff / Klim Grigor'ev
	Ivan Loginov
	Efim Stepanov
	Egor Gregor'ev
	Schitoff / Ivan Shchitov
Servants:	Stepan Matveev
	Ivan Andreeff / Andreev
Ambassador and Chamberlain:	Nikolai Petrovitsch Resanoff / Nikolai Petrovich Rezanov
His Suite:	Major Hermann von Friderici / Ermolai Kortitsch Frideritsi
Lieutenant of the Guards:	Count Fedor Tolstoi
Adviser:	Fedor Pavlovitsch Fosse / Fos
Artist:	Stepan Kurlandzoff / Kurliandtsev
Doctor of Medicine and Botany:	Brinkin
Supercargo of the American Company:	Fedor Schemelin / Shemelin

Selected Contemporary Events During the Nadezhda's *Voyage Around the World*

1802

Peace of Amiens is signed between Britain and France.
Napoleon becomes First Consul for life, annexes Piedmont, Parma, and Piacenza.
France puts down a rebellion on Santo Domingo.
The Duke of Richmond starts horse racing at Goodwood.
The British take control of central India.
Ludwig van Beethoven realizes he is going deaf.
Georg Friedrich Grotefend deciphers cuneiform writing.

1803

Napoleon undertakes military activities in Italy, the Netherlands, Switzerland, and Germany.
United States completes the Louisiana Purchase from Napoleon for $15 million.
War is renewed between France and Britain.
French occupy Hanover, a possession of the king of England.
Britain gains control of southern and eastern India and occupies the islands of St. Lucia, Tobago, and Dutch Guiana.
Czar Alexander I invades southern Georgia and eastern Alaska.
Joseph Lancaster publishes *Improvements in Education as it Respects the Industrious Classes.*
Johann von Herder, a collector of folk songs and ballads, dies.

1804

Haiti declares her independence.
The Senate and Tribunate proclaim Napoleon emperor. He is crowned in the presence of Pope Pius VII in Paris.
Code Napoleon is promulgated.
Franz (Francis) II takes the title of Emperor of Austria as Francis I.
Russia's war with Persia begins, resulting in the Russian annexation of the Kingdom of Georgia.
Spain declares war on Britain.
Serbs revolt against the Ottoman yoke.

The White Lotus rebellion in China is finally put down, leaving the Qing dynasty, however, much weakened.
Serfdom is abolished in Denmark.
Meriwether Lewis and William Clark begin their journey to the Pacific Ocean.
Friedrich Schiller: *Wilhelm Tell* is performed in Weimar.
Immanuel Kant dies.
Alexander von Humboldt publishes *Travels to the Equinoctial Regions of the New Continent during the years 1799 to 1804.*
Beethoven's *Symphony No. 3 in E-flat major, Op. 55, The Eroica* is premiered.

1805
Thomas Jefferson begins his second term as the President of the United States.
Napoleon is crowned King of Italy.
Austria and France sign to the Peace of Pressburg. Austria relinquishes Tyrol and her Italian possessions. Bavaria and Würtemberg become kingdoms. Baden becomes a grand duchy.
The Battle of Trafalgar secures British supremacy of the seas.
Napoleon defeats an Austro-Russian army at Austerlitz and enters Vienna.
Russia begins a war against Turkey.
Mehemet Ali is proclaimed Pasha of Egypt.
The Lewis and Clark expedition reaches the Pacific Coast.
Beethoven's *Fidelio* is premiered.
Schiller dies.

1806
British occupy the Cape of Good Hope.
William Pitt the Younger and Charles James Fox die.
Joseph Bonaparte is named King of Naples.
Louis Bonaparte is named King of Holland.
Britain blockades the French coast.
Prussia declares war on France.
Napoleon crushes the Prussian Army at Jena and then enters Berlin.
Napoleon forces the end of the Holy Roman Empire.
Saxony is made a kingdom.
Kitagawa Utmaro, the painter of the *Floating World*, dies in Tokyo.

1807
Napoleon, Czar Alexander I, and the King of Prussia conclude the Treaty of Tilsit.
Jerome Bonaparte becomes King of Westphalia.
Baron von Stein, as Prime Minister of Prussia, emancipates the serfs.
The Portuguese royal family flees to Brazil after the French invade Portugal.
The first Ascot Gold Cup horse race is run.
Sierra Leone and Gambia are made British colonies.
U.S. Congress forbids import and export trade.
Importation of slaves into the U.S. is banned.

- 1 -

Kronstadt to Falmouth

After being appointed, I traveled to Reval[1] to take charge of the sailors Mr. von Krusenstern had chosen from the command there and to receive the supplies ordered for the voyage, Geneva gin and spirits from Hortig and butter from Küster. The transport ship *Catharina Magdelena* was to take me to Kronstadt.[2] Only with great difficulty was I able to avoid having to command the ship myself since Admiral Tet[3] said very naively: "The cargo, the crew, and you belong to the expedition. Take that transport ship, and may God sail with you." Finally, through Captain Krusenstern's negotiation after he came to Reval for a short period, Baret[4] was given the command, and I traveled as a passenger. Espenberg[5] loaded his things onboard so I also took them along.

May[6]

Fri. 15/27 May 1803, I sailed from Reval, and on the morning of **Mo. 18/30** May, I reached Kronstadt. In Kronstadt, I unloaded all of my things, rented quarters and moved on land until 22 May and left the transport ship in the hands of the besotted Baret.

Sun. 24/5 Ratmanoff[7] and Espenberg arrived from Petersburg bringing the news that the emperor[8] had granted Krusenstern's wife an arende.[9] I became acquainted with the Director of Customs Wirst.

Tues. 26/7 Lisianski[10] arrived in Kronstadt with the ships *Nadezhda* and *Neva*. The worst complainer was Gamalei,[11] who was ill-tempered because he could not make the voyage.

Wed. 27/8 Captain Krusenstern and Romberg[12] arrived from Petersburg and transferred to me the job of taking over the ships and cargo from the English.

June

Tues. 2/14 After everything had been taken over, I was put по шчиперской [in charge of the ship], Bellingshausen[13] по комисарской [in charge of the cargo], Ratmanoff the riggings and Romberg the hold. In the afternoon, Count Rumianzoff, Resanoff, and the Directors of the Russian American Company[14] Деларов [Delarov] and Булдаков [Buldakov] visited us.

Thurs. 4/16 Bellingshausen and I traveled by way of Oranienbaum to Petersburg in order to purchase various things, met the people who are supposed to stay in Kodiak, and returned to Kronstadt on the ninth with my drunken detachment. During my absence, the *Nadezhda* had been totally unloaded, lost her equilibrium, and capsized in the canal so that only her masts had prevented her from completely overturning. The foremast, which had already been damaged by two cartouche balls, was damaged even more and rendered unusable.

Sun. 14/26 We pulled ourselves to a crane, removed our old masts, and replaced them with new ones.

Mon. 15/27 Emperor Alexander came to Kronstadt and did us the honor of visiting our ships, found the tubs to his liking, was surprised to hear Krusenstern maintain that the Russian masts were better than the English, and permitted us, after he had wandered through Kronstadt and the Admiralty, to continue our work in his presence and observed us putting the shrouds and stays on the new masts and in the evening, apparently satisfied with us, [he] returned to Oranienbaum. Everything needed for the expedition is being paid for in cash. The Admiralty sends us everything we request and calculates the amount. We are grateful to Captain of the Port Мяцоедов [Miatsoedov] for his many kindnesses.

Sat. 20/2 Romberg, who came to work too late in the afternoon, was reprimanded by Krusenstern, although Golovatscheff[15] had earned it because he was dejour.[16] Lisianski's only concern is dividing up the things he brought from England, and Василии Николаевичберч [Vasilii Nikolaevich Berkh][17] is his creature.

Sun. 21/3 Since the men received schabasch [шабаш: liberty],[18] we drove to Oranienbaum. An easterly wind had come up upon our return, and about eighty merchant ships hurried at full sail out of the harbor. Through their unnecessary haste, they were blocking the merchant entrance. It was wonderful to watch all of that rushing about and carrying on.

Sat. 27/9 I visited Crown at his little place. His wife has taken the children to England in order to put them in *Boardingscools* [sic]. We have visitors daily. Matzneff's anchor tows are going to be of great use to us because they are very good. While he was a lieutenant of the Fleet, he enjoyed visiting every possible ropewalk in England, bought his own equipment, and upon his return handed in a plan for a new ropewalk establishment to the minister. Since his plan was approved, the minister named him the director of the ropewalk in Kronstadt where he is of great use to the Fleet.

Mon. 29/11 Our provisions from Petersburg, our galley kitchen, and thirty large crates and chests with the gifts for the Emperor of Japan arrived today. At this time, all of us officers of the ship moved onboard and put our cabins in order. The young Kotzebues[19] came too.

July

On the second, twenty more crates of gifts for Japan arrived.

Fri. 3/15 Today, the captain received the news from Petersburg that the emperor is permitting us to sail under a flag of war. According to Lisianski's calculations, the repairs to the ships have cost 6,000 £ sterling, both ships 24,000 £ sterling, and the entire expedition will cost 700,000 rubles.

Sat. 4/16 We do not have any more room on the ship; otherwise, the directors of the Company would really load us down. Councilor Fosse, Friderici, Okuneff, and the painter Kurlandzoff[20] brought us 20,000 Spanish *Dahler Extraodinair Summe* [sic].[21]

Sun. 5/17 Today I went to Хаников [Khanikov] and requested a longboat to pull our ship out of the harbor. "Душенка [Deary], I'm not letting you out of the harbor before Tuesday. You may complain to the emperor if you want to, but I'm not letting you budge from the spot—Че рный день [Save it for a] rainy day."

Tues. 7/19 At seven o'clock, we dropped anchor in the roadstead, and immediately afterwards another boat arrived with more crates—presents for Japan. And then three large apothecary chests. And thus it continues endlessly to a point where you cannot move on shipboard.

Fri. 10/22 We finally washed the ship—and that just in time because Captain Krusenstern came onboard around noon with Чичаков [Tschitschagoff], Хаиков [Khanikov], Греиг [Greig], Кроун [Crown] and Каронка [Karonka].[22]

The tall masts, the low deck in which one has to stoop, the windlass, the amount of cargo, the small amount of space for people, since the chests and crates had taken up all of the room, were sufficient cause for criticism. After the admirals had all eaten breakfast, Minister of the Navy Чичаков [Tschitschagoff] kissed us all—and the gentlemen took their leave.

As long as the command is divided into two watches, we officers will have to stand three watches, i.e., Ratmanoff the first, Romberg the second, Головачев [Golovatscheff] the third.

Sat. 11/23 Mrs. von Krusenstern and a large group of guests from Petersburg and Kronstadt dined on the *Nadezhda*. Count Stroganoff[23] visited the ship in the afternoon. Today, Mr. von Krusenstern gave his first written order in which it is stated that I am to take over the fourth watch as soon as we have sailed through the canal. I have been put in charge of dispensing clothes to the sailors.

Tues. 14/26 The Emperor is supposed to come to Kronstadt once again and probably will visit us. It was a false rumor. Espenberg, who had not been sick during stormy weather, went on land. He had just barely stepped on firm land when he became seasick.

Wed. 15/27 Count Tolstoi,[24] Завяскен [Zaviaskin], and Romberg's brother arrived. They did not deny themselves the opportunity of staging a drinking bout late into the night.

Our crew was inspected for the state of their health. Некинелов [Nekinelov] will be left behind, and Яаковлев [Iakovlev], even though infected, will nevertheless be taken along. Impatiently, we are awaiting the arrival of Чичаков [Tschitschagoff] and Румянцов [Rumianzoff], who are to determine who of the ambassador's suite should stay here, since there is not enough room on ship for all of them.

Sat. 18/30 Washed the ship. The amount of trash swept and washed out of her is indescribable. During the morning, Окунев [Okunev] brought 14,000 piasters of *Nessessary Money* [sic]. At lunch, he became drunk, loud, stormed about, laughed, and acted like a lout. Tolstoi was at fault because he toasted him and did not call for moderation.

Sun. 19/31 The прикащик [prikaschtschick: supercargo] of the Company came with a load of crates, one as large as a cabin, in which he probably could set up living quarters. It will indeed be hard to find room for everything. The volunteers who have nothing to do are a lively bunch—jumping around, laughing, climbing, running, making noise, talking, etc. until tired and befuddled they go to bed. Count Tolstoi is primus [head of the class].

Mon. 20/1 Since our voyage was mainly being promoted by and Румяицов [Rumianzoff], Minister Чичаков [Tschitschagoff] did not really want Captain Krusenstern, and we officers, after our return, really began to feel it. Krusenstern submitted a petition with the question whether he would be permitted to advance Naval Guard Bistram[25] to the rank of officer if he should be chosen for the voyage. Due to Чичаков [Tschitschagoff's] absence, Krusenstern had to submit the petition to Румянцов [Rumianzoff]. Upon Чичаков [Tschitschagoff's] arrival he was informed that his decision was: Every naval guard who has participated in two campaigns[26] will be promoted to officer. In the afternoon, we went to the Рибебанка [Ribebanka], and in the evening Чичаков [Tschitschagoff], Румянцов [Rumianzoff], and Резанов [Resanoff] came onboard the *Nadezhda*. They inspected the ship, drank their tea, and only then did Captain Krusenstern arrive. Now was to be decided which members of the ambassador's suite would stay behind and where the ship should be reloaded. Seven men were stricken from the list; as expected we heard the choice was painful for them. Everyone thought that he was among the stricken.

Лисиански [Lisianski] fought hand and foot against taking the priest[27] but had to in the end as well as some of the промышвенников [agents for transport]. At twelve o'clock, our guests ate their evening meal and took leave in order to communicate the results to the Emperor. The ones who were eliminated are in a bad state of affairs, having equipped themselves for the voyage and taken leave of their loved ones only to discover they will be left behind. The gentlemen who will probably remain behind are: young Козин [Kozin] from the mining corps, the Ambassador's secretary, Naval Guard Окунев [Okunev], Resanoff's nephew, and the two Kotzebues.

Tues. 21/2 Five Japanese, to whom the Emperor had given watches, came onboard.[28] All afternoon the *Nadezhda* was crawling with officers who wanted to take our leave. The captain and his wife with several guests came onboard in the evening. Later a courier for Resanoff arrived from Count Румянцов [Rumianzoff], saying that Козин [Kozin], the miner Паулсон [Paulson], the secretary Чачков [Chachkov] and Naval Lieutenant Окунев [Okunev] were to stay behind. The Japanese are ugly people, guzzle like hedgehogs, and have a lot of pretensions.

Wed. 22/3 Lisianski is continually working on dividing up his things and is becoming a burden to us all because of his greed. Окунев [Okunev] is getting befogged in the end, picking a fight with Fosse, wants with might and main to knife him or shoot around with him. We certainly are all glad that we are getting rid of that crazy fellow.

Company at table on the *Nadezhda*: Captain Krusenstern, the Lieutenants Ratmanoff, Romberg, Golovatscheff, Löwenstern, and Bellingshausen, Chief Quartermaster Kamentschikoff, Doctor Espenberg, Naval Guard Bistram, and the cadets Otto and Moritz Kotzebue, in addition, Ambassador Resanoff, Councilor Fosse, Major Friderici, Naval Lieutenant Count Tolstoi, Natural Scientist Brinkin, Painter Kurlandzoff, and the прикащик[supercargo] Schemelin.[29] In Copenhagen, Horner, the astronomer, and Tilesius,[30] the natural scientist, will join us. In all, twenty people. In the evening, Окунев [Okunev], who cannot get over the fact that he has to stay behind, is said to have got in a fight with his uncle Resanoff; for it cannot be called a dispute since he did not let himself be silenced until Resanoff sent him out of the cabin. This useless fellow is leaving us tonight.

The sailor Василии Алевсеев [Vasilii Alekseev], who shows the onset of a bad case of scarlet fever, will also be left behind. I have the unpleasant task of claiming his clothes, listening to his begging and complaining, and not being able to help him in any way.

Thurs. 23/4 We had the Russian priest bless the *Nadezhda*. At the end, we had quite a lot of visitors. We weighed our moorings.

Абдул Абузаров [Abdul Abuzarov], a Tartar by birth, volunteered when the voyage around the world was announced. Afterwards, he fell in love with a pretty Estonian peasant girl. When I brought the detachment from Reval to Kronstadt, he absolutely wanted to stay behind. Since I could not permit him to, he had to come along. He took his wife, since he had already married her, along to Kronstadt. Now began the sailor's battle between love of his wife and the desire to travel or not. Every day he expressed new desires, and, when Mr. von Krusenstern left it up to him, he was given permission to go to Petersburg. There he placed his wife as a maid in the home of a merchant and returned. Overcome by longing, he became ill and now against his will has to be left behind.

Sat. 25/6 Lisianski had traveled with Schellichoff, the Director of the Company, and ship architect Rasumoff to Hamburg in order to buy ships for the voyage. The Company had allotted 70,000 rubles for the purchase. In Hamburg, they were offered two ships. The Hamburg City Council had issued an attest to their quality and they appeared to have no faults. Lisianski wanted to pull a fast one on the gentlemen, suggested going to England because he would have a greater choice there, and the worst case would be that they could still take the ships in Hamburg. The gentlemen agreed, and Lisianski traveled to England alone and bought, without asking anyone, the *Leander* and the *Thames* for 230,000 rubles. Repairs to the ships cost, in addition, 30,000 rubles. Upon his return, he was impressed with himself, since he had filled his pockets with the money of others. He demanded tents. They were ordered, but he did not like them, and they were returned. He sent back the old iron that was to be used in trade with the savages because he likes being unobliging and discourteous. His behavior has all of the appearances as if he wished they would take the ship away from him and leave him home.

Sun. 26/7 We weighed anchor and began our voyage. Хаников [Khanikov] visited us with bread and salt[31] when we were already under sail and gave us his blessings.

Wed. 29/10 Councilor Федор Павлович Фоссе [Fedor Pavlovich Fosse] is our steward,[32] lets us starve from the outset. Толстой [Tolstoi], Resanoff, the Kotzebues, and Bistram are seasick. I have taken over Ratmanoff's watch for the time being. We sailed past Norgen on the night of the thirtieth.

Fri. 31/12 A tale from Resanoff: "My free speech on several occasions against the emperor has made me many enemies. The miserliness can only be attributed to chicanery at court. My determination made it possible to obtain from the emperor the things necessary for carrying out the Embassy to Japan since the Japanese view gifts as very important. Even you, my dear gentlemen, would not have gone away empty handed if Rumianzoff and Чичагов [Tschitschagoff] had not mutually intervened. I was denied any opportunity of being introduced to the emperor. Only with a great deal of trouble did I achieve the emperor's granting me the Order of St. Anne.[33] Upon a successful completion of this voyage, we can hope for a great many things; and, if court intrigues should bring all expectations to naught, then the happy conclusion of the voyage will be sufficient reward." (This is what he said and demonstrated to each one of us seamen.)

August

Sat. 1/13 Because the ship is very overweight on the deck, she lists unbelievably to one side. In Copenhagen, we will have to reload the *Nadezhda*. During the evening, Resanoff and Tolstoi trumped each other in telling tales of important and rich Russians' follies, for example, that Count Strogonoff, in an attempt to become maitre de plaisir [master of entertainment] to the emperor, squandered his entire wealth consisting of 50,000 rubles income a year and failed in his attempt. Young Bistram is continually seasick. During the confusion and jostling of people on our ship, Ratmanoff's gold watch, Tolstoi's gold box, Шимелин [Schemelin's] pipe, and several other small items were stolen.

Sun. 2/14 A sailor onboard the *Neva* fell overboard and drowned. We practice as often as we can making observations with the sextants. My fellow shipmates do not like Espenberg. The Japanese we have onboard were pampered in Petersburg and are also being pampered on our ship. They have expressed their gratitude toward us several times: "You should already be trembling in fear of us. Just wait until we reach Japan." They however were surprised that we were not afraid of their threat but instead laughed in their faces.

Mon. 3/15 Captain Krusenstern had the keys taken from the entire crew. We did a general search but did not find any of the stolen objects. The Japanese's things were not searched, at Resanoff's order. Today, after the evening meal, after Resanoff, the captain, and several officers had left, Tolstoi told several tales among others of duels he had had. Fosse told him, "You are lying. You officers of the guard do not have that much courage among you."

"Алтынник" [niggard] answered Tolstoi, "that may be the case that you fellows don't have any courage, but that is not the case with me, never!" (Fosse had served in the police in Petersburg.) At that Fosse stood up and said, "в сей час Николай Петрович тебя намоет" [At that time Nikolai Petrovich, you'll get what is coming to you] and left. Resanoff came to the Company cabin a minute later and called in "перестан" [Lay off, Count!].

Now we began to debate dueling, and Tolstoi did not utter a word. Resanoff appeared unexpectedly and said to Tolstoi, "You are to stay in Copenhagen." Tolstoi answered, "If any one stays, then the two of us." The argument continued for a while, and then we went our ways. Ratmanoff and I had watch. The Count came up to speak with me. Suddenly, Ratmanoff interrupted our conversation and said, "Enough of that! You don't have to argue on the quarterdeck!" That irked us, and we nevertheless separated. A little bit later, Resanoff appeared on deck and saw Count Tolstoi talking softly with Espenberg. "Stop talking about that!" said Resanoff to the Count, without knowing what they were talking about, and then everyone went to bed. Ratmanoff tried to make a joke of the whole tale. Maybe he will succeed.

Tues. 4/16 Sailed past Bornholm. There is no more talk of the goings-on yesterday. Resanoff, Fosse, and Tolstoi however are sunk in thought. I was standing on the deck with Krusenstern when Resanoff came up to us and said very candidly, "Tolstoi always eats a second time with the officers on duty in order to empty the remaining wine and brandy. We will have to leave such a man in Copenhagen."

A little bit later, he spoke with the captain again and said, "We have to leave that restless man behind." That evening, we dropped anchor in Kjöge Bay.

Wed. 5/17 We dropped anchor at Drago and at Copenhagen in the evening. Tolstoi, who had greatly reconsidered his behavior overnight, at my suggestion, went to Resanoff early this morning and asked him for forgiveness and straightforwardly, and whether he would be making the voyage or not. This question hit His Excellency unexpectedly. He began hedging and finally said, "If Иван Федорович [Ivan Fedorovich] has no objections, you may stay with us." (Resanoff believed that Krusenstern would also like to leave Tolstoi behind.) At that moment, the captain came into the cabin and that ended that tale. Fosse was sent for and peace was made with the condition that Count Tolstoi never again should call Fosse an алтынник [niggard]. Horner and Tilesius have been in Copenhagen for the past two weeks. We are expecting the French brandy from Helsingör and will go into the harbor there in order to reload.

Thurs. 6/18 We unloaded our gunpowder and entered the harbor. Fosse, who is in charge of table, does not consider it worth the bother to worry about the lower end of the table and thinks he has done enough when he has taken care of His Excellency. That has already caused dissatisfaction, and we have already been here for two days and still do not have any fresh foodstuffs. That caused us to ask Krusenstern to talk to Fosse about the matter.

Fri. 7/19 After having worked ourselves to death the whole day, a very strong thunderstorm with gusts of wind, even at night, did not grant us any peace and quiet. The gusts followed each other with such frequency that we were all blinded by the blows. We are leaving part of the flour here. Only two or at the most three people eat meals onboard, since all of those who can are living on land.

Sun. 9/21 Young people are ashamed, and rightly so, to gallivant around in uniform into every corner of a strange city. That's why Resanoff's behavior is all the more striking. He is not ashamed to visit places with his Star[34] (which he does not know how to wear since he did not earn it through merit) whose names I am ashamed to mention. On the streets, he opens his yap at every sign as if he were seeing a rarity. This behavior says a lot. Today, the captain received a letter from a French doctor that gives rules of treatment for snake bites, dog bites, pox, savages' poisoned arrows, etc. Probably we will all prefer to follow Espenberg's treatment.

Mon. 10/22 With permission, we viewed the Danish Admiralty and did Resanoff the favor (despite the fact that he had invited us to eat with him at an inn) of turning down his invitation and returned to the ship.

Tues. 11/23 Two Danish ships from China arrived. The one had a very strong leak. Krusenstern has installed Ratmanoff as an English eldest lieutenant—that is not a usual practice in Russia, and today Ratmanoff and Romberg had a heated argument about it.

Ritterschaftskapitän [Knight Captain] Berg had arrived on his way to his daughter's in Sweden.

In the afternoon, we visited the art gallery, which has suffered from theft and fire, because I had seen the art gallery before the fire.

Thurs. 13/25 I visited Berg. He, his wife, and two eldest daughters had an unhappy voyage. Their ship landed on a sandbank, sprang a leak, and was in danger of sinking. Instead of sailing to Copenhagen they had been forced to go to Lübeck, from where Berg and his family had traveled by land to Copenhagen in order to continue their trip to Sweden today. After unloading the ship, we now have to load it again. We are leaving a lot of flour here.

Resanoff asks everyone to go totally without Compliments and nevertheless remarks, wherever he can, that he likes it very much if he is shown proper honors. The second mate was fresh enough to say to the captain that he could not work the scheduled days. Especially he, Каменщиков [Kamentschikoff], had diversions on land and was doing nothing, and he nevertheless only received a third of his pay. Полозов [Polozov] is not completely wrong to complain about Каменщиков [Kamentschikoff], who reveled four days in a row on land and not satisfied with that brought a girl of the cheapest kind onboard.

Sat. 15/27 Tilesius has a private tutor's Tournür [attitude] that annoys everyone. Fosse is like a dog that is being teased and picked at by a lot of other dogs. We are all somewhat indebted to him for buying the provisions. Every conversation with him ends up with ambiguous remarks that he can take as good pills. As a police officer, he is used to swallowing pills and digests them even now without difficulty. If it happens, and that is seldom the case, that he finds one hard to swallow, then he reacts with so little *grace* [sic] that he makes himself a laughingstock, and over and above that gets a mouthful of pills to swallow.

The trouble and work we have with unloading and loading is great and seems endless: continually вечный Шпиль [an eternal capstan]!

Par curiositet [out of curiosity] Resanoff is visiting all of the dance halls and wh[ore] houses. He had better be careful that it does not land in the newspapers.

Sun. 16/28 Brinkin[35] and Kurlandzoff are sensitive to the fact that Tilesius and Langsdorff[36] no longer seek their company. The German academics cannot speak the dead language fluently enough to use it with Brinkin, who is very fluent in Latin; and they cannot understand each other in the living languages. Over and above that, Resanoff behaves coarsely and harshly toward his own fellow countrymen and is polite, well behaved, and obliging toward foreigners. It is impossible to imagine being on a ship for a long time with him, only too often does Resanoff's false character break out. He has often enough been thoughtless, mean, partial, and roaring.

Today, we drank to the health of Krusenstern's son whose birthday it is. For me too, this day was a happy day.

Mon. 17/29 Everyone got letters, but not me. We had to re-salt the Hamburg salt meat. We still have so much work piled up that we do not know what we should do first. We have to turn down all invitations on land in order to stay with the work. The Danish boats in which we put our personal belongings are indispensable. I also had to turn down the invitation of Commodore Bilau, the Head of the Cadet Corps, because of the work. The people the American Company sent here to conduct their business are not very knowledgeable.

Wed. 19/31 Our volunteers act as if our people have to do whatever they want. I had it out with Fosse on that account today. Still cooking, he told Friderici about it, who then passed it on to me: "You know that Löwenstern. You dare not argue with him at all. He immediately becomes biting and hotheaded" is what he said. All the better.

Thurs. 20/1 Went on land and could not decline Resanoff's polite invitation to eat lunch with him. In the afternoon and evening, we walked around the city; and, had I not seen it with my own eyes, I would not have believed it. In the summer garden Resanoff forgot himself so completely that he, with Star and Order ribbon, ran after street girls and later climbed to the top floor of several houses. We followed as if pulled by the hair. I could not stop myself from saying straight out to him, that one is often glad to be able to get the troops out of similar garret rooms without getting a thrashing. His Excellency remained friendly, and, in order to put things back in order, I dined with him that evening as well as the following noon.

Fri. 21/2 In the evening, the Japanese set the ship on fire. Thank goodness, it was seen and extinguished. During this incident, Romberg had grabbed Mazara roughly by the arm because he was mouthing off; now there was no getting the fellow to shut up. He threatened with Japan, saying he was glad they would be going to Japan, where they would avenge this insult. Resanoff and the captain delude these common people too much.

Resanoff takes his commonness too far. From the balcony of his inn, he does not let a single girl cross the market without throwing her a kiss, calling to her, and even laughing loudly about his own joke. At about noon, a young girl with her handwork went by. Resanoff called and waved her in. I was also present. Then Resanoff began to get the girl for Friderici; and, since he did not want to and we had got out of it by a hair, she had the honor of being kissed by His Excellency. That takes the cake! Resanoff can talk about nothing else but girls and bawdy.

Sun. 23/4 We filled our water casks and finished loading the ship. Tilesius moved onboard today and was more than a little angry that no one took notice of his importance. Angrily he put several boxes and bundles on his back and carried them down. Since that did not help, he excused himself because of important business and went on land again. After the voyage is over, one will be able to write Theophilius Tilesius' conversion story, for this is a good opportunity to get educated. Horner is a reasonable, likable Swiss.

Mon. 24/5 We put all of the trash overboard and washed the ship clean, since we could not do it while unloading and loading. The Russian ambassador at the Danish court Lisenkewitsch and Count Kounitz and his wife visited us. Even though the weather was bad, Resanoff came onboard and not much later Count Kounitz with his wife and Count Bernsdorf. The sea was high and frightened our guests more than a little bit. I had trouble getting the Countess in the chair so that she could be raised onboard. The pretty woman was trembling all over, but, as soon as she was safe on the quarterdeck, her good spirits and cheerfulness returned. After our guests had been with us for some time, the captain took his guests in the shallop back on land again.

Our bombardier Карпов [Karpov] was more than a little frightened today. In the evening he was standing on the pristan [пристань: pier] waiting for our boat. Several Danes came up to him and said: "Russian from the *Nadezhda*, come!" Karpov climbed into the boat with six others. Halfway out the boat stopped at a merchant ship. "в пот бросила!" [boy did I sweat] said our artillerist, because he now recognized that he had put himself into foreign hands. The boat dropped off several people and than went to the *Nadezhda*. The fellow was happy when he heard Курганов [Kurganov's] voice. This example will make our people careful.

Lisianski is not yet finished because he had water fetched instead of renting a water boat, and with a longboat it takes time to fill the ship with water.

Tues. 25/6 Compare our undertaking with a grain field. Last autumn, a competent man called attention to the fact that a quite large unworked fallow field could be used. Selfish men began plowing in hope of a fruitful harvest. The workers they had chosen were also selfish and did not understand things. Instead of carefully working the land, they only plowed it. Instead of spreading the manure on this land, they took most of it and spread it on their own fields so that, despite all of the efforts, the land was badly worked and provided little hope of a rich harvest. Over and above this, the land belonged to several gentlemen and, as is usual, one depended upon the other, and only a little was done for the advantage of all. In the spring, the grain was finally to be sown.

Lisianski was sent to England to buy seed, even though the gentlemen could have bought it much more cheaply in Hamburg. That undependable man wasted such a large quantity of money on the purchase that the gentlemen, even if the harvest is ever so great, can expect no great treasure. In May, the seeds began to sprout, in appearance not as desired, since a lot of Japanese weeds were mixed in. Finally, in July, the grain shot up. In Copenhagen, however, it was restrained by reworking. Let's hope that in Tenerife the field will have grown substantially; in Japan it will begin to bloom, and after our departure, the bloom will begin to ripen; in China fill with seed; at the Cape of Good Hope that the seeds will fill out, and finally upon entrance in the Channel at our return ripen so that they can be harvested at our arrival in Kronstadt. How good the harvest will be depends upon time and conditions.

Tilesius and Langsdorff brought the news that there was theater today. We put on our uniforms and hoped that our Ambassador would keep us free and get tickets. On the contrary, Resanoff had not thought of us, and the tickets were sold out, so we were left standing in the street, where the merry waltz flowing our way from the dance floor awoke in us a desire to dance. We did not want to do it in uniform, so we put on any greatcoat we could get a hold of. Romberg put on Tilesius' and was also called Mr. Councilor. We went and stayed a little while, and got out of there. (We would have a lot of fun with this moral philosopher having seen his coat on the dance floor.)

In the evening, when Tilesius found out that we would be sailing the next day, if the wind were good, he said, "How then? Tomorrow? That is not possible. My cabin is not yet ready." With his importance, he dislikes his housing on the konstapelikoi [gun deck]. Poor fellow, for better or for worse, he'll have to get used to his housing.

Wed. 26/7 We left our фетоин [moorings]. Strong contrary wind. Tilesius, to our joy, is musical and has bought himself a violin and viola. Since we were all tired today, the fiddling was a nuisance.

Fri. 28/9 We took on gunpowder, raised the longboat, weighed anchor, and reached Helsingör in the evening. We had a lot of fun in the evening. Tilesius' night-swarming greatcoat was made fun of, and its owner took it very good-naturedly. Then one after another, everyone did his part, telling anecdotes, etc.

Sat. 29/10 Tilesius considers himself an important person in Europe. He and Langsdorff are continually at each other because Tilesius considers him his subordinate. Their disputes nevertheless always finish humorously.

When Emperor Paul[37] raised Lupukhin to Светлейший князь [worldly prince], he received a letter of patent and a coat of arms from the Senate, but a motto was needed. Several were suggested to the emperor. After a little consideration he took a pen and wrote the motto блалодать [bliss, grace, paradise, heavenly gift] under the coat of arms. благодать is Анна [Anna], and that was the name of Lopukhin's wife. As a result, the following verse was composed.

> [Light is generated from light.
> But for him the light is generated
> By such backside parts
> Where light does not penetrate.][38]

The captain was kind enough to give me a sextant and chronometer from Pennington.

Sun. 30/11 The Russian priest reminded us today of Alexander Nevski's Day.[39] I found it a pleasure to see how our people participated in the service. Through the service, we can forget the equinoctial storm we had today. It also continued to blast on the 31st.

September

Tues. 1/13 Today, since the weather had got better, Resanoff was happy to be able to go on land to run around with girls of easy virtue, to make a fool of himself and then to talk about it for two weeks. As luck would have it, they ran into an innkeeper by the name of Erasmus Spang, whose reading matter consisted of descriptions of voyages. When he heard that the gentlemen were voyaging around the world, he did everything to entertain the gentlemen and closed with the words: "If you publish your voyage, you will not be able to complain about hospitality in Denmark."

Wed. 2/14 Mr. Erasmus Spang came onboard in the morning with several melons. Resanoff set out with several gentlemen and went ashore. This acquaintance is totally according to Resanoff's taste.

The justification for taking Langsdorff along was sent from Copenhagen to Petersburg. Probably he won't get any news of his employment until Kamtschatka.

Tilesius gives himself airs that are not his to have, calls Langsdorff Er [German: he, as used with a servant], and treats him like an underling. Then he took it upon himself to proscribe rules of conduct for him. That was too much for Langsdorff. "Ey!" he said, "You have nothing to do with me. You are a natural scientist hired by the emperor and have to fulfill your contract. I, in contrast, am here on my own good luck, going along through the goodness of the Ambassador and the Captain, and will be collecting only for those two gentlemen. If upon our return, the emperor wants something from my collection, it will be at his service. Furthermore, we are totally different people. You get your pay, I none. You do natural research as an obligation; I do it of my own free will. Please spare me the assumption that I am along to be at your beck and call."

Thurs. 3/15 We weighed anchor, got rid of Чернявени [Cherniaveni] belonging to the embassy in Copenhagen, and left Helsingör under a flag of war, saluted Kroneborg, passed Kol Fyr at nine o'clock, Anhold at five and at eleven at night, Lessoe. September wind of nine knots.

Fri. 4/16 We sailed past *The Skaw*. We won't go past *The Nase* [sic].[40] Our course leads us straight toward Christiansand. All of the gentlemen are seasick. Bistram cannot stand the voyage. Instead of twenty, only eight ate the noon meal. The wind is becoming brisker and brisker.

Sat. 5/17 The passengers' seasickness is becoming unpleasant. The barometer is falling very fast. We seamen have caught slight colds.

Sun. 6/18 The barometer prophesies cold. We hauled in the topsail with difficulty and placed ourselves on the drift because the stormsail was not up yet. Even though the ship rocked very lightly on the waves, she listed nevertheless so strongly to one side that she took in water with every wave. The angle of the masts was around 35 degrees. Only in the evening were we able to lower the topgallant mast because we had not done so earlier, and now the ship was being thrown around too strongly for us to dare take in the top shrouds. The main topyard was thrown to the side out of the support studs by a wave. Only with difficulty did we become masters of that yard. The moaning and throwing up is endless. Even Ratmanoff is seasick, and I have to change my watch. The wind let up some in the night. The cabins were filled with misery; everything lying chaotically all over the place. The passengers would barely hurry on deck when they would be frightened by the roaring of the elements.

Mon. 7/19 The weather was better, and, even though the ship still rocked a great deal, everyone was healthy because the movement of the ship today was less than yesterday. Dr. Horner made several observations. Tilesius does nothing, finds everything uncomfortable, and for that reason is continually seasick.

Tues. 8/20 We saw very beautiful northern lights. The lights were strong. Even though the mist appeared so thick, you could nevertheless see the stars very clearly through it. The good weather resulted in everyone being healthy and appearing at tea and at breakfast and digging in with double the appetite. At eleven o'clock, we passed *The Nase* and left the *Skaggerak* behind us. We could indeed say we hopped over the Jutland Reef.

Wed. 9/21 We sailed over eight knots with reefed main topsail and foresail. The waves often hit over the deck to Resanoff's and the painter's horror. Yesterday morning the wind quieted down, and the sea became higher. We threw out our trawl for the fun of it but caught only some sea urchins. Tilesius, as if possessed, wanted to put it in spirits but was too lazy to get the equipment himself, tried to get someone else to do it, etc. He got to hear a lot of truths and then had to help himself as best he could. The prikaschtschik [supercargo] Schemelin, who lives next to the powder, was burning a light there very carelessly. I told him so, and, since he didn't want to hear what I had to say, I put the light out before his nose. I did my duty and so "Holla."

Thurs. 10/22 All of our poor passengers have lost weight from seasickness, fear, and discomfort. We have already sailed past Doggers Bank.

Fri. 11/23 The English war ship *Antilope* under Commodore Sir Sidney Smith forced the *Nadezhda* by a cannon shot to be put on the drift. To put things back in order, he gave our captain a present of rum and a lot of apologies, but we lost a lot of time.

The *Rubec* with 64 [cannons] under Captain Gardener is under sail and will undoubtedly leave us unmolested. At eight o'clock in the evening, the frigate *Virginia* under Captain Berrisforth stopped us. All of the English ships thought the *Nadezhda* was French and hope to capture a prize.[41] Berrisforth, an acquaintance of Krusenstern,[41] offered to put a pilot onboard and to take Resanoff and several gentlemen with him since he was sailing to Sheerness.

Sat. 12/24 Resanoff, Horner, Friderici, and Bistram went over to the English frigate that was sailing very extraordinarily. Captain Berrisforth was so kind as to fetch our gentlemen himself. Just before their departure, Resanoff had the misfortune of losing his Star in the commotion while they were getting their bundles

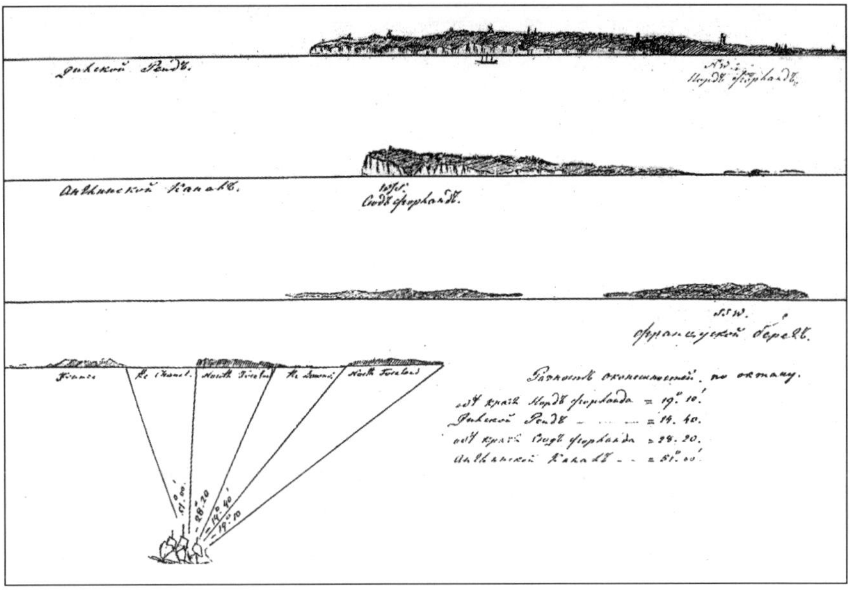

1-1. *View of England, France, and the Channel and the Roadstead at Deal*

together. All the better.[43] Bistram took his leave from us with tears in his eyes because he had to go back to Russia from London. Later we sighted North Foreland.

Langsdorff had studied medicine, traveled with a little German prince to Lisbon, was employed there by a crazy Portuguese, traveled to England and from there back to Lisbon, lived there for a time from his practice, was employed again as a surgeon major by the English troops, mustered out with the peace agreement, traveled by way of Paris to London and from there back to his family, heard soon afterwards that Russia was undertaking a voyage around the world, came by way of Göttingen to Copenhagen, applied, and was lucky enough to be accepted.

Sun. 13/25 We passed Dover in the night. Tilesius has related too much about the vocations he has had.

Mon. 14/26 We passed *Beechyhead* [sic] and put the pilot onto a custom's boat. And in the evening, we passed swimming fire near Portsmouth.[44]

Wed. 16/28 We arrived in Falmouth, where a fisherman piloted us in at seven o'clock in the morning. We found the *Neva* from whom we had been separated in the Skaggerak. She had already been there for two days. Falmouth is a nice roadstead, except for Black Rock no shallows. At ten o'clock, the captain sent me on land to speak with the commander. The armless warrior answered that he was happy to be able to answer the Russian salute. Trade also enlivens remote Falmouth.

Thurs. 17/29 We saluted the fort with nine shots at flag raising and were answered. Thereupon, we saluted the fire watch with seven shots but were not answered. The captain sent me to the warship on the roadstead. I received the very

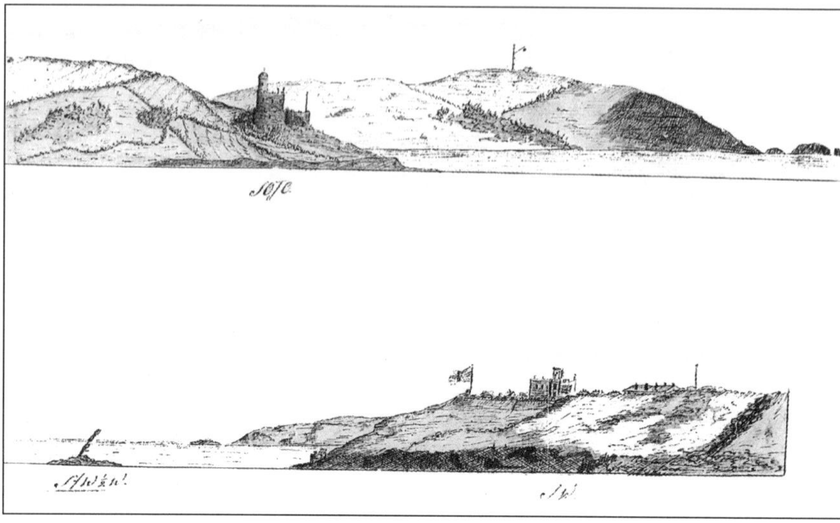

1-2. View of the entrance to Falmouth. The town is not in view.

polite answer that the captain of the frigate was the senior officer and should have answered the salute and that the lack of doing so probably was the result "*of your Captain's not having been onboard the frigate, at Captain Matzens*" [sic]. I was then sent to the frigate, where I found that the captain was not home. The Lieutenant told me he had known nothing about it, but "*I will be answerable of your Salutation being answered*" [sic]. And in the afternoon our salute was answered.

Toward eleven o'clock, Colonel Lord Rou came onboard with several ladies and officers. The lord invited us all to dine with him at noon the day after tomorrow. Romberg went on land with the Englishman and enjoyed a very pleasant ball in the evening.

We are hurrying our work so that we will be finished by the time Resanoff returns from London.

The Danish pilot, *a good for nothing fellow* [sic] was dispatched today.

Fri. 18/30 The lack of brick and tile is the reason why almost all of Falmouth is built from fieldstone or granite, which gives the entire town a gloomy appearance.

Sat. 19/1 At four o'clock, we dined at Lord Rou's for lunch. After we had eaten our fill of roast and several delicacies, the bottles were put in motion. We drank to the health of George [King of England][45] and Alexander [Emperor of Russia] and then toasts. The lord had drunk a glass too many. There was a lot of singing. Lord Rou started it. At ten o'clock in the evening, we drank tea. Krusenstern went onboard ship. Romberg, Count Tolstoi, and I stayed on land for the night. The other officers went onboard with the captain.

Sun. 20/2 We drank tea at a soldier captain's. The captain and Count Tolstoi were invited to dine with the general at noon.

Tues. 22/4 We were invited to dine in Penryn for lunch at the army officers' mess. Because we were expecting Resanoff at any time, we had to decline. Only in the evening were we certain that we had to stay. Therefore, Romberg and I went on land to take advantage of an invitation to go to a ball. We rented a postchaise (two-seater carriage). The moon cast the shadow of the carriage to the side so that the coachman could see the shadow of anyone trying to take a seat behind without permission. Every unwelcome passenger got a well-placed whack of the whip. At nine o'clock, we finally arrived at Penryn where we found the little ball very badly attended. The politeness of Major Lyn and Captain Bawse made up for the emptiness of the room. We took the chance of dancing several englois one after another. We seemed like an apparition to them, since we had not come at noon; and they had not expected us to appear for the ball. After the ball, that ended very soon, Captain Falk invited us to his place Hobson's Choice; and, after we had drunk a few glasses of wine, we set out on our way and returned to Falmouth.

Wed. 23/5 We had barely drunk our tea in the inn when Красияников [Krasiianikov] came into the room with the news that Resanoff had arrived. I hurried immediately out to him to tell him that we were having a favorable wind and went onboard. At three o'clock, everyone came onboard with sack and pack, and at five o'clock we weighed anchor. Krusenstern thought that General Kowell was going to visit us again. Since he had not come, the captain reproached him on land. "I would have liked to have visited you," said the general, "if I would not have thereby insulted Captain Norway of the fire watch, since you had not visited him." Krusenstern answered that Captain Norway himself was the reason, since he had not responded to our salute and, in addition, through me had sent very impolite advice.

In the evening when we were passing the *Lizard*, Krusenstern ordered me to take command of the fourth watch.

Thurs. 24/6 Horner has brought very nice instruments from England. Everyone likes the snuffbox sextant. Count Vorenzoff[46] is said not to be too inclined toward our expedition. Our natural scientists returned to Falmouth with a lot of booty, Langsdorff with a lot of minerals, dried plants, and stuffed fish, Tilesius with very similar minerals, fish, plants, etc. We like the painter's work the least. Thanks to Espenberg, we have left Falmouth healthy, and we are all happy about the favorable wind.

Fri. 25/7 Up to now, we have not sailed under six knots. Everyone is seasick, even Ratmanoff, the cabin quiet, and the table unoccupied.

- 2 -

Falmouth to Tenerife to Santa Catharina

Sat. 26/8 We sailed around Cape Finisterre.

Anecdote: On the day we lunched in Falmouth at Lord Rou's, Espenberg went on land intending to return onboard with us after the meal. The lunch took so long that he, in a bad mood, decided to spend the night on land. A pretty girl in the inn riled the old man so much that he got up in the night several times and knocked on her door, but without success. No one opened up. The painter Kurlandzoff spied him on one of his excursions, and, in an even worse mood, Espenberg went back to bed.

Our lunch finished at 12 o'clock midnight. Mr. von Krusenstern sent someone to him to ask if he wanted to return to the ship. Since Espenberg was already in bed, it was of no use and only increased his heat. The next morning, a boat was sent on land to pick us up, since Romberg and I had also stayed overnight. (Espenberg and Kurlandzoff had not lunched at Lord Rou's.)

The tide was going out. In order not to be grounded on the sand, we had to leave without the doctor who was unnecessarily delayed. Just after we pulled away, he appeared at the pristan. Since he could do nothing at that point, he went back into town to an apple stand where Степан Семенович [Stepan Semenovich] Kurlandzoff had just bought a large supply of apples. Unfortunately, there were only some leftover apples still available. The painter had already bought all of the good ones. Espenberg began to complain about it. (Espenberg did not understand much Russian, and the painter knows no other language but Russian.) Espenberg became heated, blamed him for having bought all of the apples in order to make him angry. The painter answered coldly, "First come first serve." His coldness made Espenberg even angrier. In the heat of the argument, he bought a scarf full of apples, threw them one after another on the ground, and kicked them with his foot against the wall or into the air, so that people stopped to watch the spectacle. His excessive hot-headedness is undoubtedly the reason that he is so reserved onboard.

Sun. 27/9 A wagtail rescued itself by landing on our ship. Shy in the beginning, happy to have found a place to rest, it became so tame that it was not afraid of us at all; and, undisturbed, it searched the ship for food. That little bird used the cabbages hanging at the back of the ship for its nightly resting place; and there it whistled, totally unafraid, its innocent song.

I was delighted that we would be taking that little European bird to the Canary Islands. How surprised our little fellow traveler would observe the objects there, flit from one unknown tree to another, when to all of our sorrow one of our Japanese, like a predatory animal, grabbed our darling and squeezed it to death.

We are continuing to sail nine knots. In the evening, we passed Lisbon.

Tilesius and Friderici have set up camp in the shallop, where neither wind nor weather nor waves washing over and getting them wet can drive them out. Horner and Langsdorff are doing so-so. Resanoff is off of his legs. Count Tolstoi is sometimes seasick and then again not. If the wind is strong, he is healthy. If the wind lets up somewhat, the fun is over, and he has to pay his dues for the rolling. The painter is continually afraid and thinks he can prevent misfortune coming only when he houses day and night on the deck. Espenberg tries in vain to drive off nausea by reading and gets angry at the word. The two Kotzebues amble around fair to middling, at any time of day, whether by storm or calm. Brinkin and Schemelin are a pair of shining lights who no one pays any attention to. We seamen take care of our quarters, are happy about good wind, and enjoy the variety of moods displayed by our passengers.

Tilesius happened to be sitting in the shallop opposite one of the Japanese, whom he drew amazingly well in pencil.

Lisianski had arrived in Falmouth two days before we did for our rendezvous. He immediately wrote Voronzoff that he had come without us and would wait for five days and then sail without us. If he finds a possibility of leaving us, he will undoubtedly do everything he can to do so.

Mon. 28/10 It was Resanoff's own fault that the trip to London [several illegible lines of German]. We make observations every day. The reviving of the fellowship in the company cabin is an unbearable sign of good weather. And the music that can be heard in there! Romberg plays violino primo, Resanoff secundo, Tilesius basso, Langsdorff viola, Friderici flute primo, Horner flute secundo. The rest of us are listeners and judges at the same time. The music is often, however, inconvenient.

In the evening, we saw a beautiful ball of fire traveling slowly in a horizontal direction trailed by a strip of lightening that glowed for half an hour after the phenomenon had disappeared.[1]

Tues. 29/11 The barometer has fallen, and, in high seas from the southeast, we are glad that we are out of northern regions. The *Nadezhda* and the *Neva* continually carry the same sails. A lot of small birds seek refuge and a resting place on our ship, all in vain. They can land wherever they want to, and they get pursued by the Japanese, the Kotzebues, and the cats. They are only safe among the cabbages because none of their persecutors dare go overboard.

Today, we passed Gibraltar's latitude. The wind, some of the gentlemen say, is good, because the rolling bothers them. Little does it occur to them that, if there were less wind or even that if it were contrary, the rolling would double.

In the afternoon, Resanoff wanted us to fire the cannons in salute of the Russian flag waving for the first time on the ocean. Krusenstern refused and said we would fire all of the cannons when we crossed the equator. "Ч оти веча не памяти!" [Of course, that will be forgotten] said Resanoff, becoming spiteful and angry.

Wed. 30/12 Resanoff is bickering with Krusenstern. And Tilesius with me. Horner, on the trip to London, would not have personally spent so much if he had not traveled with that fool of a Resanoff, who found a way of getting them all to spend money. Resanoff could not, however, resist trying to persuade Horner to pay for half of the costs of the entire voyage but under conditions, which Horner under no circumstances could agree to. Resanoff has such an instinctive urge to be paid from the extraordinair sums and that at the expense of others.

In Copenhagen, Romberg bought himself a lapdog famous for its ugliness. A sailor bought a young cat in England. Those two animals sleep, eat, and drink together and play so hilariously that we often form a circle around them and simply enjoy it all. In three months, we have sailed 8,000 versts, a twelfth of our voyage. Thus, three years will certainly pass by before we have completed our voyage.

October

Thurs. 1/13 Last evening, we had a beautiful concert accompanied by sheet lightening, squalls, and downpours.

Since Fosse won't give us an accounting of our money, all of us are fermenting, especially since he is still letting us starve. Soon the ice will be broken.

Fri. 2/14 We conducted several experiments with the *aireometer* [sic] to measure the density of the water and with the six thermometers to determine the temperature of the water at the surface and at a depth. Amusement during a calm.

At table, I made the suggestion, to get order in the company cabin, that we follow Emperor Paul's rules. My suggestion was accepted.

Tilesius finally now sees that the voyage is not being undertaken on his account, but that he was given a place on the *Nadezhda* on account of the voyage. He still has not come to terms with his cabin and thus wanders around the ship like a nomad.

Sat. 3/15 Resanoff really would like to be seen as the head of the expedition. Mr. von Krusenstern told him in England, very dryly, that it would sound ridiculous to entrust a chamberlain, undertaking the first sea voyage of his life, with such an expedition. Today, Resanoff was angry because we maintained that we would not be sailing to Madeira.[2] He could not understand wherefore and why, and that made him even angrier. Krusenstern said in a conversation that Lisianski will be sorry because Count Voronzoff has asked him to buy several anchor of wine in Madeira for his table.

"What reasons can you give for our not going to Madeira?" asked Resanoff, "I have to know in order to be able to report to the emperor."

"No other," said Krusenstern, "than ones I have considered good. By the way, the emperor will not care at all to know why we sailed to Tenerife and not to Madeira." Resanoff fell silent.

In the morning, we threw six пуд [pud] of spoiled Hamburg salt meat overboard. As far our meals are concerned, we have agreed that the majority decides who should take turns providing for it. Fosse has had to promise to account for his expenditures, so that we can decide what should be bought in Tenerife. It is Fosse's own fault that we are demanding changes in the way business is carried out.

Sun. 4/16 We passed the latitude of Funchal. It was agreed upon for the voyage that every Sunday clean tablecloths had to be put out. Today, it was Tilesius' turn. He said very coldly that it was not in his contract. I made a lot of coarse remarks to him. Through Horner's mediation, we were getting along with each other again by the afternoon. The group's problems have thus been put off.

Mon. 5/17 We have cleared everything up. I was the main mover behind the decree because I cannot stand disorder. The following was agreed upon: Weekly, two of the company are responsible and provide bills. All difficult matters will be determined, rejected, or changed by a majority vote. Conditions and everything necessary to maintain order will be determined by the entire group and will be written in a book as law. Fosse's bill was very large, but to keep the peace we are overlooking a lot of things.

Tues. 6/18 Every eight weeks, we have to defray costs. We have a great deal of difficulty keeping the things that are subject to spoilage from being declared totally unusable and to determine what should be bought in Tenerife.

At noon, we passed the latitude of Solvages [Savage Islands], and in the evening, we caught sight of the Pic on Tenerife.

Lisianski and Doctor Laband[3] ate lunch with us today.

Today, Horner made a very apt comparison for Tilesius. He compared him with an Orthodox preacher, who puts a very important expression on his face for trivialities while forgetting the main points, someone who acts like he seeks to deny himself all of life's pleasantries, yet quietly is indeed the greatest epicure, despises orgies while being the greatest indulger, strains his face and acts as if he had to use his entire strength, for example, to turn a key where no strength is needed at all, does not know how to use his strength when necessary; in every way and manner he acts childish and ridiculous because, for lack of brains, he never knows how he

2-1. A view of the Piek of Teneriffa, distant from 12 German miles bearing SW declination of the compass being 15′ W [sic]

really should behave in order not to compromise himself. These always touching exertions induce him to commit stupidities that make him ridiculous and give him a worse image than he really deserves.

Wed. 7/19 At the northern tip of Tenerife, a French frigate, armed as a privateer, stopped us and asked us who we were, said the ship was called *l'Egiptien,* was sailing back and forth here, and hurried to catch other ships appearing on the horizon.[4] During the night, we sailed around between the islands of Tenerife and Canaria.

Thurs. 8/20 At eleven o'clock before lunch, we arrived at Santa Cruz' anchorage, were visited by a Spanish officer, who interrogated us and told us where we could fill up water and when fresh provisions could be bought. The French frigate anchored next to us soon afterwards. Tenerife is very civilized, and the city looks quite good. (*See color plate 1.*)

A hurricane is recently supposed to have caused a great deal of damage in Madeira; over 1,000 people are said to have been killed.

In the afternoon, the captain sent me on land to bring his regards to the Governor Marquis Casacagigal [Marquis de la Casa Cahigal]. I was received with the utmost respect. Resanoff did not await my return but rather went on land. Immediately, an officer came onboard with the news that without the strict order and permission of the governor, no one would be allowed on land. Resanoff wanted to have it. Horner had gone with me. Together we happened to visit Mr. Caillieux and Conseque, merchants. There are almost no inns at all in the city. The houses are proper and the streets clean. The inhabitants are either very rich or very poor. Here I saw my first palm trees. The wine is good.

In order to protect the anchor cable from damage, it floats in the water on buoys so that it will not be cut on the sharp rocks sticking up.

I obtained a geranium stem with flowers from Conseque and put it in a pot for Krusenstern to take to Kamtschatka.

Fri. 9/21 Horner is taking advantage of the governor's kind offer to put up an observation post in the city. Today, he went ashore with the chronometer and instruments.

In the afternoon, the French privateer made prizes of two English merchant ships.

We are anchored opposite the fort where Nelson lost his arm.[5] The act of daring did not succeed, and the English were surrounded and taken prisoner but released again by the Spanish without animosity and with a gift of refreshments.

Resanoff went on land again and took all three natural scientists with him, probably in order to have guardians along so he could charge the costs to the Crown. Since, however, Friderici had had to pay his own trip to London, the gentlemen did not go along until Resanoff ordered them to in writing.

In the evening, you get overrun by the rabble. It would be dangerous to venture out alone among them, especially among the bold women.

Sat. 10/22 In the morning, several of our sailors were punished. They had been sent on land to buy bread and fresh greens. All of them left the boat. They had barely left when some Spanish stole our boat and rowed away with it. The Spanish officer at the main guard post was kind enough to return our boat to us.

In the afternoon, Horner, Bellingshausen, and I surveyed the bay by using our ships, the *Neva* and the *Nadezhda,* as a basis.

We had a lot of guests at tea: Mrs. Armstrong with her mother, Mme Couves with her two daughters. The latter had come with her entire fortune from Jole de France and fled to Tenerife when they heard that war had broken out between England and France again. We danced quite a lot in the evening. Mme Armstrong is a frivolous donna. We dined at 9 p.m. and danced a few dances after dinner and accompanied the ladies on land. Tomorrow we are invited to the Armstrong's for tea.

I spoke with Armstrong and his wife before supper. Then Lisianski came up to us and said: "Whoever doesn't want to go to supper has to dance."

"*Go to supper, I like to see you go down* [sic]," said Madame to her husband. Armstrong went down completely satisfied having been caressed on the cheeks, and his wife now really hit him behind, and that was it.

Mr. Linsey, whose brother is a captain in English service, found the wine very much to his taste.

The day before our arrival the governor or viceroy received word of our expedition and at the same time the power of life or death over the lives of the inhabitants of the Canary Islands.

Sun. 11/23 Resanoff returned today from Orotava. Friderici had been kicked by a horse and returned because of his injury. That had annoyed Resanoff, for the bigger his entourage, the more important he thinks himself to be. When he heard that we would not be sailing until Tuesday, he said to Krusenstern: "I am like a prisoner on your ship. Why have you been rushing me unnecessarily? Your original intention was to sail today, and now we are staying two days longer."

They argued with each other for a long time and then went up to Armstrong's together. Madame is a coquette of the highest degree. We played Vingt et un. I won. There was music and singing. Amalie and Delphine Couves conduct themselves very well.

Every one of us has written letters to Russia, and Romberg took over the task of writing Karamsin.[6] That is an expedient idea in order to ensure that our arrival in Tenerife gets into the newspapers.

Mon. 12/24 Today, while standing my watch, I suddenly was robbed of my voice and after coughing a little bit, I spit out a great deal of clotted and fresh blood. I did not feel any pain in my chest, but it was very unpleasant to say the least.

Tilesius does not begrudge Langsdorff anything, did not want to give him any spiritus [alcohol] that he needed. I tried to convince him to give him some, but in vain. Tilesius persisted in his stubbornness. I therefore went to Krusenstern, who finally convinced that mulish chamberlain by polite moralizing to be obliging, even though the spiritus did not belong to him at all.

Casacahigal took no notice of our captains, received them in his office when they called upon him. When Resanoff had returned from Orotava, he was invited to the governor's for lunch along with the captains, who, however, declined the invitation.

Count Tolstoi said at Armstrong's this evening: "We will be sailing tomorrow since everything has been taken onboard ship—water, wine, livestock, and vegetables."

"No," said Resanoff, "We are staying here tomorrow because I still have several matters to arrange with the governor." Lisianski is Mrs. Armstrong's favorite. He is like a cat prancing around a bowl of hot porridge with her.

Tues. 13/25 Krusenstern and Resanoff held an explanatory session in which a lot of truths were said. The discussion was heated enough. Krusenstern went on land and soon afterwards Resanoff and the count. We had barely finished eating on the *Nadezhda* when Tolstoi arrived with a request that we should go to Armstrong's for lunch. We had to turn down the invitation, but we did go in the evening. Played Vingt et un again while Resanoff was talking with Casacahigal, who also had come. The governor treated Resanoff very well, gave him a copy of the ukas [указ: edict] he had received on our account at the Spanish-American possessions, where we would probably arrive before dispatches came from Spain, gave him a special map of Tenerife, a mummy, etc.

Wed. 14/26 We left our фертовины [moorings].

The Spanish here are exceedingly unneighborly. There is an oversupply of fruit and wine but a dearth of bread and meat. Milk, geese, ducks, and wild game are not to be had at all. Goats and chickens are only available at the market. There are enough fish. I paid four Spanish dollars for 25 pieces of laundry. Tenerife is said to be for Spain what Siberia is for Russia. One also finds here more rascally faces than anywhere else.

The work in this heat, especially weighing anchor, is exceedingly strenuous and difficult. Tolstoi stole one of Mrs. Armstrong's handkerchiefs yesterday, and it won't be his fault if today he asks every lady for a souvenir and if she turns him down.

The bills, which Krusenstern has to liquidate, have been held up a bit, and tomorrow the governor has promised to come onboard.

In the evening, we rowed around the roadstead to observe the fishermen while fishing. There are six to eight fellows in every boat and at the end of the boat a big fire. They move like a perpetuum mobile. Every so often they throw some bait to the fish.

We had barely returned onboard when we were brought a letter from Krusenstern, in which he asked us in Armstrong's name to go on land. Since there was to be a ball, we went and happily enjoyed ourselves until midnight. The music was bad, so Romberg took a violin and played a Scottish reel. The Spaniards tried to outscream the violins with their clarinets, so that I spontaneously called loudly: "Piano!" Armstrong's coquettish behavior infected all of the other ladies. I was freer than usual and had a right good time with Delphine. We did not become acquainted with a single Spaniard in Tenerife.

Thurs. 15/27 At ten o'clock, Marquis Casacagigal visited us with a large entourage of officers, and under the Spanish flag. At his departure, we had our sailors по вахтам [at alert] and saluted. The governor went from us to the *Neva,* and the fort answered our salute. Linsey and Smith also visited us, and at two o'clock in the afternoon, we weighed anchor.

The explication between Krusenstern and Resanoff, which had begun on the ship, ended in the following way on land. Resanoff showed Krusenstern a secret указ [edict] of the emperor's in which he named Resanoff the head of the expedition, and he boasted and put on a lot of airs with it. The captain, however, said to him that it was wrong of him to have accepted this указ from the emperor, since he was in no way able to fulfill its conditions, since he should have asked the captains whether they also would have wanted to sail under the command of a chamberlain. Thereupon, Resanoff said in a very friendly manner that he was sorry to have been misunderstood and asked to be pardoned, if anything offensive were contained in his remarks.

One of the prizes that the corsair took belongs to an old Englishman, who had spent his whole life in the West Indies; put the wealth he had acquired in a ship, and was sailing to England to finish his life there. This old man has been robbed of all his hopes and gets his charity bread at the Armstrong's. His white head looks venerable.

Moritz Kotzebue has fallen so in love with little Delphine that, with tears in his eyes, he climbed up to the top of the mainmast so that he might possibly see that beloved girl one more time.

A Spanish merchant ship intended for Rio de la Plata, that was to be kept in quarantine because of several sick crewmembers, decided rather to sail with us, but, since it sailed so poorly, we soon lost it from view.

Fri. 16/28 My spitting up blood has stopped and the hefty dancing at the Armstrong's did me no harm at all. In Santa Cruz, there are two monuments: a big stone cross that gives the city its name and an obelisk to Saint Maria de Pantelaria. The Guanches,[7] as they were called, inhabited the Canary Islands earlier, but now there are absolutely no natives left. Casacagigal, they say, is supposed to be Guanche—a priest's fairy tale.

Sat. 17/29 Our map of the roadstead at Santa Cruz is successful. Even though we are at 26^0 latitude my cloth coat is not too warm. Our sailors are staying very healthy. To all of our joy, they are full cheeked and frisky. Drawing maps is tiring work.

Sun. 18/30 Today, our sailors were divided into three watches. Our housekeeping, done on a weekly basis, is better than expected. Our table is better; expenses have gone down, and general satisfaction has replaced the continual grumblings.

Mon. 19/31 In the evening, we passed the Tropic of Cancer. At noon, Krusenstern had gone to the *Neva*. He related to us that one evening in Santa Cruz the supercargo of the *Neva* had been a bit late, surrounded by common women, and undressed to nakedness.

Every day all possible kinds of observations are being made. On the trip to the botanical garden in Orotava, our traveling companions came across a Moor. Tilesius stopped the African and began to speak Latin with him with such decorum, as if he would have had to understand him. The other gentlemen laughed so hard they had to hold their sides.

To the same degree that our atmosphere is a happy one, it is said to be quiet on the *Neva*. Lisianski, the tyrant, has introduced a strict moral code so that everyone sits in his cabin and broods.

Tues. 20/1 The care which Krusenstern gives our sailors is exemplary. Illnesses are being prevented by good food, appropriate work, dry clothing, clean undergarments, and fumigating under the deck. Here's to contentment; how can you then become ill?

Wed. 21/2 The trade wind is very weak. Flying fish, called bonitos, swarm around our ship. Espenberg always has a complaint; first the tea is too strong for him, then the coffee too weak. When everyone else is dressed, he appears in his dressing gown and shaves where the others are eating breakfast, even though after eight o'clock this is no longer permitted. Today, he used an emetic and acted so wretchedly that we all had to laugh despite ourselves. He thereupon went into Krusenstern's cabin and threw up in front of him. He has his own cabin where he could have thrown up. He alone uses the captain's gallery, but that is the least of what I have against him. No one else finds the inconveniences as unbearable as Espenberg. If the ship rocks a little, he is in a bad mood. He is not on congenial terms with anyone and subject to continual tension, which he himself finds unpleasant and makes him even crabbier. In Tenerife, he overloaded his stomach

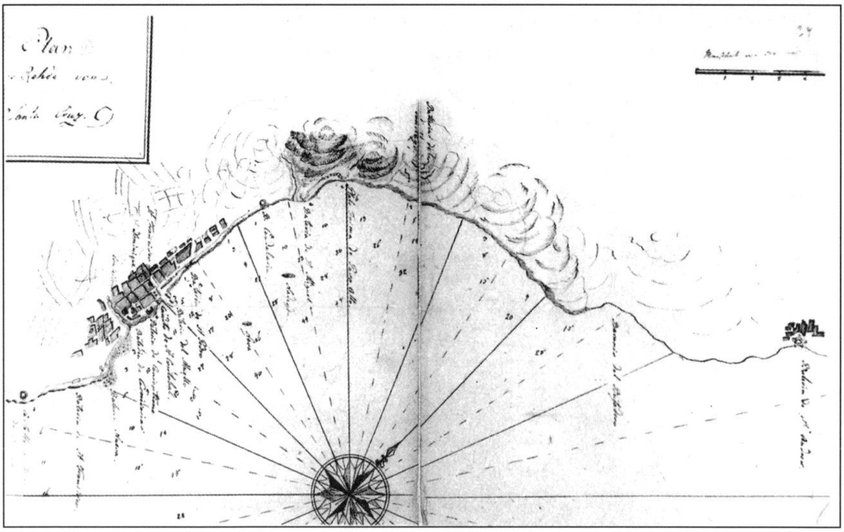

2-2. Plan of the roadstead at Santa Cruz

with fruit and that is why he is now sick. He feels he has learned more than the rest of us but lets us feel it too much through his self-conceit. He is the most unbearable when he becomes angry with himself.

Thurs. 22/3 Still no trade wind. The northwesterly wind is blowing a pleasant coolness our way, but the sea is wearisomely choppy.

Fri. 23/4 As long as you don't need the sun and the moon, they are shining bright and clear. You barely get your instruments out, and the clouds cover them up immediately. If we carry our sextants below, then the roguish moon immediately shines from behind the clouds and makes fools of us. Krusenstern of course had calculated a couple of distances that were worthless because Ratmanoff had written them down incorrectly. Calculating distances is a dreadful business if it has not been practiced enough. The images of the sun and moon dance maddeningly in front of your eyes, then the ship rocks, then a line, then a sail gets in the way.

A little fish, called a pilot, actually quite a few, are always swimming around the ship as if they wanted to show us the way. The ship can sail as fast as she wants to, but our pilots are always ahead of us, playing in the foam in the water caused by the ship. If the sun shines on the flying fish, they are rainbow-colored. Today, we saw a lot of brown fish, a kind of dolphin. They were about one and one-half ell long and jumped man high out of the water in an arch and came so close to the ship that we tried to harpoon one, but in vain.

Sat. 24/5 Lisianski, Laband, and Povalischin dined with us at lunch. Krusenstern doesn't like Ratmanoff reading while on watch. He interrupts him often by giving him petty orders, but our first lieutenant refuses to understand.

Espenberg held his own today and went out for fresh air—in dressing gown, slippers, without trousers, bare throat—on the quarterdeck, probably to catch cold again. It was generally considered inappropriate, and Espenberg went very wretchedly back down below.

Kämpfer's *Voyage to Japan* interests us all at present.[8]

Sun. 25/6 We got a view of St. Anthony, the most westerly of the Cape Verde Islands, about 20 English miles in the distance.

At noon, Resanoff and Krusenstern went over to the *Neva* in order to take part in the church service since we have no priest. I spoke with Horner about our animosities and discovered that there is no place else where men can become so estranged from each other as on a ship. Little annoyances build up; vexation grows bigger and bigger; the necessity of having to deal with the other men causes you to begin to wish they would land at the other end of the world. That can never happen on land. You can prevent it only if you, through strict behavior, prevent disputes and quarrels from arising, see the injustice of your behavior at the right time, and reveal the germ of the discord. If mistrust has crept in, then the step to discord is not very large, and lost is any hope of lifting the tension.

Our loafers Count Tolstoi and Chamberlain Fosse turned the first gambling cards today.

Mon. 26/7 A complete astronomical day: clear skies, pure horizon, sun and moon beautifully in view and at a good distance.

The little puppy came into heat today and a decision was made to throw her overboard. In the dark of the night, the sentence was carried out, and that was the end of our amusement.

Tues. 27/8 Since the small cabins are too dark, everyone works in the company cabin. Today, the following sat around the table covered by a green tablecloth: Resanoff, who was studying the Japanese language and now and then recited loudly. Langsdorff, who was teaching Count Tolstoi and Fosse English, as if they were alone in the cabin. Friderici was drawing a map of Santa Cruz. Tilesius was writing in his journal. Doctor Espenberg was giving the two Kotzebues a lesson in arithmetic and finding they were making a lot of mistakes. Horner was making astronomical calculations. Bellingshausen was drawing the *Nadezhda*. Romberg was leaning against his cabin door playing the violin with a damper. Brinkin was reading Latin half out loud. The painter was leaning against the wall staring vacantly at the goings-on. Since the cacophony was unbearable, I went to my cabin and put everyone's activities on paper. The product of Tilesius' spirit won't amount to much. To his right Romberg is playing something; to his left English is being spelled while at the same time Espenberg is admonishing his pupils to pay attention. Furthermore, everyone coming in and going out has to ask or say something. Then Ratmanoff comes in with the checkerboard and challenges Espenberg to play a game of chess.

Our natural scientists occupy themselves every day with the glow of the water. They still have not reached an agreement about its cause. Glowing animals, fluorescent little pieces of decayed fish, and the like are probably the cause. They cannot say for sure since we still have too little experience. What else is there to do but! but! to argue!

It has been proved that water does not glow. We took a neck scarf and filtered water through it. The water lost its power to glow and the scarf was glowing and covered with small transparent animals, jelly fish, etc., which Langsdorff observed microscopically.

Wed. 28/9 The little cat does not stop looking for the little dog in all of the cabins and crannies of the ship and ends her journey usually with pitiful meowing, as if she were calling her playmate. You're looking in vain, good little animal.

One of our pigs happened to get loose and jumped overboard away from the ship. Курганов [Kurganov] quickly took his jacket off and jumped into the water, caught the pig and rode it back to the ship. The animal swam so easily and washed itself so clean that we decided to bathe the rest of the pigs. The obscene squeals of the pigs would have been enough to drive anyone away, but one after another the others pushed forward to watch the others swimming. The wind was very still, and one after the other the pigs went overboard. The animals were very frightened when thrown from that quite high distance into the water, but we were doing them a favor to clean them up from all the filth and let them cool down in the water.

Thurs. 29/10 Finally, the trade wind is blowing. The heat is quite intense all day and all night so that we never stop sweating. 13° northern latitude. Since we have so little movement, we have introduced the last tack that has to be done before sunset. Then, totally exhausted and tired, we flee into the company cabin to rest up in that sanctuary.[9]

Fri. 30/11 In the afternoon, a lot of bonitos swam in front of our ship. Tarass, born in Archangel, practiced in catching meat, harpooned one. While cleaning it, we found a fresh flying fish in its stomach.

Langsdorff has discovered 10 kinds of microscopic animals that glow, have, however, no scales whatsoever, or lifeless bodies. If the water is warmed up, the glowing stops.

Tilesius is busy drawing and doing it well; indeed, on a good day, he never fails to empty several cups of punsch[10] at tea.

Sat. 31/12 We are sailing 7 knots in the most beautiful of weather on a very calm sea.

November

Son. 1/13 Espenberg is in optima forma. He is playing cards.

Mon. 2/14 Lightning reached from here to the zenith. Today, a butterfly that probably came onboard as a cocoon flew out of a head of cabbage. That poor thing must have been surprised the day it saw light to find itself in a flowerless world. Ignoring the friendly motions of its feelers, Langsdorff stuck it on a pin. Without having enjoyed life, it was robbed of it.

Tues. 3/15 Thunderstorms and variable weather. We had very strong thunderstorms with gusts of wind and endless rain. The squalls that tattered our light sail made us nervous in the evening. The work on the deck, the raging elements are making our passengers more than a little nervous.

Wed. 4/16 Today, Resanoff reprimanded Tolstoi, because on account of the heat, he came to table in his shirt. Horner made the remark today that, if we live in peace together in this hot climate, we will stay good friends for the entire voyage. True enough, we have all become more irritable in the heat.

Tilesius argued very heatedly with Horner and Langsdorff about physics, something he knows nothing about; and those are always the most heated arguments.

Espenberg fumigated the hold or фор люк [fore hatchway]. The smoke caused the navigator's watch and the painter's silver buckles to turn black. Barely had he heard about it when Resanoff was beside himself, since he thought that all of the presents for the emperor of Japan might have been damaged. Luckily, inspection showed this was not the case, and His Excellency calmed down again.

The painter painted several landscapes that we of course also saw, but he did them so poorly that none of us could recognize them, not even the Pic de Teide on Tenerife.

Resanoff let the word drop at table today as if he were начальник [commander of the expedition]. Everything suddenly was silent. As if on signal, without saying a word, everyone got up from the table.

The little cat has also fallen overboard.

Resanoff was the assistant to the head of the Russian-American Company. Even though the emperor knew him, he had no particular advantage through rank or intrigue, tried to damage Novosilzoff,[11] perhaps even topple him. Because of this, the ministers took notice of him and Rumianzoff suggested he be sent as ambassador to Japan. Resanoff accepted the post and said he would gladly serve his fatherland without salary or reward and landed in his own trap. Then he began to ask for support. From only a few did he get any salary and table money. Academics and officers were to accompany him. He obtained for himself an ukas from the emperor naming him head of the expedition and yet was only presented to the emperor after he had received the Order of St. Anne. Instead of making the ukas known in Kronstadt, he first showed it to the captain in Tenerife. Despite the fact that the emperor had signed the document, Krusenstern told him, "I shall never recognize you as my superior because you do not understand the requirements of the post."

Thurs. 5/17 After a very strong downpour, countless numbers of fish were swimming around in the water. With a lucky cast of the harpoon, we got a big shark with two small suckers attached to it. It wasn't enough that we had harpooned it; we had to hit it over the head with an axe before we killed it. When we began to clean it, it snapped at one of the sailors and scratched him on his leg. Intermittent calms, downpours, and gusts of wind with oppressive heat. After a downpour, the whole ship smokes. With each downpour, we collect several casks of water that can be used for washing. Our natural scientists caught a frigate medusa today. This jelly-like polyp kind of creature is very beautifully colored.

My sisters had shirts made for me to take on the voyage. Jettchen[12] had left her own mark on one she had sewn herself. Today, I put that shirt on and sank into sweet reverie, and through memories my imagination became so active that I forgot to stand my watch.

Fri. 6/18 The change in the temperature during the day and at night probably can cause a trade wind that has to blow toward the sun or behind it, and [another cause can be] the faster movement of the earth at the equator than at the poles. That is why in the north a northeasterly trade wind blows and in the south a southeasterly; otherwise, the wind would have to blow straight from the east. At the equator, there is rain, cloudy skies, squalls, and calms. That is the quarrel of the northeasterly and southeasterly trade winds when they meet, driving mists and clouds together which mutually check each other and do battle in rain, squalls, and calms. The quarrel of the trade winds stretches from 5^0 to 7^0 on each side of the equator.

If you capture an animal, you are happy to be able to satisfy your curiosity but even happier when you set the animal free. That is not done here. If a fish is caught, Langsdorff stuffs it. If a bird is caught, the hunter gets it to stuff. Insects and worms are immediately stuck on pins and anything that cannot be stuffed, pinned, or dried is put into *spiritus*.

Sat. 7/19 The подшкипер [mate] complained today about the sailmaker Павел Семенов [Pavel Semenov]. The latter had said to him, "What counts as justice here, I'll take you and throw you overboard." The sailmaker got 12 blows of the cat[13] for this misdemeanor. The shame of it is worse than the punishment, for he carries the name cat until someone else takes it over from him. Since our people are ruled by forbearance, it is practical, if punishment must be meted out, to use an appropriate procedure, as was the case today.

Because of calms, we have only sailed 20 English miles in three days.

I sleep seven hours, use an hour for lunch, one for supper, six hours a day for my watch, two hours pass in drinking coffee and tea and smoking. I need three hours a day for observations and to write in my journal, but often I have to count on more time. If I have had night watch, I sleep for an hour in the afternoon. A couple of hours are spent in talking and walking around, etc., and I am continually interrupted so that not much time is left over.

Sun. 8/20 Even though the sea is running high, no one is seasick, and everyone has a healthy appetite. The horizon is always filled with threatening clouds that frequently wet us through. Evenings, the lightning plays around on the entire horizon and in the dark of the night is doubly beautiful. I made a mistake in thinking that there always has to be good weather at the equator.

Today, Tilesius just happened to be presented with a platter of meat from both sides. He turned down the one with less on it, but just at that moment the servant continued with the other one. I then said: "You are taking the bird in the bush for the one in your hand." My Aulic Councilor held that against me, even though he normally takes a joke well, and began to rail and became impolite. After the meal, I told him that that was the last time there would be any jokes between us; he should kindly leave me in peace. I would no longer be on speaking terms with him. Today, the first hand of Boston[14] was played.

Mon. 9/21 Today, our passengers were united in the opinion that service at sea is much more difficult than service on land. Right after that there was a hefty downpour, and our gentlemen, like the swallows, crept back into their cabins.

Tues. 10/22 The humidity caused by the frequent rains and murky weather has become unbearable. Everything is rotting, molding, rusting, and spoiling. Most of the clothing is wet, and there is no dry weather to help dry them out. If the sun comes out from behind a cloud, then everyone carts out his belongings to let them dry out, and the whole ship is hung with clothes and bedding.

Today is the eighth day we have been working on two degrees latitude. It looks bad with our rations. Before we reach Brazil, we will certainly be on a diet of salt meat.

We met an American ship whom we gave a lot of letters. The ridiculous thing about it is that the American ship from Baltimore is sailing for Batavia[15] and will deliver our letters at the Cape of Good Hope. This little diversion was very useful. Everyone could shake out his heart's desires in a letter and felt relieved. And forgotten were calms, downpours and squalls. Barely had it been said whoever wanted to write a letter should do so when all were busily writing. And in a flash! fifteen letters were finished!

Wed. 11/23 The results of the hot climate and continually sweating at night in the tremendous heat and the necessity of getting out of bed to go on watch in a downpour are that I feel tired, sleepy, listless, and incapacitated; and the pipe tobacco also tastes bad.

Thurs. 12/24 Hiazinth Murat, who made the voyage with Marchand as lieutenant[16] was in Santa Cruz, the captain of a French East Indian ship. We made the acquaintance of this kind man in Tenerife.

The whole morning the sky was covered with black clouds that brought us a lot of rain and a favorable wind. We filled six large casks with water. Since arriving in rainy regions, not a watch has passed on which I did not become completely wet. I do not even try to protect myself from the rain any more. I also do not have any dry clothing left that I can put on.

Resanoff read to us part of his instructions today, which are very clear and written by him and confirmed by the emperor. Probably he wants to let us know how important he is.

This cloudy, wet weather at the equator must appear to be a stripe, which divides the earth in two, like Jupiter's stripe.[17]

Fri. 13/25 In the beginning, the restless, unsettled life on shipboard prevented our passengers from working. They did nothing. If one got busy, he was surrounded by the idlers who bothered him. Now all are busy: Kiseleff is teaching Resanoff Japanese; Langsdorff, Fosse and the Kotzebues English; Espenberg is giving Friderici and the Kotzebues French lessons; Bellingshausen is giving Horner Russian lessons; even Count Tolstoi is taking lessons in arithmetic and geometry from Bellingshausen. Krusenstern, Horner, and I are making astronomical calculations. Tilesius is drawing his fish and the painter his handiwork and paints us an x before all.[18] Watches pass like hours.

Sat. 14/26 We waited impatiently for noon today. After we had calculated our latitude, we found that we were six minutes south of the equator. The ship's bell had barely rung when the *Neva* turned, sailed past us, and gave us three cheers which, touched, we returned. Why we were all moved to tears we did not know ourselves. Kurganoff was dressed as Neptune, and, after Krusenstern had baptized him, he was given the duty of baptizing his comrades. You could see from the costume that our Neptune was a Russian, because he had decorated himself in sheepskins that had been put out to dry on the forecastle; and, ignoring the fact that he was dying from the heat, he did not turn down the brandy offered him by others. The first to drink a glass too much and have to lie down was our Neptune.

Resanoff gave every sailor a Spanish dollar in the name of the emperor. Lisianski was invited to lunch but did not come, and so everyone went to eat except for my little self because I had watch.

Eleven cannons were fired to the emperor's health and seven to the empress' health. No health was forgotten, and everyone had several to drink to. After the meal, Krusenstern was raised on hands for three cheers. Then Resanoff had to have the same honor. And unexpectedly we watch-keeping lieutenants also got our turn to be whipped into the air like we could have turned a salto morale.[19] Resanoff was completely drunk, and "Hurrah for Krusenstern!" was the only thing he could babble. Everyone was happy and joyous, and only the *Nadezhda* was sober. The noise lasted until late into the evening when finally everyone threw himself into Morpheus' arms.[20]

Sun. 15/27 Beautiful southeasterly trade wind with an unusual current to the west which forced us to hold to the wind.

Mon. 16/28 A cold reef topsail wind. Ignoring all advice, the gentlemen who have been sleeping on the quarterdeck were very stiff early this morning and warmed themselves up with great difficulty by drinking warm tea.

Large numbers of mackerels, tuna fish, sharks, and flying fish are swimming around the ship. At night, they light up like fiery points in the water. Our trident is not succeeding in hitting a fish.

According to an order Krusenstern issued us officers in Kronstadt, Ratmanoff was to fulfill the duties of the eldest lieutenant. Ratmanoff did not know what was meant by *first leutenant* [sic], had also never been in England. His absurdities and lack of education made Krusenstern's intentions inappropriate in trying to use him as an assistant. He also had little theoretical knowledge. But then the order had been given. He tried to encourage our passion for work. Golovatscheff, a hustler and flatterer, gained the captain's attention by seemingly being industrious. Romberg and I, we often felt the captain's partiality but did not let ourselves become discouraged. Golovatscheff's biting answers and his remarks, as if he were the one doing everything, have caused a coldness between us that is oppressive. Bellingshausen, who could very well take over his own watch, is still on my watch, and that is cause for dissatisfaction. We all find the tension unpleasant and yet one that none of us can do anything about.

Tues. 17/29 We have had to reduce our rations because we only have a few animals and poultry left. Three times a week we have salt meat. That's why today was doubly pleasant since five tuna fish or mackerel were caught.

The ship lists strongly to the side because of the brisk wind and prevents activities in the company cabin.

Gulls and albatrosses swarm around the ship even though we are very far from land.

Wed. 18/30 Since the ship lists continually to one side, I am robbed of the daylight in my cabin, because I dare not open my port—I miss it [the daylight] very much.

The tuna fish or mackerels are actually called bonitos—in French santeurs.

This morning we all felt exceedingly hungry, got a knife, and set to work on a ham that was hanging on the back of the ship. The fun of cutting off a piece, the battle for the peppershaker, the greedy grabbing, the lack of manners in the affair (since we could have had the ham put on a plate and taken into the cabin) spurred us on even more. I am afraid that that poor ham will feel how good our breakfast tasted, for now not even the devil keeps us from visiting that ham as long as a scrap of meat is still to be had.

Thurs. 19/1 The population of the water must be indescribably large and exceed that of land by a great deal. Fish swarm around us. How large indeed is the ocean!

The flying fish, a kind of herring, rise out of the water in swarms and fly quite a stretch along the surface of the water. Pursued by bonitos, they try to save their lives by flying away but find open mouths again and again in front of them when they plunge into the water. In the air, they are pursued by frigate birds, gulls, and albatrosses which gulp down many a fish in the air that wants to escape its pursuers.

On a ship at sea, arguments dare not be carried on very long. We are too dependent upon each other. The quarrel between Resanoff and Count Tolstoi in Copenhagen had been followed by several others. In Tenerife, Tolstoi had a complete falling out with our Chamberlain, and several abusive words had completed the break.

Today, Resanoff, totally unexpectedly, went up to Tolstoi and talked everything over in such a very polite manner that all past incidents were forgot and harmony returned once again.

Fri. 20/2 Krusenstern became ill this evening. Immediately, Resanoff secretly met with Ratmanoff and told him he should ask Krusenstern for the instructions and orders so that no duties would be neglected. I heard this conversation by chance because I had watch and the gentlemen could not talk secretly any place else but on the quarterdeck.

Sat. 21/3 Everyone is happy and satisfied because Krusenstern is well once again.

In the morning, we hauled in all the sails, ванты [shrouds], and штагы [stays], which had become very badly buffeted in the heat and strong winds.

Sun. 22/4 Ratmanoff babbles incoherently so much stupidity that it is becoming irritating. Today, the captain, who had watch and whose turn it was to provide for the table, had curry made, i.e., rice with mustard, pepper, and spices with the meat, a kind of pilaf. Ratmanoff made all kinds of improper jests about the food, so that Krusenstern, after the meal, stated that his duties were piling up and he would have to be pardoned for giving up providing for the meals in the future. That is exactly what the redhead wanted![21]

Mon. 23/5 Today, Resanoff demanded that Tilesius give him a duplicate of every specimen he had researched and the same of Horner. "Friderici," he said, "I am demanding the sea journal from Krusenstern." We'll see how his orders are carried out.

At noon, Krusenstern, Tolstoi, and Golovatscheff went over to the *Neva*. Because Tolstoi had forgotten to ask Resanoff for permission, His Excellency took strong offense, and Tolstoi received a reprimand upon his return.

Tues. 24/6 Today, Resanoff, who would like to get at Krusenstern, said in a very loud voice: "The American Company has promised the captains 10,000 rubles upon their return. The gentlemen will however have a great deal of trouble getting anything, because their accounts are so confused and complicated that the auditing that will have to be done will cost even more."

Resanoff judges others indeed by his own behavior. Krusenstern, who got wind of this remark, has become more attentive and keeps accounts much more exactly.

In the morning, there was a shapeless short rainbow on the horizon: a prophet of the winds, which indeed brought us quite strong favorable gusts of wind.

The provisions bought by the American Company are bad. Since prikaschtschick Schemelin had not looked after them at all, Krusenstern gave him a reprimand today. That fellow is in every way a complete Russian shop clerk, whom Resanoff uses according to his desires.

Anecdote: Lisianski's creature is Mitschmann[22] Berg. In a written order Lisianski had given a specific day on which people had permission to wash their clothes. Afterwards, Lisianski discovered that during Kovedeeff's watch a sailor had done laundry at another time. Kovedeeff received a reprimand for not following orders. Then Lisianski had the entire crew and all of the officers called to the deck; the scribe or клерк [clerk] came and read his приказен [orders] aloud. While this was done, Arbusoff paced back and forth on the deck.

Lisianski, very irritated, went up to him and said to him very brusquely: "You know that your captain's orders are being read; and it is your duty not to disturb attention by walking around; and it is your duty to follow these orders." Without waiting for Arbusoff's answer, he sent for the mate and had the incident put in the ship's journal. He took Arbusoff's watch and gave it to Mitschmann Berg. He had the incident entered in the journal and by name stated that Arbusoff had been taken from watch due to rudeness toward the captain. Mitschmann Berg signed the journal. Kovedeeff and Povalischin said straight out that they considered the captain's behavior unfair and therefore would not sign. Then Lisianski came and asked Arbusoff to pardon him: nice satisfaction, especially since Arbusoff only undertook the voyage after Lisianski's earnest and urgent supplication.

Wed. 25/7 We looked in vain today for the Isle de l'Ascension or Trinidad whose existence La Pérouse doubted.[23] After we had reached the latitude of the island, we sailed to the west with a very brisk wind, but completely in vain.

The surest way of taming Resanoff is if, when the wind is brisk at the time, I (as the good Juttchen[24] likes to say, from the desire to tease) tell him when the wind is brisk at the time about the dangers at Cape Horn. If we have good weather and the ship is quiet, then you cannot get anything going with him. Then he immediately has status or rank and intrigues in his head.

My geraniums are coming along nicely.

The only ones complaining about boredom are Ratmanoff and Councilor Fosse, the former quartal officer.

Horner brought out his compendieuse [compact], iron lathe, in order to repair a screw that was damaged. In vain, he was not able to do any work at all. All of his tools were examined, tested, and damaged. Fosse behaved shamelessly. Horner asked him not to ruin his tools after he had broken the point of a chisel, and then Fosse became very defensive.

The whole night we looked ourselves blind for the Island of Trinidad; but God knows where it is, just not here.

Thurs. 26/8 Resanoff (the Russian Pinetti,[25] as they call him in Petersburg) has told several of us confidentially that he had complained about Krusenstern from Tenerife and reported that the farther we are from Europe the more the proper respect that he [Resanoff] deserves is lost.

Our society can be divided into three groups: 1. The intriguers Resanoff, Ratmanoff, Fosse, the painter Kurlandzoff, and Friderici against his will. 2. The workers: Krusenstern, Horner, Bellinghausen, Espenberg, and my own little self and Romberg. 3. The phlegmatics Count Tolstoi, Golovatscheff, Brinkin, Tilesius, and Langsdorff. The ones of no consequence are Schemelin, the two Kotzebues, and Kamentschikoff.

Every day, Resanoff seeks out something new to anger our captain with. The result of that is that Krusenstern has a headache again today and does not feel well, certainly the result of suppressing his anger.

Resanoff now gives his instructions to everyone in secret. Several of us have requested the captain to bring the matter out into the open and to demand that the Japanese scoundrel put in writing what he has been claiming in secret—we'll see what happens.

Schemelin, at Resanoff's instigation and on his orders, as he admitted himself, went to Krusenstern in his cabin and demanded from the captain an accounting for boards, which had been purchased at the expense of the American Company in Tenerife. He had observed that the officers used them as if they were their property and he considered it his duty to inquire about them. You have to know Schemelin in order to judge the effect of this speech on Krusenstern. At first, he laughed at the impertinence of the question, rebuked him heftily, forbade him to make any similar remarks in the future, explained to him in no uncertain terms the difference between a reputable man and a scoundrel, became however silently very angry about the incident.

Fri. 27/9 In the evening, Krusenstern gave up trying to find the island of Ascension.

Golovatscheff has flattered himself into Resanoff's confidence, and they often share secrets. I know from a third party, Bellingshausen, that Resanoff said to Golovatscheff: "We have some hotheads here on the ship, who take a lot of liberties. In the short or long run I will catch them and show them whom they are dealing with." (Horner and I undoubtedly belong to the hotheads.)

Resanoff is a big braggart and plagues me with his tales. When I stand watch, very often using some kind of pretence, I leave him standing there without enough time to finish his tale. He would get a peevish look on his face, tell me again on my next watch about his heroic deeds.

Today, we heard by chance that the emperor had graciously granted officers permission to buy goods with their little bit of money and bring them on the shipboard. Resanoff has still not told a one of us about this permission.

Sat. 28/10 Krusenstern had another altercation today with Resanoff about what power that the paper with the emperor's signature might have. Resanoff answered: "You may do or not do whatever you want to. You are the master of doing or not doing. I'm master of these papers." The discussion, or rather, argument continued for a long time.

Count Tolstoi, who came into the cabin and was drawn into the conversation, told Resanoff straight to his face: "You told me yourself that you had complained about the captain from Santa Cruz and that the audit upon our return would show a larger sum than the promised one and that the captains would count more upon their illicit business dealings than upon the promised sum."

The chamberlain denied the first charge by his protocol letter. He was silent about the second charge and said to Tolstoi: "I told you that in confidence."

"You can say that about Friderici if you want to," answered Tolstoi, "but not about me."

We were all happy to see the captain come on deck without inner anger and vexation. He had said what he had to say. Resanoff shies from the daylight like envy and appears less often.

We hauled down our old meritorious sail in order to replace it with a steadier one. In several places, the old sail was like gauze, it was so frayed.

Sun. 29/11 Krusenstern was the originator of this whole expedition and is recognized as its leader in all of Europe. He left his wife and child and a happy life for the sake of renown in order to make a name for himself and to be useful to his family. Only with Krusenstern's agreement could the embassy to Japan come about, and we left Russia in the firm conviction that Resanoff was a passenger onboard. For the first time, in Tenerife, Resanoff produced the ukas with the Imperial signature, in which he was named the leader of the expedition, thereby suddenly robbing the captain of the incentives on whose account he had left his fatherland. Despite the lack of meaning of this piece of paper in Resanoff's hands, it was nevertheless still unpleasant. If Resanoff should be of a mind to use his full authority and our captain would call upon his instructions and not want to turn over the ship to him, then Resanoff will be on the short end of things for the time being, for we all would willingly sign anything Krusenstern requested.

It is tricky to determine the meridian if the latitude of a place equals the divergence. The azimuth of the meridian changes quite quickly, and the sun, supposedly standing still, does not do so. Our shadows are completely covered by the hats on our heads. The speaking trumpet between my fingers casts a ring as a shadow.

At eight in the evening, we found bottom at 120 faden, fine sand with little pebbles.

Mon. 30/12 Early in the morning, we caught sight of Cape Frio thirty English miles away. We were surrounded by dolphins, which in good weather we had observed in our spare time. It is not possible to describe the changing colors of these fish: blue, green, golden yellow, and countless mixtures of these colors continually alternate with each other. A dolphin or blue fish was harpooned. It was over three fuss long, but soon lost its beautiful colors. To Langsdorff's joy, we also used a capture sack to get a lot of very tiny zinobarred crabs.

Yesterday and today, the sun did not let us determine the meridian.

Langsdorff and Friderici are greedy for animals and plants. If someone captures something and gives it to them, they are not ashamed of to claim that they caught it, as if that would make it theirs even more. Today, Bellingshausen caught a water insect. Friderici took it to inspect and kept it. A dispute arose and turned into hard words: "You are lying" and "Shut up!" which, granted, sounds better in Russian, as if Friderici were ashamed to thank a man who had gladly given him the little animal for a friendly face. Friderici stood by his claims: "I caught it and claim it. The insect belongs to me, etc.," he said.

Lisianski dined with us today at noon.

Resanoff did not stir from the company cabin because he was afraid of an altercation with Lisianski.

December

Tues. 1/13 Although a summer day, it is acting quite Russian. On my night watch, I had to wear my capote [soldier's greatcoat], proof enough that the Southern Hemisphere is colder than the northern. If the air till Cape Horn cools down, we will undoubtedly welcome furs and tulubben [sheepskin coat] in the summer there.

We saw two fishing boats today that made no move to come out to us.

Wed. 2/14 Shortly after noon, one of our sailors caught a 3½ -fuss-long dolphin. We bought it from the sailor and left the fish. While we were discussing how we should prepare it, in full view on the deck, Langsdorff and Tilesius, like a couple of hungry wolves, threw themselves all over the fish. Langsdorff, for the life of him, wanted to have it stuffed, but the hungry ones of us would not have that. Then the fish was inspected for lice and insects that had attached and sucked themselves onto the fish. Langsdorff collected over a dozen of them and did not want to give Tilesius, who was busy sketching the fish, even one of them. That is how jealous and selfish those two are toward each other.

In the evening, we practiced shooting muskets with the sailors and discovered that they know almost nothing about muskets.

Card playing has become livelier. The players are Espenberg, Ratmanoff, Golovatscheff, Tolstoi, and also sometimes Fosse. In half an hour or less, they win from each other 50 dahler in горка [gorka]. There are often little disputes.

Thurs. 3/15 Krusenstern has asked Tilesius to sketch his canary birds so that he may send their likeness to his wife.

We absolutely cannot convince our painter, who is mainly a portrait painter, that the main thing about painting a landscape is the accurate portrayal of nature. He always sticks in so much of his own composition that we cannot recognize the spot again.

Tilesius only uses watercolors, remains true to nature, and paints very rapidly.

We irritate Kurlandzoff a great deal by saying, if he does not paint a true picture of nature, then none of his pictures will be able to be etched in copper.

The determination for St. Catharina is wrong by two degrees longitude. We cast our lead without success.

Fri. 4/16 We are busily lashing down our anchor cables and making our longboats that have dried together useful again. Today, we still have not caught sight of land.

When we anchor, the officers among us are looking at a lot of work in order to prepare the ship for Cape Horn: checking tackle and sails, taking two months worth of provisions out of the hold, filling the hold with water, lowering most of our cannons into the hold, procuring fresh provisions for us, etc.

Our passengers are extremely happy to be going on land soon.

- 3 -

Santa Catharina

Sat. 5/17 During the night, we tacked around, and in the morning at 9 o'clock we sighted land. Since we do not have a map of St. Catharina, we felt like we were before a newly discovered land. Only La Pérouse and Lord Anson[1] are in agreement about St. Catharina. Thus, we had to sail along the coast to inspect the country more exactly. At 12 o'clock, we were just as smart as before. Then the skies clouded over and it began to rain and the fog robbed us of the view of land. At five o'clock, we caught sight of the northern tip of the island but had to spend the night at sea again in order to be safe in case bad weather set in again. Our passengers kept asking endlessly if we would soon anchor, especially Espenberg wouldn't quit asking, even though he turns sour if you ask him how his patients are doing and similar things.

Our entire wealth consists of twelve chickens. We caught a frigate medusa today whose feeler-tentacles were over ten faden long. The animal resembles a hand-sized blister and is decorated with the most beautiful colors. The long tentacles are used for obtaining food and for defense. If you touch them with your hand, they burn like nettles. The tentacles were filled with half-digested sea insects caught in them.

Sun. 6/18 We approached land in good weather but too weak wind. At noon, we were located at 47° 3' west longitude and 26° 52' south latitude; and we discovered that the islands we had seen yesterday were Alvaredo and Galles; and behind them is the land that must be St. Catharina. The air filled with approaching rain and a thunderstorm, and an approaching squall forced us again to take our distance, *to clear the Lee shore* [sic]. The map we have drawn is quite successful since all of the angles and measurements we took came together.

Today is Неколин день [Nikolin Day],[2] once again a day that is not easy to forget. We had set all of the sails when we heard a strong thunderstorm developing, and the entire land was covered by a black cloud. Countless numbers of butterflies fluttered around our ship; even gulls and other sea birds sought protection

3-1. Santa Cruz in Brazil

from the approaching danger. We quickly hauled in all unnecessary sails and headed toward the east. We had just lashed down the topgallant sail when a gust of wind tossed the ship on her side. With difficulty we had just hauled in the mainsail and foresail when we had to lower the topsail, because the wind was howling so unbelievably strongly. In less than two hours, we had all sails hauled in, let down the topgallant and upper masts, had the stormsail attached and raised, and sailed as best we could in that wind, glad that the land was at our backs. Around twelve at night, the *Neva* came для перовору [for a conference] because her foremasts had been damaged, but she also came so close that we did not miss crashing into each other by much. In such high seas, we probably would not have been able to sail apart again.

Mon. 7/19 Toward noon, the wind died down. We exchanged our sails tattered by the bad weather for others, attached them, and sailed onwards with them so as not to fall prey to the swollen seas. Our passengers were inconsolable. Instead of amusing themselves in Brazil, they were letting themselves be unpleasantly knocked around.

Resanoff said: "I am surprised that it is possible to sail along a coast for so long without finding the harbor entrance. What is going to happen in Japan, if we are having so many difficulties in a known area?" Romberg had heard Resanoff's remark and loudly tightened the screws on him in the company cabin, because he knew that Resanoff was sitting with Friderici in his cabin. When he heard that, he came out and could not stop praising our successful voyage, that we had lost no sails, no ropes had ripped, etc. The false dog!

Our Japanese have been healed of all their pretensions, have friendly expressions on their faces when we greet each other, and carry on a quiet life to themselves.

Since the weather has improved, we are again sailing westwards.

Tues. 8/20 At morning twilight, we caught sight of land, found ourselves about twenty English miles to the north, and had contrary winds. Only at about two o'clock in the afternoon did we again reach the spot we had had to leave before the storm and inspected the coast more exactly; and only now will we be able to attempt to sail into the entrance.

Today, I finally worked. In the morning, we determined the height of the sun and the determination of time. At noon we calculated the height of the meridian, and for both we put a point on our map. From three spots on the ship, we surveyed land and immediately calculated it, taking the azimuth of the sun with the land, observed the several distances of the moon and the azimuth to determine the deviation of the compass. Then I had my watch and enjoyed the evening, since I had been on my legs continually since sunrise. It had been a long time since my pipe tobacco had tasted so good.

At five o'clock, a boat came sailing up to us. The captain had a cannon fired. Not long afterwards the boat tied up to the *Neva*. Krusenstern sent Bellingshausen over to the *Neva* and had the people brought onboard. They were Portuguese, even though in shirts, proper and clean. Their boat had been hollowed out of a tree trunk. Langsdorff, who speaks Portuguese very well, acted as interpreter. Two of the Portuguese remained onboard to act as pilots to direct us into St. Catharina. Since it was, however, already too late, we spent the night at sea. We had judged the land very correctly. A lot of comments will be made about us for sailing in with pilots.

Wed. 9/21 I had night watch. At sunrise, we sailed with a brisk wind straight for land. I went to bed in the expectation that, when I woke up I would find the *Nadezhda* in front of the entrance. I had just lain down when the wind changed, became contrary; and upon waking up I found the *Nadezhda* in full tack. Our pilot assured us that the wind would become favorable toward noon. Soon we will have dear trouble with our passengers, as if it were possible to give each one his own boat.

Our pilot was right. We had barely determined the latitude as 27°6' south when the wind turned. All of our passengers were tying up their bundles before it was time. Packing is going on all over the company cabin. Dr. Espenberg pulled out one of his old vests; and, when he put it on, it almost went around his shrunken body twice, he had lost so much weight.

We passed the Island Alvaredo and Galles, sailed down the bay, and anchored at seven in the evening in 7 to 10 faden opposite the little fort of Santa Cruz, twelve English miles from the city of Nossa Senhora do Desterro,[3] because foreign ships are not allowed to sail closer. The captain sent me to the fort from whence an officer came out to meet me. The officer asked me for the name of the ship, etc., and told us we could not begin to do anything until the following evening, because we first had to be visited by customs and obtain the permission of the governor to go ashore. We began immediately to unrig the ship. Even though foodstuffs are offered for sale, the inhabitants immediately raise the prices if they believe that one absolutely needs them. Two Englishmen, anchored here in their privateer, gave us this news. In addition, it is not the season for green goods and fruit. Neither the Portuguese nor the Englishmen knew which country they should assign us to. One of the Englishmen, who has been living here for the past ten months and claims to be bursting from the fat of the land, lives here *for the benefit of his health* [sic]. Self-interest is probably the driving reason, as well as privateering.

Thurs. 10/22 Lowered all of our boats into the water.

Resanoff, by virtue of his power of attorney, issued the captain an order not to permit Count Tolstoi to go on land without giving a reason for his being so severely punished. Fosse and the painter began loudly to complain about Tolstoi from the quarterdeck, saying: "He has earned being left here," etc. The captain rejected Resanoff's demand immediately. No one could be surprised that the strife (since you could no longer call it a dispute) between the two had never before been so heated. Among other things, Resanoff said: "If this is the way you act, you won't say anything if someone hits me in the face" and several other such absurd remarks. Resanoff angrily went into town with his entourage when Lisianski went to pay respects to the governor.

In the afternoon, I stepped for the first time upon Brazil's very fertile shore in order to find a place to pitch our tents and seek out useful fresh water. Climbed around for a long time in the wilderness and returned onboard after a couple of hours, exhausted. Brazil is a beautiful country!

Fri. 11/23 Today, to our great joy, we got two steer carcasses.

The fertility of the land is admirable. Everything that can only be grown at home in greenhouses grows wild here: lemons, oranges, pineapples, aloe, cactus, etc.

In the morning, Senhore Adolpho, a German who has been living here for twenty-five years, arrived onboard with several turkeys and fruit. To our joy he is taking over the task of having our black laundry washed.[4]

At noon, the captain returned from the city; he had had to row for six hours.

In the afternoon, Mr. Lang gave us a guided tour of the area. Our Adolpho is named Lang.

Cultivation has contributed nothing. Everything grows wild: coffee, indigo, and an excess of plants and trees that none of us had ever seen before—the countless quantities of unknown objects made it even inhospitable. We will undoubtedly fill up our water supply at a quite good overshot stampmill.

The *Neva*'s foremast is rotten and damaged. She will undoubtedly have to have a new one made.

Sat. 12/24 At ten o'clock, I went into the main city on St. Catharina Nossa Signora del Desterro; and, since the current and wind were favorable, I arrived in two hours. Near the city, the Island is divided from land by a 200-faden-wide channel filled with scattered rocks and reefs that make passage from the south impossible. The governor is named Curado. The black slaves offered for sale at the marketplace like cattle are an unpleasant sight.

Life here is expensive for Tilesius and Friderici. Per day they have to pay five Spanish dahler for housing and maintenance in a private home, since the inns are so bad. At noon, I ate with them and saw that the two pretty daughters of the house would probably bind my shipmates to these quarters with their friendliness. The houses are all poorly built, and you can only call them temporary housing from necessity. Only the church and the governor's house are built of massive stone. The whites are indolent. When the talk is of work, they say: "Why do we have the blacks?" The Moors are treated like cattle. Landowners pay about five percent in taxes. The Negroes would escape more often if they were not at war with the savages or Indians. If a Negro is captured by the Indians, they prepare a feast and enjoy consuming their catch, or else they fatten him ahead of time because they consider Moors to be a kind of monkey. That is the same reason why the Blacks spare no Indians.

We climbed around so much that we were dead tired and indeed actually found in beautiful Brazil an emptiness or kind of desert, so that we were glad in the evening finally to be able to leave. Since by day the wind always blows from the north, you have to wait until evening to begin the trip back to the ship.

At 2:30 in the morning, we arrived back at the *Nadezhda*. We already have several monkeys and parrots on the ship. Resanoff is living at the governor's. The governor also gave one of his officers the task of helping us with purchases. Today, a large quantity of provisions arrived whose cost we do not yet know.

Sun. 13/25 We saluted the fort with eleven salvos and were answered by the same number.

On the ship, we are running around like ants in an anthill. In order make room for ourselves, we have transported a lot of things on land. The large numbers of chickens, turkeys, ducks, pigs, sheep, fruit, and vegetables, which people have dumped on our heads prematurely, cause the most problems.

Horner and Bellingshausen have moved completely into the small fort with all of their astronomical instruments. Langsdorff and Tilesius are climbing through bush and field collecting specimens.

Today, Resanoff explained to the Russian priest Едион [Edion—Gideon] that it is the emperor's will that he be left in either Kamtschatka or Кодияк [Kodiak], that Едион had had the choice of going with the ambassador to either Madrid or Japan. He chose the former and now regrets it since he will never see Japan. In a certain way, this man is being sent astray, and by whom? By Resanoff, the object of our general hatred.

Mon. 14/26 Our nice Norwegian boat ripped loose as a result of carelessness. Luckily, it was noticed in time to be towed back again.

Five gentlemen are on land with Resanoff and not one of them is interested in doing anything for the general good. Today, 75 head of livestock arrived, and 25 were already dead.

Horner is outdoing himself with carpentry, turning, and metal work. I bought myself a parrot today.

When we arrived at the inn, we found a Moor in chains as attendant. I have no idea what he had done, but we found it unpleasant. The following day, the fellow was without chains, but the spots where the chains had been were all swollen, and his back was swollen and bloody from lashes. You could not look at the fellow without shuddering.

At the governor's country house where some of our gentlemen are staying, there is a slave as guard. This human being takes the place of a housedog, but with the difference that a housedog gets fed and cared for, and this one, naked, has to lie under the open skies and find his own food and nevertheless never dare be absent. Killing a black man is not murder.

Tues. 15/27 The foremast on the *Neva* has been taken out and declared totally useless. Lisianski intends to take the mainmast that is also damaged and make a foremast out of it and have a completely new mainmast made here. Since the kinds of wood found here are very beautiful and Resanoff is always threatening to check accounts subsequently, Lisianski is being so generous, in order to earn 100% on the deal, as to have the mast put on his account. The prikaschtschik [supercargo], overjoyed, gave his consent.

A steer on the hoof costs 8 Spanish dahler here and weighs about 13 pud.

Espenberg is treating Chirugius [surgeon] Sidham[5] unfairly, so that he can always stay on land himself. He does not permit him to go ashore. At least up to now, his requests have been fruitless.

Wed. 16/28 We no longer have any idea where we should stow the bananas. We are buying pineapple (the size of two fists) for four copecks apiece. The *Neva* will need a lot of time for her masts.

Langsdorff came out from the city to pick up a few things today. That continually scurrying fellow gets on my nerves. To our relief, the whole sauce of the Embassy is living on land, for there is now peace and quiet on the ship.

Brazil is a country for botanists. Trade is very narrow here. There are a lot of products available for trade: cochineal, indigo, coffee, sugar, rice, rum, all kinds of wood, especially colored woods, etc.—everything in superabundance. The Portuguese, however, are all too indolent. The viceroy put a lot into Rio [de] Janeiro, but the government became too popular and was relieved for that reason.

Stomachaches are the order of the day. Probably the water is at fault. Even though the sun has reached its height, it is not overly hot here and as the inhabitants say, it is now spring.

The only mistake you can hold against the captain is his kindness and obliging nature.

I bought an anchor of rum for Равл Иванавич Кошелев [Pavl Ivanovich Koshelev], during my time [1800–1801] the commander in Sevastopol and now the head of Kamtschatka.

Thurs. 17/29 While we were hauling up the shrouds, our newly acquired cordage broke. Now we have to unrig the foremast again and raise the masthead.

The weather is very stormy and the northwind (which is supposed to be warm) very cold, probably because it is blowing from the mountains.

The difficulties on a voyage around the world outweigh the pleasantness. From the beginning, Bellingshausen, a recalcitrant man, has found it unpleasant to be Horner's aide. Yesterday they quarreled about a misunderstanding. Horner did his best to be reconciled with him. Bellingshausen kept to his stubbornness. Time will heal things again. I tried to mediate but in vain. You cannot do anything with Bellingshausen.

The emperor is going to be surprised to get so many petitions from Brazil. Resanoff is writing on land. The captain is requesting justice and protection. Resanoff is making no secret at all of his intention to denounce us all. That is in character for him. May the hangman take him!

Fri. 18/30 Today, Krusenstern showed me a letter or petition he is thinking of sending to the emperor. Espenberg had written a very nice letter in French, and Krusenstern, after weighing his own effort, put one on paper completely in Russian. May the emperor receive the letter!

Tilesius mentioned at a meal at the governor's that we have sketched the islands and entrance. "Quietly! Quietly!" said Curado, "That is not allowed." But indeed Tilesius brought us a Portuguese map of the island today which he had secretly obtained from a Portuguese officer. That made us very happy. The Portuguese can be assured that we will not betray him.

Sat. 19/31 Bought myself a very beautiful parrot, and green he is!

We are caulking the poop decks, and I am digging around in the hold like a mole.

Golovatscheff had a hard dispute with me today. I had raised the water casks in the front hold in order to make room for the crate in which the pumps were to be placed. Голдовачев [Golovatscheff], hoping to ingratiate himself with the captain, became angry because I was indispensable for the job, saw that one cask had been left behind in the hold, preventing the crate from being lowered, and said to the captain: "Löwenstern ordered the crate to be shoved to the side"; and, upon my coming up, he adds with a scornful smile: "That simply does not work."

I had not given the order and told Golovatscheff the hard truth. We argued heatedly with each other for a while until Krusenstern asked us to declare our argument a misunderstanding and to reconcile. In the last six months, I have not talked so much with Golovatscheff.

There are getting to be too many cats onboard. We have no cockroaches, can get along very well without vermin. One of the English privateers is supposed to be teeming with them.

Sun. 20/1 New Year's according to the New Style. Damned wet. In order to keep the rain out of the cabins, we had to close all of the hatches and sweated like mad in the hold. What a difference in climate and location: we are almost antipodes. I am sweating in my jacket, and my brothers are wrapping themselves up in furs so as not to freeze on the hunt. I think about or rather dare not think

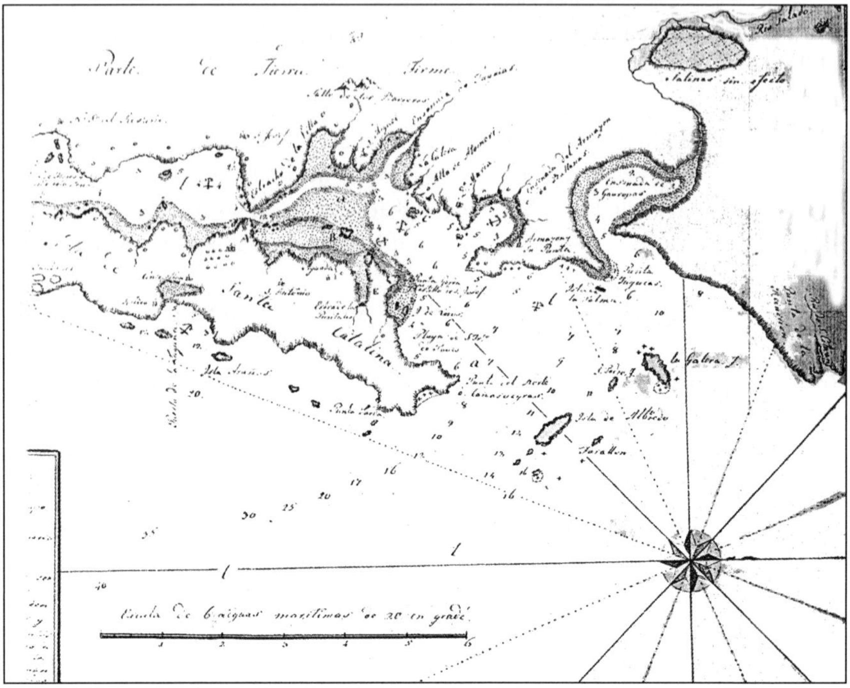

3-2. Map of Santa Catharina

about any holidays and am working like a day laborer. My brothers and sisters are preparing themselves for a happy Christmas drive, and I can think only of trouble and works; and all of you, who perhaps don't think about your lost brother, have your heads filled with fun. Enjoy life! After surviving this voyage, used to hardships, I will know how to appreciate the peace and quiet more than you spoiled Epicureans, will be satisfied with little and not fed up with enjoying home life and striving for something new. What a feeling it would be if I could unexpectedly appear before you now in Selli.[6]

Tilesius brought us another map of St. Catharina today and wants to try to get the special map of Brazil hanging in the governor's office.

Mon. 21/2 Every day, we become more proficient in measuring angles, drawing and copying maps. Toward noon an English sloop arrived. Krusenstern sent me onboard. The raw character of the captain, who seemed to be a privateer, answered all of my questions unsatisfactorily, so that I left having accomplished nothing. At the fort, we heard that the Englishman claims to come from Liverpool, to belong to the South Sea Company, and to have been sent out to catch whales and walrus. Were he heading for the northwest coast of America, I would be more inclined to believe him.

Tues. 22/3 Today, all of our stinking sauerkraut, all of our pickled beets, and a large barrel of spoilt salt meat were thrown overboard.

My beautiful parrot! A certain nobody tortured it so long until it flew into the water and drowned because its wings were clipped.

Lisianski still does not have his mast, and the old one has already been sawed into boards.

The captain of that recently arrived ship came over at noon in order to get some advice about one of his sick men from our doctor. He now says he is sailing to Otahiti [Tahiti] and from there to the American coast to buy furs. He told us that the Portuguese mail is untrustworthy, that he would send one of his prizes to St. Helena; and, if we wanted to, we could take the opportunity to dispatch our letters. The captain is a Swede by birth.

Wed. 23/4 Cleaned up the vessel and we have finished our work. The first pleasant day since our arrival. Everyone likes my musket. Since we have more peace and quiet, my comrades have gone hunting, took a fishing net along, brought us also a dozen birds and a lot of fish back. Tolstoi caught a humming bird alive, like a butterfly, with his hat after the bird had been stunned by a shot.

Thurs. 24/5 Bad thunderstorm and heavy rain.

Espenberg, who is treating a sick man on the English ship, had to go over, and I went along to act as interpreter. The man was suffering from an obstruction. The ship's doctor was drunk, the medicine chest empty, not even linseed oil or plasters, spiritus, and camphor were to be found. Espenberg had brought all other medicine along. We found ourselves, after Espenberg had explained the use of a salve, having to go back and prepare this salve to send over. Undertaking so long a voyage without a proper doctor is very risky.

The English captain brought Krusenstern the description of the voyage Frisius made to the South Seas 90 years ago.[7] I am now busy copying a large number of maps of estates in Chile.

Count Tolstoi, Brinkin, the painter Kurlandzoff, and Tilesius had gone with the pilot Kamentschikoff in the longboat to St. Michel where Adolpho lives. The pilot, who made himself self-important at the wrong time, left in the evening with the painter without waiting for the other gentlemen who had asked him to. The pregnant wife or mistress of the English captain, who was also on land, became ill and took the room, the hoped-for night lodgings of our gentlemen. The remaining party, our ship's comrades, then rented themselves a boat and arrived back at the ship before the longboat. Impatiently we awaited Kamentschikoff's arrival. Barely had he come aboard when he went to the captain and lied to the high heavens and finally finished by saying that Count Tolstoi requested that he be picked up the next morning. What a surprise that was when he walked into the company cabin and found all of those who had been left behind quietly eating their supper. He stopped and stood there as if made from stone. The mate had not paid for his lunch on land, and the count had made good this foolishness from his own pocket. And to avenge himself he said: "You undoubtedly left without us, so that we would have to pay for the noon meal."

The painter, to whom the remark was not addressed, very coarsely said to the count: "You don't need to holler so much for your dahler. If it is all right with you, I'll give you twice as much if you will then keep quiet."

This coarseness caused more to follow, and, if we had not been present, then the painter would have got a right good thrashing, the least of which were the swear words that do not belong to the finest. Finally, Count Tolstoi, after cussing and abusing him in a very unheard of way, said, "You can now request any satisfaction you want and choose anything from a cane to a keg of powder." The painter who is a big poltroon saw his life in danger and went pale. To avoid a duel he went to the captain and complained about Tolstoi. We were called as witnesses, and all declared that the painter had begun the strife and was at fault. Before we all went to bed, the whole matter had ended.

Fri. 25/6 Today, I drank to the health of those at Selli. Yesterday, we finished our work. The officers of the *Neva* visited us today, and you heard no other topic of discussion but of absent friends and acquaintances, whom everyone of us sent the warmest wishes.

Oh, how sympathetically you good people would look down upon us, if you knew how bad the man is we have to deal with, and would certainly admire our patience, steadfastness, energy, uprightness, and our sense of morality; for these are the only effective weapons against vileness.

Sat. 26/7 In Tenerife, the strife between Resanoff and Krusenstern had ended with Resanoff groveling submissively, begging for pardon, and very sincerely adding: "I am at fault!" The following day he sits down and writes the emperor complaining about Krusenstern. Now he is not ashamed of saying, when he hears reproaches for his behavior: "Who directed him to let himself be deceived"; and filled with glee he brags with his умная штука [clever maneuver]. He begged the captain's pardon at that time to prevent a counter-complaint.

For the first time in my life, I am eating pineapple, bananas, watermelon, and oranges at Christmas. And you brag of rabbit and game, so we put a parrot pie and a fine boiled dolphin on the table for you.

My little Jacko calls "durak" [fool] so often that I will have to go in to stuff the fool's trap.

Here you find white and black people, yellow, copper-colored and olive-colored. Mulattos have European fathers and black mothers, Mestizos European mothers and black fathers. The children of two Moors born in Europe or America are called Creoles. Kakerbakken are white Moors.

For my black laundry, 90 pieces which I got today, I got a bill for 3,000 rees, and this large sum came to barely four Spanish dahler. These rees are imaginary and almost 1,000 of them are one dahler.

On the first holiday, the priest Edion, at the captain's request, read a mass on the *Nadezhda*. In the evening, the priest had secretly talked with Tolstoi for an exceedingly long time. Today, Tolstoi told us the entire discussion. Здион [Edion], at Resanoff's request, sought to sharpen Count Tolstoi's conscience and hoped through his eloquence to get that lost sheep to confession. He pointed out to the count how bad things were, how much he had failed in his duties to his chief, what consequences that might have, etc. He preached on deaf ears and had to muster all of his patience and perseverance not to fall out of his role, for he himself cannot deny that Resanoff needs spiritual chastisement more than Tolstoi.

Sun. 27/8 In the night Lisianski, who was in Dodesterro, sent his boat with a letter for Krusenstern; at the same time the captain received a letter from Resanoff. Resanoff writes, "Since you do not want to recognize my authority, I have found it necessary to give Captain Lisianski orders, etc." (This letter was written only for the purpose of getting an answer and something in writing from Krusenstern that could be sent to Petersburg.)

Lisianski has sent a letter to Krusenstern requesting him to go into town because some very unpleasant things have occurred, especially concerning the count.

An hour ago, Krusenstern left for Dodesterro. In order to increase our supply of wood, the captain bought 20 faden of kindling. Oh, what a calamity! Rosewood, mahogany, palm wood, etc. are being burned indiscriminately in the kitchen.

We have so many parrots on the ship that it goes unnoticed if a couple fall overboard and drown or die.

I visited Horner in Santa Cruz. He has had nothing but bad weather, and his apartment is a shed with bare earth for a floor. The roof is not watertight. The wall is green with dampness, and at night it teams with innumerable tarantulas, cockroaches, spiders, and other insects.

In the afternoon, we raised the mizzenmast with shear legs in order to shorten it by around four fuss and put it back in place.

In the evening, an English shallop brought our clerk Чугаев [Chugaev] onboard stinking drunk. He had gone on land and voluntarily stayed there. Dead drunk, dead asleep is how the Englishmen found him lying on the shore. Two Portuguese had crept up and just taken his bags as the English arrived on the scene. They wanted to flee with his hat. The English took it away from them when they caught up with them. A glass of brandy and a thank you were the reward we gave the *tars* [sic tarheels].

Mon. 28/9 The captain returned from town in the night. The painter, who had complained to Resanoff about Count Tolstoi and the captain, is the reason for the repeated strife. Resanoff is on his high horse and repeats ad nauseum, "I am by the grace of the emperor the absolute commander of both ships as well as of the entire expedition." The orders Resanoff issued to Lisianski concern only Kodiak.

Mr. von Krusenstern wrote a civil, informed, honest letter with truthful reasons, which he let us read. Resanoff left it unanswered. (Krusenstern had done it, had written only to Resanoff because he hoped that the disagreements could be mediated more readily in writing than orally.) Krusenstern will send a copy of the letter to the emperor. Today, Krusenstern wrote Resanoff for a second time and was kind enough to read the letter to us.

Count Tolstoi has asked us all to give him attests [recommendations], which he needs for his own vindication.

Yesterday, I told Krusenstern, before he left for Dodesterro, to be careful because I suspected that Resanoff would provoke the matter to an extreme. Today, the captain told me that was the case. After Resanoff had asked the captain repeatedly: "So, you do not recognize me as your unlimited head," and each time received "No" as an answer, Krusenstern finally asked: "So you are leaving me only the command of the sails? This duty belongs to my officers; and I do not believe that was the will of the Emperor; for I would then be superfluous, etc., and more."

We provided Tolstoi with the following attest: "I deem it a special pleasure to say of Count Tolstoi, who is sharing our journey's labors, that this man has earned, in proportion to his sacrifices and love, my love and respect as well as that of our entire company."[8]

Resanoff had attempted to win over Lisianski but stopped talking when Lisianski answered him (which I would not have believed him capable of), "If Krusenstern returns to Russia, then I will follow him" (because Resanoff threatens to return to Russia). We have not yet been asked, but without the captain we are not moving from the spot.

Today, they caught a young crocodile on the *Neva*. It was only four spannen long. (Old ones are said to grow to 30 fuss long). Even as young as that animal was, it had devilish sharp teeth. Wherever that animal bites, bones do not stay easily in one piece.

Tilesius has moved back with us on shipboard, because Resanoff does not support his business and collecting at all and does not want to defray his costs at the Crown's expense nor give him money to be deducted from his pay. Langsdorff has received money from Resanoff in order to motivate Moorish boys to bring him all kinds of natural historical objects. That also was done in order to sow discord. Krusenstern continually sits there writing duplicate letters to the emperor in order to convey to the monarch through Tschitschagoff, Rumianzoff, and several others the detailed history with Resanoff. Tschitschagoff especially will find himself touched by the matter since Resanoff said to the captain: "Tschitschagoff himself confirmed the emperor's power of attorney and added another point in front of the signature." Since Tschitschagoff never does anything secretly and, after several discussions with Krusenstern in which he mentioned no such thing, it is probable that this story is Resanoff's invention. Krusenstern reported everything to this man with full understanding. These letters for Russia will be sent at various opportunities, making it impossible for Resanoff to intercept them all.

Tues. 29/10 Our boat from Dodesterro that took the captain's letter to Resanoff returned early with no answer. Now Mr. von Krusenstern, who had up to then conducted everything privately with Resanoff, felt obligated to call us fleet officers together. "Resanoff," the captain told us, "has proved to me so often that he disclaims today what he said the day before, that I find it necessary to let you know about Resanoff's conduct." At the same time, the captain pulled out his own instructions (in which he is called by name the head of the expedition) and asked us to read it through. "Resanoff only tells me his claims orally," the captain continued, "and supports them with his paper and now and then repeating to me: 'you know the Emperor's signature? I am head of the expedition, of both ships and commander over them and everything that belongs to the expedition.' "

"When I then answered him," said Krusenstern, "that I, in matters of seamanship, could never recognize him as my commander, Resanoff told me, 'You have command of the sails and nothing more.' "

We were united in our opinion that Krusenstern should laugh about Resanoff's stupidity and that he had to continue absolutely as before.

"He always compares himself with Lord Makartency [Macartney][9] (He has it like the donkey in a lion's skin)," continued the captain. "According to the laws in Russia, everything runs by command. Resanoff gives Lisianski orders before telling me about them. The result is that Lisianski dare not carry out the orders. Resanoff wrote his instructions himself in Petersburg and gave them to me unsigned to read, so that I know quite well what Resanoff added afterwards. 'The Emperor was kind enough to give me these instructions,' says Resanoff, 'and I have always been accustomed to carrying out the emperor's orders most punctually.' In Tenerife the Chamberlain said to me, 'I feel that I am incapable of being the head of the expedition, and, if you wish, I will give that to you in writing.' "

"Now," continued the captain, "he gives me no written answer to my letters, as he is according to the law obligated to do, so that he can keep everything ambiguous in order to be able to turn and twist everything according to the time and circumstances. If something happens where he thinks he can act as head, then he throws orders around, and, in situations where his advice would be necessary, he withdraws, always in order to have the law on his side and to do damage, etc., etc., etc."

How ridiculous! Resanoff threatens with Japan and says, "When we arrive in Japan, then the proud captain will take orders from me every day, which he will have to carry out and which I will force him to obey."

To Lisianski he said (he wanted to move to his ship and Lisianski answered, "Without Mr. von Krusenstern's consent I cannot receive you on the *Neva*"), "The officers openly insult me on the quarterdeck; and I believe that, if these men were to attack me physically, then Mr. von Krusenstern would remain silent." The result of our consultation was that we all assured the captain and maintained our conviction that we should not react to Resanoff's baseness and absurdness and not obey any of the ambassador's orders that were not to the advantage or service of the emperor, the expedition, or the American Company. The captain called us together because Resanoff is putting nothing in writing and his words disavow reporting the whole matter to us, so that we may not think that there are secrets between the two of them and judge our captain falsely.

Resanoff tried sounding out whether he could go around the captain and give us officers orders directly. None of us takes orders from Resanoff and dare not accept them.

When we are at sea, Resanoff does like all of those whose conscience is not pure. He chooses the night to forge intrigues and slander others. Among other things, he said to Espenberg one fine night: "There sits Romberg sleeping and certainly drunk. How is it going to be at Cape Horn if the officers already are so remiss? If Philip Ivanitsch (the dumb mate) weren't there, there could certainly be many a calamity." Unfortunately, it was the truth because Romberg at supper had drunk one glass too many, something that happens rather often, so that he usually peters out on his watch if the weather is good. Such incidents always make Resanoff maliciously happy. I am surprised that Resanoff has not told or invented any stories about me because I have up to now done too little to please him. We have known for a long time that he hates Romberg and me.

In the afternoon, I wanted to go to visit Senhore Adolpho Lang but didn't because of a thunderstorm. It rained for over four hours with gusts of wind, thunder, and lightening, poured as if splinters. I had watch and felt as though I had come from a cold bath when I was relieved.

That Lang was born in the Cologne area, Catholic, has already been here for 25 years. He carries on in all possible arts, sciences, and handicrafts to earn his bread. He is highly respected as a doctor among the common folk. He is very proficient at pulling teeth, bleeding, and knows a lot of healing herbs that he applies for the good of the people and his pocket. For the lack of a deacon at St. Michael's church where he lives, he does that job, too. Since he speaks German, French, Portuguese, and a little English he is the general podraideur [procurer] for foreign ships. He has his little garden he uses for his own needs. His wife is from here, nothing particular, unlike his sister-in-law who turned all of our heads and got our blood churning. He has only a daughter. He is also a kind of schoolmaster. With all of his activities, he must have amassed a tidy sum. We all have to praise his honesty. He took on the job of having our black laundry washed and serves us, the *Neva,* and the English ships punctually and exactly with everything we need. Our officious Adolpho finds us things that you can't get yourself in Dodesterro.

Wed. 30/11 I went to St. Michel where we are filling our water casks. The area there is quite nice. The main attraction is a waterfall that drives a stamp mill.

The water falls in steps from the high mountains and forms at each step a basin which time has hollowed out and filled with fine sand, so that one could not build a more beautiful place for bathing. Both sides are shaded by tall ancient trees that stop the burning rays of the sun. We arrived in our longboat around ten o'clock in the morning. After giving our people orders about how many water casks they should fill, we climbed up the mountain and bathed in that beautiful cool water. Afterwards we visited Adolpho, who was playing the role of schoolmaster with ten boys whom he was teaching reading and writing.

The wind at this time was growing brisker and brisker so that we could only depart with difficulty. Our rudder, which we could only put in place with a great deal of effort, held us up for a long time, because the surf was so heavy that the waves ripped the rudder out of our hands every time we tried to put it in place. Despite all our efforts, we did not reach the ship. The current played havoc with us. Hoping for better weather, we fled into a little bay where the *Neva* had pitched her tents. The captain, who had seen us from the ship rowing in vain, sent his shallop in the evening for us, and we returned to the ship at eight o'clock in the evening and left our longboat anchored by land until the next day. Even though I had not eaten since yesterday, I felt no pangs of hunger because I had developed a very sharp headache from bathing, which I only got rid of by a lot of retching.

Madame Eckstein, the wife of the English captain, is in a very bad state. The woman is toward the end of her pregnancy and indecisive whether to continue the voyage with her husband or stay here. Life here has nothing attractive about it, because only a few of the Europeans are people one would want to have anything to do with. Despite that, however, the situation of the poor woman is even worse on a ship without a doctor (better to have none at all than one like the swine they have on that ship) in case help is needed. It is difficult to decide to go to sea. They really should have thought about that earlier; now she has no choice but to choose one of two evils.

Impatiently, we are awaiting the departure of Captain Smith *of the Swallow* [sic], who has promised to take part of our letters along. He is sailing from here to Rio Janeiro and will send the letters from there, as opportunity presents itself, or with the mail, or then again if he should sail from there to St. Helena.

Thurs. 31 / 19 The English captain came to us and took the letters, which are to justify us against Resanoff. Count Tolstoi was given attest from our captain, us five officers, Espenberg, Horner, and Tilesius. The mate refused to give the count one, because he claimed there was an ukas preventing it. That is of no account; an attest from a common unimportant man is no recommendation. I only feel sorry for Count Tolstoi that he did him the honor of asking him for an attest. Tolstoi needed these attestate because he correctly assumed that the emperor would give Resanoff's complaint more weight than his justification.

Our signatures can do us no damage since Resanoff did not publicly have himself recognized as head [of the expedition]. I have not yet received his instructions to read, the others only secretly; therefore, none of us is going against his superior but rather bringing together the unsanctioned actions of one passenger. Our letters are gone. That they are securely on the way is a great comfort.

War on the hummingbirds. The sweet little animals have bewitched us circumnavigators. Everyone wants to have one, and, if he has one, then he looks around for another one. Horner brought a little mother with her nest. The nest had been built with great care, and that little bird sat there lifeless with her long tongue, or rather butterfly proboscis, hanging out over her eggs. It is very difficult to stuff such a small dainty bird.

Description of Brazil: Upon arrival, we considered it that promised land—pineapples, bananas, oranges, water melons, etc., pleasant smelling herbs, beautiful overgrown mountains, magnificent forests. All of nature seems to be competing to bewitch man: hummingbirds, all kinds of parrots, quantities of birds with the most beautiful plumage, and butterflies flattering fearlessly around you. One is full of admiration for the climate and the beauty of nature. Suddenly! What horror! Surrounded by poisonous snakes, lizards, toads, crocodiles, scolopenders [millipedes], and tigers. You stand there petrified and think only of fleeing. Only too gladly do you not begrudge the Portuguese their Brazil, and happy and satisfied climb back on that sociable ship.

The poor Blacks are the object of general contempt and are, however, the Brazilians' pack animals. All of them are branded on their chests. This brand P indicates that the slave tax has been paid to the Portuguese court and that the owner is master of this human life.

Langsdorff returned from Dodesterro with a large quantity of specimens of natural objects, and, as he says (or rather threatens), soon several of the gentlemen from Resanoff's suite will be returning to the ship.

This year is ending. In the New Year, we will undoubtedly expect less damage from storms and bad weather than from Resanoff's intrigues. These are the coral snakes, the coral reefs that poison good moods, satisfaction, and health.

Well, my dear ones, you who in the future will leaf through my diary have to be kind to its writer. I have written for me. My passionate character has led me to conclusions that I have written down only as they occurred to me. You know me too well to need a diary of my life in order to get to know me and will therefore soon distinguish between what has been said in passion and what has been composed calmly.

As far as spelling and legibility are concerned, you may criticize as much as you like. If you understand what I want to say, then I don't care if I hurriedly write an x for i or not. Have you had enough of this first part of my diary? Can't do anything about it, for now comes the new second book or the New Year. Everything helter-skelter as it occurs to me, a quodlibet [what you please] of its kind.

1804—January

Fri. 1/13 Best wishes for the New Year, in which we can only expect unpleasantness. Today was a holiday for me because I turned my thoughts to my family and asked myself: What are my dear sisters, my old father, brothers, aunts, and uncles, etc., doing? Where are they now? What time is it in Estonia? What kind of weather do you have? I spent a large part of the day with comparing your New Year's Day with mine.

In the morning, the priest read mass. Priests are the same all over, whether on land or sea. Ours told us, мир всем [peace be with you or everyone] more often than is usually customary. The captain invited the Commandant of Santa Cruz and his Fähnrich [midshipman] and assistant of forty years' service to lunch. Arbusoff and Kovedeeff also spent the first of January with us. The wind was very brisk. I cannot say any more about our New Year's. The future, which lets us expect little happiness on account of the ambassador, hovered before all of our eyes, and all of us, as if we had agreed upon it, were sunk deep in thought, all of us.

Sat. 2/14 A Portuguese brig of war arrived. We do not know where she comes from or what her purpose is.

Ratmanoff, Tolstoi, Espenberg, and the two Kotzebues went to Dodesterro. Those Kotzebues' education, because of this voyage, is being exceedingly neglected, and to their disgrace, I have to say, the two brothers live together like a cat and dog.

Langsdorff related today that Resanoff was beside himself because Lisianski had sent his orders back to him with the answer that according to the law, he had to receive them through Mr. von Krusenstern and he (Lisianski) therefore had to return them to him.

Langsdorff and Tilesius must have a natural antipathy for each other. At any time of day, they can talk when and about anything they want to, and they are always arguing, always of different opinions, always heatedly against each other.

Sun. 3/15 My comrades who had gone to Dodesterro yesterday returned. Ratmanoff brought us the following news. Captain Smith *of the Swallow* [sic] had boarded and taken prizes of two Portuguese ships on his marauding, seized their cargo, and sunk the ships with man and mouse, sailed into St. Catharina, where he illegally took two French whalers as prizes. The Portuguese knew nothing about his misdeed with the Portuguese vessels. It is suspected, however, that the French captain, an American by birth, had sold his ship to the privateer and found this suspicion confirmed by several sailors who had fled the whaler. The governor here sent the Englishman a message: he was to leave the Brazilian shores within five days. Since he answered that it would be impossible in fewer than 19 days, yesterday the governor received orders from Rio Janeiro through the brig of war to arrest the two Englishmen, i.e., Smith and Dicken, who had been living here for over a year. They had learned through the American, who was quarreling with

Smith and wanted to duel with him, what had happened to the Portuguese ships. (The American had regretted selling his whaler to such an unscrupulous man and thereby becoming himself a scoundrel.)

Our gentlemen were sitting in an inn in Dodesterro when little Kotzebue came running into the room and behind him a Portuguese officer with drawn sword and several soldiers. The first person the officer saw was Count Tolstoi, whom he immediately grabbed by the chest. Count Tolstoi was disconcerted and said, "But I am a Russian!" while reaching for his pistol. The Portuguese let loose of him with many apologies and arrested the two Englishmen who also were there. And they, after Captain Smith had turned over three loaded pistols, were led off to prison so that they could be sent to Rio Janeiro at the first opportunity. The count became frightened because, at that moment, the possibility occurred to him that Resanoff could have him arrested in Dodesterro. Half an hour later, Lisianski and Friderici also arrived from Dodesterro.

We commissioned a Portuguese officer, whom the governor had recommended, to buy provisions for us. We can only hope we don't get the same treatment as Count Tolstoi did. He wanted to buy coffee, sugar, rum, tobacco, etc., gave the commission to another Portuguese officer, and paid him 100 dahler in advance. After Tolstoi had received approximately ten dahler worth of goods, he found it necessary to consider the rest of the money lost, so as not to get in a quarrel about the purchases.

Lisianski's masts are not ready.

I hadn't thought that our painter was such a bad fellow up to now. On land in Dodesterro, he said publicly to Mr. von Krusenstern that a person's life was not safe on the *Nadezhda* and that it looked like a kaback [tavern or colloquially a pigsty] and was one. Today, the painter came onboard from land. The captain repeated the painter's words and accusations in our presence and added, "Either you ask my pardon as well as that of the whole group, or else you avoid the company's cabin when I am in it."

Thereupon the scoundrel said, "Then I will have to eat with the sailors. Send me on land!" That stupid man does not even admit his offence and thinks he is protected because Resanoff told him, "Be afraid of nothing! Come what may, I will protect you."

Resanoff also said during this incident, "There is no discipline at all on the ship if I am not there." After Lisianski had returned Resanoff's orders to him, he turned the whole thing around the next day during our noon meal and wanted to maintain that he had only sent the orders to Lisianski solely for him to read.

Lisianski, who was present, said, "I stand by my opinion contained in the letter I sent you."

"I will send your letter to the emperor" was the ambassador's answer when he saw that his deceit did not help.

"You are welcome to do that if you wish," answered Iuri Fedorovisch. Notwithstanding that, I do not completely trust our кaypa,[10] as they call Lisianski.

They are saying that Resanoff is also supposed to have reported the incident between Tolstoi and the painter to the emperor. It throws no favorable light upon Resanoff's love of justice that he is capable of reporting to the emperor something he only knows one side of, since he has not asked Count Tolstoi at all about the matter and thus has taken the painter's word, all of his calumnies, be they so absurd. I therefore find it hard to believe.

Mon. 4/16 Last night, Langsdorff killed a xiraracca, one of the most poisonous snakes. How beautifully marked that animal is with brown and green shadings, slim body, and the regular scales lying sleekly upon each other are superb. The two movable poisonous fangs were about half a zoll long and of indescribable sharpness. This coral snake's bite is incurable. (The snake was over three fuss long.) In less than ten minutes, every animal bitten by this snake dies. The poison distends the entire body. Bloods pours out of the nose, ears, and even under the nails and no rescue is possible. The inhabitants fear this snake most of all. Our Sinhore Serganto compared it with the devil and said that, if we kill a similar snake, we should bury it deep in the earth because even the sharp scales are said to be poisonous. Our natural scientists contradict this, but nevertheless this precaution is praiseworthy since most of the people here go barefoot. It is a wonder that they are not bitten more often by snakes, since there are only footpaths in the whole country and people have to squeeze through the thickest brush to get deeper into the country.

In the afternoon, we went to the fort of St. Cruz to bring Horner his lunch and to see the military preparations the Portuguese are taking against English privateers. Unfortunately, the cannons on their carriages looked as though they have been unused since being put in place and would hardly withstand much bombardment, for they are very rotten and rusty.

The Swallow and a prize have already been seized and the crew on the ships arrested. The brig and the other prize are, however, already under sail in flight. They say that a Portuguese cutter is sailing to the south around the Island of St. Catharina to intercept the two boats and seize them, too. The Portuguese are especially wanting to apprehend Captain Smith (the one arrested in Dodesterro was a different one), since he had taken the brig under Spanish flag as a prize despite the fact that England at that time was at peace and without permission to make a privateer out of the prize.

Some of the sailors from *The Commerce*, Captain Ekstein's ship, are being held at the fort because they are English and, emboldened by alcohol, got into a fray on land. The captain of the cutter that escaped was on *The Commerce* when a guard came onboard and demanded he should be turned over. Since this was not done, they began to prepare for war at the fort. They wanted to get with force what they could not get with good will. The Portuguese must have changed their minds, however, since everything is quiet again at the fort.

Tues. 5/17 Early in the morning the incarcerated sailors from *The Commerce* were set free. Finally we got the news that the masts for the *Neva* have arrived. They were lying quite far inland on the hills. Now we only need hoops. Romberg, Friderici, and the painter are going into Dodesterro in the afternoon. The latter no longer takes meals with us, if the captain is there, because he is afraid that we would slam the door on him (which certainly would happen). Nevertheless, the painter was pert enough to set up his easel in the captain's cabin. Mr. von Krusenstern told him very coldly: "Once and for all, I have forbidden you to be where I am, and I beg you not to be so bold as to enter my cabin again."

After the painter had spread a panic fear on land and talked of death and destruction, kith and kin took him at his word. They went in corpore to the rattlesnake, that is, Friderici (I hope from curiosity), Fosse, Brinkin, the mate, Kamentschikoff, and the painter as leader and requested from their beloved head protection from us cannibals. Lisianski was present during the complaint and told us about it.

Resanoff is set at driving Tolstoi to his limits and making him unhappy whenever he can. Resanoff has written the emperor (his creatures are saying, if to frighten the count? or for other reasons.), as if Count Tolstoi were guilty of using bad language and slander against the emperor. That is what is called hatching lies to inflict damage. If that is the case and true, then Resanoff's slanderous tales and stories against Grand Duke Constantin[11] and the emperor should also come to light. (Resanoff says he only did it in order to investigate our intentions.) That will be a nice bit of scandalous tale bearing.

Three year's worth of eating poisonous gall without being in a position to air any of it out, get it off of his chest—Can a human body really hold up under that? Must we always yield and watch as malice and spite triumph over us? Care and reason! direct us along our thorny way! and allow us to overcome and fight all the difficulties that are put in our way for us to stumble over. We do not need anything else other than to place the whole story, as it really is, before the world in order to unmask our enemies and to show their true light and to justify ourselves.

Wed. 6/18 Shortly after our departure from Russia, we had a dispute at table that occurred to me again and bode us well to be careful. The talk was of the postal service and mainly of letters being broken open, etc. "Ey!" said Councilor Fosse (who had served as a police officer in Petersburg until our departure), "This art (he called it nothing else and that with veneration) of unsealing letters is done nowhere else so perfectly as in Russia. I can open a well-sealed letter for you, read it, and reseal it, so that no one can easily discover it, and am willing to bet that they will not notice and discover which letter has been unsealed."

Wonderful prospects! Yesterday, Horner brought us the unpleasant news that Captain Ross, the American who had taken our letters, has also been seized. Our captain did not waste a moment but requested that our letters be returned, and we received our letters at ten o'clock this morning and have to think of new means and opportunities to send them, for they dare not fall into Resanoff's hands.

In the forenoon, we went on the nearest land, because we could not think of any better way to entertain ourselves on Three Kings' Day: [12] Krusenstern to measure angles with Horner; Lisianski, Langsdorff, and I to run along the beach looking for mussels, capturing insects, etc. All work for today was put off. We had relaxed during the day, however, in order to work the whole night. Toward evening, the ship moved, as if always in a little current. We therefore had to raise the anchor, which we already knew was not in good condition or could not be in good condition. But an anchor has perhaps never been as tangled as ours was when we raised it. Our anchor cable had wound itself around the shaft and stock nine times and was, in addition, through innumerable turns, tangled around the buoy cable (our mooring buoy had been ripped away eight days after our arrival). Furthermore, the cable of our stopanchor had made so many twists around the cable and anchor shaft that we had to work until morning to get everything repaired and back in order. In the evening, we cast anchor. It was backbreaking work raising the combined weight of the mud clinging around the anchor and cable. Our precautions and continued effort helped us happily to complete the job earlier than we had hoped.

Thurs. 7/19 Raised our stopanchor and hauled in all of our sails, sent the longboat to St. Michel for water, and from Dodesterro received a boat load of chickens, ducks, turkeys, pigs, *pumpkins* [sic], corn, coffee, onions, garlic, etc.

Our boat has not yet returned from town.

Langsdorff proposed to the captain that a chest of butterflies be ordered and dispatched to Lisbon. I took the opportunity to order a chest full, pay in advance so that they would be sent from Lisbon to Kronstadt.

Several days ago, a group of us went on land on the Island of St. Catharina. During our walk near a house, we met a rather cleanly dressed man whose face made us think we had seen him some place. The fellow looked so damned saucy that we simply could not resist bantering him a bit. I asked him in broken Italian as best I could for his name and pro casa (this word means something entirely different in Russian, which made it all the more fun for us). The man, who in the beginning had paid no attention to us and looked proudly down upon us because we were all dressed in nankeen jackets, found it strange of us to ask a man in unison for edicts, especially the mixing in of the words, Dodesterro and Goubernatore disconcerted the man. He did not know what to do with himself and finally wrote, with trembling hand, what we were requesting on a piece of paper we gave him and was happy to be rid of us again. That proud man will have had a sleepless night on our account and think we were informers and rack his brains why we could possibly need his name and the name of his house. (You're lazy enough, can't hurt if you for once have had your peace and quiet disturbed.) Especially the names Dodesterro and

Goubernatore hit him in the nose, for you have to know that the viceroy and the governors in Brazil have absolute power. (That was the return of old tricks.)

Even though the heat often climbs to 23°, we still cannot complain about the heat. The cool winds from the mountains don't cool the air off so much as make the heat bearable.

The sun however burns intensely. If you are in the rays of the sun for only a quarter of an hour, it burns your skin so much that for a couple days afterwards you have a wound where the rays of the sun have burned. We therefore watch very carefully that our people do not go around without a hat, because, if the sun can fry the skin in such a short time, what horrible effect must it have if it burns a man's head (sunstroke).

In the evening, Romberg returned from Dodesterro. He had been sent to deliver a letter that the captain had written to His Excellency, in which he spelled out his injustice and how much discipline would suffer if he continued to ignore laws and give orders that cannot be issued по команду [by command], etc. Resanoff greeted Romberg very coldly and did not speak a word with him. Before Romberg left, he had gone again to see Resanoff in order to ask him whether he had any orders to issue. As answer, Romberg got a countless number of scrape legs. Good paths ahead! Cape Horn will teach Resanoff manners and gentility.

Fri. 8/20 We weighed anchor early in the morning and kedged ourselves into deeper waters.

The seawater here or the bottom must have something very caustic in it. Everything made of iron scales off in layers, and our rudder chains, especially the hooks, are completely filled with holes. The iron is peeling off our anchor in thick plates.

After we had cast anchor again, a fresh wind arose from the south. For a long time, we had wanted to go to Alvaredo. It was too far to row there. The best thing we could do was to use this wind.

We asked the captain for the use of a boat, took provisions, muskets, and other such articles and left the ship just after noon. Ratmanoff, Langsdorff, and I. First we went to St. Cruz and picked up Horner. Then we sailed with the wind. The wind, which became brisker and brisker, prevented us from daring to sail far out to sea on the same evening. Therefore, we turned into a bay where the boat was protected from the wind and spent the night. Local dinghies under a roof served as a camp for the night. A little house not far away, where we found people willing to help us, made camping easier. We ate a duck and some eggs for supper, and the friendly faces of our innkeepers spiced our meal. Our innkeeper was a former English sailor who had married here and settled down permanently. He knew the area very exactly and did not give a favorable description of Alvaredo. We especially did not want to hear that you couldn't land there when the wind is blowing from the south. Myth has it that the whole area, even the mainland, but especially the islands are filled with ghosts—Catholic fairy tales.

Sat. 9/21 We got up with the sun. The hard beds especially woke us up. Right after getting up, we bathed, bought some breakfast, a portion of eggs, and set out on our way. The wind, which had not let up today either, prevented us from carrying out our plans, and the high breakers hitting the shore made landing very difficult. Finally, with a lot of effort, we landed on the northern side of Aromazunt del Balleyas, mainly to see the establishment. It is for the most part a whale wharf. In September, whales, mostly koschelotten [cachelots or sperm whales] near Alvaredo and to the south, are thrown on shore and their fat is boiled in this rendering works and refined; 28 large kettles or pans set in a row on foundations, and the containers show how profitable the catch here must be. Several years ago around 500 koschelotten and whales were slaughtered. The slave huts, the sails for the boats, warehouses, shelters, etc., give the whole place the appearance of a small city. After we had become tired of the place, we set out on our way. The sea was running so high that we did not dare to put out to sea; and because we had the wind, waves, and current against us, we reached the northern point of the Island of St. Catharina only with great difficulty. We did not arrive until evening, and, since we had not eaten the whole day, our first concern was to satisfy our hunger. A couple of chickens and grits from cassava and manioc roots were very suited to our taste. (The island, in contrast to the mainland, is much more cultivated and the inhabitants better off.) In the hope of finding a softer resting place in the home of one of the locals, we spent the night at his place, were however disappointed, for even there a board served us as a pillow, the floor served us as a table, a clean mat as tablecloth and wooden spoons that were nicely made that we bought them from our innkeeper.

Many, especially Spaniards, have eaten themselves to death on the manioc root. Raw, it is the purest poison, and, if it not used when completely ripe and properly prepared and cooked, it causes a kind of dropsy and other diseases if it is eaten. Ripe and well baked, it is a nutritious tasty food. The locals prefer it to Turkish wheat and all other kinds of flour.

Sun. 10/22 We began our wanderings again before daybreak. Horner and I established angles; Langsdorff dug in the sand and ran around in the bushes chasing insects, and Ratmanoff fired his musket at everything he came across. Even though I had a musket along, I left it in the boat so that I could more easily look for mussels along the shore. The boat followed us slowly along the shore. Since we were so tired and it was already very late, we gave up our plan to visit Alvaredo, even though the wind had died down. It was a holiday, and all of the locals in the neighborhood we met were dressed in full regalia coming from mass in Punta Grossa. We had wanted to visit this fortification for a long time, so we rowed toward it. The commander in a torn jacket, whom we did not want to believe was the commander, met us on the beach and said with a proud mien: "Foreigners are forbidden to land here." We answered him that we had permission from the governor to land anywhere we wished. The fellow in the jacket still caused difficulties.

Since we longed to get back to the ship and we did not want to get into an extended discussion with this fellow, we climbed back into our boat. Now the rascal started asking us to go on land. The invitation came too late, and the best punishment for him was our departure. That was at noon, so we rowed straight for the *Nadezhda* and arrived very tired. We had had a lot of plans but carried out few of them. The best part of it was that our toil and trouble had done us good, and our exhaustion and hunger caused us no further discomfort.

Lisianski is in optima forma. In order to tow the mast to the *Neva*, Krusenstern was kind enough to send his shallop to the *Neva*. Our people had forgotten to take hardtack along. They could just as well have got it from the *Neva*. But no! Lisianski sent our shallop back against wind and current to get hardtack and then ordered it to return so that the masts could be transported. Mr. von Krusenstern could not stop himself from uttering: "Какая глупость!" [What stupidity].

Romberg went over to visit the *Neva*. After tea, Povalischin offered him a glass of punsch. It will, however, be put on his account because Lisianski has forbidden giving out rum. It is the officers' own fault that Lisianski tyrannizes them so and has expanded his lust for power to include their personal property.

We killed a beautiful coral snake on our excursion. The mosquitoes, as small as they are, bit in a most lively fashion.

The *Nadezhda* is lying very quietly on her moorings, and I wish all a good night.

Mon. 11/23 Eckstein came to thank our captain for the help given his sick men. Eckstein has also been forced to leave the bay. In order to tease the Portuguese brig of war, he released his topsail with a salvo of his cannon. Eckstein half admitted today that his main speculation is that there would be a war with Spain, which, as he had hoped, would soon break out between Spain and England. He now intended to sail to the Straits of Magellan and winter there and build a ship for which he has along all kinds of tools and things; then there is a sunken ship near the Falkland Islands, which he plans to take (the braggart).

Thunder, lightening, and unruly rain disquieted us for the whole afternoon into the evening and our longboat transported water to the *Neva* for Lisianski, while he left his longboat unused on the bulkhead. The thing that angers us is that he does not give our people any hardtack if they need some. Today, they went without eating the whole day because Lisianski protested, "You are going to Japan and will have an excess of everything. We, on the other hand, are going to barren Kodiak and need our hardtack ourselves." But then, why not at least lend it?

Tues. 12/24 Put the *Neva*'s masts in place, and finally it looks as if we can sail.

Anecdote: Lisianski could not praise the *Neva* enough upon his arrival in Kronstadt. But even there the officers found flaws in the masts and the ship (so that the *Neva* in all probability has to be older than the *Nadezhda*). "That is nothing," said Lisianski. "If the ship is new, the masts certainly also have to be good." He let his crew know that, if anyone ventured to find any defects, he would seek revenge and the cat [-o'-nine-tails] would be the infallible fate of the violator of this order. Now and again along the way, officers have found that several important spots in the ship are rotten and shown them to Lisianski. He only answered them, "I don't like your snooping!"

Lisianski played under the same hat as the seller of the ships *Neva* and *Nadezhda*, that is for sure. But he had also calculated very well. Had he changed his masts and tackle, which were not the newest and best, in Kronstadt, then the costs of repairs would have been so high that the people of the American Company would have smelled something rotten. Lisianski would have hardly remained the captain of the *Neva,* for, in order to establish the additional bills and their cause and why they were so high, Lisianski would have been forced to stay behind.

Wed. 13/25 Krusenstern, Horner, and I went to Punta Grossa and made a base camp in the sand, returned at noon in order to put our work on paper. We had measured countless angles. Bellingshausen and Espenberg went to Dodesterro.

The *Neva* is fully rigged. At Lisianski's request, Krusenstern sent six men to help, and Lisianski goes on land every day with his shallop looking for mussels for the fun of it, so little does it bother him that his rowers are taken from their work—the egoist.

Thurs. 14/26 Resanoff is the authorized agent of the American Company. The directors told us in Kronstadt when there was no more room left for stores, "In case, Captain, you and your officers should need provisions, you have the right to take them from the ship's provisions and stores for their original price." On the contrary, Resanoff now says that we should get everything at the prices current in Kamtschatka. We have nothing in writing, and Resanoff can determine the bills, but they will certainly not be paid. Thus does Resanoff, through his intrigues and schemes, make the alliance between us officers all the closer, resulting in something good, because without this disunity we certainly would not have become so unified.

Fri. 15/27 Espenberg and Bellingshausen returned from Dodesterro without any news. Some people are possessed of a spirit to torment. Golovatscheff is one of them. As if it were his duty, he teases and picks and pokes and pulls. No matter what kind of animal is brought onboard, he is not still until he has tortured it over board or to death. Several dozen parrots have already ended this way. Among the few we still had on the ship was a small sparrow parrot that I had received as a present from Lang's eight-year-old daughter for my gift of a travel necklace. The little bird was very tame. My little Perokito made wild from teasing until it was no longer tame. To make it behave, I hit the bird several times. The little bird misunderstood and wanted to fly away. In my hurry, I grabbed it somewhat too harshly. My little parrot's eyes began to roll and, so that I did not have to watch the misery any longer, I threw it overboard.

Krusenstern has divided his cabin in half, so that he does not have to be vis-à-vis Resanoff, and can still have a corner for himself. Resanoff would certainly vex him by inviting the painter into the cabin quite often, and that would be the cause of renewed strife.

Sat. 16/28 This morning at nine o'clock Ratmanoff and I went to Punta Grossa to investigate whether the point is an island. We rowed up the river until we could go no farther, climbed out, and went on land. We came to a hut. The unexpected appearance of strange, armed men surprised the locals and frightened them. Undoubtedly, they thought we were robbers. One woman who met us at the door was totally frightened and barricaded the door and handed us from inside the house everything we asked for, even watermelons, which they had a surplus of, since there were quantities of melon rinds lying around the hut. We then returned to our boat, shot a few birds, and headed back.

Clouds covered the mountain peaks, and the sound of distant thunder foretold bad weather. We had not gone quite half way when a rain shower caught up with us and accompanied us to the ship. Onboard, we quickly jumped into dry clothing and into our berths, because we were so tired from climbing around on half-empty stomachs from morning until evening.

Sun. 17/29 Lang was given the task of bringing the remaining provisions we had bought from Dodesterro. Since part of them had not yet been paid for, Lisianski sent over to the *Neva* to request 200 dahler from Korobitzin, the supercargo on the *Neva*. He refused, however, to do it by answering that he would not hand over even a heller without Resanoff's direct order. How clever Resanoff is with his chicanery and spite! He is going to have to pay the money anyhow.

Our carpenters are busily working on the dividing wall in the captain's cabin.

A hummingbird fled to our ship just before the rain we had today and was caught. Sehnore Serjanto then said very importantly, "That is a happy omen." Let's hope so.

Mon. 18/30 Resanoff, who since our arrival has been a burden around the neck of Governor Curado, will probably want to give a party for him onboard ship before we leave. Since he knows nothing about the division of the cabin, he is going to be wide-eyed when he arrives. Krusenstern had intended to put a dividing wall in the cabin in Kronstadt. Since Resanoff is now saying loudly that the captains are enriching themselves with the ships' provisions at Company cost, he is harvesting hate and the desire for revenge. His having said in Petersburg, "I will keep a sharp eye on the captains, so that they do not do anything behind the backs of the American Company while running the ships," shows a corrupt man who judges others based on himself.

A boat with watermelons arrived. In order to purchase them more cheaply, I climbed down the side of the ship and bargained for one at two vintiins. Unexpectedly for me, Golovatscheff saddled me with a sailor with two baskets, telling the sailor to offer three kopecks. One does not outbid someone else on the ship, and moreover it was gross to compromise me with a sailor. I let him have the battlefield, climbed back up, and told him a few truths. The desire to buy watermelons also hit Espenberg. He called: "I gladly will give a petako for a watermelon (and very pitifully) if I can only get one."

"Overbidding," I said to him very dryly, "must be avoided, for it is the best means for buying nothing." Hardly had I got that out of my mouth when little Moritz shouted, "Ah, my brother!" Otto Kotzebue had also climbed down along the length of the ship, had slipped, hadn't been able to hold on and fallen into the water. Luckily, he was pulled out immediately. That frightened the Portuguese. They hurried off with their watermelons. Only with difficulty were we able to convince them through pantomime and shouts to come back onboard. Thus, we almost did not get any watermelons.

The ship's reckonings can only be determined to a tolerable degree of accuracy because the current, *the Swell* [sic] (high seas) and *Leeway* [sic] (drift) can only be noted down approximately in the journal and leads us seamen astray. Without observations, we would be lost. Enough effort has been put into devising *Logs* [sic] that are supposed to determine a ship's course, but a lot of what seems clear on paper is impossible in practice or at least very defective.

screw type log

a similar one

typical log

the so-called new log of Bouguer[13]

None of them meet expectations, etc. Navigation owes its thanks to astronomy that it has reached its present perfection.

Dominant weather in St. Catharina—with northeasterly clear skies, at night quiet, toward noon fresh. If the wind shifts to the south, then we have overcast weather, gusts of wind, thunderstorms, and heavy rain. The weather is very variable and also the temperature of the air. The current is irregular and maintains itself the longest downwind. Flood tide comes from the north and ebb tide from the south. The anchorage is good though somewhat slimy. The depth of the water along the roadstead is a uniform 5 to 6 faden.

The *Neva*'s masts have been put in place and almost rigged. At the governor's orders, no payment is to be taken for them. Aye Curado! Mutto Politiko. We cannot repay the kindnesses this cultivated man has shown us and especially Resanoff, through public ceremonies and courtesies. He treats our shark of an ambassador coldly in his house; something our king of quills also deserves.

Tues. 19/31 Raised the longboat and hauled in all of the stays and shrouds. The sails are all lashed. We need to weigh anchor only as soon as Resanoff and his suite arrive in order to leave Brazil. I have had enough of the place, and that is the way most of us feel. We are impatiently awaiting the moment we weigh anchor.

The time without constraints is over for us, unfortunately, with Resanoff's arrival. Among ourselves, we could talk freely, but soon we will be damned to put our words and actions on the gold scale, because we are surrounded by spies and backbiters. After the evening meal, Schemelin, the American Company's prikaschtschik, arrived from Dodesterro. With him our plague begins again. Tomorrow, the other gentlemen are supposed to move from land onto the ship.

The dividing wall in the captain's cabin was finished today.

Wed. 20/1 Krusenstern sent his shallop for Resanoff, who, they say, is to come onboard today in the company of the governor. It's being whispered around that, when Resanoff goes past the fortifications, he will be saluted. Then we have the possibility of returning the salute with only four cannons—we did not put anymore than that in place. The captain of the Portuguese brig, an Irishman by birth, ate with us at noon. They say he is a cunning smuggler. Mr. von Krusenstern made his acquaintance in order to give him letters, since he is staying six more days here, so he feasted with us.

Thurs. 21/2 We weighed anchor. We had barely finished our work when we saw our shallop arriving with the ambassador. The shallops were saluted as they approached the fortifications. Upon their arrival, we put our people on the shrouds. (Resanoff found little joy in the cold reception and the divided cabin.) His whole suite arrived with sack and pack. Curado stayed barely an hour with us. Upon his departure, we gave him five cheers and saluted with eleven salvos. Despite the fact we had only four cannons in place, the salvos followed each other quite regularly. Krusenstern made use of an auspicious moment and before his departure entrusted the governor with all of our letters.

Fri. 22/3 Adolpho came and with him a lot of boats with oranges, lemons, watermelons, etc. The chaos they caused on deck was great. Everyone was buying, counting, bargaining, and making noise, especially our passengers, who have only their own bellies to take care of, and therefore are the forestallers and noisemakers.

Resanoff sits for the most part in his divided cabin (thus, we have the company cabin free). The *Neva* is not quite ready yet.

The cold at Cape Horn cannot be colder than what meets Resanoff from us.

Friderici and Berg had made several acquaintances in Dodesterro. A boat full of guests came to the *Neva* to take leave. As the guests were ready to take their leave, everyone was in tears. A young Portuguese in the group took advantage of the situation to steal Lisianski's pocketbook and etui. The theft went unnoticed until all of them had left.

In Dodesterro, there is a soldier captain known for his stealing, and for this reason is not invited to any gatherings and is only admitted to the governor on business matters. Resanoff had an inclination toward this man and was in his company almost daily, even though Curado and all of the locals wrinkled their noses at his behavior.

Today, we have in practice excluded the painter Kurlandzoff from our group at meals. Resanoff has not yet mixed into the matter, probably will let it alone.

Sat. 23/4 Among the animals that we have caught, shot, or received, the toucan has aroused my attention the most—because of its beautiful feathers. Its incredible bill surprises you; its lightness is even more remarkable. The large spider bird has caused a big argument between Langsdorff and Tilesius. The one maintains they live on hummingbirds and the other the opposite (Tilesius is for hummingbirds). They have not come to any agreement. The small white stork, the black-necked swan, and several beautifully feathered woodpeckers, countless parrots—for butterflies, bugs, and all kinds of insects Brazil is the true abode. Crabs, snakes, bullfrogs, lizards, etc., live in very great numbers and diversity here. I indeed believe that a botanist will reap the biggest harvest here. We have onboard two live American raccoons, whose fur is used for carriage blankets.

Right after table, during my watch, the wind shifted to the south. We did not waste a moment. The captain gave the signal to weigh anchor, and half an hour later we were under sail. Golovatscheff, who had gone on land in the little boat to get water, held us up a bit, but, before the sun went down, we had sailed between Alvaredo and St. Catharina and were in open sea. As is customary, we congratulated our captain (and that from our hearts) on the successful departure. We ignored the ambassador because, without any discussion, we had agreed to pay no attention either to him or to his suite. (He is kind enough to reward us with mutual coldness.)

Sun. 24/5 Contrary wind. We are impatiently awaiting the time when we sail around Patagonia, Tierra del Fuego, and Cape Horn in order to add our tidbits to the multitudinous rumors about the area.

Our people are used to the good life on shipboard. The hearty soups, the fresh meat—even chicken—their tea, grog, and punsch have made their palates so dainty that they did not live otherwise on land. When our people were on land in St. Catharina, they always drank their coffee at breakfast and ate eggs and fruit. They often think about their return and ask each other whether they will like life on a ship of war again.

Anecdote: In Brazil if a young man wants not only to court a young woman but also to have some fun, he takes a thin ball made of wax filled with pleasant smelling water and flattens it on her bosom. Since the ball is the size of an apple, the flood may not bring forth a pleasant reaction in the Dulcinea. This happens often at Carnival, but it is used for amusement at other times. The beau has in addition the pleasure, the right, to dry the lady off. Friderici tried it. I am very sorry that I did not know about it earlier; otherwise, I would have gladly had the fun of washing the bosom of a Brazilian lady. While at work, the sensation may not be so bad, depends upon the bosom. If the perfumed ball is big, then you get a bit much to wash.

- 4 -

Brazil to Nukahiva

Tues. 26/7 We are spending quiet times right now. Resanoff does not risk joining us because he fears sharp remarks. The other gentlemen are also still and quiet, and, since we have excluded the painter from our group, his stupidity and poltroonery no longer make us laugh.

Since this is the longest stage of the voyage, our captain has rationed water for all of us. Everyone without exception gets two kruschka of water, about four bouteilles [bottles] a day for meals, cooking, tea, and drinking. According to our calculations, this way we will have enough water for four months.

Langsdorff bought twelve large pineapples in Brazil for a quarter of a dahler, that is 8 vintiin.

Wed. 27/8 Xaviel Curado let himself be paid for the costs he incurred in feeding our ambassador. After refusing to accept anything for a long time for the masts for the *Neva,* he asked to be paid 1,000 Spanish dahler. Now these costs will be charged to the American Company. If they had been, as we originally thought, only 300 dahler, then Lisianski would have gladly put them on his bill because there would have been some profit in it.

We assume that the difference between our observations of the ship's position we make and the ship's reckoning is caused by the current, and, nevertheless, the incorrectness of our and every ship's reckoning is a large part of the difference which we, from egotism and for simplicity's sake, blame on the current. If we are in areas where there is no current, the ship's calculation very rarely indicates the correct position on the map. However, we find then immediately some other excuse. Then it must be the fault of high seas, the waves, the drift. Seldom can we determine our position with certainty on the map without having made an observation. Several degrees' difference in our course through the deviation of the magnetic needle over a short distance are not noticeable. If we sail several degrees off course for days, it does make a big difference. The current carries everything. That is the way it is with the log line and the hourglass. A mistake of ten miles a day in the measurement of our course sneaks in easily if we have a good wind. The log line is the leash that can become longer or shorter, the hourglass, a sand clock. These deficiencies can be attributed to the fact that no definition of the current is made. In addition, the pilot plays his part. I would like to see the seaman who could prove to me that he is capable of sailing straight along a rope in a strong wind. The course or path we sail is a continual zigzag. You can set the sails whatever way you want, and the ship is inclined to sail more to one side than the other. Even this mistake is blamed on the current. Our clock's mistakes have become irregular since we now determine our longitude with all three chronometers. That is the reason we are so keen on the distances of the moon.

Thurs. 28/9 During Romberg's watch last night, a leeward squall hit us under alee. Nothing is more dangerous at sea. We were sailing with the wind. Suddenly the wind blew from the right. We had not yet finished bracing when a gust of wind from the left hit into our sails, so that the topsails and masts creaked. Because we had been carrying four sails, the jib was also standing, and, because we had been tacking to the right, the line of the блиндарея [sprit yard] also had been brought around to the side. With the gust of wind from the left side, the jib boom was greatly bent, and Golkeeff, one of our sailors, without waiting for the command "кливер долой!" [jib duty], tried to loosen the sheets a little in order to relieve the jib boom. The wind, however, tore the line out of his hands, and in a few minutes the entire sail had been ripped into a thousand pieces and disappeared. We were able to haul in the rest of the sails in one piece. The sailor's good intentions protected him from being punished.

Around noon, we reached the latitude of the Rio de la Plata. Up until now, we have been holding straight south, but because of the expected current from the Rio de la Plata we have begun to strike a westerly course. Only for tea and at the noon meal is Resanoff to be seen in the company cabin. On deck, he usually avoids the side on which we go (windward).

We still have some water left over in our rations because of the cool weather. In the hot climate, we will then yearn for it.

The wind is becoming brisker and brisker, and the barometer has fallen. That is why we have prepared ourselves for a storm, lowered the topgallant masts and yards and our main topgallant and foresails, and hauled in the foretopsail, foresail, and forestaysail, all of our sails. Along the American coast the dominant winds blow from the northeast and southwest, and, the farther one is from land, the more variable they are. Krusenstern therefore decided that it would be good to sail five degrees closer to land than any ship up to now had sailed, and we are happy to have continual, favorable winds. The captain gave the order that if the entire crew is called to work, the rest of the officers likewise have to come on deck to help those on watch.

A miracle! Resanoff spoke with Romberg and me today. (The weather is bad today. That is the cause.)

Fri. 30/11 The wind shifted to the southwest; the barometer is still continually falling.

In Brazil, worms called bischu bore into Count Tolstoi's feet. They are so small that they crawl into human pores, gnaw into the skin, and lay countless numbers of little eggs. If one does not cut them out in time, they cause a lot of abscesses on the feet, which often make it difficult for the Negroes, who all go barefoot, to walk, and are very painful. Langsdorff operated on Count Tolstoi and cut out innumerable eggs.

Sat. 31/12 The Rio de la Plata's current has driven us strongly to the east. We have 15° according to Réaumur's [scale],[1] and everyone is complaining about the raw south wind.

Colds, stomachaches, and sores are the order of the day on shipboard.

February

Sun. 1/13 A beautiful, dry fall day.

Ratmanoff is very rude, and he may be right or wrong, with his "You are lying!" or "It is not true!" is how he tries to hit the other fellow in the face. Today at table he said that and then something coarse to Romberg. Romberg couldn't stomach it and returned equally well the same kinds of truths and coarseness. It was left at that. This discord, however, left behind a coldness that is lower than our thermometer.

Our clocks make great jumps now and then.

Mon. 2/14 Cool dry weather with clear skies.

Moritz Kotzebue is a tormentor. He has trained his nice little parrot to death.

Tues. 3/15 Our captain is so considerate of our sailors that one can say he is weak for all his fairness. He looks after their health in a fatherly way. Since leaving Brazil, our sailors, up to now, have had salt meat only twice, and we have twelve big, live pigs for our sailors, so that they will still have fresh provisions when we reach Cape Horn.

Wed. 4/16 At home! What is meant by that? We mean our part of the world. If we are in Europe, we mean Russia; if we are in Russia, we mean—at home! the district where we were born; if we are in that district it means the county; in the county, the parish, and in the parish, the estate or the house in which we were born, where we live or feel at home. When will we be home again, at our place?

Thurs. 5/17 The weather was like one of our beautiful fall days. We made a lot of observations, since the sea was somewhat quieter and the skies clear.

We are already at 43° southern latitude, and the weather was pregnant with more gusts of wind at the equator than here.

Fri. 6/18 A favorable northwester. We are not sailing less than six knots.

Sat. 7/19 Wet, foggy weather with favorable winds. Espenberg exposes himself to a lot of jeers and has to listen to a lot of truths about his eating voracity, and that doesn't solve anything. His body is possessed of an uncontrollable gluttony, greed, and impatience with food and drink. When we sit down at table, it seems as if our doctor has been starving for several days. He flings himself at the food and drink; others follow his example, causing an unbearable grabbing and gobbling, and there is no correcting this disorder. The offenders of good manners are no longer schoolboys, and no one wants to take up the matter of their education.

During the day, the fog was now and again so heavy that we could not see the *Neva* as she sailed close by us.

The nights were all the nicer. With a fresh wind, the *Nadezhda* cut playfully through the waves. (We were sailing seven knots.) The sky was clear, the moon shone and the stars twinkled, not a single little cloud to be seen. Suddenly, the *Neva* sent a signal that we did not understand. Since the sea was quiet, Krusenstern had a boat lowered and sent the mate over. He returned with the news that the *Neva* had hit a sleeping whale that gave the ship such a strong jolt that they thought they had run into a sandbank.

Sun. 8/20 Today, Tilesius was supposed to write a receipt for spiritus he got to preserve his specimens. Since, however, he had had to give Langsdorff a couple of stof, he fought hand and foot saying that they were demanding of him he sign for things he had not received. He became so loud and got me involved in the business, too. He makes me angry, and I let him know how absurd he can be. I could have been a bit more calm and composed about it.

Mon. 9/21 We observed our barometer, which fell today, like a trustworthy friend who gives us good advice, and we are glad to follow that advice.

Tues. 10/22 We reached the latitude of the Falkland Islands. Large numbers of whales and porpoises are swimming around our ship. The dolphins rival the *Nadezhda* for speed, swim in front of the ship, and, if they hit the ship, they hurl themselves into the waves or throw themselves into the air, only to fall with a crack back into the water.

The *Neva* sent a signal that she had damaged a large topsail yard. We had to stop and wait for her until the work was finished. We were held up for two hours.

The unpleasantness we have had, the cold water, and permanent stress (even though time passes very quickly) have converted our voyage into an eternity. I shudder, as does everyone else, at the thought, "You have to spend three more years together with these people." Each one of us will find the other loathsome before the end of our voyage and be glad finally to have other faces to look at.

Wed. 11/23 From last evening until early this morning, we have had calm. The barometer has however fallen.

Our next anchorage depends upon our successfully sailing around Cape Horn. If we sail through quickly, then we will go to Chile; if not, then the Mendoza

Islands are our next stopping place. Going to Chile is the general desire, since on the South Sea Islands we might experience what Portlock[2] did. He had to battle so many difficulties at the *Sanwitsch* [sic] Islands [Hawaii] that he had to buy fresh water in bottle gourds so that he could go to sea again.

Today, innumerable whales played in view, blew their fountains while breaching the water, then cracking the water every time with their tails. They swam barely fifteen faden from the ship and satisfied their curiosity about this large animal in their vicinity. A huge lump breached next to us, and with his tail that he raised high in the air he would have been capable of smashing our longboat. Another huge lump, looking like a flat on which a lot of sea swallows had landed, swam past the ship. The albatrosses also like the nice day, because for the first time we are seeing them swim on the water. They have approached our ship boldly. When the bird had become shy from our loud calls "Look at them!" it ran a couple of cable lengths on the water before it could give itself enough momentum to lift itself into the air.

Since the evening was so nice, Lisianski and Povalischin visited us for half an hour. Thank goodness everyone on the *Neva* is healthy.

Thurs. 12/24 In the morning, we passed the latitude of the Straits of Magellan. Krusenstern prefers a stop on the South Sea Islands to one in Chile. As far as that goes, he is right in that he robs Resanoff of the means of doing us damage. (I pointed that out in my cabin.) Resanoff goes around the ship like a water-shy dog, with lowered head, and seeks out opportunities to do damage to the captain and us and to give a bite of death. He has time and leisure enough to brew new attacks, to invent new lies, so that he can once again complain about us to the emperor. That will not be possible from the South Sea Islands.

Irresponsible of me but I nevertheless have to admit it! I am hoping for a storm at Cape Horn.

We reduced our sails in the evening because we are afraid we are too far to the west and headed to the east so as not to reach Staatenland in the night.

Fri. 13/25 Staatenland came into view at sunrise, but we still had to sail to the east in order to double Cape John. The thermometer was 7° warmth (that is, the middle of summer). At noon, the latitude was 54° 12' South. The longitude 63° 40' West. A brisk north wind is driving us forwards. At six o'clock in the evening, we had Cape John (the eastern point of Staatenland) to the west and headed again to the south. The current was very strong against us. We had been sailing eight knots and, according to our observations of the stars, been driven 15 miles backwards. At midnight, we were at the latitude of Cape Horn! Sailed however farther southwards in order to gain windage or sea.

Sat. 14/26 The wind was variable all morning, and with gusts of wind, rain, snow, and hail it shifted to the southwest. We hauled in the sails and prepared ourselves for the wind's fury and to be ready to take on a storm. The barometer had fallen sharply. The wind stayed reef topsail and shifted again to the west. You good people who are carrying out your March tasks perhaps think we are lost. On the

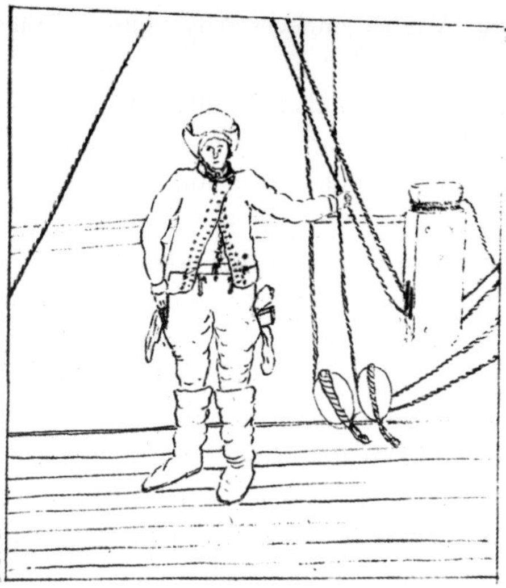

4-1. A view of the ambassador to Japan at Cape Horn, Resanoff, in optima forma [sic]

contrary, we are quite well, freezing like the devil, and waiting longingly the time when we once again may put our winter clothing away.

Sun. 15/27 We have chosen the best time of year for doubling Cape Horn. Today, we once again put up as much sail as the weather and the movement of the ship allowed, so that we would sail forwards.

Everyone for himself and God for all of us! is the watchword on our ship.

During the afternoon, we took a heavy gust of wind. Our jib ripped to pieces, and we were forced to set our storm sail. The *Neva* must have had it worse. She was overshot by a whirlwind and therefore had to turn again immediately with the wind. Half an hour later, the wind calmed down a bit.

Recently, Mr. von Krusenstern has been giving the subaltern officers orders that the officers on watch do not know about. That causes disorder and has already left us peevish. We are tacking to the right. The captain went to the pilot and had the ship tack to the left. Naturally, the sail came out of the wind, and Romberg, who saw it from the waist cried, "To the right!"

Krusenstern went to him and said, "We want to sail a bit farther away from the *Neva*."

"If we," answered Romberg, "were part of a fleet in this sea and stayed so far apart, then the last ship would be on the horizon." (Romberg could have refrained from saying that.)

Mr. von Krusenstern retorted: "You do not need to get hot at all about things I want to have done!" I'm sorry about this incident, and it would be better if it had never happened.

Resanoff, who eavesdrops on everything, had barely heard that Romberg had had a dispute with Krusenstern when he went up to him when he had watch again and asked: "Which rhomb are we sailing?"

"To the south," answered Romberg. "We are unnecessarily cautious," said Resanoff.

"Which course would you then take?" asked Romberg in turn. The question came unexpectedly, and he broke off the conversation with a lot of excuses. (Resanoff hoped to be able to make Krusenstern look bad and to proselytize Romberg.)

The *Neva* lighted a false fire in the night during my watch. I ordered the mate Филип Иванович [Filip Ivanovich] (Kamentschikoff) to see which rhomb they were at. Since he did not want to do it and in addition was coarse about the matter, I had to look at the compass myself and complained to the captain, who also came on deck. In the morning, I will pursue the matter further. (The rascal hopes by doing such things to ingratiate himself with Resanoff.)

Mon. 16/28 Today, the captain told Kamentschikoff the following: If he behaved in such a way again, so that the officer of the watch found it necessary to complain about him, then he (Krusenstern) would remove him from service.

Tues. 17/29 Cape Horn asserts its rights. (A fool if it doesn't.) Intermittent gusts of wind, snow, hail, icy, snowy cold, and rain. The wind is brisker and brisker, and the waves grow higher and higher. (Up to now, I have always experienced worse weather.)

Our passengers are all very quiet and hover between fear and hope. We are busy defying the violent storm. Moritz Kotzebue, a useless boy, got in it with Tilesius today, and they got in a tussle in which Moritz of course got the short end of the stick. Instead of Espenberg's giving Moritz a reprimand for his misbehavior, as he should have done, he began an argument with Tilesius. (Moritz is Espenberg's favorite.) Tilesius, angered by this, did not know any more what he was saying. Espenberg got to hear enough.

Wed. 18/1 Wind and weather are better. We joined the *Neva* again, from which we had been separated for 24 hours, only to be separated once again by the fog. It is unbearably wet and cold. My arm has caught cold. It is as if paralyzed, and that was a result of the rainwater coming through the deck and dripping on my arm in my berth. I asked Espenberg what I should do about it in order to prevent ill consequences. Our egoist was much too much concerned with himself and to get rid of me said that he found it much worse when it leaked through the moldings, as was the case in his cabin. And he claimed this so fervently that I said nothing, went to my cabin, and put on a flannel waistcoat with the intention of not asking him again.

Intermittent southwesterly and westerly winds. The cold weather has caused my parrots to lose their good humor, and they do not want to eat right. Their feet are swollen (frostbite) and they will probably die one after another. By chance, we fleet officers were eating our evening meal together. The food was carried out. We were still engrossed in our discussion when the passengers ate up the food. There was nothing to be done about it. We all got up from the table again without having eaten, since not a one of us wanted to be a teacher of morals.

In the evening, we were reunited with the *Neva*.

Thurs. 19/2 Becalmed. (We had not expected it at Cape Horn.) We unlashed our last anchor cable. We had a leak in the ship, a zoll of water per hour. We plugged the spot. It was at the front of the ship under a mirror. The ship's seam had burst, probably through the heat. It was caulked, and our leak stopped.

Espenberg had bought several piglets and chickens in St. Catharina for his own use. That is not permitted here or on any ship. (What is good for the goose is good for the gander.) Otherwise everyone would be smart enough to provide for himself. Since no one has said anything, my comrades plan to follow Espenberg's example the next time to force the return of order.

Not only my parrots but also Krusenstern's canaries are suffering from the cold. They are now hanging in the company cabin where it is somewhat warmer at tea and meals.

We are sailing at nine and ten knots. Superb wind. Whenever Resanoff condescends to speak with us and talk about something, then they are always stories about Irkutsk and of Emperor Paul.[3] Today his tale surprised us, for he said, "Before my departure from Russia, Tschitschagoff advised me to abandon the voyage and offered me a position in his department, sent for me, and told me he wanted to make me his assistant."

Resanoff wants to impress us with this story because he knows that we seamen all respect Tschitschagoff.

Fri. 20/3 Again contrary wind from the southwest. We sailed past the longitude of Cape Horn in the morning.

Sat. 21/4 Nice, brisk northeasterly wind, but high seas to the west. The western tip of Tierra del Fuego has a very fitting name. It is called Cape Victoria, for, when one has passed this promontory, one has overcome all difficulties that the southwesterly wind puts in the way of a seafarer.

Sun. 22/5 We were at 60° latitude. The currents flow to the west with a mild wind, with the wind from the east.

Mon. 23/6 The equinoktium is not much farther, and I nevertheless still wish for a non plus ultra of a storm. It just seems to me that we have not been at Cape Horn if we have no storms to remember.

Tues. 24/7 My beautiful parrot has gone crazy. In this cold weather he is molting, the poor bird.

Contrary wind. Moritz is a capable boy. Otto is more solid but also more phlegmatic. The latter has unfortunately attached himself to Tolstoi and Ratmanoff, who teach him only smut. Had I the patience, I could well decide to give them lessons in geometry and navigation. It is deplorable to see the children wasting their time. In actuality, they spend the whole day doing nothing.

Wed. 25/8 We were becalmed in the night. These calms at Cape Horn are the most unbearable for all us because the continual high seas toss the ship around murderously.

I impatiently awaited a wind on my watch. The horizon was surrounded by black, threatening clouds. Finally, a wind arose, but again an accursed southwester that will probably plague us for its full eight days.

Thurs. 26/9 Calms, changes in the light (new moon), the threatening skies, and the slightly falling barometer bode nothing good.

Our passengers have used their idle time to read descriptions of voyages by Cook,[4] Marchand,[5] Anson,[6] La Pérouse, etc. If something unusual happens, then judging, arguing, and blue-apron statesmanship starts up in the cabin. They have not correctly digested what they have read and argue into the day. Espenberg, who has a very good memory, exaggerates things the most.

Fri. 27/10 The wind is blowing out of the same old hole, always from the southwest with gusts of wind, rain, and hail.

My beautiful parrot died this morning. It was everybody's favorite.

Sat. 28/11 Finally, a south wind with innumerable gusts of wind that are unsettling but have moved us nonetheless forwards.

Before noon, the painter Kurlandzoff went to Krusenstern with his diploma and a medallion from the Academy of Sciences and complained that a man who had drawn so many things was being excluded from the group. Krusenstern answered him that all these honors were no guarantee of good conduct and that he therefore could only, through asking for pardon, make good what he had spoiled. At lunch, our delinquent spoke again, though with very few manners, and asked to be pardoned; thus, he was given the right to participate in our company again. Resanoff used it to show his authority. Ratmanoff followed his lead and told him in his coarse way some rather ticklish things. Resanoff answered "fine" and left. I am glad that I was not present. I had watch.

We got an east wind in the evening, the first wind we have wished for since Staatenland. We sailed past the longitude of Cape Victoria, and, if God wills, we will soon be in warm climes.

Sun. 29/12 General joy over the nice wind. We have not been sailing under eight knots. Right after the meridian, we congratulated the captain with Cape Horn, since we have now reached a sufficient longitude that the dear west wind, no matter how big an effort he might make, wouldn't be able drive us backwards.

What will I do if we get back safely? Go on a new voyage, stay in the service and cruise around the Baltic, or take leave of the service. The latter is what my good sisters would say, "Take a wife and stay with us." The second thing is what I have to do in order to get an order of St. George,[7] and the first thing is driven by my ambition. The future knows better what is to become of me.

After we had congratulated Krusenstern, he invited us to drink some schnapps and eat breakfast with him, with the exception of the painter whom he had told to avoid his cabin forever. Despite that, that fresh fellow came anyway. Mr. von Krusenstern told him as he came in, "I have not sent for you." He acted as if he had not heard and stayed. The captain repeated his words again and said to him: "You know that I have asked you to avoid my cabin." The rascal did not even react to this and approached the breakfast table. Whereupon the captain said to him: "You force me to tell you that you are to leave my cabin this very minute." That the painter could not say he had not heard and was forced to leave the cabin immediately.

I spoke with Krusenstern about his plan for Kamtschatka on the 25th. The captain had not yet told Resanoff. Golovatscheff, however, is so ready to be of service that he told Resanoff. (He could have left that alone.) To excuse himself, Golovatscheff now claims he did it at the captain's request—very believable indeed!

March

Mon. 1/13 Resanoff has taken over the role of fiscal attorney, and his creatures are his quick scribes. Everything in our discussions that might do us damage, that might later be used, de facto is booked. That is the way we are spending our March.

Tues. 2/14 We passed the latitude of Cape Horn with a fresh topsail wind.

Resanoff is busy finishing a complaint about Ratmanoff, or so his creatures are saying. Because Ratmanoff, as eldest lieutenant, is the eldest in the company cabin, and Councilor Fosse and the others are treated and titled as passengers, and because of his recent dispute with Resanoff that also had its origin in his position, Ratmanoff considered it his duty as eldest lieutenant to speak.

I have completely forgotten to mention that Fosse has been ill since our departure from St. Catharina and has not appeared even once in the Company cabin. Not one of us naval officers has visited him since our departure.

Wed. 3/15 The wind caused us all to take in reefs, and the waves were high. We immediately cursed the rolling of the ship and the waves, but we were glad that we could still maintain our course. Lamenting indeed does nothing to improve the weather.

Thurs. 4/16 On my watch during the night, I did not want to take in reefs without the captain's permission. I sent him word that the wind was increasing, and he ordered taking in a reef in the course sail. Since I took all possible precautions, nothing was torn or broken. The sailors, however, acted as if they were crazy. I had to show them in the dark every rope that had to be drawn in or let out. Krusenstern, who was also present, even became angry with the men. Since he had resolved to command humanely, they received only a reprimand. We were carrying more sail than the wind permitted, causing the waves to toss the ship about so very strongly that the entire vessel trembled, and, since the front of the ship is heavily loaded, it resisted the waves and pounded our prow. In order to take advantage of the wind, we sailed right on.

Our fresh provisions decrease daily, and the lust and brashness of our sluggards also increase daily. Last night, Langsdorff almost tore the mustard jar out of Bellingshausen's hand. The baron lay hold of him so cordially that he considered it advisable to let go of his booty. We are the ones who suffer. It would be terrible if we also wanted to dig in. Only through flexibility is it possible to maintain peace here. That is what Krusenstern has requested of us, and we are willing to do anything to please our captain.

Fri. 5/17 I'll try to describe the way it is at tea and at meals on our ship. Two of us, a naval officer and a passenger, are in charge each week. Since the gentlemen have nothing to do, they are in agreement, even though there is no formal agreement, that it is their duty to pour the tea. Every morning at eight is teatime. Even though the gentlemen have had plenty of time to sleep, they always are the last to appear. If one voices any objections, there is discord. Finally, the host appears and takes up his duties. Nothing is easier than to misjudge taste. One of the society therefore requests another piece of sugar, or the tea is too strong or too weak; he wants hardtack, etc. The answer he receives is, "One cannot serve everyone all at the same time"—or the question is diligently ignored. After repeated requests, the beggar finally gets a piece of sugar, but with an expression and manner that puts salt in his tea more than it sweetens it. I have few needs, and no one has been inclined to treat me that way, but it is unpleasant to see others treated in such an indecorous manner.

The tea things have just barely been cleared away when one of the long sleepers demands the leftovers from the evening meal. Since we usually have things to do at this time, everything has been eaten up before we can even dream of getting something for breakfast. Then we wait impatiently for lunch. Finally, at 1:30, soup bowls appear. Usually I have become so overhungry by that time that my appetite has disappeared. The smell of the food passes over my taste buds, and I sit down at the table with a ravenous appetite. As is well-known, sea air makes you hungry. Since our stops are far apart and the group is large, we have to use our fresh provisions sparingly. The number of chickens slaughtered each day is not large enough to satisfy the group's hunger, and salt meat and grits often have to help still our hunger. The soup is passed around. Often, because of the rolling of the ship, the strong wind, etc., it is not always good—edible. The gentlemen who have laid up their hoard at breakfast therefore spurn this fare and wait for something better. Now comes salt meat. The smell itself is repulsive to the gentlemen, even though salt meat cannot be any better. While we are satisfying our hunger, the learned gentlemen amuse themselves with the wine bottles. The bottles are empty before we have come to our senses. It happens all too often that our captain gets to drink no more than one glass of wine, for all of the gentlemen drink from beer glasses even though wineglasses are standing in front of them. (Langsdorff once said to Stepan, "Why are you giving me such a small glass? I cannot drink wine from small beer glasses.") Since the gentlemen know which side will be served first, before the table has been set, they have taken all the seats. In order to make up for the spurned fare, they take a double portion of the roast. The last in line gets almost nothing and has to be satisfied with the chicken's neck. One of us [officers] draws that lot for sure. No attention is paid to this fact but rather tomorrow will be like today. Then come grits, a pudding, or some other kind of satisfying dish; always a large portion is prepared in order to quell our hunger. The bowl is barely carried away when we get up from the table. Usually after a meal, the group is in high spirits, and a good mood reigns in the company cabin. No wonder! Each one of the gentleman passengers has eaten and drunk for two.

At tea in the afternoon, it is just like in the morning, with the difference that they unrestrainedly go after the bottle of brandy, the lemons, and oranges. And without a sense of shame they are capable of using rude language over a lemon, etc. Since each one of us has night watch, we usually sleep after tea and therefore miss the evening meal. To fast from noon until the next noon is really difficult. Now comes the evening meal, which is very frugal and can only be considered a snack. Usually, it consists of a piece of salt meat and a bowl of vegetables. Since the gentlemen cannot stand the smell of salt meat, let alone eat it, they consider it their due to make themselves masters of the bowl of vegetables, and in a flash the bowl is empty. Since the portions they have heaped up on their plates are indecent even for them (especially since they see we have nothing), the gulping and secretly looking around (from a bad conscience) make me, at least, feel nauseous. If per chance one of that gang has nothing, then a ruckus is raised, and he thinks it his due to take an even bigger portion the next time as indemnity. Six to eight hands reach out for the bottle of brandy served at the evening meal before the bottle can even be set on the table, because each one of them wants to be first in order to have the privilege of filling his beer glass half full. None of them care whether his neighbor also gets some. With his mild nature, our captain ignores all of this so as not to compromise himself. And we follow his example out of respect for his extraordinary character.

Sat. 6/18 A tricky matter with Japan: Resanoff, with his secret machinations, will undoubtedly make demands of Krusenstern there that our captain will have to reject and, in case the Embassy is unsuccessful, will use these refusals to claim that Krusenstern was the reason for the unsuccessful embassy, in order to wash himself clean while at the same time indulging in his desire for revenge.

Prikaschtschik Schemelin's duties are to take care of the ship's provisions and cargo and while dispensing them to record receipts and expenditures. As result of Resanoff's instructions, the fellow does nothing and messes up the calculations. Rats are doing a lot of damage. During my watch, I was told that rats had eaten up four sacks of hardtack. I sent the lieutenant on watch to Schemelin to tell him he should look into the matter. He gave as an answer that he did not want to come. I had this dereliction of duty written into the journal and asked Krusenstern to have the officer of the watch sign the journal every time in order to prevent trouble. Schemelin finally appeared—very fresh and pert—the captain bawled him out, nevertheless bore patiently his stupid evasions and talk. (These people want to cause us to make mistakes through haste.)

A lot of albatrosses had encamped around our ship this afternoon and pulled in their large wings. We shot at them with coursing balls that whistled around their ears. They only shook themselves a little, raised themselves slowly into flight again, and flew unconcernedly around our ship as before.

Sun. 7/19 Krusenstern issued a written order that every lieutenant is duty-bound to sign for his watch. The helmsmen find the order unpleasant, and Resanoff's suite has a wide variety of opinions about the matter. But now our journal becomes authoritative, and, since the smallest detail gets put in it, it can be used to justify the captain's actions—that is the way it has to be.

Mon. 8/20 The captain provided the ambassador with the plan for the voyage to Kamtschatka. His Excellency did not have enough time to consider this because he was studying the matter with Fosse and Schemelin (those two simpletons). The shortsightedness and one-sidedness of the whole bunch is therefore not yet finished with deliberating, and no answer is forthcoming.

Tues. 9/21 The wind is unparalleled.

We sailed to the west past the latitude of the Straits of Magellan. Joys of this kind are imaginary at sea, since the power of imagination can only imagine our point on the map.

Wed. 10/22 The wind continues to be kindly inclined toward us.

It seems to me as if I were hired to ferret out the mistakes in the ship's reckonings. At present, we are sailing with gusts of wind. The first quarter hour at ten knots, the second at five, the third at eight, and finally at the end of the hour at nine knots. The *Loglin* [sic: log line] is cast, however, when the hour strikes, cause enough to suspect mistakes that are blamed on the current. In addition, one rarely finds two people measuring the speed of the ship at the same time who count the same number of knots, especially if the wind is brisk. Bad weather often prevents a seaman from taking the azimuth, and the rolling of the ship often prevents an appropriate exactness in these observations, and the deviation of the compass is incorrect. In addition, the determination of drift is very inexact and nevertheless has a great influence on the course of the ship.

Still no answer from Resanoff to the captain's letter or suggestion. The long deliberation suggests chancellery tricks are coming.

Thurs. 11/23 The full moon is capricious, for the strong reef topsail wind drives us around the Pacific in a very unfriendly way. The barometer, our soothsayer and prophet, lies during the equinoctium. We made this discovery in the last eight days.

Fri. 12/24 It is three years ago today that our benevolent and good emperor took over the throne. May God grant him help. The bad weather does not permit us to celebrate today, as our hearts would like to.

Sat. 13/15 The result of sailing so far apart is that we are separated from the *Neva*. We have been very happy every time we find each other again; will that be the case this time? The weather is foggy, and we have been separated for a day now.

Now I want to tell a stupid tale.

My watch was in the morning at four. At ten o'clock, I was hungry, so I drank a glass of my coffee liqueur and ate a piece of hardtack because I could get nothing else. Half an hour later, a full plate of ham was served. I said, "I'm sorry I did not know that each one of us can request something. Had I known I would not have just had hardtack for breakfast." I said it without any designs, having forgotten that Espenberg is the steward this week. Our doctor took my remark the wrong way, and we ended up in an argument. I strongly defended myself and mentioned that we souffre douleurs [whipping boys] got short shrift with food and drinks and for the sake of peace kept quiet.

Espenberg said, "Proof that I have not looked out just for myself is, if I wanted something to eat, I would only need to send for my студин." (He meant the pork jelly or aspic he had made from his pigs.)

I answered, "If everyone had bought as many pigs for his breakfast as you did, dear doctor, then we would not have found enough space on the ship to keep them."

Now Tilesius, uninvited, got into the dispute. (I wasn't in good standing with Tilesius and avoided him wherever I could.) That irked me, and I said to him, "Where two are arguing with each other, a third should not join in uninvited." This answer enraged Tilesius, and he vented his anger at me by threatening to complain about me to the captain. And, when I tried to tell him something, he wouldn't even listen to me. Therefore, I went to Krusenstern, told him the story, and asked him to straighten out Tilesius's false impression and to tell him that such incidents could only be settled between the two people involved, and in such situations unnecessary complaining did not help. Returned to the company cabin and told Tilesius that we now had to deal with each other alone, and he had to act accordingly. The dear councilor behaved well. I, however, asked him to show his bravour [gallantry] when necessary, and now he had better be quiet.

Mr. von Krusenstern told me a few hours later that he had spoken with Tilesius and hoped that the whole incident would not lead to any further problems. We will see!

Sun. 14/26 Nothing is to be seen of the *Neva*. If Lisianski is sailing to Chile, then our separation is deliberate.

The wind is not blowing from the best direction north-northwest, deviating from that almost northwest.

The two Kotzebues are in a bad school as far as decorum is concerned. For example, if someone needs something lying at the other end of the table, he doesn't ask his neighbor for it but rather reaches himself across the entire table and wipes the other person's nose with his sleeve. One sits more comfortably above the wind. These seats are taken before the table has even been set. We would grant them any seat they wanted if only they did not force us to move from one side of the table to the other. The way this is done makes the whole matter impolite and ill-mannered.

Mon. 15/27 The wind has become quite strong.

The continual pressure, the unpleasant, inhospitable calm, which is only interrupted (like gusts of wind) by discord and arguments, makes us all of us surly.

During the night on my watch the wind changed with an unbelievable force from north-northeast to west-southwest. We were carrying very little sail and traveling nine knots. It was a pleasure to see the ship working her way through the waves; and since the sea was from the north-northeast and the wind from the west-southwest, every third wave went over the ship, sometimes more often. Within an hour, however, the new wind's fury had replaced the old waves with new ones that hit the sides of the ship violently.

We had to haul in some sails.

Tues. 16/28 Using this nice wind, we had traveled two and one-half latitudes since yesterday.

Golovatscheff is, as ever, false, sanctimonious, and suspicious.

Wed. 17/29 The equinoctium is catching up with us. This causes Espenberg the greatest vexation because he is almost the only one who cannot get used to the ship's movement.

The painter was bragging today that one could hardly name twelve artists in Russia who could be compared with him. (He may well be the 100,000th one who can claim to be an artist.) Brinkin lazes around and literally does nothing because he is conceited; and since he speaks Latin, is cleverer than everyone else.

Ratmanoff is prouder of his healthy lungs than many another of his inventions. Fosse thinks himself in his stupidity more cunning than all of the rest of us. Resanoff is proud of his bad qualities. Kamentschikoff thinks he is old enough to speak ineptly about stupid things with the happy conviction that no one can better judge things than he, and brags about his supposed experiences.

Count Tolstoi is actually an ignoramus; acts worldly wise and thinks he is superior to all of us in breeding. If one takes stupid boldness and coarseness for decorum, then he is right.

Schemelin does not deserve to be counted among civilized men.

Thurs. 18/30 Self-love has, thank goodness, been granted all of us. Therefore, we should not judge too severely.

A rainbow in the morning is the sailors warning.
A rainbow before night is the sailors delight [sic].

Today, Ratmanoff took it upon himself to fumigate his cabin. The weather was very bad and the smoke so strong that he drove everyone out of the company cabin (as if he had wanted to play a trick on those idlers). Espenberg, who immediately got in a bad mood, made the most noise because he is also Ratmanoff's neighbor. But Ratmanoff paid no attention and continued fumigating; thus ended this affair.

Fri. 19/31 Rain and gusts of wind. Since the weather cleared up intermittently, we made observations.

Sat. 20/1 The captain had given the order, in case the weather was good, to wash the berths.

Sun. 21/2 The morning was nice, and at four o'clock I had things washed. Soon afterwards, we got rain. Now I awaited Ratmanoff, who was to take over for me and criticizes everything: Right I was; Ratmanoff came up on the deck very ill-humored with the words: "What a time to wash berths!" The weather, however, cleared up and our cabins dried out. That happened on Monday. Ratmanoff has dared up to now to criticize the captain's every step and order. To our chagrin, Krusenstern always takes it patiently.

Mon. 22/3 Today, Resanoff gave an oral positive response in answer to the captain's written plan, first to sail to Kamtschatka, leave the cargo there, and then sail to Japan. Since Resanoff has broken his word so often, he certainly did it this way to leave his back free and to give the appearance of correctness in case something did not go as wished. Privately, during the discussion, he said to Krusenstern with tears in his eyes, "I am so sorry that there has been so much discord between us. Everything is Count Tolstoi's fault (naively). You must have seen yourself that the count has behaved badly toward me, and it was wrong not to follow my demand to arrest him. You could have taken action against me as a result." That is, Resanoff wanted to be reconciled with Krusenstern at Tolstoi's expense, to be sure of Krusenstern in order to be able to avenge himself more pointedly. Then Resanoff complained about our behavior toward him, about our lack of attention, etc., and said that this treatment was not proper toward a man who possessed the authority to prescribe laws for an entire district in Russia. In answer to the captain's question, that he should provide an example where he had not been given his due respect, he had no answer. Then he assured the captain that he had not complained to the emperor about him either from Tenerife or from St. Catharina but only about Count Tolstoi. (You lie and the devil, too; so two of you are lying.) "The rumor has been spread," said Resanoff, "that I intend to avenge myself against you in Japan. You need not worry. No one means it so well toward you as I do." Krusenstern did not owe him an answer.

Descriptions of voyages have piled up. One would need years to read them all. The entanglement of names in the South Seas causes a lot of errors, and, since every country calculates longitude based on its capital city, it also leads to errors in determining a spot's location. Krusenstern has begun to severe this Gordian knot and has already filled several notebooks.

Tues. 23/4 Good old Horner is continually plagued by a toothache. That man enjoys the love and respect of all.

Wed. 24/5 Even though at 30° latitude a reef topsail wind, we are used to the rolling, but the *Nadezhda* still overdoes it sometimes. Today, we took in water several times with the foresail. The channels are continually under water because the ship lists so much to the side, and we catch a wave now and again with the forecastle. This strong movement of our ship is nevertheless very easy!

Thurs. 25/6 The high seas are attacking our ship even more. The *Nadezhda* has had a leak since the Falkland Islands. We have to pump once a day. We suspect that the leak is above the waterline because the leak is stronger as soon as the ship lists to the side.

Fri. 26/7 Up until now, we have always had autumn days.

Sat. 27/8 The first nice day, and let's hope we have withstood all of the storms. Today, Fosse appeared in the company cabin for the first time since St. Catharina. That patient has gained weight in his cabin. I saw him for the first time today after nine weeks—I'm not lying, but that is nevertheless hard to believe.

Sun. 28/9 Only twenty chickens left in our store of fresh provisions. That's why we are hurrying impatiently to Easter Island.

Mon. 29/10 The stubborn winds come from southwest and northwest, and it probably is impossible later in the year to double Cape Horn.

We have been put on water rations since Brazil. Each man gets two kruschkas. Up to now, everyone has got along on his quantity because the weather was cool. Now, with warmer weather and salt meat, the consumption is greater and some are complaining that the quantity is not sufficient. Our small quantity of water does not permit increasing the ration. Our doctors are not able to show moderation. In the evening, Espenberg and Count Tolstoi made a racket about the lack of water, acting as if they would die of thirst. The captain stared very nearsightedly at his plate with a piece of salt meat on it. We all said not a word. And! the noisemakers shut their traps! If the water jug is brought in, Espenberg, Langsdorff, Tilesius, and Tolstoi all raise their glasses at the same time. Each one wants to be the first to empty his glass full of water in order to ask for a second one, without stopping to think that they are taking water from others. They are used to being that way. Yesterday, they got no more than their allotment and were bold and fresh enough to make a racket about it. Every one gets two kruschkas of water. He gets handed out one kruschka daily, and the other is given to the kitchen, and whatever is left over is drunk during the meal; and fights ensue over this water.

Tues. 30/11 Starting today, to help end the disorder, everyone will get a bouteille of whatever is left after the kitchen takes what it needs and for tea. And then everyone can do whatever he wants to with his portion. This measure had to be taken with the wine, and probably the hardtack will end up the same way. We had to take these unsociable measures in order not to have those idlers making fun of us in the end.

Good weather has arrived, and with it we have again raised our topgallant mast with our flagstaff. That gives the ship a completely different appearance. We have repaired our old sails in order to save the present ones for bad weather. We probably will not get to Easter Island. The wind is too contrary. The Marquesas Islands are no doubt going to be our next nation.

Wed. 31/12 The wind is continually from the northwest. It blows like a trade wind. We sailed past the latitude of Easter Island in the night.

April

Thurs. 1/13 On my watch in the night, the wind changed from northwest to southwest. The change in temperature was indescribably great. The cold blew into my face like the warmth streaming out of a baking oven.

Fri. 2/14 The high seas make life very difficult for us and throw everything topsy-turvy in the cabin. Poor Horner, still plagued by a toothache, had his water bottle broken, soaking him, including his clothes and books. You need to know that the continual storms have smashed most of the bottles and glasses.

Mr. von Krusenstern suggested that we make barometer observations between the Tropic of Cancer in order to determine accurately the ebb and flow of the atmosphere, since the sun and moon must have just as much influence on the air as on the water. We were able to do only experiments. Let others figure out theories. Our natural scientists did not understand much about physics. The rest of us are dilettantes and often know more than these doctors. If one imagines a spot under the water, then one would feel as little of the ebb and flow of the water as we do of the ebb and flow of the air. Now we know that the rise and fall of the water cannot be noticed under water, and the current of the water can be compared with the wind. The theory of the movement of water is still underdeveloped, and how much more do we need to know about the atmosphere whose changes control us daily? At the equator, the sun and moon are almost perpendicular; consequently, between the Tropics, the results of observations must be most noticeable.

Sat. 3/15 All of the seafarers before us and also we, starting at 27° latitude, have had high seas from the southwest, which no brisk northerly, northeasterly, or northwesterly wind can tame. The poor ship is therefore being inhumanly thrown about. High seas are already so well known that they are marked on the map.

Sun. 4/16 For a second time, we have passed the Tropic of Capricorn. The weather is foggy and wet.

Mon. 5/17 Bellingshausen is happy to provide diversion during every storm in the cabin with his Russo-German impromptus and funny jokes.

Tues. 6/18 For the first time we saw tropical birds. I did not see them in the Atlantic Ocean. Today, an attempt was made to brew beer. We are, oh, so happy that up to now we have not had to take any anti-scorbutic measure. At night we calculate distances with the planets and stable stars.

Wed. 7/19 Does the power of attraction of the earth also influence rays?

Thurs. 8/20 When I have spent the night on watch and then am relieved, tired and hungry, and imagine all of our thin pots and bowls and bottles, inevitably I think about one of the tables of food at Neuenhof.[8] Had I one of them here, what more would I need?

Fri. 9/21 Our last pig landed on the table today. Espenberg did not let the roast get away from him. He piled so much on his plate that several others got only a bit. He could not possibly eat it all at once. Thus, he was clever enough to save the rest for the next time—very praiseworthy!

Sat. 10/22 The southeasterly trade wind announced its arrival today with a heavy rain.

Fosse, Resanoff's bosom buddy, let the cat out of the bag today with Romberg after a glass of punsch and several bouteillen of cognac. Fosse said that Resanoff planned to stay in Kamtschatka for a whole year and use the sailors to build barracks (and at the same time not to forget his private interests, I would say). It is a good thing that a Fosse chatters about that school.

Krusenstern finally got something in writing about the voyage to Kamtschatka from Resanoff.

Sun. 11/23 Earlier there were a few who could not drink tea and were surprised that others liked the taste. Now these finger-pointers drink two full cups and don't have enough. Several of them could not stand the smell of salt meat. Now you seldom find a piece to eat in the morning because the former complainers have already happily pulled everything over to themselves.

Mon. 12/24 The wind is good, the rain unbearable.

Tues. 13/25 True April weather. It has just stopped raining, and the sun is shining again.

Wed. 14/26 Espenberg's favoritism toward Moritz Kotzebue embitters both of the brothers, one against the other. Bellingshausen has taken the trouble of giving Otto lessons. I am also going to do my part, too, since he is assigned to my watch. Espenberg, who teaches both brothers, screamed at Otto and told him he did not have many brains. No wonder! Otto has always seen his brother preferred and himself put down. Ambition now spurs him on, and within a short amount of time he has passed his brother in geometry. The actual perpetrator of discord between the brothers is Count Tolstoi. Last night, Otto overheard the count talking with Moritz, and he could not prevent himself from saying, "I am here. Stop your secret machinations."

Thurs. 15/27 Everyone bought sugar in St. Catharina, and the captain ordered Schemelin to buy 400 pfund for the *Nadezhda* and 400 for the *Neva*. Schemelin had taken such poor precautions with the chest that, when weighed once again, there were barely 250 in it. A great loss.

We did not get issued knives, axes, and hooks for trade with the savages. Our smithy is therefore now converting old iron into articles of trade. If the knives, etc., are not as good as shop-made, we are not on our part trying to deceive them, since we will be giving the savages the best we have.

His Excellency has been out of sorts for several days. During the night, he took a walk on deck for *Motion* [sic]. If only there is no discord again.

Fri. 16/28 Moritz told Espenberg what Tolstoi had told him, what he was teaching him, and the kinds of advice he was giving him. Ratmanoff has the job of getting Moritz out of the claws of that depraved fellow. Out of boredom, Tolstoi has played several bad pranks. Most everyone now looks upon him with contempt.

Sat. 17/29 Put our anchor cable on the anchor again and raised the cannons out of the hold and put them in their places, four in number. Night and day, a sailor sits on the trestletrees and looks for land. Up to now in answer to our question, we have got the answer, "Nothing to see!"

The sun is burning again so strongly that we have to pour water over the ship every day inside and out. Since they are painted black, the sides of the ship are so excessively hot that you cannot hold your hand against them.

The *Nadezhda* is 117 fuss long, 28 fuss 4 zoll wide, and 13 fuss 6 zoll deep in the water.

Sun. 18/30 Theory is very necessary, but without practical use it is boring and useless. Of what use is a lot of knowledge if one does not know how to use it?

Mon. 19/1 Sailing with the trade winds is an easy game. Beautiful weather, mild good winds, and quiet seas are continual.

Tues. 20/2 The sails (the old ones) that we have up now are so thin that the sun, moon, and stars shine through them. In Kamtschatka, we are going to have to get rid of them all. Langsdorff has added to his collection an almost thumb-sized animal of the medusa family that glows like a lantern.

My impetuous character comes to forc involuntarily wherever unfairness, caprice, and egotism come into play. In such cases, I am not master of myself. At the beginning of our voyage, I was full of good intentions. My hot-headedness took me often farther than I would have expected. Even though my comrades tell me I do myself justice, that I am always looking out for the interests of the whole group, I still reproach myself. Even though experience has made me smart, I am not able to calmly watch unfairness without saying what I think. Indeed, other people's weaknesses involuntarily grieve me. The best thing for me to do is therefore to withdraw and avoid it all, witnessing scenes that do our company no honor. Our behavior toward each other is something less than upright. There is little pleasure in conversing with men who display falseness so often. It is quieter and more profitable for me to spend my time alone in my little cabin. Conversation, the spice of life, is completely gone of course, but there was little of that in the company cabin. But the group is rid of me who, through my hot-headedness and often saying the truth at the right moment, found me annoying, also the story with Tilesius that has been stretched out to the point of being ridiculous even to mention it. It is then better that I withdraw.

Wed. 21/3 Observations that we could make three days in a row have proven that our chronometer shows 25 German miles too far to the west.

Thurs. 22/4 Tirelessly, Langsdorff has been enriching the natural historical knowledge about phosphorescent animals in the water. He has been sitting night after night with his net on the gundeck, fishing in the wake of the ship. He has found a lot of often microscopic small animals. Langsdorff has also taken it upon himself to observe the barometer, thermometer, electrometer, hygrometer, and the wind. We have discovered that the water's phosphorescence has nothing electrical in it as such. He has described and drawn in the smallest detail all of the little microscopic animals.

Today, Tilesius asked Langsdorff to show him his drawings. He barely had hold of them when he began copying them, giving the animals which Langsdorff had named and described new and unsuitable names, and saying very loudly that he intended to write and publish a monograph about these animals. (That would have formally been robbery.) A heated argument was unavoidable. The coarse behavior of the two doctors, their coarse expressions, their swearing caused us all to be silent and thus to stop this feud too.

Bellingshausen has caught a bad cold and cannot hear in one ear. It is not right of Espenberg to pay him so little attention. He says, "I have too few Spanish flies[9] and therefore am letting nature take her course."

Horner's suffering must have settled into his teeth because his toothache has not gotten any better. The poor fellow is plagued night and day. Resanoff is still calling himself ill. He'll be sitting in his cabin with a scorbutic neck.

Fri. 23/5 Resanoff compares himself with Lord Makartency [Macartney]. Our voyage has more similarities with that of the d'Entrecasteaux;[10] only we better hope that ours will end more happily.

Since Tolstoi may not have anything to do with the Kotzebues, the two boys live together in harmony, as brothers should.

Since we will probably see land tomorrow, today we have made preparations to defend ourselves against the savages. The cannon have been loaded with balls and cartouche, muskets, pistols and sabers cleaned, cartridges filled, etc., and all of our trading articles put together. We knew that we had along a crate of axes, saws, knives, scissors, buttons, etc. We did not, however, expect such a nice collection of useful things as we found upon opening the crate.

In order to maintain order, the captain has appointed Romberg and Espenberg to trade with the savages, because, if everyone wants to buy for himself, that will cause disorder and the prices, especially through outbidding, could be ruined. Gusts of wind with squalls of rain. Proof of land nearby.

- 5 -

Nukahiva

Sun. 24/6 On Easter Sunday at sunrise, we caught sight of Hood's Island. All of nature is alive. The sea is teeming with fish that are reflected on the surface of the water. Frigate birds, tropical birds, gulls, etc., crisscross through the air. All of them are hunting the multitudes of flying fish rising out of the water. Everyone is on deck full of expectation. We are making observations, taking angles, putting points onto the map, maneuvering with the ship, and preparing to drop anchor. Our passengers observe the goings-on and enjoy watching our sailors as they try unsuccessfully to harpoon the masses of fish swimming in front of our ship.

During the night, we sailed with little sail between the islands of Nukahiva and Rios, so that we could look for an anchorage in the morning.

While you, my dear brothers and sisters, are enjoying Easter Sunday and have an oversupply of eggs and all of the rest, we have to be content with a piece of salt meat and got, in honor of the day, a double portion of half-rotten water. We had too much to do to be able to think much about the holiday. The sight of land was enough to delight us, and the hope of soon having an oversupply of fresh water gave us renewed courage. Nevertheless, you epicures, your colorful eggs don't cause as great joy as our extra portion of water. The day was very hot, our work exhausting, and the salt meat caused an insatiable thirst that nothing refreshes more than a drink of water.

You have to have experienced it to judge what it means to do without food and water. Our size and weight determine our human needs in these matters; thus is the craving twice as much, and, therefore, hunger pangs and burning thirst turn into pain. I advise anyone who has not learned forbearance not to sail around the world.

Mon. 25/7 At the break of day, we set sail and sailed along the island. Rough cliffs covered in green with rivulets spilling down through gaps and at their base the breaking of the roaring sea lend the country beauty. Two of our armed boats

5-1. A Tabu man [sic]: a fellow who made himself taboo

rowed ahead of us in order to measure the depths. Then a canoe set out from land straight toward our boats, and Golovatscheff, who was in one of the boats, brought the savages onboard. We were more than surprised to discover a naked tattooed Englishman[1] among the savages. He had been living on the island for seven years. For the time being, he served us as pilot. He had been a steward on an English ship on which the sailors had mutinied, and, since they intended to murder him, he had found it advisable to stay among the savages. The savages are exceedingly beautifully tattooed, all regular geometric figures. We had barely dropped anchor in Taiohai when we were surrounded by a swimming legion bringing breadfruit, coconuts, bananas, and plantain. Their childish behavior, the noise of these savages, and the strange appearance of these amphibians were unique. (*See color plate 2.*)

Right after lunch, the man called king visited us. He appeared dark blue, almost black, so completely was he tattooed. After a short stay on the ship, he returned to land promising to send us fish, crabs, and pigs. Handsome people, each savage could serve as a model for an Apollo in Belvedere.[2] [*Kätenuä.*[3] *See color plates 3 and 4.*]

A Frenchman,[4] who had totally forgotten his French, a complete savage, came onboard with the king. The Englishman, who is respectable, and the Frenchman are enemies since he, to all appearances, is a good-for-nothing.

Golovatscheff got our anchor all entangled when we wanted to put on our moorings. I had to shout myself hoarse today until his mistake was corrected, worked like a horse encumbered by our sailors' curiosity, the noise of the savages and all the running about and the noise of our passengers.

The captain handed out a large number of presents, when, what, how, and to whom is too extensive to list.

The Herrenhüter[5] sent missionaries with Captain Cook to the South Seas. The female savages, naked, came onboard and, as customary, were only wearing a few leaves to cover their privy parts. The goats on the ship smelled this greenery and hurried over to rob the naked girls of their last bit of cover, and the women showed the Herrenhüter the way God had made them. This abomination was not enough to frighten them off, and one Lamb of God decided to stay on land. The king who had taken him in went to another island and left his wife with him for good keeping. According to the customs, the missionary therefore had a man's rights. But he did not want to have anything to do with that. . . . but take. . . . was surprised. . . . She consulted with several of her girlfriends. . . . No sooner said than done. The missionary . . . horrified.[6] He tied up his bundle and hurried to catch the next ship, had, however, everything stolen by the savages on the shore and was stripped naked. He undoubtedly lost all desire to stay as a missionary among the savages. In the evening . . . changed. . . .

Their ability to swim deserves admiration, and the ease with which they climb shows how strong these people are. The women are by far not as beautifully built as the men.

The bay is open to the south. The wind blows very rarely from that direction. The anchorage is very good. Good night.

Tues. 26/8 After a long voyage of thirteen weeks, how pleasant the sound of water lapping against land, how sociable. The morning was very beautiful. The deck, where our gentlemen[7] had camped topsy-turvy with those wild girls, looked like a lazaret.

Yesterday, Krusenstern issued a written order that no one except Espenberg and Romberg is to barter with the savages so that trading will be orderly.

The Englishman promised to make the source of water and the observation place taboo.

The people control violence here through taboos. Otherwise, there is no rank order. Whoever ignores a taboo or breaks one according to their belief dies. Every savage has a woman who is duty bound to be true to him as long as he is around. "That is the reason why," said the Englishman, "that I also gave the queen a child five years ago." The people are deceitful and wily. The island is divided into several valleys that are continually feuding with each other.

The sun had barely come up when droves of savages came swimming up. We sent the girls . . . who felt themselves rewarded enough with scraps of sailcloth or a piece of iron out to meet them.[8] The men had the women show them the things, and from their pantomime we concluded they were satisfied and happy. The Englishman claimed they considered it an honor for their women to have been applauded on our ship.

At daybreak, the noise began again. Only by gunshots could we keep the bothersome savages away from the ship. We were visited by several men called kings and priests who brought gifts of bananas, pigs, and coconuts and were the only ones permitted onboard. For the whole day a lot of them swam around the ship without taking a rest. At eleven o'clock in the morning, we raised a red flag upon the captain's order, and by a cannon shot we put a taboo on the ship. Even though

5-2. The watering spot on Nukahiva

the savages did not appear to pay much attention to it, they nevertheless kept their distance from the ship. Not long after that, the captain with two armed boats went on land. An hour later our shallop returned, and the longboat was sent ashore with empty water casks.

The savages are becoming burdensome. One of them stole a washbasin and a pair of scissors out of Resanoff's cabin by climbing up along the side of the ship. Other thieves followed him. We have had to chase them off with a shallop. Flies are the same all over and just as troublesome as at home.

Wed. 27/9 We have duty on land a day at a time. Today, I was in charge of filling up water and chopping wood and got to rest only after sunset.

The next morning, I hurried on land to begin work before the savages could gather. Barely an hour had passed, and I was surrounded by savages, some of whom carried slingshots, spears, and clubs. Their curiosity and crowding are troublesome.

The savages helping us fill up water couldn't have been paid enough for the eagerness and quickness with which they did the work. The surf was so strong that we could not bring the boat close to land. Therefore, we filled small casks with water and had the savages get them to the longboat. We could not have repeated the agility with which they took the casks through the surf. After finishing our work, I climbed onboard with my six armed sailors. Then they began making a racket before it was time to give every savage a piece of old iron as payment, and each one tried to get two pieces instead of one.

His imperial majesty paid me the honor of a visit. His brother and other relatives did not find it beneath their dignity to help me with filling up water as well as floating the felled wood to the longboat. I bartered myself a few decorations and little things from the savages. These people are obliging and eager to serve. Only one of them went after one of my men (a tiny sailor) and made a face with a balled fist as if he wanted to give him one. When chopping wood, they were much more respectful because the effective blows of our axes amazed them. One fellow had raised a beam onto his shoulder and acted as if he wanted to let it fall on one of our men who had slipped and fallen. This scene caused general laughter among the

5-3. The landing spot on Nukahiva and the distribution of tokis

savages. I took an ax and acted as if I wanted to split the beam on his shoulder (I cannot call the thing that Hercules was carrying away anything else). Now the object of their laughter changed direction, and my savage, laughing loudly, carried his burden to the boat. The most difficult thing every time was handing out the pieces of iron (hacked up from old cask rings) as daily wages. All of the savages crowded around the boat, grabbed it, held it tight, so that I found it necessary to hit their fingers, and all of that to cause chaos in order to get two instead of one piece of iron.

In the evening from a height on land, I saw the *Neva* arriving and sent word to the captain. She is still far away.

In contrast to the men, the women are very small of stature. Even ten-year-old girls are nubile.

We kept Милой [Miloi] onboard and served him food in our manner. The people behave so naturally and unaffectedly that we have to admire them rather than deride them. He ate all of our dishes with a knife and fork as he saw us doing. When, however, it was a coconut's turn, he did not know how to get at it without using his teeth. After we had let him know he should do the customary thing with the nut, he did in a wink of the eye, to our astonishment. He split the husk with his fist, ripped it off with his teeth, knocked a round hole in the nut with the knuckle of his first finger, drank the water, and then held the whole nut between his knees and broke it with both hands—all of that in the wink of an eye.

Thurs. 28/10 Golovatscheff went out to meet the *Neva*. Yesterday and the day before yesterday, our ship was taboo. Today the captain let them have it. Everybody concentrated on trading articles, trying to show the savages something new, since they are all keen for something new. It is always supposed to rain here during the full moon. It was like timbers falling, it rained so hard. It was my bad luck that on my watch I had the ship washed. If it continues to rain, I am risking having everything rot.

The *Neva* arrived at ten o'clock but could not anchor before evening because of contrary winds. She was at Easter Island, but the high surf had prevented her from anchoring near land.

The savages are very clever at stealing. It is almost impossible to prevent petty thefts.

I had my arm tattooed today. The savages are very adept at it.

Espenberg had a hefty dispute with Langsdorff because of a skull that they both wanted.

In the afternoon, Kätenuä, the king, brought our captain a pudding made from breadfruit and coconut. At first, there were prejudices against this dish, but it tasted quite good. His Imperial Majesty was very angry with Roberts (that's the name of the Englishman) because he wanted to have a pair of scissors and did not get them. We continually ask for pigs, and the savages do not bring us any. And he wanted the scissors for the pudding.

Fri. 29/11 At sunrise, Bellingshausen, Horner, and I went out to chart the inlets and their shores. The rough steep cliffs cannot be climbed. The surf prevents entrance into the little bays.

We found only one inlet surrounded by cliffs that could probably be used for a ship in need of repairs. We charted the inlet. The change of food had its effect upon our health because all three of us were sick. And, after having worked the whole day, we returned to our ship from our journey at six o'clock.

Pigs are very spoiled here. They want to eat only coconuts. They spurn hard-tack and rice.

A savage came swimming up with a piece of white as decoration wound around his neck. Moritz thought it was a tooth and gave him a sack needle for it. The trade had barely been completed when the savage broke out in loud laughter, since what he had bought was a cleaned banana peel that the fellow had deceptively hung around his neck. After he had laughed himself out, he came swimming back to the ship and was honest enough to give back the needle. It was given to him as a gift.

Sat. 30/12 We have filled our empty water casks, and it looks as though we will have to continue our voyage without pigs and with only a small quantity of breadfruit and coconuts. Kätenuä came onboard today with a piece of cloth and a pig. Since Krusenstern was just eating his lunch, I asked the king through the Frenchman to wait a bit. However, it took too long for him. The savages in the canoe lost their patience and rowed back to shore. I told the captain, and he immediately came on deck. The king, who was still onboard ship, sent a savage to call back the canoe, but since they did not obey, the king went on land in one of our boats. We suspected no unpleasantness. The canoe, that had gone back to shore without the king and the fellow who was supposed to call it back, had spread the rumor that Kätenuä had been arrested and held on our ship.

The people immediately armed themselves. Everyone appeared with slingshots, clubs, and spears in their hands, and, as a signal to do battle, they threw skipping stones they had in their hands one after another. The *Neva*'s longboat was on land filling water with one officer and no more than six sailors. The savages wanted to

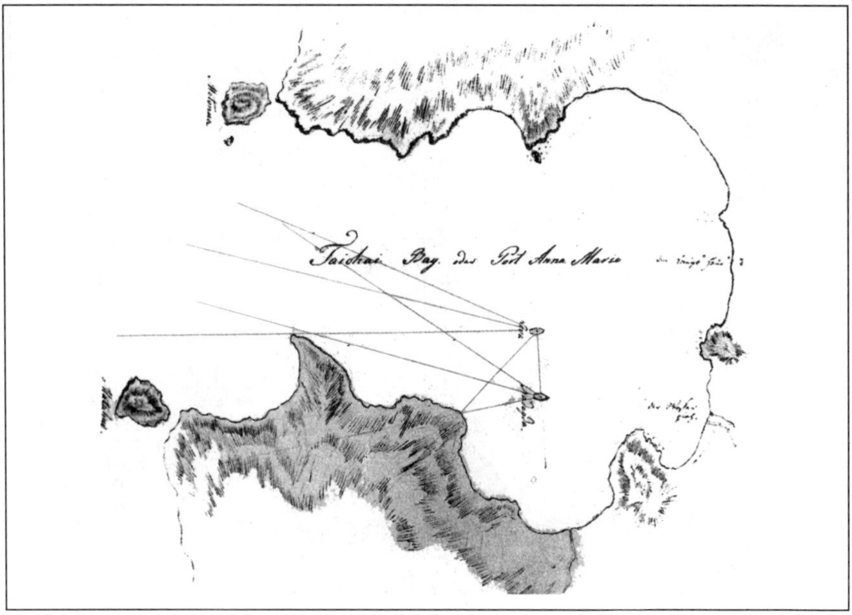

5-4. Taiohai Bay or Port Anna Marie

kill the Englishman Roberts, who was also there, and put the *Neva*'s officer in a ticklish situation. Luckily, the king arrived, and his presence calmed everything down again. However, the anger was so great that it could not be stopped at once. The longboat had to return, proof how careful one has to be in dealing with these children of nature. We suspect that the animosity between the Frenchman and Englishman is at fault for this incident.

May

Sun. 1/13 The ruckus yesterday has made us cautious. I went together with the *Neva*'s longboat on land. We landed fifteen men strong. The savages were peaceful and helped fill water and brought all kinds of things to sell. At 8 o'clock, Krusenstern, Resanoff, and Lisianski came together with a large entourage in order to go into the interior and inspect a morai. Unfortunately, I did not dare leave my post. When my casks were filled, I ventured a little way inland so that I could look at the savages' houses. Their houses, if you can call them that, are situated very pleasantly and surrounded by breadfruit and coconut trees. Their equipment is very ingeniously put together and carved. Upon returning from my walk, I discovered our boat had lost its anchor shovel while I was gone. The cable had torn apart. We looked for it without success. I returned to the ship, and not long afterwards the other gentlemen arrived onboard exhausted from their walk.

5-5. *Morai; Nukahiva; houses*

The Frenchman was the cause of yesterday's ruckus.

The swimming legions leave us only when we frighten them off of an evening with a puhi (cannon shot).

On the way to the morai, Krusenstern visited the Englishman, who is supposed to be very comfortably situated, that is, in the manner of the savages. The tattooist has the upper hand on the ship. The savage works from morning to evening. Even Krusenstern has had himself tattooed.

Today, from the longboat, I had a falconet fired when we were filling up water in order to restrain the savage's pushiness. The shot had barely gone off when a whole bunch of them dropped to the ground from fright, and, when I showed several how unnecessary that was, they got up again and began to laugh and went after those who had streaked away from it. They have a lot of respect for the puhi.

Our sailors do not deny themselves anything. They even try it out in the water to see if it is possible.

Every savage who owns property can make a taboo. Public taboos, however, can only be prescribed by priests. The freshest and pertest of the savages are those decorated with feathers.

The concept of trade is just beginning to form here. Our savages possess great ability for theft. That is a very respected ability among them. They demand a toki (piece of old iron) for a red bean just as for a club and often prefer this piece of iron instead of a well-scoured knife. We tarred all of the ropes and sheathing today.

We have had gusts of wind and rain, but never from the south, since the high mountains protect ships in the bay. The anchorage is good overall. The best place is, however, on the eastern shore of the bay because the cable is always straight there. The *Neva,* anchored on the western shore, has already had an entangled cable several times, we not once. We are anchored in a wide spot in the bay and have a straight cable toward land.

During the night, the wind blew from land, fresh, often with rain. During the day, it is very hot, often with calms and soft breezes.

Today, we had on shipboard 25° warmth according to Réaumur. This temperature causes the coconuts to decay rapidly.

Mon. 2/14 Mr. von Krusenstern had ordered and repeated several times that only foodstuffs should be bought for old iron. Schemelin, ignoring this, bought (even though we have few axes) several things for axes, as he says, for Resanoff. Everyone has permission to buy whatever he wants for knives, scissors, mirrors, buttons, etc. For that reason, Krusenstern gave Schemelin a reprimand. This morning, after the captain had had coral fished for yesterday, he went to Resanoff and told him, "If you would like, you may chose some of the best coral."

The offer was well-meaning; Resanoff's answer consisted of reproaches, "I'm the only one you forbid to buy things! You ignore the Emperor's orders. I am collecting for our monarch, and you want to prevent me from doing that! etc., etc. etc." Then Resanoff and Krusenstern went on deck. Resanoff allowed himself more freedom than his rank, the emperor's order, and the carte blanche would permit him. He was coarse, swore, etc. Schemelin, who was present, went up to Krusenstern and said to him openly that he would have nothing to do with him and viewed Resanoff as his boss.

The open threats, measures, insult, and wrongs toward the captain that Resanoff pertly committed are going to have to be straightened out publicly. The decks have the same rights as in a courtroom and who dares to caste insults into a captain's face on his own ship in front of his entire crew. That Resanoff is going to have to justify himself. His Excellency has already held a council in his cabin—today there will undoubtedly be another raging racket.

Lisianski came onboard at 11 o'clock. Mr. von Krusenstern had gathered all of his officers on deck and said, "His Excellency, Chamberlain Resanoff has said to me publicly, 'You are acting childishly! You are going to be degraded to a sailor.' In view of this, I cannot continue with the command."

Then, we officers sent Romberg down to Resanoff to be so kind as to read our instructions publicly. Resanoff very politely drove Romberg out of his cabin, came soon afterwards, pale and white, with his instructions, stopped on the stairs, and read them out loud.

The whole incident was written down, and Resanoff got to hear a lot of truths that made his hair stand on end, and we would have been bold enough to tell him that to his face with the emperor present. Resanoff's instructions and Krusenstern's contradict each other from beginning to end.

Count Tolstoi intruded in the conversation, began to talk where he should have been quiet. Ratmanoff told him straight out, "The matter is none of your business, and you have no right to say anything here."

Krusenstern went over to the *Neva* at noon, and Ratmanoff stayed behind as eldest officer (and of course acted in the captain's stead). Then Count Tolstoi went up to him and said a lot of crudities and challenged him. Ratmanoff is a brave fellow, but it was his duty to deny the challenge. He only said to the count, "You are to avoid my cabin, or I will have you removed." After the captain's return Ratmanoff handed in a written protest against Tolstoi. That Tolstoi does not know himself what he wants goes with his nose in the air insulting everybody all over the place.

In the afternoon, I rowed with Horner around the inlet in order to chart it.

Krusenstern can do whatever he wants to later, but he has to stay our captain.

After Resanoff had driven Romberg out of his cabin, Ratmanoff said in a thundering voice, and we agreed, "You have to think that he is a самозванец [someone who gives himself rank and title], and, if that is the case then, he should be considered crazy and locked in his cabin." Since all of the doors and windows were open, Resanoff must have heard it. And that was undoubtedly the reason why he obeyed and came out pale and white.

Tues. 3/15 In the morning, the captain had the longboat armed, and Krusenstern, Golovatscheff, Horner, Tilesius, Langsdorff, and I went to inspect the newly discovered inlet more carefully and possibly to buy pigs there. Lisianski with Povalischin, Laband, the pilot, and the prikaschtschick from the *Neva* followed us in a shallop.

The inlet is a good German mile from Taiohai. Since the wind was favorable, we soon reached it and took a pleasant walk in the beautiful valley. The shadows protected us from the sun, and we could admire the boundless beauty of nature. We bought a large number of bananas. We saw enough pigs, but couldn't buy a single one. The dance-floor place in this valley was a roomy square raised by stones and surrounded by huts. Every valley has a free house for poor girls with nothing to their names. The deceased from a house is its protective spirit.

When we wanted to return, several expressed the wish to go back by land. Lisianski talked a lot against it. Tilesius and Langsdorff decided nevertheless to go on foot. I would have liked to have gone with them, but I had come with the longboat and had to return with her.

We charted the inlet and began our return trip without having bought any pigs. We had the waves and wind against us. The exertion of rowing really got to our people. Mr. von Krusenstern and the others had joined Lisianski in the shallop, and I reached the ship with the longboat only at eight o'clock in the evening. Onboard, we heard that Tilesius, tired from climbing over the rocks, had fallen and injured himself, and that the savages had carried him on their shoulders to the king, where the two researchers of nature had decided to overnight.

The eldest son of the king here is married to one of the daughters of a neighboring chief. This marriage has made all wars on the water taboo (i.e., also these two tribes); after the death of this princess, her spirit will be the protective spirit for this island, and alive she is considered a saint. This saint Dulcinea has, nevertheless, for a piece of iron brought her allurements to market on the *Neva*. This marriage was carried out in a patriarchal manner. The man buys his wife and gets a trial night gratis.

The Frenchman is a complete savage. Only his nasty character and the few vulgar French ballads he still knows show that he may well be a Frenchman.

Wed. 34/16 In time of war, the savages eat their prisoners and the slain. So that their festive meals are not too *splendid* [sic], the animosities end each time as soon as several prisoners have been taken so that they have time to eat them.

The thievery has not been too great for us. While filling up water, the savages tore out some cask bands with nails (which our cooper had forcefully driven in) and stole them and several shirts.

The savages especially like our forge. The smithy always has something to do. The king can watch the work for hours, especially when he has brought an old hatchet to be repaired.

The hot buying passion has died down on the ship. We now get a lot of things cheaper than in the beginning, because we offer them something and stick by the offer. The savages give us their wares for that so that they do not have to swim back with them.

After Tilesius and Langsdorff had slept on land, they came to the watering place where Golovatscheff was working. Tilesius immediately demanded of Golovatscheff a boat so that he could go to the ship. Golovatscheff had to deny him his request. As a result, the councilor became coarse. Upon his return, Golovatscheff lodged a complaint with the captain about Tilesius.

Shortly after noon, I went on land with Horner to take the noonday reading. We did not have the hunter with us. He shot several birds. The savages considered him someone worthy of respect. They watched him with awe and served him as pointer dogs. Since all of the savages were running after the hunter, we two were able to make our observations undisturbed.

The savages' features are not all unpleasant. Omai, the king's son, is an adroit young fellow with a fiery look. I have seen many of the savages with Roman noses.

In the evening, we raised our longboat, shallop, and topgallant mast.

We have bought and eaten innumerable coconuts during our stay and will buy still more. One-fourth of the ship has continually been heaped with coconuts, i.e., the poop deck.

In the evening, we sent up a couple rockets. It is too bad that we cannot find out what effect their appearance has had on the savages. The savages swarmed like bees, hummed, sang, and clapped all evening on the shore—as soon as the rockets went up, they were quiet as mice—until one of them became emboldened, and then the noise began again.

Everything that we have written in the big books of law is covered here by the word taboo. Everything is permitted except the taboo. If a savage knowingly breaks a public taboo, then he has to die, certainly lose his land, be damned to bondage, or must flee so that he does not die of hunger. If he breaks a private taboo, he risks being killed on the spot, or the spirit of the place defends his own rights and afflicts him with illnesses. Taboo means dedicating something to a living or dead spirit.

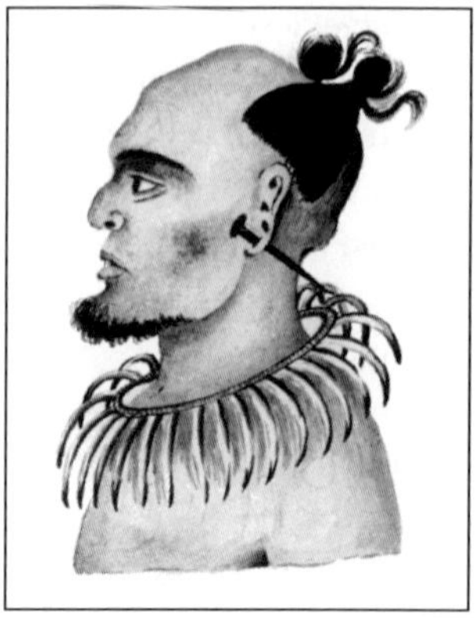

5-6. A Nukahivan

Drought and war often cause starvation here. Then they eat each other. Every taboo is over, and the women and children are eaten first.

The king is taboo; i.e., he may not be killed, and everyone who has exchanged names with him has the same rights as he does. That is the case with both the Englishman and Frenchman and protects them from assassination.

Thurs. 5/17 This morning at four o'clock, we had to work on the anchor, i.e., take it off according to procedures.

The names of our acquaintances: Muhau, a big fellow and the king's fire builder; Tuti Budona; Eduard Roberts, the Englishman; Jean Joseph Cabri, the Frenchman, is called Ehou. Kätenuä is the name of the king; Tamotai, his brother, has the name of a slain enemy. Dovatia is the name of the high priest; Nukahiva, the Island; Tajohai the inlet where we are anchored. Motonua and Matahuo the two little islands at the entrance to the inlet. Vuaboa the southern island, Gekauve the newly discovered inlet. Puhi a firearm. Natatu the soul, that is, if a savage eats something, then he throws a piece away every time and says, "Natatu, also something for you my protective spirit." My list is short, have had no time; the other gentlemen have collected more words and phrases.

We hope to set sail today and did not dream of having such an irksome day ahead of us. Exhausted, I am now setting down in the night to write superficially about the work that we did from four in the morning until nine in the evening.

After we had lifted the moorings, Krusenstern warned the Englishman and Frenchman and gave the order at eight o'clock to weigh anchor. A half-hour later, we were under sail. We had barely gone a couple of lengths of the cable when a variable wind came up and shifted the ship first to the right and then to the left. We continually had to brace on the other side, and, even with two boats towing, the ship, as if she were crack-brained, obeyed neither the tow nor the pilot nor the rudder nor the sails. We did not notice that we were being driven to the right (west-

5-7. Nukahiva; taboo tree

ern) shore, and there was no other way to save ourselves but to drop an anchor that held immediately. And we were driven so close to the steep cliffs that everyone could see the danger hovering around us. The gusts of wind, coming quickly one after the other, threatened to smash us at any moment in the surf. The only means of getting our ship away from the shore was by kedging. In calm weather, that is very hard work. Wind and waves made it three times more difficult. We had to carry the kedge out three times and drop anchor three times in order to be under sail again. Finally, the wind helped us a little bit. We had barely raised the kedge and set sail when a strong gust of contrary wind hit the sails, so that we found it necessary in the dark of the night to cast anchor and spend the night there. The *Neva* suffered a similar fate, only she was not driven so close to land.

It was irresponsible of Lisianski to force Krusenstern to resort to a cannon shot to request his shallop that was being pulled unused astern. Would it not have been better if Lisianski had been willing to help us and sent his boat?

The danger is over, thank goodness. We could have suffered a catastrophe today. Everyone is lying in Morpheus' arms. Only I sit here and smoke my pipe of tobacco half-drunk with sleep. The work begins again tomorrow at daybreak and, let's hope, more the way we want it to than today. We are not going to forget Taiohai very easily.

Fri. 6/18 This morning, we cast two cable-long kedge anchors from the ship in order to pull the ship out of the inlet. We had barely cast our kedge and raised our anchor when a favorable wind came up and gusts of wind, stronger than yesterday, drove us out. The captain ordered the kedge cable cut because we had no time to save it, and with the loss of our kedge anchor and a couple of nice cables we left Taiohai. Our shallop was ripped away from the ship by the strength of the wind and our sailors' carelessness. We had to wait a long time for them, since we had sent the other boats after them, and, with a great deal of effort on account of the high seas, we got them all onboard. Now it was back to the usual work: measuring angles, taking soundings, making observations, etc.

The *Neva* set sail last night. The Frenchman came swimming up to the *Nadezhda* very late and missed the moment this morning when he should have returned ashore. For better or worse, he now has to stay with us. It was too late and too far from land to give him a boat. We offered him a board, but, since he was too afraid to risk using it because of the sharks that could eat him up along the way, he stayed with us. He appears not to like having to leave Nukahiva.

At eleven o'clock, we joined the *Neva*.

Mr. Joseph cried for a time, while continually looking back toward the island, which gradually disappeared from view, and became very quiet when it could no longer be seen. That Joseph is a frivolous man. He forgot French easily but took over just as quickly the customs of the savages. It will take time until he again can be considered a European.

Sat. 7/19 I am not for severity, but the captain's meek manner toward his crew is excessive—that was clear yesterday and strikingly so the day before yesterday. Today, due to the carelessness of the second mate, our last barrel of tar tipped over, with the loss of over half of it. Even he got only a reprimand for it.

The Frenchman flatters himself with the hope of being taken back to Nukahiva from the *Sandwitsch* [sic] Islands on an American ship. He is nevertheless in a good mood and works as a sailor quite adroitly in the hope of being able to earn his bread in Europe as a sailor, in case he cannot find a way to return to Nukahiva.

Sun. 8/20 With this brisk wind, the old sails we have up are singing their swan song. Three sails have already expired. It won't be very long until the voyage will get the others.

Mon. 9/21 We are living as best we can without fresh provisions. Everyone is busy catching up on things left undone. Landscapes, plants, animals, fish, etc, are being sketched. Bellingshausen, Horner, and I are charting our angles that we measured and putting them together as best we can. A couple of maps are finished, but there is still enough work left to do.

The savages are masters at climbing. Since they always go barefoot, they have strength and agility in their feet and dexterity with their toes, so that their feet are as useful as hands. Ape-like, they climb up the high coconuts as if they were steps. We often dropped them a line over the side of the ship to urge them up the side. They would grab the line with one hand and a foot and with one swing they were on the ship as if we had lowered a ladder. Muhau stayed on the side of the ship for a whole hour, while holding himself with one hand, the toes of a foot on the line, and conducted trade, counted tokis, and received coconuts and breadfruit.

All of the savages here are white in color, and we only saw a few copper-colored ones. Smearing themselves in coconut oil probably protects them from sunburn. The Spanish are much darker than the Islanders are; even the children are white.

We have not caught sight of Resanoff since the last incident in Taiohai. He is probably thinking of revenge.

The number of idle bread-eaters is fifteen. And, since they all are good eaters, we find it necessary to divide the salt meat into specific portions so as not to run short.

By the sweat of our brows we have finally finished our maps. Nothing fills us with more joy. With our hearts filled with vexation toward Resanoff we have become dulled to anything that could cause us joy.

Tues. 11/23 We are not far from the equator; for the alternating calms, gusts of rain, and gusts of wind announce the presence of the equator.

Wed. 12/24 Mr. von Krusenstern went over to the *Neva* today. Lisianski also had maps made, which, however, the captain says are very defective. That is something that Lisianski's suffisance [self-importance] will not permit him to admit. Qua faire [in character]!

Our provisions have been much reduced. The brandy casks are leaking. The rats are eating the hardtack. A lot of barrels of salt meat have spoiled. There are fewer grits onboard than we expected. The peas are almost inedible. We have a little butter and no fish any more.

The prikaschtschick only bought a third of the sugar he had been ordered to. We are in bad shape and do not know at all what and how much we still have of things.

Krusenstern ordered Schemelin to report to him about the provisions onboard. Schemelin did not obey the order. After Krusenstern had returned from the *Neva*, he asked that common fellow why he had not carried out the order.

That prikaschtschik answered the captain on the quarterdeck, fresh and loud: "Your orders are none of my affair. I only recognize the ambassador as my commander. And you have to give me a reason why and wherefore you want something from me, before I will carry out your order, or you have to give me a formal order, etc." In answer to the captain's repeated question whether he intended to obey him or not, Schemelin said very pertly, "I am not going to obey you and have nothing to do with you"—went and brought his instructions, which then completely broke his neck.

Krusenstern went to Resanoff and told him, "You are here as authorized agent of the American Company. I consider it my duty to inform you of the prikaschtschik's failure to carry out his duty. And I am telling you after this incident that I neither want nor can have anything more to do with that insane man."

"Why are you coming to me?" was Resanoff's answer. "You have taken over the command from me." Then he followed this with, "But I will punish him for his coarseness." (It is clear that Resanoff instigated the incident.) Schemelin's age and his infirmities alone can cause forbearance toward him; otherwise, he would have to be treated as insane.

Thurs. 13/25 Just after lunch, we very quietly sailed over the equator for the second time.

Fri. 14/26 Lisianski ate lunch with us.

Horner had Sydham pull one of his teeth. He, however, pulled out a healthy one, but there was nothing to be done about it; the other one had to be pulled, too.

Sat. 15/27 Krusenstern named the newly discovered harbor in Nukuhiva Tschitschagoff.

At noon, we sailed past the latitude of Christmas Island.

Sun. 16/28 We saw a large log with green leaves swimming past with a lot of unknown sea birds fluttering around it. Fish are not to be seen at all, so welcome they would be for our slim pickings.

Our fare consists of salt meat, grits, peas, and hardtack. We are, nevertheless, healthy, thank God. Only Fosse is ill. Secretly, in his cabin, he has had the falling sickness that plagues him every other day, in the throat, according to what is being said. Espenberg related today that he had had eight paroxysms [fits] in a period of ten days. The falling sickness has to stop or else Fosse has had it.

In order for someone to make himself taboo among the savages he has to jump around in the valley like a dwatscher Mensch [queer/crazy man] shouting the king's name. That means that he is possessed by the king's spirit and taboo. Only a foreigner has the right to play the role of a taboo man or one possessed. *John* [sic], the Frenchman, was smart enough to have made himself taboo in all of the valleys and inlets.

Mon. 17/29 The savages are masters at swimming. In Nukahiva, I threw a piece of iron into the water for a savage. The fellow dove like an arrow, came immediately up again, and showed me his empty hands. I therefore gave him another piece. Then he raised his foot into the air and had simply caught the iron and held it between his toes.

The taboo fellow we saw in Taiohai was a foreigner who had to play the role in order not to be killed.

Count Tolstoi bought a sea-cat [long-tailed monkey] in Brazil. Upon its arrival onboard, it was put on a leash and was a lot of fun. It was new, and everyone took an interest in the monkey. As time passed, the interest disappeared, and our Makako was forgot. Then the monkey got loose and drew attention to itself through dumb stuff (*mischievous Tricks* [sic]). The count was the monkey's owner and as a result no owner. If he had pulled a prank on someone then, without any questions being asked, an execution would have taken place. The Japanese had taken a particular liking to that sly animal, and he had pulled many a vexatious trick on them. Kisselev, one of the Japanese, took him under his protection to ensure for himself monkey-business and laughter; so nothing had been heard from Makako since he had been tied up again. A little while ago, he got loose again and brought disorder in the cabin by his uninvited visit. Since the harness he had had around his body had torn loose, it was difficult to catch him. One morning, Dr. Horner caught him by the tail when the monkey was trying to play the uninvited guest in his cabin. Tolstoi, who wanted to tie a rope around its body, got bitten, and he threw the poor animal so hard onto the deck that, because of strong contusions, the monkey was dying, and the count had to kill it. The cotti (raccoons) have damaged almost all of our tobacco boxes. They eat, dig around in, and spill the tobacco and are by far not as amusing as the monkey. I wish we were rid of them because those animals are of no use to us.

Proof of how long you can keep lemons stored in a net is that today I ate a quite good lemon that I had bought on Tenerife, whose outer skin had become hard, as a result of lying around for over seven months.

Tues. 18/20 At noon, Krusenstern went over to the *Neva*. While he was gone, our cook Neumann, a Courlander by birth, died. He already was suffering with consumption when we hired him, and at Cape Horn his health did the rest. He died today, completely eaten up by consumption. The only thing we could give him on the way into the depths of the sea was a blessing as part of the burial ceremony, for we had sent word to our captain on the *Neva* that our cook had died. Krusenstern, upon hearing this, suggested to Priest Gideon that he go along to conduct the burial ceremony. "How can I do that?" was his answer. "He was Lutheran, and it is against the laws." We were angry about it and gave the blessing ourselves.

Neumann spit up blood for the first time in Brazil. That's why Krusenstern suggested he should stay there and offered him a year and a half's worth of support. Our cook refused everything and insisted upon sailing with us and upon remaining with us come what may. The beautiful climate on St. Catharina would have prolonged his life for some time. With his poor health, he would not have made it there for very long either. That his life ended here in the middle of the ocean is a great consolation. For the past eight days, we have had to watch his approaching end every day. If he had died near the *Sandwitsch* [sic] Islands or shortly before we arrived in Kamtschatka, then we would have had trouble about his funeral. Instead of that, now with his burial also the thought of him is obliterated. May God bless him.

Wed. 19/31 The current is driving us strongly to the west.

That the islanders eat their enemies' flesh is all too true. They preserve the skulls and hair as a sign of victory. We bought several such skulls. If it is indeed true that in the rage of war civilized Europeans are not ashamed of eating their enemies' flesh, then woe be to him who angers the savages by whom it is law.

Equatorial winds, alternating sunshine and rain, calms and gusts of wind, and now and then even wind from every direction.

Thurs. 20/1 Four days of continual rain. Being continually wet without the possibility of drying oneself out is nasty. Twice a day, I have been having to stand in the pouring rain. Totally soaked, I was not able to dry myself out by my next watch. Add to this the bad fare and dissatisfaction and it has to get at you. In less than two hours, I filled ten casks of water from the tank on the quarterdeck. You can well imagine that I had to help with the work. It was not worth wearing a coat on my watch. I was always soaked through to my shirt.

Fri. 21/2 In order to shatter heavy rain clouds and to quiet the variable winds, a brisk northeasterly arose in the night that, despite Cape Horn, is blowing into our sails. We never neglect making observations. In the afternoon, our deceased cook's possessions were auctioned off.

Sat. 22/3 A nice east-northeasterly trade wind, too brisk for a tropical wind. In Taiohai, we caulked our ship over the waterline. Despite that, the ship continues to leak, and we have to pump once a day, sometimes more often. She leaks up to two zoll an hour with a strong wind; in calm weather, the leak is hardly noticeable. In Kamtschatka, we hope to find the leak, since we have to unload everything there, and our leak must be under the waterline.

A new law: Our passengers, who could just as well tend to their business in the daytime, had got used to sitting up at night and were burning up three wax candles a day. Since our supply of candles was being used up too fast, the order was given that no candles were to be burned unnecessarily at night. The person in charge of household supplies at a given time is to see to it.

Sun. 23/4 During our stay in Nukahiva, it would have been impossible to prevent our people from fraternizing with the savage girls, and to keep this from happening in secret the captain permitted the girls to come onboard every other day. This was done with the greatest orderliness. After the ship had been made taboo with a cannon shot, loud calls went out from the ship: "Wahina e he!" (Come, girls!) Half an hour later, thirty to forty girls and women came swimming up, were let onboard in an orderly fashion, and stood facing forward in a row. Now everything that had hands and feet onboard came and picked a couple out for himself. Those remaining had to go overboard again, did not help when they showed enough of their uka eh! And, insulted, they swam back to land. Not much sleeping was done during the night. In the morning before the taboo was raised, the women folk were put up front again, counted, admired the presents they had received, and then they swam like ducks toward land. About half way there, the savages came to meet them and took their acquisitions, etc.

We were on land standing in a circle in Nukuhiva deliberating, when suddenly a female savage came into the circle and stared at Krusenstern because he is the tallest and pointed to her uka. Since he did not react, she went away and came back immediately smeared with coconut oil, and we could see that she believed herself irresistible. Since we all began to laugh, our sailors laughed too, and they are no scorners of fare. Krusenstern had barely said to one of the rowers, "Well, if you want to, then take it," than my sailor was off with her, and five steps from us, behind a bush, he sacrificed to Venus.

Mon. 24/5 The savages' concept of shame is unique. Some wear a belt made from the bark of the paper mulberry, but most of them go about completely naked. They bind up their foreskin with a ribbon. If it is missing, then the fellow is undressed and causes general laughter. If our sailors bathed, then there was no end to the savages' laughter.

If on land a savage's ribbon came loose, embarrassed, he immediately went into the bushes and tied it up and returned out of the bushes with the very saucy conviction that he was dressed. In front and behind, the women have a bunch of leaves on a string to cover their privy parts. Their lack of reserve causes them often to shove this covering aside or even to remove it. This worked like coquetry with our sailors.

Tues. 25/6 The *Nadezhda* continues to leak regularly, two zoll an hour.

26/7 A year has already passed since I started serving on the *Nadezhda*. At our departure we did not suspect that we would suffer more dissatisfaction from men than from the weather and the elements with which we continually have to do battle.

- 6 -

Owaihi to Kamtschatka

Fri. 27/8 Sighted the Table Mountain on Owaihi [Hawaii], the Mowna Roa [Mauna Loa], as well as the Mowna Kaah [Mauna Kea].

The savages believe that the heart and soul are in the stomach and are not, as children of nature, totally wrong.

Mr. von Krusenstern does not want to anchor in Owaihi but rather, in sailing by, to try to buy pigs and fruit, because the savages here are full of foul practices and the anchorage is very bad.

We hope that curiosity will toll out Resanoff, as fear did, when we almost shipwrecked on the shore in Taiohai. There, he was frightened out [of his cabin]; here probably he will put on his Hipocriten Larwe [hypocritical mask].

The island of Owaihi has the appearance of a beautiful amphitheater and must be very fertile. In the afternoon, we were three English miles from land. Three boats dared to come out to us to satisfy their curiosity, because they turned around without coming on board and went back. Головачев [Golovatscheff] made a mistake that caused the ship to turn even farther from land. Despite this, ten boats came out to us from land bringing us a piglet, half a dozen coconuts, and other small things. The people are ugly colored, tiny of stature, all scabby, and almost all of them are missing their two front teeth. Many of them had open sores. Our John found this view so unpleasant that he does not want to stay here but intends to sail on with us. The craftsmanship of these islanders is better than that of the savages on Nukahiva. The ropes they brought us were better made than our loglines (they were so thick). The fiber from the paper mulberry is strong, tight, and more colorfully dyed than on Nukuhiva. The savages also brought a pretty, good-natured girl to trade, one whom we could not compare with any of the Marquesan girls. I use the savages on Nukuhiva as my measuring stick in order to have a comparison with the Sandwitsch Islanders.

During the night, we stayed at sea under little sail and somewhat away from shore.

Sat. 28/9 Mr. von Krusenstern did not want to stay any longer on the eastern side of the island, so we sailed along the western coast, unfortunately too far from land.

Yesterday evening, I had a dispute with Horner and Langsdorff about purchases. Langsdorff was talking out of self-interest and faulted our captain for no reason. When Horner and I maintained that trade is absolutely not forbidden and the purchase of pigs was the reason for our stopping, we finally silenced him. To tell the truth, all of us find it unpleasant that we are not going to anchor here for a couple of days.

Around noon, we reached the southern tip where most of the people live. The strong wind let only two boats come out to us. One of the boats had a piglet that was bought. The other boat had a big pig, but from arrogance the savage did not know what he should have for it. After a lot of bargaining, to our regret, he left with it.

Lisianski had his Henkermahlzeit [last meal before his execution] with us today. The sailors on the wheel, through their lack of attention, had almost brought us against the *Neva* by steering to the right instead of to the left. Finally, they got several mild blows for that one. The *Neva* is sailing from here to Kodiak and we to Kamtschatka.

The savages' boats are exceedingly well built.

In general, the savages here speak a little English. With the big pig came a girl who greeted us with "*How do you do* [sic]?" and similar things. The savages are bold here. The wind was extremely brisk. Fearlessly, the savages sailed out into the sea. To maintain balance, the savages had put an outrigger on the boat, and thus they could return to land with unheard of swiftness.

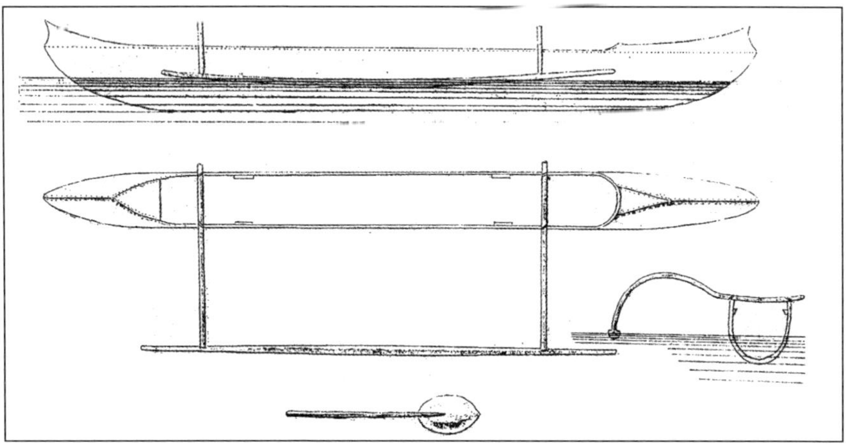

6-1. Design of a boat of the Sandwitsch *[sic] Islanders*

Sun. 29/10 Everyone is unhappy with Krusenstern because upon his orders we are so far from land (with too much запас!) [supplies in reserve]. It is already ten o'clock, and we are 25 miles from land. Only in the afternoon will we come closer to land, and before sunset we are going to be heading out to sea. The time is short too for us to be able to do any trading with the islanders. In the past couple of days, we have had a brisk wind, which has prevented the savages from coming onboard. Today, we have nice calm weather, but we are too far from land. Now the nice weather only slows down the course of the ship. Charting this island is very difficult because it is round. Therefore, we have been satisfied with just establishing the height of Mowna Roa.

Krusenstern went over to the *Neva,* from which we will now separate. He is also in a bad mood. We sailed from the Marquesas Islands with a detour by the Sandwitsch Islands in order to buy pigs and fruit, and, now that we are here, we are leaving Owaihi again without having been close to land. We have already spent so much time; what difference would a couple of days make?

At seven in the evening, Krusenstern returned from the *Neva,* and with *Three Chears* [sic] (three hurrahs)! we separated from our traveling companions.

May God grant us health since salt meat, peas, grits, and hardtack are our food.

September[1] alone can excuse Krusenstern's behavior. As consolation, we got the news that our sugar is gone. We probably have several tons in the hold that we cannot get at. Luckily for us, the raw sugar will last until Kamtschatka.

All of us are curious what we will find in Kamtschatka, how much of what we still have of our provisions.

Mon. 30/11 Krusenstern puts too much trust in Lisianski, who will sell him and us out if it is to his advantage.

The Sandwitsch Islanders were tattooed but very irregularly and mostly with animal figures, e.g., lizards, goats, fish, etc.

Tolstoi will, without a doubt because of the last dispute with Ratmanoff, be left in Kamtschatka, because the latter has undoubtedly said, "Either Tolstoi or I have to stay behind; we are not going any farther together." Fosse, who is doing better, will perhaps stay because of his illness. The captain wants to leave Schemelin behind, and so we will get some room.

Tues. 31/12 Nice weather. Tilesius has got hemorrhoids and is in bed.

Our supply of mustard is gone. That caused a great sensation, but there is nothing to do about it. Thus, one foodstuff after another goes.

On the last day before we separated, Lisianski went to Resanoff and told him that Krusenstern had ordered him to ask His Excellency for instructions. Resanoff answered: "Since you did not want to follow my instructions in St. Catharina, I have none for you now."

"In St. Catharina, I did not accept your instructions because I did not know at that time that you were head of the expedition," said Lisianski.

"What?" asked Resanoff. "Didn't I show you my papers there?"

"No!" answered Lisianski.

Resanoff was startled then because he was seeing himself beaten by his own weapon. "There were witnesses present," called Resanoff after several moments' consideration.

"Are you trying to force me to be candid?" Lisianski interrupted him. "We have so many examples of your not keeping your word, etc., etc." In a word, Lisianski did not get any instructions, and that was what he was after. He delivered a written description of the incident to Krusenstern and in return got a written order from Krusenstern to follow the instructions the captain had sent him in Kronstadt. The instructions contained the following: Upon arrival in Kodiak to unload all of the wares taken along, to load a selection of pelts, and then to sail to Kamtschatka, and wait for us there. Resanoff has sent a packet of orders from Baranoff to Kodiak, which will also cook Lisianski's cabbage. Probably Lisianski plans, if he can finish with the cargo in Kodiak, still to sail straight for China this year.

Ratmanoff's situation is also becoming confused. In Nukahiva, when we demanded of Resanoff that he publicly read his power of attorney to us and he had driven Romberg impolitely out his cabin, Ratmanoff said on the quarterdeck: "If he has so much trouble with doing that, then he is very well a самозванец [one who gives himself rank and title]. In that case, he deserves, as a disturber of the peace, to be locked in his cabin or he is crazy!" Resanoff heard this remark or someone told him about it. In a word, Resanoff's creatures are talking about it as if sentence will be passed on Ratmanoff. Ratmanoff therefore will use an opportunity to talk with Resanoff himself about it. In any case, he is going to hand in a petition against Resanoff in the name of the emperor in Kamtschatka. In Kamtschatka, there is going to be a racket.

June

Wed. 1/13 The tattooed Frenchman is staying with us. He did not like the scabby Sandwitsch Islanders.

Thurs. 2/14 Nice weather, envious climate between the tropics.

Fri. 3/15 Tolstoi is crazy. He hatches new stories every day. First, he wanted to stay on the *Sandwitsch* [sic] Islands; now, he is saying that he is going to kill Resanoff and then set fire to the Nadazhda and some such crazy stories.

In the evening, Torras harpooned a dolphin but it tore loose.

The wind is very even, the main topgallant sail is not taken down at all, and we are sailing between six and eight knots.

Krusenstern, made aware of the count's etourderie [fits], advised Tolstoi today to stay in Kamtschatka on account of his illness and thus prevent problems and difficulties. The count rejected this suggestion. The captain convinced him that

Resanoff would certainly use the opportunity in Japan to let him feel his authority. The count gave Krusenstern a long, wide tale about how grateful he would be if he let him live his life and concluded, "And, even if I lose my head by doing it, I'm going to nevertheless." Then Tolstoi again said in a very loud voice to Brinkin in the company cabin: "You are wrong if you think the crew is satisfied, not at all! Your officers cannot stand you at all, and then you are dying of hunger (and our people now have better food to eat than we do). "By the way," he said, "I'm not afraid of anything. The other people agree with me and will do whatever I want them to."

Ratmanoff and Golovatscheff, who had also heard this reasoning, asked the captain personally to observe Tolstoi's behavior for himself; and Brinkin's observation was also conveyed to Krusenstern. All that Krusenstern said to Tolstoi was, "I am surprised that you act differently from what your words and statements would lead one to expect."

Then Tolstoi related that Resanoff at various times had sent, among others, Friderici, Brinkin, and the painter to him, in order to prevail upon him to be reconciled with them. He, Tolstoi, however, had rejected this each time. Now he bragged and boasted as if it were meritorious and as if he had done Krusenstern a favor.

Sat. 4/16 Count Tolstoi has not stopped playing his bad tricks. Since his designs for the Kotzebues and several sailors have not worked, he now has undertaken to teach the half-tattooed John European customs. Fosse overheard him last night on the observation post where he had encamped because it was cooler.

Sun. 5/17 May God grant that we get rid of Tolstoi in Kamtschatka. A nice trade wind.

Mon. 6/18 Our leak is now two to three zoll an hour. Unfortunately, we are going to have to resupply ourselves from the Kamtschadals' plenty. God grant us that their plenty will be large enough.

Thurs. 9/21 Bellingshausen has sketched an inlet we charted in Nukahiva very well. Today, for the first time, we again caught and ate bonitos.

Fri. 10/22 Schemelin, without asking anyone, treats the cargo and everything on the ship as his property. He takes wine, brandy, etc., as much as he wants. Krusenstern, to whom we reported it, asked him what right he had to do that? Schemelin answered with his usual coarseness, "That is no one's business, and that all belongs to me." Ratmanoff then handed in a report about his antics in which he demanded that either the misuses that Schemelin was permitting himself be curtailed or that his name be removed from the list of stockholders. After that, we officers of the watch received an order from the captain not to let anything be handed over to Schemelin. "No fear! He gets nothing more!"

Sat. 11/23 The first total calm since Kronstadt, but despite that the water oscillates so that we cannot say that it is like a mirror; that is probably impossible here. That happens often in the Baltic Sea.

We caught two sharks during the calm. Each one was 8½ fuss long and weighed over 200 pud. Unfortunately, sharks are unpalatable.

Sun. 12/24 Today, our sailors refused to eat the sharks that we caught yesterday.

Resanoff accepted Ratmanoff's stocks, but at the same time wrote the captain a letter, saying that it was not worth all the noise over a bottle of wine. Ratmanoff wrote, as a counterpart to this letter, a defense that was just as coarse as he talks.

Mon. 13/25 Resanoff used the expression in his letter that it is ridiculous to take a bottle of wine into consideration since indeed the American Company had placed so much trust in this man (that is, Schemelin).

Ratmanoff delivered his petition to Resanoff in which he defends and justifies his behavior and demands justice according to the law.

We are rigging our ship during this feuding. The longboat is becoming a schooner; the others get lugsails.

We had the sun at the zenith during the calm. Langsdorff with bare arms fished for sea animals for a while from one of our boats. The rays of the sun burned his arm so badly that it was covered with blisters. Langsdorff's burned arm is very painful. The thermometer in the shade is 22°. The side of the ship was so hot that you could not touch it.

Tues. 14/26 Resanoff has not answered Ratmanoff's petition.

Wed. 15/27 Tilesius continues to loll about his cabin.

The sailor Черной [Tschernoi] is the first one to come down with scurvy. Tilesius had better watch out that he does not get scurvy.

Sat. 18/30 The nice days are over. Fog, rain, gusts of wind, and strong winds are now the order of the day.

Sun. 19/1 A wet, cold day with contrary winds and high seas.

Tilesius thinks that if he has told a sailor this has to be fastened down, preserved, or put away, that he has done his part and does not need to concern himself with the matter any further. Who is, however, from necessity, going to look after and be responsible for his specimens in bottles, glasses, etc., filled with spiritus? Since this counselor himself in no way looks after the things, they are noticeably rotting, spoiling, and breaking. Soon, he will wake up from his dream.

Determination of the height of Mowna Roa: a and b are specific spots on the ship determined by longitude and latitude. The distance a b is thus known. The angles a and b are points determined by the compass according to which the height of the mountain c was observed. Therefore, the distances are known from Mowna Roa a c and b c from the ship.

The dip, i.e., the curve or reduced refraction according to the condition of the atmosphere, has to be corrected, and through the measurement of the angel d a c and the diameter of the earth, one obtains the height of the mountain, then Z a d = 90° – dip, a f = the distance and z a = the diameter of the earth + the

6-2. 21 June 1804—discovery of Silver Island, Riko de Plata

height of the eye. That is how one finds the angle a z c. The triangle a z c have the angles z, z a and z a c through which one finds z c = z f + f c, thus f c or the height of the mountain.

Tues. 21/3 The captain had a piglet slaughtered yesterday for the sick men and gave it to Espenberg to distribute. Quite a few people thought it was a case of the billy goat being made the gardener and said very loudly at table that we were not allowed to have food in one's cabin other than at meal times. (Espenberg kept the roast in his cabin.)

Damp, wet, cold, rainy weather. We set our course to the west in order to look for the supposed Silver Island, Riko de Plata[2] so that we do our part in discovering a clump of earth. I certainly hope we do not find it because in such dreary weather one does not see land until one is sitting on it. The wind is increasing. We hauled in one sail after another and in the night had a storm so that we sailed nine knots for discovery.

In the night, I walked up and down with Krusenstern and thought about Reval and talked about Reval. (He is indeed often homesick.)

Wed. 22/4 In the morning, we gave up looking for the Silver Island and headed again for Kamtschatka. Nice headwind.

Espenberg leaves everything to nature. People are asking why he brought along so much medicine. The quantity he had requested according to his catalogue and received was foolish. Officers and sailors through the change in climate got sores. No one can brag about having got a plaster from Espenberg. First this one and then that one asks why he has his apothecary's chest and gets nothing.

In the evening, we saw several whales in the distance.

Thurs. 23/5 We sailed past a large turtle, lowered a boat, but came too late to catch it.

Fri. 24/6 Continual fog, bad weather for discoveries. A whale frightened me in the night by surfacing next to the ship and noisily blowing his fountain.

The difference of longitude now is twelve hours.

Soaked through to my shirt in rain and fog, I measured the quarterdeck and thought and thought of all of you and of St. John's Day [midsummer]. I have no reason to cry but just as little also to laugh. A dry honesty is midways between the two. That's why I feel rather sour about walking up and down the quarterdeck.

Sat. 25/7 Fog every day and so thick that you cannot see your hand before your eyes.

Son. 26/8 We are greatly concerned about the rarity of observations. The wind is brisk, but the fog doesn't go away. It is very quiet in the cabin and on the ship. Resanoff sits in his cabin like in a prison. His suite patrols around the ship with lurking eyes, and we do our duty without anyone worrying about them.

Mon. 27/9 Finally today, we had a few furtive moments of sun. Resanoff gave us to understand that he would collect all of our papers upon our return. Kus Lammas!—wer giebt![3]—[who cares!]

Tues. 28/10 Thick fog and cold air. Unhealthy weather. We are not used to it and therefore find the climate rawer and colder than it is. We are not yet in Kamtschatka and wish we were already away from the place. There we will certainly have to deal with Resanoff again.

Wed. 29/11 At the last minute, Boreas[4] gave us another one today. The air just as cold, and the *Nadezhda* is being tossed around just as at Cape Horn. We will have unbearable fog pribafka [прибавка: in addition].

Our taste has been totally spoiled. The Brazilian rum that we found disgusting now tastes delicious. Spirits with water, drunk as grog, are much favored. Salt meat seems like a delicacy; and if the hardtack is not spoiled, it is eaten whether it has mold in it or not.

The sky cleared up in the evening. We had only four degrees of warmth. Golovatscheff's glass of punsch to celebrate his name day was very opportune. Our Frenchman never loses his good spirits.

Thurs. 30/12 Nice, clear day that permitted us to determine our astronomical location on the map.

Flocks of puffins, sea swallows, gulls, etc., are flying around our ship.

- 7 -

The First Stay in Kamtschatka

7-1. Kamtschatka

July

Fri. 1/13 In the morning from the crow's nest, we saw land which was, however, totally covered by fog.

Today, Tilesius appeared again for the first time. Several people are claiming he reported himself ill so that he could get roast pork. In the afternoon, a bank of fog gave the illusion that we were surrounded by land—the power of imagination. By the refraction of the rays, light and shadow appeared here and there in the fog, and only our telescope convinced us that it was a fogbank and not land. Toward evening the illusion disappeared, and before sunset we saw to the west the eastern promontory of the Kamtschatka Peninsula.

Sat. 2/14 Until ten o'clock, we were kept by calms and variable winds far from land. A gull landed on our gig and was shot down. A little time before that, it had carefully cleaned its feathers and not without cause, for the gull was full of large wood lice. I had never seen a bird plagued by this vermin before.

The calm prevented us from entering Avatscha Bay. The charts are not completely correct here either. The tips of the old volcanoes in Kamtschatka appeared in the distance before sunset.

Sun. 3/15 The beautiful, clear morning, the nearness of land, and the good wind also cheered me up on my watch from four o'clock. The fire-spewing peaks of the snow-covered mountains could be seen only in the distance. At eleven o'clock, we clearly saw the entrance to Avatscha Bay. At one o'clock, we sailed into the bay, and at two o'clock we dropped anchor in the Peter-Paul Bay (or Harbor).

An artillery officer came out to meet us, and we were greeted by seven salvos which we answered.

Today, Resanoff appeared on deck for the first time since our departure from Nukahiva and went ashore in full ornata.

After Resanoff had climbed on shore, he said to the rower, who had helped him out of the boat, "I thank you! I thank you! You know that I have always taken care of you and am convinced that you will not desert me. You yourself know what is going on onboard ship." Romberg, who had gone along, overheard the rest of this speech because he had been speaking with the major who is acting commander.

The *Nadezhda* was unrigged before sundown. Today, Resanoff has already written a letter to Krusenstern: "I am leaving Count Tolstoi as your responsibility on the ship in case he should do something illegal, especially since Tolstoi does not count himself as under my command."

The highest degree of poverty. Only Russians (military) live at the Harbor of Peter-Paul, who in addition to their wages, as a result of shortages, receive only half of their paiok [паек: monthly allowance, rations]. They have no meat dishes at all. Fish has to replace every shortage.

General Major Koscheleff is in Nischnoi Kamtschatsk. He is General Governor here. In fourteen days, eight steers are supposed to be driven here for us from there.

On land, Krusenstern addressed Resanoff as представиелъ главое лицо американской компании (that is what he calls himself: the representative of the upper management of the American Company) and requested of him that he procure help and boats for the unloading or to order the prikaschtschik here to do so. Resanoff's answer was, "Do whatever you want to; I have nothing to say about that."

Mon. 4/16 The people here, after saying не ловится [there was no catch of fish], brought us a whole boat full of salmon, the work of barely half a night. Yesterday, the chest of one of the Japanese was broken open and his clothes stolen and in addition 80 rubles. While checking (промышлеников) the people who are to stay in Kamtschatka, that is Новоселов [Novoselov], Кулаин [Kuliain], Андреев [Andreev], Моноков [Monokov], and Воробиев [Vorobieff], several stolen items were found among the latter's things; those of the Japanese, however, could not be found. Since these people, as well as the Japanese, are totally

7-2. Klaerk's grave; the tomb; castle

dependent upon Resanoff, Krusenstern sent them all on land with a letter to the ambassador. Resanoff sent Воробиев [Vorobieff] back with a letter directing Krusenstern to punish him.

At the same time, Schemelin wrote a letter to the domestic Ivan ordering him, in Resanoff's name, to send on land eight days' worth of provisions for the gentlemen. Especially since the captain had already ordered this done, the latter was a lie. The messenger was sent back without an answer, and in the afternoon that lazy Schemelin came himself. He got to hear quite a few things about his correspondence. Krusenstern had him sent to him and reprimanded him for using his domestic who had no say, since that only caused confusion which was his duty to prevent, etc.

Krusenstern wrote Resanoff, suggesting the separation of his suite from our company at table, and sent this letter along with Schemelin, especially since the division of provisions could be accomplished very easily while unloading the ship.

Tues. 5/17 Captain Clerke's[1] grave marker is a wooden box at the foot of a half-dried-out birch tree. La Pérouse had a copper plate with the following text put there.

> At the root of this tree lies the body
> of Captain Charles Clerke, who
> succeeded to the Command of his
> Britanic Majesty's ships, the
> Resolution and Discovery on
> the death of Captain James
> Cook, who was unfortunately
> killed by the Natives at an
> Island in the South Sea on
> the 14th of February in the Year

7-3. Peter-Paul's Harbor [Petropavlovsk] in Kamtschatka

> 1779, and died at Sea, of a
> Lingering consumption the 22nd
> of August in the same year.
> aged 38. Copie sur linscription
> anglaise, par Order de Mr.le Cte.de la
> Pérouse, Chef d'Escadre, en 7^{an} 1787 [sic].

La Pérouse had barely sailed away when the plate was stolen. The priest spread the word that the spirit of the dead man had become very restless and demanded vehemently that the plate be returned. The thief, made afraid of the avenging spirit, put the plate back in its place again at night. Since then, the plate lies unnailed on the grave and more secure than previously. The grave of Delisle de la Croyére[2] is supposed to be together with Clerke's.

The high grass growing in the valleys shows that Kamtschatka is capable of being cultivated.

In the evening, we unloaded the gunpowder. We are working on charting the bay.

Wed. 6/18 We have built ourselves a pristan so that we can land more comfortably and repair the old longboat of the *Slava Rossia* (the ship Billings[3] had built in Ochotsk) that lies sunk in the middle of the harbor.

Thurs. 7/19 Every morning we have a thick fog, during the day clear skies. Today the fog rose and we had rain, which prevented work.

The bugs are so onerous, that we do not know where we can get away from them.

7-4. (Tongue of land) Kamtschatka

The peasant traders here are bloodsuckers; the prikaschtschiks here excel in it. For a glass of strongly steamed brandy, he buys a sable or fox pelt from the Kamtschadals, the only asset of these poor people.

That the prikaschtschiks can count is proven by the price that the American Company paid for a magazine (looks like our hay sheds) and three small huts (in comparison our honeycomb houses are large), that is 10,000 rubles cash. In the evening we tried our hand at fishing, three casts and we had our barrel full—turbot, cod, salmon, herring, and a dozen crabs.

Fri. 8/20 At six o'clock, we begin our work on the ship. A half-hour is spent eating breakfast, an hour for lunch, and at seven o'clock we have schabasch. We stand watch for eight hours.

Most of the dogs here are castrated. That is why they live together so peacefully.

Romberg, Golovatscheff, and Friderici went to Avatscha today. In the next few days, I am going to take a trip to Avatscha and Paratunka. The latter has been uninhabited for a long time and is a place where large numbers of bears stop to catch fish and wander around.

Sat. 9/21 Even though it was Saturday at home, we celebrated Sunday here because we count the longitude to the west, and the Kamtschadals count the one to the east. At noon, the officers here ate with us. All of them seem to be under pressure.

At the last revision [census], Kamtschatka was still rather populated. Pox and fever have however decimated the people, so that where otherwise one hundred people lived now barely five can be found, and those few have to pay for the iasak [ясак] (levy in pelts) for all the dead. Formerly, the crown had a cheap tax on the

7-5. *Tongue of land at Peter-Paul's Harbor, Kamtschatka*

pelts, and the poor Kamtschadals paid their tax with money. Now the taxes have been raised. The old revision, however, remains, so that the poor Kamtschadals cannot afford the taxes at all.

No soldier goes out of his house without taking a Kamtschadal along as a companion. The post has to furnish these people without pay, and, if a commando or baggage has to be transported from one place to another, then the Kamtschadals have to carry all of the burdens without pay. Thus, he does not see his hearth (house, wife, child) for months at a time because, due to the lack of inhabitants, he is continually requisitioned. The time for fishing is seasonal. If he misses it, he is without food. His joy and happiness are his dogs and a glass of brandy, for which he has to pay fifty rubles for a stof. That is how the last Kamtschadal is going to be rubbed out. Every Kamtschadal is a good shot and has a rifled barrel with a caliber the size of a pea.

Large numbers of wild bears are all over here so that you cannot step ashore without meeting several of them. Since the Kamtschadals have to pay four rubles for a pfund of powder and two rubles for a pfund of lead, they are always in debt and pay everything with pelts and can never say this pelt now belongs to me.

Sun. 10/22 For the time being, the unhappy lot has befallen me to provide for the company table. Resanoff has taken Langsdorff formally into service and completed a contract with him.

Mon. 11/23 Romberg and Bellingshausen have been put in charge of viewing and inspecting the ship's provisions. The weather is the same as at home with us in the country.

A whole sail became totally useless during the voyage and has to be thrown away. We have to sew new sails to replace this loss but don't have enough sailcloth.

There is however in the cargo для отвозу [for the embassy] a lot of sailcloth. Krusenstern went to Resanoff as representative of the American Company and got (as usual) an ambiguous answer. The shed or magazine on the shore is in a very inconvenient location. Krusenstern requested Resanoff to hire people to get the goods because it is impossible to do the work using only our sailors. Again an unsatisfactory answer. If it should begin to rain, a lot of things will be spoiled and lost, probably a trap that Resanoff is putting out for our captain—over and above that, he is demanding that all the presents for Japan should be unloaded (that is one complete придирка [cavil]).

Tues. 12/24 The gifts for the Emperor of Japan are in large crates which we could well unload but because of their weight are not able to transport. Resanoff however accepts no reasons and speaks of the crown's work and demands nosily all of the things should be unloaded (all deceitful tricks).

Wed. 13/24 Rumor has it that Koscheleff is to arrive soon. Mail arrives five times a year. We loaded the first longboat with stone ballast. Since our company table wants to disband, we let the gentlemen on land know that the remains (leftovers) of our victuals were on the deck for viewing.

At ten o'clock, Fosse, Friderici, Schemelin, Brinkin, and Kurlandzoff came on board. The first question was who was to be in each company. The first one consisted of Resanoff and his suite, the second of Krusenstern and of officers. Two causes for concern remain. Tilesius, who has had a strained relationship with Resanoff for a long time, has not fulfilled any of the conditions of his contract and has been left in uncertainty in every way. The poor fellow does not know where he is and, since he does not even know if Resanoff is going to take him along to Jedo [Tokyo], he went with Fosse on land in order to request a binding answer from Resanoff. As usual, he got an ambiguous answer and decided to join our group without calculating his costs if he would be absent from our table for months.

No one said anything about Count Tolstoi, and that matter remained undecided.

It was twelve o'clock, and only then did we begin our calculations with Schemelin. This representative of the American Company bargains with us like a niggardly merchant. Finally, prices were settled for the provisions that already had been used up, and now it was a matter of completing the task.

Up to now, Krusenstern alone had made the disbursements. Only he could therefore say how much we had used up. The haggling, estimating, reviewing, and searching in all of the tangled account books of the passengers was irresponsible and insufferable. Stoic patience was necessary to watch all of that impassively. Only Ratmanoff and I said anything. Our comrades remained silent and let this police servant (Fosse) and Schemelin act freely and do whatever they wanted to. Finally, even the two of us were silent. Then the captain lost patience and said angrily: "I curse the moment I had anything to do with the American Company" and left.

After calculating for a long time, we discovered finally that even though our income was 16,000 rubles, we had indeed made 1,000 rubles in debts. (Unfortunately for this expensive money, we had been reduced to salt meat and peas half of the time.) Finally, at three o'clock, we got to eat lunch, and the gentlemen of the ambassador's suite went on land to gather advice at His Excellency's.

At five-thirty, the gentleman appeared again for the actual division of the provisions in empty crates, barrels and bottles. (Several of the gentlemen used the expression извощики, meaning cartmen, to designate us naval officers.) Fosse's impertinent behavior angered me. I told him a lot of coarse truths and dared to use the expression извощик [cartman]. As a result, Ratmanoff had it with Fosse and I with Friderici. After a lot of pros and cons, the matter ended without hurry and will be forgotten, like lots of other things in the world. Finally, the remains of the coffee, sugar, tea, spices, and flour prevailed; and there was no thinking about an actual division, since Count Tolstoi did not belong any place and also did nothing to end this doubt. I therefore suggested weighing out each person's portion. Since it was already too late, it remained a suggestion.

Resanoff's suite drank tea with us and went back on land at night. May they take to heart the truths that they had to hear today from Ratmanoff and me. As far as the sugar and brandy are concerned that we will need in the future, Resanoff has often tried chicanery with the prices. He will not let things go without exorbitant demands and overcharges.

Our group consists of Krusenstern, Ratmanoff, Romberg, Golovatscheff, Bellingshausen, Kamentschikoff, Espenberg, Horner, Tilesius, the two Kotzebues, and me, thus twelve people.

The other group consists of Resanoff, Fosse, Friderici, Brinkin, Kurlandzoff, Langsdorff, and Schemelin, thus seven people. Count Tolstoi plays solo.

You cannot hold it against any of us if we wish, "If only the voyage were over!"

Thurs. 14/26 Everything is still lying chaotically around on the deck. And there is no point in thinking about dividing things up. Krusenstern has written a letter to Resanoff, as holder of the power of attorney for the American Company, to set a norm according to which the prices for the provisions should be determined—no answer.

Resanoff granted Langsdorff ahead of time по данной мне влаети [through the power granted me] the title of aulic councilor.

Fri. 15/27 Tolstoi has moved completely on land and is living there peacefully and quietly; Golovatscheff is increasing his deceit daily. Romberg would rather cast aside anything other than the friendship with Count Tolstoi. Bellingshausen is entre deux [in between]. Mate Kamentschikoff is known as a common creeping soul. Espenberg, Horner, and Tilesius cannot become involved in anything. The two Kotzebues are—children. That is the reason that Ratmanoff and I have to battle everything through, daily to bite the bullet, and wage continual skirmishes. Good

Krusenstern stands there alone subject to Resanoff's traps and snares. He does not deserve this hard fate. The end will however have to crown the work.

In the afternoon, we finally divided the remains of the provisions—peacefully (since we said yes to everything, how then could strife occur?). We discovered to all of our sorrow that the rats had snatched away one and one-half piepen of port wine by making a hole in the cask, where the hole for a spigot had been corked up again, and had let the wine run out into the hold.

Sat. 16/28 Since we had no more brandy, I was more than a little happy about the little provision of spirits that I had in the hold. I had already drunk a little cask and thus still had three left. Unfortunately, there was hardly half in one barrel, in the second very little, and the third one had almost been totally emptied. Thus, I have been reduced from three to at the most one. I will treat the little supply of rum like gold, in case Resanoff refuses to let us take any brandy from the cargo, so I won't have to starve. If it were up to Resanoff, he would maliciously let us starve to death for lack of food.

Among other things, it was discovered on land that the brandy casks had been freshly tapped by a gimlet. No wonder our crew was drunk now and again (Russians have to be treated somewhat strictly so as not to go to ruin).

Since today was Sunday, our people in Kamtschatka had no desire to work. I could say whatever I wanted to; more and more of them found objections. (In other words, I thought that they must have tapped the brandy casks). Федосей Леонтев [Fedosei Leont'ev] was fresh enough to answer me when I ordered him to be quiet, "I'm going to talk to the captain and tell him that." I complained myself about the matter to Krusenstern and told him, "I would rather be relieved of the watch than to have to command a watch in which my orders are disobeyed." It was hard for me to say this to Krusenstern, but his fairness bordering on weakness forced me. Oh! Miracle! Федосей Леонтев [Fedosei Leont'ev] was punished and immediately followed my orders.

Today, we divided the tableware. Let's hope we will soon see the end of the dividing up.

At noon, Major Антон Иванович Крупской [Anton Ivanovich Krupskoi] and artillery officers Prokofei and Василии Федорович [Vasilii Fedorovich] dined with us.

We put the ship on her side so that the damaged copper could be replaced.

Sun. 17/29 We divided the remaining little things. Wine, flour, and kitchen equipment and sugar still have to be divided up.

Character trait of Fosse: In Falmouth, Fosse bought two dozen knives and forks at the cost of our table group. Now, at the division, he was asked about them since they were missing. "I do not have them," said Fosse, "Ivan must have them."

Ivan told him however, "You undoubtedly remember that you did not want to entrust the knives to me and put them into your chest." Fosse nevertheless did not want to hand them over.

Then Ratmanoff interrupted his servant and said accusingly to Fosse, "Look under your linens; perhaps the knives are there."

"Maybe," said Fosse, chicken-heartedly, went and fetched the knives. Fosse is practiced in overcounting and overweighing. This is the experience we had during the dividing up. A man has to be as base as Fosse in order, with a brazen face, not to blush, to be able to act as basely as Fosse has done.

Mail arrived today, and the news we have received for the time being: Kamtschatka is to be considered an oblast (separate region of the Empire) and placed under Koscheleff, who has been made head of this oblast. As a result, our chamberlain's conceited importance drops in this isolated region. Koscheleff, who is still in Nischnoi Kamtschatsk, cannot come soon enough.

Tues. 19/31 In the morning after tea, we went to Раковая бухта [Rakovaia Buchta], which is comparable to Peter-Paul's Harbor in quality. It is uninhabited like the entire area around Avatscha; only the remains of villages can be seen if you look around among the bushes and in the luxurious grass. We rowed up the bay very slowly and were surprised not a little to see two bears on the shore. Not long after that, we caught sight of a third, and it appeared that there were more of them there. We landed at the place where they had disappeared into the bushes and found that the bunch of bears had been refreshing themselves on a quite young, large, stranded whale. The whale had probably gotten lost in the bay, stranded on the sand; ebb tide was past, and the animal had died. The whale had not been lying there longer than four days; it was that fresh.

While Krusenstern, Ratmanoff, the Kotzebues, and I walked around in the bushes with our muskets and admired the bears' wrestling place (all of the branches were broken off; the ground trampled flat and not a blade of grass grew on it), Horner and Bellingshausen charted the bay.

The battle we saw between a hawk and a sea eagle was exceedingly interesting. The speed with which the latter turned and moved in the air was admirable. The hawk had started the attack. We arrived back at the ship at teatime.

After the evening meal, Stepan came to me, since it was my watch, and asked for permission to go on land to get milk for Golovatscheff. Since it was late, I asked Golovatscheff himself whether it was true. Recently, Golovatscheff has been taking a lot of liberties and always has his caprices. I did not let him go unanswered. One word led to another, and we had a good argument. The best of it is that it stayed at that.

20/1 Since relationships are such, Mr. von Krusenstern, after his return from Japan, in no case wants to stay any longer under Resanoff's orders and would rather undertake the trip to Petersburg by land than be dependent any longer upon a man like Resanoff. I also found it necessary for me to seek my recall in case Krusenstern should give up his command. With this intention in mind I have written a letter to Krusenstern and one to Tschitschagoff.

In Rinaldo's detachment[4] was found more honest blood and uprightness than in this black guild.

My letter to Krusenstern:

> Dear Sir, Ivan Fedorovich,
>
> I am convinced, in view of all the unpleasantness you have suffered at the hands of His Excellency Nikolai Petrovich Resanoff, that you are planning to request to be relieved this command. As you know, it was my wish to join this voyage to be under your guidance, for which I received assurances. Therefore, should you receive instructions to leave your command, I also am unable to remain without your leadership. I humbly ask you to inform, in writing, those whose concern this might be. For the rest, I have the honor to remain, with respect and loyalty, etc., etc.

My letter to Tschitschiagoff:

> While abroad, outside of our fatherland, I learned about the dispatch of an expedition around the world under the command of Captain-Lieutenant Krusenstern. The idea tempted me so greatly that I immediately abandoned my intention of entering the [French] Foreign Service and instead participated in this expedition so as to improve my knowledge and thus be of greater service to our fatherland in the future. With the help of Your Excellency, I [re-entered] the [naval] service and was appointed to the expedition, for which I had wished so ardently.
>
> After departure from Kronstadt, I believed Captain-Lieutenant Krusenstern to be my sole commander. However, while in the Marquesas, His Excellency Nikolai Petrovich Resanoff declared himself to be in command of the expedition. I know also, that having been subjected to much unpleasantness, Captain-Lieutenant Krusenstern intends, upon return from Japan, to ask to be relieved of his command. Therefore, I ask, in case the Captain-Lieutenant should be instructed to relinquish his command and return [home] by land, that I, too, be permitted to accompany him. I realize that it is not seemly [for someone] of my rank to choose a commander, but Your Excellency knows that all of us, in accordance with [His Majesty's] executive edict volunteered for this voyage under the command of Captain-Lieutenant Krusenstern. Thus, it is permissible to wish to return under his command without exposing myself to any kind of misfortune.
>
> I remain, with deepest respect and loyalty etc., etc., etc.[5]

Thurs. 21/2 We hoped to buy furs here, but furs can be obtained from the natives only in winter. The American Company has already bought everything and is asking of us the prices of furs in Petersburg.

Bolschersk now consists of only a few huts. Paratunka is deserted and inhabited by wild animals. In Avatscha are only a couple of huts.

Resanoff's indolence betrays teasing. The magazine is full and has no more room for cargo. For the present, we have to put a large part of the cargo under the open skies, have of course made tents over them out of sails, but how long can they protect cargo against the continual rain. Resanoff, as representative of the American Company, gives us only ambiguous answers, or no answer, and also does not write in answer to our captain's inquiries, whether we should continue with the unloading or not, since, in order still to go to Japan, we have to hurry with the unloading so that we can fill the ship with ballast.

Koscheleff's arrival will change conditions here radically because the rumor is spreading that Resanoff would have a lot of people arrested, that nothing would come of the voyage to Japan in this year, and we will have to winter in Kamtschatka.

Fri. 22/3 After eight days, we have had our first clear day. I took a walk with Krusenstern to inspect the source of a brook, where we are going to fill our water casks, in order to look for stone ballast. Along the way, we started to talk about our inexhaustible supply of picks, and we talked open-heartedly with each other and rather loudly. Look! there at the end of the koschka [кошка: sandbank at low tide that looks like a cat's back] was sitting Friderici with a camera obscura, and Fosse, as police do, in order to eavesdrop, had come up behind us and was not ashamed of himself at having been discovered eavesdropping. Let him listen! He'll get to hear only a lot of truths, which we can and will openly tell all over and which he undoubtedly will watch out about repeating.

Sat. 23/4 We celebrated a Kamtschadal Sunday. How wearisome! Friderici sets so many conditions and is so stingy with his camera obscura that Horner, who has an objective glass along, has given it to us, so that we intend to fabricate a camera obscura ourselves. Admittedly, the glass has a very large focal point but also displaces more clearly and will work all right. We need it especially for Tilesius.

Every day, there's louder talk about wintering here. If it is not true at all, then Resanoff is digging his own grave. Today, Krusenstern was again with Resanoff to get an answer from him about the unloading. Thereupon Resanoff ordered him to wait with the unloading. When our captain requested a written order from him, Resanoff said, "You can and must expect something written from me." This impulsive order, Resanoff's behavior, and his answers are all of a nature that make us have to believe that we'll have to winter in Kamtschatka.

Kamtschadals often come to view our ship. Today, an old graybeard was here whom I treated to a glass of rum, because he looked so much like an Estonian. In the afternoon, while on a walk, we found the same fellow sitting in the grass with his whole family. I asked him where he was going. "I'm spending the night here," he said, "and am going to Shipunskoi noe where I live." (a distance of three hundred versts) Then he told us, on the way here, he had killed a bear. We inspected his rifle barrel with a caliber the size of a pea on a fork. When we doubted that you could kill a bear with so small a ball, the old man said, "Доволльно" [good enough],

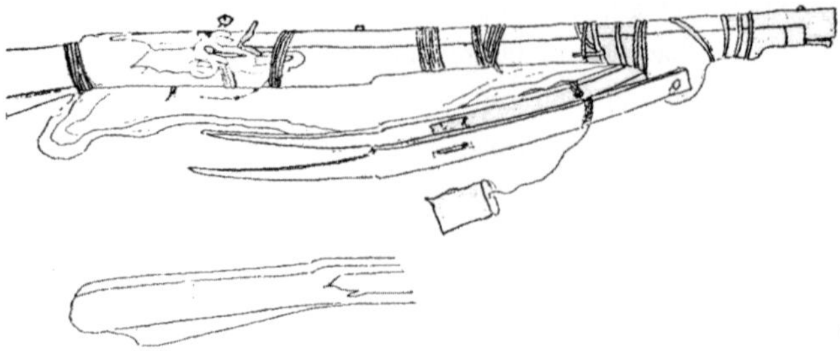

7-6a. A Kamtschadal's gun

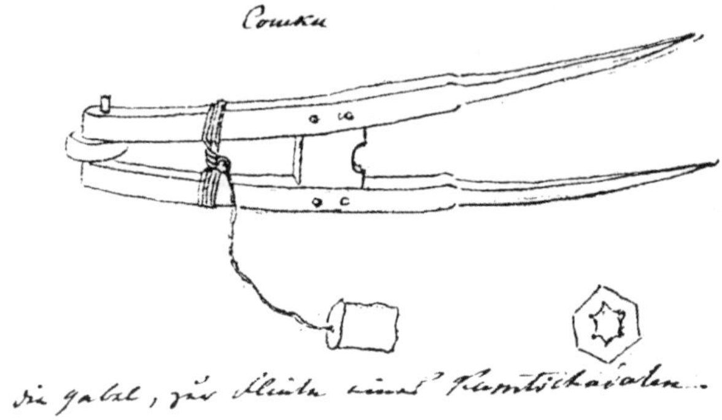

7-6b. The gun support of a Kamtschadal's gun

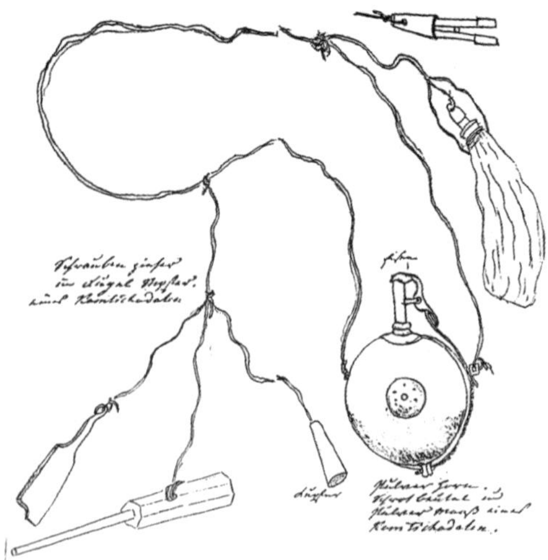

7-6c. The turnscrew and ramrod of a Kamtschadal's gun

7-6d. A Kamtschadal's copper powderhorn, pellet bag, and powder measure

totally happy about his rifle barrel. I gave the old man some gunpowder and tobacco and left him. In the beginning, he did not want to accept my gift at all, because he honestly assured me that he had nothing he could pay me with. I pointed to a carved piece of wood on which he carried his bundle. "I need that myself," he said, and I went on my way. The surprise of having been given such a large amount of gunpowder caused the old man a little bit later to run after me, hug me, and kiss me to pieces and give me the piece of wood. I was so amazed because I did not know what the fellow wanted from me. My comrades laughed a long time about my generosity and my tale.

On the way back, we visited officers here who permitted us to hook their dogs up to a sled. The sled and harness are light and strong. It is a pleasant sight to see the dogs running. In winter, they cannot to be stopped.

The officers here came on board ship to have tea with us.

Resanoff trumpeted out, "I intend to set the prices lower for everything because I intend to benefit this area. Even if it is not to the American Company's advantage, the bill can be sent to me. I'll gladly pay it out of my pocket and purse."(The American Company is going to really scratch the back of their heads for having elected such a generous representative.)

Koscheleff, since becoming general governor, has forbidden the merchants to travel inland and trade with brandy. Resanoff wants to repeal this order. Resanoff said today, "If Koscheleff does not come, I'm going to go to him." May he indeed come so that Resanoff will finally stop his secret machinations.

Sun. 24/5 The priest from Bolschersk has gone back without having taken the trouble to visit our ship. They are saying Resanoff had advised and ordered him to do it.

In answer to Krusenstern's request to have hardtack baked, he heard from Resanoff: "I cannot do anything until Koscheleff Павел Иванович [Pavel Ivanovich] has returned. And to Krusenstern's request to have various necessary things delivered to the ship before the entire cargo is on land, Resanoff answered: "I cannot do anything until the prikaschtschik's bill has been completed and reviewed." All excuses! Always a useless waste of time!

The impatience with which Koscheleff is awaited lets us expect no good intentions. Resanoff has requested military personnel, and a company is supposed to be marching here, probably to arrest all of us. Krusenstern dare not and we are not going to give a step.

Mon. 25/6 It was Макар Иванович [Makar Ivanovich] Ratmanoff's name day. According to Russian custom he had a pirog baked and a mass read in the church. From church, he went to Resanoff and invited him to his pirog. Resanoff, surrounded by his admirers, came up to him with a friendly sweet expression on his face (schadenfreude), did a thousand scrape-legs and answered his invitation with: "Makar Ivanovich, you do not want to serve under my orders."

Ratmanoff interrupted him and said, "My pirog has nothing at all in common with a commander." This was followed by a long silence during which Ratmanoff extended an invitation to the gentlemen of the suite then, turned to Resanoff, and said: "If His Excellency were so kind as to do me the honor of coming to my pirog, then I request most humbly that he appear on shipboard at one o'clock."

Resanoff answered, "Since you do not want to serve under my command, I cannot come to your pirog."

7-7. A sled for carrying loads

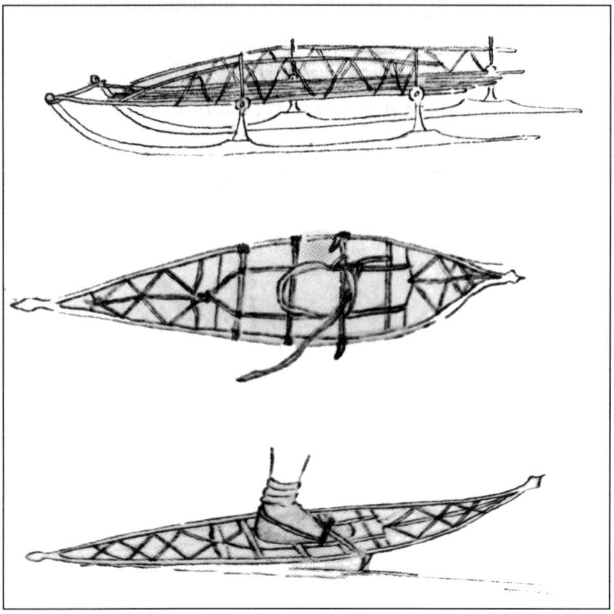

7-8. Five-fuss-long snowshoe

Resanoff and his entire suite are moving on land with pack and sack. Would that Resanoff hit upon the idea of sending the *Nadezhda* to Kodiak—then we would be rid of him.

All of the passengers and officers of the garrison dined with us today at noon.

Prices in Kamtschatka given me by Artillery Officer Volkoff: a pud of flour from 20 to 40 rubles, 1 pfund of lead 2 rubles, 1 pfund of gunpowder 3–4 rubles, 1 stof of distilled brandy 20 rubles, I pfund of sugar 3½, 1 pfund of tea 12, a small coarse towel 10 rubles for an arshin. Very coarse nankeen 1¼ rubles for an arshin. Iron that was 30 kopecks a pfund a short time ago is now 15 rubles a pud.

A clay teacup is two rubles, a teapot up to five rubles, tobacco, common, that was 1½ rubles a pfund a short time ago is now 1 ruble a leaf, a coarse pair of scissors three rubles, several faden thread seven to ten kopecks, soap two rubles, sewing needles two to four kopecks a piece, a bad knife five rubles, a homemade knife two–three rubles, butter three rubles a pfund, etc., etc.

A sable pelt costs five to ten rubles, a red [fox] pelt 7½ rubles, black, blue, and cross fox in relation to that are very expensive. An outfit made from reindeer hide from 20 to 200 rubles, etc.

Tues. 26/7 Romberg brought the news that Resanoff has given the order to seize all sailors who try to come ashore with brandy. We only know about such things from hearsay, even though it nevertheless is of concern enough for us.

On the koschka (tongue of land) lives a woman who is rather old. Our sailors did not disdain this sparse fare either and visited the hag. After satisfying their drives, they said goodbye without leaving a gratification. That made the woman mad. She therefore invited Щитов [Schittoff] to stay the night. When he believed he had obtained his desires, the hag began to scream terribly, calling for help, running to Major Krupskoi and complaining that our sailor had raped her. What makes us mad is Щитов [Schittoff's] bad taste. It is being said Resanoff intends to utilize military laws in investigating the matter.

Mr. von Krusenstern left the iron bars and iron wedges in the ship, and, since the iron is on her keel, it has already been covered with ballast.

Today Kamentschikoff comes and says Resanoff wants the iron taken out of the ship too. Why does Resanoff not tell our captain that, and why double the work? Couldn't he have informed the captain in the beginning of his desire and wish?

Today we put the ship on her left side in order to replace any spoiled and missing copper.

Krusenstern issued an order—to prevent unpleasantness and problems—that if a sailor is thinking of selling anything, whatever it is, he should have the buyer brought on board and give him on shipboard the things he has purchased. (This order is especially meant for brandy.)

A year ago today, we left Kronstadt. The prikaschtschiks and Resanoff are complaining that they have no storehouse. One of the crown's storehouses is standing empty, and Krusenstern, at his request, got from Major Krupskoi another one that was also empty. There must be a catch to why Resanoff is not issued a crown storehouse. The truth is that the American Company has a very bad reputation here.

Today, Resanoff demanded orally from Krusenstern the list of his crew in order to disburse their wages, and today Krusenstern sent him a communiqué with the requested list. Got the same back an hour later with an impertinent letter from Resanoff, because Krusenstern's signature was missing from the list. This letter can serve as a document—that is also why Resanoff does nothing in writing, so that there is nothing in black and white that might bring his dishonor to light. Krusenstern's calm and composed firmness of character angers him the most.

Wed. 27/8 The names of the officers in the garrison: Krupskoi (Антон Иванович) [Anton Ivanovich], major in the infantry; Koribin (Иван Василвич) [Ivan Vasilivich], second lieutenant; Kalmakoff (Прокофей Микайлович) [Prokofei Mihailovich], artillery lieutenant; Volkoff (Прокофей Федорович)

[Prokofei Fedorovich], chief customs guard; Vuichotzoff, prikaschtschik of the American Company.

In the morning, we put the ship on her right side in order to repair the copper there, that is, on her left side. Despite all of our efforts we could not get the ship as deep in the water as on the left side, proof that the sides are not of the same construction. The ship at sea also lists more to the left than to the right side. Today, the inclination was 14 to 15° and yesterday only 13. Yesterday, more than six copper plates were above water and today not even a full six copper plates.

Fish and again and again fish. We are supposed to get several head of cattle. They will undoubtedly be served at Resanoff's table. The few gulls we have shot ourselves are the only meat dishes we have had up to now.

Langsdorff has undoubtedly come to believe that he is an aulic councilor, since Krusenstern titled him thus today. I met Resanoff for the first time today. It is hard to meet him, since he knows quite well whom he should avoid and is also very careful about it.

Thurs. 28/9 Most of my ship's comrades went to Paratunka. Krusenstern, Romberg, and I stayed onboard. The gentlemen returned in the evening. They had rowed into the River Paratunka with high water. The water flowed out, and our shallop remained on the sand. Now good advice was expensive. Several bears appeared on the shore, and the desire to kill them drove everyone out of the boat into the water. Boots were pulled off, and then all of them waded on land with their guns, oars, and boat hooks in order to hunt the bears. Only Tilesius and an oarsman stayed in the shallop.

Our officers and sailors made a lot of noise on land, shot, chased, and drove the bears that go in herds there. During this time the water flowed out completely, and the shallop was on dry land. To Tilesius' horror, a couple of bears must have taken the shallop for a stranded whale and came slowly waddling up. Our aulic councilor was beside himself; he had no oar, no stick with which he could have defended himself; and the bears came closer and closer until they were scared off by his screams and the return of our gentlemen. Tilesius had a fever when he came on board.

All contracts are left unfulfilled and arbitrarily ignored, new ones drawn up arbitrarily, instructions cast aside and invalidated that the emperor has approved, acquisition of advantages that others have obtained through effort and work, condemning everything that can be of help for our expedition simply because he hopes thereby to do damage, using and inventing every possible trick, lie, and deceit to take fame away from a correct and deserving man and to stamp him a bad fellow, stooping low and acting common in order to cause discord, swearing revenge on anyone who does not want to have anything to do with the bad business: this is a sketch of a man who seemed to have been born to bring us bad luck. Other people have joined this man, who trump their boss in their actions and carrying them out, hatching greed, revenge, envy, and fraud and an inclination to do damage to others. Should these men triumph? The whole world will and must justify us. Let these men ignore us in the belief we are only cartmen. It takes a lot of gall to be that way, but it takes even more to bear everything calmly and with composure. Our only wish is justification.

Aside from his peculiarities, Espenberg is an upright man and in the main a knowledgeable doctor. Today, Resanoff sent for him and asked him in Russian, even though he knew that Espenberg speaks no Russian, why he does not visit him. Espenberg answered him in French. After a lot of childish and ridiculous questions, Resanoff ordered him to hand over to Langsdorff as much medicine as he would need, because he was curing a woman here on land.

Krusenstern has hurried with the unloading and reloading in order not to pass up a timely departure for Japan. Since last Sunday, we are subject to Resanoff's demands and orders for our work. We are loading only ballast, and, to get it on the keel, we continually have to roll the flour barrels back and forth and live with the fear of shaking them apart. So many obstacles prevent work from progressing.

When our gentlemen returned late in the evening from Paratunka, they were very satisfied with their hunt, had shot at a lot of bears, but not killed any.

Fri. 29/10 Finally, Koscheleff (Павел Иванович) [Pavel Ivanovich] arrived half an hour ago. Krusenstern sent someone to Major Krupskoi to ask when and where he could pay his respects. And at eleven thirty we all went with Krusenstern on land. Krusenstern introduced us to General Koscheleff. He recognized me at once and asked where Ungern[6] was now and how he was. Resanoff must have probably quickly told him of all the disputes and plans because Koscheleff was more thoughtful than he tends to be. We only spent a little time with him and took leave. At first, we had gone to the quarters where Resanoff is staying. Since Koscheleff had stopped at Kalmakoff's, he sent word to us through his adjutant that we should go there. Not long afterwards, he followed us. A guard of 36 men has arrived with him and several soldiers and people with 20 packhorses, the first horses I have seen here.

Sat. 30/11 Last evening, Golovatscheff was coming out of the bathhouse and met Koscheleff and Resanoff, who were talking. (Anyone else would have sought to avoid meeting them.) Resanoff turned immediately to Golovatscheff, as if he wanted to call him as witness and said very loudly, "Isn't it true? That I was held a prisoner on the ship for seven months."

"That is hard," answered Koscheleff and—and Golovatscheff remained silent and took his leave.

Early this morning Krusenstern sent me to Koscheleff (where I found Resanoff in full ornata and the general in a housecoat) in order to ask him, since he is to visit us today, when we should send our shallop for him, etc.

At eleven o'clock, Golovatscheff on his own went to the general's and at eleven thirty both feather hats arrived on board. Koscheleff went around the ship with Krusenstern and Resanoff (as companion). They had breakfast with us and went their ways again, after we had given three cheers along the shrouds. Golovatscheff did not miss the opportunity of accompanying the group back on land. We were surprised to see him returning with the shallop. He only wanted to go to Krusenstern and tell him his bad luck that he would have to dine with Resanoff at noon—that false fellow likes doing such things.

In the afternoon, Krusenstern finally went ashore to get a definitive answer and his final decision. Koscheleff's presence gave him hope. When Krusenstern entered the room, Resanoff met him extremely (affected) politely. Krusenstern thereupon said, "Since His Excellency had put everything off until Павел Иванович [Pavel Ivanovich] (Koscheleff's) arrival, I now hope that you will be able to make a decision in our case."

Resanoff answered, using several turns of phrase (which one can call politenesses), "I am going to winter here." Then Krusenstern asked if the embassy's presents and things should be unloaded. In answer to his questions, Resanoff (suddenly) began to curse Krusenstern in the coarsest way and forced him through his insults to leave the room. His expressions were: "Don't butt into another's affairs! You brigand, mutineer, etc."

After Koscheleff had gone home, Krusenstern went to him and explained the whole affair and the strife with Resanoff. Krusenstern will without a doubt have to travel overland. I'm going along.

Horner is right when he says, "Today is a nice day because everything is being talked about."

Sun. 31/12 Yesterday, Koscheleff told Krusenstern as he was leaving Resanoff's room: "After today's occurrence you cannot continue in command any longer," and early today at Koscheleff's demand, Krusenstern went ashore at nine o'clock. Everything is quiet on the *Nadezhda*. All the work is finished and we impatiently await the result of these vexations.

The voyage is over because Krusenstern is giving up the command and the majority of the officers are going to follow him overland to Petersburg. Koscheleff sees the matter from the correct point of view: The emperor's will, as concerns the voyage, has to be put above all else. "В колотку!" [ruffian!] called Resanoff after our captain yesterday. "I'm going to have gallows built here, and one of the two of us has to hang from them." Resanoff said to Espenberg, "There are good paths ahead for you. You are going into the mines for the rest of your life and never getting out of Kamtschatka again." He said of Tolstoi and turned him over to Koscheleff: "That one has to cool down his courage in the mines and finish his life there." His judgement of Ratmanoff is still to come, and he won't forget me either.

In the afternoon, Krusenstern was with Resanoff and Koscheleff again. Resanoff himself intends to return overland so that he can defame us and, if possible, make all of us unhappy.

Mr. von Krusenstern's only wish is to be interrogated in St. Petersburg and not here. The emperor will and cannot deny him this just request. He has to be judged in Petersburg and nowhere else. It is heartbreaking to see Krusenstern crying, and indeed today he was moved to tears by thoughts of his wife and child.

At noon, Димитрии Иванович [Dmitrii Ivanovich], the full brother of General Koscheleff, and five other officers dined with us. We are too filled with care to prevent coldness and compassion from determining the tone. Everything was also very quiet.

August

Mon. 1/13 Resanoff would like to begin something with Tilesius and where possible oppress him, but since Tilesius is such a pedant in everything and conducts himself according to his contract with Resanoff, Resanoff cannot begin anything with him. Tilesius however has the right to complain about Resanoff in a lot of matters. Yesterday, Resanoff said to Tilesius, "The expedition is ended, and you are free." Tilesius came on board and asked Krusenstern what he should do.

Krusenstern answered, "I'm dishonored and can and may not advise you." Tilesius went back on land and asked Koscheleff for protection, since he, as a foreigner, did not know what his position was. Without a doubt, Tilesius will be the first one to return overland to Petersburg. Koscheleff sent him to Resanoff, and he repeated his request.

Resanoff, who could not contain his rancor, gave him a lot of coarse words and finally *une dupe comme vous* [a dupe like you].

Tilesius replied very decorously and calmly: "An imperial aulic councilor and professor of natural history cannot be a dupe!"

Koscheleff, who had lost all patience, gave Tilesius his hand and said: "My word of honor, I will protect you." Our Mr. Aulic Councilor conducted himself quite well to our joy.

Krusenstern went to Resanoff today with a report in which he demanded that Resanoff take over the command. Koscheleff was present. After Resanoff had read through the report, he said, "I'm going to travel to Petersburg, and you are remaining as captain of the ship." Krusenstern requested of Koscheleff, after Resanoff had said a lot of things to him, to act according to the laws and protect him according to the laws. Then Koscheleff said to Resanoff in a firm voice, "You have to take over command." Resanoff then blabbed away in his impetuosity, could not save himself any more from his own contradictions, did not dare lie and slander. (He tried to give his swear words a different turn. The captain and Koscheleff's presence, however, did not allow him to do that.) He finally admitted that it was his duty to take over Krusenstern's command.

Resanoff accused Tilesius, with whom he has always had run-ins, of starting the strife with me and was long-winded about it. He did not suspect that I had long ago made peace with Tilesius.

We are standing here like a slender tree; bad men can bend it but not break it; the tree is too strong for that. And let's hope that we can steadfastly fend off all attacks. Alas, Krusenstern is leaving us, is giving up the command. God be with him! We have justice with him. Our fate is hard, having to winter here amidst uncertainty. What will happen to us, not to be able to imagine how everything will end? Giving up the command! To whom? No one wants it. No one likes it. Nevertheless, neither the ship nor the crew can remain without officers.

Resanoff intends to go overland to Petersburg! May he return unsuccessfully. If he also has the power to destroy contracts, to annul instructions, he may again determine his own instructions. I am still hopeful that everything will turn out differently.

Today, Resanoff accused Espenberg, "You should have looked after your sick men better and had less speculative trade in your head, and your advice, which you were always ready to give, you would have better kept to yourself." Resanoff also accused us of speculative trade and threatened to forbid us from doing it. Our trade has consisted, up to now, solely in buying small things from the savages. Our trying to buy pelts here and paying our washer woman, instead of 25 rubles for the wash, a couple of stof brandy are indeed not criminal actions, but we are supposed to be subject to military justice on account of this trade.

Tues. 2/14 Resanoff is now trying to get Koscheleff involved in this dirty business. In answer Koscheleff said, "I am not your judge but a witness to everything I have heard."

Espenberg has justified himself with Koscheleff today and disproved all of Resanoff's accusations too, so that Koscheleff has obtained some insight in the affair and has to be distrustful of Resanoff.

Count Tolstoi has admitted his wrongs to Resanoff in writing, formally listed all of his offenses, and, in so doing, has spoken his own judgment.

Resanoff is once again supposed to be playing with the idea of continuing the voyage to Japan. May Krusenstern do that? Can the law force him to?

Resanoff, among other things, has said, in the presence of Golovatscheff and Kamentschikoff, "Except for these two officers, all of the others are rebels"—a nice recommendation for the two.

At noon, General Koscheleff and his brother, the Major, a captain, an auditor, and two artillery officers dined with us on shipboard. (Kamentschikoff had gone on land to give Resanoff his report as pickthank.) Unpleasantness was not even mentioned. Koscheleff was in a very good mood, and one funny remark was followed by the next. Koscheleff stayed with us until the evening meal and let us know, again in a very fine way, his thoughts about our strife. Today, Ratmanoff renewed his old acquaintance with Koscheleff, whom he had met in Sevastopol eleven years earlier.

Wed. 3/15 Early in the morning, Krusenstern went to General Koscheleff and requested he be so kind as to induce the ambassador to make some kind of decision to determine our fate and to remove us from the unpleasant uncertainty, that is, either to take away our captain's command or to give him the order to complete his remaining instructions and to continue the voyage, to determine whether we winter here or not and whether unloading should be undertaken, (Resanoff had forbidden the unloading because he had found out that the flour barrels in the hold got in the way), and whether the gifts for the Emperor of Japan should be left on shipboard or whether Resanoff wants them unloaded, too.

Perhaps Resanoff will decide, as his advisers are saying, to make the voyage to Japan with a new, two-masted ship commanded by *Midshipman* [sic] Steinheil[7] and will keep Golovatscheff and Kamentschikoff for that purpose. The latter has done that service and is a common fellow.

Resanoff has really lowered the prices for the goods and wares we brought along. In the beginning, he wanted to offer the goods in general for 3 to 4 rubles less than they cost in Ochotsk. The following are the prices that Resanoff now has almost set. The American Company will have a difficult time being happy about having made Resanoff representative with the power of attorney.

Koscheleff's description of the prikaschtschiks does not sound good and does not speak well of the trade. These prikaschtschiks are said to be human dregs.

A comparison of the prices in Peter-Paul's Harbor in Kamtschatka before our arrival that the American Company had set and Resanoff's lower prices:

Earlier Price	Ruble	Copeck	Present Price	Ruble	Kopeck
Fruit brandy with water 1 stof	20	–	Spirits 1 stof	6	–
Fruit brandy with water 1 stof	–	–	French brandy double stof	8	–
Sugar 1 pud	140	–	Refined sugar 1 pud	48	–
Tobacco 1 pfund	2	50	Tobacco 1 pfund	–	75
Thread/twine 1 pfund	2	50	Thread/twine 1 pfund	1	–
Soap 1 pfund	2	50	Soap	1	50
Russian canvas 1 piece	14	–	Russian canvas 1 piece	7	–
Half canvas 1 arshine	4	–	English canvas 1 arshine	2	–
Half canvas	–	–	Same width	2	25
East Indian cloth	3	50	East Indian cloth	2	25
Canvas 1 arshine	–	65	Canvas 1 arshine		30
Coarse fustian 1 arshine	1	50	Fustian 1 arshine	1	15
Distel 1 arshine	2	50	Distel 1 arshine	1	80
Plush 1 arshine	4	–	Smooth plush 1 arshine	2	25
Plush 1 arshine	–	–	Striped plush 1 arshine	2	50
Demicotton 1 arshine	3	50	Demicotton 1 arshine	1	20
Teacups 1 dozen	40	–	Teacups 1 dozen	30	–

During Somoff's time (when he was the head commander): Money: 1 pud flour from 20 to 40 rubles, 1 stof brandy 30–50 rubles, 1 pfund sugar 5–12 rubles, 1 pfund tea 10–18, 1 pfund led 4 rubles, 1 pfund gunpowder 6 rubles, iron 1 pud 15 rubles, tobacco 1 leaf 1 ruble, soap 1 pfund 5 rubles, twine/thread 1 kopeck an arshine, sewing needles 4 kopecks apiece, etc.

Other events: Resanoff wants to make peace, and Koscheleff is to be the arbitrator. When Koscheleff told Krusenstern this, he answered, "I can and may not do anything only for me and make decisions only for myself."

The conditions we can demand are: 1. That Resanoff in a letter to the emperor state that he is at fault and report our having made peace with one another; 2. That Resanoff name the tattletales; 3. That since he has threatened us with Japan, he clarify our relationship with him as ambassador before our departure; 4. Since Resanoff maintains that the duty of the captain is only to look after the sails, we demand a clarification of his instructions. In addition, he has to show us all papers that he might have in petto [be contemplating].

Krusenstern has to agree, as we also have to, that all private insults, all arguments have to be put aside in favor of the emperor's orders and the purpose of the expedition. Time, place, and conditions leave us no choice. Peace has not yet been concluded. Without Koscheleff's uprightness and love of justice, the matter would not have taken such a sudden turn. We are greatly indebted to General Koscheleff, for we could not see clearly what would come of this chaos.

Today in Koscheleff's presence Resanoff asked Espenberg for forgiveness and straightforwardly admitted to having done that honorable man an injustice. The only one who is despised, rejected, and damned by all is Count Tolstoi. He is staying behind.

Today, Espenberg told me that at sea when, after a very long time, a bonito had finally been caught, Tolstoi bought it secretly, had it cooked for himself, and invited Horner and Espenberg to breakfast. He put gin (Geneva) in front of them for schnapps, a drink which none of us had any more. "Alexander (Resanoff's servant) had stolen it from Resanoff," was the answer and "I bought it from him." (That was at a time when Tolstoi had become totally at odds with Resanoff.)

Koscheleff is thinking about sending his brother in Count Tolstoi's stead. It is Koscheleff's wish, and there is nothing to be said against it. We have experienced well that lazy bones aren't worth anything on shipboard. Young Koscheleff (Димитрии Иванович) [Dmitrii Ivanovich] is an educated, polite man and will no doubt get along well on shipboard. In any case, we can accept the exchange.

Kamentschikoff has gone to the dogs, and if Resanoff says he is extra, we will try to leave the old cabbage head behind. It is being rumored that Schemelin is not supposed to go along. We can congratulate ourselves on being rid of those three.

Thurs. 4/16 Early in the morning, Krusenstern went to Koscheleff to give him the conditions for making peace that we are of a mind to demand and to hear his opinion and advice about the matter.

Golovatscheff is and continues to be a flatterer who has earned our disdain, even though he is a useful officer.

Our story has a beautiful theme: The victory of justice over vice.

At eleven o'clock, Krusenstern returned and brought us the news that peace has been concluded and requested of us all to go to Resanoff and put an end to all disagreements.[8]

We went to Resanoff's and found that only Fosse and young Koscheleff had arrived before us, and not long afterwards Resanoff appeared with General Koscheleff. Upon entering, Resanoff turned to Golovatscheff and went up to him and said and requested, "We should forget and forgive everything," since he had already made peace with our captain. We all remained silent because Resanoff had spoken with Golovatscheff. Not long afterwards, Resanoff turned to Ratmanoff, found fault with his behavior, and said, "It is not enough that you wanted to lock me up in my cabin; you also said, 'I don't consider him worth two kopecks.'"

Koscheleff did not permit any further accusations by saying, "If everything is supposed to be forgiven and forgotten, then all accusations have to stop."

Then Resanoff turned to Romberg and said, "You always answered politeness with coarseness." For me he had apologies. He told Bellingshausen, "You were wrong not to acknowledge me as your head." He only said to Golovatscheff, "Only the two of us have always worked harmoniously together."

Then Golovatscheff stepped forward and said with tears in his eyes, "Your Excellency has to justify me to a comrade. I have suffered because I have been treated in such a friendly manner by you. Have I ever said or done anything that could have been construed as a disadvantage to either party, or have I been a bearer of tales?"

"No," said Resanoff very indifferently. ("Yes!" said everyone of us to ourselves.) Then Schemelin came into the room and got a true reprimand and was told that he should never again disobey Krusenstern or otherwise be remiss in his behavior. Golovatscheff tried a couple of times to say something. Resanoff made a joke of it each time, and that is how it remained. Then breakfast was carried in, and, after drinking schnapps, we separated like friends. General Koscheleff recommended his brother to us, who will be making the voyage with us to Japan. We turned down Resanoff's invitation to dine with him. At lunch, Krusenstern, however, went back on land to fulfill conditions that had been set. On the spot, we began to work again, that is, to unload flour, to fill up water, to bake hardtack, to load provisions, to check riggings, to repair our boats, and everything with hands and feet got into motion.

I have just returned from a walk where I met Resanoff conversing with our three doctors. They did not seem to be in agreement. Resanoff still does not want to fulfill the conditions of Tilesius' contract, and only under that condition is Tilesius going to sail to Japan. Resanoff has spoiled things with so many and insulted so many that it is going to take time until everyone has once again made peace with him. Resanoff, Koscheleff with his brother and the Soldier Captain Fedoroff (Павел Иванович) [Ivan Ivanovich], who is also going to make the voyage to Japan, came to us and also stayed on shipboard for the evening meal.

There was a lot of drinking during the evening meal, even more after our guests had left. Everyone drank to his health and that of his comrades. At midnight, we were all finally somewhat befogged, were happy that we soon again will go forwards with cheerfulness and in a good mood.

Golovatscheff alone sat there introspective and full of problems. Finally, Ratmanoff said to him, "Why the self-reflection?" Golovatscheff stood up very moved and began to apologize to Ratmanoff, and after a lot of talking, apologies, assurances, etc., they made peace with each other. Then, Golovatscheff went from one to the next, came to me and Bellingshausen, Horner, etc., and found we are sympathetic, friendly people, who made his difficult position easier and gladly made peace with him. When however he came to Romberg, who had already looked too deeply into his glass, there was no talk of reconciliation. Golovatscheff had to listen to the bitterest accusations; events long ago forgotten were brought up by Romberg, and Golovatscheff refuted everything and apologized as best he could with the greatest calmness and humility. We entered the conversation, tried to reconcile them, in vain. It stopped just short of our arguing with each other. Bellingshausen and Horner got in an argument. I wanted to stop the argument and—Look here! It did not take much, and the three of us were in each other's hair. Congeniality won: We began to laugh at our own foolishness and strife ended, but not between Romberg and Golovatscheff, until Romberg ended with, "No! No! I cannot get along with you. Stop the noise!" (These are not his actual words, rather an indefinite, unkind putting off, that he should be left in peace, etc., which was so painful for Golovatscheff.) Golovatscheff, in tears, contrite and completely unhappy, went into his cabin after he had silently shaken hands with each one of the others of us, as if he wanted to say, "I thank you for your feeling hearts." It then became suddenly quiet in the company cabin, and everyone went to bed.

- 8 -

The Voyage to Japan

Fri. 5/17 (Димитрии Иванович) [Dimitrii Ivanovich] Koscheleff has taken it upon himself to supply us with everything available in Kamtschatka, and Captain Fedoroff is forming a bodyguard for Resanoff. Count Tolstoi is staying behind. Schemelin is questionable. The painter Kurlandzoff claims to he is suffering from [gall] stones and for better or worse has to stay behind, and, for humanitarian reasons and as a favor to him, Brinkin is also staying behind—все к лучему! [All for the better][1]

In order to gain room in the cabin and the kitchen, we have decided to have separate tables again. The dividing wall in Krusenstern's cabin has been ripped out, and from the two cabins we have one again. All are at work—whoever dares to stir the old cabbage gets his eye punched out is our motto. Only Golovatscheff and Romberg don't want to take our motto to heart.

Today, Kamentschikoff received a hard reprimand from Krusenstern. Our captain has also suggested to Resanoff that he should be left behind. That incorrigible man has to suffer some kind of punishment.

Up to now, we haven't seen hide or hair of Friderici, and Langsdorff is ashamed of himself for himself.

We have taken back all of our petitions and letters and destroyed them; even I got mine back, had nevertheless a great desire to dispatch it with a note attached.

General Koscheleff has even sent out orders to Upper and Lower Kamtschatka, 600 versts from here to provide us with all kinds of possible goods.

In the evening we, and even the sailors, were invited to a vetscherinok [evening gathering]. And at least one of us had to stay on the ship, and I volunteered; and I was glad to do it because all of the events had made me pensive.

Sat. 6/18 Our entire crew returned at two o'clock in the night satisfied with their diversion. Kamtschadal dances graced the ball; a small fireworks show lit up the night, and the happy singing of our sailors broke up the stillness of the night.

Rainy, cold Kamtschatka weather.

Koscheleff, Resanoff, and our two new comrades had tea with us, also stayed on shipboard until the evening meal. We are now living in such great harmony that no one would suspect that neck-breaking quarrels have occurred among us.

Resanoff has given his entire suite embroidered coats to grace his entrance into Japan with this worn-out tawdriness. We talk about the voyage to Nangasaki [Nagasaki] as *partie du plaiser* [a pleasure trip].

The warm or rather hot springs not too far from the village of Matka have given Koscheleff the idea of building a bathhouse there, which in time could become a hospital and a beneficial establishment for the poor. All of us got together about 4,000 rubles for the construction of this establishment. Koscheleff plans to report his intentions to the emperor and petition the dowager empress for patronage. Until approval, these hot springs are called Alexandrovskie Kluchi.

Golovatscheff is busy receiving the necessary goods from the prikaschtschik, that is, brandy, sugar, sailcloth, riggings, etc.

It looks like we only quarreled with each other so that we find our peace even more pleasant. Each one of us treats the other politely, so as to give the appearance that everything has been forgiven and forgotten.

Sun. 7/19 Tilesius was at Koscheleff's today and read a statement to him, in which he describes the inappropriate authority which Resanoff exercises over him, since it is not possible for a man of science to be forced to fulfill his duties and still to be useful to science.

Koscheleff does not understand German. Thus, Tilesius had to use French, and, since he does not speak it very well, it did not work very well and took a lot of time, but they laughed enough during the whole process. The best part of it was that Koscheleff understood Tilesius and promised to carry out his demand with Resanoff.

We absolutely need Tilesius because of his ability to sketch quickly and well. Resanoff is putting the screws on poor Tilesius, so that he can claim all of his sketches at the end of the voyage.

The two Kotzebues are to make the voyage to Jedo as letter carriers, that is, of course, the letter to the Emperor of Japan, in the procession.

Resanoff granted a soldier and a denschik [orderly], a medallion for their skills at farming.

Filled with worry, we are loading our provisions. They will barely suffice until our return from Japan. Poor as church mice and hungry as wolves is undoubtedly the way we are going to arrive in China.

We had divided and separated both tables with difficulty and exactness. Now that we have once again united, we come together without calculation—a useless effort and Fosse's tested honesty lets us expect that we will once again come out on the short end. What's to be done about that?

I truly do not know how things stand with Kamentschikoff. One thing is certain, out of desperation, he is doing nothing and is drunk all of the time.

Golovatscheff is friendly in a forced way. A man cannot hide his character on a ship and in his heart be a cutthroat. The restraint even seems to embarrass him.

I like Captain Fedoroff better than young Koscheleff. They brought their musicians along for tea today. We had a lot to do, and you are not always in the mood to listen to fiddling; and the entertainment didn't seem to want to work right either, so that our guests soon left again.

Mon. 8/20 Rain again. The nice weather was spent in idleness. Resanoff has not yet finished his letter to the emperor. He has, however, assured Krusenstern that he will soon give it to him to read.

Resanoff told us today that he had asked Tolstoi (when he settled with him and agreed that he would go overland to Petersburg) what had caused the strife with Ratmanoff. "I wanted," said Tolstoi, "to explain to Ratmanoff how wrong he was acting toward Your Plenipotentiary, when you were reading (orally) your instructions on Nukahiva. The cause of the strife was my good intention of warning Ratmanoff to be careful in word and deed."

In Petersburg, at Tischtshoff's home, Tolstoi was known as a man who pretended to be disciplined. Tolstoi, in order to paint himself white, has used as a pretext life on the *Nadezhda,* which he claims has ruined his good manners, etc. That's what Resanoff is telling everyone.

Tues. 9/21 Even though we have little time, we are going to have to repaint the *Nadezhda,* since there is no trace of any paint on her any more.

We have been touched by the advantage of our famous strife that lasted an entire year, that now everyone knows what he should not do, and that we have been raked over the coals with each other and now know each other. And, nevertheless, each one of us has the secret wish that we were indeed already home!

The climate here is unfriendly, continual fog, rain and overcast. Our masts are swelling a little.

Today, Resanoff, Koscheleff, and their officers dined with us. Tomorrow, General Koscheleff has been invited to lunch. One festivity follows the other. Today, for the first time in seven months, we ate beef, that is, fresh. We dug in inhumanely. One hundred men could have been fed with what 25 of us ate.

I have an involuntary inclination to loneliness. I would like it if my watch were from twelve noon to eight o'clock in the evening so that, duty-bound, I could wander around the deck alone.

Today, Krusenstern ordered Kamentschikoff not to leave the ship, a much too mild punishment.

Koscheleff is always in a good mood. Resanoff is his old self, that is, I am polite to him, and I cannot demand any more of myself.

Thurs. 11/23 Even though Resanoff is very generous with the property of the American Company, its profit is nevertheless being calculated at 150%.

Our boat brought three barrels of salt salmon we caught ourselves.

At noon, we ate at Koscheleff's in a tent. There is an instinctive coldness among us. Krusenstern is the most unabashed. In the evening at a dance, I could hardly believe my eyes: Krusenstern dancing a polonaise with Resanoff. The soldier Monakoff played the main part, that of a court fool. Stupidity and coarse jokes can amuse you for a while, but having a drunken peasant clod (that's what Monakoff was) dancing in front of you the whole evening and a drunkard I find an impossible situation. (Monakoff's very witty in his own way because he, in his stupidity, is better than many another when sober.) Earlier, a couple of sleds with dogs hooked to them were demonstrated, etc.

Fri. 12/24 We returned to the ship for our evening meal. Rain, continual rain. Koscheleff came unexpectedly on board at 11 o'clock, and in a short while Krusenstern sent for all of us. Resanoff had come to read Krusenstern and us officers the letter he had written the emperor. The report was several pages long. The following is approximately its contents.

1. The route of our voyage from St. Catharina until Kamtschatka.
2. The number of people who will be staying behind and will go overland to Petersburg and the reasons for it. (Here Tolstoi is strongly taken to task.)
3. A treatise about Kamtschatka. A detailed description of the lack of people, especially women, and salt, the difference in prices for products before his arrival and those set by him (Resanoff), about the founding of a bath at the hot springs and the establishment of a hospital there.
4. Apologies and petitions to forgive past happenings, where he petitions our emperor to have forbearance with him, that passion for glory had led him to foolishness and Count Tolstoi was the main reason for the strife, etc. The whole thing was very well written.

At the end of the letter, Fosse was recommended and Krusenstern praised.

After having read the letter to the emperor, Resanoff's satisfaction with himself shined out of eyes with a volubility of his own.

Resanoff asked us if we had any criticism of the letter and asked us to state our opinion freely. We all were silent, and our silence was interrupted by the appearance of schnapps and breakfast.

No one really had anything against the letter. Resanoff should nevertheless have handed the letter over to us for mailing. Krusenstern could demand that. From us it would have been official, but Resanoff put his letter away again and went on land in order to seal it (as he claimed?) together with his other dispatches. Krusenstern excused him by saying that Resanoff's friendliness, his flattering personality, sealed through his frequent kisses, were proof of respect and friendship that give his appearance the varnish of sincerity. Does Resanoff understand and know how to be sincere? Doesn't he have new tricks and traps lurking in the background?

For our own peace of mind—it is to Resanoff's own advantage to get along with Krusenstern. We have too many witnesses, and a repeated breakdown of the good intentions would only have to be to Resanoff's own disadvantage.

Sat. 13/25 We used the good weather today to put a new coat of oil paint on the *Nadezhda*. We also still have a lot of work to do on the rigging. I went for a walk before our meal in the tidal lake not far from Peter-Paul's Harbor. I met General Koscheleff there, who said he would be visiting us at noon. Fedoroff and his brother came with him. The latter two looked at their cabins. Fedoroff got the painter's cabin where Kurlandzoff had broken everything breakable and hacked up his former cabin. A base man, Kurlandzoff, as ill as he is, couldn't suppress his resentment and let himself be paid for trifles that did not belong to him.

Even though Resanoff had set prices, the prikaschtschik Viuhodzoff does not shy away from raising Resanoff's prices. (The prices were lowered for the advantage of these people.) He was recently caught at knavery. Koscheleff complained about it to Resanoff and said, "If he does not shy away from cheating while we are here, what will happen when you have sailed off?" The punishment that rogue got was a mild reprimand from Resanoff.

Krusenstern had sent, with Resanoff's permission, a net and a barrel of salt to Koscheleff. Today, that hypocritical rogue, that Vuihodzoff, went to Resanoff and demanded the two things be returned. Koscheleff was present, could not stop himself, pointed to his cane, and said, "This man needs to be given a natural correction." Resanoff let it go again with a reprimand. (That is how much Resanoff protects his own kind.)

Today, Tilesius had another long explication with Resanoff and is in the same place he was; for, instead of a specific answer, Resanoff brought him a lot of stuffed birds the hunter had shot and collected, and all of them have not yet been named, inspected, and described, because no one had seen them since our departure from Brazil. The hunter had stuffed them all and under the express command not to show them to Tilesius under any conditions—strange behavior.

Golovatscheff found a gaff in the main topsail broken this evening. Now comes the question: whether it happened during Romberg's or Golovatscheff's watch? Because Romberg raised the topmast and the topmast shrouds and Golovatscheff the lower shrouds, he therefore naturally has to blame and paint Romberg black. Stuff enough for strife between two men who normally cannot get along.

Sun. 14/26 All of the gentlemen belonging to the ambassador's suite are as happy as children about the uniforms they invented for themselves, in which they want to shine in Japan.

The *Nadezhda* looks quite good in her new coat of paint. Our work is quickly going forward and we hope to be finished in five days.

Romberg is continuing his correspondence with Karamsin. He has sent him a page-long description of our voyage. It is interesting that Karamsin does not know any of us personally. Therefore, this letter will come as an unexpected surprise for him.

Every nation since our departure from Kronstadt has marked itself through favorite songs and expressions. From Kronstadt anglaises and polonaises were the measure; in Copenhagen, they were forgotten. They were replaced by the shouts of Danish fish and fruit women and our own anecdotes, especially Erasmus Spang's stories, and from Falmouth English words and songs were in style. From Tenerife, Madame Armstrong and Amalie and Delphine Kuwe entertained us adequately. From Brazil, we were totally Portuguese and that *Rrrrrrr* accompanied us until Nukahiva. From there we imitated the savages, played their music, hitting our hollow hands against the angles of our bent arms in accompaniment to the sailor's songs, etc. Now that is forgotten and the bachio sounds all over, even the dog call "Kach! Kach! Kach!" and "Huga! Huga!!" (right and left) will probably accompany us to Nangasaki.

Today, Koscheleff gave Ratmanoff, Romberg, and Golovatscheff, as a present, very cleanly worked outer coats (камлейки), for protection against the rain, very nicely made from the intestines of fish. I did not get one because Koscheleff did not have any more of them. The gentlemen here know from experience that no drop of water can get through a similar coat, even if one also is subjected to rain for days. There has to be a hole in it, which can easily happen, since the whole thing looks like a blister.

Mon. 15/27 Krusenstern is very fair with his crew but also indulgent with us officers. There have already been times when an order was given in the evening and not fulfilled by morning. One man tried to make good the other man's failing, and thus everything was all right again. Only Golovatscheff tried, in a similar situation, to make himself look better through another's error. Yesterday, Krusenstern ordered several crates that were standing in the way on the deck be put in the crew's quarters. Romberg had delegated the order to Golovatscheff in the presence of several of us. (Granted, earlier Romberg had forgotten to carry out several orders.) Krusenstern, who saw that the order had not been carried out, asked at tea whose fault it was that the order was not done. Romberg answered that he had told Golovatscheff to do it. And Golovatscheff then answered with a spiteful smile, "I did not hear anything about it," and, alluding to Romberg's correspondence with Karamsin, Golovatscheff said, "You always speak so pompously that you cannot be understood at all."

Romberg was silent, and Krusenstern went into the other cabin without saying a word. Such incidents make for bad blood and in all probability mean that Romberg and Golovatscheff will be unreconciled from now on.

Kamentschikoff has finally appeared again in the company cabin from which he should be banished.

Resanoff has a plan to make Peter-Paul's Harbor into the emporium of the American Company and has reported and conveyed his intentions to the emperor and the directors of the Company, of having it as a stopover between Kodiak and Ochotsk. Resanoff has canceled prikaschtschik Vuihodzoff's contract, according to which the scoundrel was supposed to have half of the profit on all goods as his wages. That contract had been made in Irkutsk. If trade with Japan comes about, then with time Kamtschatka will become quite a lively place.

For the first time since I have been on the *Nadezhda*, I hit a sailor. Быченков [Bischenkov] was so impertinent that I could not keep myself from giving him one across the mouth. It was my luck to hit that impertinent fellow on a growth he had on his cheek that broke open from the box on the ears and began to bleed. I am more than a little angry at my own hastiness, but, to prevent the matter turning into an incident, I told Krusenstern myself about the whole occurrence.

Today, we brought on the rostrum (supply of topmasts, yards, boards, poles, etc.), and tomorrow we are going to raise our sails.

Resanoff plans to return to Kamtschatka from Japan. From here we will take Resanoff to Kodiak, where he will stay, so that he can visit the American coast and then go back to Petersburg overland. From Kodiak he is sending us with the *Nadezhda* to China. I like the plan, since we finally can see the time when we are rid of Resanoff.

Tues. 16/28 Madsiura, one of our Japanese, whose money and clothes had been stolen, lived with his comrades here in Kamtschatka very quietly in the country without any further complaints about his loss. Resanoff, who wanted to replace a part of his loss, especially his clothing, sent for him. Madsiura, however, did not come. The next day Resanoff went past the house in which the Japanese are living and saw Madsiura standing in front of the door. He called him over, so that he could admonish him for his disobedience. The little Japanese acted as if he did not hear him. Resanoff therefore went up to him and asked him what was the cause of his strange behavior. Madsiura threw himself down in tears before him and said, "How can you expect me to do anything, after we have had so many benefits heaped upon us, that we are lying under the burden? The Russian emperor was our father, our everything. How could I think for a moment about the lost things, since all of the other benefits are so fresh in my memory?"

Not too long afterwards, Madsiura said, "We have another memento from your good emperor that no one knows about," and produced a portrait of Emperor Alexander, which the Japanese had bought for a total of 27 rubles in Petersburg. "This," he said, "is to remind us of our Father, our Protector, after we have been settled in our fatherland for years. And we will never forget our stay in Russia." That was the first nice gesture from our callous Japanese.

It is possible that I could decide to sail on a second voyage around the world.

The cooper and Tschitoff, who live near Paganaia Retschaka, and repair water casts, live a very loose life. A lot of scheremicha (wild garlic) grows there, whose job it is for the women to collect. For entertainment, they spend time with our people who do not let them suffer from boredom. That is why the work is also not getting done. We are going to have to put an end to their handiwork.

Wed. 17/29 Fosse came on board early this morning. I told him that Resanoff had assured us that he, Resanoff, wanted to stay in Kodiak. I therefore thought it better to avoid all further division of the provisions, to leave it as it was at present and said, "You should be so kind as to bring on shipboard a list of everything that belongs to you." With a cynical smile (as if he wanted to say, "What do you know?"), he answered that he knew nothing about Resanoff's wanting to stay in Kodiak and that he totally doubted the truth of the rumor, that it might also be an incomplete plan that Resanoff has made. That the gentlemen from Resanoff's suite do not want to give us a list of the provisions that they still have can be easily explained—they wasted, gave away all of the provisions when they appeared to have the certainty of going overland to Petersburg, and are now sending their remains, uninspected on board, so that they may again partake of our table, and with the next division they will once again request a full portion. We are almost finished with the work on board ship.

Espenberg has weakened nerves from the affair with Resanoff. Weeks on end, he has not done anything with the Kotzebues, and then suddenly it occurs to him to reprimand them and bawl them out, as if he did not want to have anything to do with them, etc. He is methodically trying to make the boys wayward.

Thurs. 18/30 Recently, at the exit to Peter-Paul Harbor, we had a buoy lying on the tip of a sandbank, which was driven off by the wind and the current. No wonder that in the morning, when we had everything finished, weighed anchor, and sailed out of the harbor, we hit 2½ faden of water unexpectedly. Luckily for us, we had observed everything with great care, so that the surprise did not have dire consequences for us; and at six in the evening we dropped anchor in Avatscha Bay opposite Rakovaia Bay.

The Japanese Kiseleff, who voluntarily wanted to stay behind, now once again absolutely wants to go to Japan. We'll see if he can soften up Resanoff.

The subchirurius here, the only one in all of Kamtschatka, is a fine fellow. During our stay, drunkenness and disorderly behavior have landed him in the guardhouse six times. He knowingly gulled our Sydham and Tilesius into letting him wash their black laundry. Unfortunately for both of them, they never got a piece back, because he had sold it and had already drunk it all up. Dmitrii Ivanitsch Koscheleff was kind enough to rescue what could still be saved.

Fri. 19/31 Early in the morning, we brought the powder on board, and we hope that the whole gang will come on board today or tomorrow. We have to pay 50 rubles for the milk that we drank during our stay. We got four bouteillen today.

Our table was divided. From the gentlemen who are still on land, three are staying and keeping their part of the provisions, and, of the two who are replacing them on board, nothing can be expected. Over and above that, Fosse has already seen to it that not much will be brought back from land; and we will have to provide for the gentlemen from our remaining provisions. Resanoff indeed said, "I am taking them along at my expense." That, however, was a gesture of generosity that is soon forgotten.

Brinkin and Kurlandzoff are beside themselves, and both complain about Resanoff's injustice and Fosse's lack of honesty. As long as Resanoff could use them, he mollycoddled their dishonesty. Now that they are going back overland and he no longer needs them, he does not bother with them any longer.

In the afternoon, I rowed around the bay with Ratmanoff looking for shallows. We shot several puffins and gulls, rowed and sailed so far over to Tareinoia Bay, so that we reached the ship again at only 7:30 in the evening. We did not find anyone on board because they had all gone on land at Koscheleff's invitation to a vetscherinok. Our comrades returned on board only at one o'clock in the night.

Sat. 20/1 The gentlemen mildly enjoyed themselves yesterday. They especially applauded Jean Cabri's dance of the savages on Nukahiva.

At noon, we are expecting Koscheleff, Resanoff, and their entire suite on board. We will receive them with all the ceremonies.

At one o'clock, the gentlemen arrived. We placed our people along the yards and the grenadiers on the quarterdeck in order to give His Excellency a full roll [of the drums], and, when Resanoff went back ashore, he got a full salute.

Koscheleff, who is always joking, laughed so much over all of the events and ceremonies today that Resanoff said very sensitively, "You are turning me into a complete child." At noon, Koscheleff and all of the officers here dined with us. In truth, the officers are very languid. At sunset, they took their leave after we had also given General Koscheleff a salute.

Resanoff has paid Count Tolstoi 1,500 rubles table money and his full pay in advance. He does not do anything for Brinkin and Kurlandzoff, probably because apparently Kurlandzoff is not ill at all, and it is claimed that he only acts ill to get away from Resanoff. Stupid idea.

Sun. 21/2 The Japanese Kiseleff is staying behind. Resanoff told me that today and added, alluding to our past strife, "Pangloss[2] is right when he says, 'и все чудое к лучему' [good can also result from bad]."

In the morning, Krusenstern went on land with our letters. Never before has a Kamtschadal estafet [messenger] been so loaded down as ours was. Krusenstern returned at noon, bringing the news that mail had arrived. No letters.

We congratulated Ratmanoff after he had received the prikas for his appointment to captain lieutenant. He was promoted for age after having served as a lieutenant for fifteen years.

Kiseleff is a thief. He stole 12 shirts from the Kotzebues, which Madsiura took away from him again when he found out about it.

Mon. 22/3 We are not waiting for a favorable wind. Even our longboat has been raised. In the morning, Resanoff with his suite moved completely on board. Koscheleff accompanied him. Brinkin also came along to say good-bye to us. His eyes shone with satisfaction that his plan to stay behind was successful. Kurlandzoff claims to be sick now, cannot come to say good-bye for that reason.

Tilesius took his letters on land today to give them to the post. (Why didn't the fool give them to Krusenstern?) Resanoff met him on land looking for an excuse for a reprimand, took his letters, scratched his name off of the one he was looking for, and wrote instead Novosilzoff's address on it. Isn't that the craziest behavior? What business is it of Resanoff's what Tilesius wants to write? Novosilzoff will be astonished to get a letter addressed to someone else. Tilesius, absolutely beside himself, answered Resanoff very freely, asked him to send him back overland. Resanoff made a joke of it, and poor dumbfounded Tilesius was left standing there.

Delaroff, the old man, one of the directors of the American Company, has arrived in Ochotsk.

According to Krusenstern's order, Ratmanoff has the position of captain lieutenant from now on (that means he has nothing to do), and Bellingshausen got 4½ watches. Up to now, Bellingshausen always has been on my watch.

Tues. 23/4 Since the ambassadorial clique has come back on board, everything is as it used to be. Bad weather!

In the evening, Krusenstern went with Resanoff and his whole suite on land. Resanoff's behavior is totally the way it was during the time when we sailed away from Copenhagen. He says nothing with his smoke screen of words. The main sense of his conversation is smut and the counterpart to Erasmus Spang's tales [in Copenhagen].

If one of us by chance gets up (because he has been sitting too long or has something to do), then Resanoff requests, full of importance, that he should sit down again. His Excellency makes his entré into the company cabin with a thousand scrape legs in the morning, so that all of us are made aware of the arrival of the Ambassador to Japan. We get to hear from Resanoff himself, scalding hot, all of the new (often unreasonable, unjust) arrangements he claims to have made in Kamtschatka and is thinking about making with the addition, "The emperor may do with me whatever he wants to. I must and intend to make this area happy, etc."

Wed. 24/5 Brinkin took along a letter from Tilesius to Suchteten, in which he relates everything that took place between him and Resanoff. Brinkin said to

Krusenstern yesterday when taking leave, "From necessity I have had to act differently from the way I really am. After your return, you will certainly have a different opinion of me in Petersburg from what you can have at present."

The painter Kurlandzoff, who is no less ill, said to Krusenstern, "I have not presumed to speak with you in order to avoid mistrust. You may believe that I have had, however, the best of intentions. Brinkin and I gave that appearance when things were difficult, and you and we were making ready to travel overland. Since Resanoff had chosen me and Brinkin as his companions, we thought we could serve you, Captain, in no better way than to play hypocrites in order to tear off our masks in Petersburg and reveal Resanoff's injustices and incredible demands there."

I have no idea what Tolstoi is thinking of doing at present. It is certain that Resanoff has sent him nice Job's messages.

Thurs. 25/6 Early this morning, a favorable wind arose, and we used it to weigh anchor. Full of gratitude we departed from General Koscheleff, who came out at the very end. We saluted Peter-Paul's Harbor and with a gentle breeze approached the very narrow exit. We will sail for Nangasaki through the Straits of Dieman. At noon the wind turned contrary, and we had to anchor in the entrance.

Kamtschatka is now very happy to have Koscheleff as commander, a just, civil man. His predecessors Kosloff and Somoff laid waste to that poor land. The injustices and oppression that these men committed in order to enrich themselves are incredible. Precisely those tyrants have been heaped with rewards and now live in luxury (even though they should have been hanged). According to the latest newspapers, Captain Lieutenant Bucharin, who, in the same way, is responsible for baseness, knavery, and suppression, has been transferred to Ochotsk and promoted to captain and given an order.

Fri. 26/7 We weighed anchor with a favorable east northeasterly, and now with the will of God we are headed for Japan. We barely had Avatscha Bay behind us when the high seas began to take their toll of our old and new passengers.

Anecdote: Brinkin is a tall, strong, fat fellow with shining white skin. The people on Nukahiva, who came on board, found that fat bosom so much to their liking that they could not stop running their hands over him, and, according to their words, their mouths were watering. This made Brinkin so fearful that he was the only man, who did not go ashore in Nukahiva, so that he would not be eaten by the cannibals. Neither curiosity nor persuasion could move him to go on land.

Sat. 27/8 The *Nadezhda* was thrown around a lot in the night. The wind is favorable, and everything is bearable. We are, however, pumping once again. Let's hope we can find out in Japan for sure where that leak is.

Sun. 28/9 His Excellency is in a very good mood. He intends to publish or at least write about our voyage, travestied. He paints the devil on the wall, but Resanoff must not do the writing, so that he, as a main character, will be put in a proper light, something Resanoff, as a favor to himself, would not do.

Mon. 29/10 An exceedingly large crate in which gifts had been packed that Resanoff needs first upon his arrival in Nangasaki had been loaded in the ship at his request, so that he could have them on hand upon our arrival in Japan. That was done. Today, it occurred to our ambassador, while he was bored, to admire the materials and stuff, etc., in the crate. Despite the fact we are at sea and do not like to touch a packed hold, for better or worse, we had to haul around half a dozen cables in order to get to that cursed crate and satisfy the childish desires of His Excellency, (otherwise, there would have been a fuss immediately).

Ratmanoff, Golovatscheff, and Espenberg have recently been playing a round of Boston almost every day (since Ratmanoff, as captain lieutenant has nothing to do). First one and then another watches the game. Yesterday, I was sitting next to Ratmanoff and could see his cards. Espenberg said in the course of a completely normal conversation, "They are saying that I have been gambling away the two Kotzebue's money and that can be no one else but either Ratmanoff or Löwenstern." For me that came out of the blue, and I said to Espenberg that I was surprised how he could come to think such a thing. "Moritz told me that," answered Espenberg. I sent for Moritz Kotzebue. Moritz said he had heard me talking with Fedoroff, and I had said Ratmanoff had won 500 Spanish dahler. "That is true," I said "and let Krusenstern decide if I am wrong in telling the truth or not." I mainly wanted to prevent future gossip, so I told Krusenstern all about it so that our strife and playing Boston would stop. There were a lot of apologies to appease me. (Espenberg's accusations and Moritz Kotzebue's gossip were not totally unfounded. Bellingshausen, who was instructing Otto in mathematics, navigation, and astronomy, had really said that about Espenberg. Moritz was jealous that his brother Otto was more advanced in the sciences than he was, and could not stand Bellingshausen for that reason, and I also often taught and instructed him, thus Moritz undoubtedly mixed up our names.)

Wind and weather are bad. *Never mind*! [sic] Things will be all right again.

Tues. 30/11 The equinoctium is near and with it the storms and bad weather are raging around us. Even if the wind is rather favorable, then the waves caste the *Nadezhda* around like a ball.

Wed. 31/12 The wind had died down, meaning that we were in for it even more, because the waves were then free to do whatever they wanted to with us. Everything in the ship creaked due to the exertion (and force) that were throwing the ship from one side to the other. Fosse is the only one on board who was injured because, while he was sleeping, a chair fell over and hit him in the mouth and split his lip. The most unpleasant thing about the rolling of the ship is the moving around of everything that is movable or badly attached. Here men are falling; their chairs are smashing up; the fireplace fell over; an entire wall of the company cabin ripped loose; four cabins were demolished. In a moment, bottles, glasses, and pots were smashed by the dozens. You did not dare take a step without being in danger of cutting your feet because of all the splinters of glass. Over and above that everyone was seasick. On deck, we had too much to do to help below.

What a calamity!

September

Thurs. 1/13 Everything is quiet again. The sky is clear, the wind favorable, and the high seas have gone down. We have hardly had such bad weather during our voyage as we just had and, honestly, have to say of the captain and the officers and crew that work on the ship was carried out with the greatest orderliness and punctuality.

It is leaking in Schemelin's cabin, as if the ship were in danger of sinking—that's how much noise that weak man was making, especially that a couple of dozen shirts got wet. We acted as if we did not hear him, and Resanoff gave him in his way a reprimand for making so much noise about nothing.

Fri. 2/14 We were at the latitude of the Straits of Sangar, which are still so little known. With the reefed topsail, we were making eight knots; it takes a sharp puffer for that. If you are in unknown waters, afraid of sighting land, you look yourself blind. Today, we still have nothing to be afraid of. Tomorrow evening, we will get to an area where the sea is strewn with badly plotted islands, reefs and shallows. This time of year does not let us expect good weather, and in a storm and fog a ship is ever so easily in danger of wrecking. We have to take all possible precautions not to increase the number of shipwrecks by stranding our ship. Over and above that, the *Nadezhda* is leaking six zoll an hour after that storm, and we unfortunately cannot find the leak. At the fore and aft stem, we can hear water trickling, but all of the spots are so deep below water that it is impossible to do anything about them. Ratmanoff, who always likes an argument, claims the leak is at the forestem and comes from the chalkier, when caulking a crack, having driven the joints apart with the wedge. Be that as it may, Ratmanoff knows how to find reasons but not to help, and we have to pump water out of the ship five to six times a day. The *Nadezhda* has to serve us for two more years. No wonder we are concerned about the leak.

Sat. 3/15 The wind is very still again and the high seas our master. Since our departure we have had continual stormy weather and restless water and are so used to the rolling of the ship that the movement serves us well. The wind is favorable. Preparations and plans are endless. I am afraid that Resanoff blabbers more than he will actually carry through with.

Sun. 4/16 In order to help the ship, Krusenstern had four cannons put in the hold today. The difference in the leak was noticeable, that within the short time from six zoll an hour we have 1½.

The wind is unpredictable and threatens to blow against us. The flat seas also influence our leak a great deal.

Mon. 5/17 Resanoff talks extremely zealously against the old general governor in Siberia, "because the borders are so long that it is impossible for an old man to be acquainted with all of them, just as Silifontieff does not get out of Irkutsk, etc. A forty-year-old man of my age would behave totally differently and use his authority better, etc."

Tues. 6/18 With the wind eight knots. The weather is clear but the horizon blurred by clouds and fog. We are satisfied if we are able to see a couple of versts ahead of us, since the islands, reefs and shallows that have impulsively been spotted on the chart could cause us trouble. The long nights are the hardest for us. At sunset, we spotted something that looked like land on the horizon. On closer inspection, they appeared to be clouds that in several places deceived us, except for several places that always looked like land. The captain had us sail straight at them in order to establish what they were. It is already eight o'clock, and we have come no closer to land.

Wed. 7/19 In the night the wind became quieter, and the high seas once again had free play with us and threw the ship about without compassion. In the morning, we caught a six-fuss-long shark, the first fish the Russians have caught along the Japanese coast.

After so many years the Japanese on board are impatiently awaiting the moment when they catch sight of Japan. No one else looks more diligently for land than our Japanese.

Fosse has started the card game lamouche. There are enough disputes during the game.

Thurs. 8/20 Nice wind. Madsiura, who is very inquisitive, bought himself a lot of maps in Petersburg, which he has asked Bellingshausen to illuminate, so that he can more easily distinguish the countries.

Resanoff wearies us all with stories in which he always plays the main part, and, for politeness sake, we have to listen to him. In order to have something to do at table, I began to scratch various names into my spoon with a fork, since he leaves you alone if he sees that you have something to do; but, the moment you look at him, you are forced to listen to him and cannot get out of it for the time being.

Fri. 9/21 The wind is very strong and the waves are rising higher and higher. There is a full moon and two days after the sun. Then the moon goes over the equator and is closest to the earth. Bad physical signs. We cannot expect good weather.

In the evening, an exceedingly strong downpour suddenly changed the wind and weather. As if Neptune had swept the sea clean with a broom, the quite high waves were very much like froth and appeared to tend toward the north.

Sat. 10/22 As necessary as clear weather is for us, so seldom have we had it on this voyage. We are again sailing at seven knots with the wind and can barely see 1½ versts ahead of us. A bad situation in an unknown sea.

Sun. 11/23 A wind, blowing stronger and stronger, threatened us early this morning with a bad situation. The waves had grown higher than we could remember having experienced on our entire voyage. We were glad we had passed Fazisio and had room in which to weather the storm and made use of favorable winds. The wind died down in the afternoon as, according to our expectations, we, however, were not caused any difficulty at all by the high seas, undoubtedly because we must be nearer land than we thought. In the evening we saw clouds similar to land in the distance and sailed toward them to find out what they were in reality. The evening and the night were nice. No greater contrast is imaginable than between the weather we had early this morning and the weather this evening.

Fazisio is the exile of the Japanese. Last evening, the gentlemen musici gave a concert they had composed themselves entitled "The voyage around the world." The fun caused a lot of laughter. The creaking of the ship however outshouted the instruments so much, that forte and piano got totally lost and the music could often not be heard at all, especially since the continuing storm blew a counter-basso now and then that threw around everything movable and our musici lost cadence and continence. Indeed, the desire to play got lost and put an end to the concert.

Mon. 12/24 Nice weather. At ten o'clock, Krusenstern had the entire crew called together and read publicly the letter he had received from the ambassador concerning Japan.

The main points of these directives are as follows: We are to conduct ourselves with decorum and not make any outward signs of the Russian Church services. Everyone without exception is to put his crosses and saints' pictures in deposit and to carry their religion in his heart and not to laugh at Japanese customs, to give no reason for trouble, not to speak Portuguese,[3] and that any violations will be judged by Japanese laws.

Tues. 13/25 As nice as the weather was yesterday, so little does it have today any tendency that direction—calm and unprecedented gusts of rain.

According to our calculations, we are only 15 German miles from land. Despite the rain, several dragonflies and butterflies have fluttered onto our ship, a sure sign of nearby land, but we, nevertheless, have not caught sight of any land.

There are a lot of activities and ideas at work, so that we may quite happily celebrate the anniversary of the emperor's coronation.

Wed. 14/26 Николай Петрович [Nikolai Petrovich] Resanoff is planning to distribute medals to our sailors.

Dreary, wet weather, and in the evening a dead calm—something unusual in September.

Thurs. 15/27 At 9 o'clock, our entire crew gathered on the quarterdeck, the grenadiers in front, and, when our ambassador appeared on deck, he was given honors. Immediately afterwards, Resanoff gave the following speech and distributed coronation medals to all of the sailors and soldiers, to the great joy of our people. During the noon meal, there were salutations when we drank to the health of our monarch. And with a favorable wind we sailed toward Japan after having been held up for almost 24 hours by calms. Sydham, the subchirurius, is the only person who did not get a medal, they're saying because Resanoff considers him an atheist. In the afternoon, Kurganoff, a subaltern, pulled our clerk Tschugaeff, as Bachus sitting on a barrel, all around the deck to the shouts of the ship's folk, who were inclined to joy through a couple of schnapps. In the evening, Bellingshausen and I lighted a transparency which we had hurriedly made. In the end a rain shower forced everyone to flee to his cabin. Time passes unbelievably quickly.

A translation of Resanoff's speech[4]

Russians!

After sailing around the world, we finally find ourselves in Japanese waters! Love of fatherland, skillfulness, dignity, disdain of danger, subordination, mutual respect, and meekness are the main characteristics marking the Russian seaman, virtues that are characteristics of Russians in general. You leaders versed in navigation have earned the recognition of your fellow citizens. You have already gained fame, which even jealousy will never be able to rob you of. You, my worthy associates! There remains still the completion of our glorious deeds and the discovery of new sources of wealth! And you, dear children of the naval service, be exceedingly happy about the success of your zealous efforts! Let us unite our hearts and souls to fulfill the will of our monarch, a monarch, whom we so correctly honor. We have been united now for a long time. Now let the gratitude for our lofty ruler enliven all of our senses!

The present day, my friends, is festive in our fatherland, but even more festive because today his sons for the first time push forward deep into the Japanese Empire to establish the friendship of our glorious Russian flag in the waters of Nangasaki. As representative of our most gracious emperor and witness of your great accomplishments, it has been so flattering to share your concerns and dangers with you, as it now is for me to display the festive recognition which awaits all of us in the lap of our fatherland. I am celebrating the Coronation of His Imperial Majesty in Japanese waters and am making this day for all of you, as a result of your services, forever memorable. See here the image of a great emperor, take it as a reward and decorate yourselves with this adornment that can be obtained only through great effort and zeal. Never forget that this obligates you more than ever to stay true to the virtues of which your ancestors were proud, and in the ecstasy of fame time will bless the services even of the most minor subject in the farthest spot in the world, and he will not go unrewarded before the throne of our monarch.

All of our sailors were brought to tears by this speech.

Fri. 16/28 At ten o'clock, this morning we sighted land at a great distance. The current drove us strongly northwards, and at noon we caught sight of and clearly recognized the Japanese mainland instead of, as we had thought, the Van Diemen Straits.

In the evening, we had been smart enough to use the mild winds, so that we had sailed only a little bit forwards. The land in sight must be in all probability Sikoktt.[5]

We can, however, only say that we have seen land in that direction, for it could just as well be the island of Likeo.

Resanoff is taking up his pretensions again. He is demanding of Krusenstern that he should report to him every morning with the sergeant. Krusenstern answered, however, "You will get a written report every day. You cannot put me on the same level as a sergeant." And that was how it stayed.

Sat. 17/28 Concerning the medals—there is a lot to say for and against them. The place, the reason, for what reason and why, etc., is a subject that won't remain without criticism in Petersburg. Resanoff received 300 medals in order to reward industry and agriculture. Did he therefore have a right to distribute them to our sailors? And why exclude Sydham, who deserved to receive a medal as well as the others? And could and did Resanoff have permission to distribute the medals to our sailors without first asking our captain whether they are deserving or deserved them?

Resanoff says, (не скажуть едена мать [They won't say anything, mother fuckers]) "They will bawl me out, and that is all, and our ship's fold has their medals."

Sun. 18/30 We are used to the storm, so that we do not even notice the howling of the wind any more. Our passengers, thank goodness, are managing.

The wind let up some in the evening. I had watch until 12 midnight and Krusenstern was just giving me orders for the night. The ship was hit hard by waves. Suddenly, a wave smashed into the stern of our ship. I didn't see anything wrong on deck. The disturbance among the passengers in the company cabin caught my attention, and immediately afterwards I heard water rushing over the entire deck. And Tilesius, who had just headed up the stairs from the gunner's cabin and was met by the stream of water, let out a murderous scream. A window in the captain's cabin did not have its mock window in place (so that it would not be totally dark), and Krusenstern had forgotten to put the mock window in for the night. A wave smashed the window to pieces, and in a moment over a fuss of water spread over the entire ship. There was no further damage but a great many things that the water reached were spoilt. Damage enough!

It finally ran itself complete out on the ship. This man was pale and pallid; another one screamed, "We are sinking! We are sinking." The fright stopped quite soon because the window was closed immediately, and the water ran off, and we had to let ourselves be rocked by the *Nadezhda* as before. Everyone was ashamed of his fright and fear and went to bed. The Japanese Sea is and remains cursed waters. The wind became first stronger and then weaker during the entire night. The seas were, however, continually high.

Mon. 19/1 There was a calm in the night, and the ship was tossed around inhumanely by the waves. It was impossible to stand on deck without holding onto a line. We had to put up lines the length of the ship so that we would not be swept overboard. The wind began to roar again toward morning, and the somewhat quiet sea rose anew and grew into mountains. By chance, the screw under the barometer had fallen out, and Ratmanoff fought strongly against our prophet [barometer] which was very low and still continuing to fall. Krusenstern, who is always very careful, had the anchor, which had been lowered, raised again on board (without letting himself be led to err by Ratmanoff's talk). At 12 o'clock, with a great deal of difficulty, we lashed down the mizzensail and the top foresail. The wind was becoming stronger and stronger, forcing us to haul in the mainsail, but prevented us from doing it, since all of the sail lines and clue lines ripped from the force of the wind. Finally, with a great deal of difficulty we got these sails lashed down. And Krusenstern ordered the main topsail hauled in. Our main braces were ripped by the raging storm leeward and our cross frame was smashed about. We were afraid of losing our sail with its yard when we watched, with fear and amazement, the sailor Ivan Jakovleff, of his own volition, climb along the trembling jogging yard. He lashed another line to it, and the yard and sail were saved and lashed down. The sailor deserved a reprimand for putting himself into a dangerous situation where he might have lost his life. We nevertheless had to praise him for doing the job so successfully, because none of us would have dared to order a sailor to climb up there and do what he did so successfully.

I have to say in all justice to our people that they behaved very bravely when doing this kind of dangerous work, even though all of the braces and lines on the main topsail had ripped loose and there was danger to life and limb. The foresail was not in any better condition, and we can say we were lucky enough to lash down all of the sails without losing one. At five o'clock the mercury in the barometer could no longer be seen, it had fallen that much. We had set our storm staysails.

Since I had night watch, I took a moment to go into my cabin and fill my pipe with tobacco. Only when I went back into the company cabin did I become aware of the frightened, pale, desperate faces that had clung to the posts to which the table has been fastened. These ghost-like faces looked at me astonished, and my countenance also gave them hope. The blood returned to their faces, and we began to talk. Resanoff and his suite did penitence for their bad consciences. At six o'clock, the wind had become so powerful that I went back on the deck again. Not one of the sails withstood the wind's anger. One staysail (these handkerchiefs of sails made of the strongest sailcloth) after another ripped to pieces, either the sheet, halyard, or the sail itself. The staysail whose sheet ripped wound itself with its blocks in the six sectors, ripped them all out, took three studdingsails along, and flew overboard with them. You can judge the force of the wind by that. Those sectors were made of bolt iron in order to protect the cabins in them and bound with rope and covered with sailcloth. Luckily, there were no berths in them. The bolts were driven into the side of the ship, and two braces of strong iron confirm how supernaturally strong the force of the wind was. In less than half an hour, we were lying on the drift with only the masts. Wind and water seemed to have passed their boundaries; the elements obliterated each other, they raged so horribly. I have experienced lots of storms, but none comes close to comparing with the one that raged around us here. It must have been a typhoon. You had no desire to, and it was impossible to, hold your face into the wind. The preventer on the yard was lifted up by the storm so that the hook was raised out, and suddenly the yard came flying down. It was lashed down and saved. At eight o'clock in the evening, the wind suddenly changed direction from east to west to west to east and raged from the opposite direction with an even greater force. With a great deal of effort, we had hauled up the storm mizzen, but it was left to the wind, and waves and the wind capriciously blew it around.

While the ship was turning, a wave crashed over the stern and into the stern of the ship with such incredible force that the whole ship literally was totally under water. And we can happily say that no one was swept overboard.

The gallery on the left side was smashed by a wave and torn loose, the door with the wall pressed into the cabin, and the cabin and ship were full of water in the wink of an eye. Our boats hanging at the sides were smashed. You could swim on deck. The best proof was that a large crate in which muskets, pistols, and swords for the whole crew were stored was ripped loose from the quarterdeck and was floating back and forth without touching the windows in the middle of the quarterdeck or the company cabin. Our sail yard, hanging rigged in reverse at the side, was ripped off and floated away. Everything that was moveable was ripped loose and thrown around until it went overboard. That moment was terrible. Our barometer was also broken in the tumult.

Krusenstern, very pale, lashed to us with a rope, deliberated with us what we should do, and, filled with fear, we expected another wave that would bring us closer to sinking. In the cabin, all were at wit's end. All were preparing for death. They held on to each other compulsively asking for pardon and forgiveness. This one was preparing to give up his ghost and praying; that one was sitting like a stone as if he had already given up the ghost. Everything in the cabin was wet through and through.

The following proves how close we must have been to land. We did not have a grain of sand on the ship; yet after the storm every cranny of the ship was filled with sand and shells, even the mast basket. In several cabins, water had swept in sand and shells two to three hands high. There was sand in all the crannies and on everything you touched.

We expected at any moment another blow of a fresh wave and worked in the sweat of our faces to stuff up the hole in the captain's cabin. Because the wind had so suddenly and so strongly changed direction, the waves quieted down a little in the beginning. The continued raging of the wind from west-southwest made the sea, however, soon even more restless. The waves rose house-high upwards like mountains. One wave after another, so to say, hopped over the next. A heartening view it was to see this nutshell against the elements. First, she was between the waves in a valley; then immediately afterwards, the *Nadezhda* was thrown on her side on top of the wave like a glove. The binnacle with our compasses was also torn loose and swept overboard. In a word, everything was topsy-turvy. On my watch during the night, it was somewhat quieter. Since Krusenstern's cabin was very wet, he went to bed in mine (my berth had stayed dry because I raise it up every day on blocks). Toward three o'clock in the night, the wind began to quiet down, and the sky began to clear. The *Nadezhda* however was still so heartlessly cast about that I was always deathly afraid that the masts and topmasts would go overboard. I could barely keep my hold and still work as we continued with the greatest exertion to prevent something disastrous from suddenly happening. The nearby land was a danger that could become most dangerous for us because wind, waves, and storm would drive us straight into it. Luckily for us, the wind suddenly turned and let us hope we have now withstood the danger.

Tues. 20/2 In contrast to yesterday, nice weather. Yesterday, Resanoff thought that his last hour had tolled because he had lost his ring in all the terror (which he assured us was supposed to be a bad sign).

Today, to Resanoff's great joy, the ring was found under the ruins of the tables, chairs, crates, boxes, and splinters. He, more than anyone else, was very diligent in looking for it because that superstition bothered him so much.

We have our hands full repairing everything that was spoiled in yesterday's typhoon, as it is called here. It is heartrending to see only ragged pieces of sails; all ropes have been ripped apart. A ship without sails is desolate like after a funeral. Our passengers are putting life on deck by taking over the whole deck to dry their clothes. It is a calamity that Krusenstern's books and maps also got wet. Indeed, only a few things stayed dry, so great was the flood yesterday.

Yesterday, when the wave smashed into our ship, no one had a thought in his head of eating and drinking. Immediately afterwards, the clerk Tschugaeff went to the captain and asked him calmly, since no salt meat could be raised from the hold, what should be cooked for the people the next day. He forced all of us to smile—and was excused in a friendly way.

According to our ship's calculations, we were turning around in the same spot.

Resanoff suffered a lot of damage because of his caprice. All of the things he had taken out of the large crates, which had been in the hold, are wet through and through. The nice muskets, swords, damasks, yard goods, etc., are all spoilt.

We lost mostly riggings. In the evening, we spotted land and therefore put ourselves on the drift for the night. Calm.

Wed. 21/3 We sailed toward the land we had sighted last evening. Quiet wind. With a great deal of trouble we managed to repair all of the mischief caused by wind and storm and put riggings and sails back in order. The drying of clothing still continues without end. My beautiful tobacco is also completely wet. Luckily, I had only Oronoco tobacco wrapped in lead left and therefore only its ends got wet.

Thurs. 22/4 During the night, the wind was brisker, and in the morning we headed toward land again. The Arrowsmith[6] map is very good. In the evening, we found ourselves in a very quiet wind at the entrance to Van Diemen's Strait. The Japanese on our ship, who had always looked so sour, have finally put on friendly faces, undoubtedly the result of the Japanese air. During the day, we saw clouds of smoke rising in various places on land, and after sunset fires were set in various places on land. At 1 o'clock old Zudei and Madsiura came on the quarterdeck and asked us to answer the fires that had been set on land. At their request and Resanoff's and the captain's order, we lighted a false fire.

Resanoff's order concerning the ceremony to be observed in Nangasaki:

The ceremony to be observed aboard the ship *Nadezhda* upon entry into Nangasaki harbor:

1. Upon entering Nangasaki harbor or at the approach of Japanese vessels to the ship, all crew and officers are to be in full uniform and the lower ranks in their best dress.
2. A guard with drummers is to be stationed up on the quarterdeck.
3. Two guards with rifles are to be stationed at the hatch.
4. Captain Fedorov is responsible for the orderly appearance of the guard.
5. After entering Nangasaki, cannons are to be fired mornings and evenings and reveille drummed.
6. Whenever the ambassador enters the quarterdeck, the honor guard is to present arms and "forward" is to be drummed.
7. Both Kotzebue cadets are to be stationed, each one in turn, in the ambassador's cabin as messengers.
8. The embassy cavaliers, Messrs. Fosse, Friderici, and Koschelev are to arrange watches.
9. The guard on watch is to report the arrival of the Japanese to the ambassador. He then conducts them to the company cabin where he questions them about the reason for their visit and then is to report to the ambassador. Then, having received instructions from the ambassador, he either escorts them to the ambassador's cabin or gives them the ambassador's answer. After that, they are to be treated to vodka, wines, and smoking tobacco.

10. When the governor visits, the guard is to present arms and 3 drum rolls are to be given. Two members of the embassy guard are to meet him and, walking in front of him, conduct him to the ambassador's cabin. Here the guards bow and exit, leaving him with the ambassador. The same ceremony is to be observed at his departure.
11. When the ambassador goes ashore, the sailors are to line up on the yards and give three cheers. The ship is to fire an 11-cannon salute.
12. The Japanese returning from Russia are to be on the quarterdeck in their [Japanese] dress and act as interpreters.
13. When the Japanese arrive, every one on board is to be polite but maintain distance so as not to give any impression of curiosity.[7]

- 9 -

Arrival in Nangasaki

ON LAND, FIRES BURNED NOW and again throughout the night. In the morning, we sailed in very nice weather and with good wind into the labyrinth of islands that make up Van Diemen's Strait. The island of Likeo, which we sailed past, gives the impression that the countryside is very populated, since even the infertile cliffs have been planted.

Numbers of boats have been coming out as we sail along the shore, but not a one of them has dared to come close to us.

Resanoff called out to them (he could have let others do that), but it did not help.

Horner, Bellingshausen, and I have been working on a map of our course. Seamen have seldom taken as much trouble as we have to chart exact maps.

In the evening, we were through the strait. Mild breezes and a contrary current held us, as last evening, in the same place. Very pleasant for our charting. Since early in the morning, we were able to take up the thread of our angle where we had left off. The consistency of our measurements rewarded our trouble and made us very happy. Seaman sailing this way will thank us for our trouble.

Sat. 24/6 A beautiful bright night. Today like yesterday, we are seeing a lot of boats along the shore. But not even one soul from this unfriendly country comes near us to tell us the way. The water is dangerous here, and there are large numbers of hidden rocks and sandbanks. Krusenstern is therefore very careful, and we sailed last evening and night around known islands instead of straight ahead. This anxious precaution is now being criticized laughed at, etc., even in Krusenstern's presence. It has often enough made me angry that he takes it—his patience and forbearance are indeed too great.

Sun. 25/7 All during the night, we sailed with a northwest wind without tacking. At sunrise, yesterday's land disappeared and, in the north-northwest and west, we caught sight of islands so we sailed toward them. The weather is unparalleled. We suspect that we have sighted the Gotte Islands. The wind is calm and contrary.

Today, we will undoubtedly not catch sight of the mainland, even though we have left the Gotte Islands and have once again sailed toward the mainland. A couple of small islands that we charted today must be the Assescars.

Resanoff has formulated the following answers to Japanese questions and given them to us so that our answers are all in agreement.

Question: How large is the Russian Empire?

Answer: Russia, as far as territory is concerned, occupies half of the world and is the greatest Empire in the Universe. There are cities 12,000 versts or more from the capital.

Q.: What are the borders of the Russian Empire?

A.: In the south Japan, China, Turkey, and Greece, in the east the American States, English possessions, and part of the Chinese Empire, in the west Prussia, Austria, and Denmark, in the north a most minuscule part of Sweden. As for the rest, it is all Russia. There is no other land but her own.

Q.: How is the Russian State governed?

A.: By the Autocratic Great Emperor, in whose person is united both the civil and spiritual authority.

Q.: How is Russia subdivided?

A.: Russia is composed of 50 very large regions or governorships and encompasses various great kingdoms, whose rulers appealed for protection to the Great Russian Lord and consider it a blessing to be among his subjects. They have joined their kingdoms to Russia forever, that is, the Kingdoms of Kazan, Astrakhan, Siberia, Tavrida, Georgia, Poland, Armenia. In addition there are other peoples such as the Kirgiz, Kabarda, Kalmyk, Cherkess, and others who are under the protection of the Great Russian Monarch.

Q.: What is the population of Russia?

A.: Russians by origin over 50 million, the rest who are under Imperial protection have not been able to be counted, but they are always ready to do service for their overlord.

Q.: What is the faith in Russia?

A.: As Russia is very large, all faiths, divine services, and rituals are permitted and have public temples [places of worship], but the dominant faith is the Greek one.

Q.: Are you Christians?

A.: Christian, but of the Greek confession, not of the Portuguese or Spanish one. We do not acknowledge the Pope, as our Great Emperor himself is the authority over the entire clergy. It is at his mighty will that spiritual personnel occupy positions within the Empire. He also can deprive them of their status at his arbitrary will.

Q.: What is the difference between your Christian faith and the others?

A.: A great one. 1. Many Christians are subordinated to the Pope, whereas Russians do not acknowledge any other spiritual authority but that of the monarch.

The Great Russian Emperor conducts relations with the Pope, not as with a spiritual man but as a lord over a territory. 2. All faiths such as the Japanese, Chinese, Mohammedan, Hebrew, and others are permitted; and many conduct divine services in their temples according to their own rites, which is not permitted in other Christian lands. 3. In Russia, no one is forced to become a Christian. 4. The very dogmas and rituals are different, but the main point is that our monarch is the authority over the clergy.

Q.: How large is the Russian military?

A.: Within the State there is a regular army, always ready to meet the enemy, of 700,000, a Cavalry of 200,000, in addition, irregular units composed of light Cossack cavalry, Bashkir, Mesheriak, Mugal, and other people under Russian rule. Russia has many fleets: the Baltic, Black, and Caspian named for the seas. The first two always maintain 50 battle ships, whereas the Caspian has 25. There is a multitude of frigates, ketches, and other naval vessels, as many as the monarch wishes to build since his lands are rich.

Q.: With whom does the Russian emperor conduct wars and who are his allies?

A.: He—with no one, even though he has the power and the unlimited might. After having ascended to his ancestral throne and understanding the widespread borders established by the victories of his forefathers, he has undertaken to rule in tranquility and peace with the entire world. Using his might, he maintains a balance with all foreign countries and states, as it is his wish that peace should be obtained in the entire universe. The Great Russian Emperor unites in his person meekness with manly courage. Having been given these divine gifts, he values highly human life and peaceful existence and cares not only for his subjects but also for all mankind in general. As evidence of this, he is returning, as a gift to the Great Japanese Emperor, his subjects, whom evil fate cast upon the shores of his possessions and who wished to return to their homeland.

Q.: Why were the Japanese not returned long ago?

A.: Because all of Europe was at war, and, thus, no embassy could be dispatched to His Tenzin Kuboskoi Majesty.

Q.: What are the relations between Russia and Portugal?

A.: The same as with all nations with whom we trade. The Great Russian Emperor, seeing the deficiencies suffered by other lands, out of human compassion, permits the use of his State's ample resources, and our borders are open to all merchants.

Q.: Where have you come from?

A.: Around the world from the capital city of St. Petersburg.

Q.: What have you brought with you?

A.: We are carrying no merchandise, only gifts for His Tenzin Kuboskoi Majesty. Our ambassador knows what these gifts are.

Q.: What kind of people do you have with you? Are there any merchants?

A.: There are no merchants. All are either military personnel or members of the embassy, and naval officers of our Great Imperial Majesty.

Q.: What is the rank of your ambassador?

A.: His rank is that of a general. In addition, he is a Kammerherr [Chamberlain] and from among the ranks of those closest to our emperor.

Q.: What kind of officials are with you?

A.: They are from among the highest nobility of our empire.

Q.: Why do have a guard?

A.: This is to honor our ambassador. In Russia he has an even greater escort. He brought along just a small one, as there was no extra space.

Q.: Where did you stop en route?

A.: Denmark, England, Tenerife Island, Brazil, the Marquesas Islands, and Kamtschatka, where we took on provisions and fresh water. In Kamtschatka we left supplies needed in that region.

Q.: Did anyone die en route?

A.: A cook died en route from the Marquesas Islands.[1]

The following is the answer the Japanese government gave Laksmann.[2] He was here about twenty years ago, also returning stranded Japanese to Japan, but landed in a northern harbor. The translation is the document from the Japanese government giving Russia permission to send one ship to Nangasaki in order to deliver the suggestions for which Laksmann had been appointed, which, according to Japanese laws, however, could only be accepted in Nangasaki. As a result of these papers, our emperor was sending Resanoff as ambassador to Japan—only a little late.

Copy of the translation from the Japanese:

The list of instructions from His Majesty the Tenzin Kuboskii about the regulations pertaining to the Japanese State in regard to the arrival of foreign ships.

From most ancient times up to the present, the law of our Empire has remained firm and no changes whatsoever may be made. You, escorting our people whom fate cast out by the sea have, unknowingly, arrived from your country not at Nangasaki but at a different place. Foreign ships are forbidden to approach our land elsewhere from the sea, and this has never happened before in Japan, should any arrive, they will be taken captive, no matter how numerous they may be. Furthermore, if they proceed by sea, they are to proceed without any kind of firearms. Thus, the people who have resided in friendship since ancient times with our Empire, i.e. the Dutch, sail with their ships to the harbor of Nangasaki but not to the interior of our Empire.

Since our people have guided you to this locality, and up to now you have not had any friendly [relations with us] and you have come with [armed] people on an armed vessel; therefore, we should detain you for a long time, as you have arrived without our knowledge and more importantly contrary to our laws. Those who violate our laws are never let return to whence they came. Nevertheless, since you are bringing our subjects from your own country, and in doing so, faced many difficulties, and, in addition, were ignorant of our laws, you shall be permitted to return under one condition: you are never to return, since it is forbidden to come to this place.

Since from ancient times we know nothing of friendly relations or of the degree of worthiness of your Imperial State or of your language or writing, the majesty and lowliness, the manner of behavior and customs, it may appear that our empire offers neither respect nor disrespect of your empire. And even though we have accepted the letter you have sent, because of insufficient knowledge, it is impossible to act upon it at all, except to accept our people whose fate brought them to your country. We expect no further negotiations. As for establishing friendly relations, it is impossible to do so locally and it is forbidden to travel from here to the Capital city of Edo. The subjects of many nations with whom we have friendly agreements that were concluded long ago, trade only in the one designated place; otherwise, if they land at any other harbor or place, they are to be dealt with strictly; no dialogue is to take place and no excuses accepted.

Since we have been sufficiently informed that previously, on orders of your Higher Authority, you had even intended to approach the capital city of Edo from the Kuril Islands, we declare that this intention should not be carried out by your authorities and not considered in the future, so that foreign ships that are sighted do not cause themselves even greater difficulties because of the strict regulations governing harbors and even more so for armed persons, even if friendly relations exist. No statements that they are acting upon higher authority will be accepted. On the contrary, in such a case they will be in even greater danger. If written commands and oral, you will be permitted to enter. Without this edict entry into the harbor is forbidden. As regards establishing explanations are not obeyed, they will be bound and dealt with according to our law, regardless of justifications they offer. Two officials are being dispatched from the capital Edo to inform you about our law. I shall inform them of your arrival from a distant foreign country, and that it was a great assignment to return our people, whom fate brought to you. They have also been ordered to make it known that you have safe passage. The above-mentioned people may be turned over either to the two faithful officials sent from Edo or to local officials. Furthermore, according to our law, these officials may not accept any other communications from you, even ones concerning our people. Regrettably, according to our laws, we cannot force you to return them and should you not return them voluntarily, we cannot accept them. Therefore, you are to listen carefully to instructions and remember that, if in the future the two remaining [shipwrecked Japanese] return to this locality, they are to go unaccompanied. Instead you are to use the established route to Nangasaki Harbor and sail at a sufficient distance from land, since it has already been amply explained that landings elsewhere are prohibited, even for those who have friendly relations, and it has been ordered, in view of potential danger, any approach is to be prevented. With a single ship, you are to proceed to Nangasaki Harbor carrying the edict. Upon showing it, you will be permitted to enter. Without this edict entry into the harbor is forbidden. As regards friendship and a trade accord, an official has been appointed in that place [Nangasaki] who is acquainted with all of the above in the most minute details and will return successfully.

Edict

Regarding permission to enter Nangasaki:

One ship belonging to the Great Russian State is permitted entry into Nangasaki Harbor. As has been explained and noted by them, foreign vessels are prohibited from landing anywhere else. It was repeated that the Christian faith is not tolerated within our State. Therefore, upon arrival there are to be no such services. No acts are to be undertaken that are contrary to our laws in accordance with the instructions on procedures we have issued. This edict was also given to Adam Laksman.

The following is the letter that the Emperor of Russia wrote the Emperor of Japan:

Copy

To His Majesty Tenzin Kuboskii, who rules by the Grace of God, the Lord Autocrat of the extensive Japanese Empire, most excellent Emperor and Lord, from the Lord Emperor and Autocrat of all Russians, the most sincere wishes for good health, long life and all possible prosperity in His Realm.

Having accepted the rule over the Empire, whose borders were expanded through glorious victories by my forebearers Peter I and Catherine II, and seeing Holland, France, England, Italy, Spain, and German lands involved in a general war, I deemed it my duty through friendly counsel to influence them toward a general peace. Since I consider peace and quiet the greatest benefit for my county, I put my entire efforts into establishing friendly relations with all nations upon this earth, and especially with my neighbors. In 1791, recognizing the merits of the Japanese Empire, the late Empress Catherine the Great, as a sign of goodwill, returned Japanese to their homeland, who had the misfortune of being shipwrecked by fate on the shores of my Realm. The Russian subjects dispatched to return them were treated in a friendly manner and received an edict from the Japanese government permitting one ship to sail unhindered to Nangasaki.

I feel that even now Your Majesty Tenzin Kubskoii has a well inclined disposition and taking into account the benefits accrued from mutual trade and also the desire to know the government of other areas of the world, I decided to dispatch a part to

Japan to return several Japanese subjects to Your Majesty, who through ill-fate, through shipwreck, found themselves within my borders where they were saved. I chose for this purpose my apparently worthy subject, my Active Chamberlain at Court Nikolai Resanoff, who is to approach your Autocratic Person with due respect and dignity; and I desire that he deliver to Your Tenzinkubosk Majesty this epistle with appropriate ceremonies and with sincere respect. Under all circumstances He is to behave in a manner that would please you. He is to inform Your Tenzinkubosk Majesty of my continuing diligent work and reaffirmation of the unshakable rules governing my friendly disposition toward you. He is to carry out anything you may request as a sign of my gratitude for the acceptance of my proposals. These consist in the request that Your Tenzinkubosk Majesty grant permission for my merchants, and even more for the inhabitants of Kodiak and the Aleutian and Kurile islands, your neighbors, to sail to Nangasaki Harbor not only with one ship but with many, and also to enter other harbors with products that may please you. On my part, I am opening up my entire Realm to your subjects. As far as the basis for establishing trade between our subjects and deciding at which ports my traders may land, I am entrusting my Ambassador, the above named Kammerherr [Chamberlain] Resanoff to enter into appropriate negotiations with Your Tenzinkubosk Majesty's Ministry, and in addition about the appropriate procedure to be followed for the return of Your subjects in the future when ill fate or shipwreck casts them upon the shores of my Realm, thus saving their lives.

I am sending as presents to Your Tenzinkubosk Majesty a clock in the shape of a mechanical elephant, mirrors, fox furs, ivory vases, guns, pistols and steel and glass artifacts. All of these items were produced in my manufacturing plants. Even though they are not of great value, I hope that you will find something from within my borders suitable and to your liking.

Given at St. Petersburg in the third year of my reign.

The original was signed personally by the hand of His Imperial Majesty Aleksandr [Alexander]

(M.P.) Countersigned by Count Aleksandr Vorontsov [Vorontzoff][3]

Mon. 26/8 At sunrise, we caught sight of the mainland of Japan. At eight o'clock, we were still some 20 English miles away when about 30 boats came sailing out to us. Only one headed toward us. It had fishermen, eight of them in a rather large boat, all naked like savages, with belts on. They had their clothes lying in a heap in the boat. They showed us where Nangasaki was and took leave after telling us we had been expected for four days and troops had gathered in Nangasaki. Our Japanese, who served as interpreters, said that the fishermen had been sent expressly to turn us away, but since we had Japanese onboard they could not detain us.

Everything has been polished and washed. Everyone has his parade uniforms on and the cannons are loaded.

Shortly after twelve o'clock, an armed boat with a black and white striped flag and two Japanese officers came out to us. Neither one came onboard. After having read the permission given Laksmann, they told us that we had permission to enter Nangasaki; but we, however, had to wait until they had reported to the governors of Nangasaki and they would come back. In addition, they asked for the day and year when we had left Russia and when we had arrived here. Madsiura is our interpreter. The Japanese officers also said that one of the Japanese, whom Laksmann had returned to Japan, was now in Nangasaki. The Japanese also indicated the spot we were to sail to. According to Kämpfer, it is actually the spot where, according to Japanese custom, enemy ships and vessels are burned.

The entire bay is full of islands, which are going to be all kinds of trouble for us to map.

At sunset, we reached the spot we had been instructed to sail to. The spot is open to the sea and a bad anchorage. The water is 40 faden deep. At the orders of the Japanese rowing next to us, we had to cast our anchor. Immediately afterwards, two boats came out to us, questioned us once again; still no one came onboard but rather they tied their boats to the *Nadezhda*. Then several more boats arrived, and in a short time their number had increased to ten that tied themselves up to our ship or one of the other boats. They lighted their lanterns and began to eat their evening meal, to drink tea, and to prepare themselves for the night. But no one came onboard. One of the Japanese officers, when asking (there was no end to the questions) how many officers, sailors, etc. we had, also asked among other things if and how many pieces of sailcloth we had brought along.

Resanoff was very happy when we congratulated him upon arriving in Nangasaki. He hugged us for joy and kissed me and Bellingshausen.

At nine o'clock in the evening, we saw a lot of lanterns moving in the distance. Half an hour later the sea was strewn with lanterns (probably the Japanese had put shutters on their lanterns), and two large boats followed by an endless number of

9-1. Japanese boat approaching the Nadezhda

little boats came up to our manrope (on the side of the ship). The boats carried Japanese of rank, the Dutch resident Duff[4] and the captains of two Dutch ships, etc. (*See color plates 5, 6, 7, 8, 9, and 10.*)

9-2. *An old friendly banjos*

A Japanese climbed up and asked if they were permitted to come onboard. Upon receiving a positive answer, about 30 men, each with two swords, came on deck, and a lot with only one sword or without swords, and covered the entire deck. Then an old man climbed up who was said to be the head of the Dutch. With a lot of ceremony and Compliments, the Japanese finally all came onboard and with just as many Compliments they went into our ambassador's cabin, where a lot of questions were asked through the Dutch interpreter. The first demand was not to shoot without permission and then the Dutch, who were waiting in their boat decorated with a Dutch flag, were sent for. They demanded we turn over our muskets and gunpowder, cannons, and steering rudder, etc. These fellows know how to demand. It was not to their liking that we had dropped our anchor. The old banjos[5] is supposed to be the governor's revisor [inspector] (can also be that he is the governor himself incognito). Finally, the Dutch came on shipboard and bowed at right angles to the Japanese. When the old man, through an interpreter, spoke with the Dutch, they were standing at right angles, immovable, with outstretched hands. The interpreter tried to make Krusenstern understand that he should bow in the same way. The only thing missing was taking him by the nap of the neck and forcing his head down. When this position took too long for Duff, he hazarded to ask the interpreter, "Kan ik all upstaan?"[6] [May I stand up again?] and was given permission.

The Dutch Captain Musketier, who had previously been in military service, did not want to do it and was talking with us. Just as he said, "Wi hebben well caarten, wi wollen se man nit weisen" [We have maps. We don't want them to know it], the interpreter ordered in a loud voice, "Captain Musketier! Compliment maken for de Grote Herr!"[7] [Do a Compliment for the Great Gentlemen!] And as punishment the poor devil had to stand bowed even longer.

Questions without end and everything was written down. When Resanoff tried to use his little bit of Japanese, Duff said that Japanese of rank are only permitted to speak with Europeans through an interpreter. The Japanese drank their own tea and smoked their own tobacco from nice little pipes and acted as if they were at home. They left very late in the night with the promise to take the ship closer to the harbor tomorrow. Seven large boats patrolled around our ship the whole night.

9-3. The first departure of the messengers

Tues. 27/9 When Resanoff came on deck early this morning, he was given honneurs and the drums rolled. Immediately a Japanese boat set out for land to report this event. Duff chided us for the gifts yesterday by saying, "The people here do not deviate from their customs, and they will hardly concede you anything."

Resanoff announced today that he would also take a naval officer with him in case he had to pay the governor here a visit. Espenberg only talks and thinks about fresh provisions. Whether to wear swords or not was an important point yesterday. Mr. Duff doubts very much that Resanoff will be granted permission to travel to Jedo. At five o'clock, the governor sent the ambassador a present consisting of fresh provisions. The present consisted of a basketful of eggs, five chickens, three ducks, fish, rice, radishes, and onions.

At five-thirty in the evening, a big group came out from land. You could hear their big drum from far away: Bum! Bum! Bum!—announcing the Grote Herrn.

The interpreters came onboard and demanded that the ambassador go down to the Japanese boat and meet the representative of the governor. Resanoff rejected this demand, saying that the captain and several officers would welcome the Grote Herrn. Krusenstern and four of us went down to the Japanese boat and paid our respects to the important man, but not à la Captain Musketier. Then a banjos came to see the cabin and chose seats for the distinguished gentlemen. He was presented arms. After the seating order had been determined, the interpreters—several of them were always present—asked if our ambassador would come to meet the distinguished gentlemen on the stairs to the cabin and greet him? Resanoff agreed to this. Now with a great deal of ceremony, large stairs were placed from the Japanese boat to our ship and the distinguished gentlemen climbed up. They were presented arms with drumming. Resanoff met them on the stairs and they went into the cabin. The conference began with the Japanese demand that gunpowder and arms be turned over. After an hour in which yesterday's questions were repeated and several new ones added, the Dutch received permission to come onboard. As painful as it was for them, they once again had to, in our presence, humiliate themselves before the Japanese Grote Herrn by standing at right angles with outstretched hands for over a quarter of an hour while the interpreters, barely audible, lying on all fours, conversed with the Grote Herrn, who were sitting on the sofa in Turkish fashion.

Only the Japanese's breathing in could be heard it was so quiet. The Dutch were Resident Duff, Captains Musketier and Belmer and a Baron Papst, a curious Dutch traveler.

We began, at the request of the Japanese, to load our gunpowder to the very last grain into Japanese boats. After several debates, the Grote Herrn allowed Resanoff, Krusenstern, and all of the officers to wear their swords. They even permitted the soldiers to retain their muskets after a dispute lasting over two hours during which Resanoff, in the presence of the Dutch, displayed a lot of weaknesses. Among other things, Resanoff said that every ambassador had his own guard along, that the Russian Emperor had given him this protection, that his importance did not permit, etc—he got however answers that made us blush. All of the remaining arms were turned over to the Japanese down to the smallest kortik [dagger]. After receiving the gunpowder and arms (The Japanese also wanted the cannons, but Krusenstern got through to them that, since they had taken all of our gunpowder, they could well leave us our cannons. The Grote Herrn agreed to this and

9-4. Kan ich all up staan? [May I stand up?]

9-5. *Ossi! Oss! Ossi! Oss! Ossi! Os! Ossi! Os!*

we kept our cannons). The Grote Herrn took leave with just as much ceremony as when they had arrived. At their orders, we weighed anchor. More than fifty boats towed the Nadezhda with the beat Ossi! O! Ossi! We headed toward the Papenberg.[8] (*See color plates 11 and 12.*)

Resanoff requested of Duff that he help him with business matters. Duff apologized and said that he could not be of service. It was not correct of Resanoff to become angry with this answer, to insist and refer to letters from Holland and to threaten, "I will use all of my connections; they may then do and have done whatever they want to."

Wed. 28/10 At four in the morning, we arrived at Papenberg and cast anchor upon orders of a banjos who had accompanied us in his boat.

Our emperor's letter to the emperor of Japan is said to have been translated into such bad Japanese that it is hard to understand. That's why the Japanese demanded a French translation, undoubtedly then to have the Dutch translate it once again. Resanoff answered, however, he would consider it an honor to translate the letter for the governor himself. "Well thought out," said the interpreter and fell silent. As Duff stood bowed in front of the Groten Herrn, he asked the interpreter very peevishly, because the Compliment was lasting too long for him, "Kan ik all upstaan?" [May I stand upright again?] "Jah! He kan upstaan," [Yes, he can straighten up] answered the interpreter very commandingly. Even Resanoff had to do a Compliment. Our stiff necks did not seem to want to permit such a thing.

The Japanese have geist and knowledge but the strict discipline among them goes too far. Gunpowder is kruit, muskets snaphan; and if Resanoff does not like something, he immediately gets the answer, with emphasis and importance, "Das is Japander Manier?" [That is the Japanese manner] or "Hier mot mien Herr en Compliment maken!" [Here my gentleman must make a Compliment!]

Early this morning, the Japanese excused themselves for not having brought us pork.

We are still anchored outside the harbor. At noon, with Japanese permission, we put on moorings.

At five o'clock, the governor's revisor, actually of the Dutch, an old man and another Grote Herrn arrived in a big boat. The ceremonies were the same. Resanoff had to answer a lot of questions again. Our ambassador requested our ship be taken into the harbor because the leak might have got the gifts wet and they have to be seen to. And our ship needs repairs herself. It cannot be done tomorrow was the answer; because it is an important Japanese festival, and no people can be brought together to tow us in. Krusenstern offered to tow the ship in himself. That was, however, immediately rejected because "Mar! [but] Das is Japander Manier!"

Resanoff requested an interpreter. "You yourself have brought along Japanese," was the answer of the tolk. "Use them!" "They want to but they say, they may not," answered Resanoff. Our Japanese were immediately sent for, were sharply reprimanded, and ordered to serve us as interpreters in the future.

The Japanese's geographical knowledge is better than I expected. The old banjos liked a little English pocket globe very much. Today's visit was much more friendly than the previous ones. At nine o'clock, everyone took leave. When we were intending to take our evening meal, Resanoff invited the remaining Japanese to join us. They declined saying that they had already eaten and requested that we not feel embarrassed on their account. When Krusenstern, however, stayed in the cabin for politeness sake, so that they would not be left alone, one old man asked if it would be possible to observe our evening meal, ate a few canned things, and at nightfall went to his boat, which is stationed next to our ship after he had courteously taken leave and said to Resanoff, "If you should need anything, ask me."

To the right, to the left, behind us, and in front of us are anchored a lot of guard boats which, as the tolks say, are not going to leave their posts as long as we are here.

Thurs. 29/11 Since today is a Japanese festival, no visits were expected. Horner, who had caught a bad cold, decided to prevent further evil by putting on a nightcap and going around the company cabin that way. Resanoff, who suddenly hurried into the cabin, took offense and made a lot of unnecessary noise about it. Resanoff cannot stop his provocation. Otherwise, the day was very quiet.

Fri. 30/12 As usual, Resanoff came rushing into morning tea. (He acts as if he had so much business, that he hardly has time to eat properly.) We were all already sitting around the table, raised ourselves a little and wished our ambassador a good morning. Resanoff thought Tilesius had not straightened up enough and not bowed low enough; thus, Resanoff bawled him out coarsely, called him a coarse, impolite man, and added, "I will teach you manners."

At eleven o'clock, a large boat arrived with an upper banjos [head administrator] onboard. The ceremonies, as well as the questions, were the same, only the person was not. The emperor's letter had to be translated again, etc.

Tilesius, who is never careful, showed the Japanese a drawing of the Papenberg with Japanese boats in front of it. The drawing was immediately taken to the banjos.

Resanoff was angered by our aulic councilor's imprudence, came into the company cabin and made an incredible racket. Krusenstern had, during this period, observed the facial expressions of the banjos, etc. and only found admiration of the drawing in them. In the meantime, noon came. At Resanoff's orders, the meal was served and we sat down at the tables. The Japanese were completely astonished to hear Resanoff making so much noise, since for them patience and calmness are the first virtues of a distinguished man. Resanoff poured his gall over Tilesius, called him, for no reason, and again for no reason, a coarse man, a scoundrel. He called for the guard several times (who was smart and did not come), threatened with lock up and arrest and said, "Now you can no longer refer to your contract. I'll get you yet, etc." A general silence followed this raging.

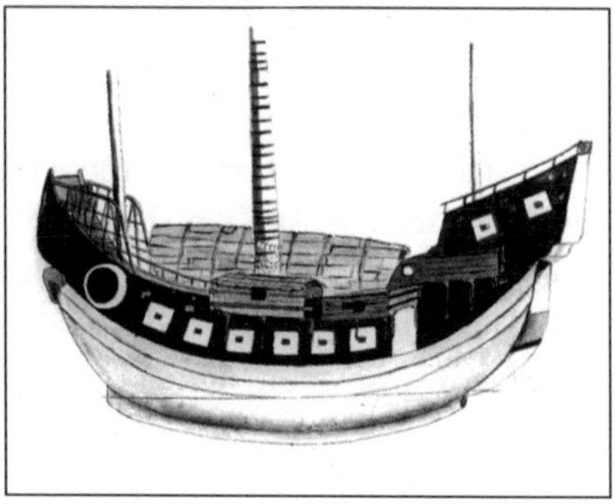

9-6. Chinese junk

After the noon meal, (as if the Japanese wanted to punish Resanoff for his noise) Resanoff had once again to translate the letter to the emperor of Japan. Our Japanese had to dress themselves in silk and were presented. We will not be going to court. Tomorrow is another large festival and nothing can be done. Among other things, the Japanese asked if the emperor of Russia could give the emperor of Japan or the governor of Nangasaki an order of distinction?

We may not row around in our boats.

Five Chinese junks wanted to set out to sea today but had to turn around, because the wind was not quite favorable, since the vessels can only sail with the wind. (*See color plate 13.*)

Horner is still not well.

The guard around us belongs to the Prince Fiesen.

In the evening at six-thirty, the Japanese took leave. The climate here, the pork, or something else is giving all of us without distinction stomachaches and diarrhea.

October

Sat. 1/13 Rainy, bad weather. We cannot for the life of us make heads or tails of this diffuse nation. The Japanese were more than a little surprised when they found out that we had four doctors onboard. Langsdorff is Resanoff's obertolk [head interpreter]. The Dutch told us that one of their ships is leaving for Batavia [Djakarta] on the tenth and promised to take our letters along. Undoubtedly, they will keep their word.

We are lying on our stay anchor moorings. The wind has changed direction and is blowing briskly from the sea. In order not to drift, we had to let out our cable, causing the ship to change its position a little. Immediately, there was movement among our guard. The flotilla that surrounded us weighed anchor and set in motion; and several messenger boats or estafets were readied for Nangasaki to report that our ship had moved, now had her stern toward land, and no longer was exactly in the same place.

Sun. 2/14 We had a brisk wind from the northwest and the sea was rather high. The Japanese flotilla guarding us could not stand the rocking and, for better or worse, all of them had to leave us. Now and again, one of the boats darted out, rowed around us once and hurried back because the waves always landed in the boat. One of these patrols called to us and said they were sorry because the weather was so bad they could not send us any provisions from Nangasaki. (Why then didn't that extensive patrol bring the provisions themselves?)

Resanoff wants to order a table for the emperor and have a map of Japan put in it as an inlay. Tilesius goes around like a dog that has been wet down and comforts himself with the thought that he now has the complete right to back out of the trip to Jedo.

In the evening, a boat came out to us with the news that in case we needed anything, we should raise a flag on the mainmast, and then the boat left us.

An hour later, Resanoff had a flag raised. Not long afterwards, a boat arrived with two Penkin [officials]. Resanoff had several items of food ordered for tomorrow. This boat passed the news on to another boat, turned around, however, and stayed with us for the night as sentinel. We were given the news through the officers that tomorrow is again a holiday and nothing can be undertaken.

I will not soon forget the tolks' expressions when they consider something and don't quite have an answer, "Mar! Upper Banjos well begreift! Mar! Japander Manier nit Permettier!" [Head administrators will understand. But! Japanese custom does not permit!]

Mon. 3/15 In the night when the wind died down somewhat, the guard boats took up their posts again. I have yet to count less than 35 each time.

Resanoff does not feel quite well. Three banjos visited Resanoff today, expressed regret at finding the ambassador not well. Anyway, this visit was just pro forma and of absolutely no use to us. Resanoff had to answer questions until he lost patience, and the more impatience he displayed the more persistently they asked him questions. Finally, Resanoff said, "I'm very sorry that we are treated with so little consideration here. We have already been here for eight days, and we still have not been given permission to go into the harbor. That is not the way in which a friendly neighboring nation should be treated."

"Well, begreift!" [Well understood] said the tolk, "Mar! You could not go into the harbor five or six days ago because your wish had not yet been put before the governor, and nothing can be done without his permission."

Resanoff said, "If we get a storm, then we stand in danger from this position of shipwrecking or having to go to sea." Resanoff said angrily, "We would hardly come

9-7. Prince Fiesen's flottila; guard boat

back since I am not granted even this small request. How can I then expect a good reception at all?"

The tolks became somewhat more accommodating and said, "One would try everything possible to give our ship a safer spot tomorrow, in any case, to bring a more definite answer tomorrow." Then the Japanese left us. Resanoff had also angrily stated that the Japanese make a lot of promises but keep few of them. Probably that is the reason why soon after their departure, a boat arrived full of provisions. The tolks assured Resanoff that the flotilla that guards us has been posted around us to honor the ambassador. Today, the fleet of the Prince Tschikusen arrived, the tolk say, as relief for the guard of the Prince of Fiesen that surrounded us until today.

At eight o'clock, three boats suddenly arrived completely unexpectedly with a tolk onboard. He had been sent expressly "van de Goodheit van de Gouverner" [as the expression of the governor's kindness] to communicate to us the promise and permission to move from our place and to anchor behind the Papenberg.

Golovatscheff, who is now in charge of table, had the strange idea of shifting the tea hour from five to eight. Today, the change was unanimously rejected and the old order for eating and drinking continues as before.

The fresh provisions we got consist of fish, pork, goat meat, eggs, pears, radishes, leeks, turnips, young cabbage, potatoes, etc.

9-8. Prince Tschikusen's flottila

The three Chinese junks that wanted to set sail a few days ago and could not, tried again today in vain to go to sea, turned around but also did not get back to Nangasaki, but were driven capriciously by the wind into a bay to the south. It is quite something that such a large number of people could not control the vessel and only ended up wherever the wind blew them.

The Japanese meal caddie is a very beautifully lacquered cabinet with several compartments in which the courses are put, everything nice and proper, everything fits together.

I became hungry every time I saw a Japanese eat one grain of rice after another with his two little sticks. *(See color plates 14 and 15.)*

Tues. 4/16 Early in the morning, we readied ourselves to leave our spot, completely raised the moorings and the holding anchor. We are not yet heading for the harbor because, as the tolks say, the city is not yet clear. We will now take over the spot where the Chinese junks were. Ships of war and merchant ships can never be together according to Japanese law. Thus, we can only go into the harbor when the Dutch have made room for us. "Well begreift. [Well understood.] Curses!"

The Japanese boats that are to tow us collected at nine o'clock, fifty in number. At eleven o'clock, the banjos together with the mayor of Nangasaki arrived, whom the governor had sent to attend our ambassador. The mayor offered his services to our ambassador, especially as the fulfiller of his wishes if he were in need of anything.

After making Compliments, about sixty boats were ordered to tow our boat and we immediately weighed anchor. (*See color plate 12.*)

The well-tended land, the numbers of boats, the decorations of the so-called forts, and finally the city of Nangasaki in the distance are a very beautiful panorama. We had barely come about five English miles from Nangasaki when once again, at the order of the banjos, we dropped anchor. We were surrounded by boats driven by curiosity out of the city. They all circled our ship, but not a one of them dared come onboard. Now we are anchored behind Papenberg. It's going to take a lot of time before we get to Nangasaki.

Wed. 5/17 Today, Tschingosin's largest boat or yacht went with great pomp from one fort to another.

The governor asked about Resanoff's health today and sent him a box of confections. In the evening, Mr. Duff sent, as he himself wrote, with the permission of the governor, 500 pfund of granulated sugar that Krusenstern had asked Duff for.

The black teeth of the beautiful sex, a sign that they are married, ruins the mouths of the Japanese women; and they must be proud of them because if one of them has black teeth, she always keeps her mouth open. Her hair-do is done with great effort, shines as if lacquered, and has long hairpins stuck through it. Her clothing is very comfortable, one nightgown put on over another, like a book one can open. The Dutch are awakening hope that according to Japanese law, everyone will be given a girl, the officers two and the Captain four, as soon as we have finished trading with them. We have already, ahead of time, subscribed for Krusenstern's four.

9-9. Fine Japanese ladies and naked rowers

We dare not leave the ship and no one may come onboard without permission. It is a kind of incarceration. We are being provided superabundantly with fresh provisions, at the governor's order, as Duff writes.

Ten degrees is the difference between the temperature by day and at night. Everything we have learned about the Japanese has been obtained by using the telescope; à la distance is the only way we know it.

Thurs. 6/18 Today was spent quietly, even though everything around us was alive. Innumerable people are discreetly spending their time on the water. You have to admire the industriousness of the Japanese when you see the very highly cultivated countryside, even the barest highest tops of the mountains are not uncultivated. I am happy to find a nation that, totally without foreign help and influence, lives, as it seems happily, in superabundance; and I do not hold it against the Japanese that they do not allow all other nations, even the Chinese, open admission to their country; so that, as the Japanese themselves say, foreign influence, foreign customs, etc. do not disturb their peace. Japan already has an extremely large number of people. Nangasaki conducts a little trade with China and Holland. Only a few junks and a couple of Dutch ships come every year. The Japanese, aside from one-mast boats, have no trading ships; and despite this the choice here is nevertheless extremely large. The Japanese, through the strictness with which they treat foreigners and even more their natural location, are totally isolated. They do not have to go to war with anyone. The healthy pleasant climate encourages population; and one can say no wonder that it makes giant steps and even increases too much; and despite that no Japanese according to the laws dare leave the country and all of them find a living in this fertile country.

This country's ceremonies are offensive to Europeans. These ceremonies, however, are only exaggerated in the presence of foreign countries. In the short time we have been here we have already seen a big difference in the behavior. The constraints of the banjos were much greater at the beginning than now. They have said that distinguished Japanese are not allowed to speak with a European without an interpreter. Despite this the old banjo, the so-called revisor of the governor, answered Resanoff very politely in Japanese when our ambassador addressed him

9-10. Interpreters

in Japanese, without using the obertolk as interpreter. The Japanese hold us Europeans in contempt and that correctly so. Their first acquaintance with Europeans came through the Portuguese, who misused their friendly reception in Japan, and made the Japanese hate the Christian religion and them. The Dutch, driven by business interests, subjected themselves to all possible humiliations. As a result, what kind of concept can the Japanese possibly have of us Europeans, when they see how much we let ourselves be ruled by passion. The uniformity of the Japanese customs, clothes, habits are sanctified by their age. We have found everything just as Kämpfer described it, including the strictness of the police. All of the Japanese, with whom we have dealt so far know, their geography through the European factory goods; they are becoming acquainted with a lot of unknown things. Their curiosity, thirst for knowledge, displays no insignificant level of culture.

The Japanese are now learning Russian with all their might. Some of them are already greeting us in our mother tongue and asking some questions. Several already can write the Russian alphabet. This learning of languages is the result of distrust and self-interest. They are learning Russian in order to get the advantageous position of an interpreter with the future Russian ships that will be trading here.

Fri. 7/19 Shortly before noon, a boat brought us 70 pfund of meat and said that the provisions ordered yesterday would soon be arriving, also said that the banjos would not be coming out to us today.

A Chinese ambassador had to sit, that is, locked up on his ship for eight months so that the Japanese had time to prepare his reception. If Resanoff is even higher in rank in their eyes, then he will undoubtedly have to wait even longer.

In the morning, about eight pfund of meat were missing. Two boats came express from Nangasaki in order to replace the missing meat, to bring us this trifle.

Sat. 8/20 We got another suitable quantity of fresh provisions. When we asked when the Upper banjos would be coming again, we got the answer, "Not morge, en ander Dag, nit so fast" [Not tomorrow, another day, not so soon]. Resanoff has absolutely no patience. We are sketching, writing, measuring angles, etc.; and the rest of the gentlemen are playing lamouche or gorka and winning their money from each other. The worst that can happen to us is if the Japanese suddenly chase us away without giving us fresh water and provisions beforehand, and if they hold us up with their praiseworthy ceremonies so long that we only can sail next year in September, and it is already so late that we dare not turn back to Kamtschatka in the approaching winter. (*See color plate 16.*)

We had played plumsack[9] with the two Kotzebues for several evenings in a row and again today after our meal chose this game to pass the time (that is with cards).

Since I had watch, I went around the quarterdeck alone and listened to the sound of the whacks being dealt out and enjoyed myself in the light of the moon and the softly shining Japanese lanterns that were burning nearby, despite the brightness of the night, all around us—about 300 lanterns and lights. Suddenly, the game in the company cabin ended for the following reason: Koscheleff lost and was supposed to get plumsack. Several days ago, the Kotzebues had distinguished themselves by giving too hard of blows that got out of hand, if not stopped. Today came the opposite extreme that they hit too softly and the game lost interest. The gentlemen therefore made the rule, that if the one getting hit were dissatisfied, he had the right to give it back. Langsdorff was the first one to take the plumsack in his hand in order to punish Koscheleff, gave him two blows on the hand that were harder than usual. Koscheleff pulled his hand back and did not want to let him give him the third blow.

Then Horner said, "If the rule does not apply to everyone, then we don't need to hit at all."

The game was continued without the plumsack. The game became boring as a result and Horner, who was put in a bad mood by this prudery said, "If the game only consists of hitting, then we could take a stick. It is all the same whether we hit with a stick, plumsack, or quill. If it is a rule of the game, then we have to follow it punctually."

"That is no way of being!" shouted Espenberg and did not let anyone get a word in edgewise by his loud reasoning and moralizing.

That became too much for Horner since the talk was directed at him. He got up and said just as loudly, "I do not intend to have a tailor like you teach me how to live and my skin is certainly worth more than yours." Then they all went their separate ways and the game was over. Langsdorff and Koscheleff had stayed quiet as mice during the whole episode. I was glad that I had not been present.

Sun. 9/21 Shortly after noon, we once again were brought fresh provisions and a tolk gave us some news: According to Japanese laws, we could not buy anything and that the provisions we had received up to now and would still be receiving were therefore a gift of the governor of Nangasaki, that we would be taken to Nangasaki when an answer to the governor's report was received from Jedo and then we could buy everything we wanted to, even get girls, as many as we needed.

At the same time, the tolk asked us not to become frightened when the Dutch saluted, as they did every time they left Nangasaki. And since the Dutch would be leaving Nangasaki tomorrow, we should not shoot. We told the tolk, "We have no gunpowder. You have absolutely no worries. We won't be shooting."

"Ah! ah! That is indeed true!" answered the bald-headed man and all of that by "de Gudheit" and "Belovtheit von das Gouvernör" [the generosity and pleasure of the governor]. He added that since the Dutch would anchor next to us, we should not send out any of our boats. The Dutch themselves have already been ordered not to meet with us in any case.

Every time fresh provisions are brought to us forty people are set in motion. First comes the boat loaded with provisions from Nangasaki accompanied by another boat in which the provider is sitting. These two announce their presence to the imperial guard boat or custom's boat. Accompanied by a guard boat they row to one of the bigger boats with the Fiesen coat of arms and announce there that they are going to come onboard. After all of that they then come out to us. The provisions boat is unloaded. An officer of the guard boat reads the articles off that have been brought and checks exactly that everything is turned over; and after receiving the empty containers, each one, after delivering a report at the big boat, goes back to its post.

No strange boat is permitted without permission through the cordon formed by the Fiesen boats around us. The minutest event that occurs onboard is immediately reported to Nangasaki. The Japanese, who bring us provisions, frightened us with the news that the Dutch probably will be staying on the roadstead for another three weeks before they set sail, and they will hardly be able to tow us into Nangasaki before their departure.

I have seen many a pretty face among the curious girls and women who go around our ship every day. Unfortunately, the pretty mouths are too often disfigured by a row of raven black teeth that, as if bewitched, are always visible.

Mon. 10/22 The two Dutch ships approached us with an endless cannonade beginning in the morning and only ending in the night. The boat that brought fresh provisions gave us the news, that we would be anchoring here for another month and that the Dutch would set out for Batavia in twenty days.

Since we only had a thin cable on our holding anchor, we had it raised today by the longboat in order to attach a thicker cable. Immediately, a boat left for Nangasaki to report our behavior. When we sent the longboat out again to drop the holding anchor with the new cable, again an estafet with the news was sent to Nangasaki. We only had to move and immediately all of our surroundings set into motion.

9-11. Nangasaki Harbor according to Schenitzer

In the evening, the Dutch fired an evening round and we drummed to it. The two Dutch ships are anchored across from the Imperial Guard on land.

The surgeon on one of the Dutch ships had sold his watch without the permission of the governor, (one of the tolks told us) and received a reprimand for it and has not been permitted since then to go ashore. The Ober Hoft Duff received a strict order from the governor forbidding this man's return to Japan. Everything "van de Belivtheit" [at the pleasure] of the governor.

The illumination on land is wasteful and that every night. When Japanese boats left the Dutch boats late in the evening, the Dutch in turn were wasteful with their gunpowder. Probably, it was time for Ober Hoft, etc. to make their Compliments to the banjos. The Dutch do not have any guard ships or boats. Resanoff may consider ours an honor guard. I consider them a sentry that holds us under arrest.

Tues. 11/23 The day passed very quietly. The Japanese haven't the faintest notion that we have charted the entire bay in our time here. That cost us more than a little calculation.

Even though we have the possibility of sending letters with the Dutch to Europe, there is a big question whether the Japanese will allow it.

No meat was brought today. The Japanese were asked why and, as an answer, they laughed in our faces. Resanoff sent word to the banjos that he needed to speak with them and asked them to come tomorrow. It is a mystery to us what the Japanese really think of us. It is possible that the Dutch might well hold a grudge against us.

9-12. Ambassador Resanoff shows himself to the people of Japan. This position is not invented but true.

Resanoff behaves very badly. His behavior when the Japanese are present contrasts sharply with his behavior when they are absent. Our Excellency, in the presence of the banjos, who never lose their composure, is importance itself. They barely have left the ship when our Grote Herr appears in a jacket despite the swarm of boats moving around us that have been able to recognize his face for a long time. Resanoff thereby loses a great deal in the eyes of the Japanese, who observe their etiquette so strictly, and fools away the respect of a nation that has no reason to deny it. Even when the boat with the provisions comes, Resanoff is not ashamed to appear in front of the Japanese in this sailor-like slovenly attire. And he nevertheless knows that the minutest little event is reported to the Governor of Nangasaki.

Even though from the very beginning the Japanese were told that it would be necessary to unload our ship in order to see if the gifts for the Emperor of Japan had suffered in the typhoon and to repair the ship, up until now, there has been no reaction.

Wed. 12/24 At Resanoff's demand, obertolks appeared rather than banjos. Our ambassador complained about everything and demanded that the tolks present the governor with the following petition and demands or report to him: What was the reason for the Russian ambassador receiving no answer? Since he, Resanoff, wanted to write to the Russian emperor through the Dutch and several officers wished to send letters to Europe, he requested that the governor be informed of this. Since Krusenstern's request to visit the Dutch ship was unanswered, then to seek permission, if not the captain then at least one officer with the letters be allowed to be sent to the Dutch, to tell the governor, that since the Dutch shoot salvos in the evening and the morning and we are not allowed to that, this displays bad manners and that the governor has to permit us to shoot salvos or else to deny the privilege to the Dutch, that the governor, for the sake of exercise, should permit us to go ashore, if only on an empty island, that a house on land should be arranged where the gifts for the Emperor of Japan could be carefully stored, that our ambassador should receive more news about the governor's health and if the answer is expected soon from Jedo, that the untertolks should be told not to be so shy and to come on deck in order to receive orders because the bad translations would lead to big misunderstandings. "Yes," said the tolk, "The provisions are all van das Belivtheit [at the pleasure] of the governor."

"We thank the governor very much," said Resanoff. "Furthermore, I hope that he will not prevent us from paying with cash. For two days now, we have had no fresh meat."

"That must be a misunderstanding," answered the tolks, "because since the Russians had shown Kodei[10] and the Japanese so much kindness, it is our duty to return this kindness to the Russians in Japan."

Resanoff then answered, "If the kind reception does not improve from now, then the differences to imprisonment are only minimal and that is not in the spirit of friendship. By the way, it is my duty to return to Russia if my reception is not of the kind that I would hope would please my emperor. Up until now, I am unable to speak of a reception in the spirit of friendship."

Hereupon the tolks took leave and returned to Nangasaki. Resanoff asked in addition if he were permitted to present the governor with gifts?

"No," was the answer. "When the answer arrives from Jedo then we can accept all of the gifts." Shortly before they left, the long-nosed obertolk (Skiseima) said that the ambassador must think that the governor has no ears or is deaf, otherwise he would not ask the same questions so often. Every word is written down that the ambassador has asked or said as well as the governor's answers.

The governor may not do anything until he receives an answer from Jedo. When Krusenstern received permission, through Resanoff, to visit a Dutch ship for the first time, the reason given was paying the Dutch a return visit according to European customs. Several days later, Resanoff requested permission to send a boat to the Dutch ship to deliver letters. When today complaints were made to the tolks through Resanoff that Krusenstern had not received permission to go to the Dutch, the tolk answered, "Mar! The captain wanted to go to make a return visit. If the captain has an additional reason, then we intend to report that to the governor." Thus, these people have written down everything word for word.

At four o'clock, a boat with fresh provisions arrived and two boats with fresh water. They brought only 15 pfund of meat and several ducks. Resanoff therefore had a larger quantity ordered for tomorrow, which was carefully written down by the untertolks, who for the first time had climbed on deck. The untertolks made a Compliment before our ambassador even though he was going around the deck in his jacket. Resanoff was not ashamed of his clothing.

In the evening, the Dutch shot off their evening salvo. Undoubtedly, the tolks have not had enough time to convey Resanoff's demand to the governor.

The obertolk Skiseima said, "The governor is himself greatly embarrassed because he does not know how he is supposed to receive and treat them until the arrival of an answer from Jedo, since this is an extraordinary case and he has no instructions for the arrival of a Russian ship of war and a Russian ambassador.

Thurs. 13/25 Even though provisions had been ordered yesterday through the obertolks, we waited in vain for them. Resanoff called to the guard boat, that he wanted to speak with a banjos and requested he come onboard ship tomorrow. Very late in the evening, the provisions that had been ordered arrived with the apology that they were being sent so late because the governor had been busy receiving a prince who had recently arrived. The untertolk received the following answer from Resanoff. The ambassador requested answers to yesterday's questions and requests and thanked the governor for the things that had been sent. Resanoff would now like to ask that yesterday's hasty invitation of the banjos be taken back; but it is already too late.

Resanoff has to make bonne mien to mauvais heux [a good face at bad fortune], for that is just like the Japanese, that we may ask for anything we want until an answer comes from Jedo; but none of them can be carried out except for food and drink. Until then, we will go neither forward nor backward. The many guards around us are there to prevent anything contrary to Japanese laws from happening; and we, according to Resanoff's threats, will not slip through their fingers if the time becomes too long and we lose patience.

Resanoff is thinking about unpacking the concave lantern mirror in order to dazzle the Japanese with illumination. He could save this childishness until his arrival in Nangasaki. It won't hurt anything anyway, if this children's game is lighted. The Japanese will open their mouths wide in the beginning, stare at us and send an estafet to the governor and that is all. The upper class Japanese are on a higher level of culture than Resanoff thinks. Unfortunately, our ambassador speaks of the Japanese as if of half-savages.

Fri. 14/16 We have had continual nice weather. When we were eating lunch, the obertolks arrived. They brought Resanoff an answer; if we wanted to write, we all had to write a letter together and this letter had to be handed over to the Dutch openly. We would be allowed to go on land and at the same time given a spot. Concerning the salvos in the evening and in the morning, they said, "The Dutch have been our subjects for over three hundred years and therefore could never be compared with the Russians. They have had the right up to now to shoot. Instructions for you Russians do not yet exist. We will, however, see whether the Dutch can be forbidden to do it."

Even though a spot on land has been determined to which we may go, we have to wait once more until a Huis [house] has been built for our Grote Herr and a fence put up around it to keep the people away who would bother our walks. Since we may not write individually, we want to let our friends and relatives know that we are well through our Hamburg correspondents. Every sheet of paper is too small for Resanoff, as if the importance of his letter to the emperor depended upon the size of the paper. In a couple of days, banjos will come to get our letter.

In the evening, Resanoff read to us the letter that he plans to send the emperor. It contains our voyage from Kamtschatka to here with a description of the storm we suffered, our arrival, etc. as usual, very extensive. Now Resanoff wants to copy the letter, so that each ship has a letter, and then to send a copy in Russian to the governor of Nangasaki and to have the letter over and above that translated into German and Dutch. That is useless verbosity without purpose that can only cause the Japanese to be distrustful.

Neither last night nor early this morning did the Dutch shoot a зоря [evening and morning salvo].

- 10 -

Rat Island: Megasaki

Sat. 15/27 The obertolks Skiseima and Sakusabura brought some news, that the place on land intended for us would be prepared tomorrow and that we would be able to go on land the day after tomorrow. The preparations consist of cleaning out an old shed and fencing in the place.

Resanoff handed over two letters to the emperor and a third letter for the governor. Krusenstern wrote a letter to Captain Musketier asking him to address the letter as it is to his wife in Reval. Krusenstern told the tolks this and they liked the idea very much. Resanoff began to talk again about the Dutch firing off their cannons. "No talk! No talk!" interrupted the tolks. "Yesterday was answer." That was as much as to say that the Dutch have not shot any more since yesterday.

Duff, whom Resanoff had sent an offer to pay for the sugar, requested today that Resanoff accept this small token at no cost, and, in case we should need coffee, he could serve us in the same way. Resanoff is in very good spirits and is happy that HE!! has put everything back on track again.

If the weather is very quiet (it is always good), then we have a large guard surrounding us. If a little breeze arises, then we are immediately left alone. Everything with life and breath around us flees into the inlets and hiding places so that they are not rocked unnecessarily. Today in calm weather, suddenly all of the boats left us and went without exception to the place designated for us to take walks. In the evening, they created a big illumination with their lanterns and ignited in addition a big fire even though the night was bright. The following morning they gathered around our ship once again.

Sun. 16/28 The Prince Tschingusen took a ride around the bay, around us. His train consisted of four large and a lot of little boats towing the big ones.

Right after table, two banjos and the obertolks came onboard. They brought along yesterday's letter well protected in a package, sealed with the governor's knot and seal. Resanoff opened the package but had to give the paper ribbon with

10-1. *Tatekiro, Sakusaburo*

the governor's seal to the banjos. He sealed the letters once again and returned them to the banjos who promised as soon as possible to order the Dutch to receive our letters. The obertolk brought Krusenstern the news that Captain Musketier had received his letter and would answer it tomorrow. We are getting provisions regularly now and the governor and Duff sometimes send even little things. Mehle heaks! [Estonian: how nice]

Mon. 17/29 The banjos came in the afternoon to accompany our Grote Herrn on land. Resanoff went in our shallop under the Russian flag followed by innumerable Japanese boats. We put our people along the yards.

Ratmanoff asked the tolks in the presence of the banjos and Resanoff whether girls would also be there. Resanoff found that very funny. The Japanese however took leave by drawing in their breaths and remaining silent.

Resanoff had been on land barely half an hour when he and his suite returned. The banjos went straight to Nangasaki after having given Resanoff the assurance that he could go to that designated place as often as we wished, that is, during the day. Resanoff had been treated with sweetmeats on land at the governor's orders. Krusenstern received a polite letter from Captain Musketier.

Tues. 18/30 One of the guard boats came to ask if we were going on land today. Resanoff sent the answer "Maybe!" That was not to their liking. We finally came to an agreement with the Japanese that, if the ambassador intended to go on land, we would raise a red flag.

Wed. 19/31 Several gentlemen went ashore. Unhindered, Dr. Horner measured the height of the sun from land.

In the afternoon, the tolks brought greetings from the governor and said, "Since the other time, such a large number of people had collected around our spot on land and their curiosity probably was bothersome, in the future, the governor had ordered no one to approach the place without permission, and, since the boat leaked, the governor intended to send three big boats, the first boat for the ambassador to live on, the second for the gifts, and the third for the ballast. Resanoff rejected the offer, and, after a lot of deliberation, half-and-half was determined that after the departure of the Dutch we and our ship would take their position. The gifts should be unloaded there, and, after news was received from Jedo, our ship should be taken to Nangasaki.

We have been allowed to row around the bay. Fosse swore today, when a large lantern was lighted as a test, that Rutibin was the inventor. It is a lantern with a concave mirror made of small squares of mirror. A true piece of childish play that only a Fosse could call important and rare.

Thurs. 20/1 Krusenstern went on land. Up until now, I have not set foot on Japanese soil. There will be time enough for that, since the tolks claim we will spend several weeks more at this spot. The weather is incomparable. Time passes incredibly fast for me.

Fri. 21/2 Every day, the Japanese asked why the ambassador and the captain do not go on land, whether something is wrong there, something that they do not like. The weather is nice, etc. And they always get vague answers or often none at all.

Sat. 22/3 Resanoff went on land. The ceremony was the same as the first time he went on land. In less than an hour, he returned again.

Sun. 23/4 Last night, we had a heavy thunderstorm. The Japanese say the continual nice weather is unusual here at this time of year.

Mon. 24/5 The obertolks brought the news that the Dutch are to sail soon and that the governor will allow us to take over the position where both their ships are anchored, and they made the suggestion to our ambassador that the gifts be unloaded into a Chinese junk. Since the Chinese have a bad anchor, we should give them one of our anchors. The things would then be loaded from the junk into a Japanese vessel and then taken on land. In order to avoid this unnecessary ceremony, everything was put off until an answer arrived from Jedo, and nothing specific was decided.

Resanoff is behaving childishly. He belittles Rat Island [Megasaki] that he hardly visits himself, finds fault with Kibatsch—the name of our spot on land where no grass grows—and wastes a lot of words on totally irrelevant details instead of demands and petitions for more important things.

The water glowed in the evening unusually strongly. That fluid element seemed on fire, so full of shining animals was the surface of the water.

Tues. 25/6 Raw windy weather. The Japanese are predicting strong winds. In twenty days, an answer is supposed to arrive from Jedo.

Appearance must mean everything here, and Resanoff's cursed behavior means that appearance is not in our favor, especially since the Japanese are always on the watch and careful always to be proud toward their subordinates and never to lose their composure. Resanoff shows the tolks and banjos so much honor and makes such an ado and unnecessarily lets them know too much, so that there is nothing left if he should be visited by men of still higher rank. These men have barely left when our ambassador puts on a jacket and is not ashamed to parade around that way.

Wed. 26/7 It seems raw weather is beginning, since colds and coughs generally rule the *Nadezhda*.

Thurs. 27/8 The Dutch weighed anchor. Musketier sailed ahead; Belmer was forced by a calm to anchor next to us. In the evening, Musketier also returned because the wind had become contrary. The tolks brought us the news in the afternoon that we would be towed to the spot tomorrow that the Dutch had left today and said a second Chinese junk would be readied so that we could unload our ballast. Now and again, people go ashore; otherwise, we live very quietly on our ship.

Fri. 28/9 The Dutch weighed anchor in the morning. Musketier was driven into an island and dropped anchor. The wind rose stronger and stronger, and he drifted or was driven a pretty piece. Belmer returned a short time later and anchored next to us. Musketier set sail again, passed us, and anchored opposite the imperial guardhouse. Apparently, he had lost an anchor since he had a spot missing.

He had anchors ready to cast out and over and above that a warp on the bow.

The banjos came at three o'clock. We weighed anchor immediately after their arrival and were towed farther in the evening. We cast anchor again between the two imperial guards—that was the fourth station.

They are all very clean. Every time a Japanese pays his dues to nature he washes himself very well. Instead of handkerchiefs, which they don't have, they use whole packs of paper and blow their noses with them and then fold the paper carefully together and throw it into their extremely wide sleeves.

Sat. 29/10 The Dutch set sail again early and finally left Nangasaki. We put down moorings. The tolks who came to us today confirmed our suspicion that Musketier had lost his anchor. Tomorrow, the Japanese want to take our rostrum on land to Kibatsch—that was the main reason for the tolks coming. The junk is stranded on shore. With the next full moon, she can be put afloat again. When the tolks come alone, they are quite communicative and friendly. We took down all unnecessary riggings today.

Sun. 30/11 Put our rostrum into the water. Everything was taken down so that the bare masts are all that are standing. Krusenstern sent me on land to get the rostrum dry as quickly as possible. That was the first time I stepped on Japanese soil. It's a shabby spot the Japanese have given us. Toward evening, Krusenstern also came ashore to bring me my noon meal. Thus, I am the first one to lunch in Japan. We went onboard for the night.

Mon. 31/12 We are sketching and writing, measuring, and observing more in the short time we have been here than the Dutch accomplished in three hundred years.

November

Tues. 1/13 The tolk brought the news (that always van de Belieftheit von das Governör [as an expression of the governor's kindness]), if it should be necessary, the whole crew could be provided with bread. Naturally, the offer was accepted. When the tolk made the suggestion whether we could not take our ballast to Kibatsch, Krusenstern gave reasons not to, and then the tolk planned to ask the governor if we might not unload our ballast on the shore opposite the ship.

Wed. 2/14 A tolk took a leather sack full of our flour on land in order to try to make bread from our flour, and, since the junk had floated with the rising water, the Chinese tolk came to ask for an anchor from us for her.

The Japanese swords are exceedingly shiny and sharp—a joy to look at.

Thurs. 3/15 The big Chinese junk was towed up and anchored just in front of us. The colossus lies like a camel in the water. Then the tolks came riding up to us and requested that Krusenstern inspect the junk. I went with Krusenstern and Bellingshausen to take a look at the monstrosity. No ship so illogical, fat, and big can exist elsewhere. It had four winches to raise the sail. The masts were inflexible and thick and long, the water containers—large boxes—and the cabin so bad and low that it would be almost impossible to live in it, and that is the cabin the Japanese intended to be used as our ambassador's apartment.

Krusenstern told the tolks, "You have to move the junk farther away or else we will collide."

The tolks answered, "Japanisch Manier, nit nier" [Japanese manner, not closer]. We then left, and barely had we gone onboard when that machine came toward us and forced us to let out our anchor cable because we were in danger of suffering damage.

The Japanese saddled us with that junk for Resanoff's amusement, because, when the answer comes from Jedo, we will be towed to Nangasaki and be able to unload our cargo more comfortably directly on shore. It also can be that the Japanese thought the junk would save us from sinking, since upon arrival, Resanoff had so insistently complained the *Nadezhda* would leak and the gifts would be in danger of getting wet.

Resanoff felt offended that the Japanese wanted him to live in the cabin on the junk and gave his tongue free reign against the tolks and told them with coarse words how impolite they were, and finally told them that he wished to speak with the banjos. That Resanoff cannot temper his behavior in the smallest way.

Fri. 4/16 The tolks came, acting very friendly, with the apology that they had not seen that the junk's cabin was so bad and that the answer from Jedo would be here in about eight days.

Thus, the junk would not be needed any more because we would be towed closer to Nangasaki. The tolks promised to tow the junk away today or tomorrow, and our hearts were lighter with this news, because the Japanese wanted our captain to take responsibility and answer for that filthy building if he would accept the junk.

Sat. 5/17 The junk was towed back with a lot of good effort to the spot from where the Japanese had towed it to us, and immediately afterwards our anchor and cable were brought to us.

Sun. 6/18 Raw, cold weather. You would think we are destined to live and die anchored before Nangasaki surrounded by land and water.

Wed. 9/21 Horner repaired Resanoff's broken watch. When he brought it, His Excellency said, "Write the year and the date on the leaf in the watch so that

I can remember your friendship." Resanoff has either cheated Horner or wants to cheat him. He is not so sweet toward him for nothing.

Fri. 11/23 We are even getting firewood by weight. That's how exact the Japanese are. We are going to calculate the height of the moon in Kibatsch.

Sat. 12/24 The obertolks came with the news that the answer from Jedo cannot be expected for another fourteen days because the governor had received a courier from Jedo yesterday, at whose departure the courier from Nangasaki had not yet arrived. The roads are said to be bad and the rivers swollen. Then the tolks said, "Mar! Van de Believtheit von das Gouvernör!" [but! as an expression of the governor's kindness], so that the ambassador would not find the wait too long and, to protect the ambassador's health, the governor was having a little house with a storeroom at the water's edge cleared, where the ambassador would have all possible comforts until the answer came from Jedo; and at the same time the gifts for the Emperor of Japan could be put under a roof. For diversion, the ambassador can go to Kibatsch on our ship.

De Believtheit von das Gouvernör at the same time sent the message that he was doing everything he could, even more than the strict Japanese laws allowed, to show our ambassador his good intentions. As soon as an answer however arrives from Jedo, the ambassador ought to make a brilliant entry into Nangasaki. In my opinion, it's all excuses. That impatiently awaited answer from Jedo arrived long ago. Soon again, there will be a lot of work drawing, measuring angles, making observations, writing and describing. In all fairness, we have to admit that the Japanese are feeding us well. We get enough to eat.

Sun. 13/25 The obertolks came to Resanoff with the request. It was necessary for the ambassador to ask the governor in writing to be taken to Nangasaki, because of his health, to live on land, and that our ship had to be brought closer to land because she had suffered damage in the storm and needed repairs. When Krusenstern asked the tolks, "when do I go to Nangasaki?" old Sakusaburo answered, "Ik soll first een moie Frau for him sieken" [I should first find him a beautiful woman].

Mon. 14/26 Today was that old sinner Philip Ivanovitsch Kamentschikoff's name day.

Tues. 15/27 I went with Horner to Kibatsch, where we, unhindered, measured a basis with the measuring chain and calculated a large number of angles. If the Japanese did not notice today that we are mapping the area, they never will.

Wed. 16/28 Today, the officers of the Imperial Guard changed with a lot of pomp. I have got into sketching flags to the point that I will soon have a whole book full. (*See color plates 17 and 18.*)

Thurs. 17/29 The playing of lamouche has stopped because Golovatscheff, firstly, lost a very great deal and, secondly, twice caught Fosse cheating. That is the reason these two men, who were otherwise very intimate, are now totally at odds.

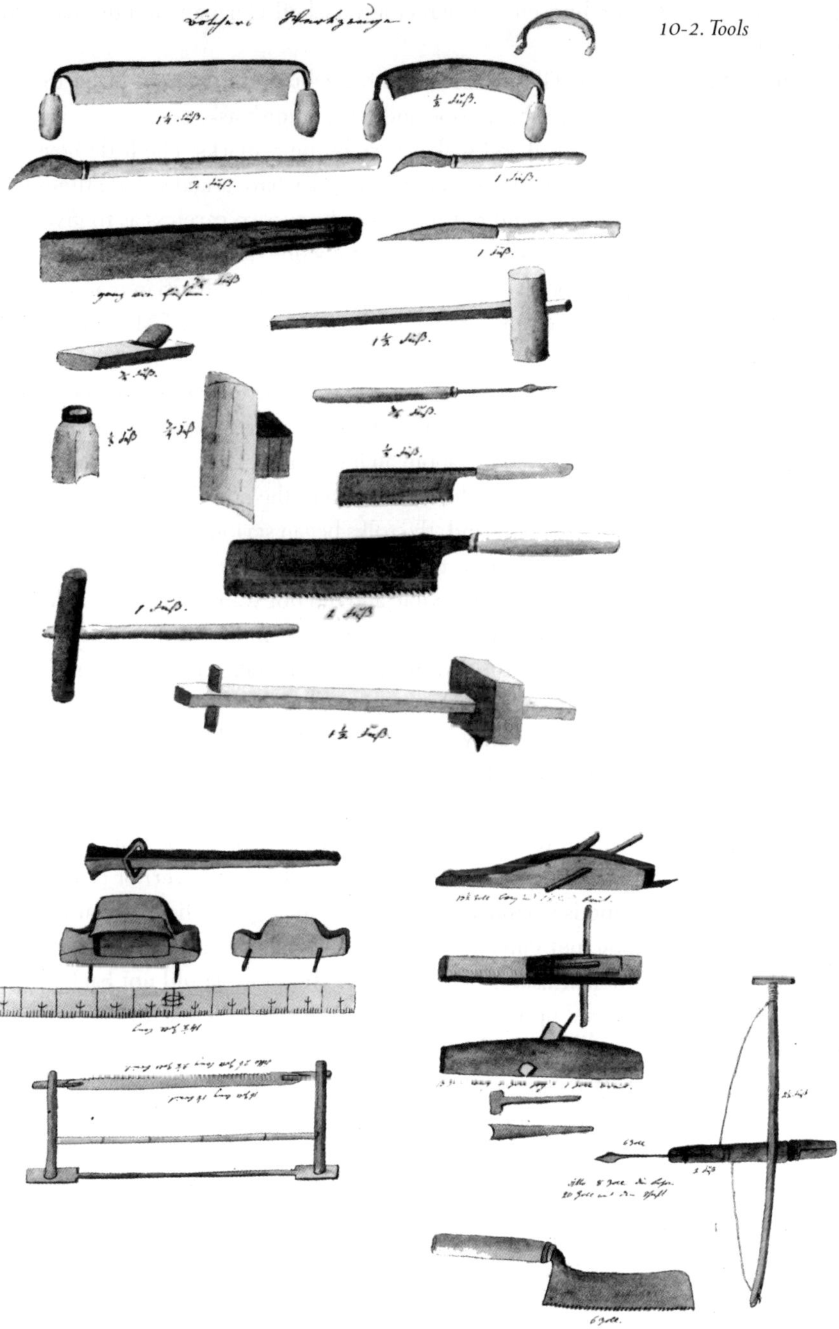

10-2. Tools

Fosse had taken it upon himself to teach Golovatscheff German, and this has also stopped.

Fri. 18/30 Councilor Tilesius and Otto Kotzebue got in a fight off to themselves in the gun cabin. For what reason and why, I didn't ask.

Madsuira is a sneaky rascal and makes very biting remarks. The little boys on the Japanese boats that bring our provisions every day have asked several times for buttons and gotten them. I could not find out who was so careless as to give out buttons. Madsuira had seen it and today said totally unexpectedly, "It's a bad thing to do something the banjos have forbidden. That is the nice Russian manner. You are going to have to behave differently when you are on land, etc." Madsuira is not totally wrong!

Sat. 19/1 Even though van die Believtheit van das Gouvenör was announced that the ambassador was to get a house on land, nothing more has been heard of it.

Sun. 20/2 Krusenstern told me about an incident that probably can influence Resanoff's future reception. When the tolks brought the news that a house would be readied for the ambassador on land, the tolks began seriously talking about our ambassador's honor guard, which for them from the beginning has been insufferable and repugnant. Resanoff was inflexible and did not want to leave a single soldier of his eight-man guard behind. "What can eight men do? That's my honor guard, which the emperor gave me. I won't let them be taken away from me," said Resanoff and added even more absurd objections.

Sakusaburo answered completely logically, "You have indeed brought the people along from Kamtschatka, and we have no need to fear either your eight soldiers or even fifty or more. We know all too well that you are not in a position to threaten us. It is, however, the appearance we have to avoid, especially since it is against Japanese laws to bring foreign soldiers on land." "The governor is so kind," continued the tolk, "and is permitting you a three-man guard. If you want to take the other soldiers along, put Pinken [?] in their hands. They may keep their swords. They have to leave their muskets behind." Since Resanoff would not back down and, stiff-necked, insisted upon his honor guard, the tolks left with the promise they would report everything to the governor.

The governor won't be able to decide the matter himself, will send an express messenger to Jedo; and Resanoff, through his own fault, will have to wait several weeks longer.

In addition to that is the fact that our emperor's own wish was that we should use a merchant flag in Japan, since the purpose of the whole expedition was trade, and, despite his efforts, Resanoff got no soldiers from St. Petersburg, because it was known that the words "foreign soldiers" offended the Japanese.

Early today, His Excellency came raging on deck with his servant behind him, who, having gotten up an hour later than his master, should be punished. I called a couple of subalterns—that they had their cats [-o'-nine-tails] so quickly at hand softened Resanoff—lucky for the servant who stood there turned to stone. As if

10-3. Kibatsch drawn from land

fallen from heaven, Resanoff remembered in time that it was Sunday and generously pardoned his faithful servant.

Mon. 21/3 Even though Resanoff sent for first the tolks and then the banjos several times during the day, no one appeared. They have had enough of his caprices.

Espenberg is and stays a strange fellow, who is too old to change his offensive habits. Langsdorff is the greediest man I know, and Fosse is a swine.

Tues. 22/4 Mien Herr [My Sir] Skiseima, a Japanese by birth, and a high-ranking obertolk appeared. In answer to the question when the promised house would be ready, Resanoff got the answer, "About five days." Resanoff reacted very violently when the tolk began again to talk of "van der Gutheit" [from the generosity] of the governor.

"Die Gutheit of both governors goes so far that I cannot make heads or tails of it and do not know how I should understand die Gutheit."

Skiseima asked a lot of questions and talked a lot but never got to the point. In order not to have made the trip for nothing, he measured the large mirror and our ship's kitchen and asked whether the ambassador would also take the kitchen ashore. When we said no, he asked how many casseroles, kettles, and pans the ambassador would need in his kitchen, etc. The tolks will probably come again in five days to inquire if the ambassador drinks tea or coffee, if he wants to sit on chairs or benches, if he'll be wearing shoes or boots, if he requires Japanese servants, if and how many girls should be held in readiness for him, etc. To fulfill all that will take another eight to ten days. God grant us patience to bear Japanese and Russian caprices and ceremonies.

Fri. 25/7 Nice clear skies. Because of the name days, we quite often have a drunken ship's crew. Today, we discovered that one foreshroud was torn and a long crosstree broken, probably during the storm.

Sun. 27/9 We are waiting for the tolks in vain. Resanoff will hardly make the trip to Jedo. He acts too absurd and behaves in his violence with too much scorn toward the proud Japanese.

Mon. 28/10 Even though Skiseima was here today, we are as smart as before. The only thing we learned is that he will bring an answer in four or five days for sure. He said today, "Japan is a small island and has small Manieren; Russia is a large land and has big Manieren. Therefore! it is taking so long for the house. The house would have been good enough for Japanese, but for the Russian ambassador a lot of things had to be changed."

Wed. 30/12 Everyone gets up at eight o'clock on the *Nadezhda* and goes for tea and coffee. Resanoff rushes in! Everyone gets up and pays him a Compliment. After tea, until eleven o'clock, everyone is busy with sketching, writing, reading, translating, drilling, correcting, etc. The quiet is only broken once in a while by remarks and discussion. When schabash is whistled, everyone goes on deck. Espenberg teaches fencing. The motion each person makes consists of jumping and hopping over marks. At three o'clock, everyone is busy again, and all work until tea. After tea, activities become irregular. The music forces us to listen to it and whistling, singing, noise, and card playing hamper work. After the evening meal, one after another disappears, and by 10:30 everyone is already asleep. Thus passes one day after another.

Since our wine has been rapidly disappearing, especially through the loss of one and one-half piepen the rats tapped off, it was decided today not to drink any more wine but rather to save it for worse times. Instead of wine, in the future we'll get the larger portion of brandy. Good, too!

December

Thurs. 1/13 Resanoff carries on truly childishly as if he wanted to tease the Japanese. Today he ordered guards to stand on the gangway, so that the Japanese could get used to the sight of our soldiers. Up to now, we have not had guards on duty there; that has to alarm the Japanese seeing a grenadier suddenly going up and down the gangway (schkafut). Resanoff will certainly be asked for the reason, and he will have trouble finding an answer. *(See color plate 19.)*

Sat. 3/15 Lots of news! Tamachatschira, the tolk with glasses, and several others brought the news that the ambassador's house has been ready for two days. The preparation for transporting the ambassador over to it had taken time, and that's why he (the tolk) was sent the news only today. If it were agreeable to the Russian ambassador, he could move the day after tomorrow or in two days.

Resanoff answered, "I have to have the house inspected first!!"

"To whom does the ambassador intend to give this mission?" asked the tolk.

"I'll send four or five officers," answered Resanoff.

Then the tolk continued, "A large boat is ready to take the ambassador to Nangasaki, and I have the task of asking how many soldiers will accompany the ambassador ashore." He then wrote the number down, did not ask, however, if they would take their muskets along or not.

When the tolks asked why the ambassador wanted to have the house inspected first, Resanoff answered sharply and peevishly, "If a man has been cheated once, then he takes care not to fall into the trap a second time—that is what happened with the Chinese junk." In answer to the tolks' question why the ambassador was angry and in such a bad mood, "If I had expected a reception like this, I would have turned around and gone home immediately after my arrival."

Among other things, the tolks asked if the officers would be carrying the gifts when they were unloaded, who would be standing at the helm and steer the boat taking the ambassador to Nangasaki, etc., etc. All of these questions were answered exactly.

Tomorrow or the day after tomorrow, gentlemen from the ambassador's suite are to go ashore to take a look at the house. Before departing, the tolks observed our sentinels very attentively, as if they were something new, but did not, however, utter a word.

Sun. 4/16 The tolks came at twelve o'clock. Tamchatschira, the three-haired one (with glasses), was along. They informed the ambassador that the big boat would come tomorrow to pick him up.

"The house has to be inspected first!" said Resanoff very sharply and insolently.

"The banjos are coming tomorrow," said the tolks in a very well-bred manner, "to pick up the ambassador. If the ambassador likes the house, then he can stay there; if not, he can return to the ship. The big boat belongs to Prince Fiesen and will be rowed by sixty rowers."

Finally, after a long debate, the tolks and Resanoff reached an agreement. Early in the morning, several officers would inspect that house and the ambassador would be taken there in the afternoon.

Mon. 5/17 At sunrise, the whole bay went into action. A lot of decorated boats collected around the houses and they stood in rows at the forts. At eight o'clock, the banjos arrived with Compliments from the governor. (The Japanese always have two banjos, two gouvernörs, two tolks, etc. That is their plural.) They reported to Resanoff that the house was ready and that it was up to him to send several officers to inspect it. Then they said, "It is against Japanese laws for foreigners to go into the city. Even the Dutch, as long as they have been living here, are forbidden to do so. However, as soon as an answer arrives from Jedo, the Japanese will prepare a larger house for the Russian ambassador."

At nine o'clock, the ambassador's suite went on land to inspect the house. The banjos stayed onboard and said very humbly that the governor would not be in a position to fulfill the Russian ambassador's requests without permission, that is, concerning repairs to the ship and a definite answer concerning the ambassador himself. Resanoff answered, "The Russian requests are not great. Friendship and freedom are what we wish. The way the Dutch and Chinese have let shackles be forged and conducted themselves is something Russians will never understand." Thereupon, the Japanese related how much damage the storm we had suffered had also caused in Japan.

At eleven o'clock, our gentlemen returned from their inspection with great praises, and immediately after our meal our ambassador set out with his entire suite, guard, standards, etc., from the *Nadezhda* in the large, superbly lacquered boat belonging to the Prince Fiesen. (May God grant forever.) All of the boats were ready to go before Resanoff climbed aboard, and all of the other boats followed the big ship like a current.

Suddenly, it was lonely and empty on the *Nadezhda* and around us. I had the feeling that I would finally have some time to recover. I am continually afraid that Resanoff has already spoiled everything with the Japanese. The well-bred tolks have even become cheeky.

Tues. 6/18 Since we had received the order to unload today and since no Japanese boats were in sight, Krusenstern ordered us to load our longboat with riggings, and at nine o'clock she set out. She had barely shoved off from our ship when she was surrounded by Japanese boats and conducted back, and our captain was given instructions not to send anything ashore from our ship without a banjos or his permission. At two o'clock, two banjos came and with them an unusually large entourage. The Japanese almost crowded us off the ship. They brought two boats which were bound together and five Japanese longboats to be used to transport the gifts on land. We did not waste any time and immediately began to unload and load. The large boats, which were bound together, were dispatched on land with the enormously large mirrors[1] with second mate Spolosoff and artillery sergeant Raefski and at the request of the banjo with a sailor in each one of the smaller boats. The captain gave the oldest Kotzebue a written report and sent him on land. Resanoff is said to have been very angry that none of us naval officers went ashore with the gifts and goods. Fosse was exceedingly surprised that we dared to dispatch the gifts ashore without him.

Resanoff and his entire suite walk around their new quarters without shoes or boots in bare stockings because all of the floors are covered with neatly woven shiny straw mats, and they boast, "That is the Japanese Manier!"

In answer to the question how the mirrors would be transported to Jedo, the tolks answered, "Last year, we carried a live elephant to Jedo, which the Emperor of China had sent as a gift to our emperor. Why should we not be able to carry mirrors?"

The tolks have prescribed the following procedure for our ship. In order to send even the smallest object ashore we first have to notify an unterbanjos, on a guard boat, that we would like to go to Megasaki or send something there. The unterbanjos will report this to the governor. The governor will give an oberbanjos the order to come to us, and only then, accompanied by an oberbanjos, may we go to or send something to Megasaki. "That is the Japanese Manier," was the concluding sentence.

Resanoff's behavior, since he has been on land, borders on insanity, as everyone claims.

Friderici, Koscheleff, and Fedoroff share one room; Fosse, Schemelin, and Langsdorff share another; and Resanoff has a separate bedroom. The sentry only stands at the door for the sake of appearance and has no purpose, since the house is said to be overflowing with Japanese, who come and go as they please. Everyone goes about in stockings, and, if Resanoff goes outdoors during the day, even ten times, then just as many times, drums do him the honors. Actually, in reality, no Japanese Manier is as absurd as our ambassador's newly invented ceremony.

Resanoff was angry that Kotzebue brought him the report and not one of us officers.

Wed. 7/19 We unloaded all of the goods belonging to the embassy and some more additional parts of the riggings. Today, our ship was as full of banjos, tolks, and Japanese as yesterday. Every day one of us has to go ashore to dejour to receive goods and put everything under a roof, to look after things needing repairs or to be mended. Bellingshausen went ashore today.

Thurs. 8/20 A brisk northeasterly probably prevented the banjos and tolks from coming out to us; therefore, our work stood still today. One more reason to take our ship closer to Nangasaki. Bellingshausen brought the following news from land. Resanoff says, as a predicate for all the gifts, "Everything was made in Russia." When the golden elephant was unpacked, London was written on the case. The tolks who were standing there saw it and asked why that. "In Petersburg," said Resanoff, "they write London on things made there and the other way around in all of Europe."

Resanoff bothers less with the Japanese than his own subordinates, and, with almost everyone, he has already had disagreements and strife. Schemelin received a coarse reprimand because he dared to keep his hat on his head in his (the Grote Herrn) presence. He goes into every cranny of the houses and magazines, into corners where the Japanese and his suite are ashamed to follow him.

The Japanese are saying the answer from Jedo should come in eight days. When none of the officers wanted to believe it, the tolks said that the tolks to accompany the ambassador have already been appointed. I don't believe it.

Life on shipboard is now pleasant and quiet. The plague of the embassy is now raging on land.

Fri. 9/21 The banjos arrived only at eleven o'clock in the morning. The day was raw, cold, and cloudy, mixed with hail and snow and made the Japanese and us too frosty. Krusenstern went ashore for the first time today. Resanoff, who greeted him in a very friendly way but with disdainful importance, was wearing shoes himself and claimed Krusenstern should remove his shoes before entering his room. "No!" said Krusenstern, "In that case, I prefer to give you my report over the threshold and go or travel back onboard in my shoes."

A Grote Herr from Jedo is expected, and a large house is supposed to be ready for Resanoff. One of the small boys, to our Resanoff's great joy, reached for his: c..ck. That was water on the mill wheel for our great swine because he once again has something he can talk about. No cake is baked in Megasaki without the banjos immediately hearing about it.

The governor sent his regards and requested Resanoff to let him know if he needed anything. Thereupon, Resanoff answered that, for the time being, everything in his house was fine. "There are indeed so many little things one needs, and I don't want to trouble the governor who has already bestowed much kindness upon me."

"You need girls?" interrupted the tolks, who had also noted his weakness. "As many as you want and need will serve you as soon as we receive an answer from Jedo." After our Grote Herr had told smutty jokes for a time and had the tolks tell smutty jokes, the Japanese said, "The ambassador will have to give a ball later for all the ladies of pleasure in Nangasaki," and Resanoff is already happy about the sensation the ball has to arouse.

Sat. 10/22 It was my turn to go ashore, "to de Wall" [the rampart] as the tolks call it. I arrived in Russian Desima [the Dutch factory island], i.e., Megasaki, at eleven o'clock. The house is clean, light, and nice and also the storehouse. The house is so cold and airy that the drafts blow around all of our ears because the season has become raw. His Excellency was in a good mood. Friderici and Koscheleff left for the ship, and in their absence I found my stay somewhat boring. Our cannon were unloaded today and sent on land. Resanoff was present when the Japanese workers carried our anchor and cannon from their boats on land. The ease with which they carried those heavy things surpassed our expectations; nevertheless, Resanoff could not let well enough alone and needled the Japanese about their fortifications and maintained that they were only for show and without cannons.

The discipline and order among the Japanese are wonderfully great. A lot of paper is being filled up with registering our load. On shipboard, at the landing in Megasaki near the magazine and the main guard, each has its own registry.

Friderici and Koscheleff had barely left when Skiseima came with the news, the awaited Grote Herr with orders from the Emperor of Japan had arrived from Jedo. Therefore the tolk demanded that Resanoff, at his interview, should bow and stand before him as Duff did. That did not go down with Resanoff and he said, "I am much more eminent and important than Herr Ober Hoft Duff, because I have the complete authority of my emperor to conclude trade agreements with Japan, to declare war, and to make peace, and he cannot do that."

Skiseima's demand that Resanoff, during the interview with the governor, should bow before him on all fours and sit on mats did not go down with Resanoff either. He said, "I'll take my chair along."

"That won't work," said the tolk.

"Then I will also be satisfied if I can sit next to the governor on the same mat," said Resanoff.

"That is contrary to Japanese laws," said Skiseima and pulled a lot of written documents out of his archive (his wide sleeve) and proved that Portuguese and English ambassadors had all bowed and crawled in front of the governor. Nothing could soften Resanoff up and the tolk took his leave.

Not long afterwards banjos, came with the news that by the grace of the Emperor of Japan the Russian ship was to be granted permission to travel closer to Nangasaki, so that she could have a more secure anchorage. After mutual expressions of thanks, Resanoff said, "I have an explicit order from my emperor to do everything according to the Japanese ways, to adhere to all laws, but especially not to transgress the honor of the Russian nation and the Russian emperor. I have a great opinion of the emperor of Japan and expect only good of him." Then the banjos were entertained with wine and coffee and the elephant, electric machine, and large mirrors.

In the evening, Resanoff conveyed the order to me, that we should weigh our moorings early tomorrow morning, because the *Nadezhda* would be towed tomorrow before evening to Nangasaki. I of course communicated this order to Krusenstern.

The tolks wanted to know the purpose of the beautiful ivory vase. Resanoff answered totally indifferently, "It is a rarity." The hole in the big mirror, said that characterless man, was used by the ambassador to plug a hole in his purse. Resanoff enjoys making the Japanese look ridiculous and bantering them and doesn't suspect that actually he himself is the plastron. He said to Skiseima, "When are you going to add an even higher bamboo palisade (to the already high one)? They can indeed still peek into Megasaki, etc."

Skiseima remained silent and looked at him with a mien as if he wanted to say, "перестань шалить" [stop being ill-bred].

Sun. 11/23 The weather was so bad that we were afraid the Japanese would not keep their word. We had barely weighed our moorings when banjos appeared, and at two o'clock in the afternoon we set out on our trip with forty towboats and anchored several hours later in Desima (the Dutch place of residence) opposite Megasaki (Resanoff's residence) before Nangasaki.

We had barely cast anchor when the swimming guard around Megasaki left, but we retained ours. A tolk said, "That was proof that, through the report from Jedo, our ambassador would be permitted, according to his charge, to travel to the residence." The tolk smiled while saying this. I would have bet he was lying, since the guard around our ship can also guard Megasaki. Krusenstern wanted to send a boat ashore, "No!" said Sakusabura very guilelessly "The harbor is closed on all borders, and, since there are no banjos here, no one can be admitted to Megasaki." Last night, a Chinese junk arrived, and not long after us another one was towed past. Both are anchored in our neighborhood.

The Japanese eat a lot of radishes, hang them in bundles on trees to keep them for the winter. The trees look like black alders in bloom. We were mistaken for a long time, until we used a spyglass to be sure they were bundles of radishes.

Mon. 12/24 Very early today, we heard our drums on land, a trio drumming with Chinese and Japanese copper plates. The Chinese junks were totally unloaded today. Boxes and crates were thrown helter-skelter like sacks from the junk into the haul boats. Chinese and Japanese swarmed all over. Five junks are expected these days. The rats have increased so much that they are almost eating us up.

Today our officers stayed on land longer than the Japanese thought necessary. Under no circumstances may someone from the ship sleep in Megasaki, nor can someone from land sleep on shipboard without having obtained permission from the banjos. Therefore, a tolk went to Resanoff and said, "Since the banjos would like to set out for home, we request the ships' officers go onboard."

Resanoff answered, "The banjos have indeed been ordered to wait and to stay as long as we need them. Why then are you in such a hurry?" A short while later, the tolk came again with the question whether the ship's officers would depart from land before nightfall or not. Ratmanoff then thought it advisable to take leave.

Tues. 13/25 We unloaded the rest from the hold. Now we won't get to see banjos on our ship so soon again. (I was wrong. There were no Chinese helping unload the junk.) When a junk arrives (that's the Japanese Manier) all of the Chinese are taken on land. The Japanese take over the junk, unload it, guard it, and load it full again, and shortly before departure the completely loaded junk is again turned over to the Chinese. That is the reason, while unloading crates and pots, baskets, and sacks, etc., all are thrown into the boats like *old junk* [sic] (old ropes hacked up). The Chinese, in the meantime, are being entertained in their detention area with good food and girls.

Now, by the permission we received, we need to raise a flag only when we want to send a boat ashore, and the extensive procedure is no longer necessary because of de Gudheit von das Gouvernör. We are however totally forbidden to go to Kibatsch.

In the afternoon, in the hold of our ship, we killed 200 big rats with the heaviest Kamtschadal ballast. We threw baskets-full overboard. Large hawks collected in droves and fished the dead rats out of the water. It was a merry chase.

Krusenstern dined at noon with Resanoff and returned accompanied by Koscheleff, who wanted to spend the night with us. Through oversight, it had been reported that the full number of men was present. A Japanese boat came out to us later, demanding that a sailor had to sleep on land instead of the absent Koscheleff, so that the number was complete, they took a sailor along to Megasaki. Now everything was in order according to Japanese Manier. Even though a great many couriers have arrived from Jedo and Nangasaki with orders and assurances and accompanied politeness and good manners as Japanese laws permit, nothing has been said about Resanoff's trip to Jedo.

Wed. 14/26 Langsdorff came onboard with Romberg. He was in a hurry for absolutely no reason (this creature of our Grote Herrn) to get back on land and did not even bother to ask Koscheleff, who had spent the night on our ship, if he wanted to go along. This disobliging behavior is ripening among our embassy's lot.

In Japan, you have to have patience. In accordance with Resanoff's pretensions, one of us officers delivers a report from the ship every morning. We willingly do it to prevent vexation. Resanoff is full of whims and seems to be impatiently waiting for an opportunity to unleash his rancor and resentment at us. On land, he sometimes behaves so that you cannot make heads or tails of him; is he crazy, or isn't he? He is petty with little things the Japanese generously bring us. Daily, we turn red and are embarrassed by his behavior and nevertheless can do nothing about it.

Anecdote: Often in the afternoon, when Resanoff is drinking tea with his officers, the banjos on duty on land send a message to Resanoff requesting a little cup of tea. Usually, they get none because Resanoff says, "Don't spoil the banjos!" It is the same thing with the (truly enlightened) tolks, who stand there when our ambassador and the banjos are handed tea and who, for the same reason, get nothing. If, by chance, there is an extra cup and a tolk asks for it, he gets the same impolite negative answer from Resanoff, and, in reality, we are living at the expense of the Japanese.

The day after Resanoff's arrival in Megasaki, the gifts were taken on land. Resanoff, who is always in a bad mood, wanted to have all of the gifts and valuables unpacked all at once. Fosse (his man in everything) explained the impossibility of doing that. But talking did no good; he soon wanted this or that. Finally, the quartal officer (Fosse) lost patience, even though he otherwise always apes Resanoff's words, and coarsely told him the truth that time and added, "If you want to have things all at once, then take them yourself into your keeping. I have no more patience left for your whims."

This unexpected answer made Resanoff fly into a passion. He fought and argued loudly with Fosse in the presence of a lot of Japanese. (They are said to have quarreled like fishwives and babbled some things from their school of knavery in their hot-headedness.) Thus was Resanoff's entry into Megasaki, actually his entry into Japan.

After this strife, Resanoff—dogged by rancor, for, if he had given his rancor more reign, Fosse would have blabbed even more from their school—found no peace in his four walls. He went out among the common Japanese porters, so that both Russians and Japanese were struck by it. Since Resanoff, in laudable courtly manner, always carries his nose up high and made room for no one, it was no surprise that he was taken hold of on all sides, because he got into the middle of a lot of porters who had more to do than to make room for our fool. Finally, Resanoff, bent, pummeled, and shoved and thumped, went back into his house.

Schemelin (Schemelin!!! Schemelin???) made clear to him the unseemliness of his behavior. Resanoff reacted very nastily toward his well-intended advice or this kind of moral. Happy to have found an object of his rancor, he let his rancor run rampant to his heart's desire, cursed, abused, and insulted his *supercargo* [sic] for an hour. Then he was consoled.

Since he has been on land, he repeats almost hourly—he has repeated to me, Bellingshausen, and several others, "I'm doing the right thing with the Japanese . . . I'll cope with them—if we only keep peace among ourselves and no new incidents occur."

The chamberlain's key that he never takes off attracts a lot of attention from the Japanese. The Japanese forget the ambassador's person completely because of the golden key. In the beginning, as soon as he appeared in Megasaki, he had an entourage of curious people behind him admiring the chamberlain's key. That amused Resanoff, who said, "You have to be popular," and called the Japanese's attention to his key even more by wagging his most worthy backside back and forth very indecently and, to make it even clearer, adding pantomime and calling to the curious, "Keiser Kammer! [Emperor Chamber] Keiser Kammer! Keiser Kammer!"

Many modest Japanese turned away with facial expression as if to say, "The Emperor of Russia has bad taste indeed!"

Friderici and Koscheleff, who wanted Japanese pipes, asked Resanoff for permission, since the governor indeed permitted the tolks to bring pipes and tobacco for him and our Japanese, and, since Resanoff allowed it, they ordered both. The next day ten pipes and as many little tobacco pouches and a reasonable amount of tobacco were brought. The tolks took everything straight to Resanoff and said, "Since yesterday, the ambassador had ordered them, the governor was sending the order as a special Believtheit."

"Who? Me? I have not ordered anything!" said Resanoff excitedly and sent for all of his officers, reprimanded them all without exception in front of the Japanese and said, "I'm going to order the Japanese not to listen to anything you say and not to fulfill any order you request and to impress upon them and request of them solely to execute what I personally order, tell them, etc."

Koscheleff and Friderici correctly took responsibility for this sharp reprimand and answered Resanoff by saying, "We have to request of Your Excellency not to burden us with any orders that you are convinced ahead of time will not be fulfilled. It does Your Excellency little honor thus to weaken the *Credit* [sic] of your officers, especially since the pipes and tobacco were ordered and brought with your permission." (If this black soul meets resistance, then he immediately becomes pliant.) He therefore tried to repair the damage with a dense smokescreen of words, and, since that did not work and he took delight in his rancor, the *Nadezhda* had to be at fault.

Resanoff said, "I am continually afraid of new incidents from the *Nadezhda*. They are beginning to defy me again, are disobedient, and have only mutiny in their heads, etc. I will not be treated like a fool for a second time and therefore have already taken other measures."

These words startled Koscheleff and Friderici, and the latter said, "Is not Your Excellency the one who has now started the strife and discord? Can you really complain in the slightest way about the captain and the officers of the *Nadezhda?* His Excellency has said more than you can take responsibility for, etc."

The entire incident ended with conflict. Resanoff reprimanded Friderici, accused him of not showing his superior proper respect, that he neglected him, etc., enjoyed quarreling and criticizing, and that was why that strife survived. Resanoff, who himself may feel and know that he has blabbered too much to the Japanese without considering enough what he is saying, without paying attention to the consequences of his foolish eloquence and feels he has said a lot of things for which he cannot take responsibility without giving a denial, chose the following way out in order to blame others. He complained about a poor tolk, vilely tongue-lashed the interpreter Voloksisoimon, blamed him, saying he cheated him and painted him black; whatever he said he didn't translate correctly, etc.

The tolk answered very coldly, "I am a tolk bound by oath. If the ambassador so desires, then I will translate everything I have to for the ambassador into the Dutch language and deliver it in writing with my seal as signature to the ambassador for his perusal and revision." Thereupon, the tolk went to the banjos and complained on his part. The banjos had their presence announced to Resanoff, and after many Compliments, the whole matter was amicably regulated as a misunderstanding. An hour later, the banjos had their presence announced once again with a request, "One should please show them the golden elephant."

Resanoff sent the answer, "Not now, but in the evening." In the evening, Resanoff sent a message to the banjos, "If you wish to, you could come now to view this miraculous animal."

The banjos answered the invitation, "We do not want to see it now!" This answer forced Resanoff himself to go to the banjos and extend a personal invitation and to beg his pardon. The banjos were so polite and well-bred that they went with him to view and admire the gifts.

Thurs. 15/27 Through the banjos the Governor of Nangasaki has requested Resanoff to arrange the gifts, so that if the Grote Herr sent by the Emperor of Japan in Jedo should arrive, they could take a look at the gifts more easily and comfortably. Resanoff said in answer, "The house in which I'm living as ambassador, except for the magazine filled with riggings and casks from the ship, is too small. Therefore, I request a larger, more suitable apartment so that I can fulfill the governor's wishes. (You need to know that the greatest part of the gifts were already in the house, and there was still enough room to arrange the rarities in it) As far as the transport to Jedo is concerned, I'm not going to concern myself with that," Resanoff told the tolks, "but will leave that totally up to you Japanese."

Today, Duff made Resanoff a gift of a beautiful lacquer stand. Fedoroff, who told us about it, praised the beauty of the Japanese lacquer. The Japanese assess this stand as worth 500 *Dollar* [sic]. That is probably a price which the Japanese addiction to exhibitionism may well have put on it.

Today, we shoveled all of our ballast from up front to the back and found that the bung of the front stem caused the leak. The caulking was totally fusty and incapable of preventing water from pouring in. We repaired the damage with force and are happy to have found part of the leak.

Fri. 16/28 It was my turn to take the report to our ambassador. Krusenstern gave me the additional task of asking Resanoff to request paper, copper plating, copper nails, etc. There are things that simply have to be repaired on the ship—and in what manner Krusenstern should make his request, with a report or orally. Resanoff laughed about my choice of words. "Report" and said, "If your captain wrote a Billiet [memo] that would suffice." (For sure, Resanoff would have made a big racket if Krusenstern had not had me ask him this question.)

The gates around Megasaki all have locks on the inside and outside that are taken off only when our boat goes ashore and are locked again immediately after we leave. All of the keys are in different hands. If our ambassador needs anything, he has to notify a guard standing at the gate to send for a tolk, who now, unlike earlier, may only go to the ambassador with the governor's permission.

Stake upon stake is being driven deep into the water around Megasaki. It is uncertain when the trip to Jedo is to be and very doubtful whether it will ever happen. Resanoff has designated the stand or lectern from Duff for the dowager empress. It is very nice. The woven portrait of our emperor, the woven bouquet of flowers, the rugs, pitchers, and shawls are expensive gifts; and the Japanese like them very much because they are useful. Discord crushes the knees of every good mood among our ambassador's suite on land.

Anecdote: Count Rumanzoff gave Resanoff, before his departure from Petersburg, a horn to take along, which Resanoff called a unicorn, that looked like the horn of an incredibly large billy goat. Rumanzoff had claimed that the Japanese desired this kind of horn very much and asked Resanoff to take it along, show it to the Japanese, and find out if that were true.

Upon our arrival in Japan, Resanoff gave the horn to Schemelin and ordered him to show it to the Japanese and to report what the Japanese said about it and what expression they had on their faces.

On the day of our ambassador's departure for Megasaki, Schemelin used the horn as a walking stick. The unusual shape and decoration caught the Japanese's attention. The tolks, who had to view and to inspect everything, were there immediately, viewed and inspected that remarkable walking-stick, showed it to the banjos and several Japanese, and gave the horn back to Schemelin with the words, "Heil moi" [very beautiful].

Yesterday, Resanoff happened to ask about the horn, after he had been discussing business matters with Schemelin for a time, and probably was angry about his stupidity. He asked Schemelin what he had done with the horn, since it was not to be seen any place, and why he had not carried out his orders. "I have," answered Schemelin, "shown it to the Japanese; even the banjos have seen it and given it back to me with the words, 'Heil Moi.' "

"You did not tell me about that," interrupted Resanoff angrily, bawled him out, cursed him "подлец ебиснаматьб солдатами в перед нушник посадить велно" [dastard, wretch, order the soldiers to stick their heads into the privy], etc.

Schemelin, angered by these insults said, "You are making too much out of something that is not at all important, because it is neither a rarity nor can it be used as an article of trade."

The mercantile interpretation of his curses completely provoked Resanoff. The argument became so heated that Schemelin missed by a hair getting a whipping, because they cursed each other like fishwives, until Resanoff finally threw the shameless store clerk out of his room and got the object of his anger out of eyesight. During the evening, Resanoff's whole suite was gathered in Friderici's and Koscheleff's room. Schemelin drove away his low spirits and entertained the others with a harp which he played quite well, and, in order to make spirits happier, the group drank a glass of punsch. Fosse and Schemelin were besotted. Suddenly, Resanoff came into the room, cursed Schemelin anew in the most despicable way, and said to the others, "Don't give this drunkard any more punsch. The old sinner is already so drunk he can hardly stand up." Schemelin tried as he might but could not convince Resanoff of the contrary. Nothing helped. Resanoff forced him to put the harp away, drove him to the door, and ordered him to his room to sleep off his drunkenness and to guard in the future against such an inexcusable way of disturbing a Russian ambassador's peace and quiet.

Quite a bit of time had passed calmly and quietly, and, since it was getting late everyone was preparing for bed. Suddenly, Resanoff entered the room and said, "I am afraid of that drunken man. He can, drunk with courage, do God knows what, damage the expensive gifts and cause us all an unpleasant night and perhaps do, God knows what. Order two soldiers to get dressed and stand guard duty for the night at Schemelin's door, to take precautions to prevent all kinds of trouble." The order was carried out immediately and reported back to the ambassador, and he was wished a good night. No one noticed when Resanoff went to bed, since he wandered around the rooms, as if possessed by the devil and cursed to himself until late at night, and "everyone heard" [illegible].

The two guards did not let Schemelin through the door and held their gun butts in front of him [illegible] with Schemelin [illegible]. Resanoff, who had heard the dispute from afar, came into the room just as Schemelin, [illegible] foaming from rage, his wrath left him and turned into desperation. He ripped his cap or English wig from his head and stamped with his hands and feet as if he would have [illegible] but rather [illegible] a beautiful rug belonging to the gifts and other things lying in the entryway [illegible]. He would have gladly killed Schemelin if he could

10-4. Resanoff; arrest; Schemelin

have gotten him. He, however, [illegible] had in desperation fled from Resanoff. The next day, Fosse did footwork for Schemelin, and Resanoff forgave him generously with a glass of punsch. The scene of reconciliation is said to have been utterly ridiculous and a counterpart to the whole quarrel.

Our good goat had to die van de Believtheit of the governor because his Believtheit did not send any fodder for it. We threw the blessed one overboard. Now he is insisting, in accordance with a praiseworthy Japanese ceremony, that the dead goat be sent back on land even though the tide has long since carried it away.

Today, we found a leak, a borehole that was completely loose and covered only with copper. The borehole had been put in the wrong place for a bolt that had been hammered in next to it.

Sat. 17/29 Unpleasant weather. In the evening, two junks arrived. These clumsy vessels are all as if from one mold, and, upon the threat of death in China, it is forbidden to change or improve anything in the way of building the riggings or sails. They are outfitted as if the Chinese had racked their brains in order to make the junks quite clumsy.

Sun. 18/30 Romberg asked when the Grote Herr would come from Jedo. Skiseima answered him, "Perhaps in one, perhaps in two months, maybe, he can come earlier."

The tolks allotted a quite good spot for us to take our longboat ashore for repairs. We have been working in the hold like in a mine putting the iron from below on top of the ballast because the iron is to be left in Kamtschatka. This work would have held us up in Kamtschatka, and we have time enough here. If the iron is on top of the ballast, it will be easy to unload in Kamtschatka, and, since we have nothing else in the hold but ballast, we have enough room and the hope to finish with the work in a few days.

Mon. 19/31 Friderici and Koscheleff visited us. Resanoff's peculiarities are making life difficult for the two. Before dawn, Resanoff makes a racket, and for better or worse the entire suite has to climb out of the sack. Often, Resanoff shakes them awake himself; otherwise, he usually sends the soldier Monakoff and his servant Alexander to wake the gentlemen. The result of this getting up so early is boredom.

A few days ago, a Chinese junk saluted very early in the morning. Resanoff was still in bed (and his conscience not pure). With unbelievable yelling and noise, everyone in the house was suddenly awakened by Resanoff, who had believed the *Nadezhda* was in a gun battle with the Japanese. (He must have dreamt it.) When the gentlemen had all gathered, ripped from their peace and quiet for no reason and yet again for no reason and were standing in front of Resanoff, he told them the cause.

Friderici made the following remark, "As long as the Japanese are still shooting, we have nothing to be afraid of. If they, however, erect a gallows next to our house, then we have more reason to be afraid."

This remark angered Resanoff so much that he was ill-tempered for the whole day. Today, Koscheleff, in order to flatter Resanoff and get his permission to come onboard had to sacrifice a whole hour of his time, listening to Resanoff's empty insipid, tasteless stories and tirades. Nothing can be obtained with that man in a straightforward manner.

The tolks came onboard in the afternoon and showed us the spot for our shallops and for repairing our longboat. Today, with a lot of trouble, we put up our stove in the company cabin. Ratmanoff lazed around, and his insipid, lazy, acting important is unbearable. If you ask him something, he does not answer. If you don't ask him, his criticizing is endless.

Tues. 20/1 Yesterday and today, Duff entertained us with his illumination in honor of the New Year. In the morning, I took two live rats on land and watched them being killed by the electrical machine. Everything on land is as usual, and Resanoff unfortunately is not the width of a hair more reasonable.

Wed. 21/2 We put casks on our anchor rope to keep them off of the dirty soft bottom; our ropes cannot take much; they rot in the mud, not in water.

Thurs. 22/3 Krusenstern went on land this morning and returned onboard in the afternoon with rain, a storm, and some news. While Krusenstern was there, the tolks visited Resanoff and, after having made their Compliments, told him the following news privately, as something that may not yet be announced officially. The governor of Nangasaki has issued a proclamation that the Russians are to be considered friends, and that is the reason why Prince Chikosen's flotilla left Nangasaki today (the flotilla consisted of some forty big Japanese boats), that eight days ago the Kubo Sama (emperor) had sent a messenger to the Daireo (religious leader) in order to consult with him about the Russian embassy and that in about a month our ambassador would receive a decisive answer from Jedo. Let's hope so.

The Japanese have sketched the Russian eagle, and the tolks assured Resanoff, to keep him in a good mood, that the Japanese would put the eagle in mother of pearl on tobacco boxes and make them popular in Jedo. As a secret, one tolk said, "The Kubo Sama wanted to give the Russian ambassador one of his coats (which all have the coat of arms woven in them), one of the great signs of honor in Japan and even much more important," said the tolk, "than if the emperor would give someone three of his women to sleep with." Resanoff wants to, if the tolks' rumor is not a figment of their imaginations, to ask our emperor for permission to cut the coat of arms out of the garment and sew it on his coat, so he can wear it that way.

The tolks, chatting out of their school, have told how Duff sent for a tailor and ordered a magnificent Japanese nightshirt with which he plans to honor our ambassador. Perhaps Duff asked the tolks to say this in order to find out how Resanoff would react to a similar gift. The tolks are exceedingly useful men for the Japanese government to send for finding things out and to ask questions, since only in the presence of a banjos, is whatever a tolk says irrevocable or meaningful. Those high-placed officials always stay out of the game and never have to give a dementie, since the tolks are responsible for everything. One of the tolks very secretly put a well-made, quite nice tobacco pouch in Friderici's hand with the words, "a heil moi [very beautiful] woman sent it," asked him however not to display it because otherwise he (the tolk) would be beheaded. This secrecy and way of giving is something they all do. How happy they would be to be rid of the force that ties their hands so that they may not trade as they see fit.

The copper plates here are very small and thin. Thicker and stronger ones would have to be ordered in Meako, and they would not be finished for three months. Copper nails are not to be had here.

Fri. 23/4 The Japanese said that Duff entertains quite often. Their mouths watered as they named the following dishes: terk [Venice treacle] poultry, squash, duck. A rooster from here measured with a ruler, including its neck, was 26 zoll tall. The Japanese have given our gentlemen on shore a dog that, with the Russian cat, symbolizes the friendship between Russia and Japan. They do not trust each other.

Sat. 24/5 Since the place on land where our longboat is supposed to be repaired does not have a bamboo fence around it yet and no guard house, the spot is not yet ready, and we have to wait a couple of days.

Sun. 25/6 During the Christmas holidays, Krusenstern and most of our officers dined with Resanoff on land. Romberg, Bellingshausen, and I stayed onboard and invited the pilot's mate, master's mate, and artillery sergeant for the noon meal. We had to drink toasts to our stupid guests, if any drinking were to be done; therefore, we all stood up with a little shove from the table. We consoled ourselves when we saw that our comrades, who returned onboard in the evening, had got further in drinking than we had.

Mon. 26/7 At Krusenstern's invitation, Resanoff dined on our ship at noon. Resanoff's inclination for ceremonies caused us to doubt whether the Japanese would let him come. He did come flying the ship's flag and left the standards behind. We put our people along the shrouds and had the pleasure of seeing His Excellency climb on shipboard in a good mood. Drinking to the group's health with good wine soon made our company quite happy; and our people, who did not let themselves be left behind, were not less so. Resanoff played the open-hearted one and gave the besotted courage with the following plan, "I'm ready to sacrifice myself for three years. I'm going to stay alone here in Japan. Travel on, and complete your instructions. Here in isolation, alone, I'll await a second expedition to pick me up."

We could say whatever we wanted to. It did not help. Resanoff remained steadfast in his intentions. I thought to myself, "Is the Believtheit of the Japanese going to allow it?" The swaying of hands, yelling, shouting, singing, and laughing had attracted a very large number of Japanese boats around our ship. They took in our noise but remained very quiet themselves. Even though it was the express wish and order of the Japanese that none of our boats travel around after sunset, Resanoff with his suite, although very late, were permitted to go on land without being held up.

Tues. 27/8 Only Romberg, Espenberg, and Horner went ashore for lunch, even though Resanoff had invited our captain together with all of his officers to dine at noon. Since this absence did not burden His Excellency's finances, he will pardon our absence. We will get to hear enough reproaches. We cannot get used to Resanoff's climbing around in all of the Japanese sentry rooms and crannies, even though it happens almost daily.

We pulled our longboat on land today. To our surprise, we saw that the bottom was overgrown, hand-thick, with polyps and sea grass. It covered the boat like fur. How necessary it was to pull our boat on shore and repair it.

On both holidays, Friderici and Koscheleff slept onboard. I was never close with Friderici, but we had, through Resanoff's behavior, distanced ourselves from each other. Today, Friderici began to explain things to me, his behavior, and, even though never at odds, we reconciled. I have judged Friderici too strictly and often done him injustice. He has a very difficult position as the ambassador's cavalier, and appearances were often against him without his being at fault.

Wed. 28/9 Resanoff is trying everything to move the Japanese to make us acquainted with the fair sex here, won't get anywhere before an answer comes from Jedo. Today, Duff, secretly through our ambassador's tolk, sent us Dutch newspapers from September and October last year. Of course we found little that was new in them. That the tolks like to let themselves be used for smuggling and know how to do it is illustrated by the careful and correct delivery of these newspapers; even though each time they come, even if alone, they are always accompanied and guarded by two antonis (officers). A Japanese does not even trust himself.

Thurs. 29/10 Resanoff showed me Duff's letter in which Duff calls the way in which he sent the newspapers a démarche. He considers himself sufficiently rewarded if he has done His Excellency a favor and adds, "He should not give me a reciprocal gift for the stand, since especially His Excellency has had time to get to know how the Japanese think, etc. My only wish is, to convince His Excellency that I have done and will do everything in my power to prove my readiness to help. In the future, I'll not neglect giving you all possible news, etc."

Fri. 30/11 Our departure is still so far away that we shudder at its length. We are now busy with repairing our boats that have all been pulled on land.

Sat. 31/12 Friderici and Koscheleff visited us and stayed the night. The Japanese order demands that in their stead two of our sailors have to sleep on land every time. Koscheleff, who always has mercury in his body, did not give us any peace and quiet. We had to await the New Year. Even Krusenstern had to believe in it and was ripped out of his peace and quiet. Koscheleff, who has a gift for satirizing, played the role of the banjos, tolks, and our ambassador so amazingly that he aroused real admiration, and it was earned.

After the rindo had struck two o'clock and we had drunk several rounds to our health, everyone retired to his cabin, and that was the end of the New Year's Eve.

- 11 -

January 1805

Sun. 1/13 We all went on land and wished His Excellency much luck and happiness in the New Year. During the noon meal, Resanoff had wine served, and, in the midst of hail and gusts of wind, the wine tasted even better! The various kinds of wine and drinking of them frequently caused us, when we took leave and arrived on the *Nadezhda* at five o'clock, to all have little lights lighted in our little attics, which means we were all somewhat drunk. Not long after our return, the sailors came into the company cabin and moved us to give them several bowls of punsch for their wishing us the best.

This event was rather noisy, but, after the sailors had left, we had a total sweep dance in the company cabin. Sergei Ivanoff, one of our sailors, who had been punished for disobedience, was the cause and beginning of the strife. Horner and Bellingshausen argued about that story. Both got hot. When they were at the point just about to reconcile and to come to terms, Ratmanoff stuck his nose into their argument with coarse, stupid jokes and prevented the reconciliation, irritated the heated heads even more, and put them, without intending to, at each other so that Bellingshausen finally took after Horner with his fists. I threw myself between them in time and luckily was able to prevent a fistfight.

Ratmanoff decided at the wrong time to play captain lieutenant and to show his authority. He found in me an equal opponent who answered him word for word. As hard as Horner and Bellingshausen had been at each other a short time before, reconciliation quickly followed when they saw Ratmanoff and me involved in an even harder dispute or rather strife. And the service I had done for them a little while before they now did for me by reconciling me with Ratmanoff. We had barely shaken hands when Romberg and Bellingshausen were at each other because Romberg had said to Bellingshausen, "I find myself in the situation of having to avoid you like fire and to be careful around you, because I don't like being hit in the face, and, if I have anything to do with you then, I put myself in the same situation as with Dr. Horner, with whom you were just quarreling."

Both agreed to my playing mediator, and, after a long, hard argument, we were all reconciled and satisfied that the noise was over and emptied a glass of punsch. This confusing business was still not finished. Golovatscheff came into the cabin and made impromptu accusations against Ratmanoff, brought up old stories, especially with Romberg, and got us all involved in a general quarrel that ended at one o'clock, when we all went to bed in a bad mood with rancor in our hearts, because the last quarrel had no beginning or end. Golovatscheff was the most personally irritated, and he had got to hear the most truths and abusive words, most of them from Romberg.

Mon. 2/14 Everything that happened yesterday has been forgiven and forgotten. Things were better last evening on shore. To avoid quarreling, the brotherhood, to make things better, also to drive out rancor, drank so much that they were incapable of misbehaving. Early this morning, I saw on my finger, which I had cut badly, that I had drunk my portion of aquavita. Instead of sticking the English bandage on the cut, I found the English bandage on a healthy spot, and the finger was not bandaged. Indeed, the wound had been left to take care of itself and was open next to it.

In the evening, we saw—and I for the first time—an eclipse of the moon, a phenomenon that the Japanese greet with ringing bells, pounding on plates, and bamboo cannons.

Tues. 3/15 I have begun to fill the empty hours with algebra and astronomy, at least, in as much as drawing up maps and sketching leaves time for them.

Wed. 4/16 We put the *Nadezhda* on her left side in order to caulk her and repair ruined copper plates. When we were seated at table, our small boat from shore came with the news that the captain and the doctor should go on land as soon as possible. Since this invitation came at the order of our ambassador, who requested great speed, we all held our breaths and impatiently awaited Mr. von Krusenstern's return.

The reason for our captain and our doctor being so hurriedly required to go on land is as follows: Madsiura, one of our Japanese, who has always acted as if he were better than this comrades and did not want to serve our ambassador as interpreter upon our arrival in Japan, got a reprimand from the banjos because Resanoff had complained about him. Madsiura took the reprimand so much to heart that he became ill from grief. After his recovery, he became, as a result of his restless nature, a little too noisy on board the ship. When he saw that, contrary to the banjos' strict orders, little Japanese boys had been given buttons, Madsiura became afraid that Resanoff would complain about him once again, resulting in his becoming quiet and introspective. Madsiura could be heard only when there was strife or arguments among our other three Japanese, when he played mediator and settled the dispute. Madsiura, in an introspective, morose mood, left the *Nadezhda* and followed our ambassador to Megasaki. On shore, this Japanese lived together with soldiers in one room. Our Kamtschadals were already so used to the strife and bickering of the Japanese quartet that they took no more notice of it, especially since they did not understand the Japanese language. Today, Madsiura and Schafei, the squint-eyed one, got involved in a hard dispute. One of the soldiers had shaved shortly before and left his shaving blade lying on the table. Madsiura very calmly picked up the shaving blade from the table, bound a rag or cloth around it, so that it could not snap shut, stuck the knife against his neck and hit it several times with his balled fist on the handle of the knife driving the knife into his neck. Sergeant Andreeff, who was present in the room, heard the suicide's groaning and rattling, sprang in the nick of time to rip the knife out of his throat in a stream of blood and, beside himself, ran with the terrible news to Koscheleff, who immediately informed our ambassador. Resanoff ordered the Japanese sentry be sent for immediately and also Krusenstern and Espenberg. The Japanese atoni (officer), leisurely, with the usual Japanese ceremony, examined and listened to the chain of events; only then did he send an express messenger with his report to the banjos and for a Japanese doctor.[1] At this time, Krusenstern and Espenberg arrived.

Espenberg, as well as anyone else, was not allowed to approach the wounded Japanese. For a long time, Madsiura lay, swimming in his own blood, surrounded by Japanese sentries, left to himself, until finally the Japanese doctor came and had the wound in the throat washed with warm water and ordered him, as medicine, to swallow the white of an egg. When Romberg asked Madsiura what the real cause was for his wanting to commit suicide, Madsiura answered in a broken voice, because he could not speak well with the blood flowing, "I owe Russia so much gratitude. My comrades have brought me to this." He had already been able to speak coherently with banjos. The heavy loss of blood has left him weakened.

Today, Resanoff finally received the long-awaited dressing gown but with the following condition: The dressing gown that Duff intended for Resanoff had been taken to the governor. There the Believtheit had inspected the dressing gown and had it completely resewn; that is why our ambassador got it only today. Mr. Oberhoft Duff is not allowed to give presents of Japanese material; therefore, the Believtheit von das Governör was sending the dressing gown to the Russian ambassador as if it were from him, and he was giving it to him as a present.

The tolks told us, in addition, especially Skiseima, that in Japan, people go crazy and commit suicide. An overheard rumor may have played a part with Madsiura, for Skiseima said, "According to Japanese law, no Japanese, whether by accident or by chance, who has been outside the country for some time, may see his relatives and friends and acquaintances again. Those who have returned end their lives in a house surrounded by bamboo stakes, a kind of prison, and are never free again."

Thurs. 5/17 Resanoff, who, due to yesterday's event, would like to be rid of our Japanese, told the tolks today, "I want to send the Japanese to the governor."

"No!" answered Skiseima, "That is not possible. When we asked for our fellow countrymen, you did not give them to us. That was reported to Jedo. Now we can only accept the Japanese after we have reported your present desire to Jedo and receive orders from there that we are to receive our fellow countrymen whom you have brought back."

Kodei, who returned to Japan with Laksmann, is said not to have come out from behind bamboo stakes put around his house since that time. That is what the tolks say. I do not believe them.

Langsdorff, who has been working on an air balloon for weeks, tried out his first experiments with it today and let it climb over the houses on a string. The balloon, with a Russian double eagle sketched on it, looked quite good.

The Japanese tolks visit our patient every day, each time with a different tolk, who asks the same questions trying to catch him in contradictions. That's the Japander Manier the tolks told us.

Fri. 6/18 On Three Kings' Day [Epiphany], I went on land with the report. (This daily trip on land with the report is the only communication between us and Resanoff.) The dressing gown Duff wanted to give our ambassador and the governor gave him, was, although very long, made with extremely short sleeves. Resanoff, who received the tolks shortly afterwards, had on the dressing gown, complained about the shortness of the sleeves. The next day, Skiseima appeared with news that the other governor would send the ambassador another dressing gown. (The whole affair with the dressing gown comes from Resanoff's daily complaints that it is too cold and drafty and that he is freezing. The Japanese had already brought him a coal pan, and now they were supplying him with dressing gowns.) Resanoff, always in a bad mood, is angry about the Japanese blindly patrolling around his room without seeing anything (today, Resanoff is the popular one but not tomorrow) and said to them, "Set down here or over there. I don't like such swarming around." Resanoff said to Skeseima, "What good are all of your dressing gowns if I'm making no headway with the main reason for my being here (with intense anger). I'd gladly give fifteen dressing gowns if I could buy myself out of this prison."

Skeseima, to make amends with the irritated Excellency, began to talk about a lacquer manufacturer, whom, as he said, the governor had given permission to wait upon His Excellency with samples. At this news, Resanoff was as if transformed, happy as a child, and forgot his conceited vexation with this, for him, pleasant news.

Resanoff immediately ordered two hundred snuffboxes, etc., etc., etc., of everything, a lot, a lot. Skeseima, who could not and dared not answer, turned to Friderici and praised the governor's Gutheit. Friderici answered him, "Those are only details. There has been no discussion yet of the main matter." On the same evening, the dressing gown that had been promised was brought, and it, for the moment, reconciled His Excellency with all of the Japanese. Resanoff has a habit, more and more often than we his subordinates, of complaining about our imprisonment and asking everyone who is standing around, "Isn't that the truth?" To his chagrin, everyone agrees with him. (Resanoff would like to get the following answer out of us, "Where, Your Excellency is, can that be a prison for us?")

Yesterday, when the tolk was there about Madsiura, Koscheleff and Friderici said, as if with one mouth (in answer to Resanoff's usual question, "Isn't that the truth?"), "If it indeed were that way, then we would, one after another, go crazy like Madsuira and slit our throats!"

Irritated by this answer, Resanoff turned away and said poisonously bitterly, "Dog feet, if I don't send you all back to the ship."

Duff, with whom Resanoff is conducting secret correspondence (something totally to his taste) through the tolk Sosoimon, assured Resanoff in his last letter that he (that is Duff) is not in a position and dare not reciprocate, that he would, if possible, try to get our ambassador samples and prices of Japanese goods, that however a two-hour oral conversation could throw more light on the whole matter than correspondence that could not be conducted with enough secrecy and that he hoped sooner or later to receive permission to visit our ambassador.

Our gentlemen (without exception) on land now and then are disquieted by Japanese visits in the night, a quite large number of cavalry and infantry who fill up the hall in Megasaki and make what can be called a general search of the house. They say as their excuse "that is the Japander Manier. We have been at the Dutch and Chinese, and now we are duty-bound to come to you." Every ten days, a similar inspection takes place at night.

Resanoff often intends to play a certain role but never has the fortitude to carry it out. He most often and best of all plays sick and likes that role the best. At the arrival of the tolks, Resanoff is lying in bed, has convulsions and pain, and fools even those around him with his theatrical genius.

Skeseima, who does not want to trouble the ambassador in such circumstances, conveys his business very softly to Langsdorff, who whispers them to our ambassador. Usually, the news (of the cunning Skeseima) is concerned with Resanoff's favorite interest in advantageous trade with Japan, of beautiful Japanese goods, etc.

Resanoff, for joy, forgets his intended role and answers the tolk himself in a loud voice in Japanese. Skeseima, who knows Resanoff better than all of us, thereupon flatters him some, and, before you know it, Resanoff bounds out of bed healthy and fresh. Barely a quarter of an hour later, our patient is in the courtyard having fun with the common Japanese milling around and playing with the Japanese and us (throwing an iron nail through a ring). That is the Russian Manier!

Resanoff is always busy with coffee. Recently, Alexander brought a cup less than the number of Japanese there. Resanoff went at his faithful servant for it. Alexander answered, "Skeseima has already had coffee."

Then Resanoff said, "Then he doesn't need to get any more."

Skeseima, who might have understood the quarrel between Resanoff and his faithful servant, said at once and very fittingly, "Yes! Yes! Yes! Thanks! Thanks!"

Resanoff rails against the Japanese government in all possible ways in the presence of the tolks, and what the tolks do not understand or do not want to

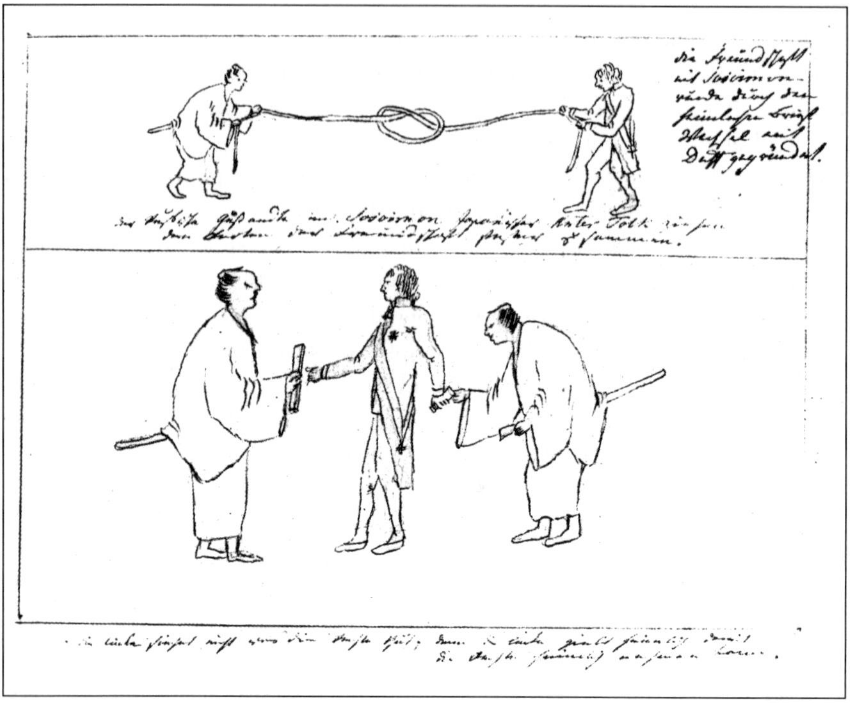

11-1. [Top right] The friendship with Soisimon was based on the secret correspondence with Duff. [Under the men with the rope] The Russian ambassador and Soisimon, the Japanese untertolk pull the knot of friendship tight. [Lower picture] The left hand does not see what the right hand does, since the left hand secretly passes it on so that the right hand can secretly take it.

understand, he has Langsdorff, Friderici, etc., translate. The smartest thing the Japanese can do in that case is—they laugh about it.

He always has schemes and plans in his head against Krusenstern and the others of us on the *Nadezhda*. Urup and Matzumai are his railing horses (Urup is a Kuril Island and Matzumai is the northern part of Japan and a large island). Resanoff, the hare,[2] always has war plans in his head.

When Langsdorff flew his hot air balloon yesterday, His Excellency was filled with fear, cursed, and railed at our Horner like a swamp snipe. Langsdorff stoically took it all and continued to fill his balloon. The balloon rose and was brought back to Megasaki by the string attached to it. Then, Resanoff was beside himself for joy, could not praise Langsdorff's patience and perseverance enough, and joyfully said to Langsdorff, "I'm happy for you." In a word, Langsdorff, who a short time before was supposed to be damaging everything and had to listen to insults, now, all at once, could not even be paid with gold.

Friderici and Koscheleff visited us again today. Resanoff finds that very unpleasant. That makes Resanoff very uncomfortable. He is unable even to keep his displeasure secret but bursts out at every opportunity that it irks him very much that Koscheleff and Friderici feel friendship and affinity for those of us on the *Nadezhda*.

11-2. Langsdorff tearing out his hair over his failed balloon in Nangasaki

He doesn't want to prevent them from going the *Nadezhda,* and nevertheless his mien and expression and actions show how unwillingly he allows them to go.

In the afternoon, right after tea, one of our sailors came running into the cabin saying, "The hot air balloon is climbing up in the air." We all ran out. The string tied to it must have broken because the balloon was free. It lost its equilibrium, however, and smoke came out, and the balloon fell into the water not far from Megasaki. A couple of Japanese boats fished it out and brought it to us. This accident caused quite a lot of noise on land and will not be without consequences.

Sat. 7/19 The balloon, which Fedoroff says Langsdorff deliberately let fly yesterday, is undoubtedly at fault for an intensified sentry around us. Our ambassador has been given more room on land. The place for walks is some 20 faden long and 6 to 8 faden wide.

Chinese ropes are very good for measuring on the water because they are made of grass and float on the water.

Sun. 8/20 Everything is calm. The weather is as in Kamtschatka, foggy and rainy.

Mon. 9/21 Langsdorff has begun trying to patch his crashed balloon. On the 17th we have the Japanese New Year, a day on which all of the Japanese fly (paper) kites. Langsdorff intends to fly his balloon on that day.

Tues. 10/22 Resanoff, always full of caprices, embarrasses his suite to the very marrow of their bones, especially with getting up unnecessarily early and always having to be there for him unnecessarily, and everyone has to appear dressed for tea, even though he himself—as a mark of his rank—runs around very indecently the whole day without trousers. Koscheleff stayed away from tea several times because he was late. Every time, he got a reprimand. Recently, Resanoff has been eating and drinking alone in his room and giving as a reason that his illness doesn't permit him to spend time in a cold dining room. Nevertheless, he wanders around outside at daybreak without his trousers.

The new place the Japanese have cleared by Megasaki is large enough to get tired from walking up and down, so the tolks told Resanoff, in order to soften his hard words, prison, etc. The governor had not given permission for it, but the Japanese sentries had created it because they couldn't stop the Russian officers, who wanted to make *Motion* [sic], and solely for this reason did we have the right to use this walkway.

This walkway is bounded by a high bamboo fence where a lot of curiosity seekers of both sexes gather to gape at us. Resanoff, from morning until evening, puts on a show for the curious Japanese, spends his time in a nightcap, without trousers, and in a dressing gown—to our anger and chagrin! How can you not have contempt for such a fellow?

On the day, when Friderici and Koscheleff were on the ship the last time, Resanoff was at his favorite place in Fedoroff's company, when Resanoff finally became tired of the gaping mob. He wanted to go home, turned around, got his feet wound up in the long dressing gown, stumbled, and fell full length with his nose in the mud, since it had rained hard early in the day.

The crowd of Japanese gaping behind the bamboo let loose with a peal of laughter. Fedoroff, who was a little bit ahead of him, ashamed, ran away instead of going back and left the ambassador lying there in the mud, and thus, for better or worse, Resanoff had to help himself back on his feet.

Koscheleff, who is always out for fun, went through a mixture of all the languages with a Japanese accent yesterday. When he was doing his act near the bamboo stakes, the Japanese standing behind the bamboo burst into loud laughter.

11-3. The ambassador in the mud

When asked the reason, it turned out Koscheleff, without knowing it, had asked if the Japanese would sell girls. The Japanese find such things very funny, and it's wrong if you call them head-hangers.

Resanoff very conceitedly thinks he understands some Japanese, speaks Japanese with the common Japanese wherever he can get hold of them, especially with the boys who daily stand in flocks behind the bamboo. Resanoff found out through them the names of the innkeeper in a nearby house, as well as of his wife, daughter, servant, maid, etc. Then he gave the tolks the names scalding hot. The tolks were surprised. They wanted to know how he knew; but Resanoff did not say, and would not, under any conditions confess through whom he had gained the nice news. The tolks tried by other means to find out but did not get anywhere. The result is that the distrust toward Resanoff must be growing more and more. The Japanese who owns that house can have problems, and free access of the Japanese to the bamboo fence is going to be restricted or totally forbidden.

According to Japanese customs on New Year's Day, Japanese have to wear new clothes, eat differently and do other work and pursue other entertainment than they normally do.

Wed. 11/23 The walkway is Resanoff's weakness. He often says, inwardly satisfied with himself and comfortably, "That's how we win little by little more and more room and freedom." The tolks came yesterday with the news that the governor had not yet given permission for the Russians to go all over the spot so freely, and the Japanese sentry could easily have problems. Therefore, we should be patient. Resanoff was more than a little angry. The tolks came again in the evening with some more news. The governor cannot actually permit use of the walkway. As concerned the ambassador and his officers, he would wink at it. The Japanese could not permit the soldiers and sailors to use it. Resanoff, again in a better mood, requested of the governor that he permit, during the Japanese festival, Japanese girls and women to visit us; and asked if the Russian ambassador might give the governors a New Year's present.

Resanoff is impatiently awaiting the lacquer manufacturer. Daily, lemons, oranges, and all kinds of nice things arrive, which Resanoff, only in Fosse's company, takes for their own enjoyment. All of the others get neither a taste nor a smell of them. Such things are always treated as important, secret government business and kept full of mystery. Resanoff corresponded secretly with Duff (it is however still a question if it was a secret for the Japanese), and the tolk Sosoimon was used as a go-between. This tolk also brought newspapers. Now Resanoff is saying, very satisfied (and not ashamed of it), "I've got that Sosoimon in my hands, because, if he doesn't do whatever I want him to, I'll threaten to betray him and say that he has secretly brought me letters."

We are awaiting permission to go to Kibatsch in a few days where our yards, topmasts, etc., are lying.

Resanoff complained again today about the long stay here and told Skeseima, "If the long expected news doesn't come from Jedo immediately, I am moving back on ship and will wait a couple of weeks and sail home again!"

Skeseima answered very tranquilly, "On the contrary, you should be happy about the length of stay because that is sure proof of your acceptance. Of all the embassies I remember that were rejected, none waited longer than thirty days for an answer from Jedo. Your discomforts and your so-called chagrin are cumulating a little and can be compared to the Japanese saying: Cut a little hay and little by little the hay wagon will get fuller and fuller, but flames eat the whole thing up all at once. Thus will all of your chagrin be destroyed by news from Jedo."

Resanoff gave the saying another interpretation saying, "Yes! After all the bother and boredom, we will have waited in vain and will be glad finally to leave this place."

"That can also be the case," answered Skeseima.

Embittered by the answer, Resanoff said impetuously and without thinking, "Japanese Manier is a bad Manier and Japanese laws and government are very bad."

Skeseima remained silent, then said, however, a little bit more, "Japanese carry out contracts and promises with the greatest exactness."

"That is good Manier," said Friderici, "and that is also the custom in Russia." "No!" screamed Resanoff, "That's a bad Manier," and gave Friderici a sharp reprimand for having mixed in the conversation (which was otherwise always the case). Resanoff finished by saying (in connection with a conversation about a northern harbor), "I'll change Japanese customs."

"No!" said Skeseima, "Just as little as the body can be reunited with its sweat, so little can the word of a Japanese once given be rescinded; just as little is it also possible to change the ancient laws of Japan, and that is why no other harbor but Nangasaki will be opened to foreigners. Laksmann had been so informed, so Resanoff has to know about it."

Thurs. 12/24 Horner had the notion of publishing the voyage to Japan under the name of the soldier Monakoff Firma in order to make public Resanoff's behavior.

Fri. 13/25 We received permission to go to Kibatsch to pick up our yards. In the morning, we put up the sheers and raised the mainmast in the evening. At Krusenstern's orders, we sawed off two fuss from the mast, made a new ram, and put an iron band around it and put the shortened masts in place again. We had taken down the shrouds and stays because they needed repairs.

Resanoff had been promised that the merchant would come today with the lacquer wares. Since he did not, Resanoff is in a very bad mood and, as Horner says, put things in his mouth that others would be ashamed to pick up with their hands. Among other improprieties Resanoff said, "I'll shit in your chest of drawers, etc."

The governor's answer to Resanoff's questions and pretensions is as follows. The governor is sorry to hear that the Russian ambassador is ill, that is, unfortunately, in Nangasaki the general situation because the season of the year brings a lot of illnesses, that he would not fail to notify the ambassador as soon as the answer arrived from Jedo, that the governor in the meantime would do everything in his power to shorten the time and to this end would send a woman, that he thanked the ambassador for his offer, but he did not yet have permission to accept gifts.

The tolks have told the ambassador so often that under Japanese law they may neither take nor give gifts without permission, but nevertheless Resanoff is demanding the monstrously small number of five hundred lacquer tobacco boxes and is swearing and hollering that the Japanese do not obey him. The governor has promised him a girl. Not satisfied with that, Resanoff demanded more girls than he can take care of, that is, for all of us without exception.

Sat. 14/26 Another detail about yesterday's story: Resanoff, peeved about the unfulfilled hope that the merchant with the lacquerware had not come, was playing svaiku [свайку: nail with a large head] in the courtyard at Megasaki with our and the Japanese officers. (A few days ago, Resanoff wrote a letter to the governors, and the tolks accepted half-heartedly the commission of delivering it.)

Then, all of a sudden we heard "the tolks are coming!" Resanoff, who had been playing svaiku, ran into the house, lay down on the bed, and played ill. The tolks said after greetings, "We have delivered the letter you had given. The governor dare not answer it because that would be against the law." (All the while Resanoff was groaning and moaning, and the tolks paused now and then while talking and called eh! eh! hai! hai!)

The tolks brought the news that the courier from Jedo could only arrive in thirty days. This news spurred Resanoff's rage.

"Laksmann," the tolks said, "was here for nine months."

"Laksmann," answered Resanoff, smiling scornfully, "Each of my officers has twenty Laksmanns under his command."

"That is why the person of the ambassador is all the more important," answered the tolks, "and therefore we need more time to prepare your reception."

Then Resanoff jumped out of the bed furious. "I shit on the governor and all of his clothes, and, when the permission comes from Jedo, I'll complain about him to the Emperor of Japan, and he will grant me justice for sure."

While Resanoff was raging so illogically, several samples of lacquerware were brought in unnoticed. "Your measly stuff!" said Resanoff somewhat more softened. "I don't want it. I want freedom, to know what my situation is." At this moment, a tolk opened a box, and, at the sight of a beautiful lacquer box, Resanoff completely changed his mood of speaking, got out of bed, and said, "Ah! Ah! What does it cost? Fedor Pavlovitsch (Fosse), look how pretty, isn't it?! Dimitri Iwanovich (Koscheleff), come closer!" and everything that had happened was forgotten.

Today, I took the report ashore to Resanoff and was invited to dine with him at noon. Resanoff wrote to Krusenstern and announced he had finally received the samples of lacquerware. (*See color plate 20.*) Not long afterwards, Krusenstern also came on land. Resanoff sent for tolks, but none came. He wanted to have the

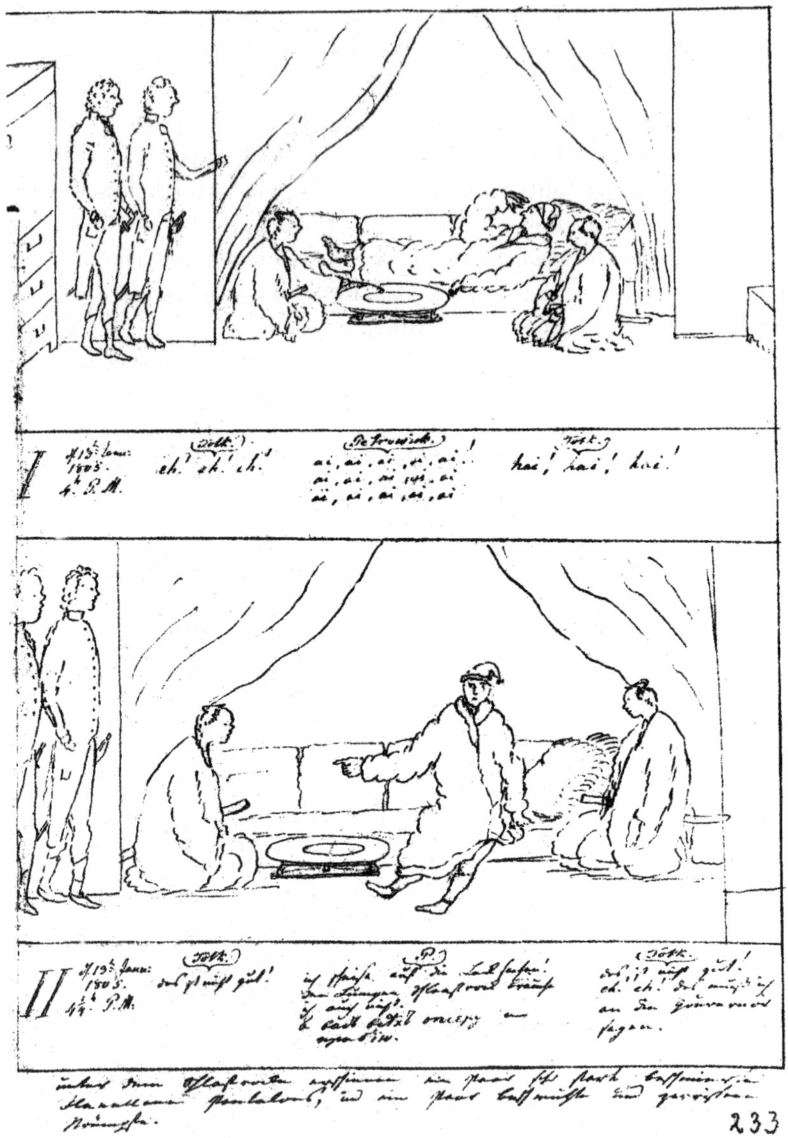

11-4. (I) 4 p.m., 13 January 1805. Tolk: "eh! eh! eh!" Resanoff: "ai, ai, ai, ai, ai. ai, ai, ai, ai, ai ai, ai, ai, ai, ai!" Tolk: "hai! hai! hai!"

(II) 4:15 p.m., 13 January 1805. Tolk: "That's not good! R.: "I shit on the lacquerware and I don't need that rag of a dressing gown." Tolk: "That is not good. Eh, eh, I must tell the governor."

11-5. (Between II & III.) Tolk: "Believtheit of the governor." R.: "Rubbish. I do not want them. I want my freedom, want to know where I stand. Ah, ah, what do they cost? How nice!"

(III) 4:30 p.m., 13 January 1805. R.: "What are you buying? How much?" Tolk: "Generosity of the governors."

(IV) 4:45 p.m. Everyone all of a sudden: "Imagine . . . Isn't it true . . . that the work is amazing?"

governors informed that he could only stay until May and therefore requested an explanation and an answer before May, that he no longer wanted to be led around blind.

At Krusenstern's request, the samples were sent on board and then a list returned with the articles each person wished to order. Since Resanoff still did not have permission to do this, the list was superfluous for the time being. The Japanese are bringing us three hundred copper plates to cover our ship and longboat.

"If they can give us that," said Resanoff enviously, "why aren't they giving me any boxes?" Even though boxes and fans have not yet been ordered and Resanoff does not even know if he will get them, he has already given them away as presents. (I'm thinking, we won't get any.) The court ladies all get fans and boxes. Boxes! He can't have enough of them. Daily arrangements are being made in Megasaki.

Resanoff told me, "Upon my return, I'm not going to the Emperor like the others. I'm going to say, 'Your Imperial Majesty, appoint a day,' and then it will be a small, exceedingly easy matter to reward you all with titles and orders." Often, plans for war are the subject of his conversations. He is so crazy he has set up a written plan for war.

One of the tolks told us dispassionately that it takes the mail fifteen or sixteen days to go to Jedo and back. Given the distance, that is probably correct.

Resanoff's behavior leads to the expectation, that we will either be sitting here for years or that the Japanese will suddenly chase us away.

If a young Japanese falls in love with a married woman and both naturally see no possibility of uniting, they give each other their word to starve themselves. If the husband sees this, he can turn over his marital rights to the other man. If he, the husband, does not want to do this, the two lovers starve themselves to death. That is the Japanese Manier!

In the evening, we shortened our foremast two fuss, lowered into the water the masts that had served as sheers, and sent them to Kibatsch.

Sun. 15/27 Even though Resanoff noisily and vehemently requested tolks yesterday and today, none have appeared. The Japanese are said to have requested, and half demanded, that we also honor their New Year's festival and stop our work for four days.

Mon. 16/28 Impatience drove Resanoff too far yesterday, so that he sent for tolks three times. The first time, the answer was they could not be found. The second time, the tolks had no time to come, and the third time they would come immediately and that immediately however took so long that Resanoff went to the Japanese sentry and complained about the tolks; the atoni then straight away went himself and finally had the tolks brought.

Resanoff, disregarding the tolks' Compliments, said to them, "I demand to know from the governors the reasons why I am being left so long in uncertainty (and with increasing sharpness) and am no longer willing to remain in this uncertain, unpleasant position, and I'm not going to let myself be led around anymore on a fool's rope!"

With the answer "Well begreift! Well begreift!" [Well understood!], the tolks took their leave.

The making of balloons is getting the upper hand. Langsdorff is going to let a balloon ascend. Friderici let one fly. Our pilot's mate Spolochoff is pasting one together incognito. The Kotzebues are also patching a balloon together, and Alexander and Monakoff are going to let one go.

Resanoff, who, because of his imaginary illness, is not to be seen except at the moment when he is superfluous, had become angry that Friderici and Koscheleff had failed early this morning to pay their respects to him, and Koscheleff got a rough, coarse reprimand.

Tues. 17/29 Today, Friderici got another reprimand for the same thing, and Koscheleff was also dismissed from his group. (Resanoff is vengeful.) Resanoff did not permit either one to ask any questions and answer. He only made himself ridiculous and petty, takes petty revenge, having the thermometer taken from their room, because he knew Friderici wrote down the temperature every day. A little later, Resanoff must have recognized his own foolishness (which is not otherwise the usual case with Resanoff), for, with exceedingly great friendliness, he himself went uninvited to Friderici and Koscheleff in order to drink schnapps with them—those are predecessors of a reconciliation coming soon.

Wed. 18/30 Yesterday, the governor sent our ambassador, in accordance with Japanese customs, several kinds of baked goods which are said to be symbolic. It is too bad that the symbolic explanations are missing,[3] for judging by Japanese sayings, they must not be bad.

The tolks brought the following answer to Resanoff's vehement, impolite question from the day before yesterday. The governor sent again the assurance of his Believtheit and word to the ambassador that the ambassador certainly could be assured that, if an answer from Jedo had arrived, the governor would have sent news long ago, that the Emperor of Japan had to confer with his whole family about such an important matter; and, since the one was 100, the other 200 etc. miles from Jedo, and Grote Herrn travel exceedingly slowly, thus that was the weakness, and no wonder the business took so long and the answer was so long in coming. In addition, the governor had already received news that a committee had been named to conclude and determine trade articles and conditions with Russia.

"I have to be there!" called Resanoff vehemently!

"I don't know about that," answered the tolk and took his leave.

In honor of the New Year's Festival, symbols are nailed on all of the doors to decorate them, and all of the Japanese, as if poured into the same form, are in their visiting clothes.

Madsiura's health has not improved in the last eight days, and he had no bowel movement for just as long. The wounds on his neck are still so swollen that he can no longer speak. The Japanese doctor has him on a diet of salted radishes which Madsiura conscientiously swallows every day. Espenberg dare not even approach the sick man. It would be unprecedented if that man got back on his legs again. It looks as if he won't make it very much longer.

Kuprian Semenoff fell into the hold on the mooring anchor and hurt himself very badly. Too bad about the useful fellow; happily, the consequences won't be great.

Thurs. 19/31 Tschernei's kubus embarrassed himself today. Tschernei (before our departure from St. Petersburg) wanted to send up a balloon but was unsuccessful, since it did not even begin to rise, and Tschernei ran away. Since Moritz Kotzebue's kubus did the same thing, he now is called Tschernei. In contrast, Friderici, who had spent the night with us, together with Horner and Bellingshausen and with my help, filled a little balloon over our stove, and it rose. This balloon rose very quickly several hundred fuss, caught on fire because of the alcohol, and rose all the more quickly; it was consumed by flames before it began to fall. The sight was not all that bad. The Japanese around us in their guard boats stared themselves blind looking for the balloon that had long since burned and disappeared.

Sat. 21/2 Everything quiet. Very bad weather for the Japanese festivals. We wanted to make banners today, but disharmony thwarted it, since each fellow knew better than the next, and no one could do it alone. The Japanese are flying large numbers of kites.

Sun. 22/3 Friderici told me today that in all probability we will not be staying longer than spring in Japan. Several days ago, Sosoimon was at Resanoff's. Resanoff, again full of zeal, had claimed he could wait no longer than the end of May.

"In Jedo, they have known for a long time that you cannot stay here longer than March," said the tolk, "since you said earlier that otherwise ships would be sent from Kamtschatka to find you."

We are now hoping that the Japanese will completely determine conditions for trade, send them to our ambassador to accept, or take over from him the gifts for the Emperor of Japan, and then that Resanoff will be taken back to Kamtschatka. At least, that would be the shortest procedure.

When the Japanese issued permission for us to use the walkway, it was bounded only by light bamboo stakes. The Japanese intended to build a guardhouse next to the gate. Resanoff however said to the tolks, "We won't go any farther than the governor wishes us to, and my word is sufficient security for you. If you build a guardhouse next to the gate, then for sure I'll not go to that area again." The intention of building a guardhouse was not carried out. The Japanese place too much trust in Resanoff's given word, for Resanoff himself does not keep his word. Friderici has complained several times about it, but that does not help any.

Resanoff said to me, "Why should we keep our word with people who don't keep their word?" and opened the gate and went out. We could say and suggest anything we wanted to; nothing helped. Resanoff did not let himself be stopped and became angry that Friderici and I did not follow him. He came back and said

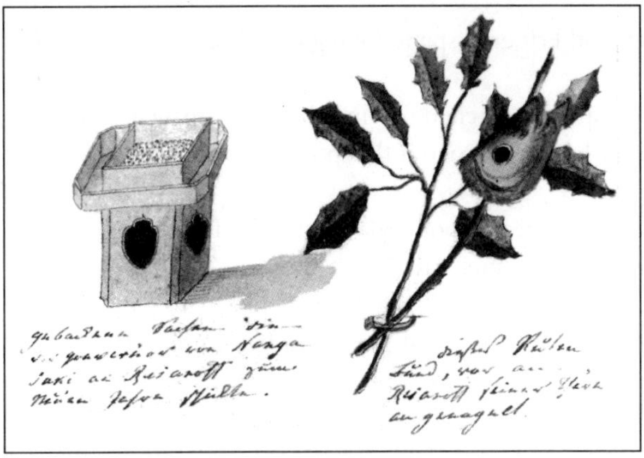

11-6. Baked goods sent by the governors. This branch was nailed to Resanoff's door for the New Year.

to me, "If *I* tell you now that you can and may go farther, then you can certainly believe me and follow me!"

I answered him, "If Your Excellency wants to, then I will go with you to Nangasaki and farther." And in order to prevent vexation, I followed him some twenty steps out of the gate. Then Resanoff was calmed down and had had his way and turned back himself. No more than a hair's width more around the corner could be seen the nearby house near the bamboo fence—all the more inexcusable is Resanoff's breaking of his word.

Part of the Japanese New Year's ceremonies consists of colorful thorny leaves and rods with a couple small fish heads on them, which are nailed on the doors to honor the household god, as well as a bowl with fried peas which should drive out evil spirits in the house.

The Japanese brought Resanoff a large quantity of peas. The graciousness of the Japanese and their readiness to serve in so far as their laws permit are badly rewarded by Resanoff's behavior and his creatures and lick-spitters. Resanoff and Fosse, his factotum [busybody, jack of all trades], are not ashamed of their niggardliness. They even permit the stupid fellow Alexander, Resanoff's servant, to snap at the Japanese if they request an additional cup of coffee more than that oxhead wants to give them. That clique does not deny themselves anything.

The low water forced me to stay on land longer than I wanted to. The police sentry was already going around with a wooden clapboard used for sounding the hour. The hour is determined by burning down a candle. Koscheleff took the clapboard from the Japanese's hands and began to beat it but hit it one time too few. The oldest Japanese officer in the main guard immediately called the Japanese, who was trembling from fright, to come to him and asked for the reason. "Horranda did the beating," he said. To justify the Japanese, Koscheleff went to the head of the main guard and indicated with comic pantomime that he was at fault. Laughter from all took care of the matter, and it is hoped that the Japanese will get away without punishment.

Mon. 23/4 Koscheleff and Friderici spent the night with us; it's a respite for them to come to us.

Tues. 24/5 Today, the Japanese fetched our masthead to repair it or make a new one. They gave us somewhat more space at the spot where our boats are being repaired.

Langsdorff wanted to send up his balloon today, but the wind was too strong for it, and he intends to wait for a calmer day.

Resanoff has found out secretly from a tolk that Duff's embassy to Jedo has been canceled (Duff, the Ober Hoft, was supposed to make a trip to Jedo this year as Dutch ambassador), that nevertheless his gifts would be received here in Nangasaki through an authorized agent from Jedo. If this rumor is true, then Resanoff has to be prepared for a similar answer. The tolk added, with a shrug of his shoulders, that Resanoff would probably still have to wait three months for an answer.

Wed. 25/6 Finally, Langsdorff decided the day was right, and it was announced that the balloon would be released today. At ten in the morning, it was really rising majestically into the heights. (It was eight fuss in diameter.) It, however, stopped suddenly and sank, driven by the wind very much faster than it had climbed—the reason—Langsdorff's lack of caution. Shortly before, he had patched a spot on top of the balloon and freshly glued it, and the glue, not yet dry when the balloon was rising, let loose, and the lighter air flew out. The balloon, driven by the wind, fell on a house in Nangasaki. Since the smoke rose out of the balloon on the roof of the house (since it was filled with smoke from straw), the people thought the balloon and the house would burn. They threw an unbelievable quantity of water on Langsdorff's pride and on the roof of the house (as we could see through our spyglass), made a lot of noise, complained to the governor (as if the Russians had intended to set the city on fire, etc.). The governor immediately sent for the guards at Megasaki to interrogate them, and, when he learned that the balloon had risen without fire, the governor laughed at the incident and had the Japanese given a reprimand, who had so hurriedly complained and had unnecessarily become very fearful themselves and made others the same way. That is what the tolks said. That baptized balloon will hardly undertake a second trip.

The reason for Duff's embassy to Jedo not being undertaken is as follows: The yearly trip of the Ober Hoft to Jedo has cost the Dutch too much during the war with France. They therefore had requested that they be allowed to send an ambassador to Jedo every fifth year. The answer to this petition had not yet been issued. Only now, in accordance with the petition, was Duff's embassy to Jedo not undertaken. Four years in a row, the Dutch gifts will be received in Nangasaki by the authorized agent from Jedo, and in the fifth year a Dutch ambassador will take them himself to Jedo.

When Resanoff complained again about the length of time he was being forced to wait, Skeseima gave assurances that everything will be clear in three months. The words "everything clear!" have many meanings.

Among other things (imprudent acts), Resanoff assured the tolks when the governor, constrained, again sent word to him that he could not and dare not accept any gifts from him: "Then I too, for my part, will accept no gifts from the governors." Disregarding this, Resanoff had (according to his principles) taken possession of the lacquerware without feeling ashamed.

The report we take to Resanoff every day cannot be different and is always the same—only the number of sick changes in the report. When Kuprian Semenoff fell in the hold, it was reported to Resanoff that he was ill. His Excellency found himself gone over and insulted because the entire history of how the sailor had been injured was not given in detail in the report. We are used to digesting such pretensions without the least amount of difficulty. If a fool is present and says a word about it, then the noise starts.

Thurs. 26/7 Resanoff, healthy one minute, sick the next minute, depending on how he feels, was ready to take a warm bath when I went on land. "May it do you well." In this weather it's not an advisable practice. Daily, Sosoimon, Resanoff's intimate friend, with whom he often spends time alone (I'd rather not hear what Petrovick chatters away about there) preaches patience to Resanoff.

Yesterday, Tamchatschira brought much Believtheit von das Gouvernör, with the news that the governor had ordered the tolks to visit the Russian ambassador every other day, in order to help him pass and shorten the time, and, in a month news, would come from Jedo, and, in three months, everything will be clear.

Fri. 27/8 One of the Chinese junks lowered its mast today (we heard it on our ship) with loud blows, by pushing and shoving the wedges that support the masts with the help of two lines fastened up front, and put the large mast lengthwise on the junk. The noise and the numbers of Chinese were enough to make you run away if you had been present. We on the *Nadezhda* became nervous at their stupidity.

Golovatscheff brought the following news today from land. The eldest obertolk, who had not been seen up to now due to illness, paid Resanoff his initial and final visit, because he has been chosen to travel to Jedo in Duff's stead. At the same time, he brought news from the governor that the courier had arrived with news that a Grote Herr, the emperor's authorized agent, had already left Jedo and would arrive in about one month.

Today, on board and on land, the tolks inquired very urgently whether it would still take a long time to repair the longboat and boats, and whether the ship herself would soon be finished. Nevertheless, Resanoff is still building castles in the sky and has a list finished of things he wants to order for himself in Meako because he wants to make a detour through that city. (Meako is in Japan what Nankin is in China and Lyon in France.)[4]

Rheumatism bothers Resanoff whenever it occurs to him and is convenient. Now for amusement, he has built a room in his room using four rows of straw mats, sail cloth, rugs, and several bolts of cloth. This newly invented bedroom is as big as a cabin. A big coal pan is put in it, making our Petrovick's sleeping cabin

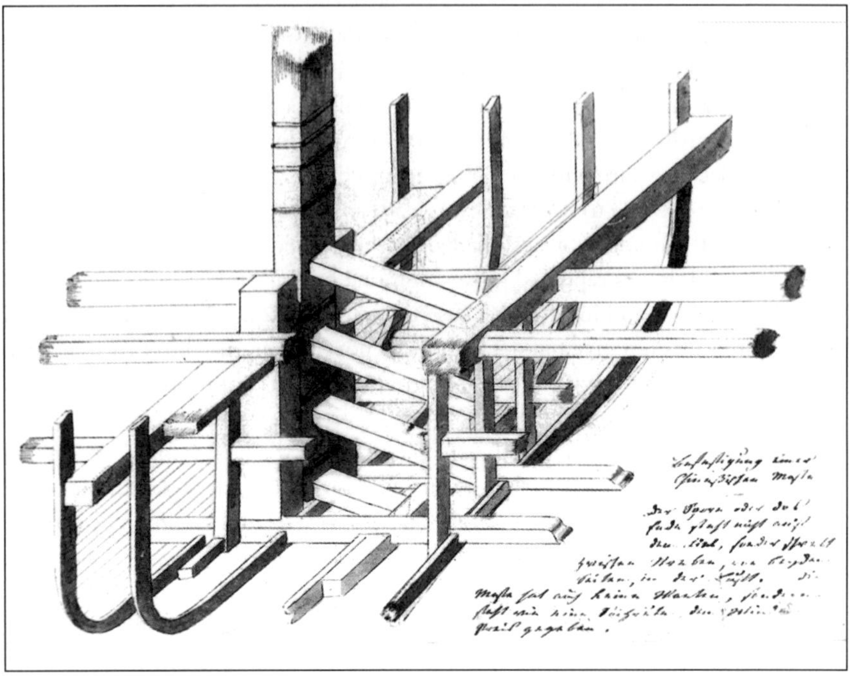

11-7. The attachment of a Chinese mast, the end of which does not rest on the keel but rather floats in the air between struts on both sides. The mast has no shrouds but stands like a pointed rod at the mercy of the wind.

as hot as a bath. Resanoff often has headaches from the coal smoke but always blames it on rheumatism. He now often runs out of his heated box into the fresh air (the weather is quite raw now). That is the way he will catch rheumatism, even if he does not yet have it.

Sosoimon, who is always preaching patience to Resanoff, said several days ago, "I like to think that it is foreign for the ambassador to follow Japanese customs and laws. But these customs cannot be changed. You complain about imprisonment? All of Japan, in that way, is a prison! We recognize ourselves that pressure and force are hard to bear—imagine that it can be no other way! Then the situation isn't so bad and much more bearable than you think. Your continual complaints could have dire consequences. Do you want our governor to receive a sword from Jedo to cut open his stomach with? Then continue to act as you have. My advice is to have patience and be quiet! And you will say Sosoimon is right. (That's preaching to deaf ears.) In this way, you can expect more love. All of Japan is talking about you, and all are saying that you indeed are different from the Dutch, prouder, more heated and-and-and- that you look down upon the Japanese. That is indeed not a good renommé."

On another occasion, this Sosoimon said to Resanoff (after praising and emphasizing our ambassador's importance), "When the Emperor of Japan sends an ambassador into the provinces, he seeks out the cleverest man among his suite." You can imagine for yourselves Resanoff's answer to this. I'm happy I did not have to hear it.

In order to make Koscheleff, Friderici, and Fedoroff sit together less idly and broodingly, Resanoff said to them that, one after the other, one of them has to play checkers with him every evening. They would have gladly done that without the remark.

Sat. 28/9 Since Resanoff does not like to see Friderici and Koscheleff visiting us, today they requested permission to inspect the place where our longboat is being repaired. "Good heavens!" said His Excellency. "You well know that I'm glad to allow anything that you wish to do to shorten the time." The gentlemen used the opportunity to drink tea with us but had to return home before sundown.

Sun. 29/10 Even though Resanoff has enough things to talk about here, he nevertheless prefers to backbite. The person who is absent always has to be the one, and it always begins with anticipatory questions, so that those present chatter from that line of talk or something similar or tell gossipy stories or twaddle or intrigues. That treatise is our Petrovick's handiwork or way and his politics. He cannot live without gossip! (He's called Petrovick because Tilesius cannot pronounce Petrovitsch and always calls him Nicolaus Petrovick.) Among other things, Resanoff complained to Friderici and Koscheleff about his bosom friend Fosse, called him an ingrate, etc. "I pulled him out of the dirt. He had nothing to vomit up, nothing to eat. I gave his wife free quarters in my house, and he doesn't recognize all of these acts of charity, etc."

Daily, the Japanese inquire about the work on the ship. A Japanese guard officer asked Fosse about it. (As important as Fosse makes himself out to be, all of the Japanese consider him a stupid fellow, because he understands no Dutch.) Fosse answered, "It's a праздник [holiday], and that's why no work is being done." The Japanese shook his head and left.

At noon, Friderici came to us, and Koscheleff and Federoff appeared after table. The latter had not been on shipboard in a long time. When he requested permission to go, Resanoff accused all three of them of going on board so often, "You're always going on board," said Resanoff. "Why doesn't anyone from the ship come to us? That's not happening for no reason, etc.," and then we were raked over the coals.

Federoff said, "Enough, every day an officer comes ashore with a report." But it did not help. Unfortunately, it appears as if Resanoff would like only too much to get in a dispute with us in order to shove the failure of the embassy off on us. His Excellency should watch out. The first time, Resanoff burned his fingers. The second time it will probably be his whole hand, since his behavior leans toward that. Resanoff now calls Koscheleff a second Count Tolstoi. Those are all bad signs. Before we know it, the noise will start up again. Не бойсь [fear not]. General Koscheleff helped in Kamtschatka, and here the discreet Japanese will help.

Mon. 30/11 I saw a norimon (post chaise) for the first time today. The box is three cubic fuss and of extremely clean workmanship.

Rats—we clubbed to death nearly one thousand on the ship. The hold is completely empty, only ballast in it. We had thrown the kindling wood in the middle in an irregular pile, then laid large boards straight across the ship, so that the rats could not get away between our feet, then placed ourselves on both sides armed with sharp Kamtschadal ballast. Most of the pile of wood was carried away, and the little bit left teemed like an anthill. Then the stoning began, and it did not take long until we were all tired. Tarass had got himself a barrel half-filled with water and was sitting at the side of the ship. The frightened rats crawled into his trousers, jacket, etc. Taras very calmly took one rat after another by the tail and threw it into the barrel. After the chase had ended (for the time being), he had caught about eighty rats in his barrel.

Tues. 31 / 12 Tamchatschira brought the news today that the long expected Grote Herr would come in fourteen days and also gave us permission to fetch our riggings from Kibatsch.

The Japanese have now placed a guard at the bamboo in Megasaki, because Resanoff did not keep his word and overstepped certain boundaries. If Resanoff should start talking of staying here in the presence of the Grote Herrn (and his wish is already known in Jedo), it would be possible that the Japanese would take him at his word and Resanoff, for better or worse, would have to stay here. The Japanese will undoubtedly guard against ending up with such a crazy fellow on their backs.

Today, Ratmanoff chased Otto Kotzebue out of the cabin and, even though both boys misbehaved, today Otto was punished as the one at fault. The two Kotzebues take turns pouring our tea or coffee. Tilesius, who never comes on time, came late for coffee yesterday. Otto, who had done the pouring, thought Tilesius was not coming at all and had poured hot water over the coffee grounds in the coffeepot, when our Domina asked for coffee. Otto said that there was no more coffee. Tilesius got angry at this answer. Ratmanoff took the pot, did not notice that the coffee was weak, and poured the councilor a cup full, turned then to Otto and scolded him for being impolite because he had refused to pour Tilesius a cup of coffee. It was actually not Otto's turn to pour. Without knowing the cause of the strife, Espenberg, who came in at that moment, sided decidedly with Otto. Otto rapidly told him everything, and Espenberg began to defend him. Ratmanoff, made even hotter by that, claimed Otto's thick-headedness was at fault and that Espenberg by his softness strengthened him unnecessarily in it, and chased Otto out of the company cabin in the presence of our captain, saying, "Such a useless boy doesn't deserve to be in our company." In the afternoon, our good-natured Krusenstern had allayed everything, and everyone was reconciled.

- 12 -

February 1805

Wed. 1/13 Japanese vessels in need of repair are floated ashore at high tide, so that at ebb tide they can easily be left on dry land. Then they scratch off the tang, sludge, polyps, mussels, etc., and dry the vessels out anew with fire. The latter they carry out by putting bamboo under the ship and kindling a fire, which often becomes so large that it engulfs the entire vessel. While burning, the bamboo sets off a loud popping that sounds like a skirmish. The crack of the thick bamboo sounds like a cannon shot.

The large fire on shore yesterday was in honor of the monthly festival, which the Japanese celebrate as follows, the first day of the first month, the second day of the second month, the third day of the third month, etc. Each festival day has its customs and ceremonies. This time, wood shavings were fastened to the door, which according to superstition, should drive away all illnesses, and fires burned on land throughout the night.

Today, we towed our entire riggings back from Kibatsch and put them at the same place where our boats are being repaired, not far from Megasaki.

Thurs. 2/14 Instead of bamboo stakes, the Japanese have nailed up boards around Megasaki, because Langsdorff had taken the liberty through the bamboo [several lines have been made illegible].

Fri. 3/15 Very common flowers give a continual beautiful, yellow color. Friderici and Koscheleff wanted to have that color. Resanoff however forbade them to order it when they asked him for permission, saying, "I have decided to send for nothing except the things we need for our table!" A quarter of an hour later, he permitted Fosse and Langsdorff to order three large balls of string so that they could fly kites. Resanoff is lying like envy on his sick bed, moans, and groans to his life's content without permitting anyone to sympathize, because he leads all astray. No one knows for sure—is he ill or isn't he?

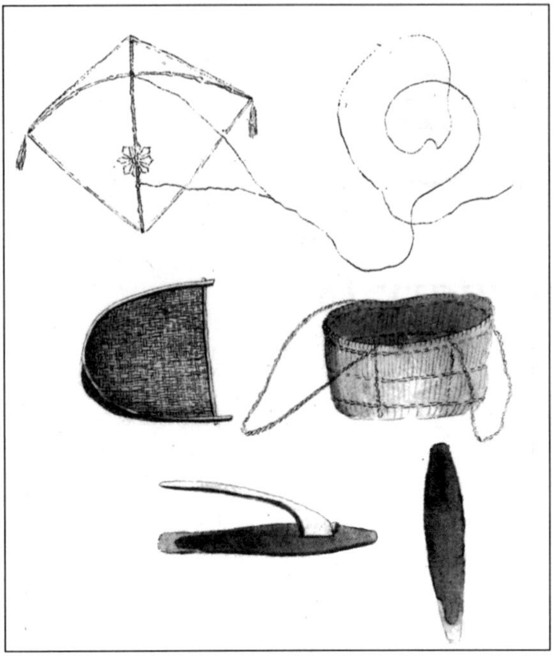

12-1. A kite made from paper

Today was the ancestor festival, and Resanoff, as he himself says, is very popular and important, which means indescribably obnoxious.

We pulled our shallop on land so that we can repair and repaint her.

Sat. 4/16 According to the saga, the Grote Herr is still coming soon. Yesterday, a banjos looked over Megasaki and inspected every cranny, as he let be known, in order to make sure that everything was in order for the arrival of the Grote Herr. These inspections are carried out unannounced. The Japanese inspect all of the rooms as if no one were in them. That angers Resanoff indescribably. Madsiura, who tried to cut his own throat, is, even though still ill, doing better.

Sun. 5/17 Last night, it hailed and snowed so much that the whole surrounding area is covered with snow. An unusual sight in Japan. Toward noon, however, there was not a trace of snow, except for the peaks of the mountains, some of which are also covered with snow and ice in the summer.

Resanoff is not ashamed, as Russian ambassador, to live at our expense. He has no furniture or household items at all. We had to give him table service, tea service, formal plates, serving plates, glasses, spoons, knives, forks, candlesticks, casseroles, and everything necessary to establish a household, and we have had to do as best we can with our remaining goods. He has emptied Krusenstern's cabin of chairs, tables, and mirrors, and, whatever we have of food and drinks, he considers his property. We have to hand over our remaining things to keep the peace, so that our ambassador can set a cup of coffee in front of the Japanese. Wine is the only thing with which Resanoff provided himself, and, since it is the property of

His Excellency, he is disgustingly stingy with it. We do not claim to want to be served wine. It is his nasty stinginess with the wine that angers us when Resanoff serves the Japanese wine. As far as clothing is concerned, we are all better equipped than Resanoff. Not one of us wears our shirts so dirty and wears such torn stockings as he does. He is the only one who needed to have new trousers made in Kamtschatka because the few he had along were unusable. He usually goes around in mechante pantoffles [shabby slippers], for appearance sake, as he says himself, because he likes them; but in reality because he does not have shoes and boots. We know that, because we loaded and unloaded his wardrobe and had, so to say, to make an inventory of it when the paltry stuff was carted on land, and he is rich only in worn-out embroidered coats, some of which may well have been used during Catherine's times.[1]

Mon. 6/18 Several days ago, Koscheleff was heading toward the room where the soldiers and our Japanese live, so that he could observe the bald-headed Japanese doctor preparing powders and salves for Madsiura. He stopped and watched the proceedings. Egei, one of our common Japanese, suddenly came up to Koscheleff and ordered, "Sit down, for you dare not stand if Japanese officers are seated." Since Koscheleff did not react to Egei's pretensions, he became insulting and with his coarseness forced Koscheleff to leave the room. Koscheleff complained about Egei to Resanoff, and His Excellency, without letting him speak, bawled Koscheleff out and drove him out of his room. Koscheleff protested enough that he felt as if he had been in his soldiers' barracks. Nothing helped at all. A very convenient method of ending strife.

Tues. 7/19 During our voyage, we have always had some kind of plague at table, first dry hay or so-called spinach with an oversupply of jagged spinach seeds in it, then tasteless rice only cooked in water, and then, lack of water, fricassees made from salt meat, blue puddings from potato starch, in Kamtschatka fish and more fish, and here brown sauce, a very tasteless kind of ragout. Even radishes contribute their part to increase our plague at table.

Thurs. 9/21 News we get from land is jogging along at the same old pace, that is, we go neither backwards nor forwards. Resanoff behaves as if possessed and now has the crazy idea of having himself cured by a Japanese doctor.

Fri. 10/22 The governor of Nangasaki sent his tolks with a message to Resanoff, when he was informed that Resanoff insisted upon Japanese doctors, that, if it truly were Resanoff's wish to have himself cured by Japanese doctors, he should give the order that his officers should sign that was the case, saying approximately, "Since the skills of the Russian doctors were not great enough to cure the Russian ambassador of his disease, he had no other recourse but to seek refuge with the Japanese."

These demands were turned down by the officers, and Resanoff gave vent by railing. When the tolks had taken leave, they once again went to Resanoff's suite and said bitterly, "It is not right for the ambassador to joke with us so irrationally! We saw quite well that before we came he was running around the courtyard, and now he is lying in bed as if he were deathly ill. He will not succeed in outwitting us."

Finally today, Resanoff received permission from the governor to have himself cured by a Japanese doctor, and now he had no desire for it any more. In addition, it was announced that the Grote Herr would probably come in twenty days.

Sat. 11/23 Yesterday, the tolks were once again sent by the governor to Resanoff's officers to convince them to sign, but, since they refused to under any conditions, the tolk had gone to Resanoff, who, without any difficulties, requested a doctor of the governor of Nangasaki in writing. Now the answer has been a little long in coming. Resanoff had become impatient and sent word that he no longer needed the Japanese quacksalver because, instead, he had seen fit, due to their taking so long, to take European medicines.

Sosoimon, who was present, told him then, "You are now contradicting what you said an hour ago, what you wished orally and in writing. How can we therefore believe your words? We cannot give any credence to your words when our big business matters begin. We may not and cannot tell our governor everything that takes place between you and us, for otherwise our friendship would have already ended long ago. Since you permit yourself to be exceedingly impolite with tolks, we find it necessary to request an assurance from you that in the future you will treat us more politely. We are not obliged to let ourselves be made fools of."

This conversation took place in front of Resanoff's entire suite. And after the tolks had finally gone, Resanoff said to his officers, "I did that quite well. Alexander, give punsch! I wanted to show the Japanese how much I trust them and requested a Japanese doctor, and, since the fools did not use the opportunity and did not fulfill my wish immediately, I got myself out of the affair very well."

Koscheleff and Friderici had been with us on shipboard these days and told us about Resanoff's crazy idea of having himself cured by a Japanese doctor. When they arrived on land, they announced their presence to Resanoff. Resanoff's first question was, "Well, Dimitri Ivanitsch, which ceremony is customary for the funeral of an ambassador? I'll look very good in a lacquer coffin!" Friderici and Koscheleff asked of him and requested that he name the person who had been telling him such lies.

Resanoff refused to give any explanation but rather made a joke of it. That remark was aimed at us inhabitants of the *Nadezhda* and not altogether incorrectly, for, in all honesty, we had hoped the Japanese doctor would do us all the favor of dispatching our crazy Resanoff into the next world.

Resanoff must have his spies, for he knows everything that goes on the *Nadezhda*. We have known for a long time that he only too gladly listens to gossip and tales. On St. Anne's Day, Ratmanoff said, when we tried to talk him into going ashore to congratulate Resanoff on the festival of his order, "I can send Ivan or Efim, etc." Resanoff knew even that.

It annoys Resanoff that Friderici and Koscheleff come out to us on the ship so often. He says, "I do not agree with what you people are doing on the ship, and how is it possible that you can pass the time better there than here? If one of you is supposed to go with me, no one wants to be the one. The captain barely steps on land, but that one after the other of you is up front, etc."

Fosse, Langsdorff, and Schemelin can do and not do whatever they want to, for they are our ambassador's benefactors. They are his. Yes! Yes!

Though a tolk, Friderici ordered for himself a conch shell, which was brought to him. Greed irked Fosse and Langsdorff that Friderici got something that they did not have. They misused Resanoff's name in order to take the shell away from him. That irked Friderici, and he asked Resanoff if that had been his wish.

Without letting Resanoff say a word, Fosse said, "Your Excellency had indeed ordered the oyster."

As luck would have it, Resanoff finally had a sense of justice and said, "No! I cannot remember that," and turned the shell over to Friderici with a great air of officiousness. Similar things happen every day but seldom have such a good ending as in this case.

When I arrived on land today, Resanoff was groaning and moaning in bed; and several hours later, without trousers, in slippers, with us in the courtyard, he was playing свайку [svaiku] (throwing an iron nail through a ring).

We have finally started repairing our riggings.

Sun. 12/24 Through a special Believtheit we had seven guns returned for cleaning. The Japanese underscored this favor done us more than a little bit. The tolks told us at the same time that in five or at the most twenty days the Grote Herr would be coming. The number twenty seems to be bewitched in Japan.

Mon. 13/25 Since the interpreters had not dared to report to the governor that Resanoff first requested Japanese doctors and then declined them, the Japanese doctors are visiting him daily. Resanoff asked one of them, "What is actually the root of my disease?"

"Ill will and ill humor," answered the bald-headed Japanese doctor very dryly.

Tues. 14/26 Resanoff's creed! He said among other things, "Duff and the Batavian Republic have to give me credit; for otherwise I will let the Grote Herrn coming from Jedo see the secret correspondence which Duff has conducted with me." With schadenfreude, "These Dutch are firmly in my claws."

Wed. 15/27 Today, I was present when Tamehatschira visited Resanoff. Since for the first time in a long time, I was present during the tolks' visit with our ambassador, His Excellency's behavior struck me all the more. His reception of the tolks was a continuous groaning and moaning. In answer to the tolks' question how the ambassador felt, Resanoff answered, "Somewhat better! But here (pointing to his heart) is ill! Your Grote Herr should come in twenty days?"

"Yes, yes!" answered Tamehatschira.

Resanoff, pointing to Fosse and Langsdorff, "Didn't I guess that?" (while declaiming with both hands and leaning out of his bed, sullied and dirty and half-naked). "You are all deceivers! Deceivers! Rogues! Knaves! You cannot be trusted! Whatever you tell me goes in one ear and out the other. That is the way all of you are! Indeed all of you! Aren't you? I still have to wait for an answer about the lacquerware? I know quite well! The governor has not sent anything at all about Jedo. Your governor sent me word that this house was for only a short time! And I have been tormenting myself here in this box for several months now, but I will bring the governor around. I will settle everything with him! He is just like you!!!"[2]

This reception had made Tamehatschira indignant. Standing up, he said, "If you talk like that, then no tolk will be allowed to speak with you any more."

Resanoff thereupon took him by the hand and forced him to sit down again, interpreted everything he had said to the tolks in Japanese to the Japanese guards accompanying the tolks. (The tolks never come alone but always in the company of a guard.) Resanoff usually speaks Japanese with the guards (who very seldom honor him with an answer) in order to have the guards as witnesses for what he had said to the tolks.

After Resanoff had talked to the Japanese in their mother tongue for a while, he ended the conversation, to his great self-satisfaction, with ябедничать! мошенники! Обманщики!" [conducting shady business, deceivers, cheats], etc., and similar Russian swear words which the Japanese have understood for a long time now.

Then Tamehatschira spoke again and said, "With the last mail we received news that a Grote Herr left Jedo ten days ago; and since he needs thirty days for the trip, he would arrive here in twenty days. This Grote Herr will bring definite answers to all of the ambassador's questions and requests. Therefore, the ambassador must be patient."

Vertrackt means depart in Dutch. When the tolk said that the Grote Herr had vertrackt, departed from Jedo ten days ago, Resanoff said, "Yes! Verreckt!" [German: croaked, died of animals] and laughed loudly.

"Verreckt! Verreckt!" yelled Fosse and Langsdorff and laughed with him. During the entire incident, Resanoff continually turned to Friderici, Koscheleff, and me and asked, "не правдали?" [Isn't that true?] Silence on our part was the best answer. This silence angered Resanoff every time, since he is used to hearing a "Yes! Yes!" from these creatures as an answer.

Fosse, unbidden, seeks to justify Resanoff's absurdities and chatters the most muddled and mixed up stuff. The tolks, calmly, always smiling, seldom leave Fosse unanswered. Langsdorff, installed as interpreter, laughs and jokes where there is nothing to make jokes about. The tolks handle Resanoff with great forbearance. They remain silent when he fumes. If Fosse or Langsdorff say something preposterous, they answer straight out, "That cannot be! I have to know that better! These tolks cannot have told you that for they are my subordinates and are informed by and do everything through me. You are prophesying too much prematurely, think you know more than we do." Or they use an appropriate Japanese saying.

Among other things Resanoff said, "I am sitting in prison. If I killed ten of you tolks, then I would know indeed why I am being held prisoner; and indeed then my business matters would go faster and better!"

"Yes! Yes! Prison!" repeated the tolks.

"I would rather take a thrashing than sit here!" said Resanoff very violently and translated what he had said into Japanese and all European languages.

"Yes! Yes! A thrashing!" repeated the tolks.

One of the oldest tolks, who had visited Resanoff at the most twice, answered Fosse's question why he comes so seldom. "I am exceedingly violent and that is why it is not advisable for me to visit the Russian ambassador."

Sosoimon, in Resanoff's presence, made a comparison between a sensible man and pure water. He said, "One may pour water into whatever vessel one wishes, the liquid takes on the form of the vessel. That is how a sensible man behaves in every situation in which he is put through duty. If the vessel is pure (and that is what all laws and customs based on experience and reason are in a country), then the water also has to stay pure. Impure water makes every animal sick and sullies the vessel."

While with our ambassador, Tamehatschira did not mention that he had been on the *Nadezhda* before going to Resanoff. Friderici and Koscheleff returned with me to the ship for the night. The tolks had come onboard with great Compliments from the governor and said that, since they had not been on the ship for such a long time, the governor had expressly sent them to inquire about the health of the captain and the officers. Then they asked whether the work on land (the riggings) would soon be completed, how long caulkers would be working, and whether our ship could be ready to sail in twenty days.

"Thirty days are what we will no doubt need," said Krusenstern.

"Mar!" The tolks asked, that is, Tamehatschira, "How is the work coming along?"

"Why not," said Krusenstern, "if the ambassador orders it, we can also undoubtedly be finished in twenty days."

"Ah! Ah!" said the tolk in a tone as if he wanted to say, "That's our business. That we intend to do."

Resanoff, who likes, all too gladly, to substitute outward appearances for what he himself may feel he lacks in inner worth, had all of his embroidered coats hung out to dry in Megasaki a little while ago, mainly, as could be seen from his expressions and comments, in order to give the Japanese an opportunity to admire their splendor. In answer to Fosse's question of one of the Japanese officers how he liked the clothing, he said, "Quite well! They are very nice! Here in Japan our ladies of pleasure wear such coats." Resanoff, who has eyes and ears all over, must have heard this anecdote red hot to his chagrin.

Among other things, Tamehatschira related how punctually Japanese laws have to be followed, that six years ago a Chinese junk, instead of coming to Nangasaki, had been driven into the Bay of Jedo and from there at great cost towed to Nangasaki. The voyage had taken a whole year.

Thurs. 16/28 Krusenstern had Golovatscheff report to Resanoff that the tolks had been onboard yesterday. Even though it must have flattered Resanoff that Krusenstern had reported that. He could not do anything without the ambassador's order, it indeed angered Resanoff that the tolks had turned to Krusenstern directly. In his first heat of anger, Resanoff immediately sent for a tolk who had been onboard yesterday, so that he could rebuke him for not having said that he had come to him from the ship. In the afternoon, the tolks had also come. We did not find out what the transactions were about. Golovatscheff only related that Resanoff himself is beginning to realize that nothing will come of our trip to Jedo, and that we will have to leave Japan sooner than we expect.

Fri. 17/1 The Japanese brought us our new topmast which Krusenstern had ordered. Every nail that had accidentally been driven in, every little piece of wood patched in, had been put in the new one the same way as in the old one. For that reason, Resanoff sent for Krusenstern to come on land.

Yesterday, the tolks formally brought greetings from the governor for Resanoff with the remark that the governor had many reasons to be dissatisfied with the ambassador. Since, however, waiting was so difficult for him and he had lost all of his patience through his illness, thus he gladly forgave him, since he forgot himself so often and had rebuked him. Resanoff then inquired if the last Portuguese ambassador had been beheaded in Megasaki or Desima.

"Yes! Yes! Megasaki!"

In order also to dampen Resanoff's desire to travel to Jedo, the tolks always related the high costs of the trip, since they know Resanoff's penchant for stinginess very well, and that the trip to and from Jedo cannot be done in less than one hundred days.

Sat. 18/2 The Chinese junks are preparing to sail again. One is already loaded, and four have been floated off of the sand. Every evening in the Chinese settlement there is a great illumination, music, and jubilation.

Madsiura is still ill but better. In order to quicken his recovery, his comrades, following the Japanese doctor's orders, take medicine. Egei burns moxsa[3] on himself daily. The Japanese are firmly convinced that it is not at all necessary for the patient to take medicine if his friend does it for him; that will help him get better. The moxsa cure is as follows. The Japanese uses a fine, highly flammable match to burn holes in his skin until he reaches the flesh and the pain has become unbearable. Only then does he stop. Every disease has its predetermined places on the body where burning has to be done and its predetermined figure given by the doctor—triangle, square, pentagon, etc., crosses, star, etc.

Sun. 19/3 Even though the tolks are always telling Resanoff about the trip to Jedo, they have said to Friderici, who asked how long it would still take, "You probably indeed understand, that we cannot determine the day when the Grote Herr will come, that he will be here however in about a month is certain. Then it cannot take longer than another four weeks and the business dealings with the Russian ambassador will be completed. The Grote Herr, however, will not travel back to Jedo before the ship has sailed away, that I can assure you."

Soon we will have no more flour, tea, and brandy. Resanoff does not want to provide himself with flour and tea here, even if he would be permitted to do so, but rather intends to let us suffer until we get to Kamtschatka or Kodiak, where he claims that we can be supplied with everything from the stores there, as if indeed the poverty in those locations were unknown to us. May he indeed do and be whatever he wants to be, if only we are finally rid of him.

Fosse, who visited us for the first time on ship, told us that Skiseima had visited our ambassador and had repeated the old news that the Grote Herr would arrive in about twenty days.

Mon. 20/4 Friderici and Koscheleff slept here with us for the night. Krusenstern gave the ambassador a report about the things that had been requested, received, and not received. Among the things not received was also a navigation chain. As concerns provisions, the tolks have assured us that we will be well supplied with everything here as well as for the voyage. For the flour we requested, they first have to bring the governor a report, because bread is not a usual food for Japanese as they are satisfied with rice, and, as a result, this article would have to be ordered.

Resanoff finally admits to himself that our departure, without our having obtained our objectives, is striding mightily closer and is happy at the thought of leaving Japan, where he has outlived his fame.

Tilesius is being richly supplied by the untertolks with fish and all kinds of animals that he draws with a very high degree of skill. Tilesius' drawing talent is indispensable for our voyage.

Tues. 21/5 At the captain's order, Ratmanoff, Golovatscheff, and I went on land today to inspect our riggings and put them in order—otherwise only one of us went on land with the report, and we usually found Resanoff in Fosse's room. That was the case again today. When, however, Ratmanoff, Doctor Espenberg, Golovatscheff, Friderici, Koscheleff, and I entered the room one after another and filled it, we could see that Resanoff was disconcerted. The only thing he said in his initial confusion, without paying any attention to the report that Ratmanoff handed him, was, anxiously turning to Golovatscheff to ask him, "You were here yesterday?" Then he reconsidered, walked up and down several times, and reproached Ratmanoff for not having been on land in such a long time. We then took our leave and went to our magazine to inspect our riggings. After finishing our work, we played svaiku in the courtyard and stayed a little longer to wait for a breakfast that Friderici had made for us. Then we went to Resanoff and took our leave. Resanoff invited us at leave-taking to come to lunch, repeated his request, especially because of Ratmanoff, who was on land for the first time after such a long time. Ratmanoff's decline surprised Resanoff not a little, and, even though we could not give a reason for our hurry, we followed Ratmanoff's example and went back onboard together. Since today was Romberg's dejour to do work on land, Golovatscheff and I were excused. Ratmanoff ordered Otto Kotzebue to stay on land instead of an officer; that, however, was not to Mr. von Krusenstern's liking. He said that our sailors never should be left on land without an officer and ordered Romberg to go there immediately after our meal. When Romberg reached Megasaki, Resanoff asked Koscheleff (whom he calls the second Grote), "Why is no one having lunch with me?"

"I do not know," answered Koscheleff (and he could not say more than that, because otherwise he would have known more than those of us who were being talked about). Then the gentlemen began playing svaiku. Resanoff sat in the anteroom, Schemelin opposite him, both loudly philosophizing, with so much energy that we could hear the discussion.

Resanoff raised his voice and said, "If I make mistakes or do not make them, if I am bad, dumb, malicious, why doesn't someone tell me? Why doesn't anyone advise me? I would accept advice only too gladly. What is the reason for everyone fleeing from me? Why am I always alone? here in Japan, where we indeed have to be viewed as one family."

Koscheleff said then, while playing svaiku, "попал!" [on the mark].

Resanoff continued, "Even less understandable for me is Ratmanoff, because where that will end, I do not know; since in Kamtschatka all discord between us was put to rest. Why does he feed it? He is enveloping the captain in new troubles. Why embitter me, since all should protect and respect me?" etc., etc.

Wed. 22/6 There is a large change in temperature in twenty-four hours from 16⁰ to 20⁰.

At Schafei's advice, Madsiura gave the banjos a letter whose content we do not know. Because of this letter, our Japanese got in a fight, and that was the reason for Madsiura's cutting his throat with the shaving blade. Even though the information is from unreliable people, that is, from Resanoff's servant Alexander, the soldier Monakoff and company, there may indeed be some truth to it, that the content of Madsiura's letter is as follows: that we Russians are especially bigoted Christians, that the Japanese stranded by a storm were forced in Irkutsk and other cities in Siberia to do hard labor, even to clean privies, and that is why, from need and despair, many stranded Japanese have become Christians, etc.

Espenberg visits Resanoff regularly every day so that he cannot reproach him, since Resanoff is ever ready to do that.

Rumor has it that the Grote Herr has been in Osaka for four days. Have patience, and we will not only leave Japan but also return home once again. Resanoff is bedridden again.

Thurs. 23/7 The fellow countrymen of our Japanese do not believe that they have really seen the Russian Emperor.[4] Concerning the theater in Petersburg, our Japanese gave such a supernatural description of it that no one wants to believe the story. Several days ago, Egei came laughing to Resanoff and said, "My fellow countrymen do not want to believe that such large metamorphoses occur in the Petersburg Theater."[5]

Today we put up a new trestletree and brought our completely repaired shrouds from land—the start of rigging our ship.

In the evening, we caught a large hawk with a hook. We had stuck a piece of salt-meat on a hook and had let the bait float in the water. The hawk grabbed it in its claws and was so fixed on its booty that it would rather be caught than let go of its booty.

Sat. 25/9 Resanoff has once again acquired from Tamehatschira four pages of a Dutch newspaper in which the route of our voyage is described in detail. The newspaper says that the Russians will be leaving Japan in 1805. No one could know that better than the Dutch. Our arrival could be given quite exactly. No one other than the Dutch could know however how the Russian embassy to Japan was progressing and that no business is completed in Japan in less than six months. That the newspaper has us, however, sailing into all of the East Indian harbors on our return voyage is something I truly wish for, but doubt it and will regret only that the newspaper's writer did not tell the truth. The intimacy between Resanoff and Sosoimon seems to have ended; otherwise, three-haired Tamehatschira would not have brought him the newspapers.

Sun. 26/10 Today, Resanoff went out alone past the bamboo stakes and behind the board fence, quite far inland toward the city. He did not meet anyone, neither in front of the houses nor at the windows, nor on the streets or in the fields, and returned. Emboldened he compelled, half by force, Fedoroff to accompany him. They had gone quite a stretch without meeting anyone and turned a corner. A lot of women and children working in a field caught sight of our indiscreet Resanoff and raised a horrid cry. Resanoff, who immediately lost his head, frightened by the noise, panicked and ran away. Fedoroff followed him slowly. At a distance, Resanoff called again and again, "Come! Come! They can throw stones at us."

12-2. Walk from Nangasaki or rather the return. "Ivan Ivanitsch, hurry up. They can throw stones at us!"

That same evening, His Excellency bragged about his heroic deed, how, despite all of the guards, he had ventured several hundred steps outside the bamboo.

Several days ago, we caught a large hawk, which we kept alive in the chicken basket. One of our sailors carelessly let it fly away. It was doubly unpleasant for us since Resanoff, upon hearing about it, requested of our captain, who had gone ashore today, that he be sent the live hawk.

Ivan Ivanitsch Fedoroff, kindheartedness itself, had ordered, more for his soldiers than for himself, four pfund of tobacco. When it was brought to him, Resanoff immediately sent for Fedoroff, gave him a reprimand and bawled him out for his audacity in ordering tobacco without his permission. Прихоты ваши [your caprices], highhandedness, etc., were the mildest expressions. Fedoroff, like all quiet men, lost his patience and then it was Resanoff's turn to listen. He recounted all the strings, mussels, paper, etc., that Fosse and Langsdorff had ordered that were more capricious. Resanoff swallowed his anger because he had no answer to Fedoroff's dry, short truths. The two separated frostily.

Resanoff was immediately happy to have the opportunity or a person against whom he could loose his bitter rage. Honey was brought, which Resanoff himself had ordered but forgot in his anger. No one knew who had ordered it and who should get the honey (for, if the embassy accepted it, each thought, then the bill would also be coming for the things which each one had ordered for himself). Friderici and Koscheleff had spent the night on ship and therefore were not present. That's why Resanoff said very violently, "Friderici must have ordered it for himself!" (So much for today.) Friderici has just gone on land. I will be curious to hear how Resanoff greets him or has greeted him!

Resanoff is thirsty for strife. His pickthanks are on our ship—Kamentschikoff and the sailors Резеб Боязитов и Клим Григориев [Reseb Boyasitoff and Klim Grigorieff]. The latter two told us themselves. In order to entice the sailors, Resanoff has promised them their discharge upon our return, promises them several rewards and favors in addition, but always while denigrating Krusenstern and us officers in their eyes. Our sailors could not stomach that, and that is why they have told us everything. That is how he belittles Krusenstern and us to the tolks, saying how little importance we have, how totally dependent we are upon him, etc. "Mar!" is what the tolks say, nothing helps. Resanoff cannot stop backbiting.

Ratmanoff behaves like a man who is divided within himself. He is everything at the wrong time, proud, scornful, and a braggart. He has less knowledge than anyone of us Чин ум не придает (Rank does not guarantee intelligence), so he has to listen to a lot of earfuls. I am afraid of a lot of strife and fights.

Our stern needs to be repaired. Bellingshausen, who lives in the gun cabin, knew the defect the best and spoke with Makar Ivanitsch Ratmanoff about it. Ratmanoff, however, answered in a tone as if he wanted to say, "What do you know? I have to know that better!" and said, rejecting him, "That is not necessary!"

Bellingshausen did not answer but did not let himself be led astray and instead spoke with Krusenstern about the matter, who, as an intelligent man, took his advice, as an intelligent man, and ordered that the defect be repaired. Ratmanoff's shallow pretensions are all the more apparent the less Krusenstern takes notice of them. If we did not have our hands full with Resanoff, we would undoubtedly have wrangling and strife among ourselves.

Mon. 27/11 Friderici went ashore yesterday expecting Resanoff to receive him with reproaches but was mistaken. There was no talk at all of the honey, since Resanoff had said as his first heated remark to Fosse, "I am going to order the Japanese that they are not, except for my and your orders (that is, Fosse's) to take orders from anyone else." Fosse, puffed up with his importance, strutted.

Friderici, in the presence of Schemelin and Langsdorff, spoke with our ambassador. Resanoff defended himself with foul language. Finally, Friderici said, "You, Your Excellency, have the right to do and leave alone whatever you want to. No one dares step on me and my honor. If anyone should dare try it, I will find it necessary to show that I can avenge myself and my honor in every possible way. Thereupon, the conversation ended completely peacefully." Friderici's last remark must have struck Resanoff. Early this morning, the pistols were missing which Friderici had got from the Japanese to clean. The pistols were searched for everywhere, but they could not be found.

Koscheleff said by chance, "Those are Löwenstern's pistols!" and, taking them in his hands, "They are also quite good. If I need them, Löwenstern will undoubtedly let me have them."

"Indeed, yes!" said Friderici.

The suite or the entire party was present during this exchange and, in a little bit, as if by magic, the pistols were there again. You should not forget that we had no gunpowder since we had given it up, conscientiously, to the Japanese down to the last grain.

Such events say a lot about character.

Monakoff is and remains the court fool. One fixed idea of Resanoff's—it nauseates—gets repeated every day, "Just imagine, the Japanese have fallen in love with Monakoff." (The blockhead) Resanoff laughs and jokes with the Japanese and Monakoff &. Co. so often that no one, from chagrin and anger, listens to him and even less wants to laugh with him. Bawdry usually replaces this pastime, for bawdry is and remains Resanoff's preferred kind of entertainment.

Resanoff now often begins to speak about the reception with the Grote Herr and only because he seems of a mind to comply with Japanese wishes and even to agree to humiliations (an extreme). In order to prepare us, he now always says to everyone several times a day, "We have to do everything the Japanese want us to do, simply so that we can finally put this cursed Japan behind us."

The Japanese pocketbooks, although not made for our pockets, are nice and practical, decorated with dainty locks, paintings, and pockets of all kinds. The outer garment of the Japanese is usually lined with white taffeta on which the beloved has usually put some kind of symbol. A Japanese showed us two crabs, very nicely drawn with a few strokes of the pen, which held their claws spread so that when the garment is put on it fits exactly on the shoulders as if they wanted to say, "As firmly as the crabs hold their catch in their claws, that is how firmly I also love you." Hidden deep in the pocketbook were drawn a rooster and a hen, which, as much as I understand of the matter, were sacrificing to Madame Venus.

Tues. 28/12 A few days ago, when Resanoff intended to go to Nangasaki without permission and was frightened back by the screams of the women and children, an officer came a half hour later, sent by the governor to Resanoff, with the message that, since the Russians are forbidden to go behind the bamboo fence, that was indeed the case today, the governor wishes to call the ambassador's attention to this fact and to request that such transgressions of Japanese orders be forbidden. The governor also requests to know who attempted to go into the city? Resanoff had no other alternative but to say, "I was the one," since there were too many witnesses when he ran back for him to blame someone else. Later, there was no further talk of this unsuccessful walk.

- 13 -

The First Audience

March

Wed. 1/13 Friderici and Koscheleff came onboard for the night and related the following very interesting scenes from yesterday and today.

Resanoff had sent for a tolk the day before yesterday in order to discuss the still missing boards, but none came. Therefore yesterday, he once again sent for tolks. Instead of only one coming, Skiseima, who never visits without a reason, arrived with two other tolks.

Golovatscheff, who was present, said, "There certainly is a reason for that."

Resanoff answered him peevishly. "And, if twenty of them came, it would be all the same to me!"

Skiseima appeared with a great many greetings and Believtheit from the governor, spoke however for a long time about a lot of unimportant things until he thought he had reached the right point in time to say, "You will hardly be traveling to the court." Resanoff did not understand him. The tolks looked at each other, surprised by Resanoff's calmness. After a little while, Skiseima said again, "The Russian ambassador will hardly be traveling to Jedo."

Resanoff: "What? I'm not to go to Jedo?"

Ski.: "If you were to receive permission to travel to Jedo, the Grote Herr would certainly not be sent here.

Re.: "I have not been sent to the Grote Herr; I have to see your emperor himself and personally hand over my emperor's letter and gifts.

Ski.: "Mar!"

Re.: "I have to go to Jedo because I have my emperor's order to do so!"

Ski.: "No, that cannot be permitted. The Grote Herr, whom we expect, is authorized by our emperor to take care of everything with you."

Re.: "In other words, the Emperor of Japan does not intend to receive any Russian ambassador at all?"

Ski.: "Yes! Yes! Not permitted this time, another time! Yes! Yes!"

Re.: "That is not possible. I have to hand over the letter myself."

Ski: "The Grote Herr will inform you about everything. It would have been very pleasant for us tolks to accompany you on your trip, to travel with you to Jedo, to share your joy and suffering." After a little while Skiseima asked, since the news had disconcerted Resanoff, "You have had enough time to examine the lacquerware?"

"Oh yes," answered Resanoff, but made no move to return them.

I would bet that the tolks are audacious enough to demand that Resanoff give them back.

Thank goodness! Now it is certain that we will be leaving Japan within a month.

In answer to Resanoff's question about the Grote Herr, Skiseima said, "Since the Grote Herr is being sent by the emperor himself, that means he is the most important person one can imagine."

In answer to Friderici's question, "Then we will not get to see Nangasaki at all?"

Skiseima answered, "Why not? The Grote Herr is going to live in Nangasaki, and, when you go to him, you will be led thorough the entire city."

Where is Resanoff's list of lacquerware now which he intended to order in Meako?

Concerned, Skiseima inquired especially about the condition of the ship, whether our work would soon be finished; since one could see that the deck for our shallop had been finished for a long time, why we had not put it on, etc.

In answer to the question whether we would be permitted to purchase various things here, Skiseima answered, "No! No! Not permitted! For what do you need so much? Your voyage to Kamtschatka does not take so long, and you can get everything you need there."

"The ship needs a lot," said Friderici, and, since no one offered an answer, he continued, "Since we will stay in Kamtschatka for only a short time, we will not have time to provide for ourselves properly." General silence.

Then Skiseima inquired what would be the best time for us to sail from here, as far as the weather and the time of year were concerned. "May and June are very stormy and wet," he thought. He was told to go to Krusenstern with this question.

The tolks had barely left when Fosse suggested, "Since the Japanese do not want to permit us to travel to Jedo, we should withhold the gifts" (nice advice!) and added to his stupidity, "This whole expedition is bringing our ambassador little honor! And—and there is little to be served by it."

Resanoff, for his part, showed an unnatural, forced joy after the tolks had left. He, who had treated Friderici and Koscheleff up to now in so unfriendly a manner, was, as if by magic, obtrusive, obliging, and candid toward them.

All of his creatures were forgotten. He took no notice of them. After Resanoff had prattled on about a lot of things confusedly, he said, "I am now determined, even though I have children whom I love, to sacrifice myself! I will travel to Kodiak. I will send Fosse overland with dispatches from Kamtschatka to Petersburg. I will give you, Friderici, the choice at the end of my embassy whether you want to travel by land or to continue your voyage by water on the *Nadezhda* or whether you will stay in Kamtschatka with General Koscheleff or travel with me to Kodiak. I have written very favorably about you, Koscheleff [Dimitri Ivanitsch], to the emperor, and without a doubt you will receive an order and a Charakter [title]. The *Nadezhda* will take me to Kodiak and continue her voyage from there. Langsdorff will stay with me."

After Resanoff had declaimed all of these unripe plans, he took Friderici and Koscheleff individually aside and said to them, "Those scoundrels! Those Japanese do not deserve to get that many gifts. We intend to do business for the crown and decorate Kamtschatka and Kodiak, and we will be thanked for that. A couple of glass tables, a pair of mirrors and chandeliers would look very good в шевском дому [in the house] of Kamtschatka's chief; and with the quantity that we have it will not be noticed that a few are missing. So that the Japanese, however, do not notice anything, you [Koscheleff and Friderici] could easily secretly pack these things in your rooms and send them onboard with the riggings and the casks." The scoundrel got excuses as an answer, since he cannot be cured.

When the tolks left Resanoff yesterday, they went to observe our cooper's work and asked, "How soon will he be finished?"

Friderici answered, "He cannot be finished soon enough, but it cannot be done all at once."

Ski.: "We have to inquire about that because the news has suddenly come that the Russian ambassador will not be traveling to Jedo."

Frider.: "Oh! Oh! We have suspected that for a long time and have thought that with certainty, since the time when the tolks told us that obertolks would be traveling to Jedo instead of Ober Hoft Duff." Friderici had barely said that when the tolks broke out in loud laughter and politely took their leave.

Today, Sosoimon was at Resanoff's on account of the boards that had been requested and said, "Indeed, we see that all of the repairs have been made to the ship and therefore the requested boards of camphor wood will not be provided because they are superfluous.

Krusenstern was luckily present and answered, "I need the wood and boards, not for my own use; I need them to repair the ship. If you wish to give them to me, then I am well served in that way; if not, then I am forced to leave without them and will have to help myself in some other manner."

By his expression, Sosoimon showed that he was disquieted at having been hasty and then said, "In order to fill your casks with water, you may have as many vessels as you want, and we will supply you with sufficient fire wood, provisions, and all

13-1a. [Left] "All is fine, Your Excellency." [Under the money bags] казна *[kazna: State Treasury]. [Right] "Here is the piece I got off!" F.p.: "All of the mirrors have holes in them. I was given 1,000 dahler . . . in place of all of them. Here are 500 dahler for you. Please give me a receipt. You accepted the goodies."*

13-1b. [Left] "Indeed, yes, Sir, Your Excellency!" [Middle] "You remember. In Siberia, where we had so many means of getting rich—long live the treasury which fell to us and permitted us to steal it—and the stupid American Company—I shall take the skin off it." [Right] "In trade, I am the first agent."[1]

other necessities." Sosoimon said, " The Grote Herr is expected in nine or ten days, and in the first days of the month of April, you will be sailing away." In the course of the conversation, Sosoimon asked, "And you, Sir, Captain, are always on the ship?"

"Yes," said Krusenstern, "because the ship is warmer than on land."

Sosoimon, "Yes, yes! You are captain, everything on the ship is under your command, and you find fulfillment in your duty. Your situation may be as whatever, may change to whatever, you act in every situation like a prudent man! Mar!" Pointing to Resanoff, "The ambassador is totally different. He does not like it here, because! Because it is too cold here."

Resanoff then answered, very ill humored, "That has become a habit with me."

When Sosoimon had gone, Resanoff explained his plans to our captain and said, as if he were happy to leave Japan without carrying out his purpose, "Now we will soon be seeing Pavel Ivanitsch Koscheleff once again (importantly), and, since we will be leaving here very early, we can do a lot of things on our return voyage—inspect Urup, Sachalin, Matzumai, etc. We will stay in Kamtschatka for only a short time. I am sending Fosse to Petersburg, and you will take me, Friderici, and Langsdorff to Kodiak, where I will stay to put everything in order. I will make that area happy. You will travel from there according to your instructions. After completing my business, I will return with a vessel from Ochotsk to Kamtschatka and back and travel from there finally overland to Petersburg." Resanoff now claims that Friderici will go with him to Kodiak even though he had left it up to him before to do whatever he wanted to when the embassy was over.

Krusenstern asked Resanoff not to forget to prepare the Grote Herr for the possibility that on our return voyage, in case of contrary winds, we might by chance once again be cast upon Japanese shores, and to ask him therefore to issue an order for the Japanese in such an event not to hold us up unnecessarily.

Normally, Resanoff did not like to let Friderici and Koscheleff go onboard, and now he even suggested it himself by saying, "Don't you want to go to the ship? Go ahead! Go ahead!"

I am of such bad character that I believe that he is misappropriating gifts with Fosse and Schemelin at this time.

Thurs. 2/14 Now, Resanoff is trying to slow down everything, just as he earlier did everything hastily. Our captain's every request, be it ever so urgent, when the tolks say, "Yes! Yes! Tomorrow! Tomorrow!" or "In three or four days."

Resanoff calls out every time, "The day after tomorrow! or in five or six days is time enough" and always adds one or a couple of days.

His Excellency is feeling very much better since yesterday. He is eating at table again and is in higher spirits. Even Fosse is very polite and ready to serve others. Today, he even offered Bellingshausen a glass of punsch.

Resanoff has always had an inclination to eavesdrop. During the incident (February 26) when Ivan Ivanovitsch Fedoroff and Bellingshausen were talking about Resanoff's behavior, he overheard it from behind the door and when the talk was of ropes, etc., Resanoff rushed in the door and said, "Как? [How?] I ordered the ropes myself, etc." Bellingshausen's witty remarks, which can be very biting, and laughter forced Resanoff to leave the room again.

Fri. 3/15 For a long time, Resanoff has sought an opportunity to speak privately with one of the tolks, not to do business but rather afterwards to be able to lie about all of things that the tolk had told him. This wish was finally fulfilled. The last time that Sosoimon was with him, Resanoff spoke with him alone for about five minutes, and, now, he is full of all of the things that Sosoimon told him. Since Resanoff does not want to hear from us that his behavior has made the trip to Jedo impossible, he now assures us that Sosoimon had revealed secrets to him, that three months ago it had been decided and even much earlier, that the Russian ambassador would not be traveling to Jedo.

Since Resanoff has an exceedingly great inclination to everything that is dishonest and is actually the only one who stepped over the boundary the Japanese had proscribed, he now seeks to force everyone to go beyond the bamboo to acquire accomplices. If someone from the ship comes on land, he shows the innocent man what he has to do, convinces him to follow him, and also goes beyond the bamboo. He does that only in the hope that we, led astray by his curiosity, will also, without him, follow his example. The Japanese would certainly complain about us, and Resanoff believes he thereby has the right to push all of the blame onto us that the embassy has not been accepted. This view is black in spirit but totally in Resanoff's spirit.

Today, for the first time in a long time, Resanoff put on a worn-out blue coat to which he had fastened the Star of St. Anne. Resanoff was looking toward Desima through a Tubus and caught sight of Duff, who was also looking toward Megasaki with a telescope. When he caught sight of the Star he took his cap off to it. Duff, even though in a yellow waistcoat with a black collar, blue pantaloons, and a green cap, was very properly dressed. Resanoff, without considering how improperly he himself had been dressed the whole time, mocked Duff's costume not a little bit, mocked him, and forced himself to laugh. When he saw that those around him really did not want to laugh, in Japanese, he asked the Japanese standing next to him, and translated his remark for me each time, "Is Duff a good Man?"

(Japanese:) "Vorui," that means he is bad.

"Do you love the Dutch?"

(Japanese:) "Vorui."

Then Resanoff turned to me and said, "Listen to what he is saying," laughed himself, and the Japanese laughed with him.

Then he began again in Japanese to talk of Kubo Sama and Dairo[2] and asked, "If Kubo sama sent you a vakisasch [a little knife, in Japanese, a dagger], "Would you cut open my belly?"

(Jap:) "Yes, yes."

"And if Dairo sent you one?"

(Jap:) "He will never send me one, for he is the first spiritual leader and a holy person."

Resanoff's loud laughter was totally out of place. He also laughed alone.

At table, Resanoff said, "The Chinese and Japanese are very similar to each other. Since I have been in Kiachta,[3] I can judge this," and often spoke quite irrationally to prove his statement; that is the reason why he should be all the more ashamed of himself for saying he knows the Chinese and Japanese exactly, when he does not understand how to deal with them.

Resanoff, who is always making plans, sent our emperor from Kamtschatka an exceedingly detailed plan for trade with Japan, China, and the Philippines, etc., which the failure of the embassy has caused to miscarry. This plan is now causing Resanoff not just a little uneasiness and to rack his brains, since otherwise he would not admit to us that he had sent the plan to Petersburg. Now, he is trying to collect various views on how the mistake can be rectified.

The consumption of coffee, sugar, brandy, and tea on land is double that of our ship. Even the quantity of soya is large. Fosse must have put back a private store of these things because not even a quarter of it is being used.

Sat. 4/16 Today, Resanoff again gave Sosoimon a secret audience, after which he sent word to Mr. von Krusenstern that he hoped to receive 3,000 pud of salt and 5,000 pud of rice from the Japanese. We do not know how this trade agreement may be concluded. Resanoff also requested a Japanese vessel manned by Japanese and hopes to receive one, for what purpose is also a secret from us.

When Golovatscheff, who was on land, said, "Since the whole quantity of salt, rice, and other provisions we have requested weighs around 10,000 pud, it will be necessary to know somewhat earlier that we will be getting it for sure, so that we do not have to reload, since the things require not a small amount of room and we would not be able to secure them."

Resanoff's peremptory answer was, "It is not my business to rack my brains about the division of work and time."

Resanoff also related, as if Sosoimon had told him, that it would be possible to load ten ships with tree resin in Nangasaki. Not a word has been said about the prices for all of the things Resanoff has negotiated. Probably, Resanoff will do everything he can to keep them a secret, since that makes drawing bills with arbitrary prices much easier.

Sun. 5/17 Romberg brought the news that Resanoff said today that he intends to be in Petersburg before the *Nadezhda*. He also said that we need not appear at all as if we were fitting ourselves out for the voyage. Why does he not say that to Krusenstern?

Mon. 6/18 Resanoff said today, ignoring Krusenstern, in the presence of a lot of people, that he would not travel to Kodiak but rather go straight from Kamtschatka to Petersburg.

As far as salt and rice are concerned, Resanoff thinks for sure that it will be a quantity of 8,000 pud. As far as our provisions are concerned, the Japanese will provide us with everything. Indeed, without being asked to do so, they have brought samples of hardtack that is of equal to the best European. They nonetheless will certainly not sell us even a needle, since every time trade is mentioned, they say, "Not permitted." I think that the tolks now visit Resanoff so often in order to examine his intentions even more thoroughly, so that they can report everything in detail to the Grote Herr, so that he knows about everything before the entreuüe [audience] and can definitely answer every question.

At night, the Japanese have their own way of dividing up the hours. Lights are designated or divided by strokes. If a light has burned to a stroke, then the hour is tolled with two little sticks.

The day before yesterday, Resanoff had no small fright. A Chinese junk washed up to Megasaki and stopped on the sand two steps away from Resanoff's apartment. The whole house full of chandeliers, tables, mirrors, etc., was in danger. Resanoff is said to have been so upset that he could not recover for a long time.

Old Zudei, to pass time, is still burning moxsa on himself; and Skiseima is thereby getting better day-by-day. The last time I was on land, I saw the old fellow over the course of one and one-half hours burning himself in four different places. He had four piles of matches (each pile as large as a big pea) on his thigh. As soon as one pile died out, he lit the next with the remaining coals that died in the flesh and so forth.

Tues. 7/19 Today at noon, I had the pleasure of dining at Resanoff's. Krusenstern was there. I can call it a pleasure because, since nothing is coming of the trip to Jedo. Resanoff has become expansive. He gave us a delicious breakfast, a good midday meal, good wine, and afterwards punsch in addition. Resanoff is otherwise not generous.

Tamechatschira, who came today, brought Resanoff little consolation. As far as prices are concerned, he contradicted the information of the other tolks and made a new transaction himself, which left us all confused.

Tamechatschira said to Krusenstern, in Resanoff's presence, "Get your ship ready. In a month, you will certainly be under sail, for the Grote Herr will be here in about six days."

Today, we raised the topmast cap, rigged the lowest yards, and continued to work on our riggings. Resanoff continually makes new plans. Now, he wants to have trade between Kamtschatka, Kodiak, and Manila, without asking the Spaniards if they will be served by it.

Wed. 8/20 Normally, I brag about my health! However, my spitting up of blood today is not to be placed on a par with the preservation of my comrades. Yesterday evening, the past night, as well as the whole day today, whenever I coughed, I always had a mouthful of blood—bad enough!

Thurs. 9/21 Today, Krusenstern made me a gift of woolen socks after he had heard that I was spitting up blood. This compassion is flattering, but it is unpleasant to be in the situation of being pitied. Krusenstern was also moved to write me because I never wanted Espenberg to prescribe anything for my spitting up blood. The old man was totally unhappy abut my disobedience and that I had not told him immediately that I was spitting up blood. For better or worse, I now have to gulp down his mixture.

Fri. 10/22 We got a Japanese boat for our use, which was given to me to transport our riggings and all of the things on land belonging to the ship out here.

Horner is now on land every day and is undertaking experiments with a pendulum. We have our riggings so far that, if necessary, we can raise all of the topmasts and yards.

Schemelin, undoubtedly not in his right senses, is busy writing a mercantile dissertation about trade with Japan and has only begun his scribbling, since he knows for sure that our embassy will not be accepted and suspects that trade with Japan will also come to naught, especially before we have gotten to know Japan.

Sat. 11/23 Equinoctial weather. Worried Chinese and Japanese continually go around the bay. We alone depend upon our anchor.

Sun. 12/24 Resanoff has suddenly become very pensive. We celebrated the Emperor's coronation day very quietly because of the failed embassy.

Mon. 13/25 As usual, Espenberg goes ashore every day. When he wanted to return onboard today, Resanoff all at once had the idea of going to the bay where our shallop is being repaired. (Krusenstern is having the shallop covered with copper and a deck made so that the little boat can also be used for short trips.) No sooner said than done! Without thinking much about it, Resanoff climbed into the boat. He was barely in it when he started and asked, "Who of the officers is there?"

Ratmanoff answered, "Espenberg." It was, however, too late for Resanoff to turn around because the gates had already been closed and locked. Resanoff was sorry that he had not taken a bottle of wine along. He now had to go there. He only stayed at the shallop a little while, was in a very good humor and promised to send Ratmanoff a bottle of wine. When he arrived back at the gate to Megasaki, it was closed. The Japanese are never in a hurry, and Resanoff, for better or worse, had to wait behind the gate. Not used to waiting, he began to make a lot of noise and to raise a ruckus, as if a fire were behind him, until the gate finally opened, and the Japanese just as dispassionately let him in, just as they do with any one of us. They looked at Resanoff, who complained to them, just as dispassionately and indifferently as if dealing with a third party.

Tues. 14/26 During the night, a strong wind arose, with frequent gusts, which turned into a typhoon around eight o'clock in the morning. At nine o'clock, our anchor moved. We had to cast a third anchor and very near Desima. In nineteen fuss of water, we withstood the raging wind. It had barely lessened at about nine o'clock in the morning, so we had been keeping the warp and cable ready to kedge ourselves away from a dangerous spot. Resanoff, using a red flag, requested a boat from us (could have waited a bit). As soon as the boat was free, Bellingshausen went ashore, got the daily provisions there and heard that the Grote Herr was to arrive the day after tomorrow. His Excellency was pleased to believe that we had let ourselves purposely be driven to Desima in order to take a look at the Dutch houses.

In the evening, we put on our moorings again.

Wed. 15/27 During my stay in Megasaki today, the mayor of Nangasaki came to look at everything himself and to put everything in order for the arrival of the Grote Herr. His attention focused mainly on the bamboo stakes, board wall, and gate. He looked at everything else superficially.

The officers of the guard said that Resanoff, as well as every officer, had been sketched and that they would now be selling our portraits engraved in copper. They said that everyone was portrayed in his usual garments. If that is the case, then Resanoff glitters in copper in his nightcap or English wig, torn, dirty stockings, and slippers (worse than my dog-eared ones). Tamechatshira came at noon and confirmed the report that the Grote Herr would arrive in Nangasaki the day after tomorrow.

Sosoimon came with a great deal of Believtheit von das Gouvernör and said that the governor was surprised, since the Russians, indeed, know that it is forbidden to go behind the bamboo stakes, that, nonetheless, someone had dared not only to go out of the gate alone but, in addition, even into the nearby house and into the garden belonging to the house. So they have found out about his tricks. Look at that! Resanoff could not resist secretly taking the liberty of going there himself.

The provision's tolk related today that the Grote Herr would come the day after tomorrow. The governor had traveled out to meet him. The Grote Herr would rest for three days after his arrival in Nangasaki, then deliberate with the governor, and only then would the ambassador be able to visit him, that is, before Resanoff's departure.

Several Japanese officers sheared off the sections of water by Megasaki. It was raining a little bit. As a result, they waded, or rather waddled in the mess with rods, with the best of hairdos, coifed at their best with umbrellas. For what we did not know. The work and the behavior of the Japanese I found very amusing, especially if one of them stumbled and was concerned only about his pigtail in the rain.

Today, Resanoff sent Tilesius two bouquets of flowers obtained from the governor. This attention surprised us because we remembered Resanoff's earlier behavior toward Tilesius, and it is striking that Resanoff is flattering all of the ones for whom he did not have a good word earlier.

Thurs. 16/28 Resanoff wrote to Krusenstern that he should, at the request of the Japanese, stop all work or give schabasch on the 19th and 20th because of several Japanese festivals. The tolks told us today that tomorrow we will receive 900 katti of hardtack from the Japanese.

Fri. 17/29 Krusenstern, who had visited Resanoff in the morning, brought the news that the long awaited Grote Herr had finally arrived. The Japanese appear not to want to keep us here much longer, since today they brought hardtack, coal, fire wood, boards, beams for the trestle trees, which Krusenstern had only requested a few days ago. Otherwise, eight to fourteen days pass before we receive requests. Now, barely three days pass after a request.

13-2. Shearing off Megasaki

Resanoff has been busy with new trade speculations. Recently, he wanted to take iron from Japan to Kamtschatka, and now he intends to take iron from Kamtschatka to Japan. Since Kamtschatka is poor, Resanoff forgets that that poor land has no other article of trade than fish and more fish.

Resanoff wants to build all of the houses in Kamtschatka from Japanese tiles and roof them with Japanese roof tile. As long as a land still suffers from a lack of foodstuffs, as in this isolated part of the earth, one cannot and dare not think of luxury.

Sat. 18/30 There are usually two flags hanging from Japanese boats, the one of the ruler or prince of the land and his sign or coat of arms, in Japanese mong [mon], which is sewn on the flag as well as on the curtains and sails. The other flag is decorated with the coat of arms of the commanding officer. Of their signs of honor that they cart around with them, there are several decorated with their coats of arms or mong. The most distinguished flag is the one with blue letters on a white field like the imperial one. The highest-ranking ones are particularly those with their mong on a red field; then follow the white ones and then the blue flags. The police or city flag has a black stripe or line in the middle. Our guard boats belong to Prince Fiesen, appear however to be manned by the imperial guard.

The crews change when the boats change. The officers change weekly since that is the time when the flags are changed. Even the horses' trappings have the officer's mong to whom the horses belong sewn on them. Every Japanese has two mongs, one for himself and one belonging to the whole family or the family coat of arms. Even the fortifications have similar mongs decorating curtains and flags. (*See color plates 21 and 22.*)

If someone receives a coat or garment from a ranking man in the area, from the ruler of the area or the emperor, he receives the garment with the coats of arms and this mong is what makes the gift valuable. Even on their possessions such as furniture, equipment, swords, pillows, etc., etc., they have their mong printed or sketched. Every Japanese has his mong woven on each sleeve and on the back of the garment.

Sun. 19/31 A Chinese junk raised its masts, which had been repaired, and put them in place. The procedure was a follows: after the masts had been pulled out of the water with a lot of noise and put lengthwise on the junk, two other junks came alongside that junk. Each one put two ropes on the mast; then they put a block or sheer legs over the mast on which, in turn, four ropes were fastened to the mast. On the lower end were fastened two lines to keep the mast from moving forwards. And then a countless number of men on all three of the junks, with an exceedingly large amount of noise, pulled the ropes on the windlass. Since the block was farther back than the spar of the mast, the sheer legs or block sank as on an incline as the mast rose and fell forwards when the mast reached its perpendicular position. The foremast was put up from back to front with the help of the main mast. Since the Chinese have neither loops nor blocks, the friction of the ropes hindered the work, so that we certainly could have raised those masts with 20 percent of the crew that they did.

One other junk lowered its masts by raising them into the air on the windlass only so much as was necessary in order to knock out the supports in the hold. Two ropes were taken forward from the end of the mainmast, whereby they moved a little backwards, because it was also being kept in the hold and finally was shoved lengthwise into the water. They raised the large mast out of the water through the port in the front of the junk. The foremast was let down along the mainmast.

The provision's tolk told us, as a secret, that on Wednesday Resanoff would make a visit to the Grote Herr (Japanese Daimeo).

Ratmanoff finally dined today at Resanoff's. When Ratmanoff asked, "Are you traveling on land or on water?"

Resanoff, who makes a secret of everything, answered, "It is all the same to me." "I am only asking," said Ratmanoff, "so that we can be ready to give the ambassador honors and put our people along the yards."

"Yes, yes," said Resanoff, "by water, by water!" And now we know what we need to know. "Now we will have to take off our shoes!" added Resanoff, without there being any reason for this remark. (I think like Duff, Resanoff will do Compliments.)

Friderici and Koscheleff were given reprimands for not lying and sitting in uniform in their rooms. Why? Because Resanoff has not taken off his star and key since the arrival of the Daimeo (Grote Herr). He does not consider that for over five months he has had reason to be ashamed of his own outfit and now embarrasses his subordinates without reason.

Resanoff has yet another new plan for trade. Two ships should leave Kronstadt every year. The one should go fully loaded to Japan where a factory should be built, sail from there with Japanese goods to Peter-Paul's Harbor, take on a load of furs in Kamtschatka, and then sail to China, where in turn a new factory loads the ship with Chinese goods and sails back to Kronstadt. The other ship sails straight to Manila, loads mainly sugar and whatever the country has to offer, also takes this load to Peter-Paul's Harbor, where it also gets furs with which to obtain a cargo from the factory in China for Petersburg. Peter-Paul's Harbor should become the emporium of the American Company, and two ships from Ochotsk and two ships from Kodiak are to be used to transport the goods, and even as far as Irkutsk everything should be supplied through Peter-Paul's Harbor. If one takes into account the costs and difficulties of establishing and building three new factories in addition to Peter-Paul's Harbor, having six ships at sea, manning, and stocking them, and just as many and even more to be kept ready to sail in order to prevent the newly established trade from not stopping, and the buying and stocking of goods in the factories, so that the ships do not unnecessarily wait around to be loaded. That would force a little monarch to go bankrupt if unsuccessful, and the typhoons would add to the miscalculations, etc.

Mon. 20/1 Prince Fiesen's boat, probably with the Grote Herr onboard, went on an excursion to the imperial guard. His suite consisted of ten big banjos' boats, which were all towed by a lot of little boats.

The Chinese junk put up its mizzenmast today. It was raised up on the mainmast, the spur of the mast directed toward the gang board and straightened up by two ropes to the back. The work was soon finished because the mizzenmast is not large. The Chinese had fastened the thing poorly, and the paltry stuff fell overboard into the water again, because the gang board of the mizzenmast is on one side of the junk, not in the middle as on other ships. Therefore, with just as much noise, they had to start the work all over again—the Chinese are very inept seamen.

Tues. 21/2 Up until now, the Japanese have not formally informed Resanoff of the arrival of the Grote Herr. Otherwise, the tolks visited him very often, and, if they did not come, then Resanoff sent for them. Ten days have now passed without a tolk paying him a visit. We get all of our news underhanded through the guard officers or the provision's tolks, who also told us today that they had brought us two days' worth of provisions because they thought that Resanoff would visit the Grote Herr tomorrow. And, in any case, all of the doors and windows in Nangasaki would be closed, and they would not be in the position to bring provisions that day.

The large boat, in which Resanoff had been brought to Megasaki on our arrival, was also towed here today. The Japanese with a supply of boards also appear to be anticipating that in case low water should catch them, they can prevent any problems by conjuring up a bridge. They have enough boats and people, also boards. I have to praise the Japanese for this foresight.

Wed. 22/3 Finally, in the early morning the long awaited tolks announced their presence to Resanoff. Skiseima, Sakusaburo, and Tatiskiro appeared. They had barely entered when Resanoff asked, "Well? Has the Grote Herr come?"

"Yes! Yes!" answered the tolks.

"Hasn't he been here for six days now?"

"Yes! Yes!" was again the answer.

"And nothing was said to me. Nothing was reported to me. Indeed, you had promised me. That is no good! That is rude! Impolite! That makes a bad impression in Europe!" General silence. Tatiskiro had not been at Resanoff's for a long time. Therefore, Resanoff asked him where he was coming from, that he had not been seen for so long, and then said immediately, without letting him get a word in, "I was always so ill. The house made me ill. Everything is done to make one ill."

Tatiskiro, with his glasses on his nose, then said very calmly, "Enough! Enough! We have already heard too much about that! We now have to go over the main thing and not get held up by minor details." Then the tolks informed Resanoff that he would have an audience with the Grote Herr (in Japanese Daimeo) tomorrow and now had to agree upon ceremonies and etiquette. "When you go to the Grote Herr tomorrow, you will indeed wear small, clean shoes?" asked the tolks.

"I will put my shoes on," answered Resanoff.

"The ambassador has to be seated and bow before the Grote Herr, according to Japanese custom," said Skiseima."

"No," said Resanoff, "I cannot and dare not. I am too old for that, and I dare not in any case."

Tatiskiro got up and said, while squatting in the vestibule, "That is very easy," and showed Resanoff how he should do it. When Resanoff absolutely refused to understand, Kakusaburo got up and showed another way, which, however, Resanoff also refused. They finally agreed that Resanoff could sit on a mat; however, he wanted to with the only condition that he was not to have his feet directed at the Daimeo. Tatiskiro, who is very biting, said before they had come to an agreement, "If the embassy is thereby unsuccessful because you did not want to bow, are you going to tell your emperor that too?"

"Oh yes!" said Resanoff.

The tolks then laughed with facial expressions, as if they wanted to say, "You are lying."

Friderici felt it his duty to say, "If it is possible for the embassy to be aborted by such a large trifle, then the Russian emperor will certainly not be angry about our return without having accomplished its purpose."

Both governors and the Daimeo will be present at the audience. In answer to the question of where Resanoff would sit, it was agreed that he would be seated the length of a mat from the governors and in front of them. They did not want to hear at all that someone would travel with Resanoff.

Tatiskiro finally said, "Are there then five ambassadors here? We thought that there was only one here!"

Resanoff answered him, "I have to have someone along who is present at the negotiations, so that if I were to die during the voyage there would be someone, one of my officers, to report to my emperor." That Friderici should be along was finally approved, and then Fosse also was permitted to be present in order to help with the interpreting (Fosse who speaks no other language than Russian). The rest of the officers would remain in the anteroom and could replace each other if the ambassador so desired.

The tolks forbade Resanoff to speak Japanese. He was permitted to speak Russian. Resanoff will travel by water from Megasaki to Nangasaki. From the landing spot, he will continue to travel in a norimon (post chaise). The officers will be going on foot and have to wait at the house of the Daimeo. When the tolks said that, Resanoff asked, "For what reason? Why?"

"Solely to go up in smoke," said Sakusaburo.

The soldiers may not go along, only a subordinate officer carrying the standard and the servant for cleaning his shoes.

Then Skiseima said, "You have to take off your sword."

"No," said Resanoff, "I won't do that."

"The governors are also going to put aside their swords," said the tolk.

"Well," said Resanoff, "I will take along two swords and put one aside."

"In that case, you will first have to have your head shaved," said Tatiskiro. (That is as much as saying, "In order to be permitted to carry two swords, you will have to be Japanese.")[4] "The governors will have their swords lying next to them," said a tolk.

"I will do that," answered Resanoff.

"Well, all of the swords are not supposed to be in the room," said the tolks in unison, and they agreed that Resanoff would also be without a sword. Now Resanoff asked, "Can I give the two governors and the Daimeo gifts?"

"Oh yes," was the answer, "Mar! Afterwards! Afterwards! Since everything is permitted, also to buy."

"Then the obertolks should also be satisfied," said Resanoff. "I will do everything so that the contracts and agreements are advantageous to Japan as well as Russia." "Tomorrow morning at eight o'clock," said the tolks, "two banjos and the tolks will come to pick you up. Tomorrow, only Compliments will be done, and you will have to answer earlier questions, that is, where do you come from? Who are you? Why have you come, etc.?"

Already in the afternoon the part of the city through which Resanoff was to be carried was hung with curtains, and that is the way the streets are also to be hung.

In answer to Resanoff's question, why they were doing that, Skiseima said, "That is an honor!"

"No!" said Tatiskiro, who cannot stomach Resanoff, "that is to prevent the people from crowding in. That is why all of the doors and windows of the houses will be closed."

After the tolks had left, Resanoff asked, "Is it enough if I give each tolk seven arschin of cloth and 100 piasters?" (He had nothing better to think about!) The embroidered coats were all brought out and cleaned and put in shape as Resanoff asked, full of interest, when the *Nadezhda* is going to be rigged? (Because he has a weakness for outward appearances; since he knows that he has no inner worth, he is not concerned that we would not have time to raise our topmast and yards; and he would have to forego the pleasure of seeing our sailors, on his account, standing on the yards.)

Thurs. 23/4 Yesterday, the tolks described in minute detail how the room, in which the audience is to take place, is divided by walls made of screens. The walls made of screens will be removed and, our ambassador will be separated from the Daimeo by the sill of the screen along with the length of mats.

Precisely at eight o'clock, a large beautifully decorated boat accompanied by a large number of other boats arrived in front of Megasaki to take Resanoff to Nangasaki. At nine o'clock, two banjos came with the news that, if the ambassador were ready, they would come to pick him up. After Resanoff had the tolks presented with a glass of wine, he set out on his journey to Nangasaki. In the courtyard of Megasaki, our soldiers stood at attention, and Fedoroff gave His Excellency the honors. Next to our soldiers were standing a row of Japanese. A large rooster had put himself in front of them and quietly watched the ceremony. The contrast between the Russian and Japanese formations was really funny.

Because the large Japanese boat, on account of low water, could not get close enough to the shore, Resanoff first had to climb into a small boat and then be taken to the large boat. He was followed by Friderici, Fosse, and Koscheleff in red uniforms, Langsdorff in an academic uniform and Fedoroff in a regimental uniform. The subordinate officer carried the standard, and Resanoff's servant was the last one to climb in. Early in the morning, we had raised our masts and yards on the *Nadezhda* and put our people along the yards as Resanoff sailed past our ship. At eleven o'clock, the audience ended, and the whole train returned to Megasaki.

In confidence, Resanoff said to me in the morning before he went to Nangasaki, "I have finally convinced them that Schemelin will stay behind as overseer or agent in Japan, and I have already engaged him for six years."

After Resanoff had returned, Krusenstern sent me to Megasaki, had me make excuses why he did not come himself, and tell Resanoff that he hoped the first audience had ended as he had wished. After I had carried out my assignment,

Resanoff related to me himself everything that had happened during the stay in Nangasaki and with both Daimeos.

Friderici, Koscheleff, and Fedoroff confirmed everything Resanoff had related. Resanoff and his suite went on land at the so-called mussel stairs in Nangasaki. There he entered a norimon (post chaise) and was carried through several streets. Two rows of about 24 Japanese went ahead of him. Our officers followed on foot, each one with a tolk at his side and a quantity of soldiers who were followed by an indescribable number of people. This train, like a funeral procession, still and slow, spread out more than one and one-half versts up to the governor's house.

Hanging from all of the doors and windows of the houses were straw mats or jalousies. All of the cross streets and alleys were blocked by board walls and the houses were decorated with curtains. Every street or quarter has its gates, and two guards stood at every gate, a police or city guard and a guard of the Prince Fiesen or Omuro. Our officers saw women and girls who could have made claims to beauty.

At the Daimeo's and the governors', Resanoff, as well as Friderici and Fosse, had to be seated on mats; and, after the Grote Herrn, who were there before them, had performed their Compliments, Resanoff had replied to this Compliment in a *simpel way* [sic] in European fashion, and Friderici and Fosse had followed his example. Instead of one mat away, Resanoff had had to sit two mats away from the governors, even though he protested, because Skesecima had the audacity to say to him that they did not remember that. Instead of the swords that the Grote Herrn were supposed to deposit in the room next door for the period, a Japanese stood behind each one holding the swords in his hands. Instead of the Grote Herr being alone, the room was almost filled with people.

After the Compliments had been performed and a lot of unimportant things asked, the Daimeo said, "You have come here to trade?"

"Yes."

"There is nothing written about that in Laksmann's letter. It says that only one vessel is permitted to come to Nangasaki, not for trade or to bargain but only to make agreements, and that only one vessel and not, as with the Dutch, a vessel every year. Japanese laws do not permit us to harbor commonalties with foreign nations. Up until now, only the Dutch have been allowed to trade with Japan. At the time that the letter was given Laksmann, the governor of Nangasaki received the order, that since a similar letter had been given the Russians that the same, with the Russian ship provided with this letter, should be allowed to have free access to Nangasaki and upon the arrival of this ship was to be carefully considered and examined whether it would be possible to permit this ship to trade in Nangasaki. We have waited in vain for twelve years. Since trade up to now has not been permitted at all, it has been a shock to us that the emperor of Russia, without reason, had something about trade put into his letter which he has had written to our emperor. Laksmann's letter states expressly that it is forbidden to conduct any correspondence with the Japanese and in no case to send or bring letters. Because Laksmann had brought a letter from the general governor of Siberia for the governors of Matmai, why then has the emperor of Russia sent a letter to our emperor?"

Resanoff answered, "Neither you nor I can determine which emperor is greater and more powerful, the emperor of Japan or the emperor of Russia. The emperor of Russia wrote the letter to the emperor of Japan to show his inclination to goodwill and friendship. Each emperor or king of Europe and Asia would consider it a great honor to receive a letter from the emperor of Russia."

Then the audience came to an end. The governor said that, since the Russian ambassador is not used to being in such an uncomfortable position, they would quickly end the present interview. Resanoff then said, since he saw that our intentions had not succeeded and the embassy was not going as desired, he requested that they not keep him any longer than necessary and permit him to use the beautiful weather and good wind. Then Resanoff got the answer, that tomorrow or the day after tomorrow, the Daimeo and the two governors, after considering the matter in detail, would inform the Russian ambassador what they had concluded about the letter, the gifts, and trade.

The tolks are supposed to have been very quiet and thoughtful. After Resanoff had made his way back to Megasaki with the same ceremony, he arrived back at his apartment somewhat introspective and thoughtful.

In the evening, Tamechatschira and Sosoimon, relaxed and satisfied, came with the news for Resanoff that he would travel to Nangasaki again tomorrow. As far as the Russian officers were concerned, probably everybody would be allowed to be at the audience. A banjos would come again tomorrow to get the ambassador. In answer to Resanoff's question when they would receive the gifts, the tolks said, "When everything has been clarified. You will hear tomorrow."

Skiseima and several tolks told Friderici with great Compliments, that he had won their trust and respect. They have enough reason to tell him that, because Friderici, during all of Resanoff's caprices and crazy behavior, has behaved above reproach.

Last evening, Resanoff asked Sosoimon why the promises that had been given were kept so badly, that is, concerning the distance of the mats, that the Russian officers were supposed to remain in the next room and then were removed three rooms distant, that so many Japanese were present at the audience and the swords of the Grote Herrn were held behind them.

Sosoimon thereupon answered, "Yes! Yes! That is the Japander Manier. Russia is a great land and has great manners. Japan is a small land and has small manners. Russia is close to the pole and Japan is near the equator. At the pole, there are 360° longitude and also at the equator."

Resanoff had no desire to ask him what he meant by that.

Fri. 24/5 We had variable strong winds the whole day with continual rain and very strong thunder and lightning. At 8:30 in the morning, the weather cleared some, and immediately all of the Japanese boats set about picking up Resanoff. At nine o'clock, the banjos and tolks arrived in Megasaki. Since it had begun to rain again very heavily, Resanoff requested that, from the landing place to the house of the governor, each officer be provided with a norimon, because it would be impossible in such bad weather to go on foot without getting muddy. The tolks denied this just request immediately. In answer to Resanoff's question whether the governor had only one single norimon in the city. And, when he said, "The emperor of Russia had your common Japanese transported in coaches, and here you deny a Russian officer a miserable norimon," a couple of tolks returned to Nangasaki to take care of the request. In addition, Resanoff requested that, on account of the bad weather, he be taken right up to the governor's house, because yesterday he had had to get out far away from the governor's house. The tolks did not want to grant this either because, they said, the governor himself customarily got out there. The tolks also returned to Nangasaki to clarify the matter. Finally, they came back with the news that at the ambassador's arrival in Nangasaki, everything would be ready.

At eleven o'clock, Resanoff left Megasaki with all of the ceremonies. They had barely reached Desima when the boats all got stuck on the sand. Resanoff had already gone from Megasaki in an open red boat to the large boat because of the low water and therefore, luckily for everyone, was provided with an umbrella. The rain was endless. The boats waited in front of Desima until almost one o'clock before they could finally leave, and at one thirty, Resanoff finally landed in Nagasaki. It appeared as if the tolks conducted the trip in order to gain time to get the norimons ready and to clarify everything.

Our poor sailors on the yards were totally soaked, since who would give them umbrellas? We waited a long time for Resanoff's return. Finally at six o'clock in the evening, the boats set in motion again. Since there was low water once again, the big boat got stuck on the sand very far from land.

Resanoff climbed into the red boat and was protected by the Japanese umbrellas from the rain. The water was so low that the red boat could not get close to land even though the Japanese had calculated ahead of time and had had a pristan [landing] built that was unfortunately too short. Therefore, Krusenstern sent Golavatscheff with our little jollyboat and, with the help of our boat, first Resanoff and then all of our gentlemen were dragged over the bar of mud to the pristan.

In the afternoon, two boats full of lanterns went to Nangasaki—we suspect to put on an illumination. Since the weather was so bad, undoubtedly nothing came of it. The Japanese are great friends of illuminations.

- 14 -

The Second Audience

AT SEVEN O'CLOCK IN THE EVENING, Golovatscheff, Friderici, and Koscheleff (whom Resanoff himself had sent) came onboard. They related to us, while they were still hot, the procedures and deliberations of the present day, which I am also putting down on paper as best as I can remember everything.

Krusenstern went with Friderici ashore and returned around ten o'clock in the evening. Koscheleff slept with us overnight on the ship.

Upon arrival in Nangasaki, after the long wait on the sand, our gentlemen found a lot of norimons standing ready. They climbed into them and were carried straight to the governor's house. The politeness and manners of the Japanese today were striking. After they had all got out of the norimons, the head secretary greeted Resanoff very politely and led him into the governor's room.

After everyone had taken his seat, the Daimeo said, "Since, for several centuries, the conditions in Japan have been such that the government has sought to avoid all relationships with foreign nations in so far as possible and trade, for this reason, has never been engaged in, thus, the government, with the intention of modifying this irreversible law, determined that only the Koreans, Ryukyuans, Chinese, and Dutch should be allowed to trade with Japan. The first two nations have given up trade with Japan of their own free will, and, as a result, now only the Chinese and Dutch are permitted to trade in Japan. Japanese needs are of course great, and our products, however, very limited, so that we are barely able to fill the ships of the Chinese and Dutch with goods, even though the Koreans and Ryukyuans have stopped trading with us. Mar! We are not in a position to load a ship as big as yours with lacquerware. All of Japan does not possess enough lacquerware to fill your ship. Furthermore, strict Japanese laws forbid us to associate with foreign nations. And, finally, since we are not in a position to offer you anything for your wares, which could encourage trade with us, therefore, you are completely forbidden to trade with us. We also are not permitted to trade because many other nations would feel insulted, which also, like you, wish to receive permission to trade with Japan and have long since received a negative answer, likewise, because our strict laws forbid it and expressly state that we are to avoid all association with foreign nations."

Then the Daimeo continued, "Through Laksmann, the Russians were absolutely forbidden to send any kind of written message to Japan. The basic laws of the land forbid us from making foreign acquaintances. The breaking of this law could disturb the peace in Japan and have bad results for us Japanese. Therefore, the emperor of Japan cannot accept the letter that the emperor of Russia has written. The embassy (continued the Daimeo) and the gifts can, therefore, also not be accepted, and, in addition, because the emperor of Japan, if he should receive them, would be required to reciprocate and, as a result, on his part have to send an embassy to Russia. We do not have the large vessels needed for an embassy. The strict laws of Japan forbid all natives to leave the country and go abroad. Therefore, it is also not possible to reciprocate either the embassy or the gifts, and that is why the emperor is accepting neither the one nor the other."

Resanoff was next given two letters. The one was from the High Imperial Council of the Emperor of Japan, which consists of 200 Grote Herrn. The other letter contained the opinion of the governor of Nangasaki and his advice.

While handing over the letters, the Daimeo said to Resanoff, "You must not misinterpret the long waiting period, for, if you consider that the 200 Imperial Counselors had first to gather in Jedo before the Imperial Council could begin its consultation, you have to admit that you have received a definite resolution more quickly than you could have expected."

Then Resanoff was taken into another room where the tolks translated the papers for him. The Daimeo said among other things, "Laksmann went to Matzumai. That is a small province where there were neither tolks nor anyone else who could have communicated with the Russians. That is why he received the letter so that in case another ship came, it would sail to Nangasaki, where the governor with the help of the tolks would be able to negotiate with the foreigners. At that time, the governor of Nangasaki also received an order that, if a Russian ship should come to Nangasaki, it should be given information according to Japanese laws."

After both letters had been translated, pipes, tobacco, and confections were offered; also the soldiers—today there were two of them, one as standard bearer, the other as shoe cleaner—received confections, and, afterwards, Resanoff was once again led back into the audience hall. After Resanoff had taken a seat, the Daimeo said. "As an expression of the emperor's special good will, he is giving your officers 24 coats."

Resanoff answered that he could not accept them in any case, since the Japanese did not want to accept the Russian emperor's gifts from him.

One of the governors then said, "I request you to accept 10,000 pud of rice and salt as a gift."

Resanoff rejected this too and resisted with all his might. Then the governor said, "You have no reason to feel insulted since the gift is neither for your emperor nor for you but for your ship's crew."

Then the third Grote Herr began speaking and said, "All of the provisions you have received up to now and are still to receive we are giving to you."

Resanoff rejected everything, but no notice was taken of his negative answer.

Unanimously, the Grote Herrn said, "Anything you need of lacquerware and other goods will be given you, but not for money."

"Now to come to something else," said Resanoff. "Since Russian ships frequently sail in these waters near Korea, Mutmai, etc., it could easily be possible that a Russian ship might be stranded on the Japanese coast. I hope," said Resanoff, "that the Japanese will treat the unfortunate ones well."

Unanimously, the Daimeo and governors said, "We promise to distribute an order along the Japanese coast that a stranded Russian vessel is to be received and treated like friends. The vessel is to be repaired and provided with everything possible and returned again to your fatherland, but nothing for money."

Resanoff said, "Since I cannot and dare not accept your gifts, you will permit me to pay for the provisions we have used, and, likewise, I request that stranded vessels be permitted to pay any costs they may incur."

The Daimeo's answer, "Trade is forbidden. It is all the same whether we sell something for one heller or for 500 dahler. If we accept something, then that is trade, and that is why you have to accept everything we have offered for free. Japanese laws can simply not be changed."

In answer to Resanoff's question whether the Russians could bring stranded Japanese back to their fatherland, the three Grote Herrn permitted it orally, but with the condition that the vessel had to come to Nangasaki without bringing letters or anything else written and without opposition to turn the returning Japanese over to the governor and leave immediately. "The Japanese are friends of the Russians, but, since Japanese laws cannot be changed, then we have to conform and act accordingly."

Then the three Grote Herrn said, "Now everything is clear." And Resanoff took his leave.

Upon leaving, Resanoff said to the tolks, "I can accept none of the governors' and Daimeo's gifts. I dare not."

The tolks answered. "You are indeed not being given gifts. You can do whatever you want to. Since this has been decided at the High Council, you are only making difficulties for yourself with your rejection. We would have to report this news to Jedo, and months would pass again before we would receive an answer from there, and then your rejection could perhaps have bad results for you."

Resanoff could not stop asking during the audience when he, or our crew, were given rice and salt, how much that was in Russian weights. Friderici reminded him in time that it was not appropriate to ask such a question at that point.

As Resanoff was leaving the governor's house, Sosoimon asked very urgently whether the Russian emperor, when he heard everything, would declare war on the Japanese. Resanoff calmed Sosoimon and asked for time until tomorrow in order to determine whether he would receive the gifts of the Grote Herrn or not. And after Resanoff had arrived in Megasaki, he immediately sent for Krusenstern to consult with him. Krusenstern returned onboard in the evening with the news that Resanoff had decided it would be better to accept the gifts than, possibly, once again to put us in control of the Japanese.

Resanoff could not stop himself from saying, "I would like to know how the Japanese know that we need rice and salt in Kamtschatka, for otherwise they certainly would not have given it to us." Resanoff said that only to make sure he got the gift, so that he could wheel and deal with the rice and salt as he wished, which indeed belonged to our ship's crew, since he has sent word through Friderici that the governors, the Daimeo, had presented the officers with 24 coats and the sailors with rice and salt.

Sat. 25/6 Early in the morning, Krusenstern went on land to find out from the tolks, who had come, how heavy the Grote Herrn's gifts would be and heard that it was 16,000 katti salt and 9,000 katti rice, approximately 1,200 pud salt and 700 pud rice. Our joy was great for not having to reload our ship. Immediately, Resanoff announced a new plan to our captain, which he had thought out overnight, that is, now to sail once again to Kodiak.

The tolks also brought us the news that Resanoff was not going to be permitted to visit a Japanese temple. Skiscima said, "The Dutch also cannot and may not walk around the city."

Duff is being denied the opportunity of making a farewell call on our ambassador. "Why?" asked Resanoff.

"Because it is against Japanese laws," answered the tolks. "The Dutch as well as the Chinese have been trading with us for over 150 years. They have never been permitted to visit each other. When the ambassador arrived, Duff and the Dutch were solely there onboard in case we could not understand them, to serve us as interpreters."

Then Resanoff requested again a definite answer concerning Russian ships that might shipwreck upon the Japanese coast and whether Japanese shipwrecked on the Russian coast could be returned to Japan and how. The questions would be answered by the governor at departure said the tolks, "Since they told you yesterday, as you yourself know, we will consider these questions."

Resanoff suggested the following plan to the tolks. Since he could not turn the gifts down without receiving permission from Edo, the gifts for the Japanese could, in the meantime, be turned over to Duff; and we could continue our voyage unhindered. If then news arrived from Jedo that we had to accept the gifts, then Duff could have them and, if that were possible, then Duff could send them to Batavia with Dutch ships and from there to Europe. The tolks were also supposed to tell the Daimeo and the governors this figment of his imagination and bring back an answer, and then Resanoff said, "Let's set about translating the two papers given me."

Now once again, Resanoff began to talk about lacquerware and asked if he could buy some, how much he wanted to have these things, etc., etc. He indeed well knows that the Japanese are not going to sell us any!

Tatiskiro said several times, interrupting Resanoff with questions, "Why do you want to go to the governors and say thank you for the gifts that you have already received?"

Resanoff did not let himself be frightened away and requested the tolks to bring him an answer to his questions tomorrow, that is, whether he could leave the gifts with the emperor of Japan here, whether, aside from the quantity of provisions we were being given, we could buy salt and rice, and whether he might buy lacquer ware. Then Resanoff talked about soya, saki (Japanese wine), salt fish, etc.

The tolks wrote everything down on paper, and Skiseima said, "According to the Japanese way of thinking, it is impolite to hold up a Grote Herr because of trivialities, and I am convinced that the ambassador will certainly not be held up by the Grote Herrn and the Japanese because of trivialities."

During this conversation, Resanoff suddenly changed his mind. He said, "Since the gifts from the Russian emperor are not going to be accepted, then I want to know if I will be permitted to leave gifts for the tolks and Duff."

Tatiskira answered, "If you are permitted to do that, then I request that you give us only a token gift, since, if you give us valuable things, that could cast a false light on us and have consequences for us."

Krusenstern asked the tolks if we would be permitted on the return voyage to Kamtschatka to sail through the Straits of Sangar and, if we could hope that the Japanese would let us sail on without holding us up in case it might be necessary to anchor near the Japanese coast.

In answer to these questions, the tolks in turn asked if we would once again come near the Japanese coast on our return voyage from Kamtschatka to Petersburg. "Not more than 100 miles," answered Krusenstern.

"We will bring a specific answer to all of these questions," said the tolks and took their leave.

Resanoff told Krusenstern, since the gifts for the emperor of Japan are not being accepted, we will have to sell them. "That is not possible," answered Krusenstern.

"Oh yes," said Resanoff, "I have a letter from our emperor which grants me full powers, in case the embassy to Japan does not succeed, to sell the gifts." (Could that really be true?)

Today, we painted our decks with oil paint, and the fresh paint makes the *Nadezhda* look young again.

Ratmanoff's pride, self-conceit, dogmatic nature, his stupid predictions, and his illogical commands are insufferable, especially since these traits are combined with a raw, coarse, unrefined character. Each one of us has had cause to complain about him. He would be unbearable if we were not all above him and did not have laughter so often on our side. He himself does not really know what he wants.

Sat. 26/7 Late last evening, the tolks came to Megasaki with answers to Resanoff's questions.

Tolk: "We spoke as much as possible to your advantage and attempted to move the Grote Herrn to fulfill your wishes. We received a negative answer to everything with the following words, that, just as little as one can buy something for a heller, if one does not have permission, just as little is it permitted to buy something for a large sum of money. The lacquerware here in Nangasaki has all been bought up by the obertolks. If you will permit us to bear witness to our services to the Russian officers, it will count as a pleasure and an honor to be obliging."

Resanoff: "What? I am giving you gifts."

Tolk: "We are not permitted to give you, as a Grote Herr, any gifts. You are too great, too distinguished, but, incidentally, that is the way we see it too."

Resanoff: "You may not give the officers gifts, you cannot! Nothing for the officers, everything to me!" (That had a double meaning, either, everything for me and nothing for the officers or I am everything and the officers nothing.) "But," putting his finger to his forehead, "there are in my possession still several lacquerware objects and trifles. Take them back."

Tolk: "It is now too late. These things have been in your possession too long."

Friderici to the tolks: "If you also want to accept gifts from us, then that is an another matter."

After a lot of useless talk, the tolks finally said that the Daimeo had given permission for Resanoff to give each of the seven tolks a token gift.

Instead of immediately getting out the gifts, Resanoff appeared to have not heard this and said, "I want to make a gift of wine to Duff. The governors will undoubtedly permit me to do that."

"No, certainly not," said the tolks. "We dare not even ask the governors for permission; for, if you have too much wine, why do you then need saki, since European wine is better than saki?"

The tolks inquired of Friderici when we could be ready to sail. "In about fourteen days."

Fosse interrupted hastily and loudly and said, "In six days, all of the gifts will be repacked."

Resanoff, who had taken a heartfelt liking to the rice and salt, argued with Friderici. He claimed that the Japanese gifts were intended for Kamtschatka. Friderici argued with good reasons against this until he got Resanoff to say, "Well! Well! I must have heard wrong." Resanoff intends to take possession of the things through Fosse.

The gifts that the emperor of Japan was supposed to receive and all of the other nice things have already been divided up by Resanoff. The portrait of the emperor,

14-1. "Nothing for the officers. Everything for me. I will indeed give you gifts," said Resanoff, when the tolks claimed he himself was too distinguished for them to be allowed to give him presents.

several mirrors, tables, and chandeliers are to stay in Kamtschatka. Several other items and cloth are to be taken to Kodiak to decorate the church there. Other things are to be given away, and another part of the things is to be sold in China. Schemelin is now taking charge of all of these things, so that Fosse can make the journey to Petersburg overland. You can see that Fosse is happy inside, that, by the turning over all of these things to Schemelin, all of his knavery will be cloaked.

In addition, the tolks reported that the ambassador's last audience would be today.

Early in the morning, all of the boats were set in motion, and, after Resanoff had eaten breakfast, he left Megasaki at twelve o'clock attended by the usual ceremony. And at four o'clock, he returned again to Megasaki.

Bellingshausen, who had gone on land, reported to us that Langsdorff and Fedoroff had been present during the audience; and, therefore, we still know nothing about what happened at this audience, because Fedoroff speaks only speaks Russian.

Sun. 27/8 The audience yesterday went as follows: Resanoff had to say he was thankful for being permitted to stay in Japan for six months in order to receive a negative answer. This was great proof of Japanese friendship because certainly every other nation would have been taken care of much faster. Then Resanoff had to say thank you for the gifts which not he but we had received. Then Resanoff asked, referring to the *Nadezhda*, "Since it might happen that we would find it necessary once again to cast anchor along the Japanese coast, I would hope," he said, "that you will not detain us or even force us to defend ourselves against attacks."

While shaking his head, the Daimeo answered, "No! No!"

Resanoff: "Since this is an important point that could easily lead to misunderstandings between two nations, I request the Grote Herrn to tell me your opinion yourselves in Japanese because I am convinced that I can understand you adequately in your mother tongue."

Daimeo (through the tolks): "We promise you to send orders to all of the coasts of Japan that, if you should find it necessary to cast anchor any place or on another Japanese coast, you will be helped everywhere, given everything you need to repair the ship if that be necessary, and, if you shipwreck, you will be brought to Nangasaki and from here sent by way of Batavia to Russia. This order has already been sent out."

Resanoff, speaking Japanese, even though he had solemnly promised not to speak any, commended the banjos and all of the tolks, praised their polite, good behavior, which he could not praise enough.

Daimeo, "These people have done what is the duty of every Japanese. They have fulfilled their duty."

Resanoff: "I have to admit, since I need and would like to buy a lot of things and you are so hard as to refuse to give me permission to purchase them. I am leaving here in great need."

The tolks translated similar unsuitable remarks. Silently, they were ignored, and Resanoff had to take his leave right after that with great Compliments.

The Daimeo also said, "We will permit Japanese, who have the misfortune of shipwrecking on the Russian coast, to be returned to their fatherland, and we request that you deal with them as we have dealt with the Russians, that is, help them in every way to have vessels repaired and sent back, but everything free of charge."

Large crates of silk padding, which had been standing in the governor's room during the audience, were carried out behind Resanoff.

The Daimeo had also remarked: "You need only to show your Japanese papers and to say that you come from Nangasaki, and you can be assured no one will stop you."

The silk padding, 25 large crates in number with 2,000 pieces of padding, followed Resanoff to Megasaki. Resanoff took possession of all of them. With Fosse, he went to the magazine to decide what to do with them. Resanoff's servant, who was present, said: "The Emperor will be quite happy about the padding."

Resanoff answered: "That is not at all for the Emperor, as if there were not enough of such things in Russia, you stupid fool."

We had mistakenly taken the 25 crates of padding for two dozen coats.

Friderici, who observed the business with the padding, believed he had to justify himself when Resanoff said that these gifts belonged to him. He went up to him and asked, "Whose gifts are these? the ship's crew? the Kamtschadals? you alone? or all of us? In accordance with your order, I told the captain and all of the officers on the *Nadezhda* what I heard at the audience, and now you are giving me a dementi."

"They belong to all of us," said Resanoff peevishly, and he and Fosse continued to unpack and pack the crates of padding.

Fosse (While working): "From 20 chests I will make ten."

Resanoff: "You can pack the mirror crates full of it."

Two crates were already in the making when Friderici and Koscheleff came up.

Friderici: "If the padding belongs to all of us, then we cannot do whatever we want to without the agreement of the ship's officers. That is not right, especially opening them, which can cause them to spoil."

Fosse: "Вздор" [That's nonsense], since he perceived that the [smell of the] roast was going out of his nose.

Friderici (to Fosse): "You do not know how to handle this padding any more than I do and, therefore, cannot tell me that I am talking Вздор" [nonsense].

Resanoff (peevishly): "Friderici is right," and the knavery work stopped.

Having been hindered in his intentions made Resanoff very angry. If only we had kept quiet until our departure, then Resanoff would have been firmly convinced that everything belonged to him. It would have been very difficult to maintain the contrary. In addition, he would have had no pangs of guilt having taken everything unjustly for himself.

Yesterday, Resanoff said to Sosoimon that nothing has come of our trade with Japan. Russia is thereby losing nothing, only Japan. Japan alone will suffer for it. Sosoimon remained silent.

Bellingshausen, who was present, said, "Then we will go warmly dressed, and you will be without furs."

"Hm! Hm!" answered Sosoimon. Bellingshausen was sorry that he had said that, because at that moment he thought of the beautiful padding that warmed better than furs.

Resanoff always alludes to animosities and war and torments the peace-loving Japanese because he cannot get at them in any other way.

That irked Bellingshausen, so that he said to Resanoff (in confidence), "Your Excellency should indeed remember the story of the Persian shah who disappeared in the Caspian Sea. A similar fate can also come to us at Papenberg. You threaten the Japanese with war and know that the Japanese have an extreme fear of animosities. It is not for nothing that thirty boats surround Megasaki, and also the large banjos boats have rowed to the Papenberg."

Resanoff took this advice very much to heart, and, to our joy, nothing more was heard of animosities from that point on, since Resanoff is always the biggest poltroon of all.

Before Skiseima left, Resanoff said to him, "Tomorrow I will take your pipe and your tobacco pouch and, ah, what a nice lantern you have there." That was as much as to say, bring me this and that tomorrow.

"Ermolai Kortitsch," said Resanoff to Friderici, "We intend to divide up the lacquerware correctly among us."

"No!" said Friderici, "I thank you, I do not need them. It would be another matter if the Japanese had allowed us to buy things as we pleased. What good are these trifles to me?" Then Koscheleff joined them.

"Why," said Resanoff to them, "Aren't you having the tolks bring a lot of things with the provisions? It is exactly the time for that."

"No," they both said, "that is not proper; we would be ashamed to do such a thing, since we know that the Japanese have been so generous to us and have given

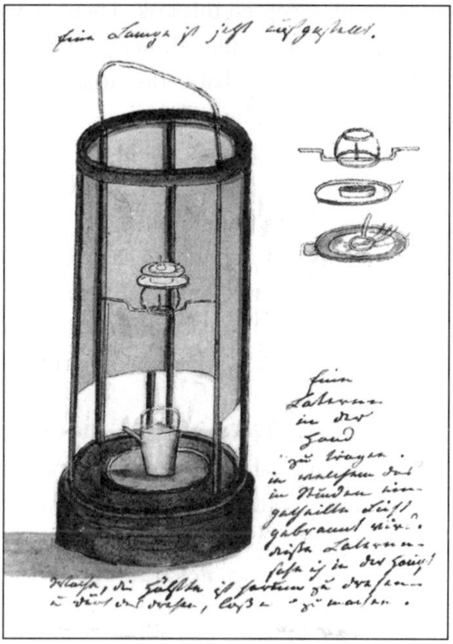

14-2 [above the lamp] A lamp now turned off. [next to the lamp] A lantern carried in the hand in which a light divided into hours is burned. I saw it in the main guardhouse.

us gifts, that they over and above that have given us everything else free, only at the very end to have them bring things we could do without. The Japanese would be right to have a bad opinion of us."

Peeved, Resanoff remained silent. After a little while, Resanoff's servant came and said to Koscheleff, "You have always wanted Japanese pipes? Why don't you order them? It takes only a word, and the tolks will bring them to you immediately." Resanoff's understrapper was forced from the room under protest.

Fosse insists, using the reasons of a true quartal officer, that, except for the things received from the Hermitage [in St. Petersburg], all of the things are to be divided, given away, and sold. Resanoff ponderously confirmed Fosse's suggestion, since all of the things Resanoff and Fosse had bought for a lot of money in Petersburg are pure rubbish and, therefore, dare not be taken back to Petersburg because then their knavery would come to light.

Yesterday, word was sent that four banjos and all of the tolks would be coming to pick up the Japanese we had brought along, the gifts for the tolks and for Duff. Resanoff only dreams about lacquerware and he is so interested in that that he continually forgets himself. That bad fellow betrays himself at every opportunity. He no longer even has his imagination under control, a characteristic which at times gives him the varnish of integrity. Early this morning, it was my turn to take the report ashore. As I was climbing into the boat, I caught sight of the tolks' flag in Megasaki. I reported this to Krusenstern, who immediately got dressed and went on land with Espenberg and me.

Upon arrival, we found the house full of Japanese. In accordance with yesterday's promise, there were two banjos from here and two from Jedo and all of the tolks with their kotskeis and magatonis.

Resanoff was busy giving the tolks their presents. From each category, the tolks modestly took only a one piece.

After we had greeted Resanoff, Krusenstern turned to the tolks and requested them to ask the banjos to thank the Grote Herrn for everything in his name. The tolks gladly accepted this task. Then we went into the dining room, and Resanoff followed us, where the following conversation took place.

Krusenstern: "What is the situation with the gifts? Whom have the Japanese given all of these things?"

Resanoff: "To all of us! All of us!" (extending his hands away from each other). "The salt and rice are for Kamtschatka" [для Камчатского края].

All of us present contradicted Resanoff and said, "That is indeed not possible. What reason do the Japanese have for giving the Kamtschadals gifts?"

Krusenstern: "I thought that the rice and salt were gifts for the ship's crew."

Resanoff: "So? You certainly do not think that I am going to keep these things from your crew? I will pay you 500 rubles and help out the poor Kamtschadals in their need."

Krusenstern: "I cannot make any decisions about that. If it has been given the crew, then it belongs to them, and I cannot and dare not wheel and deal with it as I wish to."

Resanoff: "Your people certainly won't want to trade with the salt and rice in Kamtschatka?"

Krusenstern: "No, not that, but deciding about their property capriciously—that cannot be done."

Resanoff: "Laksmann also got rice from the Japanese and turned the entire quantity over the crown's storehouse in Ochotsk."

Krusenstern: "If Laksmann acted unjustly toward his crew, it does not follow that we also should act unjustly toward our people."

Since the conversation began to be heated, I said to Resanoff: "Since the Grote Herrn have given us officers padding, please permit me to ask the tolks in my name and the name of my comrades to express our thanks to the governors."

Resanoff: "No! No! I! I! I have thanked them for all of you."

General silent, then after a little while, Krusenstern said, "It is not allowed for the Japanese to give you absolutely no gift. Indeed, these same Japanese gave Laksmann several swords."

Resanoff: "Oh! They were very bad swords, very ordinary swords."

Krusenstern: "Laksmann was also only a small light in contrast to Your Excellency. The Japanese should have given you a beautiful, large sword."

Then Resanoff went off very frostily. We followed.

"Skiseima?" asked Resanoff after a little while, "what did the Grote Herrn actually say about the gifts?"

Skiseima answered, "The padding is for the officers, and the rice and salt are provisions for the ship, for everyone!"

Resanoff then used pantomime, pointing with his hand at Krusenstern, as if he wanted to say, "Well! Wasn't I right!" and he would have gladly added, "Everything belongs to me." He nevertheless could not let well enough alone and once again considered the gifts as provisions so that he could attribute them to the American Company and think up new ways to take possession of everything for himself.

Then Krusenstern asked the tolks once again, as if he had not understood the explanation, whom the gifts actually belonged to. Then Sosoimon said, "The provisions which you have used up to now and will continue to use and those that you, Captain, have requested as a two-month supply, you have received through the Believtheit of the Grote Herrn. The Daimeo is giving all of the officers the padding, and the rice and salt are a gift for the ship, for all of you on the ship, as a replacement for the expenses and the work which you have had during the long voyage from Petersburg to Kamtschatka and from there to Nangasaki." We all were happy about that decisive answer.

Now, our Japanese were introduced to the banjos. Their things down to the smallest article were inspected, written down, and sealed. When everything was finished, Resanoff kissed each of the Japanese, and, after the banjos had handed Resanoff a receipt, they were led away. Aside from twenty ducats that each one received from Resanoff, none of them had under 300 Spanish dahler in cash and a quantity of linens and clothing. Madsiura, who as still very swollen, was carried off in a norimon, followed by his comrades, and a lot of Japanese carried their baggage behind them. Slowly, they went forwards, followed by a large crowd of people bringing up the rear of this sad parade.[1]

The tolks assured us that Kodei, who had returned to Japan with Laksmann, was very well and living in Jedo. He had to thank his good behavior for obtaining the emperor's permission to live in the capital city, and he also had been consulted in several of the country's affairs.

The banjos took a look at the gifts that Resanoff wanted to give the tolks and Duff. They were all written down, packed, sealed, and carried away. That is: two large mirrors without frames, two green and one blue chandeliers, a candelabra, a piece of bright blue cloth, a cabinet for curiosities or valuables, which had a lot of spots from sea water on it. Krusenstern could not keep himself from asking if there were a better piece available.

Fosse, a complete smatterer, fetched the piece and showed it to him answering, "Nikolai Petrovitsch picked out this piece himself." Resanoff, who heard that, said nothing, and that is the way it stayed. There were also four very simple marble tables, two of green and two of yellow marble, two small pocket globes, a set of steel coat buttons, a small dejeuncu,[2] a packet of maps, and a quantity of Russian clothing. The latter, Resanoff requested be given the governors. The banjos accepted them under the condition that they would be brought back to Resanoff if the governors did not want them. Then Resanoff secretly gave the tolks small gifts, which, to Resanoff's shame, consisted of lead pencils and children's toys. When this was also taken care of, the banjos took a good last look at the display of imperial gifts and took their leave.

Resanoff, the personification of greed, would like to have everything, to take possession of everything and begged for everything, asked when the tolks would bring the souvenirs and received as answer from the tolks, "We have taken the liberty of giving the Russian officers gifts." (Then turning to Krusenstern:) "Mar! First the provisions come onboard and then the presents, then the ambassador, and then the ship to Papenberg, and only then may be tolks come and give the officers presents as souvenirs." Once again, the tolks asked Resanoff and Krusenstern to let the ship be towed to Papenberg as soon as possible. Then they could stay if they wished for another month, but, since the Daimeo wished to return to Jedo as soon as possible and dare not leave Nangasaki before the ship was at Papenberg, it would be a great favor to the Daimeo if they fulfilled his wish and speeded up their trip to Papenberg.

14-3. "Soisimon, take this pencil quickly, so that no one else sees it."

Our Kamtschadal soldiers have gained the most and through the supply of salt and rice. They will be Croesus[3] among their comrades.

A little while ago, Friderici gave the Japanese officers a glass and a tolk a world map from Arrowsmith. The latter brought him secretly a roll of obscene Japanese paintings and the former two very beautiful fans. He had barely given them to him when he became frightened, grabbed his hair and said, "The oberbanjos is coming. Take it quickly, otherwise I will be in trouble" and ran away. There is absolutely no playing around with Japanese Manier and their strict laws.

Resanoff, who is still speculating how he can take possession of the padding, etc., divided up the crates with padding as follows today, "18 crates I will give the officers, and three are for the Imperial Court." Nothing was said about the other four crates. He was even bold enough to say to Krusenstern, "I will take the stand to the emperor, since I do not have anything better, and the padding to the empress."

Krusenstern laughed at him in his face and said, "That is no gift for the empress." Resanoff grimaced.

After the tolks had left us, promising to return tomorrow in order to translate the Japanese papers and letters, to bring people and boats to transport the large mirror onboard, and to talk with Krusenstern about when they should bring provisions, fresh water, kindling, etc., onboard, they took their leave, and Krusenstern also went onboard.

I remained on land and went with Friderici to the magazine to have the casks put in order in which we planned to pack the salt. Unnoticed, Resanoff followed us and asked very unexpectedly, "Do you want to count the crates with padding?"

"No," we said, surprised by the question.

Resanoff felt that he had betrayed his inner feelings and asked again, very unembarrassed (for he is an actor), where the two crates were that had been unpacked yesterday.

"In your room," answered Friderici.

Resanoff did not say anything else and slunk away. He had gone to the empty spot without our noticing it. Since I did not suspect him there and was famished to do something about it, I also went over there and found Resanoff deep in conversation with Schemelin. I wanted to go back, but he barely had become aware of my presence when he spoke to me.

Resanoff: "How happy I am for Kamtschatka [для Камчатского края] to be taking such necessary things as nice rice and salt."

I: "I thought that gift was for our people."

Resanoff (angrily): "No! That is for Kamtschatka."

I: "Then we have made a big mistake. What will Ratmanoff and my comrades say when they hear that things change hourly? Friderici last told us at your orders that, according to the words of the Grote Herrn, the rice and salt are a gift for our crew—and now you are contradicting that."

Resanoff: "No! No! It is for us all. It is to be considered as provisions. Your people do not need that, and that is why I am leaving it in Kamtschatka."

I: "We are getting provisions over and above that. This is a special gift and therefore belongs entirely to our people."

Resanoff: "I am the one who should know that better, and you certainly can take my word for it."

I: "Of course, Your Excellency. The Grote Herrn would have certainly also called them provisions."

Resanoff (heatedly and impatiently): "The tolks themselves said today that they are be considered provisions."

I: "The word of the Grote Herrn has greater weight than the chatter of the tolks, and, by the way, the tolks themselves have also been clear about the matter."

Resanoff: "I have asked for salt and rice so often, and only at my request alone have I received it (for sure), and that is for Kamtschatka!"

I: "That is impossible. For giving a gift to a country means giving a gift to its ruler or monarch, and the Japanese have repeated one hundred times that they cannot do that. And, if that is the case, then Your Excellency, as plenipotentiary of the emperor—you cannot accept them at all. If, however, the Japanese have given these things to our people, that is another matter."

Resanoff (irritably): "No! That's also not it. It belongs to the people."

I: "Also, our people, if there is surplus, will gladly leave it in Kamtschatka because salt is very hard to keep at sea and melts easily."

Resanoff: "Your sailors do not intend to trade in Kamtschatka?"

I: "No! We will turn over the entire quantity to Paul Ivanitsch (Koscheleff). And either he will pay us for it immediately in Kamtschatka, or the crown will pay us the money upon our return to Petersburg."

Resanoff (in rage): "Yes! Yes! I will take it! and pay your sailors! What! Do you want to?" [Что! Вы вздорить хотите?]

I: "вздорить? [Looking to trade?] What gives you that idea? I am forbidden to do that. Since I have had the pleasure of knowing you for almost two years, will you permit me to speak, to give my opinion freely?" Silence. Resanoff stifled his anger.

I: "You yourself would consider it impolite if you had given someone a present and he did not even bother to thank you for it. It is all the more our duty to thank the Japanese for this unexpected gift of rice, salt, and padding, and you nevertheless do not permit us to do this."

Resanoff (wringing his hands): "Yes! Yes! Yes!"

I (angrily): "Especially a gift intended for us alone, and the Japanese dare not make either the emperor or you a gift, because you, Your Excellency, represent the person of our emperor."

Resanoff (stifling his rage): "I do not want to have anything."

The conversation had become so heated that I said nothing more. Resanoff was not inclined to take up the conversation again, and so we parted after we had silently gone up and down a couple of times. Thank goodness! Without quarreling.

About an hour later, I was called to noon table. Resanoff remained completely still. He finally said to break the silence, "The crates of padding that Fedor Pavlovitsch (Fosse) unpacked, I am taking for my part. Furthermore, I am thinking," continued Resanoff, "of staying here quite a long time!"

"Why that!" said Friderici.

"The tolks," continued Resanoff, "said that, when the ship is at Papenberg, then it can remain another month there."

"If I am not mistaken," answered Friderici, "the tolks also said that the Daimeo cannot leave before Your Excellency has moved back on the ship."

Resanoff (short and irritated): "No!"

Friderici: "What will Your Excellency do here alone when all of the things have been transported to the *Nadezhda* and the ship herself has been towed to Papenberg? A person has trouble amusing himself in an empty house."

Resanoff remained silent, and the conversation was ended. The scene is this: Resanoff is seeking to control our departure in the hope of having more opportunities to beg little things from the tolks.

Resanoff's speculation with the rice and salt is not bad at all, for, if he can claim the Japanese gift, then he could buy furs for the load of rice and salt in Kodiak and, in turn at his cost, have the *Nadezhda* or the *Neva* loaded with Chinese goods and then sell this cargo in Petersburg and, as a result, return a wealthy man. Then he would have put everything back in order using bribery that he had spoiled by his behavior.

The motto on a Japanese officer's flag: He who aims well and hits is the chosen one! Sosoimon translated that for Langsdorff. Langsdorff showed it to another tolk. "This motto is so idiosyncratic that it is hard to translate," said that one, "Sosoimon must be the one who translated it." That tolk also has the reputation among his colleagues of having an intelligent head [on his shoulders].

The Japanese have their own way of sealing crates, boxes, and bundles. They take a roll of paper which has been folded together several times and bind it with a rather loose knot and cut the ends very short and press a stamp blackened with ink onto it. The Japanese claim it is impossible to untie and retie the knot as it was.

In the evening, Romberg went on land for a quarter of an hour and returned with the news that Resanoff had suddenly decided to move onboard the *Nadezhda* in eight days. Had he not decided to do this, then the tolks would have already gotten him onboard; then there is nothing easier than chasing Resanoff into the pump [for removing water from the ship].[4]

Tues. 28/9 Early in the morning, the large Japanese boats (longboats) were ready at Megasaki to transport the mirrors. Krusenstern had barely gone ashore when the banjos with their entourage came onboard so that they were present for the loading.

Krusenstern, who came back onboard at noon, told me the following: "Resanoff told me very touchily, 'I am not taking any gifts and am only keeping the three crates of padding for our Imperial Court. I would be very sorry if we spent the last couple of months we will be together in strife and discord. I! am going to do everything I can so that we can part in peace.'"

Tatiskiro assured us that all of the Japanese are sorry that trade with the Russians had been forbidden. Unanimously, the tolks told us that the reason why the answer had taken so long to come from Jedo was divided opinions. Part of the Imperial Council and most of the common people were for trade, and the other half, that is, the overwhelming part, was against it. (Resanoff's behavior actually squandered everything). Had the Russians come with a ship four years before, then trade between Japan and Russia perhaps would have succeeded, because four years ago a very respected man who was very much for trade with Russia died. It is also still possible (something I do not believe) that our children's children will trade with Russia. If circumstances should by chance change, we will give the Russians news of it through the Dutch, that we are doing everything to appease Resanoff."

The position of tolk is inherited. These people, who put everything down on paper, have to have a complete archive of all of the dealings of the Japanese empire with foreigners.

The crates in which the mirrors were packed by Fosse were eighteen in number. Golovatscheff asked Fosse, "Aren't there more? There must be a lot of mirrors packed together in one box."

"Yes," answered Fosse. "There are one, two, three, even nine in a box."

"Also thirty," yelled Resanoff, who had been standing not far away and had heard the conversation. (Resanoff knows well where his shoe pinches. The purchase of the mirrors may have brought him a nice sum.)

"Then there must be more than one hundred," said Golovatscheff.

"There must be 95, since two are here, and there were 97 in all," said Fosse, who had been disconcerted by Resanoff's behavior, for, if Resanoff laid himself open, then Fosse tried each time to cloak this through coarseness, since his soul knows nothing of shame. Resanoff turned around, peeved, and went away.

In the afternoon, we loaded all of the mirrors into the ship and several boats full with our salt meat. At six o'clock, we had schabasch, and the banjos left us after cordially eyeing everything we had.

Krusenstern went on land again in the afternoon to determine what was supposed to be loaded tomorrow. Resanoff took the opportunity to surprise him with two letters. One of the letters contained the following: "Since, according to my instructions, it is the wish of the emperor that I should visit the islands of Sachalin and Urup, I therefore request of you that we touch both of these islands on our return voyage. From there, we will sail to Kamtschatka, and then I will go with you to Kodiak, since, according to my instructions, it is the emperor's wish that I also view this area." The second letter had the following content: "Since, through the generosity of the Japanese emperor, the Grote Herrn had made a gift of padding, I therefore request nothing for my person but retain three crates full for the Imperial Russian Court. The remaining crates the officers may divide up as they see fit. The provisions already obtained and the 16,000 katti salt and 9,000 katti (a katti is three pfund) rice have been given your people as provisions, which I will request to receive for you."

The unterbanjos and otonis (officers) thanked Resanoff today for his good intentions, of having the governors asked if he might also give gifts, but received a refusal.

Wed. 29/10 Through a prikas, Krusenstern made known to us the content of the letters he had received from Resanoff.

Sosoimon, who knows all of Resanoff's weaknesses, is always making plans for him. Today he said, "A Russian always has to be here at the Dutch residence. Mar! secretly, so that no one knows. This Russian could then secretly trade with the tolks." These plans are only for Resanoff's amusement. The tolks assured us that the greatest gift that could be given them would be a quick and peaceful settlement of all the business with the Russian ambassador. The Japanese appear to fear us now, probably because Resanoff talked some about war and animosities. They are polite and well behaved (as they were earlier) but just let things happen; even Tatiskiro remains silent. Without a doubt, they hope to be rid of us soon and, in this short period, gladly control themselves to get rid of us with good will, since Resanoff is now really not in his right senses.

Resanoff, through a tolk, had tried to get Duff several days ago to buy lacquer ware for 2,000 dahler, for which, if it were permitted, he would immediately pay the money. In case it should be denied, then he would like to have him send the things to Russia by way of Batavia. Duff received permission for that. Resanoff, however, does not spare any effort in trying to obtain the things here. Finally, he has had to admit that it is impossible. To keep himself from being blamed, he is trying to supply himself with Japanese things through the tolks—by begging! Secretly, he puts pencils into the tolks' hands and gets lacquerware as a gift from them in return. Resanoff has absolutely no sense of shame.

Since the weather was very bad today, no banjos came onboard. Therefore, we were only able to bring our anchor and three warps from land onboard.

Thurs. 30/11 Bad weather again. We loaded our anchor cables and several boatloads of salt meat and hardtack. On shore, where our longboat was lying, the Japanese last night stole a barrel of tar. Up until then, they had not touched anything left lying at the place designated for us on land. We were not allowed to post a guard by our things. This is the first theft since we have been here. Before our departure, right now, we have to be more careful and not leave anything on land that can be stolen.

Tomorrow, the obertolks are supposed to bring the translation of the Japanese papers.

Sosoimon spoon-feeds Resanoff new plans daily. Both are so intimate that it is shameful. The Japanese are asking each one of us to write something on their fans as a souvenir, and we are glad to do this. Today, with a pen, Resanoff drew Sosoimon and himself very badly on Sosoimon's fan, both pulling on a knot with the caption: "the farther! the firmer!" That is as much as to say, the farther apart they are, the firmer their friendship will become. It would never occur to Resanoff to go to Sachalin and Urup if Krusenstern had not suggested it himself. Since Resanoff is inclined to take over other's thoughts just as unscrupulously as other's property, it makes me happy that Krusenstern finally has taken it upon himself to avoid such subjects in his discussions with him. Let Resanoff make plans himself upon our arrival in Sachalin.

Tomorrow, if the weather is good, we will get salt and rice.

Fri. 31/12 Very late yesterday evening, Skiseima had come again to Megasaki with two boxes being carried ahead of him. According to the inscription, the first box was a gift for Resanoff from Duff, and, without asking whom the other box belonged to and what was in it, he had it carried to his room and said, "Ah! Ah! Those are the things I have ordered for myself!"

Not long afterwards, Skiseima entered the room with many Compliments and said, "One of the boxes with lacquerware is a gift from Duff to the ambassador. The other box is from the tolks. I request in the name of all of the tolks that the ambassador be so kind as to distribute the things in the box among the officers so that each one has a souvenir to take with him."

Friderici: "No! I cannot accept anything since you won't let me give you a present in return."

Resanoff wanted to interrupt Friderici.

Friderici: "Since I am being talked about, Your Excellency will permit me to answer for myself. (To Skiseima) I cannot accept any of these things, because the ambassador as well as we have already declined them once."

Skiseima: "You will certainly not decline a souvenir from us?"

Friderici: "No! But then we have however to give souvenirs in return. The value of the things is of no importance. If you write your name for me on a piece of paper as a souvenir, that is of more value to me than a beautiful lacquer box."

During this conversation, Koscheleff and Fedoroff also entered room, and Friderici declined the gifts also in the name of both of his comrades.

Skiseima: "Then the ambassador intends to accept them!"

General silence.

Before Skiseima, leaving the boxes behind, took leave, he asked Resanoff in such a loud voice that everyone must have heard him. "Mar! Das Embassador, een kleen letken gist vor Das Officiers" [The ambassador is a fine little spirit in front of his officers].

Skiseima had barely turned his back when Resanoff said, completely satisfied, "Let us now divide the things up."

"Since we have no part in it, we cannot do that," said Friderici and his comrades.

Resanoff: "You, nevertheless, will need nevertheless fans to give your acquaintances as gifts."

Friderici: "My acquaintances will not hold it against me if I do not bring them anything."

Resanoff (to Koscheleff): "You certainly will also need things."

Koscheleff: "No, Your Excellency! I have few acquaintances; but the things come very opportune for you, because you now can make gifts to all of the ladies and maids of honor at court."

Resanoff nevertheless used every possible means of getting them to take something, by good and bad suggestions, by begging and ordering, but nothing helped at all. Then he said to them, "Then at least come and look over the things at least."

In the room where the two crates had been carried, Fosse was already busy unpacking things and making a preliminary division.

"Choose!" said Resanoff, pointing to the things.

Friderici: "I am taking nothing."

Resanoff: "If you do not want anything from these things, then you can choose something from Duff's things."

Plate 1. Two Spanish soldiers.

Plate 2. Taiohai in Nukahiva

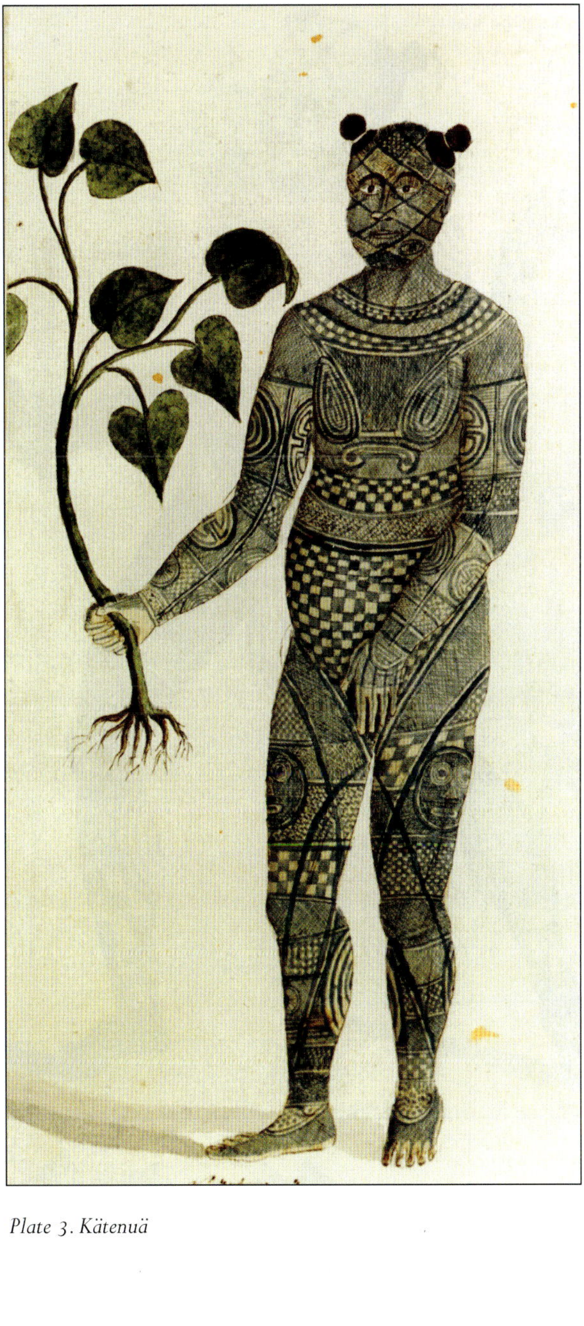

Plate 3. Kätenuä

Plate 8. Skislima

Plate 9. Interpreters

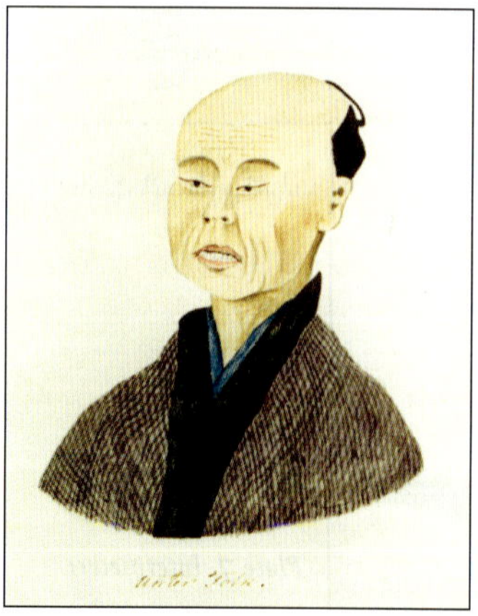

Plate 10. Assistant interpreter

Plates 11a and 11b. Papenberg

Plate 12. Preparations for the trip to Megasaki

Plates 13a & 13b. Chinese junks

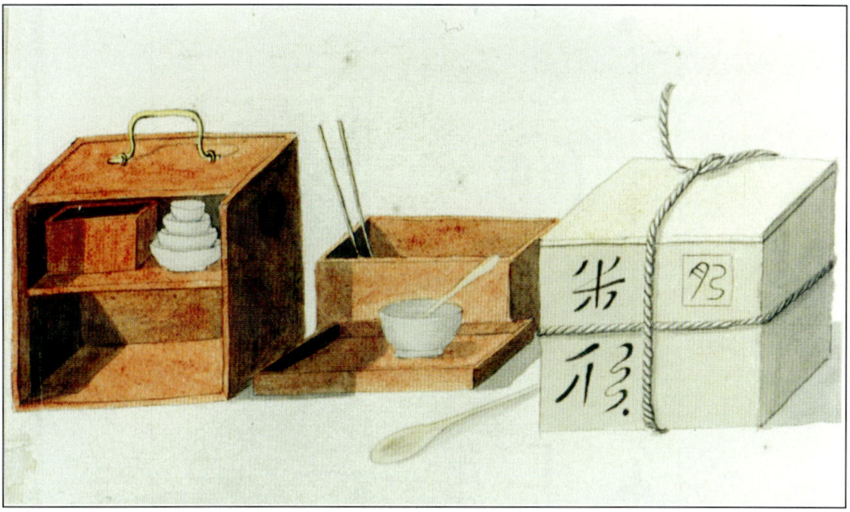

Plate 14. Ober banjos' [head administrator] meal caddy

Plate 15. A banjos' breakfast

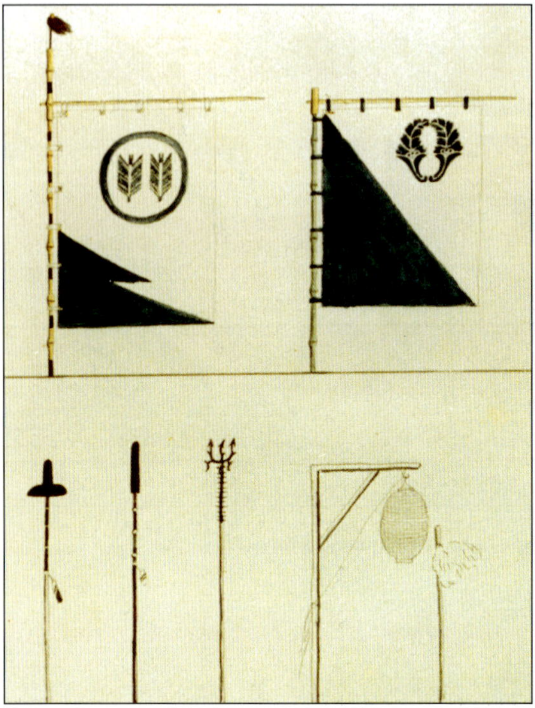

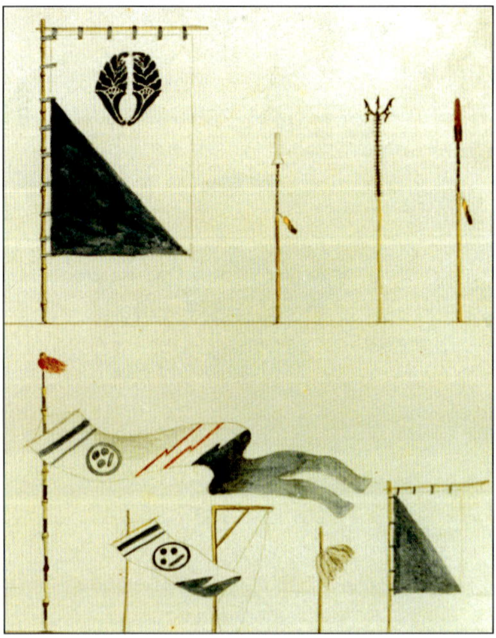

Plate 16. Flags and signs of honor [mons] on Prince Fiesen's boat

Plates 17a & b (top); 18a & b (bottom). More flags

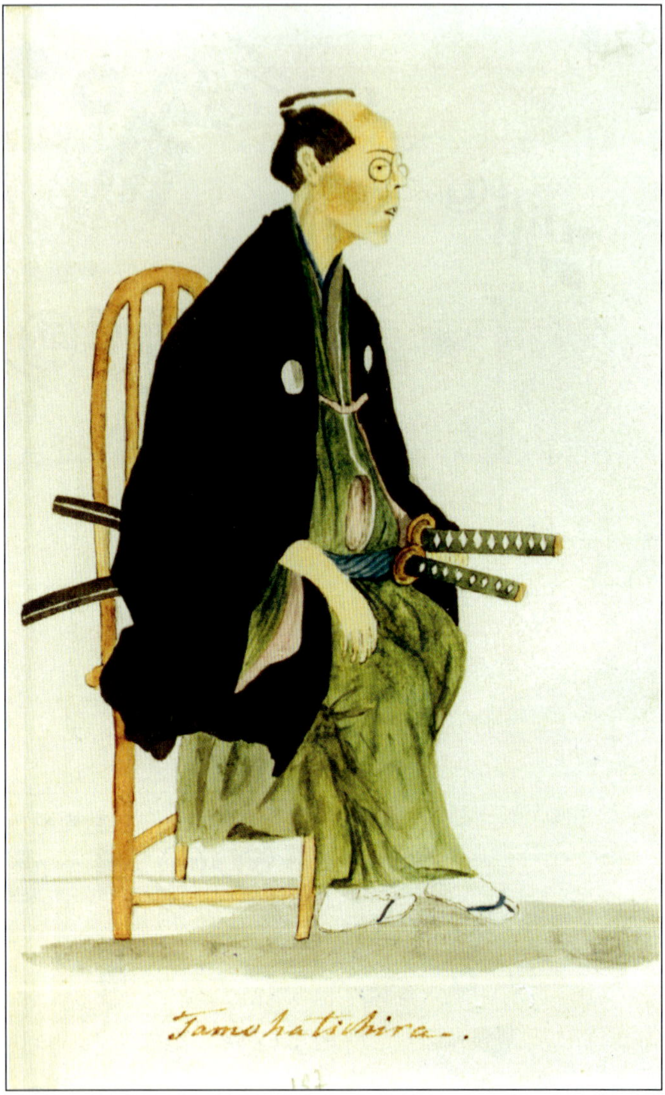

Plate 19. Tamachtschira

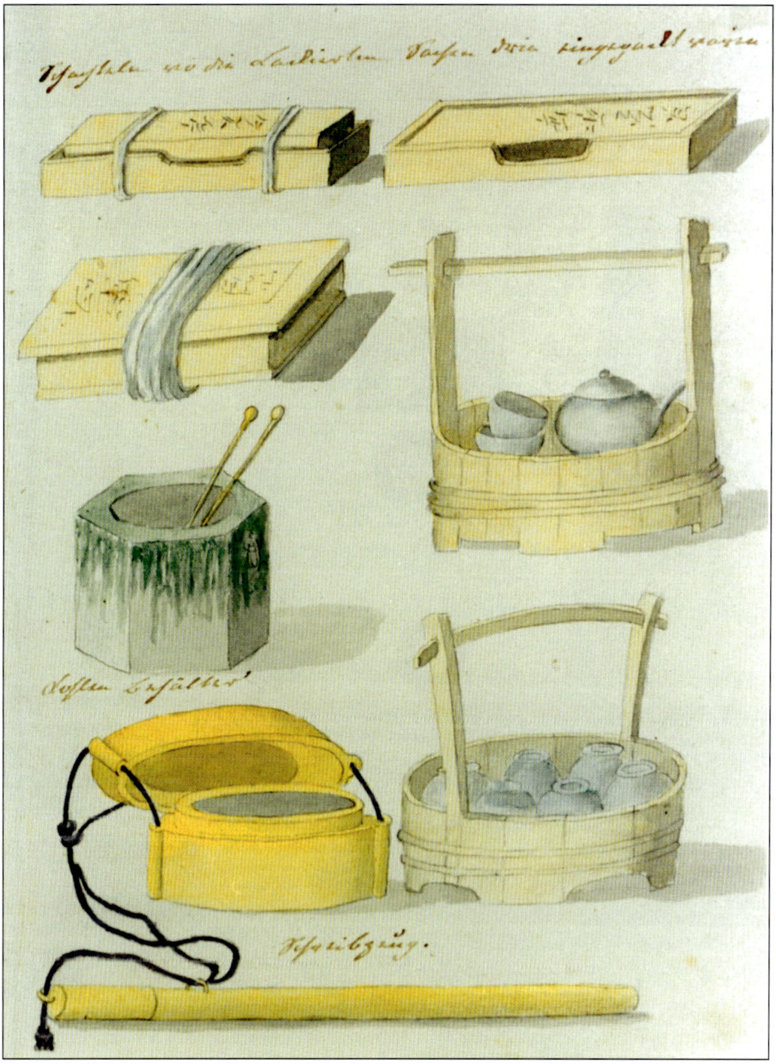

Plate 20. Boxes in which lacquerware was packed; container for coals; writing implements

Plate 21. Curtains of the forts

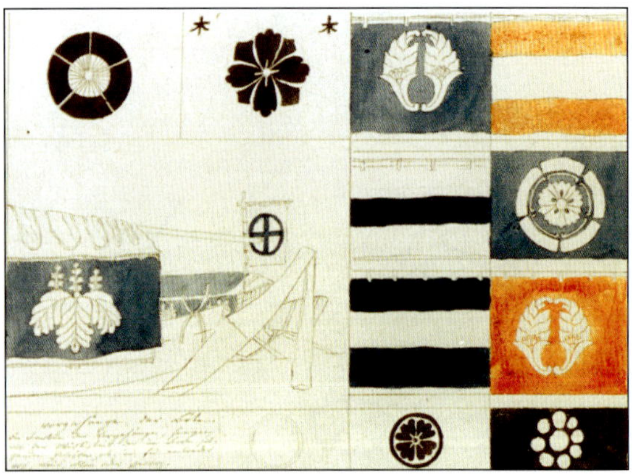

Plates 22a & b. Curtains of the boats; the color of the curtains

Plate 23. Japanese horse

Plate 24. Liberty men returning from Canton

Plate 25. Hermann Ludwig von Löwenstern

Friderici: "I have already told you several times that I am taking nothing. If I were to do that, I would be breaking my word to the tolks, and I don't like that."

Resanoff: "Well, then! So accept something from me!" and Resanoff used his complete eloquence in getting them to do it.

Since Resanoff used reasons that they could not counter without insulting him, Friderici said, "I will take the things you are offering me, simply because I have to, and I am taking them as a gift from you."—Koscheleff and Fedoroff also did the same thing. Resanoff only wanted them to take something. It did not matter how much or what, and thus each one of Resanoff's suite got a pipe, a fan, or some such trifle. The gifts from Duff are said to be nice. I did not get to see them.

Now, Resanoff immediately divided up all of the things. The emperor, the empress, the whole imperial family, all of the ladies and maids of honor, etc. got a share, because the worse Resanoff acts, the more often he cloaks his misuse in the name of our emperor.

Early this morning, Krusenstern went on land. He had barely handed over his report to Resanoff when he showed him the valuables received yesterday. Resanoff wanted to make him a present of a fan for his wife and a box for himself. Krusenstern declined both in saying, "Since you will be in Petersburg earlier than I, then, if you want to, you can give my wife the fan yourself. As far as I am concerned, I cannot accept anything that I cannot share with my officers. As long as they have nothing, then I also may not have anything."

Resanoff, peeved, stuck his preciosa [valuables] back in the box.

Krusenstern: "How am I to understand the letter I have received from you? Are the rice and salt the property of my sailors or not?"

Resanoff: "It belongs to the provisions! and I do not need to explain myself any further in the matter. Upon our return, it will be completely up to our emperor how he intends to consider the matter."

Krusenstern: "I only wanted to know what you intended to say with your letter, whether it is the property of the crew or not?"

Resanoff (very peeved): "Yes! It is their property. I intend to give it to you in writing" (and wanted to set down immediately and begin writing).

Krusenstern (interrupting him): "And another thing!" (beginning to talk about the padding).

Resanoff: "What? Don't I have a right to claim three crates for myself?"

Krusenstern: "You could just as well take twenty-two for yourself instead of three crates and, out of generosity, leave us only three. Since none of us are acquainted with anyone at court and among the ladies at court, none of my officers are considering letting you have their part. The emperor, if he wants them, may have all twenty-five crates placed at his service." (We had requested Krusenstern to say that to Resanoff.)

Resanoff: "Well! I don't want anything at all! But that could also be cause for discontent. Each one of your officers could ask why I may give them my crates of padding."

Krusenstern: "It's not the three crates of padding but rather the way in which you kept them back from us, and, to tell the straight truth, because you did it, that was the cause of our dissatisfaction."

Resanoff: "Ah! Ah! Now I see; you are making new schemes and want to cause strife. So that I can avoid all strife and conflict, then I also do not intend to go with you to Kodiak." Toward eleven o'clock, the banjos came onboard with salt and rice. Upon hearing this, Krusenstern took his leave. He had barely left when the obertolks came and brought Resanoff the following news that, because the ship was being loaded today, the oberbanjos could not come on land, that the tolks would bring the translations the day after tomorrow, that tomorrow the captain would have the use of four boats and fifteen men for loading. Resanoff then answered, "I believe that things will be clear in four days" (and added several times and yelled so loudly as if all of us in the room were deaf) "and! before! our! departure! I am still giving! the obertolks! gifts!"

Skiseima said very politely that the governor had given him the charge of telling the ambassador that, since the large boat belonging to Prince Fiesen had been sent away, he would be sending his own boat for the ambassador to take him onboard. They would give us the gunpowder only under the condition that we would not fire it.

"Tomorrow we will be coming again," said Skiseima, "in order to ask you several questions, so that we can compare the statements of the Japanese, whom you have brought along, with your answers."

Old Zudei had a box hidden in his chest in which he kept his money and preciosa. If the tolks find out about it, then the old fellow is going to have trouble.[5]

On land, I received 2,000 katti hardtack and on the ship 1,500 pud of salt and 100 sacks of rice. The Japanese brought us so much all at once that we did not have enough casks.

Today, an obertolk said to Langsdorff that the Japanese would undoubtedly give the ambassador a gift of two Japanese swords. If that is true, then Resanoff is at the pinnacle of his desires, since he is only concerned with obtaining things, the way he gets them is all the same to him. Even though Espenberg and I were both on land the entire day, Resanoff did not show us any of his valuables, since he must be ashamed of the way he obtained them, since he is also afraid if he showed them to us, he would have to give us some. And, furthermore, I would not have failed to tell him candidly my opinion.

- 15 -

Departure from Nangasaki

Sat. April 1/13 Today, all at once, we loaded more than on any day up to now. All the casks with provisions did not give us as much trouble loading, as the loose straw sacks of salt that we do not know where to put. We have already filled more than thirty water casks with salt and will have to empty another ten water barrels for storing the salt.

In the afternoon, banjos only came onboard for a short time to show the ship to two banjos from Jedo. The behavior of the banjos from Jedo was very different from that of the banjos from here. The banjos from here are always decent, indolent, patient, slow, stiff, proud, pedantic, and discreet. Very much in contrast with our phlegmatic banjos are the free, bright looks, the fresh flexible bodies, and the thirst for knowledge of the banjos from Jedo. When they inspected our ship and walked all around it, our banjos, accustomed to a slow snail-pace, could barely follow their comrades from Jedo.

The Japanese are very clever at cheating by overweighing and overcounting. It was very noticeable when we got hardtack. They delivered it in terms of katti (weight of three pfund). It was not enough that they increased the weight by hand or knee pressure, but each time they claimed to have brought several more katti than the boxes actually weighed. Since, to obtain the true weight of what we had got, the weight of the box had to be subtracted every time, they brought each time a part of it in baskets, dumped the hardtack into the emptied boxes, and continued to weigh it. In the end, we found, through the confusion, even though ten boxes full had been brought, we only had received six, because there were no more empty boxes there than the weight of four boxes when the hardtack was accounted for.

You don't look a gift horse in the mouth, and that is why I winked at them and let them enjoy the pleasure of having cheated us. When, however, one time they were too coarse, I let the tolk know that I had noticed but did not want to make

15-1. Banjos' guard house

15-2. Guards

any unnecessary ruckus about it. The tolk became embarrassed, and then things were delivered again properly.

Fosse, who has obtained everything he has illegally, is now inventing stories, trying to make us believe that he has obtained the things in a legal manner. Among other things, he said, "A little boy suddenly came running up and gave me two very nice fans without wanting to be paid for them, while saying, Mussume! Mussume!" (from a girl)—the baboon!

The Japanese officers have given Fosse the nickname ворота [portholes] because of his calf eyes—and, nevertheless, a Japanese beauty fell in love with him! If, in addition, you take into account the strictness of the Japanese guard that searches everyone down to his shirt before letting him in Megasaki and that a young boy trying to bring him fans would never be let in alone, then this fictitious story is all the more improbable.

May the hangman get him!

Two of Resanoff's strong traits: Not long after our arrival in Nangasaki, Resanoff said to the tolks, "If you are going to the ship and are going to ask a lot of questions there, then I am going to complain about you to the governor. I will answer all of your questions. The people on the ship do not know anything. They are seamen. That is why I do not want you doing that. I am the ambassador."

Tamchatschira was only onboard one single time, and this single time caused immediate unrest with Resanoff and reproach for the tolks. The tolks have now told us that themselves, so as to excuse the fact that they had not visited the ship more often and had left the appearance that we had been being neglected by them.

Yesterday, Langsdorff said. "An obertolk secretly brought me a very nice fan and told me at the same time not to show the fan to the ambassador, because he has expressly forbidden giving the officers any nice things. 'Bad fans and the like,' said he, 'you can bring them but no good ones. I absolutely forbid it.' "

Sun. 2/14 We loaded all of the things belonging to the ship. Only the crates with padding and Resanoff's and the officers' baggage were left in Megasaki.

The tolks are only going to be bringing the translations of the five Japanese letters the day after tomorrow.

We removed our four-oared boat covered with camphor wood boards from the stock slips. Tomorrow our shallop and longboat follow, which we covered with copper and have given the name Добрые намерения [good intentions].

The quantity of saki, soya, etc., is quite substantial that the Japanese have promised to bring us. They are bringing our guns and swords back to us together with the gunpowder, since they are said to be stored in a magazine together. It could only happen in Japan that guns and gunpowder are stored together in one pile.

God willing! we will be ready to sail in a few days.

Mon. 3/15 Ratmanoff had the longboat named Добрые намерения [good intentions] and newly covered with Japanese copper, taken from the stock slips. Resanoff had also been invited to the festivities. There was high tide at nine thirty, and we found ourselves with Resanoff on shipboard drinking several bottles of wine and eating two pirogs. At the same time, we took everything from the shore onboard and turned over our totally clean little corner to the Japanese.

In the afternoon, we were brought onboard saki, soya, salt pork, and fish, flour, eggs, live chickens, and pigs, everything in superabundance.

The Japanese have behaved very finely toward us. They always gave us hope that we would be able to buy, get, let us order anything we wanted, only afterwards to give us all of the things.

While we were taking the longboat from its stock slips, curiosity attracted a lot of Japanese. Among them was a Japanese doctor in his square boat in which he had put his medicine box, a pail of water, and food caddy, also a lacquer box next to him. The whole boat was six fuss six zoll long, two fuss five zoll wide, and one fuss three zoll deep above and below the water.

Tomorrow, we will receive three more Japanese boats for transporting the remaining things from land onboard.

Today, the tolks asked very urgently if Resanoff would move onboard earlier and when the governor's large boat should come to pick him up. The translation gets shoved off from one day to the next. Today, they said again that they would bring it tomorrow.

Before the tolks came, Resanoff was very candid with Bellingshausen (because he was not expecting them). He said, "At the very end, I will give the tolks all of the cloth and things I have along."

Several pieces of the most beautiful cloth, velvet, etc., were scattered around the room on chairs and boxes when it was announced, "The tolks are coming."

"Ah!" said Resanoff, "take all of the things quickly into the magazine so that Fosse can pack them." That is what you call galloping too fast [committing a blunder].

We are convinced that Resanoff would call all of these things expenses and that, with Fosse, he will send a bill to Petersburg that adds up to zero, that the tolks, however, will get barely a tenth of it. We do not even think that much.

Today, his servant brought part of Fosse's baggage onboard. Recognizable among it were some pieces from the gifts intended for the Japanese. Now that the Japanese, as Fosse says, are not accepting them, it was indeed not a sin if he took these things. They had to be viewed as given away; since they had already been entered as expenses (в расход) in the accounts book.

Yesterday and today, the Japanese flotilla has been maneuvering here in the bay under the Fiesen and Tschikusan flags, beautifully decorated, with drum rolls, and a wild but regular noise of Ossi! Os! Ossi! Oss! and now and again a kind of hurrah! It appears they are replacing each other. This evening, they put themselves quite near us, very quietly, and created a quite pretty illumination with their lanterns.

Undoubtedly, the Japanese want to impress us with the strength of their naval power, as the tolks are saying, by having Prince Tschikusan's fleet replaced by Fiesen's fleet, because they are afraid that we have become too well acquainted with Fiesen's guard in the past six months, and, to avoid any trouble, Tschikusan is taking over the guard duty for a short period, for immediately after our departure Tschikusan's fleet is to return home again. The Japanese do not even trust each other!

Tues. 4/16 Yesterday, Resanoff finally decided that everything should be brought onboard tomorrow, that even he would move onboard. When, early this morning, all of the things on land were brought onboard, Sosoimon, who was present, said, "The tolks cannot bring the translation today."

"Well!" answered Resanoff, "then I also cannot move onboard tomorrow." And looky here, in the afternoon, the tolks appeared incorpore with all of the translations and a letter from Duff. In his letter, Duff regrets not having received permission to visit the Russian ambassador before his departure, advises us not to sail through the Korean Sea along the Japanese coast, regrets not even having been given permission to send a letter to his father with us.

None of us know the content of the Japanese dispatches. Resanoff has read them secretly, even though he knows too little Dutch to understand them. If he can have secrets and can lend them weight by making important and dangerous faces, then he is satisfied, even if everything also goes under.

Early tomorrow morning, the Japanese are bringing us our gunpowder. Toward noon, Resanoff is coming onboard with all of the ceremonies, and in the evening, we will weigh anchor and be towed to Papenberg.

Resanoff repeated ad nauseam that he intended to give the tolks gifts before our departure that it made you sick. Finally, he told the tolks, "I have never had any intention of giving you any going-away presents."

The tolks could not be moved by any translation to accept anything from Resanoff. Resanoff said, "If you do not take my gifts, I will leave Japan filled with anger." Nothing helped.

Finally, the tolks said, "We want to ask the governors for permission and will bring you an answer tomorrow."

If Resanoff had given them the things secretly, the tolks would have already taken them. If Resanoff talks with the tolks secretly, the expressions he uses very often are, pai [share], love, sweet, beautiful, etc., that can be heard as a refrain from a distance. These expressions have come to make us nauseous.

Koscheleff requested permission (that is, of Resanoff) to obtain tobacco for his brother Pavel Ivanovitsch. Resanoff permitted this. When the tolks brought the tobacco, Fosse took it and said, "I will take care of it." Resanoff, who was present, even though Koscheleff protested, was satisfied and let it happen. Resanoff has to be casting a blind eye at Fosse in a lot of things, because that police officer is initiated in all of Resanoff's scandalous deeds.

Moritz Kotzebue, who had gone on land today, had the pleasure of being given, by a third hand, a Japanese picture from Mademoiselle Aphsa (a little thirteen-year-old girl in the neighboring house Resanoff had once sneaked up to). Resanoff came up as the picture was being given Moritz, took it, and kept it. At the same time, Aphsa sent Moritz a very colorful bouquet of flowers. A Japanese attempted to explain them. Unfortunately, we did not understand him. The bouquet had a white, a bright red, and a pale green ponso flower.

We wanted a boar for Kamtschatka. Krusenstern told Resanoff, who immediately said to the tolks, "The Captain wishes to have a sow and boar for America." The Japanese promised to bring them, and now Resanoff will take them for Kodiak.

Resanoff acts like his papers are so important, so secret, that we still do not know what is in them.

The tolks said, however, that the papers state that we are absolutely forbidden to anchor on the Japanese coast unless we are in distress.

Wed. 5/17 Today, when Krusenstern asked the source of the denial for us to anchor on the Japanese coast or on one of the islands belonging to Japan, Tatiskiro answered, "That is the Believtheit von das Gouvernör, since we know how many reefs there are along the Japanese coast and how easily we would be in danger of shipwrecking if we were to get too close. That is why we are requesting this of you. Otherwise, you can anchor any where and only have to show the papers received here in Nangasaki so as not to be detained."

We began work at four o'clock in the morning, weighed the moorings, drew the other anchor up perpendicular; and then five boats full of things were brought from land which the gentlemen could just as well have sent yesterday; a countless number of small boats collected around us to tow us, each one displaying the Prince Tschikusan' trappings and flag. And in the blink of an eye our armada was decked out.

At eleven o'clock, with all the ceremonies Resanoff left Megasaki in a large Japanese boat, and half an hour later he climbed onboard the *Nadezhda* again. The soldiers had been sent ahead so that Resanoff, along with the honors on his account, would not be robbed of the pleasure of seeing our sailors standing along the yards, also, in addition, hearing a drum roll upon his arrival at the ship. Banjos, tolks, otonis, katskus, or whatever they are called, came onboard with Resanoff and filled the entire ship.

At twelve o'clock, we weighed anchor, and, while one hundred boats towed us, we stored our guns, swords, and our gunpowder which the Japanese had returned to us, undamaged, onboard.

Of the things, Resanoff wanted to give the tolks yesterday and didn't, today they only accepted very few of them. Rumor has it; they got little. The governors had heard that Resanoff wanted flower seeds for the empress and were so attentive as to send him a package today and, at the same time, tobacco for the officers who love to smoke and all of the sailors.

At three o'clock, we dropped anchor behind Papenberg at the same place where we had anchored upon our arrival, and all of the Japanese left our ship with the wish, "happy voyage to Batavia."

At the end, Sakusaburo wanted secretly to give Krusenstern a box as a souvenir. Since this, however, happened secretly, Krusenstern said to Sakusaburo, "Don't hold it against me that I am not accepting your souvenir."

Sakusaburo, very hurt, answered because he had good intentions, "The ambassador takes everything we bring him."

Krusenstern then answered, "That does not mean that I have to do whatever the ambassador does;" and a sad Sakusaburo put the box back under his garment on his chest.

Even though Resanoff and Fosse have taken all possible effort to find out the prices for the Japanese provisions as well as the Japanese wares, they have not even been able to find out what a pfund of tobacco and a pfund of rice cost in Japan.

Thurs. 6/18 At seven o'clock in the morning, we weighed anchor and left Nangasaki. May God grant us good weather and good wind sailing through these dangerous unknown waters. We all are glad to leave Japan, and, even though we were guarded for six months like prisoners there, I, for my person, nevertheless cannot deny the Japanese my respect.

- 16 -

Return to Kamtschatka

RESANOFF IS QUIET AND STILL, speaks neither of the past or the present or the future. He remains still or speaks of the wind and weather. There is no talk of the Japanese papers or their translations. They are not even being mentioned.

Favorable wind but dull rainy weather. In the evening, with a reef topsail, we passed the Gotto Islands in ever-brisker winds and put ourselves on the drift for the night.

Since we thought we would have to pay for everything that we requested from the Japanese, an exact list was kept. The following is a partial list from it. The list of provisions, etc., used by Resanoff in Megasaki and requested of the Japanese and brought by them from 6 December 1804 to 5 April 1805.

Name of Item	Pieces	Katti	Pud	Pfund
White bread	–	1,982	74	13
Black bread	–	460	16	20
Ducks	85			
Chickens	88			
Fresh pork	–	1,486	55	29
Goat meat	–	844	31	26
Rice	–	455	15	2½
Eggs	1,627			
Fresh fish	–	479	17	38½
Various kinds of crab	184			
Salt fish	–	15	–	22½
Dried crabs	5			
Oysters	200			

Name of Item	Pieces	Katti	Pud	Pfund
Salt	–	91	3	16½
Red peppers	30			
Bunches of carrots	108			
Bunches of radishes	266			
Bunches of wild garlic	403			
Bunches of onions	704			
Bunches of garlic	6			
Jugs of soya	38			
Jugs of sake	2			
Jugs of vinegar	34			
Mustard	–	7	–	10½
Candles / taper	429			
Lamp oil	–	112	4	8
Oranges	810			
Small oranges	–	½	–	–
Pears	30			
Large limes	5			
Chestnuts	50			
Dried figs	50			
Potatoes	–	40	1	20
Honey	–	1	–	1½
Heads of cabbage	15			
Heads of endive	20			
Bunches of parsley	1			
Japanese cabbage	4			
Halves of salt pumpkin	4			
White flour	–	75	2	32½
Measures of peas	2			
Tea	–	4	–	6
Seaweed	2			
Hardtack for tea	–	20	–	30
Kindling wood	–	12,500	312	20
Kuhli of coal	90			
Bunches of lamp wicks	16			
Bunches of sulfur matches	15			

Name of Item	Pieces	Katti	Pud	Pfund
Bottle baskets	200			
White lead for paint	–	30	1	5
Jugs of train oil	2			
Smoking tobacco	–	29	1	3½
Leaf tobacco	–	10	–	15
Raw camphor	–	1	–	1½
Tree resin	–	½	–	¾
Pure lamb tallow	–	1	–	1½
Seed rice	–	1	–	1½
Beans	–	–	–	–
Reams of Japanese paper	3			
Balls of twine	12			
All kinds of sundries	338			
Large snails	8			
Fish for stuffing	–	128	4	32
Various birds	24			

The list of things that Krusenstern requested for use on the ship and received.

Date 1804		Number	Length/fuss	Thickness/zoll
Oct. 31	Boards of camphor wood	2	9	6
Nov. 29	Deal boards	1	21	4
Dec. 4	Ditto-ditto	6	21	4
Dec. 6	Deal boards	5	21	4
"	14 Camphor wood planks	2	10	7½
"	26 Bamboo brooms	2		
	Copper plating 15 zoll long and 13 wide	100		
	Pfund of copper nails	11	–	
	Brown paper for covering the ship with copper	580		
	Camphor wood boards	4	16	1
	Ditto-ditto	1	22	1
	30 Camphor wood boards	3	22	1
	Pfund of copper nails	8½		
	Sheets of paper	500		

1805		Number	Length/fuss	Thickness/zoll
Jan. 5	Pfund of copper nails	14		
	Ditto-ditto	11		
	Ditto-ditto	11½		
15	Copper plating 14 zoll long and 12 zoll wide	320		
31	Ditto-ditto	70		
Feb. 5	Bamboo brooms	20		
10	Camphor boards	8	15	2½
14	Ditto-ditto	3	16	1
	Ditto-ditto	2	14	2½
	Pfund of copper nails	18½		
21	The Japanese made a new foremast for us.			
27	Pfund of copper nails	27 _		
Mar. 2	Deal boards	2	21	4
6	Ditto-ditto	4	19	4
10	Ditto-ditto	6	19	4
17	Beech boards Curved wood for railings	4 8	18 8	4½ 4½
20	Small boxes of white lead	28		
26	Oak Boards	3	20	4½
	Ditto-ditto	2	17	4
	Poles and stakes	6		

The quantities of provisions used on the *Nadezhda* during our stay in Japan, which we requested and the Japanese brought.

	For Officers			For Ship's Crew		
	Pieces	Pud	Pfund	Pieces	Pud	Pfund
White bread for officers, Black bread for crew	2,493	–	–	–	53	4
Rice	–	12	33	–	62	38
Fresh fish	–	27	13½	–	21	25
Salt fish	–	1	5	–	–	–
Fresh pork	–	25	3½	–	164	16½
Fresh goat meat	–	10	14	–	42	36½
Mustard	–	1	4½	–	–	12

	For Officers			For Ship's Crew		
	Pieces	**Pud**	**Pfund**	**Pieces**	**Pud**	**Pfund**
Salt	–	2	6½	–	4	34
Bunches of onions	422	–	–	643		
Bunches of radishes 2,5,6 in each 334	–	–		12,493		
Bunches of turnips	299			413		
Bunches of wild garlic	274			446		
Bunches of lettuce	13			14		
Bunches of parsley	15			6		
Sugar from Duff					16	36
Potatoes	473					
Ducks	347					
Chickens	450					
Eggs	4,000					
Oranges	442					
Pomegranates	10					
Jugs of soya	42					
Pears	20					
Jugs of sake	1					
Jugs of lamp oil	1					
Jugs of vinegar	5					
Tea	–	1	4½			
Large crabs	18					
Scrimp or small crabs	100					
Sacks of chestnuts	10					
Various nuts	–	–	5			
Hardtack	–	–	5			
Kindling wood	1,512	20				

Things that the Japanese later gave us officially as presents.

	Number	Pud	Pfund
Silk Padding	25		
2,000 pieces in all			
Sacks of rice	100	340	

	Number	Pud	Pfund
Packets of salt, 29 pud each	2,000	1,340	
Hardtack		150	
Little casks of white flour	3		
Salt fish	–	15	
Little casks of Japanese wine, sake		15	
Little casks of soya	10		
Salt pork	–	28	5
Little casks of lamp oil	3		
Buckets of vinegar	4		
Live pigs	10		
Ditto piglets	2		
Chickens	49		
Ducks	10		
Eggs	440		
Green tea	32½		
Onions			38
Garlic			5½
Mustard			18
Bunches of radishes	100		

Fri. 7/19 Reef topsail wind and dog weather. At daybreak, we set out under sail. A lot of albatross flew around us at seven knots speed. Resanoff, as before, has a lot of respect for wind and weather. In the evening, the skies cleared, and we caught sight of a short sunset and in the distance the Island of Sutzsima.

Sat. 8/20 At sunset, we sailed along the length of the Island of Sutzsima, before which we had tacked against the wind for the entire night. The clear sky let us use the good wind. The little island which Collinet[1] noted down was to our right. In the afternoon, we hauled in our shrouds, which had become somewhat slack. We sailed freshly through this unknown sea until nightfall.

Sun. 9/21 Easter Sunday passed like any other day and confirmed the old saying, "На море празников нет" [At sea, there are no holidays]. Only Resanoff voluntarily carried out a ceremony, kissing everyone and being kissed by everyone. Our travel route is approximately as follows: In order not to break our word to the Japanese, we will sail through the middle of the Korean Sea up to the Straits of Sangar, the promontory, explore the western shores of Matmai or Jesso, sail through the Straits of La Pérouse, touch Urup and explore the eastern coast of Sachalin as exactly as possible, take course for Kurils, sail through the first best straits and head for Kamtschatka, from where the continuation of our voyage will be determined.

Today, we had contrary winds.

Everyone, officers as well as sailors, received an egg in honor of the Easter holiday. We will probably celebrate our next Easter holiday next year at the Cape of Good Hope.

Things are very quiet among us; even Resanoff is not using his otherwise so ready spies. It seems to peeve our ex-ambassador that we are not curious about reading the translations of the Japanese papers, which he would not let us read anyway.

Mon. 10/22 Forced by contrary winds to tack, we caught sight of the Japanese coast fifteen miles away. It bothered Resanoff a great deal that we were again so close to Japan. The visible land must have been the Island of Oki.

Tues. 11/23 Forced to tack because of the continual east-northeasterly wind, we again saw the Japanese coast today at a distance of 25 miles.

Since our longitude is 1 to 1½ degrees off that of the map and the land does not correspond to the coast on the map, we cannot enter our course on any one of our maps, because we would otherwise sail over imaginary land and reefs. Krusenstern, therefore, took a clean piece of paper and had us make a chart, and, on this clean piece of paper, we have nice room to tack—all the more reason, we have to watch out that we do not run into reefs.

Resanoff has become generous. I'm sorry that he has decided to do that right now, because I have drunk neither brandy nor wine since the last time I spit up blood. He was niggardly during the entire trip, and now, every morning at breakfast, a double bottle of some kind of schnapps gets emptied. At noon, Resanoff is generous with a bottle, even two of Madeira or Cheres, and in the afternoon at tea he offers a bottle of the nicest Jamaica.

It would have been better if Resanoff had been more generous with offering the folks these drinks, rather then wasting them now at sea on our ship. Ne bois [je ne suis pas de bois: I'm not a plaster saint] when it comes to it, so we are drinking it by the barrel. Even without that, Romberg, Fosse, and Kamentschikoff are drinking systematically.

Wed. 12/24 Often you overlook something for a long time until your attention is called to it by chance. Because of La Pérouse, my attention was called to the wind, and I have also discovered that the weather regularly goes with the wind. If the wind changes from west to north, then the sky is clear; from west to south the sky is overcast; from southwest to southeast or even east, then you have foggy overcast rainy weather. It is also the same case from north to east that rain and fog seldom occur.

In the afternoon, we were approximately at the latitude of the Island Dajelet.

Thurs. 13/25 Resanoff has another new plan. He wants to go overland from Kamtschatka to Petersburg, and that makes the *Nadezhda*'s return voyage easier. Since loading and unloading takes a lot of time and the food we have in the hold, because of the bad roadstead in Kodiak, could only be moved slowly (that is the unloading), since the *Nadezhda* sails more deeply than would permit her to be towed into the harbor, thus, we should leave all of the goods in Peter-Paul Harbor, where transportation vessels coming from Ochotsk can transport the iron, etc., as opportunity arises to Kodiak. We would than sail straight to Unalaschka with the *Nadezhda*—everyone would be there—load furs, and without touching Kodiak sail straight to China. The *Neva* will be expecting us only at the latest until October and from there likewise sail for China, where we would meet. Resanoff is still going to make many a plan before we are rid of him, and, before we have parted, since that is his weakness, making plans without considering them in depth and even less carrying them out.

Tilesius, swayed by Resanoff's sweet talk, who knows all too well the weaknesses of our aulic councilor, has totally made peace with him and has simply forgotten that this hypocrite put another address on his letter in Kamtschatka and that he bawled him out and abused him several times in Japan and probably will make similar jumps with him again in Kamtschatka, because Resanoff does not stop his teasing—and Tilesius is now indeed so weak that he defends him.

Fri. 14/26 According to Resanoff's instructions, the inspection and organization of Kodiak is one of his main jobs. Since he now wants to travel from Kamtschatka to Petersburg overland, he gives as his reason that the *Nadezhda* would be held up and could miss the monsoons and that a stay of several weeks for the *Nadezhda* in Kodiak would not suffice to reorganize Kodiak and that he (Resanoff) had obligated himself, if it were the emperor's wish, to travel to Kodiak and to go on land again in order to carry out the orders he had been given. Every plan suits us if it means getting rid of that snake.

Sat. 15/27 Among the gifts intended for the Emperor of Japan was also a beautiful black fox pelt. This animal is considered impure in Japan and probably also its fur, even though we place a great value on it; thus vary the views.[2]

Tscherveninoff, one of our soldiers from Kamtschatka, has come down with natural pox. That disease could not be less opportune for us since we will be visiting peoples who do not know the disease and since pox get into clothes, we will have to go into quarantine in Kamtschatka.

Sun. 16/28 Even though the barometer has dipped very greatly, we have nevertheless had no storm. The weather is however overcast, rainy, and wet-cold. La Pérouse also had a very low barometer at the same latitude on his voyage through the Sea of Korea.

Mon. 17/29 At table, the talk was of Matzneff, who, through his mechanical genius, improved the ropewalk in Kronstadt and is now its manager. (All of our anchor cables and cords were his work.) "He must have earned himself a tidy sum!" said Fosse, and, when he was asked how? in what way? our court councilor said, "Как не быть!" and laughed as if to say, "If he does not know how to steal, then I can teach him."

Even though the barometer has fallen a great deal, we are still having good weather.

Tues. 18/30 I cannot compare Ratmanoff with anyone better than with d'Escures,[3] La Pérouse's lieutenant, who drowned in the Port of François.

Wed. 19/1 At eight o'clock in the morning, we sighted land, and, at eleven o'clock, we saw thirteen Japanese vessels in the distance. The horizon was overcast, and changing winds blew toward land. We put out to sea without having seen the land clearly. Toward evening, we approached the island of Soo-Sima again and were becalmed at a distance of three German miles.

We have so many onboard who would like to be the Forsters[4] and Fleuries[5] of the Russian expedition that we already have a horror of the smeared vapor smoke that, after our return, will appear in print. The one, with quite a lot of talent, the least ability, and the greatest pretensions is Tilesius. Langsdorff will not be deficient keeping himself undamaged through the voyage in every way, even if at the cost of others. Espenberg also seems inclined through the voyage to want to be brilliant in the literary world.

Horner has to prove and make known to the world his observations and research in astronomy and the physical world in order to give our work validity. Resanoff will not be deficient, through written lies, of confusing everything even more that he spoiled irreparably by his behavior and certainly will not refrain decorating himself with others' words and others' achievements. There will be so much written, smeared, invented, and lied in this way that Krusenstern's description of the voyage will be doubted if he tells the truth.

Romberg, who works on translations, also will not be deficient (through Karamsin) in giving the world his version. There are as many journals as people onboard. Все к лучему [all the better].

Resanoff used to greet the tolks in Megasaki with the following words: "Don't give me any Mar! Anything you want but without Mar." He repeated that so often that no one paid any attention to it any more.

Tatikiro finally pointed that out to him and said, "You have an unfounded antipathy toward Mar. The law does not permit you to get this or that. Mar, the Believtheit of the Governor does not permit you to get it. We use Mar! only when it is for your well being."

Thurs. 20/2 The land we caught sight of yesterday was not Soo-Sima but a promontory belonging to the mainland of Japan. Since we are already about 40^0 latitude, we should be reaching the Straits of Sangar.

In the evening, we were carried by a calm and current closer to land than was our intention. During the calm, we saw four big boats shove off from land that had at least 150 men in them. Even though we knew that they were Japanese who came rowing up to guard us in case we should anchor, Krusenstern nevertheless thought it advisable to take a defensive stance. This armada stopped not far off, and, when we were able to go to sea again with a gentle wind, the Japanese boats returned to land.

Fri. 21/3 The wind and weather were favorable and permitted us to sail along the shore. At two o'clock, we sighted Cape Sangar and headed toward the long sought passageway that Krusenstern is now planning to use.

It was late when we approached the southern tip of Matmai. The wind was blowing toward the strait, and the current also carried us toward the strait. We therefore found it necessary to turn the ship and sail away from land. At the foot of the steep shores of Matmai, we saw a city that compared to Nangasaki in size and appearance.

Horner, Bellingshausen, and I are busier than anything making our observations, rhombuses, angles, measurements, maps, etc. Resanoff would really like to have copies of our maps. Instead of asking Krusenstern for them, he recently gave Horner the bad Russian maps of these waters and Bellingshausen pencils. He tries to use punsch and wine with me because I dare not drink any for the time being. He could spare himself the effort because he is not going to get anything. Resanoff does not like our heading so close to land because the better our maps are, the more fame we will reap; and that does not help him any. And he does not begrudge anyone anything good. Now, Resanoff is peeved that Krusenstern has given the written order to sail along Urup and Sachalin and that he does not have to arrive in Kamtschatka until July.

The Russian map of Matmai is good and needs to be improved only in latitude and longitude and details.

Sat. 22/4 Resanoff, who always made declarations of love to the tolks in Nangasaki, once said to Sosoimon, "I love you! I am giving you my heart!"

Sosoimon, who did not understand the word heart, said, "That is not permitted, can possibly, but secretly."

"No," said Resanoff, "I am giving you my heart" and made himself understood by pantomime.

"Yes! Yes! Yes!" called Sosoimon, "Hes sin Haart" and could not contain himself for laughing.

Today, we sailed along the coast of Matmai through between Kosima and Ohsima, which are both old volcanoes. From the later island, we saw smoke still rising. We came as far as the Island of Okosir, which we had to sail around, because between it and land there were dangerous reefs. The weather was terrible. Large numbers of whales are swimming around us. Up to now, our trip from Nangasaki has been very good. We have had the desired weather and favorable winds most of the time.

Sun. 23/5 Nice weather. Resanoff regrets more than a little having given the map, which Laksmann had brought and Schelichoff had taken possession of, to the map depot.

Mon. 24/6 The snow and ice-covered mountains and the old volcanoes rising up here and there give the Island of Matmai an unfriendly appearance. We sailed according to the Russian map, which is becoming more and more trustworthy. We sailed past the promontory Ozui, then past two barely visible dangerous islands, Janikisiri and Teariri, lying in the deep bay, and then the promontory Nozusiaphu. As we were passing the last one, we caught sight of high, snowy mountains ahead of us and an apparent strait across from us. We thought it was the strait between Matmai and Schischa and sailed into it, even though we are a degree more to the south than the strait given by La Pérouse. Behind the mountains, we lost the wind, and at two o'clock we became becalmed, which continued for the whole evening. The land has a wild desolate look; all of the mountains were covered with snow and ice deep into the valleys; and only in one single spot in the distance did we see smoke rising. In the evening, the inhabitants lit fire at the place where smoke had risen during the day. We tacked restlessly through the night without knowing if we would find a bay or a passageway opposite us.

Tues. 25/7 We tacked in contrary wind in front of the supposed passageway and could not be sure of it. Resanoff talked a lot about loss of time, seconded by Ratmanoff's scabs, who always uses similar situations to portray Krusenstern as afraid for no good reason. These people all too gladly criticize Krusenstern whenever they have an opportunity. Upon Fosse's advice, Resanoff has stopped wasting rum, because in Kamtschatka rum could also make a big show, and he is right.

Wed. 26/8 We finally found that we were in a deep bay, turned the ship, and hurried out of it. At the entrance, a cold fog encircled us, and, for better or for worse, we had to try to stay in one place. Ratmanoff began to argue and swear. We should have either sailed to the end or not have sailed into the bay at all. Resanoff enjoyed listening to this absurd, senseless talk because he was hearing Krusenstern criticized. Ratmanoff argued into the day because he had nothing better to do, and Krusenstern never contradicted such blather.

Thurs. 27/9 We sighted two islands, which we took for a strait from the islands on Laksmann's map. Since we, however, saw no strait, we steered farther to the north. We are at the latitude where we do not have to sail much farther to the north in order to come to the Straits of La Pérouse. Then we have already passed the Strait, which is supposed to be between Matmai and Schischa, or this strait and the Island of Schischa do not exist at all. We are undoubtedly sorry that we sailed too far from land several times, especially since the wind would have permitted us to stay closer to land. These doubts are exactly the thing that Resanoff and Ratmanoff mull over again and again, because – because they have nothing else to do.

Fri. 28/10 After being enveloped in a thick fog the whole night and the whole morning, we found ourselves at noon, when the sky had finally cleared up, almost at the same place we had been at yesterday. We were unable to scan the land very well, but we could see no strait. In the afternoon, we caught sight of a high peak to the north, which must have been at the latitude of the Pic de Langle. If there is no strait between this peak and the land next to us, then nothing will come of Schischa.

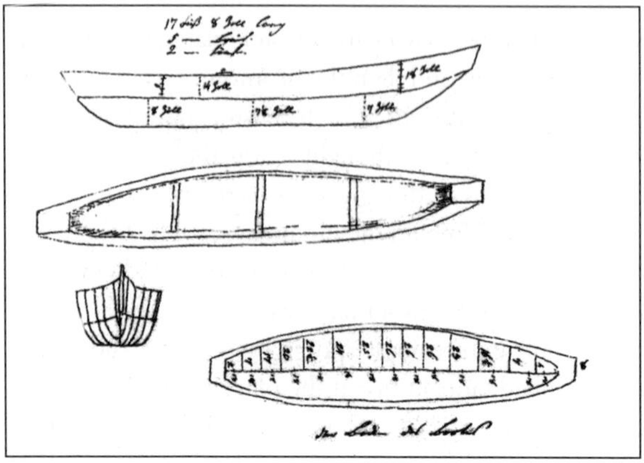

16-1. The bottom of the boat. This boat, fished [out of the water] near Matmai. The bottom is carved from on log, the rest is sewn on with tree roots, done quite regularly.
17 fuss 8 zoll long
5 fuss wide
2 fuss deep

In the evening, we fished up a small boat floating around the sea with no one in it and brought it onboard. As much as we would like to return the boat to her owner, it will be difficult to fulfill this wish.

During the night, we will tack in front of the island of Pic de Langle and in the morning sail into the Straits of La Pérouse.

Sat. 29/11 Early in the morning, we sailed with a favorable wind between the Pic de Langle and Matmai, were not able, because the overcast weather, to catch sight of the land across from us on Sachalin. After we had passed the northwestern point of Matmai, we steered into the strait. Our southerly wind turned suddenly to the northeast and forced us, as we wished, to anchor in an open bay on the northern side of Matmai. Several boats with bearded inhabitants (they looked like Estonians) approached our ship, and, at our invitation, climbed on deck showing no shyness. Their looks had a lot of good-naturedness about them. One of the boats brought us several dozen nice, large fresh herring.

In the afternoon, Resanoff, Krusenstern, and about twelve officers went on land. They had barely left when a large boat came with five Japanese and several natives aboard. The Japanese remembered quite well that Kodai had been brought back to Japan from Russia. They brought all kinds of trade goods with them and went away toward evening. Resanoff had taken coronation medals along. We hope that he will not be so foolish as to distribute them among the Japanese. The Japanese explained the bay and promontory with their names. They did not want to believe that we were Russians. They promised to come again tomorrow. They found it very puzzling that we were coming from Nangasaki. They claimed that, along with the straits of La Pérouse, there were two other straits and pointed to this side as well as the other side of the Island Schischa. (Matmai, as we suspected.) These Japanese appear to have settled here as agents. They are not permitted to bring their women with them. Their natural behavior, their trading freely, everything about them, showed that the iron hand of the Japanese government did not stretch in its full force to the shores of the straits of La Pérouse.

16-2. Ainu

Resanoff has taken it upon himself to patch together a dictionary of the inhabitants of Matmai. Obscenities already fill up the first rows in this dictionary. In the evening at six o'clock, our gentlemen returned from land and were not little surprised to hear from us that Japanese had been onboard, for they had only found natives on land. The herring here are exceedingly large.

This bay is very open, the roadstead good. We hope to find a better anchorage at the other shore.

When I told Krusenstern what the Japanese had told me during his absence and congratulated him on the new strait, Resanoff was very happy and immediately began making war plans to avenge himself on the Japanese by taking Schischa.

Sun. 30/12 At four o'clock in the morning, Ratmanoff, Fedoroff, Espenberg, Friderici, Romberg, and I went on land. The rifleman and Resanoff's servant Alexander were along as guards, and Schemelin also went along with us in order to cook us ucha [fish soup]. The vegetation is still way behind, little grass, and we saw almost no flowers at all. The trees still had only small buds. Japanese lived in the first house we went into, which was somewhat larger than the typical ones. I made them understand that they should come onboard. Not long afterwards, a Japanese officer (ontoni) with two swords came and went out to the *Nadezhda*. The houses are woven from straw, the walls as well as the roof, and covered in winter with snow to keep them warm.

A kettle hangs in the middle over the fireplace; above the roof is a hole for the smoke where a lot of herring were being smoked. The door, the sole opening in the house, has a small entry built on. In every house, we found a young bear tied up on a pile of manure in a corner, totally raven black in color with a white collar around its neck. We could offer however much we wanted to, no one would sell us his bear. The men all have beards and look like dirty Estonians and, in the summer, wear clothing woven of tree bark that looks like sailcloth and, in the winter, of dog and bear pelts. The women have stripes tattooed on their lips, also on their hands. A lot of them had scurf. Both sexes smoked tobacco. Their household utensils were sparse. Everything was lacquerware of Japanese manufacture, mainly wooden utensils, except for a copper kettle over the hearth.

16-3. Ainu

They dry their fish like the Kamtschadals in balagans [summer hut]. Towards two in the afternoon, we returned to the shore, where Schemelin had very diligently cooked his ucha, which spiced by hunger, tasted exceedingly good; and after we had eaten our fill, rested and looked for mussels along the shore, and especially paper nautiluses, we went back onboard.

The Japanese had been on the ship and had tried to convince Krusenstern to leave the coast. They had shown him, using pantomime, how we had to weigh anchor, and blew, in order to indicate that with strong winds we risked being stranded, indicated that also Schischa (or Sachalin) was under Japanese domination and that there was a Japanese guard there, and, finally, if we did not go away, a Japanese guard and a large flotilla would come and drive us away. The Japanese also related that he had heard that there was a Russian ship in Nangasaki, did not, however, want to believe that we were Russians and that the *Nadezhda* came from Nangasaki, especially because we were not wearing braids like the Russians usually do. He, in any case, would not accept gifts. Krusenstern had everything explained as well as pantomime permitted, as far as the inhabitants were concerned, the names of promontories, villages, etc. Resanoff's war plans have a catch. Karafuto or Schischa or five parts of Sachalin belong to the Japanese, the rest to the Chinese Tartery. And Urup, the Japanese said, belongs to the Russians, only the inhabitants of Urup know nothing about their being Russian subjects.

May

Mon. 1/13 At five o'clock in the morning, we weighed anchor.

The women carry their children on their backs in the fur coats that they wear. The inhabitants of Matmai are called Ainus by the Japanese, and the stretch of land on which these people live is called Jesso. The southern part of the island inhabited by the Japanese is called Matzumai with a city of the same name, the only one on the whole island. Toward evening, we caught sight of a promontory and rocks charted by La Pérouse at the southern tip of Sachalin.

Tues. 2/14 We caught sight of Aniva, sailed past the reef les Dangereuses and into the Bay of Aniva. On the rocks were lying countless sea lions and seals whose bellowing cause a horrible noise. The wind was favorable for us, and, in the evening about eight o'clock, we dropped anchor in the bay. Not far from us was anchored a Japanese merchant vessel and at some distance in another bay another one. The Bay of Aniva cuts deep into the land and must be dangerous in strong winds because it is so open and has such a large basin.

Resanoff is once again thinking of trying to pressure the Japanese by way of Sachalin into trade, by force if it cannot be done otherwise.

Wed. 3/29 Several Japanese boats with Japanese and Ainus came out to us. They asked us a lot of banal questions. None came onboard. Then Krusenstern, Resanoff and several officers went over to the Japanese vessel. They found it half full of salt fish which were packed in the hold like in a cask. The Japanese said that they were only there in the summer and every winter they returned to Japan, also stayed at the northern part of the island. Immediately after our meal, Resanoff, Krusenstern, Friderici, Fosse, Golovatscheff, Koscheleff, and I and Kotzebue #2 [Moritz] went on land. We could not land because of the surf and finally were taken on land by Ainus in a little boat which, after a lot of pantomiming, finally did us this favor. The Japanese were very frightened by our arrival. Two of the most prominent ones could not speak a word for a time and were very pale. It took a little while, but their fright nevertheless did not completely disappear. The Japanese are the masters here and treat the natives like slaves. We found several sheds full of salt fish, that is, salt fish not in barrels, stacked on both sides of the shed with a path through the middle. Other sheds were full of salt (in sacks), dried fish, rice, etc.—all the property of the Japanese. Nothing belonged to the natives. The Ainus had only erected summer housing from bark, twigs, and mats. During the winter the Ainus live far inland. We returned onboard at teatime.

Ratmanoff, who had gone with Langsdorff to a bay about twenty versts to the east, reported that there were also a lot of Japanese. Two Japanese officers had given them a noon meal and had been very friendly but could not hide their fear at the appearance of our ship.

Countless numbers of wild ducks and fish are found here. Dozens of whales swim around the bay and make it dangerous to go by small boat. Anchoring here is very difficult.

In the bay in which Ratmanoff had landed, the Japanese had a temple and two gallows, the former for themselves, the gallows for the Ainus, who appear to be good-natured, ready to serve and competent.

16-4. Ainu woman and child

Fosse, who is made up of pure selfishness, would not let Otto Kotzebue use his gun until he promised to give him a Japanese pictures for permission to shot his gun several times.

Thurs. 4/16 We weighed anchor and were happy to sail out of the bay of Aniva with a favorable wind before sunset. It would probably be difficult to tack out of it with a contrary wind.

Fri. 5/17 We doubled Cape Aniva, could not however reach Cape Vertowning charted by Friese (Vries) in the *Kastrikum* because we becalmed. The whales that throw up their fountains around us are too numerous to be counted. These whales are not large. Since they only blow one fountain, they are kaschelotten.

We will perhaps be better off in Pationie Bay if we found inhabited places as on Matmai and Aniva, because the Japanese will undoubtedly not have settlements so far up.

Sat. 6/18 We sailed past Cape Vertowning

Sun. 7/19 We reached a bay which seems to be suitable. Since, however, a rocky reef runs from the southern spit of land deep into the sea, Krusenstern sent Golovatscheff in with a boat to inspect it. During his absence, we stayed on the drift. Golovatscheff had the express order not to stay away more than two hours. After three hours had passed, Krusenstern had a cannon fired as a signal, but there still was nothing to be seen of the boats. Ratmanoff then made the remark that Golovatscheff probably was looking for mussels (could as well have not said that). Krusenstern then had the ship headed toward land in the bay as far as the water depth permitted until we finally caught sight of the boat under sail. Golovatscheff reported that the bay is large but does not offer a good anchorage. The inhabitants are Ainus but better off than those in Aniva. Their main effects, pipes, etc., were all of Japanese manufacture. Golovatscheff also saw countless numbers of dogs there. He had not, however, been able to obtain fresh fish. Golovatscheff had stayed there so long taking the measurements of the bay as well as the depth of the water.

8/20, 9/21 On Monday and Tuesday, we sailed along the shore of Sachalin (or as the Japanese call it Tschoka, Schischa, or Karafuto) and busied ourselves with charting it as best we could. Only at night did we go away from land so that we could continue our work in the morning where we had left off the evening before.

Wed 10/22 We reached a very large section of low ground stretching from east to west. We noticed several small openings that appeared to us to be the mouths of rivers, but those were only suppositions. About six miles from land, we had only eight faden of water; and in the evening at ten miles from land we found that the water was only twelve faden deep. That's why we also dropped anchor. The Bay of Patienie seems to end with this low ground, for, in the distance running toward the south, we caught sight of high ground. We counted ourselves lucky in such shallow water not to have run into any sandbanks.

When the entire crew is called to work, then Ratmanoff, according to Krusenstern's orders, takes over the command, and we other officers are distributed to various parts of the ship—that is fair. The manner, in which Ratmanoff, however, takes over his command and shouts, is characteristic. What he lacks in education and knowledge, he replaces with cuss words in his big screaming voice. (He is nevertheless a good practical seaman.) Today, he yelled with this thundering voice, even though Romberg and I were on the forecastle. "Straighten out the blind yard; otherwise, when casting out the anchor, the topsails get loose." Anyone knowing the way work is done on the *Nadezhda* has to view this as ridiculous. We laughed in his face as a way of thanking him for his zeal.

Thurs. 11/23 We could not weigh anchor because of a calm. We have our anchor up and are staying on the warp so that we can use every little breeze. At eight-thirty, Ratmanoff went ashore with Friderici. They took a net along. When Krusenstern asked, "You'll be back by noon?"

Ratmanoff answered, "Weigh anchor and set sails. I'll catch up with you in good time." The way in which he said that was as if giving an order. During all of that, Krusenstern patiently remained quiet. At four o'clock in the afternoon, a little breeze came up, and we raised our warp. There was nothing to be seen of our boat. Only after the third shot did we see by the sail that the gentlemen had shoved off from land. At five o'clock, they came onboard again. The land is flat and barren. They found a river teeming with fish. Since, however, they had been on foot and had, as a result, no net along, they could not catch any fish except for a salmon that weighed 30 pfund. Ratmanoff had also shot ducks with my gun. On the opposite bank of the river, they saw several Ainos; otherwise there was no sign of inhabitants. A favorable northeasterly wind helped us to get out of the flat area.

Fri. 12/24 The overcast, foggy, and rainy weather prevented us from seeing the western side of Patienie Bay. At two o'clock in the afternoon, when the weather cleared, we caught sight alee four Italian miles ahead of us a large surf. We immediately turned the ship to avoid the rocky reef charted by Friese. We have

Krusenstern's caution alone to thank for our having avoided the danger, and nevertheless this caution has its faultfinders. For what reason? Because Krusenstern alone is responsible for everything.

Sat. 13/25 Fog and bad stormy weather.

Sun. 14/26 Nice weather. In the morning, we caught sight of several ice floes, and, toward ten o'clock, we reached an impenetrable icefield which prevented us from sailing farther north. In a conversation with Resanoff, Krusenstern said, "It is too bad that we did not find a harbor in which we could remain for some time, then it only takes a southerly wind to break up the whole icefield, cause it to melt and disappear."

"Will we stay near Sachalin for very long?" asked Resanoff.

"It all depends upon the weather," answered Krusenstern, "four to six weeks."

"Well, since you need so much time to look for a harbor, then I would rather you put me off in Bolchoretsk and returned to your explorations," said Resanoff.

Since the icefield was not disappearing, we set sail again on the same afternoon, God willing, for Kamtschatka, where everything belonging to the embassy is to be left; and let's hope also Langsdorff, if not as a natural scientist then as a medical doctor. Fedoroff is happy because he is expecting his discharge and can sail with the first ship to Ochotsk. Friderici awaits everything patiently, and Koscheleff is sorry that he has to return to Kamtschatka soon because he likes it with us.

When we have taken Resanoff back to Kamtschatka and are finally rid of him, then the only wish we have is that we may not find him in Kamtschatka after our return from Sachalin. Today, Resanoff demanded of Krusenstern in writing that we sail to Kamtschatka.

Our soldier's pox is causing us worry. It is everyone's duty to go into quarantine in Peter-Paul's Harbor on the koschka [spit]. I think that Krupskoi (the commandant of Peter-Paul's Harbor) will have to object to Resanoff's desire to travel on immediately.

Mon. 15/27 Friderici has a difficult choice, since Resanoff is thinking of traveling through Siberia as quickly as possible, thus not giving Friderici the opportunity to stop in Siberia and permitting him also to get to know that distant land, if he travels with him. He does not, however, wish to arrive in Petersburg later than Resanoff. He finds it totally unpleasant to travel through Siberia with Resanoff and Fosse. Staying behind in Kamtschatka means a too great loss of time. As a result, he is highly indecisive.

Today, Friderici, who up to now has been our kasnotschei [treasurer], turned our books over to Krusenstern, and we immediately began to calculate and divide up things belonging to our company and to prepare everything for our complete separation.

Resanoff is thinking of leaving Schemelin in Kamtschatka, so that he can take over the embassy's gifts from Fosse while we are on our trip to Sachalin.

The precautions caused by the pox are as follows: Tschervenikoff's clothing is to be burned. We will not come together with the inhabitants of Peter-Paul's Harbor, and everyone who is staying in Kamtschatka has to be in quarantine on the koschka, and so that the quarantine is punctually completed, we will put up a cordon with Krupskoi's help.

Tues. 16/28 The wind became stronger. We had new light. The moon was closest to the earth and celestial equator at the same time, three heavenly events that do not let us expect anything good. Toward evening, we were forced to haul in all of our sails, and, last but not least, before our total separation from Resanoff, we had a very heavy storm which disquieted us because we did not know how far away we were from the Kurils.

Wed. 17/29 At sunrise, we caught sight of the tenth Kuril Island, a barren, steep volcano. Calm, choppy seas and an irregular storm did not let us sail between the islands.

Thurs. 18/30 At sunrise, we caught sight again of that uninhabited island (barren, desolate, gray, empty), which was not charted on any map. We sailed around it and sailed between the islands toward the east. The weather was very unfriendly and the barometer had fallen. Toward two o'clock in the afternoon, we sailed past four small dangerous islands, actually reefs. Two hours later, we saw an island again in the fog ahead of us. (Everything caused by the storm.) The wind had shifted to the east during this time, and the weather had become worse and worse. The torrent raging around the island made the water look like it was boiling (the Kamtschadals call it toltscheia), and the seaweed covering the entire area looked like rocks and sandbanks. We had to look for clear seas for the night. Because of the strong current, we could not go back the way we had come. We were forced to go straight ahead, to sail past the rocky islands to the north so that we could reach the Sea of Ochotsk for the night, which we succeeded in doing. That was a very dangerous evening. On our voyage, we have experienced few so restless days and have not been so close to apparent danger as today.

Fri. 19/31 The wind died down very early, remained however topsail wind. The weather was fair. It had snowed the whole night, so that we needed several hours to clear the ship of snow. Impatiently, we watched for a favorable wind, so that we could reach Peter-Paul's Harbor, where we would nevertheless be protected from the raw clime and finally could hope to be rid of Resanoff and his gang.

Before the storm, Tilesius had borrowed a book from Fosse which actually belonged to Frederici. It disappeared. Tilesius thought that Fosse had taken it. Fosse contradicted this assumption, and the bad weather passed in a dispute of yes's and no's. Fosse, just to anger Tilesius, had often asked about the book during that period. This evening at table, the talk was again about it; and Fosse, who is always coarse in his speech, got Tilesius so beside himself that he said, "Well, then you have stolen it!"

Then he got the answer, "For that, you deserve a box on the ears," and "I will drag you around through the streets by the hair, etc." Resanoff, who was also sitting at the table, took Fosse's part.

Fired on by that, Fosse swore like a mire snipe. I could not stand to listen to it any more and said, "The gentlemen may do as they please on land, but here on the ship the peace and quiet must not be disturbed." That was followed by quiet. Both parties separated with the firm resolve completely to tan each other's hides as soon as the opportunity presented itself.

Tilesius said to Resanoff, when we went up to the quarterdeck, "You undoubtedly remember the mummy's hand." Tilesius, because of this hand, accused Fosse in writing of thief, and Fosse, as an excuse, assured him that a servant had put the half decayed hand among his things by mistake. This story, like a lot of others, will undoubtedly be forgotten.

June

Sat. 20/1 Toward noon, we caught sight of the fifth Kuril island. Krusenstern's intention was to sail through between the fourth and fifth islands. A brisk wind from the northwest prevented us, however, from doing that, and we saw ourselves forced to sail between the fifth and sixth ones. Since the skies were rather clear, we also caught sight in the distance of the fourth and seventh islands, all of them high pointed rock masses like old craters totally covered by snow.

Sun. 21/2 Nice, clear weather. In the distance, we saw the eighth, sixth, fifth, and second islands. Vessels coming from Ochotsk sailing through the Kurils do not go through any other strait but the ones between the fourth and fifth islands and are thus often greatly held up.

Resanoff wants to turn over to Krusenstern his Extraordinair Summe for his disposition and then in Petersburg to have himself paid the same sum by the American Company of the Crown. In answer to Krusenstern's question, "Can I disburse with the money my officer's salaries?" Resanoff answered, "Yes!" He doesn't want, however, to put that Yes! in writing. The sum is in the amount of 20,000 dahler Spanish; one half went for paying the salaries of the embassy, and, nevertheless, Resanoff says the whole sum has to be turned over to the Crown. Thus, he contradicts himself and gets himself and others twisted up in ambiguities.

As far as the portion of monies (table monies) is concerned, Resanoff wants Krusenstern to take over the entire sum which we are indebted to the Company for provisions. Krusenstern, however, is not doing that and says, each person pays for himself—and that is the right way.

Mon. 22/3 In the morning, the weather was very unfriendly. In the afternoon, it cleared up again, and we caught sight of the Island of Alait, the Lapatka, and three peaks which are the southern tip of Kamtschatka. In the evening, we caught sight of Povorotnoi Muis in the distance, and now we are heading straight for Avatscha Bay. Everyone is flattering himself with the hope of finding letters waiting for him in Kamtschatka.

Krusenstern had the idea, if he should be allowed to, of publishing his letters and using Koscheleff's portrait as a front piece, since, without him, the voyage to Japan would have come to naught, and with our arrival in Kamtschatka our voyage would also have been over.

Tues. 23/4 At noon, we doubled Povorotnoi Muis. Since our departure from Japan, our stay there has not been mentioned a single time. Especially remarkable is the fact that every day of our stay and every detail of what we saw there would have provided such a rich content for conversations. The reasons are as follows: Resanoff's fear of the truth, and our care to avoid strife and unpleasantness.

The object causing the strife between Fosse and Tilesius was found behind the mizzenmast today.

For several days in a row now, the clothes and berths of our people have been washed and fumigated. Today, Tscherveninoff's clothes were thrown overboard, and we equipped him anew and all of the clothes, and berths were cleaned by beating on the deck and fumigated once again. On our part, nothing is being omitted to prevent contagion.

Before sunset, we saw the entrance to Avatscha Bay, cannot nonetheless enter it before morning.

Resanoff's malleability and gentility toward us all, and especially Dmitri Ivanovitsch has no bounds; even Fosse, who always follows Resanoff's example, is trying to ingratiate himself through little favors, behaves, however, so coarsely out of habit that we often have to laugh. A Siberian proverb says, Либо обманул, либо обмануть хочет [Either he has cheated us or wants to].

- 17 -

The Second Stay in Kamtschatka

Wed. 24/5 In the afternoon, we cast anchor with a very gentle but favorable breeze in Peter-Paul's Harbor. Without a doubt, at Koscheleff's order, there was already a guard standing at the majack [lighthouse]. Ahead of us, we found two vessels which had spent the winter there, the one a transport ship commanded by navigator Vasili Ivanovitsch Astafieff, the other belonging to the American Company commanded by Andrean Vasilevitsch Maschin. Nikolai Alexandrovitsch Chvastoff and Gavrilla Ivanovitsch Davidoff[1] were on the latter as passengers headed for Kodiak from Ochotsk. On the ship belonging to the American Company were eighty men, but twenty-four of them had run off.

There was plenty of news. Our three doctors have signed a certificate making the quarantine milder. We however are not permitting any of our people to go ashore. General Koscheleff is not here. Resanoff has suddenly changed all of his plans and is going to sail with the *Maria* to Kodiak. Resanoff, as well as Krusenstern, has only received private letters, which has to be contrary to Resanoff's desires, because he is completely civil and has suddenly changed all of his plans.

Chvastoff told us that Prince Gortschakoff is supposed to be living in Irkutsk in lamentable conditions. Even there, he has not been able to refrain from cheating and is now being counted as a member of the common class. He begged fifty rubles from Chvastoff.

Thurs. 25/6 Resanoff went on land today, and let's hope he will not return onboard again. Since he went on land so suddenly and incognito, our sailors were not put along the yards, an omission Resanoff could have prevented if he had let us know earlier, since he really likes these empty gestures of honor so much.

In the evening except for six men, all of the missing people came back whom Davidoff had found and brought back.

Maschin is a tight-chested man, who lets himself be lead too much by self-interest, and, therefore, agrees with the American Company and, even more, its subjects, who are known scoundrels and rascals (because who wants to go to Kamtschatka as a prikaschtschik if he can find his bread in Petersburg or Moscow). From self-interest, Maschin was also uselessly indulgent with his men and only too often acted quite vilely. Chvastoff had warned Maschin several times to take control of his people and to treat them more strictly—in vain!

In the spring, shortly before the ship was to be newly rigged (Chvastoff did not explain the reason for this), Maschin came running up to Chvastoff one morning and said with tears in his eyes, "My people do not want to obey me any more. They are rebelling and even wanted to attack me."

The crew consisted of a motley, armed eighty-man bunch. The soldiers and artillerymen at Peter-Paul's Harbor are even more spoiled and obey their officers just as little. Chvastoff left Maschin hanging somewhat and said, "Their leader has to get the cat [o-nine-tails]."

"None obey," said Maschin timidly. Finally, Chvastoff went with Maschin to the rebellious men. A fellow who had already got the knout once walked freshly up to Chvastoff with a facial expression as if he wanted to silence him. A couple of slaps up the chops which Chvastoff gave him, throwing the fellow off his feet, impressed him. The fellow jumped up again and called to his comrades who all came up growling and went after Chvastoff with balled fists. At that moment, Davidoff arrived and hit the fellow over the head with a knotty stick, causing him to fall. Chvastoff gave the rest of them slaps across the chops so fast that they had no time to know what was happening. The cat was brought immediately. The main bandit could barely be controlled. His clothes were forcefully ripped from his body and he got twenty-five blows of the cat. (Who counted them?) And, in addition, twelve other men were punished. That bandit has been sick for six weeks now, is under arrest where he continually screams about tyranny and breathes vengeance. Chvastoff took over the command, and for fear of his strictness the twenty-four men had run away. Our arrival brought peace again. During the whole occurrence, Maschin had stood there as if it were none of his business.

I am forced to be of Chvastoff's opinion that Maschin should have chased a bullet through the bandit chief's head to prevent an even greater catastrophe. Things will be quite all right until Kodiak because Chvastoff, Davidoff and Resanoff are going along. On the return voyage, however, things look bad if Maschin, who does not know how to control his people, is alone.

We are filling our water casks but do not know how long we will be staying.

Fri. 26/7 Chvastoff is a quick fellow. He already has seen through Resanoff. Langsdorff, who is to go along to Kodiak, is now concluding a contract with Resanoff. In the afternoon, our soldiers moved on land to an isolated house where they will have to spend their quarantine. We are filling our water casks without knowing whether we will not have to pour it all out again. Resanoff is living on land, busy writing letters and preparing for his voyage to Kodiak.

Our comrades here are telling us news of Ochotsk and Kodiak. I served with Davidoff on the *Helena*. With Maschin, I did the Mediterranean campaign, and I spent several years in England with Maschin.

The way in which the promischlenikis sailed to Kodiak earlier resulted in all of the vessels that the American Company launched being stranded on the first or second voyage. One vessel got so far off track that it was sailing to south instead of to the north. When, in September, the tar began to well up out of the seams, they finally admitted that they were sailing the wrong direction. They brought forth the Mother of God and said, "Wherever you have the wind blow, that is where we will sail." And after twenty days, almost without water and provisions, they sailed with a very strong wind, always before the wind, and finally stranded on the island of Kodiak. If the officers of fleet now in the service of the Company, request riggings, etc. they always hear, "Етак ли мы ходили?" [How did we used to sail earlier?] The security of the ship and cargo seems to be secondary.

Sat. 27/8 This time, Fedoroff is not getting his discharge because his petition was handed in in the wrong form, and, because of that, he will have to stay in Kamtschatka for almost two years longer. Family matters were his reason for asking to be discharged because, during his stay in Kamtschatka, his parents had died.

Sun. 28/9 The soldiers here are very spoiled. They have had mainly scoundrels for officers who made robbing and stealing easier for them, so that they now no longer want to get used to rules. Major Krupskoi was sent to Nischnoi Kamtschatsk in the winter to take over command of the Tschuktschs during Pavel Ivanovitsch Koscheleff's absence. Lieutenant Falkin did not want to accept him as commander, and the soldiers obeyed even less. Falkin, you see, had robbed several merchants and wanted to gain time to develop his knavery thoroughly. On the same evening, he even followed a merchant into Krupskoi's room where Chvastoff and Davidoff, who had gone with Krupskoi to Nischnoi Kamtschatsk, were sleeping. He stormed in shouting, "Who has decided to support this knave?!" Krupskoi had barely opened his mouth when he said, "Ah! Is that you? Major, old woman, etc." Only in Chvastoff's and Davidoff's presence was he surrounded and forced to go home.

On the following morning, Krupskoi demanded that the command be turned over to him. When he walked in front of them, the soldiers yelled, "What do we need a different commander for? We already have one."

To reinforce this remark, Falkin went after Krupskoi with an open knife and said, "Scram! If you love your life!"

With the help of several not totally spoiled soldiers, Falkin was finally arrested and he has now been turned over to the military court. Unfortunately, the military court consists of similar subjects. While Krupskoi was in Nischnoi Kamtschatsk, his house in Peter-Paul's Harbor was totally assaulted and destroyed. His wife and four small children had stayed behind, and, since she was ill, she would have perished if Chvastoff, who had returned to Peter-Paul's Harbor, had not helped her.

In the summer, the soldiers are lazy and catch no fish for winter supplies, and, in the winter, they starve to death with their dogs. Since supplying them is so difficult, they only get half pajock [rations]. Wood grows in front of their noses, but chopping it up is too much trouble. They would rather burn fences that do not belong to them and chop up sheds, balagans [балаганы: summer huts of the Kamtschadals] and houses than take the trouble of chopping wood at the right time. Abuse, even fights, are not rare between officers and soldiers; and disobedience is a daily occurrence. Robbery and theft seem to be their mainstay. That is why the Kamtschadals, those peaceful people, have been exterminated. General Koscheleff has the difficult job of establishing discipline again. (Three years after our departure, these people, through false witnesses and false oaths, caused General Koschcleff to incur the emperor's disfavor and even be turned over to a military court which investigated the matter for five years and, nevertheless, decided nothing. He could not participate in the whole campaign of 1812 because he was under military law, and, thus, through his stay in Kamtschatka, his whole military career came to naught.)

For the first time this year in Kamtschatka, they have learned to smoke fish, which Davidoff taught them. Undoubtedly, they understood how to do it, but for laziness never wanted to try it. There is an abundance of wild game here, but no one takes it for winter supplies. Codfish, which can be caught in large enough quantities that all of Kamtschatka could be supplied with them, are not caught at all. Only their heads are eaten, and the rest is thrown to the dogs. They throw butterfish, which can be caught by the net full, back into the water or on shore for the dogs. Only when they have caught herring or salmon are they happy with their catch. They always complain that they have no salt or not enough and that they have to work for the Crown, and, if one looks for work done, then one finds nothing. In answer to our question, "What kind of work do you do?" these rascals became embarrassed and did not give us an answer.

Mon. 29/10 In Kodiak, there is supposed to be much better discipline and even an abundance of the usual foodstuffs available there, which also consists mainly of fish. Even though the American Company hires the worst scoundrels and ships them there, these people are forced to behave orderly. If one of them is caught stealing, he loses trust and thus also his entire livelihood. He cannot escape because otherwise he would end up in the hands of the Americans [Tlingits] on the northwestern coast of America, who seldom let an individual Russian live. Horses, cows, pigs, goats, chickens, and dogs have greatly multiplied there and live mainly on mussels and fish, even bruin the bear joins the domesticated animals and eats his meal of fish in the company of cows. The way the American Company operates is faulty, aside from the organization. It treats the Aleuts tyrannically and treats its catch of pelts so poorly that 900,000 kottiki [fur seal] pelts are supposed to be lying in Unalaschka half ruined.

In the afternoon, Golovatscheff, Bellingshausen, young Koscheleff, Chvastoff, Davidoff, and I went for a walk. When we came home in the evening, a lot of dogs were running around the koschka ahead of us. Davidoff suggested we should force the dogs into the water. We had driven the dogs out to the extreme point of the spit of land, but the dogs did not want to go into the water. And they did not know how to save themselves any other way, so they began to break through our line so violently that Golovatscheff was tossed about. Davidoff threw his stick at the last dog, so that it hit the dog with a crack, causing it to fall over. Only a short time later did it begin to recover. We, however, could not wait to see if the dog got up on its legs again. Golovatscheff suffered no damage. We were sorry about the incident because it had happened out of want of foresight, misbehavior, and childishness.

Prospects for the future are as follows: Resanoff wants to travel with Langsdorff and the rifleman on the *Maria* to Kodiak and will take, it is being said, Kamentschikoff along at his request. Fosse is traveling with Resanoff's servant Alexander to Petersburg. Friderici is making the voyage back with us. Resanoff plans to stay here until the tenth of June. We are going to sail from here to Sachalin. After completing our voyage of discovery, we will return to Peter-Paul's Harbor, where we will then find a vessel from Kodiak filled with pelts, load these pelts, and, without sailing either to Kodiak or Unalaschka, set out straight for China.

Tues. 30/11 We had been planning to make a trip to Anvatscha but the horrible weather stopped us. The barometer is completely wrong.

In the morning, I went on the *Maria* to see the vessel's outfittings. The masts are unmanageably tall and thick. Not a rope is in proper proportion; and despite the thickness of the beams, boards, ribs, and outfittings, the vessel is anything else but sturdy, since it is leaking six zoll a day here in the harbor. The stem has a bad crack. The cabin where the people are to live is very small. The kitchen takes up half of the room; and Maschin has had anchor cables put in it, making it even smaller. The ship is going to be reloaded and fitted according to Chvastoff's directions. Up until now, Resanoff has intended to sail to Kodiak before the arrival of Pavel Ivanovitsch Koscheleff. Now he once again wants to await his arrival. He's still itching for the Japanese salt and rice. Resanoff does not want to grant the soldiers who were along in Japan their part of the salt and rice.

Vichotzoff, who is a prikastschik here, has done nothing else in his whole life but commit stupid pranks. Unasked, Fosse is now going to his defense. That certainly is not happening without self-interest.

Wed. 31/12 The day before yesterday, we had sent a fellow ahead who was supposed to shoot a bear for us, since here you go bear hunting like we go out into the country rabbit hunting. Toward evening, he brought us a reindeer instead of a bear.

After table, it was decided to take a trip to Avatscha. Since it was my watch, I could not go along.

June

Thurs. 1/13 Resanoff used the nice weather today to have all of his things sent to the *Maria*.

Today, herring streamed into Avatscha Bay in such large numbers that with a few pulls six бами [boats made from a single trunk of a tree] and two large baidaras were filled; and in addition three of our boats and everything that was alive filled Peter-Paul's Harbor.

A pud of salt is usually sold for thirty rubles, from now on, for four rubles. Now it is being sold at the price it costs in all of Russia, especially in Siberia. Since the quantity of salt acquired at Crown's expense is not sufficient to satisfy everyone, the commanding officers in Ochotsk and Yakutsk, and previously also in Kamtschatka, bought up all of the salt and had a monopoly and sold a pud for five to ten rubles to the same people for whom the Crown had imported it. That is the manner in which all common institutions of the Crown are treated in this area, since distance makes every appeal impossible. The population of Peter-Paul Harbor consists of about 120 men without women and children, that is, soldiers, artillerymen, and Cossacks. There are no Kamtschadals. For every five men there is one woman.

Fri. 2/14 Kamentschikoff's plan is to stay here has come to naught, even before it was turned over to Krusenstern for a decision, for Resanoff does not want to take him along and has denied his wish and request.

Resanoff has so much to write, that according to Fosse's remarks, he is writing day and night. In order not to disturb him, none of us visit the Grote Herr. We nonetheless see each other outside on walks every day.

Sat. 3/15 Resanoff is not well, and even though none of us intended to visit him, he sent word that he would not admit anyone into his presence.

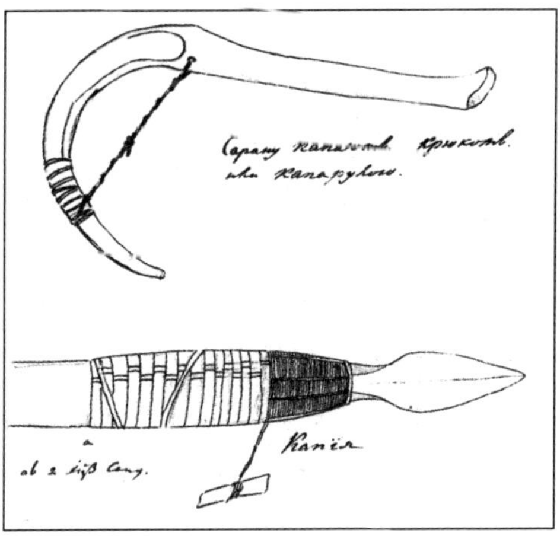

17-1. The point is one span long, the shaft 9 fuss long, the hand can barely get around the circumference. Kamtschadals kill bears with it.
[underneath the spear] longer than 2 fuss.

Fomin, who was recently the commander in Ochotsk, ingratiated himself as lieutenant with Count Tschernitscheff by drawing up a plan for his dacha. Even though he is a naval officer, he never had any desire to do sea duty; and at his request inspected the Volga and several other rivers on the Caspian Sea and mapped these rivers. With the enhancing of his rank, he was sent to Ochotsk, where he was supposed to lay out the harbor, make maps, build stocks and found an admiralty. All of his activities show a timorous, fearful man. Thanks to his good-naturedness, obsequiousness and mainly due to his weaknesses, all of the rascals there could do whatever they wanted to with him. His weakness is also the cause of his now being called back to account for his behavior. He arrived in Ochotsk as a captain and earned his way up to vice-admiral.

The *Slava Rossia*, the ship used by Billings for his voyage, lies sunken in Peter-Paul's Harbor. I think it would not be as difficult as people believe to float her again by using naval pumps. And there are no worms in her, so the ship must still be in quite good shape, since wood does not rot in water. The effort would undoubtedly be worth it.

Sun. 4/16 We weighed anchor and pulled ourselves out of Peter-Paul's Harbor, hit land with the stem, arrived nevertheless undamaged in Avatscha Bay, where we dropped anchor again. It was necessary for us to cast off; otherwise it would have taken several days before the gentlemen who are remaining here would have moved ashore with sack and pack, since no one takes into consideration that our command consists of only thirty man and all of the work on shipboard has to be done. The going back and forth from the ship to land was endless. Now, we finally have peace and quiet.

Resanoff put on several *Airs* [sic] to impress his new acquaintances. Chvastoff then said to him, "You are certainly not going to Kodiak as ambassador? If that is the case, then we are not taking you along, since we would have to learn a lot so that we might observe all of the etiquette the rank deserves. Furthermore, you would be totally superfluous in that cold stretch of heaven." After that, Resanoff behaved himself.

Mon. 5/17 Ratmanoff, on one of his excursions, set part of the woods in Pakovja Bay on fire. It is uninhabited, unused land. Such things however drive away the wild game.

Fosse, as courier, is taking along the lacquer commode, strongbox, and the Japanese house overland to Petersburg. He will present his bill, and these things will cost the Emperor more than they are worth.

Resanoff was so careless as to tell Schemelin, so that other could hear it, "Let them (that is the *Nadezhda*) go. I am going to leave them nice instructions." We do not need to worry since that man, when we are rid of him, cannot do us any more harm, but not, as this indicates, because of his lack of desire to harm us.

Tues. 6/18 Chvastoff has already traveled through Siberia twice and was prompted by Resanoff's remark, that is, that Chvastoff wanted to enrich himself by his trip from Ochotsk to Kodiak and to make a large profit. He said, when we asked him about it, "I had the opportunity but did not use it. I was given enough opportunities to make a cut of 20 to 30,000 rubles for my silence, to make me an accessory through my signature. I however took nothing from these people and forced Baranoff[2] to dispatch all of the promischlenikis to me who had served their time and did not want to stay any longer. They mainly bear grudges against me here because of my lack of self-interest and are afraid of me because I speak freely.

In Kodiak, they made attempts on my life because I prevented the rascals from stealing. I even found it necessary to protect my life by writing a petition to the Minister of the Interior in which I requested my recall. The minister considered my petition, and, at his order, I was called back to Petersburg. After having participated in the Swedish War under Bukshöden[3] in Finland, hate toward me, especially Tschitschagoff's, moved me to travel back to Kamtschatka. The American Company offered me 4,000, and I wanted 6,000 rubles salary. Through my trip, first to Kodiak, etc. and then to Ochotsk, I had made big profits for the Company and damaged the Company in Petersburg by telling the truth. Admiral Mardvinoff convinced me to take 4,000 rubles. Buldakoff and the other directors of the American Company wanted me to contract to stay in Kodiak for several years. I was not in agreement with that and Mardvinoff tried to convince me and Davidoff to do it. Finally, I told him that I serve the Emperor as a free man and can take my leave any time I want to, have at present permission to serve as a merchant without having to leave the service. It would be base of me if I were to sell myself even for months to merchants and thus misuse this permission." Mardvinoff, who realized his powers of persuasion did not help, said to Buldakoff, "Do not worry Michail Matveitch, as long Tschitchagoff is Minister, Chvastoff will be staying in Kodiak."

"What do you mean by that?" I asked.

Then Mardvinoff said, "He is a prominent man—and could force you to take your leave."

"If that is the case," I said, "and, if Tschitschagoff were of a mind to treat me so badly, then I would do like Koschcleff and would show that Chvastoff does not let himself be played with. Tschitschagoff has done me damage and can do me damage, but he will never act basely and insidiously toward me."

(Kuscheleff was in the Admiralty Collegium. One of his colleagues had a box with a tiger's eye lying on a red cloth. "That eye is so ugly," said Kuscheleff, "that can be no other than Tschitschagoff's."

Other admirals said, "Well now, and what if Tschitschagoff had heard your witticism?"

"Well then, I would meet him with my walking cane." At that moment Tschitschagoff came into the Collegium. Kuscheleff, as if scalded by hot water, smoked from fear and groveled to Tschitschagoff for the whole morning. Nips tasku sisse [Estonian: snitch into your pocket]. "The result of that was that I did not even get 4,000 rubles and had to accept it in order to be able to leave Petersburg. Last summer I arrived in Ochotsk for the second time."

Resanoff told Krusenstern today, "I am sailing the day after tomorrow." Resanoff is holding up the *Fedosia* (that is the name of the transport ship), on which Fosse is going to sail to Ochotsk because the Japanese dictionary that Resanoff wants to send to the Academy of Sciences is not yet finished.

Wed. 7/19 With the departure of Resanoff and his suite, our stem is lighter, and we are going to have to load ballast, since the gentlemen's baggage was not light.

It is being said, that, if Chvastoff is corresponding with the Minister of the Interior, if the rascals, bandits, etc., get wind of it, then Chvastoff can only watch out for himself. They would rather do him in before permitting their clandestine goings-on to come to light.

At noon, Chvastoff had a weight of fish cooked for us that we ate heartily after a walk at his place on land.

Resanoff asks every one of us he can catch hold of when we are going to be sailing? In order to gain time, under the pretext that the water was not good, he had all of the casks in the *Maria* emptied. He is indecisive to the utmost degree. Whatever he orders done today he repeals tomorrow. His permanent wish is to get us out of his sight.

Yesterday, Resanoff had the prikaschtschik Vichodzoff turn over all of the things belonging to the embassy that could be sold, and today he is forbidding him to sell them. Resanoff is keeping things that could spoil on shipboard at his place and is leaving steel objects, guns, pistols, etc. on the *Nadezhda*. Vichodzoff is having bread baked from our flour, raw and mixed with sand so that it weighs more. Resanoff, even though he is the authorized agent of the American Company, acts as if it were none of his business, even though Krusenstern has complained about it. The brandy we had left here we had to accept again from Vichodzoff mixed with water and bad liquor. Resanoff knows it and approves of it by silence. Instead of flour, a barrel of salt had been left in Kamtschatka. Even though we are certain that the barrel was full, Vichodzoff stubbornly and firmly maintains that it was ⅔ empty. We could turn him in for stealing the salt. Resanoff, however, does not take the trouble to investigate the matter. May God grant that Pavel Ivanovitsch Koscheleff arrives soon; for only then will we be able to separate ourselves totally from Resanoff without getting further instructions from him full of subterfuges, which injure Krusenstern and could cause difficulties.

In the evening, Langsdorff and the hunter/taxidermist came onboard with the news that they would be sailing in the morning. Resanoff has had this rumor passed about so that Krusenstern will also set sail.

Thurs. 8/20 Since our kettles had leaks, we found ourselves having to take our galley apart so that the kettle could be repaired. (That was a trick on our part so as to vex Resanoff one last time, for our kettles were quite good.) We had nonetheless to lie to Krusenstern, since we were ready to sail, and he would not have let himself be prevented from weighing anchor. Resanoff wants us to sail so much that he would not have stopped from leaving instructions behind that would have damaged Krusenstern, and we wanted to prevent that. We wanted to put off the voyage until Koscheleff arrived and Resanoff had sailed. The next day we confessed the truth to Krusenstern.

In the morning, we changed our position, because our anchor was rotten, and put ourselves on moorings.

The *Maria*, since she has been on the roadstead, has never leaked less than seven to eight zoll. Maschin took no notice of that until he had fully loaded the vessel. Ready to sail today, he began to put the ship on her side to find the hidden leak. That cheat is doing it as a favor to Resanoff, and according to his wishes, so that he can postpone his departure for Kodiak.

In the evening, our officers came back from land with the news that Fedorovna, the wife of a soldier here, had died suddenly and had been buried in the evening. That woman had lived more with Vichodzoff than with her husband, who had been absent for some time. During this period, the woman had become pregnant and had, on Vichodzoff's advice, taken an abortion-causing remedy, because her husband was expected in General Koscheleff's suite. Yesterday, the woman had a miscarriage, and, today, she herself became a victim of the remedy.

To keep the case from being talked about, because the medical faculty on the *Nadezhda* is rather numerous, the body was buried immediately. The woman had died in the morning, and, at one o'clock in the afternoon, she was already buried. With—with Resanoff's permission.

Fri. 9/21 Makar Ivanovitsch Ratmanoff went to Tarcinaia Bay. One of his rowers was forced to jump into the water to save himself by swimming because a large bear suddenly came upon him and chased him.

Today, Resanoff told Friderici and Chvastoff very decidedly, "I am not going to await the *Nadezhda's* departure but sail earlier."

Resanoff has had an argument with his bosom buddy Fosse. Resanoff wanted him to sign that he had received his salary, without having given him any money, because Foss is supposed to owe him money. Fosse did not agree. Resanoff became so angry about it that he publicly called him an ungrateful pig, etc., etc.

Resanoff has already turned Maschin into his creature. Self-interest and avarice are Maschin's main motivations, and Resanoff certainly did not spare promising that weak man all kinds of attractive things.

Today, Maschin was brought two reindeer his men had killed. Even though we had provided him and his ship generously with hardtack, rice, and salt meat, he did not want to turn over to us even a pfund of his reindeer meat. Chvastoff and Davidoff forcibly took away half a reindeer from him and sent it to us.

Sat. 10/22 Davidoff has promised me an essay about the work and treatment of the Aleuts and the work they have to perform for the American Company.

In the evening, Friderici brought the news that Resanoff had given Maschin the order to prepare to sail because he plans to sail for Kodiak tomorrow afternoon. Thereupon, Langsdorff asked Resanoff, if he would be waiting for Pavel Ivanovitsch.

"No!" said Resanoff.

"Well," said Langsdorff, "since you have waited so long, and the mail has to be coming with Pavel Ivanovitsch, it would be worth the trouble to put off the voyage for several days."

"No!" said Resanoff, "that will hold us up too long."

"Then," said Langsdorff, "you must not be expecting any good news in the mail; otherwise your curiosity would have to prevail." No answer and the conversation ended.

Sun. 11/23 After a long time, today, Krusenstern wanted to have a religious service held on the *Nadezhda*. The priest could not come on board for some unknown reason, and all religious ceremonies did not take place. Since the priest's self-interest should have brought him on board, we were surprised. A bad rumor has it that Resanoff had kept the priest busy so that he would not hold vespers on the *Nadezhda*. May the *** take him.

Resanoff is now trying to make anyone who will listen understand that he only forgave Captain Krusenstern on account of the voyage to Japan.

In the evening, Dimitri Ivanovitsch brought the news that his brother, General Koscheleff would arrive tomorrow or the day after tomorrow. The messenger had brought a letter for Resanoff. Resanoff was exceedingly happy to hear that Koscheleff would be coming soon, regretted nonetheless his not being able to await him, because he had to hurry so as not to miss the *Neva*. All of Fosse's remonstrations "You have waited so long, you could wait another couple of days," bore no fruit.

Resanoff is moving onto the *Maria* this evening. He said earlier, "All of my baggage will barely fill a baidara; and up to now four fully loaded ones have gone to the *Maria*; and the hauling of boxes and crates has not yet ended. The very small cabin on the *Maria* is supposed to be so full that you can hardly move in it.

A persistent southerly wind will force Resanoff to await Koscheleff's arrival.

None of our people dare spend the night on land, and they also do not do it. And since there have been fights several nights in a row on land, Resanoff blames our sailors and claims that it is being done to anger him.

Several days ago Resanoff sent his servant on board requesting a candle. Ratmanoff refused the request saying, "Possibly you are wanting to cheat us. Resanoff himself has enough candles." The needling undoubtedly makes it desirable for us to finally separate. Resanoff's character is warranty that he has nothing good in mind for us. Thank goodness he cannot do us much damage.

Mon. 12/24 Pavel Ivanovitsch Koscheleff is expected daily; and the road from Avatscha to Peter-Paul's Harbor is very bad, Friderici, Koscheleff, Moritz Kotzebue, and I went to Avatscha to await him. Immediately after table we set out in a boat after having taken leave of Chvastoff and Davidoff, who had eaten a last lunch with us, since the *Maria* had already set her topsail. The wind however was not favorable.

The little village (ostrog) of Avatscha is pleasantly situated on the River Avatscha which, though shallow, has a plentiful salmon catch. The Paratunka River is not far away, where the Kamtschadals likewise have weirs. There is plenty of wild game but no powder and lead to kill it with. We spent the night in a tent. Unaccustomed to camping outside, I was unable to sleep.

Tues. 13/25 At four o'clock in the morning when I woke up, I caught sight of the *Maria* in full sail leaving Avatscha Bay. I wish Resanoff a lot of things! on the voyage. Calmed by seeing the ship lost from sight, I filled my pipe with tobacco and took a walk in the area and went to breakfast with a good appetite.

We waited in vain the whole day for Pavel Ivanovitsch Koscheleff. At ten o'clock in the evening, we finally went on board without having had the pleasure of obtaining our goal. The taion (the eldest) had provided for us during our stay richly with wine and brandy, and we enjoyed very much eating our meals in a Kamtschadal hut. Our table was decorated with a soup and ucha, delicate salmon, schnapps, roast, and an omelet.

We arrived back onboard at eleven thirty in the night. We would have stayed overnight in Avatscha if the rain had not moved us to use a favorable wind to sail home. I am using my leisure time in Avatscha for measuring angles, taking noon zeniths, etc.

Wed. 14/26 Around midnight, the *Maria* sailed out of the harbor and yesterday early in the morning at three o'clock weighed anchor. Krusenstern had sent Romberg onboard the *Maria* to find out if Resanoff had any orders for him or had left any behind. On deck, Resanoff came toward him very deranged and pale, asking, "What is wrong?"

Romberg: "The captain sends his regards and asks if you have any orders for him?" Resanoff: "Since the captain made no effort to come to me earlier, I now have no more orders for him." That was his parting greetings.

When Resanoff had an argument with Fosse about his salary and was very bitter, he said to Chvastoff, "That Romberg is a real plague!" Romberg got wind of it.

While taking leave on the *Maria*, Resanoff asked, "What is the meaning of you, Sir, Lieutenant, being in uniform?"

Romberg answered, "Because I have come to get last orders from you."

Resanoff: "This is not the way one comes to a chamberlain to pay respects and take leave. Now, I have absolutely no orders to issue. A great deal of effort has been put into everything. How much vexation and anger I have already experienced, hindered all over; one has put everything in my way."

Romberg: "You have put more obstacles in our way than we in yours, Your Excellency."

Resanoff: "The emperor will decide that, but I would quite like to embrace and kiss Romberg."

Romberg: "And I do not dare approach His Excellency."

Resanoff: "Why? For what reason?"

Romberg: "Because I was compared to the plague."

This was followed by a pause and Resanoff asked, "What is the great Makar [великий Макар], that lever in the whole machine, doing?" (To Chvastoff and Davidoff) "I did not know who was the Captain of the *Nadezhda*." Romberg interrupted him by saying, "Krusenstern," and then the conversation became general. Before his departure Romberg got a Judas kiss from Resanoff. And a favorable northerly wind separated us, God willing, forever from Resanoff.

Resanoff's behavior at the end was totally inexplicable. In the beginning, he wanted to sail immediately. When we were on the roadstead, he again wanted to await General Koscheleff's arrival, unnecessarily held up the *Fedosia* with his papers, and then leaves Avatscha the day before Koscheleff's arrival in a noticeably indescribable hurry. The reorganization of Kodiak, which that incompetent man intends to carry out, will be original enough. Resanoff said, "One will see that injustice done one man can be disadvantageous for a whole country." He wrote Rumantzoff, using very bitter expressions, and requested of him, since he intended to move totally to Kodiak, to send his children there when they turned thirteen. Chvastoff, whom he (Resanoff) had given his letter to read unbidden, related this.

Judging by these statements, Resanoff is undoubtedly thinking of making himself the master of Kodiak. He has the power in his hands, since he can refer to his power of attorney from the American Company—and it won't be for his lack of trying.

I think all of these stories about Kodiak are lies that Resanoff is spreading so that we will pass them on and then can be charged with slander. Our wish to be separated from him is fulfilled, and with this fulfillment all of the remaining thoughts of him are obliterated. Long ago, we became tired of the continual feuding and longed for peace and quiet.

Langsdorff, the rifleman, and the servant Alexander left with Resanoff.

Early this morning, Ratmanoff and young Koscheleff traveled to Avatscha to wait for Pavel Ivanovitsch

In the afternoon, the *Fedosia* went out of the harbor but had contrary wind

Thurs. 15/27 The *Fedosia* weighed anchor today. The contrary wind forced her however to anchor again at the entrance.

It is uncertain whether we will get a cargo for Canton. All of the pelts here were sent to Ochotsk before our arrival. The *Neva* has perhaps already sailed from Kodiak with a load and might miss us in Canton. We can count little on the vessel which, at Resanoff's orders, should be bringing a load of pelts from Kodiak in the fall. We will undoubtedly set out on our return voyage without a cargo. The American Company cannot provide us with any provisions here. Therefore, it will be necessary to wait for Pavel Ivanovitsch for us to learn if we can be supplied through him after our return from Sachalin, and, afterward, we can take measures accordingly.

Fri. 16/28 In the morning, the *Fedosia* weighed anchor and set out to sea.

With the departure of Resanoff, Fosse, and Langsdorff, we finally are not under pressure and do not need to weigh every word we speak. With their departure, all of the strife has also ended that had dogged our footsteps from the beginning of the voyage.

Man is a too restless animal to be able to behave quietly. The discord between Resanoff and us was the reason for none arising among us, since a big fight usually suppresses all of the smaller ones.

I am very much afraid that we are far from ending our voyage without strife. Now, new strife can begin. We admittedly have fewer lazy louts on the ship who from boredom could begin strife. Except for Tilesius, Friderici, and Espenberg, we are all busy. Unfortunately, the former and the latter are a couple of characters, whose oddities are unbearable; otherwise every one of us overlooked little things which now will be hard to leave untouched. Work itself offers sufficient material for discord. And even though I am convinced that every one of us means well, it is nevertheless seldom possible to put such a large number of heads under one hat.

I would give a lot to see our future better halves sitting together as we do daily around our table. It would be fun, since we have got to know each other quite well, to get to know each one of them. It is a good question whether our wives (imaginary) would get along as well as we do?

Sat. 17/29 Before our voyage to Japan, Pavel Ivanovitsch gave us two steers for which, with Resanoff's permission, Vichodzoff let himself be paid. Now Dimitri Ivanovitsch Koscheleff is sending us daily free bread, which that Vichodzoff keeps track of and will also let himself be paid for. That is undoubtedly what will happen with the wild mouton and reindeer meat which Davidoff had sent.

Romberg, Golovatscheff, Tilesius, and Koscheleff have just returned from Avatscha, where they had spent the night. Pavel Ivanovitsch has not yet arrived. Krusenstern is not planning to wait any longer but rather, if the wind is good, to go to sea early tomorrow morning.

Dmitri Ivanovitsch plans to have hardtack baked for us from the flour that Pavel Ivanovitsch has been able to turn over to us. He also wants to have wood chopped for us and to have seremscha (wild garlic) and all kinds of berries picked; so that upon our return from Sachalin, we will find everything waiting for us and we will be able to continue our voyage without being held up.

Sun. 18/30 Contrary wind The ovens, the usual ones as well as the ones for baking, are built very dangerously here. The oven is made from a square of wood lined with tile and clay. The small dome is slapped together with clay. The chimney is woven from sticks and smeared with clay. The chimney is most libel to suffer from fire, since the inhabitants are too lazy to renew the clay that has fallen off and all of the blackened sticks are visible. The fish weirs in the rivers are woven of sticks, artlessly, very simply. Their fishnets are like simple wings without a sack. The mesh varies according to the size of the fish. The herring nets are thirty faden long and one and one-half faden wide. Salmon nets are the same size, only they have a larger mesh. The sable nets are fifteen to thirty faden long and one faden wide. The Kamtschadals make these nets themselves, mainly from nettles, especially the sable nets.

July

Mon. 19/1 We are setting about weighing our anchor, had already set our topsail when the wind changed again, and we were forced to stay. And look there! In the evening Pavel Ivanovitsch finally arrived. He was very happy that Resanoff had already departed, who had written him: "They tried everything possible to turn your brother against me and to set us against each other. My heart was filled with too warm of feelings for the Koscheleffs for that to succeed."

We learned through news from Petersburg that the four or five soldiers taken along to Japan as a guard were to protect His Excellency from us, as Resanoff wrote in his letters to Petersburg last year immediately after the reconciliation—characteristic of him (instead of sending the letter which he had read to us). He described his voyage from Nukahiva to Kamtschatka and said that his servant Alexander had lowered bread on a string down into his cabin to save him from starving to death. The sailors had stood guard at his door voluntarily in order to protect him from the hotheads [буйные головы]. (The letter to General Koscheleff in which he also calls us буйные головы and Ratmanoff and me бунтовщики [mutineers], he requested be returned to him before his departure, and he had torn it up.) In Brazil, Resanoff wrote that Krusenstern had paid only three hundred dahler for the Neva's masts and brought a bill for 1,000 dahler. From the beginning of the voyage, Resanoff never said what he had done and always acted differently from what he had said.

Pavel Ivanovitsch judged Count Tolstoi as follows: "He is pleasant company but an immoral dog. It took a lot of effort to get rid of him after your departure for Japan."

General Koscheleff has just come from the Tschuktschis, who had been having a fight with the Koriaks. The Tschuktschis met Pavel Ivanovitsch with gifts. Koscheleff took none of them, but, on the contrary, gave them gifts. That surprised them. "Why are you not taking anything?"[4] they asked. "You are indeed a great general. Earlier, everyone took them."

Koscheleff answered them, "I am not here to take gifts from you."

"We have been being told for a long time now," continued the Tschutktschis, "that you are a strict man when Pavel Ivanovitsch had Captain Ispravnik [исправник: police inspector of a district] and several others arrested and turned over to the court."

"I am strict toward bad people," answered Koscheleff. "If you behave badly, then I will be just as strict with you as with those people."

Then a Tschuktischi pulled out his knife and said, "My uncle gave me this knife on his deathbed and told me that I should never sharpen the point against a Russian. Now, however, I am going to break it off and give it to you as a sign of my friendship."

The Tschuktschi had killed eight Koriaks, and, as retribution, the head of the Tschuktischis, without asking Koscheleff, had had just as many Tschuktischis killed.

Tues. 20/2 Pavel Ivanovitsch dined with us at noon, remained until evening and also for the night because we were anchored quite far from Peter-Paul's Harbor. The day passed very full of noise and bustle. (Koscheleff likes pleasures full of noise and bustle.) Together with several salvos we drank to the health of our gracious emperor, etc. Ratmanoff, who only too often at the wrong time, lets his voice be heard, called too early during the salvos "Pali!" He did not wait for Golovatscheff, who was standing watch, to report, pali [fire], "The cannons are ready." Several cannons were not ready (protruding from the ship) and the sailors with the lunts, fired by Ratmanoff's thundering order, lit the cannons in the ship. The result was that a port was smashed to pieces and several were damaged. Granted, the damage can soon be repaired. Ratmanoff's indiscretion is inexcusable. That incident has left behind tension between Golovatscheff and Ratmanoff. Tilesius and Horner are also at odds. In the evening, Dmitri Ivanovitsch played the tolks and Petrovik (Resanoff) as they behaved in Japan. His manner of portraying them caused general laughter. He really played them strikingly similar to the way they were.

Wed. 21/3 Tilesius drew Pavel Ivanovitsch's portrait and hit him quite well. Koscheleff assigned our Captain sixty pud of flour, ate with us at noon; and after table we all went ashore where we found the beautiful sex collected for a vetscherinok (ball). They looked more than good in their jewelry and danced their bachin (bear dance), osmerka (a kind of quadrille), and Russian dances with a great deal of grace. Madame Nikolevna, the former favorite of Lieutenant Davidoff, played prima donna, was also by the way, to be preferred to the others. Most of our sailors had been given permission to go ashore. They watched the dance from an anteroom and now and again took part. The beauties' bending and the sailors' bowing in the crowd were amusing. Several of them seemed to be precisely acquainted with our whole crew. We spent the evening in a revel and riot of singing, playing, drinking, and dancing. We ate very late in the evening and took our leave of Pavel Ivanovitsch around one o'clock in the night. I am no friend of leave-taking and felt the pain of departure all the more, because we were taking leave of amiable good men, that is, of Pavel Ivanovitsch Koscheleff, his brother Dimitri Ivanovitsch, Captain Ivan Ivanovitsch Fedoroff, and Frederici. The rest of the inhabitants of Peter-Paul's Harbor were unimportant luminaries for us and had to be content with ceremonies without sincerity.

Pavel Ivanovitsch gave Krusenstern a very nice present with fur, which Krusenstern sent with the estafet taking our letters to Petersburg for his wife. Let us hope that we will see each other again in the fall.

Friderici is staying with General Koscheleff in Kamtschatka until our return, and Schemelin is also staying behind in Peter-Paul's Harbor to settle the bills with that rascal and scoundrel Vichodzoff. Those two good-for-nothings in their isolation during our absence will put together a nice bill to which we will have to say, "Yes."

- 18 -

Exploring Sachalin

Thurs. 22/4 We had barely returned onboard when dawn began to appear. Without losing any time, we weighed anchor and left Avatscha Bay. The day was spoiled for all of us because not one of us had slept that night. Everything will be back to normal soon enough, and time is passing for us as fast as earlier.

The *Nadezhda* is empty in comparison to what she weighed before. No one misses our superfluous passengers as much as Espenberg, who does not know what to do with his time, finds no one with whom he can talk or who would like to chat with him.

Fri. 23/5 Nice weather! Toward evening, we lost sight of the old Kamtschadal crater. All of the noisemakers stayed behind, for dead silence reigns in the company cabin. The most likely cause is undoubtedly the tension on account of Ratmanoff.

Romberg and Golovatscheff mostly sit in their cabins, where they also brooded earlier. Bellingshausen and I are continuing our work on the maps which we are finishing and have, over and above that, our watches, which leave us no time for useless chatter. Horner has enough to do with his calculations. Everyone is leaving Tilesius in peace, and, for better or worse, Espenberg has to be quiet, too. The two Kotzebues, who otherwise tend to make a lot of noise, also have to be quiet so that they cause no irritation in this peaceful atmosphere. Ratmanoff, who otherwise ripped everything apart for the sake of dispute, avoids everyone. And Mate Kamentschikoff is not seen in the cabin except at meals and at tea.

After the continual noise, this peace and quiet, for me at least, is pleasant. It may be, before we have become used to it, conspicuously unpleasant. I, for my part, would have wished a similar peace and quiet from the beginning of the voyage. Pleasant times would not have passed so unused. Krusenstern is working as before. It is unbelievable what that man accomplishes by combining knowledge with unequaled work. I only hope that the world will treat him justly, for if merit is not recognized, of what use is it then?

Sat. 24/6 Nice weather. In a little while, we will be reaching the Kurils, lying like a turnpike bar between us and Sachalin.

Sun. 25/7 We now have a whole new field of discoveries before us, for everything we have done up to now at Matmai and Sachalin, Broughton[1] is supposed to have already described in his newly published voyage, so they say.

Since Resanoff, before our voyage to Japan, wrote a report to the emperor that is to Krusenstern's disadvantage and, even though he reconciled with us, nevertheless still sent letters of complaint and now once again paints Krusenstern black, Krusenstern, in a letter to Novosilzoff requested a court martial after our return. The emperor's love of justice will not and cannot deny this petition.

Let's hope that we will finish our expedition to Sachalin, as well as our return voyage, happily and be able to speak out about just matters in our homeland.

Mon. 26/8 Impenetrable fog and wet cold bad weather. On the 27th, we caught sight of the Kurils at noon.

Tues. 27/9 Since they are exceedingly high old craters, we were unable to reach them by evening even though the wind was quite brisk.

Otto Kotzebue is very industrious and uses the opportunities he has to learn something. With Moritz, it looks more dubious. He nevertheless has more abilities. Otto, upon our return, will certainly not fail to become an officer. The question, however, is whether Moritz will pass the exam.

Wed. 28/10 Through the night, we sailed toward the Kurils with a mild wind but full sails in the expectation of a clear day, so that we will sail through this chain of islands. A thick fog enveloped us however. And the island, which we had not been able to see in the dark of the night, we could not see during the day because of the thick fog. Our situation is bad since the maps we have show the old craters of the Kurils, since you cannot call the islands anything else. Their positions as well their number are incorrectly indicated, and we therefore cannot trust them. As a result, we do not have a clear horizon and find ourselves in a dangerous situation. That we have to be very close to the islands is attested to by the sounds and the boiling seas, which are caused by the currents swirling around the Kuril Islands and have a great deal of similarity with the surf around reefs, the quantities of sea cabbage, which sometimes holds up the ship, and the innumerable seabirds flying around us.

Thurs. 29/11 At sunrise, the sky cleared up, and the fog lifted. Not very far from us, we saw the 7th, 8th, 9th, 10th, 11th, and 12th islands, and, after we had sailed between the 11th and 12th, we caught sight of the 13th and 14th islands in the distance. We had barely sailed through the strait when the fog came down again, and we felt our way ahead in the darkness, but with the difference that we had the Kurils behind us and we could set all of our sails so we could steer toward Sachalin. For once, we had clear weather at the right time. We did not need it any longer than it took to sail through the Kurils, and we also did not get it any longer. Diving birds of all kinds, especially puffins, stormy petrels, ducks, gulls of all kinds, albatross, and other birds teemed on the barren Kuril Islands and their straits, especially where the countercurrent caused the sea to boil. You do not find this kind of boiling water (толчея) any place other than here and along the Aleutian Islands. And, since it was completely light, the waves and the water broke against each other with so much force that I think it would be impossible to row or sail through the uproar in an open boat without running the danger of being sunk by the water spraying in. The water shot high up on the ship and seemed to have no other motion but for boiling. Often, nearby, the surface of the water was mirror clear which, however, always looked as if the water had been covered with fat or oil—crazy water!

Fri. 30/12 Saritscheff's[2] description of Billings' voyage was written with a great deal of forbearance. One has to be surprised that Billings got off with such a mild sentence as having to live in Moscow after the completion of the voyage. Sauer[3] writes much more candidly, nor was he able to include everything that really happened in his description of the voyage. According to Billings, he did nothing along the American coast, and the travel costs only swelled into the millions because, along with several others, that wicked man stole from the Crown. Even now, a lot of hemp and other materials Billings had received lie molding in Ochotsk, as Лоброе Намерение [The ship of *Good Intentions* by name], which Billings had built in Ochotsk, was not yet ready to be launched, and an estafet from Petersburg arrived for the Commander of Ochotsk with the order—since war had broken out with Sweden—to hold up Billings' expedition. Billings bribed the commander to suppress the news that the estafet had brought for a little while. The ship was hurriedly launched, and neither Hall nor Behring wanted to take responsibility for it because the ship was not yet finished. Billings turned the work over to a mate who left the *Dobroia Namerenia* on the slips. Without hesitating, Billings had the ship pulled to the roadstead, even though everyone told him how daring that would be. And a short time later, the ship foundered before she could be used.

Billings did that so that his malversations would not come to light. He sailed away on the *Slava Rossia* simply to see Elias, because he thereby had the right to promote his officers to a higher rank for which he had the authority. Thus ended the entire expedition, which had lasted for several years and had cost incredible sums of money and work. You have to be surprised that the empress trusted that Billings so much, even gave him carte blanche—for that is what he had.

By the end of August, we will undoubtedly have finished the expedition at Sachalin and have arrived back in Kamtschatka. In December, we can count on anchoring in Macao, in February on leaving China, and in September 1806, God willing, we will be in Kronstadt.

Who knows how long our voyage will be stretched out? We could just as easily be under sail for another year, thus arriving in Kronstadt next fall.

July

Sat. 1/13 After completing this voyage, not a one of us will be able to say that I will undertake doing this or that. When I was in Constantinople [1799–1800], I did not believe I would go to Paris, because Paris has no sea harbor. And when I was in Paris [1802–1803], I could not have dreamed of sailing around the world.

Sun. 2/14 Nice clear weather and mild winds. We have not yet reached Sachalin and therefore cannot use the nice day.

Resanoff could have damaged Krusenstern and us very much if he had worked more intelligently. It certainly was not for the lack of desire. His inappropriate behavior, claiming authority without purpose, and again, the so falsely over-hurried actions, that so inexcusable swearing and threatening in various situations, and mainly his low greed involved him in a labyrinth from which he will have trouble extracting himself; especially Koscheleff's common sense broke his neck. Since Resanoff, beginning in Tenerife, then in St. Catharina, and for the last time in Kamtschatka, had complained about Krusenstern and us and had defamed us, he needed only to find a Kamtschatkan sheep, a man like himself, to give his slander the appearance of truth. He would have spared neither money nor words if it had been possible to win General Koscheleff over to his malevolent, unjust machinations. After our return from Japan, he would have only needed to have blamed Krusenstern and his officers for the failure of the embassy and to have made any justification on our part difficult, using spontaneous additions to the strife so as to confuse the events so much that any investigation would have been impossible. We have to thank Koschcleff that the voyage to Japan took place. Only through his intercession could a seeming reconciliation take place. Without him, the expedition would have ended in Kamtschatka, and we would have had to complete the voyage around the world overland. In that case, Krusenstern would have had a lot against him; now he has everything going for him.

Mon. 3/15 According to the latitude and longitude, we have reached approximately Cape Patience, could not, though, because of the overcast weather, catch sight of it. The countless numbers of seals and sea lions, sticking their heads out of the water and looking at us, indicate that we must be near land, also the numbers of diving birds and gulls of all kinds flying and swimming around us.

Several days ago, in the night during my watch, I saw a beautiful moon rainbow, a phenomenon I had never seen so beautiful before. The arch was white. If you looked at it more exactly, though, you could also distinguish very faint bright colors.

Tues. 4/16 We found bottom first at 100 faden and soon afterwards at 80 faden. According to Vries' map such depths are found about twenty miles from land. The barometer began to fall, and a very overcast sky with heavy rain forced us to sail away from land. The wind blew more and more briskly, and the seas were rough. We had to take in all reefs and soon afterwards haul in several sails completely. Thank goodness the sea is free of reefs! It would be possible for a reef to stretch from the Kurils to Sachalin and cause us worries and distress—and to put gray hair on our heads.

A seaman seldom ceases to wish for wind. In these waters the choice is difficult. South, southeast, east, and northeast are favorable for us, always bringing along however fog, overcast, rainy weather. Northerly and northwesterly winds are contrary. Only westerly and southwesterly winds could bring us clear skies with more favorable winds. Westerly winds very seldom blow here at this time of year. It is not worth the trouble of wishing for these winds. Nothing will be gained by that.

Wed. 5/17 After the wind had raged until midnight, the weather cleared up toward daybreak, and the wind died down. We again steered immediately for land, are, however, undoubtedly so far away from it that we will probably not catch sight of it today.

I would gladly endure a storm for two weeks so that we could enjoy several weeks of nice weather afterwards. It's annoying in our situation—where we can only approach land with clear skies—always to be surrounded by fog. In the evening at sundown, we caught sight of land.

It is a true loss that Europeans, even though they brag more than a little bit of their enlightenment and culture, in general behave very badly toward the natives wherever they have founded colonies. In Europe, they preach freedom and equality and in these distant regions, where they have the good fortune and satisfaction of finding natural, unspoiled people, they are tyrants. No countries, in that respect, can condemn another; just like the Spanish and Portuguese behave in America, so the English and French in the West and East Indies. Similarly, and the worst of all is the behavior of the Dutch in Ceylon [Sri Lanka], Batavia, and the Moluccas [Spice Islands] and the Russians on the Aleutian Islands and on the Northwest Coast of America. You hear all over a lot of examples of tyranny and atrocities committed by Europeans, which are not condemned because they are done to a human race or class which in the eyes of the civilized Europeans may be compared to animals. If it happens that these proud Europeans meet a nation that is too strong and warlike voluntarily to take on the yoke that the Europeans want to put around their necks, then the Europeans are open to every degradation. You see that on the Northwest Coast of America, Japan, China, where no demand can be so degrading that the Europeans will not voluntarily use it simply to satisfy their greed, which is the driving force behind all of these evil and cruel actions. Unfortunately, in totality, human beings are quite bad.

Thurs. 6/18 At sunset, we approached Cape Patience. We were several miles away from land and intended, by using the favorable wind we had, to sail along the shore to the north so that we could continue our voyage of discovery, when we were enveloped in a thick fog and forced to sail away from this unknown land and await clear weather again.

Fri. 7/19 Through the night, we put ourselves on the drift several times or tacked with little sail, and, since the barometer had fallen rather strongly, we kept ourselves more out to sea, so that we were about thirty miles from Cape Patience. At six in the morning when the fog lifted and we could head for land, most of us did not believe that we were not closer to land and could not see it. Ratmanoff claimed we were staying so far from land that we would not be able to carry out our mission.

If in the opposite situation, through too great of audacity or lack of caution, we would come too close to land in such bad weather, then exactly these gentlemen would complain that Krusenstern came too close to land unnecessarily, since then no one would have any peace and quiet and no one would be able to sleep.

Toward ten o'clock in the morning, we caught sight of land. It looked as if the weather was planning to stay clear. A calm however did not permit us to make great progress today. The lowland at Cape Patience could be seen very clearly and also Robber Island several times. (The rocks at Cape Patience were raised by refraction so high that we could measure them, which clearly shows that the breakers we had seen while sailing out of Patience Bay were not icebergs, as Ratmanoff foolishly maintained, but actual reefs.)

Sat. 8/20 After we had passed a very quiet clear night, a brisk westerly wind rose at the reddening of the morning skies, permitting us to sail at leisure along the length of the shore and actually begin charting the eastern coast of Sachalin, since our earlier work was only fragmentary. Even though there are now and again variable winds between the mountains, we were nevertheless able to stay on a rather straight course. The clear skies held until evening. Only the wind became too brisk, and the seas began to swell.

Partie honeuse [a shame-faced parting] on the *Nadezhda*. Krusenstern had a privy next to his cabin in the galley, which only he and Espenberg, out of consideration for his age, used. The rest of us had a privy at the front of the ship next to the kitchen, which had very uncomfortable arrangements. It was a dark box hammered together from boards with a commode. That thing was always so full of smoke and steam and filth that you did not want to go into it at all, and, once in a storm, when the thing tipped around and around and caused trouble and stink, well, since then all of the passengers also followed our example and went to the galleon, where our sailors have put a seat and take care of themselves. If the sea was moving in a strong wind, waves hit up on the galleon now and again and also over it; and almost regularly every ninth wave did that. If you awaited the right time and expedited matters quickly, nothing happened to you. If however you spent too much time there, you would certainly get sprayed or a wave would hit you with a clap on your most noble of spots, or you would even get soaked to the skin. We were so used to the thing that we very seldom got wet. If the sailor at the wheel was inattentive and held too much into the wind, then almost every wave hit the galleon. Tilesius, during our voyage, has always acted gauche [clumsy] when easing nature and was the most often sprayed and soaked. The cold wet water and the continual fog were the reasons why, over his usual clothing, he had on a Friesian schariwaren and kurka.[4] He had enough to unbutton, especially since his schariwaren also had frog-bands buttoned on it.

One afternoon, I was coming happily from the galleon where I had taken care of nature, when Tilesius met me and asked, "Can you go without any danger?"

"Oh, yes," said I, "Only wait until a wave has hit. Take off your big schariwaren, and take care of things quite fast, and nothing will get you. Only pay attention to every ninth wave!" and went on my way. I said to Golovatscheff, who had watch, "Tilesius is going to have it good. He has on far too many clothes that he has to unbutton." Golovatscheff was silent, went very casually to the wheel (he enjoys maliciousness) and was so nasty as to turn the wheel unnoticed.

The ship then shook into the wind. (That is why I noticed Golovatscheff's nasty trick.) Tilesius would have gotten wet even without that. The poor fellow, after a lot of trouble, was finally sitting on the throne, when suddenly a wave hit all over him. Tilesius, as if pulled from the water, breathless from shock, with his trousers hanging down, and with a murderous scream, came climbing on deck and in the same position onto the quarterdeck, since all of his trousers were so full of water that he could only hold them up with difficulty. The sight was ludicrous. Everyone laughed and me too. That caused Tilesius, in addition to his shock, to become angered and chagrined. He could not be convinced that I had not played the trick on him, because I was the one who had said that you could go there. He lodged a complaint with Krusenstern and complained to anyone who would listen to him about me, as if I were the cause of his fright, accident, etc. I had to keep quiet about Golovatscheff's little affair, since that would have only made matters worse, and tried to justify myself with the help of my comrade to Tilesius, who only after some time recovered from his fright enough that he again finally pulled up his hundred thousand trousers. Since the wind had become even more brisk and the waves hit across the galleon more often, Tilesius finally agreed that I could not have been at fault for his getting wet. He nevertheless could not forgive me, though, that I had said, "Yes, you can go there!" Espenberg gave him a calming remedy, and the incident had no further results.

Sun. 9/21, Mon. 10/22 A couple of nice, clear days, calms, and mild contrary winds permitted us to make only a little progress, even though the discovery and inspection of the coast of Sachalin, from a geographical and nautical point of view, is the most interesting aspect of our entire voyage; and we, with goodwill and gusto, are nevertheless taking too long for a few people. The silence that reigns among us and indifference toward all possible events show only too clearly that the wet, cold, rainy, foggy weather also is endless. Large numbers of seals swam around us again. If they dived and wanted to swim on, they struck the ship under water. This barrier surprised them so much that they immediately came to the surface of the water so close to the ship that we could have grabbed them with our hands. They were shot at several times but always only as a torment. The whales also played their games. In particular, one whale enjoyed sticking his tail out of the water and waving it in the air several times. He did this repeatedly. When whales dive, they always hit their tails on the water so that they make a crack like a little cannon shot. The sivutschi [сивучи, Steller's] (sea lions), also present in large numbers, threw themselves totally out of the water and fell back with a crack, a lot of din, and a bellow, into the water again—all of this premonitions of bad weather.

Tues. 11/23 We never sail forward much. In the evening, we had a calm and rain. The wind remained favorable. Toward seven o'clock, we sailed away from land, so that we could spend the night at a depth of thirty faden. At this time the sky cleared a little, and we caught sight of a bay which we would certainly have visited if it had not been so late. At least, we would have sent a boat to take a look at it. During the night, we sailed ahead. If the wind remains favorable in the morning, then we will probably be so far away that we will no longer be able to see the bay.

Wed. 12/24 Krusenstern had counted too much on the current, which up to now had been driving us toward the south, because the noon zenith showed us that we had reached too high a latitude, and the promontory which we had seen last evening at northwest 35^0, we saw again today at noon when the fog lifted in the south. We did not recognize any mountain we could use for orientation. That will be a little hole in our map. In general, we were dissatisfied with things.

What was done was done and could no longer be changed. To err is human, and Krusenstern correctly was expecting a current from the north rather than from the south. Ratmanoff's over-loud pretentious remarks were ill placed, and you can correctly say of him that he only opens up his trap when he comes out of city hall.

Thurs. 13/25 Fog and a brisk southeasterly wind. We tacked around in position. Our discovery at Sachalin has many similarities with the crossings of a fleet in front of a blockaded harbor.

Fri. 14/26 The weather is not a hair better since a thick fog continues to encircle us.

Sat. 15/27, Sun. 16/28 Both days we had strong winds and high seas, undoubtedly the result of the new moon and the eclipse of the sun, which came together on those days. Those two heavenly bodies influence the wind, weather, and tides so very much and validate La Place's theories.[5]

Mon. 17/29 Last evening, the weather cleared up, and we caught sight of land before sunset. Ratmanoff did not know that. Today, he said prophetically that we would probably need two more days sailing to land. (You have to know that Ratmanoff did not bother himself with anything, did not stand watch, and was the greatest sluggard on the *Nadezhda*.) He left the cabin without saying a word when I told him we had long since seen land. Today, we sailed with a favorable wind along the low, shallow shore on the northern end of the island of Sachalin. We stayed so far from shore, because Krusenstern correctly did not trust the low land and was afraid of a shallow bottom. Toward five o'clock in the afternoon, Krusenstern ordered the sounding lead to be cast. "We will probably have over thirty faden," said Ratmanoff ironically. It was only however twenty-four faden. Every day, we hear similar remarks from Ratmanoff in Krusenstern's presence. Wherever he can reprove and criticize Krusenstern's behavior, that is what he does. Krusenstern smiles and remains silent—and then nevertheless does what he wants to.

The most vexing thing is the way in which Ratmanoff says similar things, that is, his lectures, sounding like a prophet about totally bizarre subjects, presupposed absurdities. That detracts us, because we have really kept a little far away from land in recent days on our voyage of discovery; and, if there were small inlets, we only noted them but could not inspect them exactly. The shore runs in such a straight line that we cannot expect any big inlets, and Krusenstern's considerations are justified. Ratmanoff's talk can little damage Krusenstern, since our captain has behaved in an exemplary fashion during the whole voyage, put himself above all of the slander. It is irksome though that he may babble unpunished throughout the day. Ratmanoff dares to do it only because he knows that Romberg, Golovatscheff, and Bellingshausen are of the same opinion, as far as the distance of the *Nadezhda* from land during the night and the holding our distance from shore during the day are concerned, are of the same opinion. And I have to admit that I too sometimes here and there agree with my comrades.

Tues. 18/30 The land we sailed by yesterday and still have in front of us today is indescribably flat and can almost be called a barren stretch of sand. It has probably been created since time immemorial by the Amur's drifting sands, because at this latitude on the opposite side is the mouth of the Amur on the Siberian coast. The mouth itself is not in sight. The bottom is formed from fine sand like drift sand (*Quicksand* [sic]). In the afternoon, even though rather far from shore, we were sailing parallel to the land at a depth of twelve faden. Suddenly, it became shallow, and, before we knew it, we had only a depth of 4½ faden of water, had, as a result, to steer away from land and seek deeper water. We can count ourselves lucky that we did not get into the sand!

Wed. 19/31 In the morning, even though clear, we could not see the low land. We had a depth of 35 faden. Toward eight o'clock in the morning, a thick fog arose which engulfed us for the entire day.

Through the night, we tried to fish on the sandy bottom with a trawl, caught only sea nettles [anemones], sea urchins, and more of the same kind of trash about which Tilesius made raving noises, formed new species, stuffed them, embalmed them and stuck them in spiritus, dried them, and drew them. In a word he could have used ten hands for all of the work, if he had had them so that he could procure them for science, an additional growth of natural products which he could not extol enough to us.

We are not already at such a high latitude that we can suspect we have discovered the northern tip of Sachalin or not to be very far away from it. If this low place is indeed the northern tip, then it certainly stretches through this shallow outlet into the sea, and so far out that, when we double it, we will have trouble catching sight of land. If the Amur carries such a large quantity of sand along like the Themes, Neva, Duna, etc., then a lot of shallows can be expected at the Amur's mouth, making it impossible to sail to the shallow spot where La Pérouse ended his discoveries. Our discoveries at Sachalin, thus, will soon be ended, and I think that we will get to sight land only at the Schantar Islands, at the most, to visit Удинский Порт [Udinskii Port] (Fomin's imaginary harbor on the River Ud) and then to return to Kamtschatka.

Thurs. 20/1 The weather is bad, foggy, wet-cold, with continual rain and a strong topsail wind from the east, which is driving us toward land and forces us to carry a lot of sail. At this time of year, this strong wind will undoubtedly not last for long.

It would be more practical to inspect the mouth of the Amur, the Schantar Islands, etc., with small vessels from Ochotsk than with the *Nadezhda*, which is somewhat too deep, thus not permitting us to make any exact map of the land in a sea filled with shallows. Furthermore, we have at the most three weeks' time, since at the end of August northerly winds dominate, which make it difficult to sail into Avatscha Bay.

Fri. 21/2 After the weather had raged through the night, it cleared this morning. At noon, we were at 53° latitude and caught sight of land in the distance. We immediately sailed toward it and found, upon approach, once again a sand hill which was strewn over a very shallow bottom. The land was not worth all the trouble and time we spent in inspecting and describing it.

Sat. 22/3, Sun. 23/4 Two days again passed unused because of fog and bad weather. The relationship of nice days to bad days is one to four. You can almost say that every eighth day you have sunshine here.

Mon. 24/4, Tues. 25/5 On these two days, the weather has been unbearably bad. We are unable to dry our clothes, and no watch passes without our being soaked through and through by the rain and fog. The fog is especially unbearable here. It soaks worse than the rain and simply runs along the lines. The barometer is still very low, and the wind is blowing from the southeast. Both are signs of continuing damp weather. Today, the 25th, the weather appears to want to get better. The rain, however, has only made up for it, and the fog has distributed itself so as to cover us even more thickly. We have been sailing these days for the most part using the sink lead, because the depths rise and sink quite regularly.

Wed. 26/7 We sailed on this day on our departure from Kronstadt. The dreary, foggy weather had put us in bad spirits. We spent the day quietly enough.

Krusenstern does not make us very happy with the news he communicated to us, that he is thinking of determining only the northern tip of Sachalin and then setting out on the return voyage to Kamtschatka. And he said in addition that he thought we could probably spend a few days at the Cape of Good Hope on our return voyage to Europe. It would certainly be annoying enough to have sailed around the world without having been at the Cape of Good Hope.

Thurs. 27/8 Even with bad weather, it was light enough to see land, and, contrary to all of our expectations, we caught sight of high ground covered with forest which constitutes the actual northern tip of Sachalin.

Fri. 28/9 Yesterday, as we doubled the northern tip of Sachalin, we had a reef-sail wind from the south-southeast. The seas had grown quite high, and at five o'clock we had only the two topsails with two reefs, the foresail, and the mizzen staysail. The rest of the sails were lashed down because the wind blew in gusts. Finally, we put ourselves under the topsail on the drift opposite a bay. Since we found ourselves at the time protected by the high ground so that the sea was quiet and the wind quieter. We could have also still inspected both of the bays that were in view and anchored there without danger, since we still had three hours of daylight, especially since the wind blew from the land. That, however, was not Krusenstern's intention. When we dropped the sink lead, it stayed under the ship. It could be assumed that the current was driving us that way. Krusenstern had us hold to the northeast with few sails, and that is how we sailed for the whole night. Early today, we discovered that the current had driven us very far to the northwest. Even though we could suspect a current to the north, since we are opposite the mouth of the Amur, the sink lead nevertheless indicated yesterday the contrary.

Ratmanoff and Bellingshausen judged Krusenstern's behavior yesterday and today much too freely, using coarse expressions. I was not of their opinion and attempted to excuse Krusenstern. That vexed Bellingshausen, and he said I did not understand how to ingratiate myself. I did not let him finish speaking but answered, "That remark is out of place here"; and we ended the conversation. I could conclude that much, however, that Bellingshausen thinks that I talk differently from what I think. I am glad that during the voyage I have always behaved reservedly toward Krusenstern. Such things always leave a coldness behind.

After this dispute, I felt very uncomfortable the next morning when Krusenstern said to me at table that I should go ashore and inspect the depths, etc. Horner and Tilesius are going with me. I thought that Krusenstern would anchor in the bay for the night and go ashore himself tomorrow. At a quarter of three, I left with the express order to be back at four and, in case Tartars or Chinese happened to be there, not to land. On my trip ashore, I cast the sink lead often and found a nice regular deep anchorage. As we approached the spot where houses were, we saw a lot of people had collected, thirty-two Ainus were sitting in a row on the shore, and three who were dressed in Tartar or Chinese costumes were standing very near the shore and waving at us with fox skins. We climbed out. These people showed no fear at all and embraced us like old friends. Their costumes had caused us to be distrustful, and since we were unarmed and these people all had knives sticking out on their belts or chests, eight of us to their thirty-six men, made me think it wise, since I thought Krusenstern himself would come ashore, to get into the boat and simply do nothing more than determine the depths. We went along the shore for a couple more versts and landed to inspect a large tidal pool lying behind a tongue of land. After we had climbed to the top of a rise, we saw that a flag had been raised on the *Nadezhda*. We believed correctly that the flag was intended for us and returned onboard. Onboard ship, we found out that the flag had been raised immediately after we had left because Krusenstern had recognized Tartars on land through the tubus. We were not able to see the flag, because the ship had been sailing with her nose toward land and the counter mizzen was raised. By the time we had climbed the rise, the sail had been lowered, and the ship had turned her course seawards—and only then did we see the flag.

Even though we had a calm and could have stayed in the bay without danger, even if the wind had come from the north, Krusenstern left the bay anyway; and everyone was unhappy with this hurry to go to sea again. His haste was and remained vexing and shocking.

It was no consolation for us that Krusenstern said, after we had already sailed out of the bay and had to subject ourselves to the will of the current, "I am sorry that we did not anchor in the bay."

Sat. 29/10 Trapped in the current and by calms, we spent the day facing land, where we could have spent our time pleasantly if we had anchored.

Sun. 30/11 Things did not go much better. The current's play moved us only a little to the south and at a greater distance from land.

Mon. 31/12 A clear day and favorable wind. Even though we sailed rather quickly, the current does not leave us unscathed. We know for certain that it flows from west-southwest to east-northeast. Nevertheless, it carried us so irregularly that we do not know how we should steer, because it does not help us. Toward noon, the wind became brisker, and with that possibility we were able to sail along the northern shore of Sachalin, which provides a more pleasant view than the eastern shore.

August

Tues. 1/13 Fresh water, shallow depths, everything points very clearly to the fact that we are in the mouth of the Amur. Too bad that La Pérouse does not speak more exactly about the strait out of the Tartar Gulf. From all appearances, Sachalin is a peninsula. Around two o'clock in the afternoon, we caught sight of land to the southwest and of a strait in the south. Krusenstern sent Romberg in a small boat out to scout and check the depths. He found that the water, even though shallow, nevertheless stayed at the same depth so far into the strait that we lost sight of him. The uneasiness that Krusenstern displayed was shocking and injurious, since it showed that he did not place enough trust in Romberg and was afraid he would carry out his assignment badly.

Wed. 2/14 Krusenstern, who always likes to move away from land for the night, miscalculated the current once again. Early this morning, we found ourselves almost forty miles farther north than we had been yesterday evening. In the afternoon, we were close to the western tip of Sachalin, and Krusenstern decided to anchor, even though the bay was shallow. Calms forced us to tow the ship closer to land, and toward evening we anchored on a bad, stony bottom. There was a village of ten houses two miles from us. The small boat was sent out to the next shore with fishnets and got such a good catch that they brought half a boat full of fish back. In the night, the wind came up from the east, and toward midnight we drifted as a result of the bad anchorage. After we had drifted about two cable lengths, our anchor held us again, and we were not disquieted again by a similar incident.

In the morning at eight o'clock, Krusenstern went ashore. Except for Ratmanoff, who stayed onboard, all of us officers accompanied him.

A boat with natives had landed opposite the ship, and we rowed toward them. When they saw us approaching, they hurriedly tried to row away. We shouted and waved at them until they stopped and landed again with us. You could see from a distance how indecisive they were, wondering whether they should trust our calls or not. On land, we embraced each other like old friends. We found them all well armed; the boat was filled with bows, arrows, spears, and large knives.

In the beginning, they did not want to show us their weapons. Since they recognized our peaceful intentions, they finally agreed and appeared to lose their distrust completely. Then we wanted to go to the village; however, not one of the natives wanted to follow us. They nervously climbed back into their boat and, with their weapons, rowed very hurriedly homewards. The village was on the other side of a river formed by the connection of the sea with a tidal pool. We stopped there to see how we could cross it. Since the water was rather shallow, we decided to wade through it. All of our acquaintances had gotten out of their boat and collected on the opposite shore. The eldest had put on his parade clothes, which were made completely of Chinese materials. Facial expressions as well as clothing, body size, and manners showed that these natives were not Ainus but actually Tartars, who had undoubtedly settled here. About fifty paces from the village, the people made a raging ruckus and wanted to prevent us from going farther. One of them was fresh enough to take Bellingshausen by the arm and lead him back, because he was going ahead. That struck us all the more because Krusenstern, a short time before, had generously given them a lot of gifts. We had barely gone ahead again when they raised an even noisier ruckus. We did not let ourselves be stopped however by their calls and noise, and then all of the natives followed us voluntarily. We were not permitted to go into the houses. Each owner put himself in front of his door and appeared determined to maintain his right to his own home and to prevent anyone from entering by force. One in particular was pale and distraught from fear we would nevertheless dare go into his house despite his dying effort.

The houses are on raised pilings, like columns, and built totally unlike those in the southern part of Sachalin or in Kamtschatka and appeared to be summerhouses.

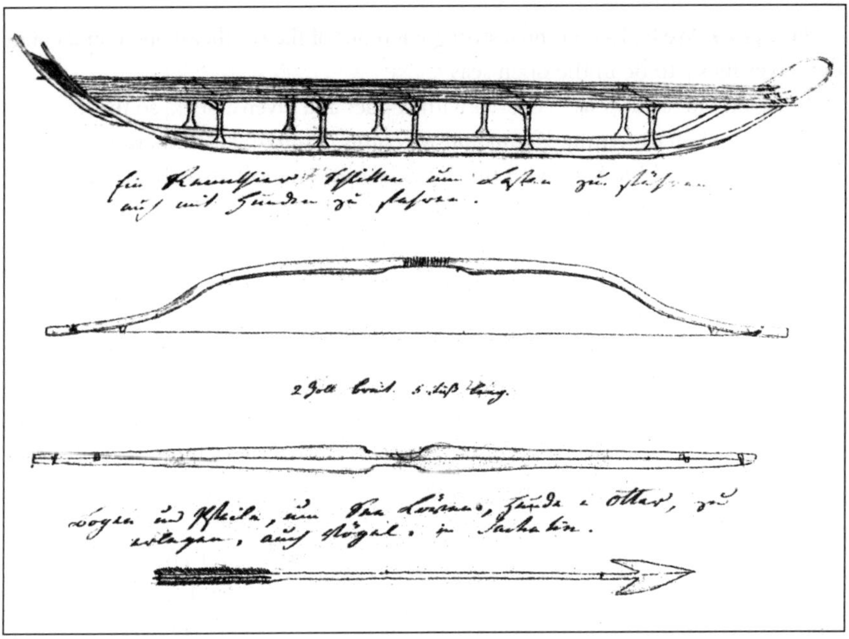

18-1. [top] 1 fuss wide 2 faden long
[below sled] A sled to carry loads and also to be used with dogs.
[bow] 2 zoll wide 5 fuss long
[below bow] Bow and arrow used to kill sea lions, dogs, otter, also birds, on Sachalin.

They had large numbers of dogs living under the houses between the pilings. Underground winter houses a little way off were uninhabited and appeared to have fallen in. After Krusenstern had given them all some more presents, we began a little bartering in order to obtain their utensils and other small objects. The greed, stinginess, meanness, and baseness which these people showed while trading was indescribably great. Krusenstern had given the eldest one or taion a great deal and gave him in addition, because he had uttered the wish to have a small object, that too, showed him however through pantomime that he would like in return for it a bunch of dried fish which he had in his hand. This man, without a feeling of gratefulness, did not do it and kept his fish, and, fearing we would take them away forcefully, distanced himself from us. I tried to trade for their weapons, but, blinded by Krusenstern's generosity, they, for a long time, did not pay any attention at all to the few things I could give them. One of our sailors, who had taken tobacco along, was surrounded by the natives. Each one of them wanted to have some. We certainly could have traded anything we wanted for that article. At one o'clock in the afternoon, we returned onboard, and at two o'clock we weighed anchor.

This was the end of our voyage to Sachalin, and, God willing, we will return to Kamtschatka.

Fri. 4/16 We had a continual strong wind out of the southeast and could count ourselves lucky to be in the open seas.

In Japan, our shallop was covered with copper and given a deck, so that the boat could be used on the Amur. Ratmanoff was supposed to explore there in this boat wherever we could not go with the *Nadezhda*. Ratmanoff also always called the shallop "my yacht." He dared not say it but shows all too much that he is very angry that he could not become famous on his yacht.

Sat. 5/17 The wind let up toward noon. Totally unexpectedly at sunrise, we caught sight of the Island Ion, which Saritischeff had discovered. Our sailor who saw it first received a reward of five piasters because we unexpectedly had caught sight of the island. It looks like a haystack. A bare rock, which is all the more dangerous, since it is surrounded by so many sunken reefs, and because of frequent fog in the Sea of Ochotsk (putrid sea, гнилое море), it is seldom seen. Too bad that we could not determine its longitude because the sky was too overcast and uncertain to determine times close to noon by several minutes.

Sun. 6/18 The Japanese count as their possession the southern part of Sachalin or Karafuto and have settled there. The Tartars have settled on the northern point, and Russia counts the entire island as her distant possession. The actual Ainus of Sachalin live only in the middle part. If Russia claims Sachalin, obtains free shipping on the Amur, and, instead of in Ochotsk, puts in a market, only then can these distant areas bloom, for that difficult dragging of things from Irkutsk to Ochotsk remains a great barrier, since only through the Amur can the communication by water between the interior of Siberia and the Sea of Ochotsk and Kamtschatka be established. Today, we had stormy, bad weather.

Mon. 7/19 Very high seas and low reading of the barometer led us to expect a storm. On the contrary, however, along with the usual bad weather, the wind had died down, and also зыб [the high seas] have become quieter.

Tues. 8/20 A favorable wind from the northwest and clearer skies, and by using longitude and latitude, we were finally able to determine our position on the map with certainty. When reading a lot of descriptions of voyages, I have to envy of the capriciousness in the division of time and changes in routes that every chief of an expedition was granted. The geographical placement of Kamtschatka, the Kuril Islands, and the Aleutian Islands is still so full of mistakes that it would be necessary to establish the correct main points. Since the main points are determined astronomically, the details can easily be filled in through later information. The year is too far advanced, and we have to hurry to Macao in order not to miss the monsoon.

Wed. 9/21, Thurs. 10/22, Fri. 11/23, Sat. 12/24, Sun. 13/25 Overcast, foggy, unbearably rainy days. Also, the wind is not to our liking. Sailing by Sachalin was boring. The wet weather, however, tests our patience anew. We hope that at the sight of the Kurils we will be rewarded by a clear day.

- 19 -

Return to Kamtschatka

Mon. 14/26 Even though the night and morning were very overcast and promised nothing good and the barometer had fallen under 29 zoll, the sky cleared up toward eight o'clock in the morning, and at ten o'clock we caught sight of the Kurils. At noon the wind became brisker and brisker, and, after a long time, we finally had clear skies again and favorable winds. Krusenstern wanted to sail between the sixth and seventh islands. Since, however, we found ourselves in front of the second island, we sailed between it and the fifth and the third and fourth. Alaid or the first island could be seen very clearly even at a great distance.

Since the wind was brisk so that we were sailing eight and half knots, we can, if it continues, be in Kamtschatka tomorrow evening.

Tues. 15/27 Our course carried us very close to land. The weather is, however, so overcast that we only now and then have caught sight of the snow- and ice-covered Kamtschadal Mountains. It is too bad that we have not caught sight of Lapatka (the southern tip of Kamtschatka) because King[1] and Saritscheff have a difference of six degrees in the latitude, and we would have liked to correct that point.

Wed. 16/28 In the morning at nine o'clock, we sailed past Povorotnoi Muis (the promontory). The wind was not very good. Since it did permit us to hold to a straight line, we are satisfied with it. We sailed very close to the steep, stony, barren shores of Kamtschatka and hit gusts of winds. To our regret, the wind became weaker and weaker; and at sunset in the evening, we found ourselves pulled away by a current, no farther than we had been at nine o'clock in the morning.

The whole day, we had flattered ourselves with the hope of anchoring in Avatscha today.

Thurs. 17/29 Earlier, we had contrary winds and tacked around in front of Avatscha. At noon, there was a calm, and then a nice wind arose from the south, with which we headed toward the harbor and at eight o'clock in the evening, we cast anchor in Avatscha Bay.

According to Krusenstern's order, Ratmanoff has the command when everyone is working. Today, when Krusenstern gave Romberg the order to call the crew to the deck and then turned the speaking trumpet over to Ratmanoff, the two of them exchanged several words I did not understand and went their own ways. Krusenstern then called Romberg to order him to hold a rhomb higher. He had already gone on deck and found it necessary himself to tell the sailor at the wheel what he should do.

Only then did Ratmanoff take over command with a tone, as if he, from necessity, had to guide the ship, because no one else would know how to do it. He does not have enough sensitivity to feel that he has compromised Romberg, since Krusenstern did not know that Romberg had already turned over his trumpet.

Leaving one's watch in a narrow passage is a bad recommendation.

Then Romberg exchanged words with Ratmanoff ending coldly.

Since we spent the whole morning tacking near land, the people on the maiak had enough time to let them know in the harbor that we were coming. We had barely entered the entrance when a baidara came toward us with Ivan Stepanovitsch Chamekoff. Since a calm held us up a little in the entrance, we sent a baidara to the former saltworks and had milk brought for our tea. We, however, made so little progress with our towing that we found it necessary to anchor in Rakovaja Bay.

During our absence, nothing much has happened. Pavel Ivanovitsch had left two days after we had and had the misfortune of capsizing on his trip along the Kamtschatka current. He was in danger of losing all of his baggage, and one of his Cossacks drowned. Whether the current also carried away our letters, we will find out in more detail from Dmitri Ivanovitsch and Friderici. Several weeks after our departure, seven Japanese, who had the misfortune of shipwrecking on our coast, disappeared in their own poor little boat. They lost almost all of their things and salvaged only a few provisions. Gertschefskii looked for them for five days and went quite far out but did not find them. Those poor people either foundered or starved.

The promischlenikis, who had run away from the *Maria*, have all returned again, except for the smithy who probably died.

Fri. 18/30 The officer, who had come out to meet us, stayed with us last evening until we cast anchor, and, since it had become quite dark by that time, he decided to spend the night with us.

The baidara's absence had caused uncertainty, disquiet, and fear in Peter-Paul's Harbor. Through useless musings, they had convinced themselves that our ship had to be a foreign ship and was coming with hostile intentions, had arrested all of the people in the baidara, etc., etc. All of them packed their possessions, so that they could cart them into the mountains if a good opportunity arose. Several had already carted away part of their things. Only this morning were they torn from their mistake when Krusenstern sent denschik Stepan on land to get milk (because we had gotten no milk at the ruins and the saltworks), and the baidara returned. Ashamed, every one of them hurried to carry their things back again, so as not to betray their unnecessary fear.

Immediately after noon, a favorable breeze came up, and, since both Krusenstern and Ratmanoff were on land, the rest of us weighed anchor and sailed toward Peter-Paul's Harbor. Halfway there, Ratmanoff came toward us, and, at three o'clock, we anchored next to the sunken *Slava Rossia* and immediately took all of the sails down and all superfluous riggings.

At our request, during our absence, wood had been chopped, scheremscha collected, and hardtack baked. There are few fish here right now. Soon, however, the herring run should be starting.

Of the innumerable peroquitos (little parrots) we had bought in Brazil, I had kept only one pair. All too often their noise had disturbed me. Yesterday, one of those pretty birds died. In order to keep the other one from dying, I gave it to Romberg, because I was afraid that it would not live very long, because it missed its pal. Even though the birds' screams often made me angry, I was nevertheless really sorry to do it.

After we had fastened the ship to the anchor cable, I went on land to visit Prokofi Michalovitsch, who was ill. On the way, I stopped by Schemelin's, who told me in detail the story of the Japanese. Three of them were sick or pretending to be sick before they left. Several days before, they had insisted on being baptized, and, on the evening before their escape, they had used their last money to purchase brandy and make everyone around them drunk. Except for about 100 fresh fish, they took along no other provisions. Even though the distances from one Kuril Island to the next are not great, there is a strong current, толчея [turbulent water], and continual fog that make the trip dangerous, and, since the Japanese also had so few tools along with which they could catch food, they are in a very bad situation. What won't be tried for the love of the fatherland!

Sat. 19/31 After we had sent everything ashore that could encumber our unloading and we had transported over the riggings, Krusenstern gave our sailors schabasch because today is Sunday. Everyone went on land but me, because I had watch. The *Nadezhda* has never been so empty. Today, I justified my behavior to Krusenstern and was happy to see that he could see my reasons, because I did not want Krusenstern, in the midst of the general tensions, to judge me falsely.

Sun. 20/1 I went with Horner to Tarcinaia Bay to determine its latitude and to map the bay. We took along provisions so that we could cook our noon meal there. The weather was very nice. The sun burned so strongly through the hat I had on my head that a dizzy spell overcame me, which by the way was not serious. Since Captain Bligh[2] mapped only one part of the bay, we had enough to do with mapping the missing part and finding depths with the sink lead. When Bligh was here, the bay was filled with ice. On our return, we met a Kamtschadal with his entire family. They had come to Tarcinoia Bay to kill seals. They had been in Paratunka to catch fish. We gave those people everything we had that we did not need. They could not thank us enough for the bread and gunpowder which we gave them. At eleven o'clock in the evening, we went back onboard again.

Mon. 21/2 We unloaded our firewood and inspected our riggings. We still have several days' work before we get the iron out.

Tues. 22/3 Mitschmann Steinheil arrived on the galliot *Ochotsk* from Ochotsk. He brought us a lot of news, a lot of letters, and some supplies. A packet of letters is missing in which there must have been a letter for me, judging by a letter written by my father. Woldemar's[3] to me was a pasquinade on all letters to Kamtschatka. With this courier, Krusenstern received the Order of St. Anne for his neck. All of the news was welcomed. Resanoff has been called back to Petersburg. His dispatches have, however, been sent back, since they learned through Fosse that he has sailed for Kodiak. The military messenger traveled the 10,000 versts from Petersburg to Ochotsk in two months and three days.

Chvastoff's behavior toward Delaroff (the director of the American Company), who also had traveled to Ochotsk, is the reason that Maschin and not he received the command of the vessel *Maria*. Chvastoff insulted Delaroff, cursed, and with drunken courage wanted to kill him, and, sober, to put an end to the noise, gave up the command of the *Maria*, since according to his contract, the first vessel to arrive in Ochotsk was to be put in his hands.

Wed. 23/4 We had enough to do reading our news and telling each other about it. We unloaded our provisions and 1,015 bars of iron and repaired our riggings.

Thurs. 24/5 I went with Horner to the maiak at five in the morning. I returned at one o'clock in the night because the boat was so hard to row.

Fri. 25/6 I took a warm bath. Yesterday and today, 1,438 bars of iron were unloaded and 1,106 pud of ballast.

Sat. 26/7 We congratulated Krusenstern upon receipt of the Order and artillery sergeant Raefski for the elevation of his Character [promotion]. 588 pud of ballast were loaded.

Sun. 27/8 I went with Horner to Avatscha. Very heavy frost in the night.

Mon. 28/9 Once again, we began to load our crates and chests, etc. Tilesius was, of necessity, forced to watch out for his bottles of spiritus and is raging diffusely with his rubbish.

Tues. 29/10 Firewood, provisions, and the silk padding were loaded. The water casks were filled at Paganaia Retschka and the riggings repaired.

Wed. 30/11 We took on provisions from the galliot *Ochotsk* and loaded them. The difficulties made by Schemelin and Vichodzoff were unbearable, since they showed only too well that they are rascals and they do not trust each other. Each one tried to make sure he has left himself an excuse open in order to cloak his future knavery. God forbid having to deal with the American Company!

Today, Tilesius made a lot of unseemly noise about a chest that he said had been lost. Since this could have only happened through his own carelessness, Romberg gave him the advice, upon our return in Kronstadt, to watch out for his things better, since there his boxes and crates could end up in the wrong hands, since it is likely that his chest is now on the voyage to Kodiak. Tilesius, with his important mien that drew a smile from all of us, said, "All of those things belong to the expedition," and left us with the clear understanding that we were responsible for them.

I then said to him, "We are just as much a part of the expedition as you are. Certainly, no one will watch out for your things, however, if you do not do it yourself." What I had said in German I also repeated in Russian and added, turning to my comrades, "We have to take precautions not to let this man cause us trouble."

Then Tilesius suddenly accosted me and accused me, since I was speaking Russian, of speaking about him. "You cannot prescribe for me," I answered, "which language I am to speak. It is, however, impolite of you to butt into a conversation between me and my comrades and, in addition, to want to tell me I should speak a language other than Russian." Tilesius became even coarser and finally told me that I should be quiet. This demand angered me and I made known quite loudly that Tilesius is crazy. Tilesius was still reasonable enough to keep still, and I also considered it better to let this half-crazy man go and not to mention the matter any further. Tilesius himself will have to want to warm the matter up again.

Thurs. 31 / 12 His chest has indeed disappeared.

Friderici and Dimitri Ivanovitsch Koscheleff arrived here. They had left Nischnoi Kamtschatka on the same day on which we arrived here.

In the evening, Bellingshausen and Espenberg made declarations of love to each other, which ended approximately with their wanting to give each other in writing a statement that they have never been able to stand each other and will always think that of each other. The cause was scheremscha (wild garlic) which Bellingshausen liked to eat and Espenberg could not stand.

September

Fri. 1 / 13 The nice weather has ended. The following is the name of the officers whom we have seen here: Prokofei Michalovitsch Kalmakoff and Prokofei Fedorovitsch Volkoff, artillery officers; Ivan Sergeitsch Gertschevski, Andrei Spriridonitsch Suchorkin, Kondratii Ivanitsch Linschtet and Chamekoff, military officers, all of them unimportant men.

Sat. 2 / 14 Pavel Ivanovitsch Koscheleff and all of those people traveling with him were in danger of drowning. Only with difficulty were they able to save their lives. They lost all of their baggage. Our letters had been left behind and therefore were saved. Resanoff's account book of the extraordinaire sum of money, however, was lost, because he had not sent it with Fosse but with the mail to Petersburg.

Sun. 3/15 We are filling our water casks and rigging the ship. Captain Ispravnik Tonin, who had come here with Koscheleff, went back again today. He had come here to collect evidence concerning the demand for a court martial.

The priests had charged the Ispravnik [police inspector of the district] with trying to convince the Kamtschadals to leave the religion and of forbidding them to go into the church. The priests had tried to support this charge with a petition from the Kamtschadals. Then it turned out that the petition had been written in the name of Kamtschdals who had died twenty years before.

Tomin strongly rebuked the priests here. The Kamtschadals blindly trust the priests, and a Kamtschadal says very patiently, "That is the priest; why should I not believe what he says?" and let him take and give him everything they have. And, in addition, they haul all of the stolen things to his house with their own dogs.

The bears take revenge for that. There is not a priest living in Kamtschatka who has not been in the claws of a bear and does not have a torn up or broken arm or leg.

One taion, a twenty-five year-old fellow, killed seventeen bears in one day and in two years around five hundred, countless numbers in his lifetime.

One cannot imagine the numbers of bears living in Kamtschatka. In the summer, they live from catching fish and hurt no one. In the fall, they are, however, very rapacious. The bear climbs into the water and splashes with his front feet in the water; everything that flies on land between his hind feet belongs to him. That way of catching fish is successful only in Kamtschatka where the herring migrate by the millions.

Mon. 4/16 Koscheleff and Steinheil, a couple of persuasive men, are in charge now, and we get to hear it.

Today, we put up our yards.

Tues. 5/17 In the morning, I took a walk around the tidal pool. Very unexpectedly I heard someone ahead of me yelling "Nerpa! Nerpa!" (seal). I hurried up and found a soldier who had killed a seal by hitting it with a stick on the nose. He had seen it sleeping on the shore and had crept up to it.

Wed. 6/18 We sealed up our letters and gave them to Steinheil, who was ready to leave.

Today, we claimed our riggings and continued filling up our water.

Thurs. 7/19 The vessel *Ochotsk* went out of the harbor and anchored in Avatscha Bay.

A monument for Captain Klark [Clerke], which Ratmanoff took the trouble to build, is almost finished. Today, we loaded firewood and hauled up the shrouds and stays.

Fri. 8/20 The one-mast vessel *Konstantin* with mate Jakoff Gepifanitsch Patapoff arrived. He had left Unalaschka on the 22nd of July, where Resanoff had already arrived. Resanoff had needed fifteen days from here to Unalaschka.

The *Konstanin* has brought us a lot of spoiled kottik pelts and 4,000 sea otter pelts (the kottiks are also a kind of sea otter). Chvastoff has written Krusenstern requesting a map of Japan and Aniva. Undoubtedly, Resanoff is building castles in the sky again and wants to conquer Sachalin and avenge himself on the Japanese.

A vessel from Sitka brought the news to Kodiak that the Americans [Tlingits] have not wanted to bear that old yoke willingly and all of them have fled into the woods and mountains. Baranoff received a wound in his hand, Povalischin one from shot, and Arbusoff, the pilot's mate, the chirurus, and several sailors were wounded quite badly. If the *Neva* had not been there, the Russians would have gotten the short end of it.

Besides the *Neva*, six other vessels sailed from Kodiak to Sitka to take back the establishment there, which had been massacred in the winter. In addition, Baranoff had also taken along a small detachment in baidaras and boats.

Sat. 9/21 Resanoff dreams only of war. Now, he intends to capture the first ship from Boston carrying guns and gunpowder and declare her a prize, since they supply the savages on the Northwest Coast with gunpowder, thus making it possible for the savages to resist the Russians, the M…er in Sitka is especially at fault.

Resanoff has taken over the command from Maschin and turned the *Maria* over to Chvastoff and plans to send Chvastoff out to conquer Queen Charlotte's Island. In his report, Resanoff requested a frigate of the emperor in order to add weight to his crazy plans.

Steinheil set sail today in his galliot.

The Aleuts possess great dexterity, and the workmanship of their crafts is admirable. They defy the strongest winds and the highest surf in their leather boats that are dangerous to use without practice, and they kill sea otter, whales, dolphins, marsh otters, sea cows, etc., from their boats and are just as clever at killing sea lions, kottiks, and seals. Their harpoons are so accurate that these animals, which are vulnerable only in one place, are killed with the first throw; that is, a sea otter has to be hit on the head; whales, dolphins, marsh otter, and sea cows under the front fin; and the sea lions on the temple; otherwise, the harpoon glances off. The sea lions move around in herds. Their leader is a male, who has a seraille of females as entourage. (Here they call him gekatsch. He weighs up to 100 pud. His fur is called laschtok.) If two herds meet each other, jealousy arises. Each gekatsch tries to steal females from the other herd by grabbing them by the throat and throwing them into his herd. If two of them grab a female at the same time, she gets ripped up every time. Two herds rarely meet each other without several females being cruelly ripped apart.

Sun. 10/22 The *Konstantin* has brought along a prisoner who killed a girl in Unalaschka. He is kept in chains. This man, who has been in America for twenty-two years, is named Kulikaloff and went with Schelichoff to Kodiak. His head for business and his usefulness had caused the prikaschtschiks to wink at many a cruelty. It was his bad luck that Resanoff came to Unalaschka and heard about the murder, because he was put in chains upon Resanoff's orders. He had undertaken several trips by baidaras with twenty or more men, for example, from Alaska to the Islands of Peter and Paul and always brought back the greatest catch of furs.

Mate Patapoff appears to play a large role. He is the chief overseer of the Aleutian Islands, Blischnia, Krissie, and Andreanofskie. Resanoff has turned the command over to Vichodzoff to give orders, also to the cutter awaited from Ochotsk, and to communicate to Bellingshausen that he is to report to the American Company upon his return so that he can to be taken into its service. Bellingshausen is spitting mad about that.

A sea cow's kidneys are supposed to weigh 15 to 20 pud. It is also the largest animal known. These animals have been driven away from here and are almost never seen.

A pair of boots made of bear paws must be very good for climbing. Bear paws are commonly used as mittens for climbing.

Tues. 12/24 Ratmanoff, Golovatscheff, and Koscheleff went to Tarcinia Bay. The strong wind, however, spoiled their trip. In the evening, Horner and Bellingshausen had a biting dispute about the mail, because Bellingshausen granted the government the right to open letters and Horner fought against that. Anything less than unity reigns among us.

Wed. 13/25 Aftstem water 16 fuss 3 zoll, forestem water 13 fuss 10 zoll, a difference of 2 fuss 5 zoll.

In the evening, before sunset, three big bears came to the koschka [spit]. We saw them from the ship and hurried to kill them, ran after them for a long time, but could not do what we planned without guns. Now a period of starvation begins, since the fish are becoming scarcer and bruin fishes poorly. The strawberries, etc. are not found as often and Monsieur Michel is forced to seek his keep in other places. The beasts came to the koschka in order to feast at the racks of dried fish (jukata). This is also the time when they pull down the cows and horses if they can get hold of them.

Thurs. 14/26 An anecdote I heard earlier, which Steinheil told us in more detail. He had read the journal of this boatswain (pure nonsense). In 1796, (back then the American Company had not yet been founded, and taking furs and trade with America was free) several merchants (lavoschnikis) sent a galliot from Ochotsk to Analaschka to get furs. The vessel was entrusted to a former Russian boatswain (a man who could neither read nor write, otherwise a good seaman, for if he had been able to do both, he would have become a master's mate (podschkiper or sailor). He left Ochotsk in the middle of September with nineteen promischlenikis (avantüries) [adventurers] and headed for Bolschertsk. He happened to discover that he had sailed past and turned to the southwest, without knowing exactly where he was heading. On this detour, he met Schalichoff on the *Phönix*. Expecting that the vessel was sailing for Ochotsk, Schalichoff asked that and where he was coming from. When the boatswain answered, "We are sailing to Unalaschka," Schelichoff put him straight. Only with great difficulty were the promischlenikis able to get the boatswain to follow the *Phönix* and give up his crazy course to the southwest. Together, they sailed as far as the first strait between the Kuril Islands. There they were becalmed. After they had sailed through the strait the next day; the *Phönix* took course to Kodiak; my boatswain, however, sailed to the south-southeast. His sailors (promischlenikis) raised objections. Nothing helped! He claimed the *Phönix* was sailing there for the first time and wanted to make discoveries. "I know the way, and we do not need to stay so close to Kamtschatka."

After they had sailed for several days in the brisk, favorable winds, he said prophetically, "Now we should be seeing land soon." The people stared their eyes out of their heads in vain. They continued to sail for a long time until the boatswain began to have his doubts. Then he began to make mistakes. First, he headed this direction and then that one and plagued his people the most by making them unnecessarily cast lead where there was no bottom. One promischlenik finally took the lead and stuck it into the grits, pulled it out, and showed with great amazement that the bottom was made of grits.

The end of October was so warm that the people were running around onboard in their shirts. This magic sign moved the boatswain to give up his command and to admit that he did not know a way out of the situation. Since no one had any advice, the Mother of God had to be called upon for advice. In procession, she was brought onto the deck, they decided that they would sail where the wind blew. In six days, a strong southerly wind took them to an unknown shore surrounded by rough cliffs and surf. They sailed into a gorge (schetschel) they caught sight of, but found themselves in a bare, dangerous bay. They lost the anchor they had cast out, because it had been on three thin hawsers (perlin) which, by their own weight, pulled the ship forward and threatened to shipwreck them on the rocks. The quiet water protected them from disaster. The next day, they left the bay and headed toward the north along the shore, until one of the people onboard recognized the Tschugatskaia Bay. From there, they sailed for Kodiak, still uncertain of their route, since no one knew the area. Near one island they met a baidara in which there was also a Russian who had gone out fur hunting as a promischlenik. He served them as a guide. He led them to a bay on Afoggriak. Not far from land they were becalmed. The people wanted to tow the ship in. The boatswain, who, since they had sighted land, had once again taken over, did not allow it by saying, "We will now cast anchor, rest, and tomorrow we will sail into the bay." Even though his people begged and maintained that it would be better if they first had the ship safe and then rested, it did not help at all. The stubborn boatswain cast anchor. During the night, the wind became brisker. They were forced to cast another anchor, but it did not hold either. They cast out another grapnel (a little anchor with four bills). Nor did that hold. All three hawsers broke, and in the morning the galliot was again at the mercy of the waves. The newly acquired pilot was asked, if possible, since the season was so far advanced, to take them to some bay. They had of course supplemented their water with rainwater. Water and provisions were getting short; they had to hurry up.

"I know a little island with a bay," said the pilot, "but there are a lot of reefs in the way." Without paying attention to the reefs, they sailed straight ahead through them past cliffs where no baidara would dare to go so close to danger, but the people said that they never hit a yard on a cliff; happily, they sailed in the bay they were looking for; and, since they had no anchor, they sailed straight for land and firmly into the sand so as not to be driven off again, tied the vessel to a tree with lines and wintered there, happy finally to have land under their feet. The travails had affected the boatswain so much that he became ill not long afterwards and died in Kodiak, where he had gone by land and baidara.

For a while, Kosloff-Ugrainin [Grigorii Alekseevich, port commandant in Okhotsk] had played tyrant in Kamtschatka. His oppression ruined the Kamtschadals. (He always rode around in a large kibitke [covered wagon] pulled by fifty or more dogs, and the owners of the dogs had to run alongside in case the dogs could not go on and they had to help themselves. At each stop, several dogs always died, sometimes people too, without the misery softening up that cruel man. During these trips, he raised the gesak [the tax in pelts for the Crown] arbitrarily, and due to his carelessness smallpox spread, killing countless Kamtschadals.)

When Emperor Paul took over the government, General Somoff was sent to Kamtschatka with a regiment. His voyage from Ochotsk to Kamtschatka is a pendant to the boatswain's peregrination. Somoff sailed from Ochotsk on a galliot with 140 men. The pilot, who was the only one who understood anything about sailing, became badly ill and could not continue carrying out his duties. Driven by storm and bad weather, they rocked around the seas for a long time until suddenly one evening they found themselves in surf and in danger of being thrown against reefs without thought of being saved. Only a hair away from destruction, a strong gust of wind drove them into a gorge or break in the reefs, undamaged, out of danger, and back into the sea. (Except for four men, all of the others were sick with putrid fever and heat fever.) The reefs had been part of a Kuril Island, since on the next morning, through a miracle and as if awakening from a dream, they found themselves at the entrance of Avatscha Bay.

Late in the fall of 1798, the galliot anchored in Peter-Paul's Harbor. Somoff was so cruel that he sent his soldiers suffering from putrid fever to the surrounding villages, as far as Bolscheretsk, and, before Christmas, the entire southern part of Kamtschatka had died out. Since then, the Kamtschadals have not recovered. Another vessel with Somoff's soldiers got to Pensinskaia Bay, thinking they were entering Avatscha. And instead of sailing into Peter-Paul's Harbor, they wintered in Tigil. Infectious diseases also raged there but not as murderously as around Avatscha Bay.

The vessels the people used here earlier were all so shallowly built that the seamen had the habit, instead of anchoring, of sailing the vessel (usually a galliot) straight on shore. Climbing out, they picked berries, fished, etc. At high tide, they floated the boat again and sailed away undamaged. They never could say where they had been. Only by chance did they reach the place they intended to.

Fri. 15/27 Last night, we had a strong earthquake here in Peter-Paul's Harbor. You could feel it very much on land. Even the *Nadezhda* shook so much that Krusenstern was afraid, since the water was so low, that the ship might have hit bottom.

This afternoon Potapoff set sail.

Sat. 16/28 Finally, the wedding business has ended. For eight days, our sailors have been made déshabillé. They always had something to do on land and could not be gotten to work. The marriage was supposed to be later, but, in order to tap the purses of our well-off sailors as wedding guests, the wedding was celebrated during our stay.

Sun. 17/29 We raised all of the topmasts and yards and loaded 15 bales of beaver pelts and 85 bales of kottik pelts into our ship.

The wooden pyramid with a fence around it for Klerk's grave is finished.

I went with Horner to find shallows with the lead, especially a sandbank at the entrance. Bligh's map cannot be improved.

Mon. 18/30 We hauled up all of the sails. Our gentlemen, last but not least, are getting the affections of the fair sex here; especially Ratmanoff, Friderici, and even the two Kotzebues do not come out badly.

Tues. 19/1 We loaded firewood and provisions and are quite ready. Today Fedor Schemelin and Fedor Vichodzoff treated us with a pirog (imennik) for their name days. Romberg, who had drunk too much, had a fit of laughing and then a fit of crying. Romberg laughed like a drunk for a couple of hours, one after the other, then cried even longer and, exhausted, finally lay down. That man is going to drink himself to death if he keeps it up.

Wed. 20/2 At ten o'clock this morning, drums were rolled. A fire made itself apparent by a thick cloud of smoke from one of the little houses on land. We immediately sent our entire crew on land. The owners got out of it with the loss of the roof. We were so happy to have extinguished that fire. The calm favored the inhabitants of Peter-Paul's Harbor, for, if the wind had been as strong as a few days ago, half of the few houses existing here would have certainly caught fire.

Dimitri Ivanovitsch Koscheleff, who celebrated his imennik today, spoiled everyone's lunch with his breakfast. I was the only one who ate onboard because it was my dejour.

Today we cleaned up our house and finished our work, filled all of the empty water casks. We have only 156 of them. In the evening we shot up ten rockets. Only four of them climbed nicely to a height. The other six had gotten damp and exploded.

The Kamtschadal sledge, which General Koscheleff gave Krusenstern, is laboriously and beautifully made.

Thurs. 21/3 We brought onboard our live oxen, which are nice and fat. In order to prevent any additional bills, Krusenstern obtained for himself and all of his officers and the whole crew a receipt from Vichodzoff stating that no one owes anything. It appears that Vichodzoff trusts us more than himself, because Golovatscheff, Friderici, Ratmanoff, and several of our people have run up debts with him, which they have not yet paid.

Krusenstern was thinking about opening the packet of letters to Resanoff, which had come with the mail, in Schemelin's and Vichodzoff's presence in order to see if letters for us were there. Vichodzoff showed him, however, a letter he had received from Irkutsk, which expressly forbade him to remove the seal on the package and, in case Resanoff had already sailed for Kodiak, to send them back with an estafet.

In the afternoon, I went on land. Last but not least, there is to be a vetscherinok at Dmitri Koscheleff's. Since it is my watch this evening, I will not be able to go to this party.

Schemelin has come onboard with sack and pack, and tomorrow, God willing, we will sail out of the harbor.

Fri. 22/4 Froloff arrived in General Koscheleff's boat. The General writes in the letters and dispatches, which Steinheil had brought along, that he has received an order from the emperor, in detail, to report the strife that occurred in his presence between Resanoff and Krusenstern, desirable from our standpoint. At Koscheleff's request, officers in Kamtschatka will be rotated or changed every five years.

We wanted to be towed out of the harbor in the morning, but contrary winds prevented us from leaving.

The mail has arrived with the *Tschernoi Orel* (a packet-boat) from Ochotsk over Tigil to Nischnoi Kamtschatsk, three batches of mail in 12 knapsacks at the same time. The quantity has prevented General Koscheleff from opening everything before Froloff's departure. Therefore, it is possible we too will get some letters. Krusenstern, however, will hardly wait for the next messenger from Nischnoi Kamtschtsk.

The vessel *Kodiak* was in danger of sinking and therefore turned back to Ochotsk. Upon his arrival, Bucherin (a base fellow), who arrived at Ochotsk as commander, put his pilot's mate and port commander Baschutski under martial law. The emperor has given the American Company permission to use two transport vessels in Ochotsk, and this is why Steinheil worked for the American Company.

Finally, all of the officers here ate with us at noon. We drank to Pavel Ivanovitsch Koscheleff's health and took up a collection for Sinizin, who, though he did not suffer any great damage from the fire, nevertheless lost enough for a poor soldier. The collection was five times more than he had ever had in his life.

Sat. 23/5 Early in the morning at three o'clock, we weighed anchor, towed ourselves out with a kedge anchor, and, since it later became completely still, we towed our *Nadezhda* out of the harbor. At eight o'clock, we cast anchor in Avatscha Bay. All of the officers from the harbor are coming out onboard at six to take leave, because they thought we would be setting sail immediately. We raised our shallop and longboats and lashed everything down for the sea voyage.

At noon, all of the officers from Peter-Paul's Harbor came to dine with us. We drank to Dmitri Koscheleff's health, whose birthday was today. Immediately after table, we took leave of all of our Kamtschadal acquaintances and set about weighing anchor so that we could leave Kamtschatka. The weather was highly unfriendly. Snow, snowy rain, rain, cold, and thick air were bad omens. Even though Krusenstern would not have weighed anchor in such unfavorable weather if he had had the time, it seemed to me that Ratmanoff was the driving force behind leaving because the wind was favorable, that he [Krusenstern] decided to go to sea. With a favorable wind, we weighed anchor with only the staysail and put up the foretopsail. The wind became ever brisker and the weather darker, so that we were unable to see the closest land.

Ratmanoff, bragging to Krusenstern, said, "We have to set all of the topsails." We had barely set them when we were sitting tight in the sand. That happened at two-thirty in the afternoon. The misfortune had barely happened when Ratmanoff said, "I said that we should have stayed higher." No one had heard that. We doubted him. He swore by God. And we stayed silent because we had too much to do and no time to argue. We were barely sitting tight when we heard a cannon shot from land. Not long afterward a baidara came out with the soldier Dorofeeff. He had just arrived from Nischnoi Kamtschatsk and brought us several letters and newspapers.

Everything with hands and feet was busy pulling the *Nadezhda* off of the sand. Only Ratmanoff reported ill at the right time. We threw two kedges out and tried to use them to pull the *Nadezhda* from the sand, in vain. She sat too tight. We lowered the longboat and put supports on both sides because we had ebb tide. Because the wind was becoming brisker and brisker and the seas more and more restless, we had the yards and shrouds lowered, emptied about thirty casks of water, and pumped the water out of the ship again. Up to then we had suffered no damage. Since we had tried repeatedly in vain to pull ourselves off of the sandbank, we were forced to spend the night in this unpleasant situation. The *Nadezhda* was tossed some but not overly strongly. At twelve o'clock at night, our sailors went to bed, and, at three o'clock in the morning, we took up our work again.

Sun. 24/6 Our first task was to put an anchor into the longboat and to tow it away with a nine-zoll hawser. We pulled and worked for a long time without success. We threw the rostrum into the water; that did not help either. At nine o'clock, a baidara came from Dimitri Koscheleff with a greeting and a question, "What is wrong?" They went back with a less than calming question. At twelve o'clock,

Gertschevski came onboard with twenty-five men to help work. Since we were expecting high tide at four o'clock and we had only about one fuss or less of water when our ship grounded, we were impatiently awaiting the time when high tide would come. During this period, we sent another 27 empty water casks on land, because they hindered us and we wanted to lighten the ship as much as possible. If we, however, with the next high tide were not fortunate enough to pull the *Nadezhda* off the sand, then we had no other alternative but to unload the ship completely.

At twelve-thirty, with the help of Gertschefski's men and with a cheer, we were happy to see the ship afloat again. Ratmanoff reported ill again today. Barely had we pulled ourselves happily off of the sandbank when our patient appeared, wanting to go on land despite the cold, windy weather. He was not ashamed of wanting to go on land so that he could court his lady, the Nikolaeva, as long as we were working. Three of our people were badly injured, two with the viboffkis (the capstan bar) and one with the anchor stock of the winch. At twelve thirty, we pulled ourselves off the sandbank, after having sat on it for twenty-two hours and having lightened the stern with the help of hawsers and ropes. The *Nadezhda* suffered no other damage but for the copper being rubbed off the keel, since the sea bottom seemed to be rocky.

Ratmanoff seems to understand that it is not a good idea to report ill during work and then immediately after we have pulled ourselves off of the sand to play healthy and want to go on land, because he did not go on land. At four o'clock, we had a lot of work to get our roster onboard again, so that it would not be driven off by wind, current, and waves. The wind was quite strong and a baidara broke loose and caused not a little bit of work to catch it again. They could not get our two jollyboats towed to the ship and had to let them drift to the Rokovaja Bay. Contrary to my expectations, our ship stopped, and we occupied ourselves with putting the deck in order instead of being towed farther. In the evening, around nine o'clock, we had low tide and only three and one-half faden depth, a bad place to be in bad weather. Krusenstern, while resting in the afternoon, turned over the command to Ratmanoff; he acts just like a billy goat. Even though he had acted very stupidly yesterday, today he is strutting around like a hero. His audacity goes a bit too far. When Krusenstern received the report in the evening, it was too late to tow the ship farther. Even though the night was nice, the weather mild, the wind weak, and the moon bright, our people had been so strained yesterday that it would have been difficult to have them work through the night without letting them rest.

Ratmanoff, in order to make himself look sick, tied three scarves around his face; thus, neither yesterday nor today has he been deficient in witty ideas.

Mon. 25/7 At daybreak, we transported our stop anchor three hawser lengths away from us and pulled ourselves free with them. Around noon, we cast anchor and finally found ourselves out of danger.

The soldiers who had come in baidaras that had torn loose from the ship yesterday continued to stay onboard longer than they had expected. Only after noon did a baidara come from land to pick them up, bringing the news that Dmitri Koscheleff had not yet left and wished to come onboard again.

Romberg left immediately for shore to pick him up. We sent the shallop to Rakovaja Bay to fill the empty casks with water. A yard and schkala [шкала: wooden blocks for supporting the mast] had floated over to Rakovaja Bay yesterday, which we are going to have to pick up.

Romberg came onboard at tea with Koscheleff. He has sent all of his baggage and people with Chamekoff and is going himself to remain with us until we set sail.

Toward five o'clock, second mate Spolochoff, who has also been promoted to officer, arrived back with the jollyboat in the longboat from Rokovaja Bay with the news that we could not fill our water casks there. Without being asked and without thinking about the many cloths wound around his face, Ratmanoff offered to go himself to the harbor and take over filling the water casks. His making the matter of especial importance befits of his way of thinking. At seven o'clock, he went ashore, and, at one a.m., the first shallop with water came onboard—as we had suspected Ratmanoff has found his Uriah[4] here. For a tip, the soldier Aksionoff was sent by him onboard with all kinds of unnecessary tasks.

Dmitri Ivanovitsch is awaiting our departure because he knows how indecisive the officers here are. Without Koscheleff, certainly nothing would have gotten all of the people to move the day before yesterday; and we would perhaps have received no help from land, and, if we had needed provisions, beams, etc., Prokofi Michalovitsch Kulmakoff would not have decided to order the things for us without a special order from the General; and since Dmitri Ivanovitsch has the power of attorney from his brother, he can be very helpful to us, if our situation becomes worse than it is at present.

Poor Romberg suffered a second attack of melancholy, hysteria, or insanity this evening, since laughing and crying for hours totally without reason cannot be called healthy reason. That borders on insanity. Exhaustion put an end to the incident.

Our people are very exhausted. Many are already ill, and all of them need peace and quiet. If only they could be permitted peace and quiet!

Yesterday, when we were still on the sand, Vichodzoff with the people who came to help us, sent a promischlenik with an empty bottle and a letter to Schemelin in which he warned him to send the brandy he owed, since he would lose it in case the frigate were to sink.

Tues. 26/8 Our work went faster then I would have thought. The help that Dimitri Ivanovitsch had soldiers provide was indispensable. We have filled all of our water casks again, today put the hold in order, cleared the anchor cables and superfluous lines from the deck, raised the top masts and yards, put everything in order, and raised the longboat onboard, so that we are ready to set sail early tomorrow morning. At twelve o'clock midnight, Ratmanoff returned from Peter-Paul's Harbor very satisfied with himself.

Dimitri Ivanovitsch Koscheleff slept on the *Nadezhda* for the last time. That young man gained our respect and love.

Wed. 27/9 At four o'clock in the morning, during my watch, with a favorable wind, we began our work, took leave of Koscheleff, and took him on land. At six o'clock, we weighed anchor, and, at eight o'clock, we had already sailed past the majack. With sincere joy, I wished Krusenstern the best с походом [for the voyage]. Ratmanoff also slept through this work, and I was happy to see him come on deck when we were already out of the entrance [to the harbor].

Ratmanoff, the day before yesterday, without being authorized to do so, had given Otto Kotzebue the order to go ashore with the longboat. He did as told and received a reprimand from Krusenstern, because he had gone ashore without saying anything to him. This reprimand was necessary, because the two Kotzebues are becoming men and, following Ratmanoff's example the whole time, were having fun with the women here.

- 20 -

Kamtschatka to Macao

Thurs. 28/9 We are seeing Kamtschatka for the last time. Only Mount Strelotschnoi can still be seen. And, soon, we will also lose sight of it. In reality, we are now setting upon our return voyage. It depends upon the *Neva* how fast we will leave Canton and Macao, but we are not there yet.

Fri. 29/11 The American Company's treatment of Krusenstern is inexcusable. The last instructions Krusenstern received from Resanoff stated that he was making him Schemelin's interpreter, and, by means of a letter to Krusenstern from the directors in Petersburg, he is to be informed that he will receive all necessary instructions from Resanoff. Actually, Krusenstern has thereby overcome all difficulties and does not need to concern himself at all with trade in Canton. From Petersburg, Krusenstern wrote, at the request of the American Company, to Mr. Torkler, who was to try to trade in China as a commissioner for the Company. If that man has traveled from the East Indies, then it is nothing more than fair that the Company should pay the expenses of his trip and his unnecessary stop in Macao.

Thus, Schemelin should conduct the trade in Canton. He is going to put up Kiachta stands in Canton. Made wise by his mistakes, he will either have to offer his goods ridiculously cheap or to give them to someone else on commission.

If we do not find the *Neva* there ahead of us or if she has already sailed on, then we are out of the way of all difficulties. Our cargo is not sufficient to take up trade there, because the costs are too great. We would thus fill the ship with water, acquire fresh provisions, and sail on.

Our group at table has increased by three, that is, second mate Spolochoff, now a pilot mate; Raefski, now gunner; and assistant surgeon Sydham. All together we are now sixteen people at table.

Sat. 30/12 Finally, a northerly wind. If we had not sailed out in the morning, the southerly wind would not have permitted us to leave Avatscha Bay, and we would have been held up for several days.

According to Tschitschagoff's directions, every officer has to hand in his journal after the completion of the campaign. This directive is appropriate. For the most part, however, copies of the same ship's journal will be handed in. The Admiralty won't be lacking in makulatur [pulp literature or packing paper].

October

Sun. 1/13 It is Friderici's turn to provide for our table. I only hope that, when he takes over from me, it will not be my turn again.

Easterly wind and thick fog. Fog is the most intolerable in unknown waters.

Mon. 2/14 We are once again sailing to Rio de Plata, probably with the same results as last year. We can only hope for good weather, so that we can at least see some things and, not like last time, set out on discoveries in thick fog and stormy weather.

Tues. 3/15 Krusenstern advised me to forget Baroche's supposition as far as Rio de Oro and Rio de Plata are concerned. I had taken all of it for suppositions and do not believe that we will discover anything. But you have to do something to please those academicians.

Wed. 4/16 A sharp reef topsail wind is inopportune for many on board because it makes the *Nadezhda* roll strongly—we are sailing briskly forwards.

We found a totally undigested silk scarf in the stomach of a cow we slaughtered, which the cow had swallowed ten days before, because the scarf was missed back then. Its green color had undoubtedly led the cow to steal it.

Thurs. 5/17 A brisk, strong, favorable wind. No one on land can imagine how difficult it is on a ship on the ocean, tossed around by the waves from a brisk, strong, favorable wind that causes high seas.

Fri. 6/18 It has been a long time since the barometer stood as high as now. Earlier, Ratmanoff chased his pleasures, and now he is a complete lazybones, eats, drinks, shouts, and utters sacrilege for a change, swears and talks smutty to pass the time, and sleeps. Since the boat was on the sand in Avatscha Bay, his behavior has changed dramatically. He has become much quieter and does not claim, as earlier, decided absurdities; even his bawdiness has lessened.

Sat. 7/19, Sun. 8/20, Mon. 9/21 Stormy, bad, overcast, rainy weather, and intolerable high seas. On Monday morning, the weather was better, and we had set sail again. Toward evening, the barometer began to fall, even though the weather looked clear and calm. Krusenstern had the sails reefed, and we prepared for bad weather. It was already dark, and the weather was still good, until suddenly about nine o'clock in the evening, the wind changed and began to blow fiercely out of the west. This time, I have to confess, I had wished for bad weather and could hardly wait for it, so impatient was I, without knowing why. The cause was probably so that the barometer, in which I have a great deal of trust, would not be called a liar.

Tues. 10/22 Finally, once again clear skies. Toward noon, we caught a large shark, which was raised onboard amidst appropriate noise. High seas from the northeast arose and grew progressively higher. The *Nadezhda* rolled so strongly that the masts creaked; the ship herself had been groaning so long that she was laboring, as they say.

Wed. 11/23 A brisk wind, high seas, and fair weather

Thurs. 12/24, Fri. 13/25 It is difficult to describe the behavior and life style of our company cabin. If a stranger were to get to know each one of us individually, he would hardly believe that it is possible among such really good men to find so little unity. Sincerity and unity are totally missing among us. That causes conversations to be boring and dry. Everyone gleefully tries to catch the next one in an absurdity, especially since several in our group are conceited enough to claim they know everything better and often in making their point become hotheaded and insulting. The result is that most of us withdraw. Egoism is the main cause of the disunity. All people are egotistical. Among us, however, some excel in egoism. Some get the short end of things; if modest ones awaken, then they rave even more than the others, for they are then egoist as a matter of principle. This atmosphere is the reason why no order in the cabin, as well as at table, cleanliness, punctuality, etc., can be maintained. No one wants to make a suggestion for doing something about the situation. Convinced that everyone else will remain silent when the talk turned to that, a lot of disorder is industriously ignored, only to be able to talk about it all the more afterwards. The respect which Krusenstern has gained with everyone still keeps the whole thing within bounds; otherwise, I would not stand for flagrant discord and strife. His gentle character is not of the kind that can keep disorder in bounds. It is a ticklish matter for the captain to mix into the business of the company cabin at all, because he can only compromise himself and help little. Since the will of the captain on the ship is outside the law, he has either to take over the matter totally or to do as Krusenstern does, not mix in or worry about it.

Ratmanoff is the eldest officer in the cabin. He could make suggestions to create order and by doing so create general satisfaction. He, however, by his coarse behavior, bawdy language, self-conceit, and imperviousness, which have aroused little love, is not qualified to do it. And, despite that, he could and would concern himself with the matter, if he had not made it his rule to censure everything connected with Krusenstern and the *Nadezhda,* and industriously to let everything take its course so that he can criticize and utter sacrilege all the louder, indeed even to attribute to Krusenstern mistakes and weaknesses that his black soul alone can discover. Well, that is then Ratmanoff's trick. In actuality, he is a dry, straight, merry man. When we left Kronstadt, all of the officers on the *Nadezhda* were the same. In Kamtschatka, Ratmanoff was promoted to captain lieutenant and the equality stopped. It would not have had any consequences if he had not appropriated authority that was not his. Krusenstern is very much in the wrong for having let him take it over, but now it is too late to change that. A coldness between Ratmanoff and the rest of us officers had to be the result.

Romberg does not want to spoil his relationship with anyone, shuts himself up in his cabin, and does not mix into anything. Often, Golovatscheff has had strife with almost everyone, which many have not yet completely ended and forgotten. We know that he hangs his coat according to the direction of the wind. Everyone is friendly toward him. Sincerity and warmth are missing, however. Bellingshausen does little to help by showing his cards. He has a lot of falseness in his character and brings little education from the Cadet Corps, has an open mind, is bitingly witty and dogmatically, he says, "путяки" [stupidities], and thus he has done his job.

I have enough to do to keep my impetuosity in bounds, often make suggestions for the well-being of everyone with self-renunciation that, however, help none, have never found a bosom friend among my comrades, have, however, their respect and affection. One can expect no better arrangement of us.

Espenberg's egoism finds its justification in this disorder. Friderici is very wise not to mix in anything. The same for Horner. Tilesius and Schemelin can do nothing, and the rest have no voice. That is the reason this general burdensome disorder will end only upon our arrival in Kronstadt. Our maître d'hôtel [chief steward] Ivan, Ratmanoff's servant, obviously takes charge of us in this chaos. No one considers doing anything about it, and just as before we are eating badly for a lot of money. Every day, Espenberg finds new whims and lays claim to new prerogatives. Tilesius has his, and whoever had no whims and passions lays claim to some by saying, "Why shouldn't I make things comfortable for myself, too?" Both Kotzebues are following the example of their mentors and are being shortchanged. We are conducting quite a bad marriage. Mutual interest is missing. Coldness and indifference take its place. Disunity and disorder prevent sociability.

Sun. 14/26 Strong gusts of wind forced us to pull in our topsail. (The шкаторина [boltrope] on the foretopsail and the марса шкота [topsail sheet] on the large topsail were torn.) That happened at eight o'clock in the morning. The sky looked threatening, and the barometer had fallen. Krusenstern ordered the topgallant mast be lowered. The wind was actually still weak. Ratmanoff could not stop himself from making allusions to the work going on, called it unnecessary anxiety, etc. An hour later, we had a complete storm and the advantage of having already done all of the work, and I gleefully laughed at Ratmanoff for his prophecy. A lot of sharks and dolphins swam around our ship in this bad stormy weather. Their freshness caused us to cast out a fishhook, and we caught six large sharks one after another. We also caught two exhausted land birds including an owl. We are now in the same latitude in which we were in that typhoon last year.

Sun. 15/27, Mon. 16/28, Tues. 17/29, Wed. 18/30, Thurs. 19/31 Very bad rainy weather and continuing high seas, which throw the *Nadezhda* around unpredictably. We have had only one clear day since leaving Kamtschatka. We caught a water raven today and had a very strong thunderstorm with unbelievably strong rain showers, which soaked us all до нитки [down to the last penny], as the Russians say, and was replaced by a nice clear evening.

Espenberg has been ill for the last eight days or more or claims to be, racks around his cabin, is now and then seasick, always however eats well, and refuses to accept any help.

Fri. 20/1, Sat. 21/2 Clear, quiet weather. We are looking in vain for the Malabrigo Islands. We have been seeing tropical birds for the past eight days. Today, we caught a shark on a hook. Since it was so large, we wanted to cast a loop around its body. The fish however broke loose; the hook ripped through its jawbone and upper jaw, and with unbelievable speed it disappeared.

Sun. 22/3 In the so-called *Hors Latitudes* [sic] we are also having calms. Today, bonitos (a kind of mackerel) appeared.

For lack of feed, we found ourselves forced to slaughter our cow and her calf. She had generously supplied us with milk up to now. The poor animal suffered a lot during bad weather, even though we had put a band or kind of berth around her body, so that she would not suffer damage through the rolling of the ship. (Cui Consilium retracted the death decree, and the cow stayed alive.)

In the evening, poor Степан [Stepan] got several holes and bashes on his head. (He fell head first into the hold.) We were afraid that he had damaged his skull. Luckily, he came away with only contusions.

Mon. 23/4, Tues. 24/5 When we have 22° warmth on deck, the heat in the gun cabin goes up to 27½°. That is also unbearable. It is absolutely impossible to sleep there, even though the windsail is continually up.

Wed. 25/6 The contrary, very quiet, mild wind detains us on our voyage. In the last five days, we have made little progress.

Thurs. 26/7 We caught sight of South Island according to King. At noon, we found ourselves about eight miles farther south than it is on the map.

Fri. 27/8 We passed South Island, to the south, so that we could determine the length of the island.

Sat/ 28/9, Sun. 29/10 Northerly wind. Saturday, we passed the Tropic and are again getting used to the warm and hot weather.

Mon. 30/11 Today, we put our anchor cables on the anchors. This evening, during my watch, Krusenstern came on deck to give me orders before going to bed. During the evening meal, Espenberg and Horner had argued. The dispute became more and more violent until it turned coarse and abusive. Espenberg's racket screeched louder than the creaking of the ship, the roar of the water, and the wind. Krusenstern patiently walked up and down the deck, waiting for the noise to stop, and went into his cabin.

Tues. 31/12 Espenberg has assumed for himself a lot of prerogatives and rights. The *Nadezhda* does not offer many conveniences. He uses the captain's gallery, with

Krusenstern's permission, of course. Since first this one and then that one is served first at tea and at table, he tries to get the most advantageous spot for himself, often sitting on his chair an hour before mealtime, anxiously and imploringly calling it his seat, if he happens to have to get up, so that no one else will take it. At tea, he has one place, at lunch another, and at the evening meal a third. At tea, he sits on the right side of the table next to the tea machine. At lunch at the top next to Krusenstern, if possible, and at the evening meal at the middle of the table on the left side. (On a ship, this is all the more noticeable, where everyone has his place that he keeps throughout the whole voyage.) If it happens that he, even though he sought out his place at the table, by chance is the last one served, he bawls the servant out, as if a catastrophe had happened and acts very wretched. At tea, he always argues with Stepan (Krusenstern's denschik [servant]). Either the tea is too sweet for him or too bitter. God forbid if he should get no milk. Of course, that is often the case for the rest of us because Espenberg serves himself generously. (These caprices are the reason why we let the servant pour tea, which we had earlier taken turns doing ourselves.) If the meal is not to his taste, he has something else cooked (from our provisions), and in order to legitimate the extra cooking he plays ill. While eating and drinking, if he is not served first, he asks the servant immediately (heatedly and touchily), "You are probably not intending to give me anything!" often simply because the person next to him receives a clean plate earlier than he does.

If at table a place is empty because someone has gone ashore or has business on deck, he tries to use the empty place to his advantage, shoves and turns the chairs until he can sit broadly and comfortably and totally satisfied and comfortably, then rubs around on his chair. If a good, tasty dish is on the table, he takes no notice of the fact that others want some of it, too, piles his plate so full that some of us get none, and, in order to keep his plate from causing a scene, he gobbles up his portion before the bowl has gone around. (Sometimes, we intended everything to be divided into portions). Only too often, he supplies himself at table with delicacies for the next day (at breakfast), undisturbed if others suffer because of it, carries his booty with very quick steps into his cabin, and hurries back because we have not finished eating. We have barely sat down at table when he shakes a supply mustard, vinegar, pepper, sugar, etc., on his plate with such anxiety, as if we were going to take the nice things away from him or he would get none if he did not hurry. He does that almost every day. With wine and brandy, he is even greedier. It is too bad that all too often Tilesius follows his example. It is however good that Espenberg comes a bit to reason and seems to comprehend that he takes things too far, but that does not hold for long.

If we are all sitting around the table busy working, he disregards the fact. If someone does not want to get jumped at, he makes room so that he can sit down mightily and give the two Kotzebues lessons in grammar, French, etc., etc. While we are drinking tea, he shaves himself at the same table and does not let anyone deny him the right, even if some of us from repulsion leave our tea undrunk, to wash his beard in the water pitcher. Mornings, he walks around in his dressing gown completely at ease when everyone else has long since dressed. If a remark is made, he immediately acts ill. In disputes, he always has to be right; if it does not go his way, he becomes angry, biting, and coarse. Since he is always irritated and immediately acts ill, he has gained the right for himself to tell everyone crudities unpunished. Whoever lets himself get in a dispute with him and does not give in has to hear coarse remarks. He immediately goes to extremes. If one pays him tit for tat, he becomes coarse. If you give up for the sake of peace and quiet, then he says either straight out or indirectly, "See there, what a dumb fellow you are, and how intelligent I am." (He has extensive knowledge but expresses it however very indelicately.)

In the presence of the Kotzebues, he does not excuse himself. That others do not want to compromise themselves he finds ridiculous. If being insistent does not help, then he puts forth his age. (He is the oldest in years on board.) His age also has to excuse a lot of other freedoms and peculiarities.

He is a poltroon. You are supposed to believe he always plays well behaved, no matter how inappropriately he has acted. (I also think that he is upright. His anxiety outweighs, however, all of his other feelings.) If there is something unusual, he always wants to be the first one to have it and pretends that you have given it to him in the first place. If he does not see something, then he says, "You are doing that deliberately. You want to make me angry, even kill me."

If you buy a rarity that he does not yet have, he claims that everyone has something except him, that everything is bought from under his nose, that we do everything to keep him from getting anything. (Espenberg is a good doctor but lazy.) If a sailor has injured himself, the ship rocks heavily, or there is bad weather, he groans acutely himself and considers whether he should go to help the person or leave the business to Sydham. Usually he goes, finishes a completed job, bawls out the victim more than a little for his having had to take a couple of steps around the deck. From laziness, he himself, though totally healthy, plays ill, has himself served in his cabin, and eats heartily of his extra food. His good appetite never fails him.

He is a bit ashamed in front of Krusenstern, but he takes no notice of the rest of us and acts as if no one were present. He is always doing battle with his chamber pot because the thing is often turned over and soils his things. He mostly grumbles with himself, growls, and is angry with himself.

If he wants something or has something made to which he has no right (his chamber pot also belongs in this category), he begs, complains, orders, and argues secretly with Stepan and Ivan until he gets what he wants. If he goes from ship to shore or shore to ship, he acts as if everyone has to wait for him. If this does not happen, then he spews fire; but, to wait himself for a moment, for that he has no patience. If he goes around the quarterdeck, then he is the only one who obstructs everyone else, because he anxiously wants to make room for everyone instead of walking straight ahead and acts as if everyone should make room for him. He ingratiated himself with Tolstoi and Resanoff, I know from good intentions, for Espenberg is a right good man, but, since he does everything for the sake of his own enjoyment and of eating and drinking well, appearances were against him. We were discussing what was more bearable, heat or cold. Espenberg was for heat, and, since he heard too much against this, he finally said very angrily, "If I knew that it was cold in heaven and hot in hell, then I would rather go to hell," and ran on deck because he could not hold his anger in bounds any more.

November

Wed. 1/13, Thurs. 2/14, Fri. 3/15, Sat. 4/16 Clear weather and favorable winds.

Sun. 5/17 We found ourselves, according to the ship's calculations, around forty miles from Botol Tabako Hsima and one degree from Formosa. The wind became variable, and the skies became covered with a bank of clouds. Since we will soon have a new moon, we were able to expect nothing good. At noon, we established the zenith. The favorable wind from the north was becoming ever brisker. At two o'clock, I had my watch. We were carrying the topgallant sail, studding sail and the jib. The fore studdingsail had become slack. The waves were rising, and I talked with Horner about the topmast's breaking, etc. Then Krusenstern came on deck and ordered the studdingsail hauled in and the awning cleared away. This had barely been done when our main topyard broke. I am thus the first one to have something important break during his watch. We immediately took the reefs, and before sunset we had a brisk reef topsail wind. Neither Krusenstern nor anyone of my comrades mentioned the incident; only Ratmanoff, who was on deck, seemed to take pleasure in it. I had, in addition, done everything possible, so that I could not be accused of carelessness.

Since we had determined our position exactly through longitude and latitude, we sailed in the night between Formosa and the Baschus, even though we could not see land in the overcast weather.

Mon. 6/18 At eight o'clock in the morning, we caught sight of several mountains on Formosa in the distance. Thus, we had entered the [South] China Sea. The dancing of the waves is very strong; nevertheless, they are not high, a result of the confined water.

Tues. 7/19 We sailed past Pratas without seeing it. There is hardly a seaman who wants to become more exactly acquainted with those traitorous reefs. The wind is brisk. We have not sailed less than 7 or 8½ knots.

Wed. 8/20 At daybreak, we caught sight of Chinese junks, and in the night we almost sailed over a junk. Since sailing through the straits between Formosa and the Baschus, we have had a strong current from the west at two to three miles an hour. At twelve o'clock, we sailed past the Island of Lema, raised the flag, and requested a pilot by means of cannon shots and the Emperor's flag on the foretopmast. Soon afterwards, a fishing boat came out, and two Chinese undertook piloting us to Macao for 70 piasters. We had to pay four piasters for a weight of fish, because we had not bargained and haggled ahead of time.

We had sailed by Pedro Branco at three o'clock a.m. and caught sight of that isolated rock only at five thirty, at sunrise. Staying on the drift while waiting for a pilot had held us up. It was already dark, and we were still far from Macao. Since we had, however, passed all of the Lee Islands, we sailed on even though it was pitch dark, and the wind was becoming ever brisker. The rain was also making the night ever darker. We guided ourselves solely with the sink lead. A number of Chinese fishing boats—countless numbers—were prevented by the strong wind from approaching us as they appeared to want to do. At seven o'clock, we dropped anchor in 6½ faden.

The wind, which was becoming stronger and stronger, forced us to let down the top yards and masts and also the lower yards. And with fifty faden of anchor cable, we withstood the wind without knowing where we were, since the darkness of the night did not let us see land, even though we were surrounded by it.

Since passing Formosa, we have accomplished the impossible. We sailed through the straits of Formosa in a dark, stormy night. Early on the 18th, we caught sight of several mountains on the peninsula in the distance. We were held up about eight hours by calms, sailed in the night of the 19th past Pratos, passed Pedro Branko at three o'clock of the night on the 20th and cast anchor near Macao last night, after having made 9° or 450 miles in 36 hours, that is, fifteen miles in an hour, the hours during calms and on the drift included, thus actually 450 miles in 26 hours. It will not be easy for someone else to do the same thing. The current and wind do not favor everyone, and not everyone has the great confidence in astronomical observations that we have, letting us venture to sail through such dangerous passages in the dark of the night.

- 21 -

China

Thurs. 9/21 We found, after a stormy, unpleasant night upon awaking, that we had cast anchor rather far from Macao.

At nine thirty, since the wind had become milder and the sea quieter, a comprador (Chinese commissioner) came onboard with a pilot, since the wind had become milder and the sea quieter. After Krusenstern had completed the proper agreements with them, he gave me the task of going with the Chinese boat to Macao and announcing our arrival to the Portuguese governor and paying our respects. While I was on my way ashore, the *Nadezhda* weighed anchor and sailed for Taipa.

Macao is a nice city built of stone but empty because all of the merchants and traders are in Canton. The English innkeeper Bodwell met me at the landing and accompanied me to the governor's, whom I did not find at home. When I returned in half an hour, I found him home and Mr. Bachmann (*Second of the Dutsch Factory* [sic]) with him, who knows Krusenstern personally—good luck for me since he served me as interpreter. I had the charge of reporting to the governor that we intended to spend some time in Taipa. The flag of war caused some difficulties.

Bachmann maintained that we could not sail in because of the low water before *Spring Tides* [sic] (the high water with the new and full moon). Therefore, the governor thought that Krusenstern himself should come tomorrow or send me to obtain permission for that. In reality, the *Nadezhda* had already arrived in Taipa, which not one of us suspected.

The governor showed me a letter of recommendation that he had received on Resanoff's and our account and was very polite. Before I left, I wanted to go to the English supercargo. Bachmann advised me, however, to return to the ship, because it could become late, and, in the evening, pirates threatened the area. I was sorry about that because I later heard that the English Factory had received letters for Krusenstern.

The pirates are heavily armed here. They have several hundred armed boats, many of them 300 ton in size with ten canons and over 300-man crews. A month ago, they took an American merchant ship, killed everyone onboard, took possession of the cargo, and burned the ship. The flotilla of fishing boats we thought we had seen yesterday at our arrival were these pirates. Only the strong wind protected us from their attack.

Not long ago, these ladronen (pirates) took a Portuguese two-mast ship and likewise massacred all of the people onboard. Another ship saved itself with difficulty, by using its cannon and выстрела [cannon shot] (spears and poles) to keep the boats from coming close to the ship. Usually, a Chinese fishing boat comes and anxiously announces that the ladronen are coming. You can also recognize them by the numbers of vessels and their boldness and especially the numbers of armed men on each boat. For Europeans, it is very dangerous to kill a Chinese—capital punishment for that. Letting the pirates get too close however is dangerous. If you want to trade in Canton, it is hard to determine what you should do. My answer: basically shoot the Chinese and not worry any further about them.

Our comprador supplied us immediately with provisions, and we put on our moorings.

The captain of an English brig also anchored here came over to us and was so impolite, that he put everything down on paper that Krusenstern told him about the Dutch and Nangasaki. Since he wrote down everything, every word, too eagerly and without consideration, Krusenstern said less and less and told him, "You are taking all that trouble in vain, since what I have told you cannot be considered official or of use for anything. It is and remains a private conversation, and I hope that our conversation will be seen from this point of view."

The Americans are supposed to have taken 15,000 sea otter pelts to the Chinese market, and a pelt now costs only 24 piaster (Spanish dahler). No ship of an English company has arrived here yet. They are expected.

Fri. 10/22 An English brig sailed into Taipa with us and weighed anchor again today. She sailed in only to find out who we were, to hear news from us, and to find out if we had seen Dutch or French ships, probably in order to pursue them. In the morning, Krusenstern and Romberg went onboard the brig. At noon, Friderici joined them, and we went on land where Krusenstern wanted to pay the governor his respects and also to stay overnight in Macao.

We have loaded all of our cannon with cartouches, since it is said that the pirates venture into Taipa. Recently, the ladronen set an English brig on fire at night.

26 English China vessels are expected here around Christmas. It is said that within three weeks of their arrival they can set sail again with the cargo they have acquired.

For the first time since leaving Russia, four of us comrades have discussed what we can do, so that those going ashore leave the church in the middle of the village and prevent quarrels. That is how intense our curiosity is.

Sat. 11/23 Krusenstern returned onboard. In the afternoon, we took our cow and calf on land. Bachmann thought, since up until now most of Germany has been supplied with Chinese wares by the Dutch, they would be the ones most afraid of suffering if Russians also were to bring quantities of Chinese goods to Europe.

Some time ago, a Portuguese accidentally killed a Chinese in a fight. The relatives of the Chinese came to terms with the murderer and took 3,000 dahler smart money, complained however afterwards to the viceroy (John Took) in Canton. He demanded, according to the law and agreements, the extradition of the Portuguese. The governor of Macao is not doing that because he considers the matter finished and resolved. The viceroy therefore ordered all of the Chinese stands in Macao be closed and forbade all deliveries under the threat of death. This caused a great embarrassment for the Portuguese. The governor of Macao, in order not to have to give a démenti himself, had the murderer hanged. And, since this still did not seem to satisfy the viceroy, the Portuguese put Macao on defensive alert. All of the cannons in the fort were loaded and the troops mustered. Several days before our arrival, reconciliation took place, because the viceroy settled the differences and explained that he was satisfied with reparations.

Chinese ingenuity is very great. A fellow sits there with a balance scales and weighs things for passers-by for 1 kopeck, even if it is only a pebble. There are large numbers of sleight-of-hand artists, etc.

The English frigate which arrived yesterday claims to have lost her masts in a typhoon. Rumor has it that a French frigate took off her masts.

Bachmann has been so generous as to promise us to get everything from Canton we need, in case we do not sail there ourselves. He also suggested loading the *Nadezhda*, if Krusenstern can give him sufficient assurances. Krusenstern, however, cannot do that, since the American Company does not want Krusenstern to mix into its affairs and no one will give Schemelin a pfennig of credit.

According to Chinese laws, no vessel may stay longer than one day in Taipa (except for vessels of war that in turn may not sail to Wampoa). Krusenstern therefore found it necessary to declare the *Nadezhda* a ship of war. If the *Neva* comes, then Krusenstern will have to give a déminti and turn the *Nadezhda* into a merchant ship again in order to be allowed to sail to Canton. Our cargo is hardly sufficient to pay expenses and duties in Canton. Krusenstern will not accept Bachmann's offer because he does not want or intend to become involved with the American Company. Neither Krusenstern nor Schemelin have instructions concerning Canton. We basically do not know what we are supposed to do. It is certain only that Krusenstern will be responsible for everything, because he alone knows the conditions here and can and has to direct our complex situation here, so that the Russian flag causes no dishonor, since its appearance here has aroused attention.

Sun. 12/24 We put ourselves on new moorings. The scholarly faculty went on land today. The English Brig *Horrier* had taken a French merchant vessel several months ago in a storm. The prize ended upon the shore (or reefs) near Pedro

Branko and Chinese fishermen completely stripped the vessel. The *Horrier* came to Canton to lodge a complaint with the viceroy. Every ship of war is forbidden to sail to Wampoa. The brig, aside from gunpowder and balls, had no cargo and got as answer from the viceroy that it is not just to demand things back that he himself had stolen. Over and above that, no one paid any attention to the *Horrier*. No one bothered with her. She returned to Macao without accomplishing her intentions. The Viceroy of Canton (John Took), however, punished the Hong[1] with an enormous sum. Panquequa[2] alone had to pay a 150,000 dahler fine (the Hong consists of 12 merchants) for the English ship of war having dared to come to Wampoa.

The Chinese add the sum to the price of their wares, and in this way the English in reality pay the fine themselves. That is the Chinese way. The Chinese merchants are punished for every breach that the Europeans commit in China and then have the right in turn to have it paid by the Europeans, because the Hong has a monopoly on all of the trade. The captain of the *Horrier* will at least get a toss in the blanket from the English government.

Our cargo consists of 400 sea otter and 10,000 kotik pelts; the former at 24 dahler and the latter at ½ dahler add up to only 14,600 dahler, little enough to afreight the *Nadezhda*.

Mon. 13/25 We have taken down all of the riggings and are repairing them. Our cannon are however always loaded because of the ladronen, and small arms are kept in repair and preparation.

Today, three Chinese carpenters began repairing our cabins. For painting the ship, they want 290 dahler.

Tues. 14/26, Wed. 15/27, Thurs. 16/28, Fri. 17/29, Sat. 18/30, Sun. 19/1, Mon. 20/2, Tues. 21/3 Krusenstern is living solely at Drummont's home. (The same house in which Macartney also had lived.) The garden is not very large, but the enormous boulders in it make it really nice. In one of the boulders, there is a Comoen's grotto. The English have turned over the company house to us. Since the house has no furniture, we prefer life in the inn (English *Punchhouse* [sic]). Tilesius is living alone in it to save money. A young Frenchman from *Isle de Frenie* has said of Tilesius, with whom he had become acquainted, "He has bought himself a ham and is living like a scholar."

The man assigned dejour works on the ship; the rest of the time we spend in Macao. Every day, the shallop returns heavily loaded from Macao, for Krusenstern has paid us our wages. And, since it is still in doubt if we will sail to Canton, everyone is trying to purchase Chinese wares here.

Horner had a stroke of genius. We would like to get a Chinese skull for Dr. Gall.[3] But how were we to go about it? We all doubted that the wish would be possible.

At the gate to Macao, hanging on gallows in wooden cages, were the decapitated heads of several Chinese pirates. Horner's plan was to steal one of these heads, the surest way of getting a Chinese skull. We talked about it a lot, but no one thought of carrying it out. Two days ago, I slept with Horner in the same room at the inn. In the morning, when I woke up, I found Horner's bed empty. Not long afterwards, Horner came in exhausted and tense—with a ladronen head, which he had stolen from the gallows, in a handkerchief. The head (still unputrefied) was tossed onboard and put in lime and then cleaned. (This incident is and remains the only one of its kind.)

It takes a lot of patience to trade with the Chinese without being cheated. They make capricious demands and change their prices hourly. They sell everything by the pound, the best way to cheat. Since the agreement with the Chinese carpenters is by the day, they are working very slowly.

Every day, you hear again and again about the ladronen. Therefore, we are continually ready for them.

Schemelin, the fool, is also beginning to make plans, if trade does not work out here, to sail to Manila and to use our money there.

The Chinese mark themselves by long nails on their fingers, and the Chinese women by deformed, small feet.

On the twenty-first, we got the unexpected news that the *Neva* is sailing past. She is however still too far away to be visited.

Wed. 22/4 The *Neva* has brought 140,000 fur seal pelts, 5,000 beaver, and 15,000 other pelts. Krusenstern intended to sail immediately with the *Neva* to Canton, but the Chinese government is not permitting that any more because we already have said that we are a ship of war. Therefore, Krusenstern has sailed to Canton to work out permission.

The *Neva* sailed shortly after her arrival last year in the fall from Kodiak to Sitka, where along with Baranoff they had a battle with the savages. Three sailors on the *Neva* were shot to death. The second mate got a smashed arm, and Povalischin and several others were slightly wounded. For this battle, Baranoff has given Lisianski 2,000 rubles, each officer 1,000, and each sailor 100. In the name of the American Company, he has promised each of the wounded their wages for life as pension. The *Neva* wintered in Kodiak and was in Sitka twice this year. On their trips back and forth, they got stuck on a sandbank in the open sea for two days at 26° northern latitude and 160° longitude and afterwards sailed into a heavy storm (typhoon), in which a lot of pelts were ruined; a lot of them had to be thrown overboard. The officers estimate 30,000. The cargo now consists of:

5,000 beaver pelts @ 25 dahler	125,000 dahler
4,000 river otter @ 5 dahler	20,000 dahler
2,000 otter pelts @ 3 dahler	6,000 dahler
6,000 fox and sable pelts @ 5 dahler	30,000 dahler
130,000 fur seal pelts @ ½ dahler	65,000 dahler
	246,000 dahler
	15,000 the cargo on the *Nadezhda*
Total	261,000 dahler

Not counting the 30,000 pelts thrown overboard.

Thirteen wounded sailors were on the *Neva*, including some who were quite badly wounded.

Lisianski speaks with high praise of Baranoff. His officers, however, are very dissatisfied with him.

Tomorrow, the *Neva* is sailing to Canton. Krusenstern and Schemelin are making the trip, too.

Thurs. 23/5 Our chronometers have been in Macao for the past eight days, and, on account of this, Horner has also had to live there. Friderici and Moritz Kotzebue have moved into the company house without telling anyone. Metkoff should have been told ahead of time. At eleven o'clock, the *Neva* weighed anchor and sailed for Canton. Ratmanoff, Romberg, and Golovatscheff brought us the following news from the *Neva*.

In Kodiak, Lisianski was very generous with wine. Since it belonged to the whole company at table, the officers requested an accounting to see how large their expenses had been up to then. On the account, which Lisianski and Berg had kept, were three bottles daily. They all, however, knew too well that one bottle at a time had appeared on the table, remarked about that, and the scribal error in the account came up for discussion. The company at table separated, and since then Lisianski no longer eats together with his officers.

Since the *Neva* has departed from us, they have found that the account which Lisianski kept never agrees with the ship's account. When the ship was stranded on the sandbank, the officers themselves established the latitude and longitude of that unfortunate spot where they had been stranded. The latitude was not much different, but the true longitude differed from Lisianski's record by about eight degrees. Since then, Lisianski has admitted that he had deliberately done that and always recorded incorrect longitudes and latitudes, so that no one else could make use of the discoveries he was making for the American Company.

The sailors on the *Neva* are very dissatisfied with Lisianski. They intended to ask Krusenstern to mitigate their situation. (Lisianski often capriciously has his people whipped with the cat.) Our peaceable sailors advised them to hold out until they are back in Russia and complain there.

Fri. 24/6, Sat. 25/7, Sun. 26/8 I left and went ashore, have, however, to stay onboard most of the time to direct the business with the compradors and the Chinese workers, especially with the painting of the ship.

Mon. 27/9 Bachmann is worried that the chance for us to do business will be taken away under his nose by our hope of getting permission to sail to Canton. In the morning, I visited Melkoff, who has invited me over to lunch tomorrow.

The Frenchman Jean Alexandres Satéles from the *Isle de France* treated us today with schampagner [champagne]. He is having his ship loaded incognito in order not to be taken as a prize by the English. He is a good-humored, happy man and amuses us with his calculations and speculations.

The day before yesterday, Horner and Romberg had an angry dispute. Romberg wanted to remove the supports from the table, and Horner maintained that they were of use and was right—always tension.

Tilesius has business piling up and does nothing, and his Chinese Sancho Panzo (paid lackey) is cheating him wherever he can. Tilesius complains to us about it and is nevertheless weak enough not to send him to the devil. Espenberg is now also living on land, cares for himself, and comfortably slurps his cups of coffee.

Tues. 28/10 Horner, Bachmann, and I ate at Metkoff's. The whole dinner was boring; huka, Turkish calian, or the smoking of tobacco through water prevented all conversation with its bellowing. I liked the schruds or Chinese cigaros better.

The Bengali splendor shoots through the bones of all of the English here and makes them unsociable. They appear also to have other basic laws here than in Europe.

Wed. 29/11 I visited Bachmann, who has been complaining for a long time that I do not visit him and received through him a letter from Canton.

Our ship has been totally painted. On 4/16 December, we have been invited to the governor's for lunch, the name day or whatever of the King of Portugal.

The Chinese are going to come onto our ship to see for themselves whether we are a war or merchant ship. I am curious to see how they will do that. The Englishman *Scheffield* [sic], because he is sailing to Canton, took along a letter to Krusenstern.

The innkeeper Bothwell has us pay mightily. The English also have horse races here and give golden and silver goblets as prizes. Also big bets are waged. Since, at present during the trading period everyone is in Canton, there is no talk of that right now.

Thurs. 30/12 Satéles and an American visited us. The table was set, and they stayed for lunch. The meal however was very bad. We had to try to make up for that deficiency with good wine. A good mood repairs a lot of things.

December

Fri. 1/13 Ratmanoff and all of us officers received a formal invitation to go to the Governor of Macao's for lunch on December 4.

Sat. 2/14 Overcast, bad weather. Seventeen English East Indian vessels arrived here today.

Sun. 3/15 We put the ship in order again and are keeping ourselves ready to sail.

Mon. 4/16 On the birthday of the Queen of Portugal,[4] we saluted with a 21-gun salute and put our people along the yards. In accordance with the invitation, we found ourselves at noon at the governor's. The party consisted of fifty people. The table was overloaded with dishes, served twice followed by tea, and at seven o'clock we departed, well fed and well loaded by the many wishes of good health. Every guest had his own servant along to take care of him, give him clean plates, etc. If a gentleman left a lot on his plate, then the rascal put it aside and enjoyed it himself. The servants in the house found this unpleasant, and a Portuguese got in a fight with a Moor, who wanted to stop him from his handiwork. It was unpleasant for all of the guests. The Moor was removed, and the practice was taken up again. We Russians were served by the servants of the house and very honored. Romberg also brought home a good crackbrain or hangover.

Tues. 5/17 I visited Bachmann in the evening, drank tea with him, and had the pleasure of hearing Madame and Mademoiselle sing a very pretty Dutch aria.

The Chinese have inspected our cargo, and tomorrow they are intending to bring us or obtain the chops (permission).

I visited Bachmann in order to make amends for my inappropriate laughter. In the morning, Bachmann came to the inn and said that Luqua (a Hong's merchant) would be coming to take a look at our cargo. "No," said the comprador who was present, "that is Auqua." Now both of them got in an argument for probably half an hour and only the words Luqua, Auqua, Kequa, Kaqua, etc., were to be heard. I could not stop myself and broke out into a loud laugh, which ended the dispute. If we get only to Canton, it is all the same to us if it is through Luqua or Auqua. Poor Bachmann has nothing to do, and that makes him sullen, since the Dutch have no trade at all here.

I had also gone to Madame Mitkoff's to pick up Krusenstern's portrait. She very kindly showed me her shell collection, which is very large and nicely arranged. Tilesius promised her a box of shells and did not keep his word. I plan to make amends for his stupidity with my own shells and will take her especially a paper nautilus.

Wed. 6/18 Everyone came onboard with sack and pack. Tomorrow we are expecting the chop. Ratmanoff, Horner, and I made our final visit at the governor's to take leave.

Bachmann has been very helpful and congenial toward us. Since we have ordered various things through him from Canton, it is nothing more than fair, since we are now sailing there ourselves, to buy the things from the merchant from whom they were ordered. He left us the choice of slaughtering the cow or selling her, since she is not giving any more milk, or he will get us another cow that is giving milk in Canton. His plan for Russian trade is as follows: six Russian merchant ships have to be in commission so that two ships can arrive in Canton every year. The expenses of establishing a factory are too large. Business could, however, be carried out through agents; and he would be most willing to be the Russian agent. He is requesting of us to let him know fourteen days before we depart from Canton because he is planning to write to Amsterdam through us, and the letters are important to him.

A French shipper named Huje, who owns his own ship, came to Canton a couple of years ago speculating he could load his ship there. He was anchored a long time idle in Wampoa. A Chinese merchant from whom he had not expected it gave him a credit of 30,000 dahler in goods and loaded his ship. He was barely ready to sail when the ship caught fire, and ship and cargo were destroyed by flames. Huje was not in any condition to pay the Chinese his debt and needed fortitude to bear the pain of his own loss. Unexpectedly, his Chinese creditor comes to him and says, "You are no longer able to pay me if no one helps you. Even if you wanted to, you do not have the means or opportunity to do so. Buy yourself the ship that is being offered. I still have 40,000 piasters in goods on stock. They are at your service for an indefinite amount of time, and you can pay me what you owe me when you can." Tears of thankfulness streamed from Huje, and he accepted the offer, is supposed to have already paid off most of his debt and in addition is supposed to have earned a nice fortune.

Scheffield, whom I have got to know here, told me his life story. As a young man he had been a smuggler, and he like many others had plied this trade for several years, until he got in a battle with a *Customhouse boat* [sic] that wanted to arrest him. A frigate that happened to be sailing past took him prisoner. Scheffield avoided punishment because he was so young and volunteered to be a sailor on the frigate. He served for several years as a sailor. Thanks to his behavior and knowledge, he was promoted to mitschmann and after a stated number of years *master* [sic]. In this position, the ship on which he was serving took several prizes. His portion came to 25,000 dahler. He left the ship not wanting to serve any more (which is not permitted in England) and went to Gibraltar to get his prize monies, was detained there, and had to serve on gunboats. When we (I) came with Admiral Korzoff and a convoy to Gibraltar in 1799, the Spanish convoy boats had done battle with the English, and the battle went to the disadvantage of the English because the cannon had cracked on the English convoy boats. At that time, Scheffield was badly wounded. After his recovery, he was promoted to *Master* [sic] and Kommandeur and was given a brig to command. He had barely left the harbor when he was captured by a Spanish frigate and taken to Livorno [Leghorn]. In Livorno, Scheffield bought himself a merchant ship, sailed with it to America, picked up his brother there; both of them loaded three ships for the fur trade, have had a quite good voyage and are now in Canton, where they are doing good business and will return to America well off people. That is the dissolute life story of an English sailor.

Shipper Chase and Supercargo Hikin (as it seems also the same kind of geniuses as Scheffield) came on the ship *Criterion* from Friendships in the Fiji Islands (Feedgee) with a load of seal pelts and sandalwood. They had accompanied a large boat from Tongatabu carrying savage men, women, and children to the Fiji Islands. Upon their arrival, the savages from Tongatabu went on land for permission to settle there. The King of the island had them congenially invited to him, allotted them a place to live and a spot to pull their boat on land.

The following day, the savages left the ship with sack and pack to go on land in order to take advantage of the king's permission. One man and one woman remained onboard to pack their things. The savages had barely landed their canoe; they had not yet had time to look around, when they were attacked by the Fiji Islanders and all killed. In order not to be killed by the rage of the Fiji inhabitants, the two savages had to stay onboard and make the voyage to Macao, where we have seen them and where Chase told me their story. He has to leave them behind in Macao because it is forbidden to take a European woman to Canton (foreign woman).

Thurs. 7/19 The pilot came onboard at ten o'clock. We weighed anchor, left Taipa, and sailed to Lintiny, where we had to anchor because of a contrary current. Ratmanoff gave the pilot 20 and the comprador 200 dahler at their request. May they not cheat him.

Fri. 8/20 We sailed to Bocka Tigris. A shallop came over from an English frigate with the question whether we were French. I answered, "No!" and without a further question my Englishmen rowed away. When we were sailing past the English ship of war *Blenheim*, Michael Ivanovitsch Minitskii, who is serving as a volunteer on the ship, came over to us unexpectedly. Minitskii, like Lisianski, has also forgotten how to speak Russian in the two years he as been a volunteer in England, since it has not been any longer than that.

Sat. 9/21 At eight o'clock in the morning, the pilot went on land in order to show the mandarin his chop, and at nine o'clock, Romberg went over to the *Blenheim*. He could have gone earlier; he had been awakened in time. He was also met by the English shallop in which Minitskii sat and was going to Canton, and thus had to turn around and come back onboard without having been on the *Blenheim*.

Two mandarins came onboard our ship in order to accompany us to Wampoa. The current permitted us only to go (*abreast of the Island* [sic]) to the Island of Lamee (Lami) where we cast out anchor once again. In the evening at eleven o'clock, the old comprador came to us whom Krusenstern had sent from Canton to get news of us. (This comprador met the *Neva* at sea when she arrived, had immediately recognized her as a Russian ship, and named Lisianski by name, before anyone on the *Neva* could dream that someone knew that they had come sailing in).

In the evening, Golovatscheff, Bellingshausen, and I wanted to find out how strong the current is. We took a log line and threw it out. In order to establish the current more precisely, we turned the second glass over four times and stopped at four knots. When we wanted however to pull in the line, nothing happened. We investigated and discovered that the pilots in the boat behind the ship had caught the log line and pulled it in as fast as we had let it out, and thus had all of the knots in their boat, and we were, as far as the current was concerned, no smarter.

It is quite something that the comprador has found us in this pitch-dark night.

Sun. 10/22 At ten o'clock, we weighed anchor. We caught up with an English merchant East Indian ship and cast anchor between the second and first bar. The whole day we spent solely in turning the ship. We drifted with the stream and had contrary winds in that narrow passage. We had to turn every three to five minutes. In the evening, when we had cast anchor, the *mates* [sic] of the English ship visited us. They absolutely did not want to believe that we only had thirty sailors. That ship was stuck with five others on a sandbank stretching from Bocka Tigris to here. It is named the *Coots,* has a draft of 26 fuss and weight of 1,800 tons. Her anchor weighs 65 *hundred weight* [sic]. Several ships came together in this narrow passage and badly damaged each other. The ships are supposed to have a lot of sick onboard.

In the evening at ten o'clock, we weighed anchor again and let ourselves drift to the first bar. The Chinese towboats are lazy and are a hindrance more than a help. Today, the comprador came from Canton with the news that Krusenstern would come onboard as soon as we anchor in Wampoa.

The captain of the *Coots* has been in the East India Service as a captain for 25 years, has already gotten 100,000£ three times, intends to retire, and has always spent his wealth in a couple of years, has entered the service again, and now is acquiring, as an old gray head, for the fourth time his plume (a fortune of 100,000£ sterling)

The mandarins accompanying us are quite nasty fellows as concerns the pilots. We now have four compradors. I hope that Krusenstern reduces the number to avoid confusion and unnecessary expenses.

Mon. 11/23 In the morning at ten o'clock, we weighed anchor. The narrow passage was filled with English East India ships. Several were on sand; others drifted with the current and took up all of the room, so that it appeared almost impossible to sail past them. We maneuvered with unbelievable tenacity. We often turned the *Nadezhda* before she obeyed the wheel, drifted, and sailed so close to the English without touching them that you could have jumped from one ship to the other, up to the first bar where an East India vessel was stranded on the sand and blocked the way. We were being driven straight at the ship. Ratmanoff yelled at me (since it was my watch) to put the *Nadezhda* on the sand. I did not answer but continued to work to get us past her and not end up on the sand. We had to pass so close to the ship that yards and ropes began to catch and tangle, turned our ship so that we were out of danger, because the current at that point flows at a right angle. And the wind, which had been contrary to us, suddenly became favorable. I could not control the ship, so we were on the East India vessel, smashed everything to little pieces, and were stuck on the sand ourselves. Now, the ship gave us the windblind luck and attention (because I have taken everything by the horns myself, since everyone was still as a mouse and awaiting what was going to happen to us), got the *Nadezhda* to turn, and, without damaging anything, we were free. Then I told Ratmanoff, "I am so worn out from commanding that I have to turn my speaking trumpet over to you." He took the speaking trumpet gratefully from me, and now we sailed with one topsail set in the topgallant sail past the ships in Wampoa like lightening. (In Wampoa the ships are all standing at anchor like a row of pearls one behind the other.)

With a practiced eye, I chose a spot for us to anchor and cast anchor like experienced seamen at three o'clock in the afternoon not ten faden from the *Neva*. (It makes quite a figure when a ship in brisk winds and under full sail suddenly casts her anchor.)

Bellingshausen went with the *Neva*'s cutter to Canton to report our arrival to Krusenstern. And I went to the Danish East India vessel to turn over letters for Europe and to ask for permission to fasten our cable to their ship. The *Neva* has been unloaded and is ready for careening.

Schemelin and Korobitzin are in Canton conducting their business.

A Chinese merchant has come to Schemelin in order to recommend himself and to give him his address. Schemelin considered it an invitation to lunch. Only with difficulty could others explain to him that the address was only an indication where he lives, so that you can find him when you need him. Mitschmann Berg of the *Neva* acted as an interpreter with Schemelin and Korobitzin, a very flattering business.

Tues. 12/24 The *Neva* moved over toward us for careening. During this period, the officers and sailors will move onto the *Nadezhda* and live with us.

Wed. 13/25 I went with Krusenstern to Canton, glad to be away during the time that the *Neva* is being careened and that insufferable Lisianski is living with us.

Halfway between Wampoa and Canton is a nice little island called the *Dutsch Folly* [sic] (the stupidity of the Dutch) and correctly so. A couple of hundred years ago, the pirates took revenge as they are now doing at the mouth of the Tigris. The Chinese government was unable to have done with them. The incorrect governmental regulation of giving the leaders of the rebellion, who accepted the government, the title of mandarin, caused a lot of others also to join in. And instead of having fewer pirates, the number increased daily. The Dutch undertook to get rid of the pirates, if the Chinese would give them that little island as a marketplace. That happened with the condition that the Dutch were not to fortify the island and also not to put any cannons at all there. The pirates were eliminated and the Dutch settled on the island, were, however, able nevertheless secretly to get cannon there. The Chinese government found it out and took the island away from them again.

Thurs. 14/26 I visited Beal and Maniok, our commissioners, and Drummond, the head of the English factory. At the latter's place, I saw Captain Hay, commodore of the East India fleet, an old, hoary head who has been serving as captain for twenty-five years, has consumed three fortunes, and now is acquiring his fourth and also Captain McIntosch, who put his ship on sand near Ceylon, in order not to end up in the hands of a French ship of war.

In the beginning, I lived upstairs at the factory, moved down, however, to make room in case several from the ship should come on land.

Tilesius, who is always a fool, had to stay behind on the *Nadezhda* because the Chinese did not want to let his voluminous baggage come to Canton. (Why these problems?)

The factories look very good. In front of every house or factory is a national flag, and all are built in the same manner and next to each other. In addition, there is an open place and in front of it a landing for boats.

Every factory has its own street with a gateway that is closed in the evening, and the houses are like a very large coil, like Breit St. in Reval; that is probably how long they are, more clearly like the Russ St.; everything under one roof.

Fri. 15/27 You have to be very careful that the Chinese, who are great pickpockets, do not steal your handkerchiefs, watches, or money out of your pocket. The number of thieves is so large that you are literally surrounded by thieves. You barely catch one who has put his hand in your waistcoat pocket and give him a couple cuffs than another one steals your handkerchief out of your hand and disappears into the crowd and gone is your hanky.

The beautifully made Chinese goods are leading me to spend money.

Sat. 16/28 The factory buildings are very large. We are living in the so-called Tschau Tschau Factory, where everyone who does not have a national factory rents space. In the house, you find bare walls, at the most tables and chairs. In less than half an hour, the Chinese compradors furnish it with dishes and food stuffs to the smallest trifle, for money goes without saying with a promptness that is only made possible by the number of people in China.

The fact that the *Nadezhda* and *Neva* were so close together caught the attention of the Chinese. The mandarins had asked how we were able to do that without having a tschop [chop] allowing it. They were sent to Krusenstern, and, since they did not inquire again, the *Neva* was careened without further problems. But Lisianski behaved stupidly and coarsely in the process and had also to hear a lot of quite coarse remarks for it. He told his officers while pointing at his plotnik [carpenter], "He has more brains than all of you." He told Ratmanoff, while taking him aside, "Don't just let everyone be the commander."

Because Bellingshausen contradicted his egotistical orders and said, "Our ruslin [chainwale] is no worse than your broadside (наш русленъ не хуше нашего борта), and I will not permit you to smash our ruslins," and he was right. That peeved Lisianski the most.

The Chinese merchant Kinlong, the only Chinese whom Krusenstern could remember having met when he made his first trip to China on an English ship, dined with us at the factory today. The Chinese in Canton hardly know that Russia carries on a lot of trade with China in Kiachta and that Russia even borders on China.

Sun. 17/29 I visited Metcalf and Sir George Staunton.[5] Krusenstern went to Wampoa.

Mon. 18/30 Krusenstern returned with Lisianski, Ratmanoff, and Minitskii to Canton. Tilesius also came to Canton. The first night was terrible for him because he was too cheap to rent a mattress.

Tues. 19/31 Here on the first of January, Krusenstern, Horner, and I dined at Drummond's at noon. Bird nests and everything that counts as hautgout [haute goût: high taste] for me was served with Bengali splendor and lavishness. The dinner party consisted of over one hundred people.

The manner of living here is as follows: at nine o'clock in the morning, you drink tea (*Scotsch Breakfast* [sic]) with toast and eggs. At one o'clock, a tiffin[6] is handed out, which consists of brandy, rum, wine, beefsteak, etc. At five o'clock, you take off your shoes and socks and go to lunch and sit at a table. Tea is served into the night. Politics and trade are the subjects of discussion. Everything is exquisite luxury. The question is whether there is greater expense at table in Bengal.

Canton has the great advantage that a new arrival with cash can get everything needed that belongs to a well-appointed house in several hours. If he wants to, he can give a party on the very next day. The compradors and hourly wageworkers understand how systematically to defraud and cheat. Without a chop, nothing can be taken to and from Canton. An English longboat with Bengalis wanted to take umbrellas (parapluis) they had bought to Wampoa. The mandarin did not let them through. The English therefore got rid of their parapluis and then no one stopped them from leaving.

Today, I visited two Swedes, Chalmers and Lingstäte, whom I have gotten to know.

As long as Lisianski was having the *Neva* careened, Schemelin and Korobizin decided to accept the price for the pelts that Beal had got for them. Lisianski came to Canton and found the deal already closed. Beside himself with anger, he raved and swore at everyone and said, "If I had been there, the Company would certainly be richer by 20,000 dahler." (I say that Lisianski would have perhaps been cheated even worse.)

When the *Neva* came to Canton and the hoppo requested an explanation because of the *Nadezhda*, especially why we have declared the *Nadezhda* a ship of war in the beginning. Krusenstern related the whole truth. "No," said Lisianski, "That is a lot. We are complete equals." Krusenstern continued to maintain firmly, however, what he had said, and Lisianski had to be quiet. At Beal's, the talk was again of it, and Lisianski began to talk in a tone, as if he wanted to say, "We have nothing to do with each other."

To my joy, Krusenstern told him firmly and loudly, "You need only to give me that in writing that we, and especially you with me, have nothing to do with each other. Tomorrow I will weigh my anchor and sail to Russia." Lisianski reacted as if he had been hit in the trap, for he had not expected that from the patient, mild Krusenstern. He became better behaved from that time on.

Drummond carries a great deal of weight here. John Took and all of the mandarins respect him, and whatever he wishes happens. It is said that he will be staying here for another year at the most. Staunton is said to be so good in Chinese that he is considered a scholar among the Chinese.

Wed. 20/1 Lisianski, who lives separately, dined today with his entourage (Berg and his mate) in our factory at noon. Lisianski again could not stop from bragging and running others down. Ratmanoff had drunk a bit too much, and that peeved him, and he held up all of Lisianski's bad traits and actions to him, unfortunately very coarsely. A huker (calian) looks so elegant. Therefore, Lisianski now smokes his tobacco from a huker. (Lisianski would know how to behave very well as a satrap.[7] He is despotic enough.) It was not correct of Ratmanoff to make him look foolish with his huker.

The booths in which dolls and such stuff are sold, the painters' and cabinet makers' booths, and the silk booths were a lot of fun this afternoon, and the thieves are scummy beasts. No thief hangs around me because they have found out that with me the handkerchief is hanging out of my pocket, so that if a pickpocket tries to take it, he will get several well-placed blows with a cane. Poor Raefski also came to Canton. We advised him to be careful. He had barely entered China Street when a bunch of people shoved around him as if that were the way it was. Soon the bunch of people disappeared. Raefski put his hand in his pocket, and they had stolen everything, his money, his handkerchief, and everything movable.

Thurs. 21/2 Krusenstern came onboard. I put my purchases in order according to their importance. The merchants Cutsching, Yingqua, and Wooschıng are cheats. They try to steal anything they can wherever they can, are however also agreeable. I caught them cheating several times. Now they have promised to trade honestly. I did not believe them and was very right in so doing, for not long afterwards they again tried to cheat me. If you do not take precautions with the Chinese, then the stealing begins at home. There is a saying here: the person who has been in China and not been cheated is still waiting to be born.

A Chinese cheated me out of my drape overcoat. I had gotten a spot of tar on it and gave it to a tailor to turn, which costs officers and sailors ten dahler. My overcoat was worth much more than that (that happened in Macao). The tailor never came, and I am without an overcoat. I gave the comprador the task of getting my coat back. "You turned it over to the tailor yourself. I do not know him," he said, even though he had seen him on the ship every day and we knew the tailor's name from the compradors.

Pautoff, one of our sailors, bought himself a chest of tea very cheaply. The following day he inspected his purchase and found a little tea on top and the rest of the chest filled with hay.

They sell India ink made from clay, etc. Many of our officers have been shown quite nice boxes painted black with this India ink and already gilded.

Fri. 22/3 Kovedaeff is the most anxious and willful of us when trading and nevertheless has often been cheated. He would have liked to have stayed quiet about it, so that he could say, "The Chinese have indeed never cheated me." We were however present, to his sorrow, when he wanted to brag and discovered he had been cheated.

The English pay what is asked and come out quite well doing this, have to pay somewhat more, but then are not cheated. The Chinese say. "*Can see can save*" [sic] (If you see the goods, then you know or recognize what they are). The English do not bite, however, and say: "If the goods are bad, then you have to know we will bring them back because I want the goods to be good."

I was with Ratmanoff in a cabinetmaker's booth to buy a stand that had been offered me for ten dahler. An Englishman came into the booth, and the Chinese immediately asked 18 dollars for the stand in our presence.

In the evening, I went with sack and pack back onboard to Wampoa.

Sat. 23/4 Krusenstern bought a new boat for 250 dahler. I cannot make myself like the thing. Lisianski immediately offered us his cutter (the rotten thing) in order to get our jollyboat and to buy himself a new shallop. Envy is the main trait of Lisianski's character.

Sun. 24/5 As strictly as it is forbidden by Chinese laws for a Chinese woman to consort with Europeans, greed for money also overcomes these laws here. At night, a mandarin always goes up and down the river in Wampoa as patrouille, and nevertheless "*fresh meat*" [sic] (girls) are brought to the ships in the dark. The boats have six rowers and the girls lie like anchovy in them so that the mandarin cannot see them. If a patrouille approaches they flee at the speed of an arrow.

An American took the liberty of flying a Russian flag, a blue cross on a yellow field so that if his people committed dumb tricks, they would not be responsible for them. I went onboard and asked about it. He gave the excuse that it was a signal flag. I asked him determinedly, in order to prevent misunderstandings, to take down that flag, which is too similar to ours, and to raise another. Since he did not do it, Ratmanoff sent the comprador to the mandarin, who immediately went out to the American and did not leave until the flag had been changed.

The compradors and Chinese speak a mixture of Portuguese and English with the Europeans here, for example, "Can see can save" (Inspect what you are buying; if you are cheated, then it is your own fault). "Me save you save: me sawe walke Luhsa Fuschin." That is how the wage lackeys recommend themselves when asking for jobs and means: "I know how to go in the Russian manner." The sense of it is, "I want to and understand how to do it the way the Russians want it done." "Save, wissen, save walke." "I know where I should go."

"Me lusi," I lose; "You täki," Take; "Chop or Tschop," the legal permission from the mandarins; "No wantje," do not have; "Me täki," I take; "Mäki bad büse," Make bad business deals; "What büse you mäki," What kind of deals do you make?; "Cou chou büse," all kinds of business deals. The Americans are called "second chop Englisch"; sanpan, a boat; ladrone, sea pirate; "You pleasi," if you like it; "You täki," Take; "You no can sawe," You cannot know that; "Less," Russian; "Pluss," Prussian; "ungari," hungry; "Please taki no please no täki," If you want it take it, if you don't want it, then leave it alone. "Musse fusse," One has to do that. "Me no save schip, me save your face last voyage," I do not know the ship, I know, however, your face from the last trip here. That is what the Chinese said to us to recommend themselves, as we are in China for the first time. "All make so much trouble," They are all causing so many problems. "Pinterman," painter; "silek," silk; "Chinamen so much afear," Chinese are so very fearful; "You no save the pleise," You do not know the price; "so much a boberi," so many rascals, etc., etc., etc.

Mon. 25/6 Our sailors were given schabasch permission to get together. All of them were drunk, but the day passed without noise. In the evening, Schigalin was caught for having smuggled a girl onboard.

Ratmanoff has invented a new punishment. Kurganoff and the locksmith Svagin had to spend the holidays at the forge because of drunkenness. Schigalin and Loginoff, for disobedience, had to tow the *Nadezhda* while at anchor against the current. Pigalin was put under arrest on the block because he had, without permission, kept company with the mandarin next to us, probably to buy schamsehn (rice brandy) and also was drunk. Pigalin reported ill. He was given a cold bath until he reported well again.

Tues. 26/7, Wed. 27/8, Thurs. 28/9, Fri. 29/10 Painting the cabin, even though necessary, is very troublesome. We have made room in the hold to load tea and to fill our water casks. The Chinese charge a dahler for every cask of water. Only the air is free in China. We have to unload ballast. The Chinese forced us to buy a spot on the wasteland next to us, where we now have permission to throw our ballast. If you need the same ballast later, then you have to buy it again.

At their own expense, the Danish ships had had a small magazine and smithy and huts built on a deserted island. We wanted to buy them from them when they departed. The Chinese did not permit that but said, if we wanted to, we could build a similar building next to them for a price. Since we considered that expense superfluous, we were content to use two large, rented boats which we loaded with the things that were in our way for the time being.

Sat. 30/11 Lisianski is greedy for everything. I told him that Captain Aikin of the *Criterion* has promised me a pike from the Friendship Islands. Immediately, Lisianski went over possibly to get it. In the afternoon, I also went over to the *Criterion* to remind Aikin of his promise and found no one onboard.

Things look bad with Golovatscheff. He is very melancholy, gloomy, and quiet. He also does not look healthy.

Sun. 31 / 12 I visited an American ship from Manila. He [the captain] told me that the rich cargoes from Aquapulka [Acapulco] to Manila were no longer transported in golconen as before but rather in small vessels.

In the morning, Minitski came over to us, and, in the evening—yes, in the evening—"*fresch meat*" [sic] was passed up. Ratmanoff also had sent for one.

1806—January

Mon. 1 / 13 We went over to the *Neva* to our war buddies there and wish them a happy New Year. We had barely been there an hour when Lisianski came up in his Aleutian boat. He barely granted us a nod of the head. When we were taking leave—we did not stay very long on the *Neva*, but long enough to watch how he had a sailor whipped for nothing and again for nothing simply because he was peeved. The sailor had recently bought a new silk jacket for the New Year, took it off after the whipping and threw it overboard while saying худая обновка [bad new little coat] (a bad new blow). When his sailors requested permission to go over the *Nadezda* today, he did not dare, however, to deny them this because we were present. It was unpleasant for him. You could see that in the quivering in his face. Lisianski is a bad man.

Drunken people are unbearable people and all of our sailors and the sailors from the *Neva* were staggering drunk today. Our locksmith was schamscha [шамша: babbling] and the sailor Nikolai Stepanoff, who had a quarrelsome drunk, could not be contained. He was coarse, disobedient, and noisy toward everyone. He only became silent when he had filled up so full that he could not move either a hand or foot.

The concept of virtue varies. The Chinese joy girls, if they are on a ship, go with one man and do not take up for that day or that visit with another. Our sailors wanted to teach them that that could readily be done, wanted to introduce wantonness. They however did not succeed.

Tues. 2 / 14 We caulked our ship and painted its outside with oil paint.

In the afternoon a small dead child floated past our ship on the current. That is often the case here. They claim these drowned children are of European fabrication.

In the evening Krusenstern came on board with the news that we will probably set sail in fourteen days.

The Chinese painter extorted fifteen dahler more for the room in which the crew lives because it was not expressly stated that he was supposed to paint it. The Chinese make a base with coagulated blood.

Little shabby boats continually go up and down the river in Wampoa and fish with little hooks (cats) everything that is on the bottom that has been thrown overboard by the ships and live from that.

Wed. 3/15 The comprador is a wily rascal and is with all of them of the same class. We were not permitted to send our longboat to Canton with the empty bottles to so that they could be filled with the wine we had bought. Nor was it permitted for the longboat from Canton to be loaded with our purchases. The Chinese said, everything had to be brought on board with the chau chau boat (the last boat) (the chau chau boat is a large Chinese boat with which everyone with sack and pack is taken onboard and leaves Canton. Povalischin told me that a lot of Aleuts die while out hunting fur and even more while hunting birds and looking for eggs by falling off the cliffs to death. Even a greater part of them starve to death for lack of food. One party had taken so little food along two years ago, but they continued to row in the hope of killing sea animals. They landed in America. Driven by hunger they collected clams on the shore and ate them. Unfortunately, the clams were poisonous and in a few hours 180 men died, only a few remained alive, returned to Kodiak and reported the unfortunate incident, that people die of hunger is said often to be the case in that area. Where? where a man can catch in one day as many fish as is needed to live for a whole year.

Anecdote from the *Neva* and Lisianski's partialness. Kovedeeff had watch. Lisianski ordered the commando called on deck. All of the sailors came except for Egoroff (Lisianski's tattletale). He was called again "вот тебя на" [that is just it], he called from the hatch, "I do not have my trousers on yet," and he, in addition, swore and railed. Kovedeef complained about it to Lisianski. He remained silent and smiled.

A half hour later Egoroff was going around the quarterdeck. Lisianski went up to him and said, "Give me a bit of tobacco." That is the discipline on the *Neva*. Exactly that Egoroff was just now in Canton with Lisianski. He met him in the factory with a bottle of brandy in his hand. Lisianski ordered him: "Throw the bottle away!"

Egoroff obeyed with the words, "That is too much, that a man dare not buy brandy for his money." He got a couple of cuffs across the mouth for his answer, whereupon Egoroff grabbed Lisianski by the chest and said: "I know how to deal with you, Baron Lauditz taught me that." Lisiansi, pale and pallid, let him go and hurried into his room and has not tried to punish the sailor, but the next day, he was reconciled with him again. Egoroff had served with Lauditz earlier before coming to the *Neva*.

When Lisianski came on board on New Year's Day and found that Povalischin had given schabasch, he asked: "Why have you done that?"

"Because the sailors had grumbled about also having to work today," and he could see that the work would not be done.

"Who grumbled?" asked Lisianski.

"All of them," said Kowedeeff and Povalischin happened to point with his hand at a sailor who then got the cat and embittered about it threw his silk jacket over board. For that Lisianski had blocks put on his feet.

"You cannot take more than my life," the sailor called after him. Lisianski did not dare to leave this determined fellow on the deck because he was afraid he would throw himself overboard into the water but send him to the hold under guard. On the following morning, the punishment was taken up again. The poor fellow is now quite ill. That all happened because the sailor would not let himself be used as a tattletale, and Lisianski since then has a grudge against him.

Thurs. 4/16 Our new cargo was brought from Canton. 824 chests of tea, 80 balls of nakin, and 15 bundles of cane. There is no nicer cargo to have in the hold than tea. The chests stand so evenly there and form a deck. In six days Krusenstern is going to have us towed to the first bar, in nine the chau chau boat is coming, and in 12 days we will hopefully leave China.

Krusenstern was so generous and turned over to me a part of the Madeira wine that he bought here. I intend to save the wine for my old father and that is why it is twice as valuable for me.

Fri. 5/17 We filled most of our water barrels, loaded our salted meat and ship's provisions. The work left for us is to clean the ship, pull up the shrouds and repair the boats. The ship is now stuffed full. When the chau chau boat comes and these things are put on board, we will no longer be able to move on shipboard. We have problems all the time with the Chinese. In the end, you lose patience if you are continually cheated. We worked until late in the night to get the two boats emptied, which were loaded with our provisions since we had to pay them 12 dahler daily.

It was beginning to get dark when a large ship arrived and cast anchor not far from us. While putting on moorings the ship came too close to us. We did not know the language. Krusenstern sent me onboard to find out where the ship was coming from. I had barely gone on deck when they let the anchor carelessly fall striking a man. He screamed so horribly and all of them were yelling and running for the doctor. I therefore did not stay, asked a sailor where the ship was coming from, and left again. It was an English ship from Bombay, mostly manned by Indians. That is why the language seemed foreign to us. All in all, the English have a lot of Indians, Chinese, so-called Siepoys, etc. on their ships.

Sat. 6/18 We did not have a holiday. Krusenstern went to Canton. Our sailor have not sense of proportion. It is not possible to keep them from buying schamsche [alcohol]. They drag girls onboard every night. It is time that we leave Wampoa.

Sun. 7/19 We painted the quarterdeck with oil paint. The painter only causes problems and rascally tricks and comprador trouble.

I visited Scheffield and Aikin.

In the evening, we received a letter from Krusenstern in which he announced that an English officer wants to travel with us to Europe, and Ratmanoff brought the news that Krusenstern had given his consent.

Mon. 8/20 Espenberg brought the news from Canton that the Englishman, who wants to travel with us, is an officer in the Husars.

He is not going with us, Krusenstern wrote today. Today poor Aikin sent me the pikes and weapons and word that he had fallen so unfortunately that he has broken his collarbone.

Tues. 9/21 When Broughton on his voyage arrived in Port Jackson, several captains and officers visited him from the ships lying at anchor there. While Broughton went on deck to greet them, two monkeys that he had in his cabin got hold of his papers and ripped them all to pieces. Broughton, as an excuse for his bad mood, invited them all to his cabin and said, "that is the report I am supposed to send to the admiralty," and pointed to the pieces of paper lying around the cabin.

Simpson and Bischop, whom I have got to know here, were present at that time in Port Jackson. Broughton, to replace the loss through the monkeys, took the journal and the drawings of his first lieutenant as a help and put a new map together. When it was finished, he asked Simpson to visit him in order to inspect them, because Simpson had been at several of the places himself. He found a great many discrepancies, brought his maps and now the greater discrepancies became apparent. A closer inspection showed that Broughton had taken incorrect variations or deviations of the compass. He put the blame on the astronomer on his ship. This person answered, "I did as the officers of the ship did and followed the Captain's orders. I will personally hand over my remarks to the admiralty." That is the reason that Broughton's maps have become known with a corrected compass (unity on the ship was also probably not very great). Before Broughton ran aground on sand near Japan, his lieutenant, sailing in a schooner next to him, warned him. Broughton's imperviousness could not stand having anyone tell himself anything. He sailed straight ahead and shipwrecked.

Flinders, upon leaving Port Jackson, did not sail to England as the commander of a vessel but rather as a passenger. His first lieutenant had received the commando through Governor King.

Flinders suggested sailing through the Straits of Torres. They had just got to *"Saturday Night"* [sic] when the ship hit a rock and stopped. The vessel had had 16 cannons. They had been sailing 9 knots. The force, after several jerks put the ship so firmly on the point of rock that it could not move any more. Aikin saved part of the crew and the ship's baggage on his ship.

The guzzling and debauchery has got so out of hand with our people that Ratmanoff had to seek the help of the cat. The little punishments returned order, and we watched out for the little Chinese boats with girls in the night and greeted them with several pails of water, so that they will also stop visiting our people. Several of our sailors are burned, others are sick from drinking too much schamsche.

Wed. 10/22 We received a lot of sacks from our comprador (oma petja) with whom I argue freely every day. Romberg and Golowatscheff are having their busts made of clay colored.

Thurs. 11/23 Arbusoff brought the news that, for unknown reasons, a lot of mandarin would be coming to guard us with the order not to let us sail from Wampoa. Also, all of the painters, carpenters, tailors, compradors, etc. have been forbidden to come onboard. Ratmanoff sent the shallop to Canton to report this to Krusenstern. In the afternoon, we received a letter from Krusenstern, but the messenger did not want to come onboard, and in the evening our shallop brought the following news. The old governor, who was supposed to be replaced, now, without reason, is not inclined toward us and is causing this difficulty on account of the grand chop. They are saying that in a few days all difficulties will be raised. Luqua, our *Security Merchant* [sic] (the Hong merchant who had represented our interests) came himself today to Wampoa in order to take care of everything, to convince them in Hoppo to give our compradors, painters, carpenters, etc. a chop so that they may come onboard again.

Fri. 12/24 No Chinese came onboard, and we did not get any fresh provisions. That is why I went to Wampoa to the Mandarins in Hoppo in order to asked them to give our comprador a chop, otherwise we would of necessity have to send word to Canton and complain about them. I got as an answer that the compradors, painters, and carpenters would be sent onboard immediately. I went from there to the *Neva* to let Arbusoff know. He had however already sent his jollyboat to Wampoa and ordered that provisions be bought there. Since yesterday, there has been a big ship near us and the *Neva* with several mandarins guarding us. We sent the shallop with our report to Krusenstern in Canton. This dumb business can take its time.

Sat. 13/25 According to a letter from Krusenstern, the mandarin guard is to stay. The comprador, the painters, and the carpenters are to get a chop so that they may come onboard. The governor who arrived several weeks ago wanted to nullify all contact between Russians and Chinese for an unexplained grudge and that is the reason for the difficulties. Since however at present, he is being replaced again by a different one, Krusenstern is hoping that everything will be taken care of in a few days. The Hong or the Plenum of the Chinese merchants have assured Drummond, who has taken up our cause, that we would not be held up.

Sun. 14/26 And, nevertheless, the Chinese are still holding us up. Upon our arrival, the governor gave us permission to trade. We paid the taxes set by law and did business. Peking however had not been told about us (that is what the others as saying). Now that he is supposed to be replaced, he has tried to redress his mistake by the sudden interdiction to trade with us and is supposed to have reported the entire incident to Peking. That is why it is being claimed that we will not be free to go until an answer on our account comes from Peking. (Our situation is rather similar to the one in Japan.)

The Captain of the *Surinam Castel* called to me when sailing by that Krusenstern, because of the difficulties with the Chinese, will not be coming to Wampoa today. Hamilton came from Canton.

The Chinese have also not released the boat with the load of tea for the *Neva*.

Mon. 15/27 (The Hoppo determines the amount every ship has to pay according to the distance between the large and mizzenmasts and the breadth of the ship. The direct amount for the *Nadezhda* was 8,000 dahler and the indirect probably was just as much. On December 22, they measured our ship with a lot of ceremony.

Since the painters had still not come, I went to the mandarin, to the *Chop House* [sic] where permission or the chop is given. Since I acted very sensitive, the mandarin put the blame onto the painter and the painter on the mandarin, so that it remained in doubt who was at fault for the loss of time.

At noon, Golovatscheff and Minitski came from Canton and related that Krusenstern has written John Took a letter which Drummond is to deliver. At Panquequa, Drummond met the Hong and convinced them to dispatch a letter to the governor. The Hong was surprised and angered that Drummond has taken up our matters. They had barely left, when they came back and had changed their minds, that is, they wanted to write a letter to John Took themselves. Drummond did not permit that saying, "If you have delegated the sending of a letter to John Took, then you have to keep your word," and then they parted.

Tues. 16/28 Arbusoff brought the news from Canton that the new John Took has returned Krusenstern's letter and requested that he give other causes. That first letter had the following contents: since the retiring governor had taken the taxes for the two Russian ships and by chops permitted trade, we could not explain the reason why trade was now being forbidden and why we were being held up and, mainly, why we had not been told immediately upon our arrival that trade was forbidden, etc., etc. and now petitioned to have the interdict raised.

Wed. 17/29 Krusenstern came on board. His letter had been sent back to him. The Hong had again suggested writing a letter which is however filled with so much chin chin (please, please) that Krusenstern had to write a second letter, in which he asks for the reason why we are being held up and hints that the incident could have consequences and requests and hopes that John Took will let us travel without further difficulties.

Thurs. 18/30 Krusenstern went to Canton again. The *Nadezhda* has finally been painted and looks quite good in her new dress.

Tomorrow, we are supposed to receive a decision from Canton.

Pox have already killed several on the American ships, and since the people are imprudent, things can get worse because almost every ship has Indians aboard, indeed on several, half of the crew.

Fri. 19/31 Bellingshausen returned from Canton. No answer has come to Krusenstern's second letter.

Lisianski almost got in trouble. He always acts arbitrarily. In Canton, he gave his Chinese servant a couple of strong boxes across the mouth. The Chinese took it wrong, grabbed his master by the collar and would have certainly thrown him down if people had had not answered Lisianski's calls and yells. The sole satisfaction that Lisianski had was that he got rid of the man.

Sat. 20/1 Drummond, who thank goodness is taking up our matter, called the merchant community together and asked them to the Hoppo and requested a quick answer to the letter. They requested within two or three days—that is what Krusenstern writes.

Sun. 21/2 I went to Canton in order to hear the good news that John Took has answered and given permission to make our chau chau boat ready and that in several days for sure the Grand Chop should be ready for us (the Grand Chop is the attest that one has left no debts behind in China and that the government is satisfied with the conduct of the ship.)

Mon. 22/3 Lisianski's chau chau boat has been dispatched. We are still loading ours.

Tues. 23/4 Today everyone left Canton with our chau chau boat. Horner and I are both staying behind because of the chronometer and to pack all of the instruments that cannot be done without until the last moment.

Wed. 24/5 The two of us also went on board and arrived as the chau chau boat was being unloaded. The boat was loaded with 120 bales of nankin and small trifles.

Thurs. 25/6 We put everything in order and have the longboat on board. The afterstem was 16 fuss 5 zoll the forestem 15 fuss 6½ zoll, consequently a difference of 10½ zoll. In the afternoon, Krusenstern went to Canton to make his final leave-taking visit.

Fri. 26/7 Drummond said when the merchants were causing difficulties, "I am sorry that I do not have sufficient influence to serve you in the matters, as I would wish." Without Drummond's help the Chinese would have taken us.

Everything in China is received and delivered according to weight. Weighing all of the things from the chau chau boats takes a lot of time, and in order not to be cheated and have things stolen, you have to patiently check numbers and weights. The work proceeded more quickly than we expected.

The loading of the things into the ship, because of her narrow hold caused difficulties, especially since in the turmoil several suspicious people opened their chests to see if everything was still in them and took up so much space that the chests and bundles had to be stacked sky high on the deck. Finally we had everything in the hold and, then since Tillesius, befuddled, does not know himself what he had packed in his chests, boxes, and bundles, wanted us to rearrange the hold again so that he could get his shoes that he had forgotten out of his chests. In answer to the question which box his shoes were in, and whether the chest was on top, so that he could perhaps get to it and take his shoes out, but if the box were down under, he would have to wait until we arrived in Kronstadt, he said that he did not know where he had packed them. We laughed at him. Tilesius became angry and was left without shoes.

In the morning, we wanted to weigh anchor. The weather was too windy for it.

Toward noon, Kursenstern returned from Canton carrying the Grand Chop.

In the evening, we took on chickens, ducks, geese, and pigs, which made more noise than all of the crew and officers together, especially since upon receiving them, I got the brood enough time to shit themselves out. I also had the satisfaction of seeing the whole deck covered so completely by the brood that you could not find a clean spot the width of your hand. The comprador ran behind me to weigh the brood, until I finally prevailed upon him to stop. I had asked my comrades and our sailors to prevent me from weighing them so that the comprador did not notice the trick, and I could gain time with it.

The compradors let the brood a day or two before delivery starve, and then a quarter of an hour before delivery, they let them eat as much as they want to of fodder mixed with sand and stones, so that the ducks and geese have stone-hard crops when they are brought onboard, and of course weigh so much more because they have eaten. Our brood was very slim when it got on the scales, and the comprador looked very concerned at the manure that was lying finger high on the deck, then that was his pure loss. The Chinese understand how to overcount and to take advantage.

Sat. 27/8 We got a lot of letters from Canton to take along. In the morning at ten o'clock, we removed the moorings, and with a favorable wind, we weighed our second anchor in order not to come together with an English ship, cast anchor again in order to wait out the contrary wind. About one o'clock in the afternoon, we weighed anchor again and pulled ourselves past one ship after another out of the narrows until the last ship, from whence we pulled ourselves with a warp a couple of tow ropes farther. At six o'clock, we stopped the warp to await a favorable wind and current. At eight o'clock, we weighed anchor again, passed the first bar, and at 12:30 in the night, we cast anchor again because of contrary winds.

After Krusenstern had taken care of all of the bills with the comprador, paid him the money owed, and everyone else had settled accounts with him, before he left our ship, he gave everyone canned ginger, oranges, and dried fruits in big pots, including all of the sailors—and the Chinese left us.

Our sailors were very exhausted. Eskelda Istrekoff, who was sent in the evening to bind the jib, was so tired that as soon had he had done his duty, he sat down on the bowsprit and immediately fell asleep. Not long afterwards, he lost his balance and plop he was in the water, caught hold of an anchor rope and came back on board unhurt and in a good mood.

Sun 28/9 Actually, it has to be the **29/10**. I have miscalculated by a day which can easily happen with our complicated way of calculating time. We reckon according to the new style, conduct the ship's journal according to the old style. Days are counted still astronomically, civilly, and nautically, all of them different. The one begins at noon, the other at midnight, the one earlier and the other later. Thus we were, due the calculation of time in Canton, a day behind. We had so much to do with dates that it was easy to miscalculate by a day.

At seven o'clock, we weighed anchor in a calm, passed the second bar at nine o'clock and at three o'clock we cast anchor half way to Bocca Tigris. The English East Indian vessels, waiting here for their cargo because they have too deep of a draught to pass the bar, only have tea in their heads. They did not even have their flag raised as we passed by. Only one of them thought otherwise and raised her flag after we had passed. In the evening at seven o'clock, we weighed anchor again and tacked with towboats through the Bocca Tigris past the *Blenheim* and finally dropped anchor at two o'clock in the night. The Chinese towboats deserved mentioning. Bonmots were not missing on their bill. The boats were rowed solely by women and girls. Many of them, a short time before, had held our sailors spellbound by their charms and were so generous not to leave them unnecessarily panting. Now they were helping us to sail down the Tigris. They did not overdo themselves, however. Many of them rowed with one hand, with the other hand nursed their children whom they often offered to sell us, or prepared their meals. Lisianski, the charlatan, could not wait until we were at sea but had his cannons cleaned today.

Tues. 30/11 Minitzki went back to the *Blenheim* at five o'clock in the morning, and at six o'clock, we weighed anchor with a favorable wind. Our rendezvous is to be at St. Helena. The contrary wind forced us to drop anchor again in the evening. We were still a long distance from Macao and therefore sailed on with a favorable current and cast anchor about eight o'clock in the evening because we did not want to pass the island leeward in the night.

Wed. 31/12 In the morning at sunrise, we weighed anchor, and toward noon, we took leave of the Chinese coast, happy to be out of the claws of John Took and his mandarins.

- 22 -

China to St. Helena

February

Thurs. 1/13, Fri. 2/14 Our people drilled because there are Chinese pirates in the Chinese Sea.

Sat. 3/15 We passed *Maibsfield's Grunt* [sic].

Sun. 4/16 We sailed past Poolo Sapata into the dangerous Andreada. These days, we have been having nice, clear weather and favorable winds. Since the monsoon is blowing, it is actually supposed to blow favorably toward Europe at this time of year. That, however, is said not always to be the case.

Mon. 5/17 "Юрка Цманит [Yurka Tsmanit]," told Ratmanoff today, "our difference is too small, and the copper has been rubbed off, and the bottom of the ship is overgrown; that is why we are sailing more poorly." The *Neva* was careened and cleaned in Wampoa. Now, Lisianski maneuvers and does a lot of tricks for us. Let's hope the difference will be better in fourteen days, and then we will not be lagging behind so much. We sailed past the dangerous Middelburg reef today

Tues. 6/18 The *Neva* had been sailing with the wind. And all at once, the sun was shining in our eyes (бельмо в глазу); then she sailed with all of her sails up almost out of view. In the evening, we lashed down the sails and sailed only under topsails. Krusenstern signaled hold more to the wind—it remained unanswered. Since Lisianski, however, saw that we also took reefs, he steered toward us, and we were united again toward eight o'clock in the evening.

Unfortunately, the *Neva* now is sailing better than we are.

Wed. 7/19 We passed Poolo Condor.

I have not mentioned the *Liberty men* [sic] in Canton at all. (*See color plate 24.*) The sailors from the American and English ships have got themselves the right—after unloading and loading the ships and after renewing the riggings to make them ready to sail—the captain is bound, except for a watch guard, to give all of the sailors liberty for three days and permit them to go to Canton. All of the boats row popping full to Canton. Everyone buys himself a straw hat (that is the style) and a cane to protect himself from pickpockets. Then the drinking begins day and night. Fireworks are burned the whole night in the free square in front of the factory, boxing matches put on, which end in a fight between the English and the Chinese, etc., and all kind of games, fun, noise, and jokes. The crew returns onboard under the national flag with black eyes, drunk and ragged. Captains, who think logically and mean well with their crews, give them rum, brandy, and wine by the barrel, make sure that all of them are drunk on the first evening, keep them in this condition, and send them drunk onboard again. That our people behaved so well was noticed all the more by everyone, since Russians are famous for drinking.

Thurs. 8/20 Nice weather and favorable wind.

Kurganoff, who until China had not gone ashore once without coming back drunk, for that reason was not sent to Canton. That insulted him. Contrite, he went to everyone and asked them to put a word in for him with Krusenstern and promised on his word of honor to fulfill his duty and return sober. After many requests, Krusenstern permitted him to go as sub-officer with the cutter to Canton. The boat stayed in Canton overnight and returned to the ship only the next night. Triumphantly, Kurganoff climbed onboard sober, showed himself to every individual in order to win trust. Half an hour later, Krusenstern sent for him again to ask him something. And he got as an answer that Kurganoff was so drunk that he could move neither hand nor foot. That man had bought himself brandy and not drunk until he had reported and made up for what he had missed all at once.

Fri. 9/21 In the evening, Kurganoff was in such bad straits that Espenberg had to be called to help. We were all very concerned on his account and not a little surprised the next morning to see him standing guard. Espenberg had gotten up earlier to find out how he was. He asked for schnapps (after the hangover). When Espenberg offered him medicine that he did not want, he claimed to be completely healthy.

Sat. 10/22 Continual nice weather and favorable winds, according to the sink lead 38 to 25 faden depth.

We have not yet had many people sick. Ten sick with us is to say a lot.

We are all occupied with the thought of our return. We are so used to speaking of years that six months seems very short. In eight days, we will be in the Straits of Sunda, the second station is the Cape of Good Hope, St. Helena is the third, and from there it is straight home. Yes, home!

Sun. 11/23 We saw the island of Titoan or Timoàn and in the evening Poolo Quer. A *Contrary Schip* [sic] sailed past us very close, alee. She had probably sailed from Canton a day after we did. We saw five other ships on the horizon heading toward the Straits of Malacca.

Lisianski is still sailing with us. It says a lot that he has not yet separated from us. It certainly is not his decision.

Castles in the sky—trading between Russia, India, and China. You would have to sail with an appropriate cargo from Kronstadt to Manila, exchange the cargo there and supply Kamtschatka and Kodiak with products from there, from Kodiak sail with a cargo of furs to China and from there with tea, etc., sail back to Kronstadt. It might be even more advantageous to take tar, pitch, wood for masts, iron, hemp, sailcloth, etc., to Bengal in order to sell the cargo there, load cotton, and sail to China where you buy tea, etc., and can return straight away—or buy goods for Kodiak, from Kodiak sail a second time to China with furs and then with a cargo of tea, nankin, and silk return to Russia.

According to the first plan—castles in the sky or fantasies of the brain—you would have to leave Russia early in the year, at least at the beginning of May. You could be in Manila in December by way of Cape Horn; two to three months would suffice to conduct enough trade. In February of the next year, you could leave Manila. At the beginning of March, you could be in Kodiak, unload there, and load furs, would still have time to sail to Kamtschatka where you would have to leave by September in order to be in Canton at the right time. You would sail from Canton in January, and in July or August, you should be back in Kronstadt. The voyage would take two and one half years.

According to the other plan, you would have to leave Russia as well early in the year. You could be in Bengal by the beginning of November and have completed business by January. You would reach Canton by March, complete business there in May, and be in Kodiak in July. You would have to leave Kodiak again in September to arrive for a second time in China in December in order to be able to reach Kronstadt as above in August. This voyage would also only require two and one-half years. One would have enough opportunities to trade.

Mon. 12/24 Shrovetide. The *Neva* now and again sails off to explore but always returns.

Tues. 13/25 We passed the equator at nine o'clock in the morning, and, toward evening, we caught sight of the Island Banka [Bangka]. Because of the darkness of the night and hidden reefs, we only had few sails for the night.

Wed. 14/26 At daybreak, we hauled up all of our sails and, using Fleurieu's map, were opposite the Island du Millien [Mindanao] in the evening, and cast anchor in the Strait of Gaspar [Selat Gaspar]. The current was two knots strong.

The jollyboat from the *Neva* with Pavalischin came very late with a request from Doctor Laband. Because a sailor was very ill on the *Neva*, he wished to hear Espenberg's advice. The current was contrary, and he had to remain the night with us. The next morning, after we had weighed anchor, Espenberg went over to the *Neva*.

Thurs. 15/27 We sailed through the Straits of Gaspar with gusts of wind and rain. This strait seems preferable to the Straits of Banka [Selat Bangka], Clements, and Billeton. According to the map, I consider it better. A thunderstorm, gusts of wind, and rain did not stop us any more since we were already in the open. We set sail to ensure that we sailed onwards.

Espenberg stayed on the *Neva* overnight. In the evening, we put ourselves on the drift in order to give Lisianski an opportunity to send our doctor back to us. He called to us "завтра!" [tomorrow], and we set sail again.

Fri. 16/28 At eight o'clock in the morning, we caught sight of the coast of Sumatra and four ships alee on the horizon. The weather is nice. About eleven o'clock, we came upon shallows, which forced us to head to the east. During this time we lost sight of the ships.

Lisianski is making "*conclusions*" [sic] again. His latitude differed today from ours by seven minutes. That he calculated a 37 and we only a 25-mile current can be explained better by the incompleteness of the ship's calculations. We communicated this to each other through the speaking trumpet.

Toward noon, we caught sight of the "*Two Brothers*" [sic], and, at seven o'clock, we sailed past them. Because of the overcast bad weather, rain, lightning, and thunder, we cast anchor at eight o'clock. In the night, during my watch, I suddenly noticed that the *Nadezhda* was drifting. We might have been drifting awhile because the sailor on the sink lead had fallen asleep.

Sat. 17/1 We sent a boat to the *Neva* to pick up Espenberg. At seven o'clock, we weighed **March** anchor. At noon, we passed *North Island* [sic] and at two o'clock we cast anchor because of a calm opposite the *Three Sisters* [sic] between North and Zülphin Islands. We sent a boat to the *Neva*. Lisianski came over to us for tea. There is talk—and Lisianski has suggested, since the *Neva* is sailing better and since we have open seas after the Straits of Sunda—that each, without waiting for the other and taking consideration of the other, should sail for home as fast as possible. Lisianski would certainly not have made this suggestion if we were sailing as he is.

Sun. 18/2 Still unchanging contrary winds prevented us from weighing anchor. No day passes without thunderstorms. Krusenstern went over to the *Neva*.

Mon. 19/3 At seven o'clock, we weighed anchor. The *Neva* did the same, cast anchor again, however, because she could not turn. We sailed on, and, at twelve o'clock, we sailed through the narrow passage between Zülphen and *Stroom Rock* [sic]. At four o'clock we lost sight of the *Neva*. Tomorrow, she will probably catch up. In the evening, we saw a brig coming from the open seas that held for Batavia. In any case, we prepared to defend ourselves. In the evening, we cast anchor between Cracatao and *Middel Island* [sic]. Krusenstern will probably wait for the *Neva* here.

Tues. 20/4 At nine o'clock, we weighed anchor, tacked with the current. Nothing to be seen of the *Neva,* even though the wind was brisk enough. At seven o'clock in the evening we cast anchor on the eastern side of Cracatao. The heat is unbearable, continually 22°.

Wed. 21/5 We weighed anchor at the light of day and caught sight of the *Neva* under full sail. Instead of holding to the north of *Princes Island* [sic], we also sailed to the strait behind the *Neva* in order not to be separated from her. Only at eight o'clock in the evening did we sail through the Strait of Sunda and were then held up by calms until twelve o'clock. The current drove us toward *the Friar* or *Java Head* [sic], where there is terrible surf. That is exactly the reason for us becoming separated from the *Neva,* even though Krusenstern was trying so hard to stay together with her.

We were glad finally to have the Strait behind us, which had cost us a lot of work and sweat.

Thurs. 22/6 In the evening, we lost sight of *Java Head* [sic], and we were united with the *Neva*, which did not sail away from us so much again, because we have improved the difference.

Fri. 23/7 The unbridled life of the sailors in China and then the oppressive, humid weather, steamy heat in the Straits of Sunda, and the piled up work of the passage are the reason that on most of the East Indian vessels half of the crew become ill there and many die. We have been lucky to have everyone healthy in the Strait of Sunda, since, thank God, we have no one ill anymore onboard.

Sat. 24/8 Gusts of wind and rain or calms alternate hourly. In contrast, in the Strait of Sunda, we had horrid thunderstorms every day during the day, which became teeming thunder filled clouds in the night, when you saw the lightning all the brighter or countless lightning bolts around you hissing into the water. Rain-spouts accompanied the thunderstorms.

Sun. 25/9 In the evening, we caught sight of *Christmas Island* [sic].

Continual downpours and gusts of wind and calms and high seas from the southeast—the skies and barometer indicate bad weather.

Mon. 26/10, Tues. 27/11 In a brisk topgallant sail wind from the south, the *Neva* signaled she had suffered damage on the topmasts. That too will hold us up.

Wed. 28/12 The *Neva* changed her masts and we our utlagar [утлегарь: jib boom].

People will say that being a lieutenant on watch is a trifle. Why? There are many who have made a voyage around the world as witnesses and have judged the matter as impartial viewers. The only complaint a lieutenant has is night watch, getting wet, and being subjected to wind and weather. That demands a good constitution. If a man has that and does not suffer from seasickness, then he can fulfill the duties of a lieutenant. He only needs to carry out the Captain's orders punctually. The lieutenant is the captain's mouthpiece. If something succeeds on the *Nadezhda*, a danger overcome, then the captain alone harvests praise. If something goes awry, and then the lieutenant of the watch alone is at fault—that is something unpleasant—it is the captain's first duty to look out for the crew's health. He, however, has to hold them to their duties and not permit insubordination to creep in. Since

Krusenstern has retained the right for himself to punish sailors for trespasses, he prevents many an unjust punishment, but he dare not permit any transgression to go unpunished. Our people know that and are therefore sometimes insolent, because they know that they will get only a reprimand; for you cannot deny common man that desire. He is too unenlightened to be able to value and to honor forbearance and liberality. He says, before committing a stupidity, "That does not mean anything. I'm only going to get a reprimand for it." You do not need many men to sail a ship like the *Nadezhd*a. With the *Nadezhda* however, as with a ship of war, more than ten men are necessary per watch. If these ten do their work sloppily, then nothing works. Now, all at once, Krusenstern has issued twenty orders. It is impossible to fulfill them all at once.

The repetitions of such orders are reprimands. On the *Nadezhda,* we are accustomed to having the orders of the officer on watch issued punctually. With us it barely suffices to repeat the same order ten times before the work gets done, if the sailors do not feel like it. Who wants to be continually complaining to the Captain about disobedience? Ratmanoff hinders more than he does any good. Krusenstern ordered that this or that rope be pulled, often at the wrong time, since he is nearsighted. The mistake ensuing from this is the lieutenant's fault, and I nevertheless cannot retract his order. If a squall comes up, everything is carried out with great order, if Krusenstern does not mix in and limits himself only to giving general orders. If the lieutenant finds something on the riggings in need of repair, then he has to wait patiently until the following morning, because the master's mate has received orders that prevent the good intentions of repairing whatever is not in order. If we have done a lot of hard work, then half of the crew reports ill, because they know the Captain can be gotten to do anything and will take care of them. I often work on the *Nadezhda* more as a sailor than as an officer does.

On my watch, the old longboat, which is totally good for nothing, was taken apart. Krusenstern ordered me to have the jollyboat lowered, to put us on the drift under the main topsail, and to furl the main and foresails. A quarter of an hour later, we became aware of the fact that distance could be taken and went immediately to work. The carpenters made so much noise that "Stop" could not be heard. Since the mainsail and mizzen staysail hindered *observation* [sic], Krusenstern ordered the crossjack be hauled on the topmast and to haul the maintop brace until he called "Stop." Four sailors had gone to the *Neva* in the jollyboat, two were repairing the blocks of the mast basket, and I was left with four men on deck. The work went slowly. A cloud covered the sun. Krusenstern put away the sextant and said irritably, "Have the yards braced."

I reminded him that he had forgotten to call "Stop" and asked "Fill the sail or not?"

"Наполнить!" [fill] he said irritably. The work, for lack of men, had to be done slowly which angered him even more. I pointed to my whole crew. He remained silent and, dissatisfied with himself, went into his cabin. He did not even notice that those four were also being lazy. On the *Nadezhda,* it is up to every individual himself to do his duty. If he does not want to, he gets no reprimand.

March

Thurs. 1/13 This evening, Krusenstern called me to him in his cabin to excuse his behavior for the incident the previous evening and asked me not to make too much of the misunderstanding. Even though my anger had not led me to put it into words, the expression and look of my face must have betrayed my suppressed anger. I therefore had to admire Krusenstern's admission and thank him for his reaction. That is the first strife I have had with Krusenstern.

Fri. 2/14 A calm the whole day.

Sat. 3/15 The American ship, visible because of the calm on the horizon, sailed out of view today.

Chickens have the worst life on a ship, a narrow cage, little water, and continual strife among themselves. They went half-crazy in the great heat, pulled each others' feathers out, picked each other bloody. Several have already been picked to death. If a hen lays an egg, it gets eaten even before the hen has laid it. A continual murderous cry batters our ears from the chicken coop.

We have finally gotten trade winds.

Sun. 4/16, Mon. 5/17, Tues. 6/18 Nice trade winds, we have not been sailing below seven knots. The *Neva* is sailing much better than we are. Even though we would all gladly spend another year so that we might stop in places which we are going to be sailing past, we all, however, have our fill of life on the *Nadezhda*.

Wed. 7/19, Thurs. 8/20, Fri. 9/21, Sat. 10/22, Sun. 11/23, Mon. 12/24 The trade wind blows like the wind around the equinox. We continue to sail eight and one-half knots with the topsails, the main, and foretopmast staysails. All of the topgallant sails have already been ripped to pieces, and on the 12th the top mainsail was torn up.

Tues. 13/25 The stir tross [штир трос: wheel cable] broke. A new one was put in without any damage.

Wed. 14/26 Continually eight to nine knots. The seas are running higher here on the ocean than usual. That permits us to see lower parts of the ship. The copper is in part totally loose and hanging in half-ripped-off tatters; the bare spots are overgrown with tang and polyps, which must be giving the ship strong support. It is therefore no surprise that the *Neva* now is sailing better than the *Nadezhda*. When we left Kronstadt, the *Nadezhda* was sailing better than the *Neva*.

Thurs. 15/27 We sailed out of the tropics and past the longitude of the Island of Rodriques [Mauritius].

I would like to make a trip to Bengal. It would not need much time and must be very pleasant and also advantageous for trade speculations. If you left Russia in June, you could be in Calcutta in five months and stop along the way in Madeira and Bon Esperenie and resupply. You could stay in Calcutta in December and January on the return trip, stop for supplies on the Isle de Frenie and St. Helena, and, in July, you could be in Kronstadt again. As a seaman, you could not spend a year any better.

Fri. 16/28 We changed the old main and also the foresail.

Sat. 17/29 We passed the longitude of Isle de Frenie.

Even though the trade winds have left us, we are still sailing rapidly forward with a brisk southerly wind. Since the 4th of March, we have done 12½^0 latitude and 44^0 longitude, a distance of 3,500 Italian miles or over 6,000 versts.

Sun. 18/30 We passed the longitude of the Island of Bourbon. High seas from the south-southeast. The trade winds are gone.

Mon. 19/31, Tues 20/1, Wed. 21/2 The winds in these waters are called monsoons. They rule the Chinese and Japanese seas and in the Bay of Bengal up to the Persian Gulf. Their change comes in October and in April. This change comes together with typhoons (orcans) and strong storms. The northeasterly monsoon rules the winter months and the southwesterly monsoons our summer months. They reach the equator, southerlies blowing with northeasterly monsoons, northwesterly or westerly winds and with southwesterly monsoons southeasterly and easterly winds, which make the eastern passage possible with contrary monsoons. To the south, there are winds blowing counter to these monsoons up to the 12^0 southern latitude, where is found, after strong gusts of wind, calms and rain, the actual southeasterly trade winds which blow year in year out. They always blow very briskly. Away from the tropics, the prevailing winds are from the south and southwest, essential for a voyage from Europe to China but make the doubling of the Cape of Good Hope very difficult, especially if you sail through the area during the stormy season of the year. During our winter months, you have here and there nice clear weather. In our summer months you have to fight storms, rain, and overcast weather.

Thurs. 22/3, Fri. 23/4 We got a fresh east-southeasterly again. The high seas are continual.

Sat. 24/5 We passed the longitude of the southern tip (*Cape Mary* [sic]) on Madagascar.

Sun. 25/6, Mon. 26/7, Tues. 27/8, Wed. 28/9 Nice clear weather and favorable winds.

29/10, 30/11, 31/12 The wind has slackened. With 145 faden lead line, we got no bottom.

April

Sun. 1/13 On Easter Sunday, the wind became contrary, and, since it became ever stronger, we had to take reefs. In honor of Easter, our sailors were all drunk, and because of that we almost lost a sailor, since he was no longer able to keep his hold.

Ratmanoff's servant Ivan gave us orders. Obviously, words do not improve the man, and no one wants to put an end to his misconduct, since both Ratmanoff and Krusenstern remain silent about it.

Mon. 2/14 We passed the meridian of St. Petersburg. Everyone is turning his experiences into law. We have now been in the latitudes and longitudes where other seafarers have felt a favorable current from the southwest. However, we still have continual contrary currents.

Tues. 3/15 Nice brisk wind. On the Bank Aquillas we found bottom at 105 faden. We have completely lost sight of the *Neva*. She is nowhere to be seen.

If men can only be taught while filled with numerous mistakes and egotism, then they can become beloved only after their deaths and famous through their written works, because their contemporaries, who know their bad personal characteristics, do not value them. Seldom, very seldom do you find a scholar who harvests the fruits of his marked understanding and ingenuity during his lifetime.

Wed. 4/16 Contrary winds from the south-southwest and high seas from the south.

We found bottom at 80 faden on the Äqüllas Grund.

Thurs. 5/17 Prerogatives and statutes of limitations.

Charitonoff: privileged drunkard (cook).

Tschugaeff (the clerk): confusion adviser.

Ivan Andreeff (Ratmanoff's servant): thief.

Kamentschikoff (mate): liar and gossip.

Tilesius (court councilor): weightiness.

Ratmanoff: idler.

Espenberg: egoist.

There are plenty of privileged eye-pleasers.

Fri. /18 We passed the Banke Ägüllas.

Sat. 7/19, Sun. 8/20 We caught sight of land, asked an American ship, and got a not very satisfactory answer that the Cape of Good Hope was blocked and probably already taken by the English. We passed the Cape of Good Hope without sailing in.

Mon. 9/21, Tues. 20/22, Wed. 11/23 The rats are causing a lot of damage again. Unexpectedly, this morning, I had a very heated argument with Tilesius, which will probably end with a duel. It had been my watch from in the morning until four o'clock. Relieved, I came into the cabin to drink tea, which the others had already had. I had barely drunk my tea when Tilesius entered the cabin and, turning to me, said, "I intended to close the window hatch-way, but not a single pane is in one piece." He said that with a jeering smile, as if he intended to reproach me.

I answered, "We are ourselves at fault. It is in everyone's way. This fellow puts it here, the next there. And the quarterdecks are not a place where you store breakable things and scatter them around."

Tilesius became sensitive about that because he had broken many a bottle, etc., in this way as a result of carelessness. "You mean me," he said and began to preach in a lofty tone. I interrupted his blather and said that it was not worth it, that it was not worth the effort of making so much noise about a trifle. Thereupon, Tilesius accused me of high-handedness. That was too much for me. I hit the table with my fist, so hard that my cup broke into pieces, and angrily and sharply said to him, "I do not permit anyone to tell me stupidities." Ratmanoff was kind enough to hold me back in time. Tilesius offered me swords or pistols, which I accepted, and would be at his service as soon as we came to St. Helena. Immediately afterwards, he went to Krusenstern and complained about me. When I heard that I asked Ratmanoff to get Tilesius to be quiet, because I would not be able to control my hotheadedness if he opened his yap again. To justify myself, I related the incident to Krusenstern and asked him to talk with everyone who had been present to ascertain whether, in my anger, I had described the events too partially. Krusenstern could do nothing better than remain silent.

Thurs. 12/24 With great strides, we are approaching Helena, where I hope that we do not meet the *Neva* once again, for I find Lisianski unbearable. Krusenstern is thinking of raising the flag of war in St. Helena, and Lisianski is not permitted to do that. If he dared to pull some dumb ones in Canton, he will undoubtedly not let it alone there either.

Fri. 13/25 On the 2/14 of April, when we passed the meridian of St. Petersburg, we were sitting around the table in the evening drinking tea. All at once, Espenberg said, "It smells like gunpowder," and at that moment the cabin was full of smoke. The powder chamber is in the constable cabin where Tilesius, the Kotzebues, and the second mate live. We ran over. It was dark there, and there was no sign of smoke; also, there was no smoke anywhere else on the ship.

Golovatscheff had the habit of leaving his cannon port open longer than necessary, and his neighbors Horner and Friderici had often complained that the waves get into his cabin, thereby causing their things to get wet. That was the case again this time. The smoke had dissipated, but the water had the upper hand. Golovatscheff, the only one with a lock on his cabin, had gone on the quarterdeck shortly after the noise and had locked his cabin. Horner asked him to have his port closed and to have pity upon his books. Up to now, we have not been able to find the source of the smoke.

Sat. 14/26 Ivan stole 45 bottles of wine from us again. Since he was caught, the cost of the wine is to be deducted from his wages. Ratmanoff said, "Here they have completely spoiled the man for me."

Sun. 15/27 We attached our anchor cables again.

Mon. 16/28 We had to throw overboard three casks of rotten hardtack from Ochotsk and several barrels of salt meat.

Tues. 17/29 The rats have eaten up one large sugar barrel full of hardtack and a barrel of peas, and we also found one barrel of butter unusable. In addition, the rats had also eaten up a barrel of rice. The butter we got in Reval is otherwise still good.

Wed. 18/30 April, by completing the voyage around the world or 360°, we have lost the longitude to the west, because we have sailed from east to west.

I have forgotten to note a main act of state. On the 16/28 of April, our company got a new look at table. Friderici had outweathered his time as steward. By lot, Espenberg has become our provider. And the result was that Ivan has been gotten rid of, and it was agreed that everything missing will be deducted from his wages. Efdokiim Michailoff has taken Ivan's place.

Thurs. 19/1 In two, at the most, three days, we will arrive in St. Helena.

Fri. 20/2 Some time ago Krusenstern gave Golovatscheff the task of cutting a sail that was needed or of having it cut. Golovatscheff has a lot of qualifications, but that he could make such a mistake and miscalculation of making all of the sails too small and short I find impossible. Krusenstern ask the sailmaker for the reason and got the answer, "Peter Trofimitsch had ordered it." If the four sides of a square have been given, then the devil must be at work if the sail does not fit. It can well have a sag here or there, but it has to fit. Golovatscheff takes the whole thing very much to heart. Now, Krusenstern has ordered a topgallant staysail sewn, and the sail is fine. Some one may be smart in the matter. I think for sure Golovatscheff did not check, and the sailmaker stole sailcloth.

Taras is a perfect fellow; he, however, has to be kept in check like all common people. Ratmanoff has taken the trouble upon himself since no one oversteps him lightly. The locksmith Svägin is a skilled, industrious man, unfortunately too much inclined to guzzling.

Tilesius is a big braggart. For that reason, I reminded him of our argument, so that he would remember that I have not forgotten him and told him, "If we cannot do it in St. Helena, then it can happen in Copenhagen." He tried to chime in, but I asked him to keep quiet in order to prevent strife.

Sat. 21/3 In the evening, we caught sight of the Island of St. Helena and cleaned all of our cannon in which the old load had rusted.

- 23 -

St. Helena

James Town in St. Helena

Sun. 22/4 At noon, we cast anchor on the roadstead at Jamestown, which is very open and good only because the wind never blows from the northwest. Still, ten miles from St. Helena, Krusenstern sent me ashore with the six-oar boat to report our arrival to the governor and request permission to obtain fresh water and provisions here. They observe a great strictness here to ensure that no foreign ship or boat lands without permission. On a steep cliff in large golden letters are written on a black board: "*Send a boat on schore*!" [sic] At five bastions, which I had to pass, I was questioned through a speaking trumpet before I was permitted to land. The whole island is a high steep rugged rock which cannot be climbed. From the northwestern side, where Jamestown is, it is fortified with heavy batteries up to the top of the rock. It cannot be climbed from the southeastern side because of the overhanging cliffs. I got the news that Lord Nelson had ended his life in glory, that Pitt also had died and that Russia had declared war on France and that Lord Grenwill [Grenville][1] has become a minister in England.

Mon. 23/5 At noon, I went on land with Raefski to go for a walk. Krusenstern dined at noon at the Governor's with Ratmanoff, Friderici, Horner, and Tilesius. We went along the street as far as our feet would carry us. I intended to go as far as foreigners are allowed to, because I had been told that foreigners are not permitted to go into the interior of the island. The way we went seemed somewhat long to me. The city was far behind us, and a brook and path bordered by small luxurious vegetable gardens meandered through a small ravine. In the distance, we saw several average stone houses. I asked a soldier we met how far it was to the sentinel. He answered us, "You have already gone over ¾ of a mile farther inland." So I turned around and hurried back to town again.

23-1. James Town on St. Helena

In a valley that quickly becomes narrow is a fast flowing brook that makes the area arable, and about 20 faden of rugged land on both sides are arable. They say that there is a beautiful valley in the middle of the island, which is supposed to be incomparable as a pleasant, arable, and beautiful area.

Most of the houses have straw and earthen roofs. The earth, as a roofer explained, becomes with time so firm that it is indestructible. On top of a roof of boards, they put a three-finger thick layer of clay-like earth that soon becomes compact. These kinds of roofs are proof of the dry climate. Around our place, they would not have enough time to dry out.

The inhabitants here are very polite. Mr. Belliam invited me to lunch tomorrow at his place. I had, however, to turn down the invitation because tomorrow is my dejour onboard.

Tues. 24/6 Everyone went on land. I stayed alone onboard. The governor has requested Krusenstern to sign assurances that we would take no one from here along or leave any people behind or conduct any trade, not go into the island beyond where the sentinel was standing, not commit any excesses, etc., etc. Krusenstern did not consent, and that is also how it stayed.

Wed. 25/7 Golovatscheff and Bellingshausen stayed onboard alone, and all the rest went on land. We had gone into *the Company Stores* [sic] (warehouses from East Indies) to buy some things. When I left the house again, Tilesius, who was coming from the ship, met me. Amicably and convulsively and almost out of breath, Tilesius grabbed my hand and said, "Don't frighten the captain." Since I was on bad terms with Tilesius, I took a step backwards. Without a lot of explanations,

Tilesius took both of my hands and said, "Let's make peace and let bygones be bygones. Golovatscheff has shot himself." I really was alarmed. I visited friend Krusenstern, told him the unhappy story, and we went onboard. Golovatscheff was already dead. He had put a little pistol whose lock was broken into his mouth and pulled the trigger. His whole face was tattered and distorted. (He earlier was always working on the lock, broke several of Horner's and my files until he himself had broken the lock.) He had lighted the pistol with a lunt made of cut-up paper, which was still burning in his hand after the shot. In order to call no attention to himself, he had lit a cigaro, which he did not smoke, and used it to light the lunt and thus carrying out his intentions. Golovatscheff never drank brandy. Nevertheless, the day before he had taken a little bottle of Rotafia and emptied it alone in the morning. Both of his образа were lying on the table in front of him.

Golovatscheff left behind a lot of letters, a big thick letter to the emperor, and a large number of letters to his relatives and acquaintances. In these letters addressed to us, he calls Krusenstern, Romberg, Tilesius, and Horner his murderers or the cause of his suicide.

Krusenstern went ashore to the governor's to obtain permission to bury the body. The governor told him, of his own accord, that a man who kills himself in a fit of melancholy cannot be considered a suicide. "I will order the body to be buried with all ceremony." When we took the casket on land in the afternoon, we were received by a forty-man commando of soldiers and funeral music, which accompanied the casket to the church. The English pastor buried him after a very nice sermon, and three salvos by the soldiers ended the ceremony. Everything was done in an orderly fashion, so that we returned onboard, consoled, having done the last service for him according to his wishes. We came together and ordered a gravestone.

Thurs. 26/8 After getting an invitation yesterday, we dined at noon at the governor's. The English, who have a post like the governor's here, live in Oriental sumptuousness.

At table, I made the acquaintance of Major Billingwhisk, who had been a lieutenant in the Dragoons, which had the misfortune of landing in Holland. The telegraph which the present governor has erected seems to be taken very much to heart. There was a lot of talk about it. Suddenly, a sentinel came into the room and reported that the telegraph in the area reported a vessel sailing in. The governor said self-satisfied, "That must be the *Neva* that you are expecting."

I contradicted him saying, "I think that it has to be the American we saw sailing by yesterday that was becalmed." An hour later, my suspicion was confirmed by a second report. That appeared to annoy the governor. In the evening, we took our leave, thanked the governor for his kindnesses and went to Major Seal's, at whose place we were lodging. He was kind enough to provide us with tea and food, etc., during our time there, since no inn exists on St. Helena. Since everything here is enormously expensive, he had us pay devilish prices. His little children, whom I always brought treats or confections when I came ashore, attached themselves unbelievably to me. Seal's wife, a pretty woman of at the most 25 to 30 years, had the misfortune of having polyps in her nose. If she sat still, you noticed nothing. If she wanted to speak, it was almost impossible to understand her. She also had a pale, weak appearance. All of our acquaintances wished us a happy voyage, and we were barely onboard when the work began. And at eleven o'clock in the evening, we weighed anchor.

Fri. 27/9 We lost sight of St. Helena. Doctor Espenberg, who is responsible for table, tries very hard. (He was the one, when the rest of us had to take care of table, who made a lot of work for us.) Efdokim, who replaced Ivan, is an honest fellow, and Charitonoff—under Espenberg's direction—cooks quite well, so that everything is carried out in a quite orderly fashion and we are now eating quite well.

Sat. 28/10 Golovatscheff must have carried the thought of shooting himself around with him. When we arrived in Kamtschatka the first time and the ruckus with Resanoff had reached it high point, after the reconciliation, he poured an anchor of rum into bottles and put a label with a name on every bottle. In China, he made several gifts and had two names engraved on all of the things he had bought, his and the name of the person for whom he intended the thing. He gave me a tortoise-shell box. If the object did not permit a name to be put on it, he determined who was to get it with a neat label, etc.

Several times, he said to our sailors, "All but one of you will arrive home well." As you can see from his letters at the time when we smelled gunpowder, he intended to shoot himself when we were passing the meridian of St. Petersburg and had gone 360°. The pistol apparently burned out, and he did not succeed. He had gone to St. Helena with the intention. Since he is of my height and stature, Seal's children mistook him for me and joined him. He gave them treats and spent so much time with them that it was too late to shoot himself, since everyone had collected to go back onboard. That he left the world unreconciled is unpardonable, especially since he names innocent people as the reason for his suicide.

Sun. 29/11 Golovatscheff's letters to us:

> April 7 latitude 31° 34' and longitude 16° 20'
>
> Tell Romberg that I, beginning in China, have not been his slave, as he seems to think I am, and that he has totally lost the bet with Horner, as if I were a weak person.
>
> Recognize! Captain, Espenberg, Horner, Tilesius, and Romberg, that beginning in Kamtschatka, you have wished my death and promised me death in the Straits of Sunda.

At the end of the letter, he forgives everyone and prepares for death.

That was written on the day Friderici smelled gunpowder in his cabin. Espenberg wanted to take a look at Golovatscheff's cabin. He noticed it and came out, put himself calmly in front of his door, locked it, and went on the quarterdeck, and did not come back down until the waves had entered his cabin. And he had to close the cannon port.

Translation:

April 14 to the Captain:

The wish all of you have has been fulfilled.

I wish you all the best even though you, every second, wanted my life. Your inventions and the plot against my character in front of Resanoff! You convinced Councilor Tilesius to blacken my character (that Krusenstern would recommend him—that is Golovatscheff—to be a sailor or to send him to Siberia). Your conscience hindered you from locking me in my cabin. Chicanery!

Pressure!

Deliver this package addressed to His Imperial Majesty. There is also a letter to you . . . in it.

This letter shows all of the events in their true light. I do not want to hide this from the Father of my Fatherland. May he see my innocence. In addition, I ask him to open up your hearts and lead you again to the true path. Let me call you tyrants, only—not all of you. (He attempts to pardon himself on Resanoff's account.) I will continue, still groaning, bear your revenge and evil until the unfortunate moment when it is then all clear.

Yours, Golovatscheff.

I am very calm. You are surprised at my tranquility of mind and composure.

As crazy as this letter is, its beginning brought Krusenstern to tears, and, seeing himself as an innocent damned, it caused him a great deal of worry and suffering.

The 15th of April.

Fedor Romberg.

Tyrant of humanity!

You are the beginning of my misfortune. You have the conceit to think that I have intended to blacken the honor of some other man or have acted coarsely in my actions toward you.

You owe me 29 rubles. Keep them, and do me the favor of giving Resanoff and my brother each a copy of the judgement and remarks made about me. And, if you do not have enough money to have them printed, then there will be enough money in my account. Farewell, you monster.

In Kamtschatka, you did not act in vain as if you were crazy.

The 16th of April. Councilor Tilesius!

That I snuffed out the light you had burning while you were sleeping in Brazil, that I did not take you onboard in Nukahiva—and the little capucan [monkey] in the cabin—those are the reasons—and you wrote against me and tried to blacken my character—others got you to do it. You are at fault for my death.

G.

Tilesius lived next to the powder room and was very careless with candles. Golovatscheff snuffed the light out once right in front of his nose when he was half-asleep and had let it continue to burn. And, in Nukahiva, Tilesius was late as always. Golovatscheff did not wait for him and left him on land because an hour later a boat was to be sent. Tilesius had raised a raging ruckus when he came onboard in the evening.

"The 18th of April. The lost day in a human life, in verse."

In this letter, he charges Krusenstern with suspecting him in Kamtschatka and accusing him of suppression, malice, and tyranny that was his fault. Finally he says,

> The 19th of April.
>
> Espenberg, note that Resanoff called me his friend.
>
> Romberg believes that I have related his drunken tricks.
>
> Krusenstern is revenging himself. Löwenstern is a good man. In the end, he agreed to my misfortune.
>
> Bellingshausen is swollen-headed by his supposed scholarliness and said in Kamtschatka, as if I had wanted to be number one, that I had been invited to sit at the ambassador's table.
>
> Ratmanoff is a straightforward man.

He asked that all of these letters be given the emperor and the whole command and that they should be read aloud.

May

Tues. 1/13 God willing, we will be in Russia in three months.

That Lisianski did not come to St. Helena, even though the spot had been designated for a rendezvous, was predictable. That he is heading for England is sure; whether, however, he will get to Russia earlier than we do, time will tell. It is typical of Lisianski that he had absolutely no interest in and did not bother much with what we did in Japan and at Sachalin. His egoism and his envious character cause him to consider worthy only whatever he himself has done.

Krusenstern's and our enemies can triumph. In addition to all of the intrigues, accusations, and slander, etc., now comes Golovatscheff's death. The letters he has left behind will play no little part, if the three-year-long strife should be turned over to a court for inspection.

The various points of view from which our strife have been presented in Petersburg only have to make things even more entangled. Every relationship is different. Brinkin and Kurlandzoff traveled overland and were glad to be free of us and Resanoff. They will wait to see which way the wind blows and, according to this principle, will tell their tales. Count Tolstoi had to do everything possible to get himself out of the dirty situation in which he had gotten himself. Resanoff's relations from England, Tenerife, Brazil, and Kamtschatka may well have been strident enough. Fosse's faces, tales, and anecdotes were learned to suit Resanoff. Krusenstern has countered these only with short reports and was supported only by General Koscheleff's impartial report to the emperor. Golovatscheff's letter makes the whole story hazardous—and can be refuted only by our testimony, reports, etc.

Perhaps Resanoff is already in Petersburg and has made preparations. Lisianski will also not fail to stick his oar in and ruin more than be helpful with idle prattle. We are approaching our fatherland with trepidation.

Golovatscheff gave Schemelin for safe keeping the illuminated bust of clay he had made in Canton and told him that Resanoff had transferred him (Golovatscheff) to Petersburg before his departure for Kodiak, even though this was very unpleasant for him and he prayed to high heaven not to be.

Sometimes at night, Golovatscheff would go on deck and smoke a cigaro, and Golovatscheff implied to Schemelin, among other things, that Ratmanoff had called Krusenstern's attention to it. He had called it disobedience and said, "You can take away his watch." Krusenstern then answered: "Let's wait until St. Helena."

The truth is that Ratmanoff told the dead man to his face that it was not right to smoke on deck.

Golovatscheff also complained to Schemelin that he never got around to having his black laundry washed (simply because he did not take care of it himself). In the beginning, he wanted to send his laundry ashore with me. I was not going. Then Romberg and Fokin went but forgot to send the laundry on land. When Krusenstern went, there was no room in the boat. Thus, his laundry remained unwashed. Golovatscheff called that chicanery.

Otherwise, Fokin had had all of Golovatscheff's things in his possession. Since Canton, however, he had had them under lock and key. Often, he went down from his watch, if he had by chance forgotten to stick in his key, in order to fetch it. If he met Fokin alone in his cabin, each time he would react harshly for no reason. He had not bought himself any clothing, shoes, etc., in China. I had to lend him a pair of shoes because he did not have any more. That is why he was also so badly outfitted.

The inscription on Golovatscheff's Tombstone:

> Defeated by his sad fate Peter Golovatscheff, second lieutenant of the Russian Ship *Nadezhda,* died on the 7th of May in 1806 in his 29th year.
>
> May Heaven grant him peace! May his remains rest in peace.[2]

- 24 -

St. Helena to Kronstadt

Wed. 2/14 Our spirits since Helena (if I may use that expression) have become more bearable. The reason is that instead of Ivan, who openly stole from us and through whose negligence we always were short of provisions, we now have Efdokim as our tyke with whom all are satisfied. Stepan was continually arguing with Ivan. Now our servants are satisfied with us, and we with our servants, and unity rules the company. Espenberg was always the stumbling block with food and drink. Now that he himself is in charge of table, all of the unpleasantness has stopped. Espenberg is also occupied and does things to everyone's satisfaction, is no longer bored, and is therefore not a burden to himself and others. Probably Golovatscheff's tragic end may have caused a lot of people to reconsider. And the truths which Golovatscheff told each one, so exaggerated and confused as they were written, appear to have borne fruit. Thank heavens the voyage will soon be over!

Thurs. 3/15, Fri. 4/16 We passed the latitude of the Island of Ascension.

Sat. 5/17 In the evening and in the night, we had fiery keel water. This illumination was caused by medusas, which swim under the rudder and the bottom of the ship.

Sun. 6/18 We threw a bottle overboard with the inscription:

Latitude 4° 38' S. Longitude 18° 40'W from Greenwitsch. Current to the SE, 10 miles a day, on board the Russian Frigate Nadeshda [sic].

A great many frigate birds (a kind of black sea bird) flew around our ship today and followed the flying fish, which are trying to save themselves from the bonitos by jumping out of the water and thus becoming booty for the frigate birds.

Mon. 7/19 We saw a fata morgana [mirage] on the horizon as if clouds of smoke were rising.

We lieutenants are taking three watches, during the day from 8 to 8 for three hours and at night for four hours. The crew has three watches for four hours, each watch except for 12 noon to 4 o'clock for two hours. The pilots also have three watches, during the day six hours and at night four hours. The sentinels at the powder chamber have two watches of four hours each. Thus the watches pass around, so that I am never on with the same crewmen twice in a row.

The swimming frigate, a kind of medusa or jellyfish, is totally occupying Tilesius. Its thread long feelers burn like nestle. Rarely does an animal have such beautiful and tender colors as this one does. What more does Tilesius need? He can have sea creatures by the bucket-full.

Tues. 8/20 A lot of dolphins and porpoises are playing in the water. It is a bit hard to have three watches. Only Ratmanoff is lazy. He eats, drinks, sleeps, and amuses himself. We report to the captain through him; that is his only job. He bathes every day in a tub, lets himself be served and does whatever he wants to, because Krusenstern winks at everything and everybody. And Ratmanoff goes too far in everything.

Wed. 9/21 At 22° 30' west longitude, we passed the equator. My strife with Tilesius has totally ended since Golovatscheff's death. It would have been incorrect of me, given Tilesius's request to forget everything and to become reconciled, to have still pushed the matter. We are now best of friends.

Since Golovatscheff's stand and boxes were sealed and lowered into the hold, his cabin is vacant. Krusenstern offered it to Tilesius—he had already turned down Friderici's cabin in Kamtschatka—and he also turned this one down and remained in the gunner's cabin. Krusenstern then offered it to Raefski, who abhors sleeping in a cabin where someone shot himself. That was Otto Kotzebue's reason for rejecting the cabin. Krusenstern wanted to give it to Moritz Kotzebue. Ratmanoff in turn, from caprice, did not agree, and then Mate Spolochoff got it.

Here we picked up the favorable current which flows counter to the wind.

Thurs. 10/22 In general, we are following the same course as in 1803.

Friderici is little loved among my comrades. And that too-intimate friendship between him and Moritz is the reason that the latter is also not tolerated quite so well. The suspicions which several of my comrades have I consider unfounded. I cannot, however, totally condone Friderici's behavior; that he is at fault for Moritz' knowledge being behind where it should be may be true, that Moritz early became introverted is probably the fault of those who give it to him daily. The hate between the two brothers toward each other is also a result of that and does not speak well for either of them.

Fri. 11/23, Sat. 12/24 An example of Krusenstern's behavior on deck especially since St. Helena: It was my watch from 4 to 8 o'clock in the morning. At five o'clock, it began to rain, and the sun had not yet risen, when I was wet to the skin. A middling wind was helping us, however, to move forwards. Several times, I had thought about filling up rainwater. Since the sailors say that the water is not drinkable and I myself found it bitter and salty, I did not do it. At six thirty, Krusenstern came up the steps, where he stopped, because it was raining too much, and called to me, "Have the three empty casks brought up. Have tubs and basins brought up. Have the awning taken down." The casks and tubs were left out for some time. Krusenstern tasted the water and found the water was not suitable for drinking. He therefore ordered everyone to wash the berths.

The boatswain came in answer to the order and said, "The berths are still completely clean." Krusenstern repeated the order, and the people began to wash the sleeping quarters. Krusenstern personally showed each sailor the spot he should wash, had the casks first put here and then there, so that the water would run in better, etc. I played a silent role in the whole thing; and since the wind did not turn and the sails had been set once, I had the satisfaction of not being ordered to have any old sail to be raised or lowered or this rope be pulled in or that one let out. Krusenstern could have given his orders in a much shorter fashion if he had told me, "Have the sleeping quarters washed and fill as many casks of rainwater as are needed," and the berths would have been washed just as clean.

Krusenstern went back into his cabin completely soaked and had to hear Ratmanoff maintain that, now that the cabins were washed, there was no hope that they would be dry by evening. He said, "Нашли время койки мыть" [You sure have found a good time to wash the berths]. Krusenstern's behavior was with the best of intentions. It, however, has to cause sluggishness. We had collected only two casks of water from seven in the morning until midnight.

Krusenstern has extensive knowledge, which brings respect, which has given him influence over us, which in the various situations in which we have been together would have otherwise been difficult to achieve. True, his goodheartedness has gained everyone's love—except for ours—since exactly his excessive softness of nature is what we fault him for. From experience, Krusenstern knows that he is his own best adviser. Ratmanoff, who would have gladly taken over this role, feels himself that he is incapable and now seeks to give himself weight by complaining, slandering, etc., Krusenstern's behavior whenever he can and spares no words.

Bellingshausen has set his stakes high (he is capable of most anything) and has a lot of natural talents and a clear head. Krusenstern puts up barriers to this conceited, one-sided person through his knowledge and lets him know, without intending to, that there are people who know more and are more intelligent than he is—and that wounds. Therefore, Bellingshausen associates with Ratmanoff and both act scandalously, unpunished. Romberg is very comfortable, likes to harvest without sowing, and makes himself important, by, together with a bottle of rum to pass the time, translating several descriptions of voyages, but otherwise carries out Krusenstern's orders laxly and often in drunken courage has been coarse toward him. Krusenstern has always stayed calm, thereby defeating Romberg. The result of this is hate. I see myself surrounded by comrades with whom I am of the opposite opinion, resulting in my keeping quiet. Krusenstern is very careful to prevent trouble, to shut up the traps of vociferous criticism. He leaves the company cabin totally under our control but in contrast gives us none at all on watch. That hurts. Krusenstern is, however, forced into acting that way to protect himself. Differences in behavior would create envy. Therefore, he meets us all equally. I have to regret that, even though I agree, I am not calm enough to see all of that without irritation. We accuse Krusenstern of spoiling our sailors and then excuse ourselves totally.

If we were to talk openly and if we were sincere among ourselves, then all of the misdeeds would have been taken care of a long time ago. I may not speak without being asked and give my opinion, because I might only make things worse and not better. We wink at the sailors' disobedience and laziness. Since Krusenstern gets no complaints, no punishment is meted out. In the company cabin the blame is shoved off on Krusenstern. As Captain Lieutenant, Ratmanoff should be the one to reprimand these things. He, however, likes his position of laziness too much to bother about that. His business is to rebuke Krusenstern, even to make him look ridiculous, to scandalize him (if his own egoism is not part of it). Krusenstern's best intentions are interpreted badly, opposite extremes claimed, fault found with the most necessary and best things; simply in order to be able to say afterwards, "I already said that earlier; I predicted that." If Krusenstern asks us for advice in order to change something or to reorder something (without having it necessary), he gets an unsatisfactory answer, finds himself forced to act on his own and no longer asks people for advice, who do not know how to give him advice or are not willing to. Krusenstern has given the cabin over to us and does not mix in with anything concerning it and our behavior. He has reserved for himself only the leadership of the ship and the care of the sailors.

Since the crew is so spoiled, it often happens that Krusenstern's orders are not carried out. The officer of the watch has to take the blame. That is unpleasant and makes for bad blood, reduces trust, and is the reason that Krusenstern relies upon himself and does everything himself if he possibly can. Open talk would soon clear up this misunderstanding. (Self-love and vanity for having done everything oneself may also lead Krusenstern to do some things.) Those are the results of Krusenstern's excessively mild character.

In that, Lisianski thinks otherwise. He says, "Treat the Russian like an animal, last of all (before the end of a campaign, voyage, or march), be tender and friendly toward him; thus, everything in the past is forgotten, and you have won the love of your people."

Sun. 13/25 Calm and rain, two things that generate boredom at sea. Bored, Espenberg did not know what to do with himself. Most people were busy around the table. First, he would go behind this chair, then that one looking to see what was being read or written (an unbearable habit). Now and then, he amused himself with Romberg's parrot or ate hardtack and intermittently went into the captain's gallery to amuse himself. We observed this for a long time and remarked about it to each other. I then had to take up my watch and was going up and down the quarterdeck thoroughly soaked. Then Horner came up totally ill-humored and said, "Gobble! And shit! Comrade! I do not want to be with Espenberg since he is doing both to pass the time." And that is the truth.

Horner, through Espenberg's useless questions, had miscalculated a couple of times in my presence, and, in my opinion, he had been so bothered that he had to do the entire calculation anew. To recover and renew his desire to work, he came on deck.

Mon. 14/26, Tues. 15/27 Calms. If I calculate eight knots, then the *Neva* is sailing a knot better than we are. We separated on April 15 and still had 106 days' voyage until the end of July to be in Kronstadt and to travel approximately 21° longitude and latitude. Calculating six days in Helena and four days in Copenhagen, there remain 96 days of travel divided into 12,600 miles giving 133 miles a day. From that, we are losing 17 miles every day and 1:17 = 96: 1,632. That is divided in 150 that the *Neva* sails daily, meaning that the *Neva* has won 12 days; add six days in Helena and four in Copenhagen giving 22 days. If the *Neva* stays in England for ten days and two days in Helsingör and Copenhagen, then she will still be in Kronstadt ten days before we are. Or the wind has to be especially favorable (we have enough calms), and the *Neva* would have to fight contrary winds.

Wed. 16/28 In the evening, we got trade winds.

Thurs. 17/29, Fri. 18/30 Our rigging (стояной, standing) is beginning to tear, and our sails are no longer of much use. We are tying a patched, old sail in the place of an old, torn sail. The damaged rigging is also being repaired as well as possible. Everything nevertheless still looks honorable.

Sat. 19/31 The topmast would have certainly gone overboard if the weather had been stormy, since two pairs of shrouds ripped at the same time.

Since we also lashed on a new topsail, it was a good opportunity to haul in the top shrouds. I had Krusenstern asked about it, and he ordered it done. Since China, we have sailed on the left tack, and our shrouds have therefore become awry on the right side. Many said that it was the fault of the crooked mast. Now, since we are continually tacking to the right, the topmast is too warped on the left side. Of course, the shrouds are at fault. It was necessary to straighten the masts and that had to be possible. But master's mate and our sailors had no interest in doing this work. They claimed that the masts were naturally warped to the right side and did not want to do the work. I did not get into an argument but had Krusenstern asked once again what he had ordered. He had ordered, "Haul the shrouds," was the answer. When he came on deck, the work had progressed quite far. I told him that I had not wanted to get in an argument with the sailors and for this reason had bothered him with the repeated question. "They have to be hauled from both sides," he answered me. That is what I had already ordered earlier. Krusenstern looked up after the work had been done and said the masts are warped to the left. The sailors had finished the work. Krusenstern remained silent and the masts remained warped; подшкипор [master's mate] deserved a reprimand in any case. Krusenstern, however, does not want to end our voyage with punishments.

Sun. 20/1 Whitsun. The weather is good. We could also get along with bad weather, since the good weather passes without any pleasure.

Mon. 21/2 Kamentschikoff and Spolochoff are both ill. Their positions have been taken by Otto and Moritz Kotzebue and Raefski, who are now our pilots. That is why Romberg made the following remark, "Now we will have a decent current."

Due to the high seas, the *Nadezhda* wallows too much in the water. (She is too heavy up front.) Krusenstern therefore ordered the fore topgallant sail hauled in. Since it is all the same which sail one uses if the rudder is lightened, Krusenstern left the upper topgallant sail alone. Ratmanoff came on deck. "That is the first time I have seen the upper topgallant left, when the fore topgallant is hauled in," he said, "You can learn new practices here." That is the way Ratmanoff remarks about everything that Krusenstern does in his candid way. A ship looks ugly under these sails, that is true.

Tues. 22/3 We are making quite good progress, but it does not go as fast as in Southern Hemisphere.

Today we had to change the fore topgallant sail.

I have been reading Schubert's *Astronomy*[1] since Helena. I regret not having used this book earlier since I had it. That big volume, almost thick as a hand, scared me off.

Wed. 23/4 The second foreshroud tore. We turned the ship immediately on the other tack and retied the line by splicing and hauled the shrouds anew, including the yard and top shrouds.

We also attached a new jib fore yard staysail and mizzen stay. After completing the work, we turned the ship again.

Our rotten bowsprit and another even more rotten large yard can cause us even more work. The cross-jack yard is so bad on the right end that the crosspiece of the schkief [sheave, a grooved wheel of a block pulley] tore it apart. At one o'clock, we attached another fore topsail.

We left Kronstadt on the 26th June 1803. If we arrive on that day, we will have been gone 1,100 days and still have to complete 1/17 of the voyage.

At our departure, not a one of us dared to think about our return. After our arrival in Kamtschatka, we heard, when we return from Japan, then we will have completed half of our voyage. After the voyage to Sachalin, we were still counting years, from China months, and now weeks, and, before we know it, we will arrive in Copenhagen, from where we have to count only a few days left. I—and many of my comrades are of the same opinion—if immediately upon our return, an opportunity were offered to make a second voyage around the world, would take it up, and three days after the completion of the first voyage would begin the second.

Thurs. 24/5 Now the talreps [риф тали: reef tackle] have begun to tear (lines used to lash the shrouds).

Fri. 25/6 The topsail also tore a line.

That I have withdrawn into my cabin surprises some, and others criticize it. I do not want to see the arguments and laziness in the company cabin any more and use my time in solitude better, am in no one's way, and do not have to sit there silently when I would like to talk, and spare myself many an annoyance.

Sat. 26/7 High seas from the northeast.

Sun. 27/8, Mon. 28/9 On the 28th, we had sun at the zenith for the last time, and then we left the hot zone. I am glad to leave it, since neither day nor night have I stopped sweating between the tropics—and that gets to you.

Tues. 29/10 Again unexpectedly we lost the trade winds at the 25^{0} latitude and have now been a toy in the wind for the fifth day in a row. A lot of seaweed and tang drifts by our ship.

Wed. 30/11 It became apparent that the end of the great yard is very rotten. We had to clamp and support it with two schkalen [шкали: blocks of wood]. We also had to attach another topgallant sail.

Thurs. 31/12 High seas from the northwest.

June

The *Horse Latitudes* [sic] are claiming their rights.

Fri. 1/13, Sat. 2/14, Sun. 3/15 Our impatience makes the calms even more oppressive. We are moving only a little bit forward.

Mon. 4/16 We observed an eclipse of the sun. It lasted from one-thirty to four o'clock. Very little of the sun remained uncovered. The shadow was very weak, and the sun cast shimmer on the water like the full moon on a bright night. The horizon was sharper and darker. The chickens settled in to sleep, and some dew fell so that the portholes were damp. We could clearly see the sickle-shaped sun through our old torn greatsail. All of the sailors satisfied their curiosity and looked at the sun through our telescope. The only ones who did not seem concerned with the eclipse were Romberg, who went around on watch, and Tilesius, who undisturbed, wrote and drew at the runduk [рундук] (locker above the wheel). We were all surprised how anyone can be so uninterested in such a rare phenomenon.

Tues. 5/17 We attached another fore topsail.

The aft stem was 16 fuss 2 zoll; the fore stem is 14 fuss; thus the difference is 2 fuss 2 zoll.

Wed. 6/18, Thurs. 7/19, Fri. 8/20, Sat. 9/21, Sun. 10/22 We broke the fore topgallant yard. Calms have been holding up for a long time. Since the 29th of May, we have gone only a little forwards. What good does impatience do! Come what may, in a couple of months, we will nevertheless be at the goal of our voyage.

Mon. 11/23 We passed the latitude of Gibraltar.

Tues. 12/24 In Kronstadt in 1803, after experimenting, we found that the second glass took 14 seconds to run. Krusenstern ordered the distance between knots to be made 46 fuss long. During wet weather, the second glass compared to the chronometer takes 14½ seconds. That is the reason for our knots measuring 48 fuss since yesterday. That must make a big difference in the calculation of the current. On Russian ships of war, the second glass runs at 29 seconds, and the log line is set to 30 seconds; that is 50 fuss [feet] 11 zoll [inches] English from each other. That shows how imprecise the ship's calculations are.

Wed. 13/25 We caught sight of a vessel in the northwest sailing to the southeast. As a precaution we loaded all of our cannon.

Thurs. 14/26, Fri. 15/27 We passed the latitude of the Azor Islands.

Sat. 16/28 Finally, a good wind. The calms had put all of us without exception in a bad mood. It is doubly pleasant to watch the ship cutting through the water with a good wind.

Sun. 17/29 Weather is still good; barely three weeks, if the wind holds, and we will be in Copenhagen.

I can twist and turn things however I want to; I have to count myself lucky to have made this voyage. Thanks goodness, though, it is coming to an end, since I and almost everyone else have become crabby and everyone from thoughtfulness and melancholy lets his head hang. I am honest enough to admit my crabby nature and for that reason excused myself today with Krusenstern and asked his pardon in case I might have offended him with my crabby behavior.

Mon. 18/30, Tues. 19/1 We caught sight of the topgallant sail of a ship on the horizon. We approached each other. First, the ship tacked to the right and then to the left, as if it were waiting for us, maintained then the same course, and was then lost from view. The ship held more to the east. We mused a long time about what the intentions of the vessel could have been.

Wed. 20/2 A long sea voyage is tiring. It is not the difficulties of the voyage that are burdensome, but the continual sameness and the little things that become a heavy burden. Wind, weather, sunshine, and rain—one has enough of all of them. If the wind is contrary, you are angry. If it is better, then you are afraid it will turn bad again. If it is good, then you regret that it does not continue long enough. It is the same way with everything we do. We could be satisfied with the food and drink, if we were not continually tense and in a bad mood and thus embitter every pleasure. There is no entertainment at all and that because everyone, being in a bad mood, puts his words too much on the balance scale.

Thurs. 21/3 Once again after a very long time—fog.

Last night, I experienced well how much you can do with ten men. At twelve o'clock at night, I took up my watch. We had a good main topgallant sail wind from the south with rain and overcast skies. We were heading northeast for east and were carrying the following sails: all of the top main sails, topgallant sail, and maintop gallant staysail. On the right side were all the studdingsails, all staysails, the foresail, the outer jib, contra-mizzen, and mizzen staysail. The wind became fuller at a quarter of one, and, in addition, I set the topgallant studding sail from the left side. Suddenly all of the sails swung back with full force. I had time only to have the topgallant lowered and the rudder turned to the left in order to hold fully until I was finished with the studdingsail, that is, had it drawn in. I sent two men to lower the topgallant studding sail and topgallant sails from the great mast, two men to the foremast in order to lash down these sails and lower them. Since the sheet tore, I sent two men up the mast in order to lash down the topgallant sails from the main mast; two men stood at the steering rudder, and thus I was left with only two men and the boatswain on the deck. With great difficulty, I hauled the top studding sail down. During this time, I had to steer toward the east-southeast. When several sailors had come down from the trestletrees, the lanyard on the lower studdingsail tore. That sail gave us a great deal of trouble. At the same time, I had the contra-mizzen sail lowered. Then we pulled down all of the staysails, and only now was I able to go by the wind. I was barely finished when Krusenstern, awakened by the flapping of the sails, came on deck, since I had had no one whom I could have sent to wake him.

He ordered the topgallant sail also to be lashed down and all of the studdingsails hauled in and in the jib hauled in halfway, since the wind was becoming ever brisker. Now, I put the sails sharply closehauled alee and put in a new schturtross [штуртрос: tiller line], because the old one was threatening to break. Then I turned the jollyboat around, which has hanging on the right side, because the wind had already become so strong that the water was streaming past very close under the boat. We barely finished with that when a barrel of beer and the large water cask standing on the deck were threatening to rip loose from their lashings. I had the barrel put allee, which had been standing at the great mast in the middle of the deck, and ordered the other to be lashed down. Then I set the apsel [апсель: mizzen staysail], raised the fore shroud staysails and took a reef in the krusel [кружок: sheave]. This work also ended my watch (on which I could have very easily lost all of the masts). I was hoarse from continually issuing commands and tired out from running around and pulling and wet through and through from the rain and cold weather. How wonderful it was to be relieved at four in the morning. I slept like a stone until eight o'clock when Stepan woke me for tea. Everything in the world is transitory, and also that difficult watch is forgotten. Many a seaman will find doing that work with ten sailors unbelievable.

Fri. 22/4 Judging a squall is difficult at night when the sky is overcast. Often, black clouds pass by without any effect, and insignificant ones carry strong gusts of wind.

In the morning, a brig sailed by and in the evening a schooner. The wind is good, but the sea is high.

Sat. 23/5 In fourteen days, we hope to be in Copenhagen. Barely arrived we will have soon left, and after half a year the whole voyage will be like a dream. Is all of human life indeed only a dream?

Sun. 24/6 It is very good if all of the sailors on a ship know how to steer. Since there also are, however, among them such stupid men, it can be dangerous. At two o'clock at night, Efim took over steering and relieved a sailor who is just as ignorant as he is. The wind had continually increased. I had already taken in the studdingsails, and we were sailing eight knots under the main topsail, topgallant sail, and fock. Suddenly, all of the sails began to flap and were out of the wind. Luckily, I was standing near enough to the wheel immediately to chase the rascal away from the wheel and to take over steering myself; otherwise, our topgallant mast would have certainly flown overboard. The stupid devils had no idea what they should do and held east-southeast for east-northeast, turned instead of to the right to the left. The noise caused by the sail woke Krusenstern, and he ordered the topgallant sail also be hauled in. I felt sorry about the nice wind, blowing so evenly, briskly from behind. At four o'clock all of the sails were set again.

Mon. 25/7 In the morning, the two sailors who deserved to be punished did not even get a reprimand from Krusenstern.

Bellingshausen is ill, and Romberg and I both have to stand two watches. That may be all right for a short period of time. If the weather is damp and stays damp, cold, and wet, then we cannot stand it very long, since neither Romberg nor I have very strong constitutions. We have been taking it now for eight days.

Tues. 26/8 Miracle of miracles, Ratmanoff decided to stand watch with us and took up his first watch at noon today.

One lazy person less in the cabin. It would have been the highest degree of shamelessness and laziness if he had not taken over a watch. Romberg let him hear quite a few things when he was relieved.

Wed. 27/9 There is nothing better than domestic joys! There are many of them on the *Nadezhda*. As different as we are from each other in outward appearances, we are just as different in our views. We all agree with that. All of our purchases in China consist of things intended as gifts. Only a few of them will be given to guests. The greatest part of them are meant for a small circle of friends and relatives for whom everyone lives, in whose company he feels at home, with whom he has similar views, and with whom he wishes to live. As much as we look forward with joy to our return, so is it limited to seeing acquaintances and friends whom we left. Without acquaintances, friends, and relatives even the fatherland is no longer of interest. Without them, all of the areas of the world are the same; without them, the country in which you feel most comfortable is the fatherland. And it makes no difference if it lies in the north, south, east, or west. As unfriendly as the climate of Estonia is, I would not now exchange it for the riches of India or the fertility of Brazil.

Thurs. 28/10 Yesterday, a big mistake was made, which Krusenstern also reproved today by upbraiding the pilots Spoloschoff and Raefski. On Ratmanoff's watch, Krusenstern had ordered keeping east to north. Ratmanoff gave this order to the sailors who were at the wheel and did not concern himself with it any further. Raefski, who did not know anything about it and was too lazy to look at the compass, wrote down the old or early rhumb, that is east-northeast, in the logbook.

This mistake was discovered only today and the negligence earned a reprimand.

Fri. 29/11 We passed Rockall in the night. At the last minute, the rain soaked us to the bone. I hope Bellingshausen gets well soon but would like him to continue reporting ill because Ratmanoff, since he has been standing watch again, has become much more humane and makes less noise and criticizes much less. He is busy.

Sat. 30/12 At three o'clock in the morning, at sunrise, we met a privateer (corsair) that is cruising around here. At first, she raised a French flag and then an English flag. We got ready to defend ourselves. I went on board and got newspapers from the captain of the privateer *Crawfuit* [sic] (*Atalanta* is the name of the two-mast ship), and he very kindly told me a lot of news. This privateer is cruising around here trying to catch Prussian ships and has already sent four prizes to Bristol. Bonaparte is master of Europe?

July

Sun. 1/13 Tilesius is angry that no one told him earlier that the Marquesas Islands had been discovered before us—that is just like him! The question, "How did the Englishman Roberts and the Frenchman Cabri get there?" angers him even more. Since then, there have been frequent arguments between him and Horner and Espenberg. The rest of us just listen and do not get into the argument at all.

Mon. 2/14 We have put the cables on the anchors. Daily there are a lot of vessels on our horizon.

Tues. 3/15 We have been seeing a tender that, however, makes no move to approach us. In the evening, we put up another fore topgallant sail.

Wed. 4/16 Held up by contrary winds, we are cruising around here and have to content ourselves with the news we get from passing ships. At six o'clock in the morning, we caught sight of two vessels downwind sailing toward us, the frigate *Blanch*e and a cutter and alee an American and a tender. The frigate forced us by a shot to go on the drift and sent, after she had splendidly sailed toward us and had gotten, in answer to the question where we were coming from, "from Kamtschatka," said "not understood," and sent a shallop with a lieutenant on board to question us. (They had been looking forward to catching a good prize.) The frigate was cruising around because of several French frigates, which they said have already taken several prizes. Krusenstern used the opportunity and gave them letters acquired in Canton to take along, and we sailed on. At five o'clock, we caught sight of the Orkney Islands.

Thurs. 5/17 We are still sailing with contrary winds and calms. The Orkneys were the first European land we have caught sight of, but we nevertheless sailed into the strait.

Fri. 6/18 After we had passed Mold He[a]d and Ronaldschay [Ronaldsay] we caught sight of *Fair Island* [sic] in the morning, sailed past the island, and made our entrance into the North Sea. The *Schetlands* and *Orknei* [sic] Islands seem inhospitable enough.

Krusenstern plans to stay only a very short time in Copenhagen. I only hope we will all have enough time to be able to go on land.

Just after noon, a fishing boat came out to us from *Fair Hill* [sic] with fish, three chickens and eggs—very poor people. There are supposed to be about 250 people on *Fair Island* [sic]. There is an agent there whom they call governor. The north side of the island is steep and has a clean shore or fairway; the south side has hidden reefs. High water is at eleven o'clock, and a strong current sets in from the northwest.

They were crazy for old shoes and boots. An old Scotsman danced for joy over a pair of old boots and had, like Scotsmen, brown hair and a red beard. Krusenstern asked them about war. "Ye!" said one, "we are not at war with anyone." They knew that Pitt[2] was dead, but they did not know Fox at all. They asked about letters, which could be sent by way of the Shetland Islands, reconsidered, however, and said the Orkneys.

The old fellow offered us gloves for sale, which in terms of coarseness and colorfulness are comparable to the ones Estonian peasant girls wear and knit and even had threads on the tips of the fingers, which had not been cut off, as proof that the gloves had not been worn. They brought us an especially large cod and mackerels. They knew how to beg and bargain as well as the Jews. Before the islanders left, we told them, "Bring us sheep." One among them, after having promised to come again if the wind did not get brisker, asked Krusenstern imploringly, "If I come again, you have to give me a pair of old shoes." At eight o'clock in the evening, we saw four boats rowing toward us bringing us sheep, chickens, eggs, coal, and fish, etc. Our acquaintances were the first to arrive and also brought us the most. Everyone crowded around to see what the people had brought to sell, even Espenberg with his usual silliness. I had a falling out with him, and we were really at each other. Krusenstern, who was present and listened to the argument, acted as intermediary and reconciled us. We promised each other to forgive and forget everything that had happened, and now we are better friends, since the reconciliation after the strife has eliminated the discord expressed in cold behavior and snideness between us, which had eroded our sociability.

The newly bought fish were cooked in the evening. The cook had not put enough salt in the water. Espenberg, as steward, sent the bowl back to the kitchen with an order to put more salt into the water and to cook the fish again. The vehemence with which he ordered it and his need to exaggerate everything, for he had anxiously said to Stepan, "The fish have to be salted and cooked five more times," was without a doubt at fault; for Tschernoi, our present cook, losing his sense of proportion and putting much too much salt on the fish, cooked them totally to pieces. When the bowl was brought again, the fish were tasteless and the ucha [fish soup] absolutely inedible. At table, we all mercilessly blamed Espenberg, who had had very good intentions. In Kamtschatka, Espenberg had preached enough that the fish had to be salted and cooked more. His advice, however, was not followed, and, except for Krusenstern, Espenberg, Horner, and a couple of others and me, all were plagued for months afterward by tape and other worms.

We mediated afterwards, but our evening meal stayed spoiled.

Sat. 7/19 Total calm. The play of the current is driving us around in view of the unfriendly Shetland Islands. Impatiently, we meet every little breeze that brings us the hope of taking us closer to our goal.

The little lambs we bought from Fair Island are so innocent, nice, and tame that it will be difficult for us to pass judgment on them and lead them to the slaughter block, but, since we are on a salt meat diet, they will have to go.

Sun. 8/20 The wind is weak. We can nevertheless still hope to reach Copenhagen in ten days. Upon our arrival there, we have more to do than the time allotted. Espenberg therefore divided up the remaining fish money to the sum of 130 dahler per man. Through a misunderstanding, he got into an argument with Ratmanoff. 200 dahler had been collected and spent, without saying when and where. Ratmanoff, coarse as usual, used his jaw. Espenberg very angrily used an expression, as if the matter were none of Ratmanoff's business. Krusenstern had to investigate the strife and decide. The mistake was found, and the strife ended and was put aside.

This morning at sunrise, I counted 28 Dutch fishing boats around us. This is the area in which the Dutch generally catch herring. Are the English going to let them continue to fish undisturbed? During the morning we lost sight of the Shetland Islands.

The military appearance of the *Nadezhda* has undoubtedly made nervous many a merchant ship quietly sailing by, since our intentions are uncertain because we rarely hoisted the flag—and that I believe very correctly so.

If we meet a ship of war, she demands through a shot that we show our flag. If she is a merchant ship, then we are not empowered in foreign waters to force her to raise her flag. We sail quietly on without bothering others and desire that others not hold us up either.

In the evening, a three-mast vessel was closing in on us. She was too far away for us to be able to tell whether she was a war or merchant ship. Toward nine o'clock, she raised a French flag with a shot. We also raised our flag then and prepared to defend ourselves. Not long afterwards the little frigate raised the English flag. Since she would have taken too long in the calm winds for us to wait until she caught up with us, Krusenstern sent me onboard to report to the English captain who we were. It took me an hour to go back and forth. The frigate was the *Lynx*, Captain Marshall. It had been cruising around for two months, had only nine ports or cannon, and appeared to be more out for boarding. The falconet on the quarterdeck was arranged very nicely and very useful in boarding. The manrope was blocked by berths, and the whole ship was hung with grapnel nets. In the beginning, they absolutely did not want to believe that we were coming from Kamtschatka and had already been at sea for three years. Marshall was also chasing three French frigates that were supposed to be in these waters. Since the captain has been at sea for a long time, I was unable to get much news and hurried back to the *Nadezhda*.

Mon. 9/21 Nice favorable wind.

Tues. 10/22 At four o'clock in the morning an English frigate sailed after us. Since we were traveling eight and three-quarter knots, we hoped to escape her. She, however, was with the wind and that is why we had to wait. At six o'clock, they sent a boat over to interrogate us, and half an hour later we set sail again. The frigate was named *Quebeck* and Lord Faulkoner was her captain. The *Quebeck* had held up the *Neva* three days before on her way to Copenhagen. If we had not been held up by a calm at Fair Island, we could have been in Copenhagen earlier than the *Neva*. There would have been general cheering among us if that had happened. Lisianski sailed with an English convoy, bragged that he had been on a voyage of discovery and had discovered groups of islands, which everyone will avoid visiting, since the groups consisted of bare sandbanks and rocks.

In the morning, we were sailing eight knots, and in the afternoon we were becalmed once again. In the evening, we saw land that we soon recognized as *the Nase* [sic], the southern tip of Norway. Where has the hope gone of being in Helsingör tomorrow?

Wed. 11/23 We sailed slowing past *the Nase* [sic] with calms.

The *Neva* did not sail for no good reason from Portsmouth with a convoy. The frigates of various countries cruising around the North Sea are not able to catch the privateers holed up in Norwegian hiding places, waiting for storms which drive the frigates from their stations out to sea. The English cruisers do not get to the Skagerrak and Kattegat at all. That is why we feared privateers the most on our trip from *the Nase* [sic] to Helsingör. As a precaution, we had our cannons loaded, balls, etc., ready, so that we could not be captured at night by privateers and could scare them off in time.

Thurs. 12/24 We drifted around in a calm in view of Dernaus, as the Russians call *the Nase* [sic], without being able to withstand the current which drove us back. At night, involuntarily turned around by a variable wind, a brig headed toward us.

In the dark we could not distinguish whether the ship was armed or not. Therefore, alarm was sounded on our ship. We had barely readied everything for defense when we saw that we had inconvenienced ourselves because of a harmless merchant ship. Everything was put away, the lunts extinguished, and everyone went back to sleep.

At eight o'clock in the morning, we caught sight of a convoy. It consisted of 38 ships and passed us at ten thirty. We put ourselves on the drift because Krusenstern had letters from *Adington* he wanted to pass on. They had not seen the *Neva*. A Russian frigate, however, passed in the Kattegat yesterday. They were kind enough to give us a packet of old newspapers. The wind does not want to be kind to us.

Fri. 13/25 Krusenstern's caution did not permit us to make a stop immediately on the coast of Jutland. We sailed for two days in view of Norway and therefore did not move from the same spot either. The continuing contrary winds forced us to hold to the south. We barely caught sight of Jutland when the current became favorable for us and we are going forwards. Even Krusenstern cannot hide his impatience and dissatisfaction with being held up by contrary winds and calms.

Sat. 14/26 The main top sheet tore while turning.

The preacher on the Danish East India or China vessel told us in Canton, very openly, that the complete necessity of having to live together, that is to say, imprisoned on the ship for so long, gets to be wearisome. If someone of the group is absent for several weeks or even days, then you are happy to see him again, even if his company during the time was ever so repulsive. How pleasant it is after a completed voyage to see each other after years of separation. This view is very true.

Sun. 15/27 Finally, at noon, we passed the longitude of Skagen (the northern point of Jutland), and the same wind that had been contrary in the past days is now favorable to us.

Mon. 16/28 We sailed past Marstrand, Winga, Nidingen, and Warberg with a favorable wind and came as far as Anholt. With the sink lead, we found 50 to 90 faden bottom and at Marstrand 25 to 30 faden. 38 cartouches with gunpowder that had gotten wet were cast overboard.

Tues. 17/29 We passed Anholt, and, because of contrary winds and current, we cast anchor near Kolmajak in 13 faden of water. The current was two knots to the south-southeast.

Wed. 18/30 Danger of shipwreck in which the *Nadezhda* was during the voyage: in the Skagerrak, at Brazil, at the Marquesas Islands, trying to find the silver islands, in the typhoon, near the Kurils, near Sachalin, in Kamtschatka, and near Java in the Straits of Sunda.

Yesterday, when we cast anchor, we requested through a shot a pilot who came on board at eleven at night. We are lying at anchor only 15 miles from Helsingör and waiting for a good wind.

At six o'clock in the morning, we weighed anchor, could not, however, because of a contrary current, reach Helsingör but rather had to cast anchor again at ten o'clock in the morning three miles away in the narrowest passage of the strait. At our request, a Danish pilot came onboard, and we released our Swedish pilot. Using the pilot's boat Espenberg, Friderici, and Tilesius went ashore in order to get us fresh provisions and send letters. Tilesius gave Krusenstern the task (who himself was planning to go ashore) of seeing after his things, which he had left scattered about the gunner's cabin. He was laughed at and, peeved, went on land—that is how blockheaded the man behaves.

The *Neva* passed here eight days ago.

The Russian consul Tolbitzer came on board at twelve o'clock, not long after that a shallop from the fire watch. Krusenstern went in the Consul's boat to Helsingör, turned the command over to Ratmanoff, and gave him to task of setting the clocks. (He has this honor for the first time during the whole voyage.)

At noon, we had fresh potatoes and grits.

At three o'clock, the wind became brisk. In order to see if it were brisk enough to overcome the current, we set sails without weighing anchor. Since it did not want to pull us forwards, we left the sails in place in order to lighten the pull on the anchor cable in the hope that the wind would become even brisker. Krusenstern in Helsingör will have suspected that we have already set sail.

Thurs. 19/31 We weighed anchor, could not, however, get to Helsingör because the wind was weak and the contrary current too strong. We had to cast anchor again.

Fri. 20/1 At twelve o'clock, we weighed anchor, and, at four o'clock, we cast anchor finally on the Copenhagen roadstead in six and one-half faden of water.

We heard little pleasant news. Our long absence has become a burden for us, and the unpleasant news has embittered our happy dreams for our futures. We need peace and quiet to strengthen our bodies that have become tired and exhausted from the hardships and diversions in order to awaken feelings that have almost been suffocated in us.

Sat. 21/2 An English frigate from the Baltic arrived here.

Sun. 22/3 Like hamsters, we are dragging fresh provisions from land. At three o'clock in the morning, the English frigate set sail for the North Sea.

At ten o'clock in the morning, the Danish Crown Prince Christian with his suite came on board. Barenflit, Löwenörn, etc. were with him. At eleven o'clock, we had a raging gust of wind with rain, and at eleven thirty the Crown prince returned to Copenhagen. We saluted him with fifteen cannon shots and put the sailors along the yards.

Mon. 23/4 We renewed the black oil paint on the *Nadezhda*. Aft stem 16 fuss 5 zoll; fore stem 14 fuss, the difference 2 fuss 5 zoll. Anyone who can is heading to Copenhagen.

Tues. 24/5 We also painted the *Nadezhda* with yellow oil paint. The mate Andreeff, who had been left behind due to illness, came on board to sail with us to

Kronstadt. He had been left behind by the frigate *Feodossia Totmenskaja* sailing from Archangel.

There are very many provisions being hauled onboard, as if we were going to set out on another voyage around the world.

Wed.. 25/6 After we had saluted, we weighed anchor and set out again under sail, sailed past Stefens and Dragoö and in the evening past Falserbon.

Thurs.. 26/7 In the evening, we sailed past Bornholm and in the night Christians Ör.

Fri. 27/8 Heaving the [sink] lead is exhausting but very necessary.

Sat. 28/9 The shrouds and fore backstays also know that home is ahead; first this one and then that one tears.

Sun. 29/10 We sailed past Gotland, damp air and fog.

Mon. 30/11 A convoy is sailing with us. It is ridiculous to watch how all of the ships in quiet waters sail past us. As soon as the weather is bad and fresh, we are up and going again and sail past all of them.

Tues. 31/12 Thick fog. At noon, we caught sight of Osterhorn, the island.

August

Wed. 1/13 We passed the northern point of Gotland. Almost daily we are having thick fog in the Baltic.

Thurs. 2/14 We caught sight of it in the morning and in the evening passed Dagerort. The wet, steep angle of the lead line has rubbed blisters in the palms of all of the sailors.

Fri. 3/15 We sailed past Odgesholm in thunder, lightning, rain, and gusts of wind, in the evening Pokerort and in the night Ravelstern. We left the convoy behind us. The wind was reef topsail.

Sat. 4/16 In the morning we passed Kaschkar, and Olaiturm could be seen in the distance; soon came a calm. The convoy caught up to us again and sailed past us, and we drifted around behind Norgen and Wulf.

Sun. 5/17 In the fog, we caught sight of Rotschkir, and in the evening we sailed past the promontory in the evening.

Mon. 6/18 We sailed past Sommers, Lavensar, Narva, and Seskar.

Tues. 7/19 We sailed past Krasnuiu Gorku, were happy about Tolbuchin Majak, and sailed into Kronstadt. Since the wind was very still, Krusenstern, Horner, and Schemelin went with the boat into Kronstadt ahead of us at twelve o'clock. And, at nine o'clock in the evening, we cast anchor in Kronstadt next to the Merchant's Gate and Harbor. On the roadstead, intended for Italy, were the ships of war Мочной *[Mochnoi]* (contr. Admiral Ignatieff), Михаил *[Mikhail]*, Рафаел *[Rafael]*, Твердой *[Tverdoi]*, Скорой *[Skoroi]*, the frigates Спешной

[Speshnoi] and Лехкой *[Lekhkoi],* the sloop Шриц Берген *[Spitz Bergen],* and the cutter Стрела *[Strela].*

Wed. 8/20 Using warps, we pulled ourselves into the harbor through the middle gate, and at twelve o'clock we entered the canal. At two o'clock, we fastened the *Nadezhda* with hawsers, and thus ended our voyage around the world.

Thurs. 9/21 Tschitschagoff visited the *Nadezhda.*

Sat. 11/23 Count Rumantzoff visited the *Nadezhda.*

Mon. 13/25 General Katagrivoff and a lot of generals and military men visited our ship.

Sat. 18/30 The emperor did us the honor of visiting our ship, was very propitious and satisfied with us.

Sun. 19/31 Upon arrival, our main business is to greet all of the guests and to satisfy all of the curiosity of our visitors. Their number is large. From morning till evening, the *Nadezhda* is stuffed full. We greet our tours of curious guests killing us with questions.

The work of unloading the ship and taking down the riggings continues in an orderly fashion.

Mon. 20/1 We unloaded the American Company's cargo.

Sun. 26/7 The entire crew with sack and pack moved on land.

As requested, I have to stay in Kronstadt in order to finish turning over the *Nadezhda* and helping Krusenstern. Everyone wants leave; everyone wants to go home. I have also taken over the task of transporting Krusenstern's and Espenberg's things to Reval.

The emperor was so benevolent as to give the order that all of our things and baggage should be let in free of customs. To prevent misuse of the order, customs, with very sour faces, put a custom's stamp on all of our things.

The *Neva* arrived in Kronstadt ten days before we did, also had the honor of seeing the Empress Mother on board. And she presented every officer with a golden box as a gift. We came later and went away empty handed.

The officers and the crew of the *Neva* get the same lifelong pension as we do; Korvedeeff and Berg of the *Neva*, both midshipmen, get only 800 rubles a year.

The emperor was also so benevolent as to promote us ahead of time and to grant us all discharges.

The emperor ordered the controversies with Resanoff to be forgotten (предать забвению) and Golovatscheff's letters to be destroyed (unread), because he doubted his being able to find justice in his fatherland.

Horner and Tilesius each received 1,000 rubles pension, which, at their request, was changed to 300 ducats.

Epilogue

AFTER THE VOYAGE, Krusenstern rose to be an inspector (1811) and then director (1827–1842) of the Naval Cadet Corps. He published his memoirs of the around the world voyage and a two-volume *Atlas of Voyage Around the World* (Amsterdam: Nico Israel, 197?). He became a founding member of the Russian Geographic Society as well as a member of the Royal Society in London. He was the impetus for the voyage around the world under the leadership of Otto von Kotzebue 1815–1818 and 1823–1826.

Löwenstern had a quite different career. He spent six months at home before returning to active duty in March 1807. Then he was ordered to Archangel with its rampant corruption among officials and its unhealthy, dank climate, yearly floods, and plagues of mosquitoes. "I got no little shock one morning when I went to the barracks and found of all of my sailors sleeping. All of them had been overcome so much by the fumes that they had to be carried out one after the other." Bouts of illness caused him to return to Reval in May 1809, where he regained his health and, at the same time, fell head over heels in love with Wilhelmine von Essen (1795–1862).

In the fall of 1810, he traveled to Petersburg to request a transfer to the Crimea. "Before my journey I returned to Reval, revealed my wishes to my future father-in-law and, in February 1811, traveled by way of Petersburg and Moscow to the Crimea in the hope of soon returning from there to take my leave, marry, and become a farmer [estate owner]. I would have preferred to stay, but that was not a possibility, and I had to leave, so better to travel to Sevastopol than Archangel."

In Sevastopol, he was promoted to captain lieutenant when the Russian Navy went to sea to take on the Turkish Fleet and then to captain and assigned the frigate *Magubei Supan,* a Turkish ship captured as a prize. His diary entries are far less informative than in earlier years. He complains of illness, his and of those around him, of the fear of the plague, and of corruption. His boredom and discontent with his life are reflected in weather reports, meetings with other ships, and waiting for peace, which came on the 13/25 July 1812. Only when he was in Odessa or Bucharest was his monotony broken. Then he wrote livelier and longer entries. Periodically, as in July 1812, he asked, "What is happening in Reval? What is Wilhelmine doing? No letter from my father. I'm in exile. . . . Recently, every commander was ordered not to accept petitions requesting discharge or leave. Since the peace with the Turks, there is nothing more to do here, but still I cannot leave."

In 9/21 October 1812, he grumbled, "Carl and Woldemar are at fault that we children have no credit with our father. Can it also be the reason for my old father leaving me so long without an answer?"

Finally on 28 July 1814, his father's letter arrived: "My joy was endless. Finally, I can request leave and discharge . . . My health is worthless. Therefore I am unsuited for service."

On 5 February 1815, he left Sevastopol and, on the 27 February, he arrived in Reval. The diary's last entry reads. "Wilhelmine Essen reconciled me with my fate." Löwenstern then registered the names of the cities and villages along his route from Sevastopol to Revel: 2,341 versts and 113 stations.

Unfortunately once he left the naval service, married, and took over the estates of Allafer, Rasik, and Campen, he then felt no more need for a diary. He grew up on and, in retirement from the Navy, owned estates during the period when serfdom was finally abolished in Estonia. He undoubtedly witnessed or knew the famines in 1781–1784 and 1802, particularly among the Estonian peasants. He was, however, at sea during most of the events leading up to the end of serfdom in 1812. Had he kept a diary, he might have left perceptive comments about the transitions taking place in the social structure and way of life in Estonia.

Appendix: Weights and Measures

UNTIL THE METRIC SYSTEM came into universal use, there were no international standards for weights and measures and reference works vary in the information they contain. Thus, a foot (fuss), or an inch (zoll), or a mile could vary from country to country and even from town to town. Therefore, I have left Löwenstern's terms for weights and measures untranslated. The information found here is taken from *A Dictionary of English and German Language* by Chr. Fr. Grieb (Philadelphia: Schaeffer & Konradi, 1866), *The Shipmaster's Assistant and Owner's Manual* (London: David Steel, 1796), and *The Oxford Companion to Ships and the Sea* (Oxford: Oxford University Press, 1976).

Anchor (anker): A Dutch or German liquid measure used for spirits. One anker equals 9–10 U.S.gallons, or 30 to 40 liters.

Arshine (arsheen/arshin): A Russian measure of length varying from 28 to 39 U.S. inches, or 71.1 centimeters, to 1 meter.

Faden (fathom): Seven fuss equal 3 arshine, or 6.99 U.S. feet, or 2.131 meters. An English fathom equals 6 feet, or 1.83 meters.

Fass: One Hamburg fass equals 1.56 U.S. bushels.

Fuss (foot): A Prussian fuss equals 12 zoll (inches), or 1.13 U.S. feet, or 34.44 centimeters. A Russian foot is the same as a U.S. foot.

Katti: Löwenstern says a katti equals 3 pfund.

Knot: This is a unit of speed equal to one nautical mile per hour. A knot equals 47 feet 3 inches U.S. on a log line marked off by knots.

Kruschka: Ten Kruschka equal 13½ beer bottles or 10 wine bottles. One hundred kruschka equal 32.4927 U.S. gallons.

Mass: It varies in size, but is approximately 1.5 liters.

Mile: An English statute mile equals 5,280 feet, or 1,609.315 meters. There are 69.042 of these miles to 1 degree of the equator. A common London mile, however, equals 5,000 feet. A nautical or English geographical mile is 60th part of a degree of the equator. A Berlin mile equals 4.68 U.S. miles, or 7.53 kilometers.

Pfund (pound): A Russian pound equals 9.03 pounds avdp., or 10.9 pounds Troy in the U.S.

Pud: A pud is 40 Russian pounds.

Stof/stoof: A square bottle for brandy for about 2 U.S. pints. Eight stof equals 10 kruschka.

Verst: A Russian verst equals .663 miles U.S., or 1.067 kilometers.

Zoll: See fuss.

Endnotes

Introduction

1. At the conference, *Meetings of Frontiers*, held May 17–18, 2001 at the University of Alaska Fairbanks and sponsored by the Library of Congress and the Russian Academy of Sciences, I was most fortunate to be able to talk with Dr. Nikolai Nikolaevich Bolkhovitinov of the Institute of World History and the Russian Academy of Sciences in Moscow. He most graciously expounded upon the basis for his view of the imbroglio between Captain Krusenstern and Ambassador Resanoff and his desire to rehabilitate Resanoff's reputation from the official Soviet one. Since Resanoff came from the highest court circles, his importance and position in Soviet historical analyses were downplayed and Krusenstern was elevated. In the monarchial hierarchy of tsarist Russia, the emperor was an autocratic ruler whose word was absolute law. Alexander I signed the decree making Resanoff the head of the expedition and even underlined the words. Therefore, it did not matter that Resanoff had never been to sea. The emperor had made him head of the expedition and Krusenstern, no matter his extensive naval experience and feelings, and his officers had to submit to Resanoff's leadership or face the consequences. Krusenstern and his officers were lucky that Resanoff died before returning to St. Petersburg. There is documentary evidence that Krusenstern drove Lieutenant Golovatscheff to commit suicide and that Krusenstern and all of the officers had to apologize to Resanoff for their behavior.

I hope my memory of our conversation does Dr. Bolkhovitinov justice. Since I have not worked with the documents upon which Dr. Bolkhovitinov bases his interpretation, I cannot comment upon them. I can only ask the reader to study this diary with an inquiring mind and an awareness of the diverging views. The diary sheds a different light upon the whole imbroglio and indicates a belief in the emperor's being a reasonable, impartial ruler interested in justice for all concerned. Golovatscheff's letters, as quoted in Russian and Löwenstern's translation, indicate that he had become deranged and irrational, but not as a result of Krusenstern's actions.

2. Sybille Schönborn. *Das Buch der Seele: Tagebuchliteratur zwischen Aufklärung und Kunstperiode* (Tübingen: Niemeyer, 1999) 1.

3. Adam Johann von Krusenstern. *Voyage Round the World in the Years 1803, 1804, 1805, and 1806* (Amsterdam: Da Capo, 1968) 1: 42.

4. Reinhold Wittram. *Baltische Geschichte: Die Ostseelande Livland, Estland, Kurland 1180– 1918* (München: Verlag R. Oldenbourg, 1954) 46.

5. Toivo Raun. *Estonia and the Estonians* (Stanford: Hoover Institution Press, 1991) 15.

6. Raun, 16.

7. Axel von Gernot. *Forschungen zur Geschichte des Baltischen Adels* (Reval: Kluge, 1893) 1: 40.

8. Raun, 38.

9. Wittram, 128

10. Axel von Gernot. *Geschichte und System des bäuerlichen Agrarrechts in Estland* (Reval: Kluge, 1901) 17.

11. Tallinn F1414 N3 51.

12. *Mit Graf Pahlens Reiterei: Denkwürdigkeiten des russischen Generals Eduard von Löwenstern*, ed. Baron Georges Wrangell (Berlin: Mittler und Sohn, 1910) Stammtafel.

13. P. Th. Falck. "Woldemar Freiherr von Löwenstern und seine Memoiren" in *Baltische Monatsschrift* 71 (1911) 314–18.

14. Tartu F 1674 N2 S128.
15. Tallinn F1414 N3 51.
16. *Denkwürdigkeiten eines Livländers aus den Jahren 1790–1815*, ed. Friedrich von Smitt (Leipzig, 1854) 1: 56.
17. According to folk beliefs, mother ravens totally abandon their young a few days after birth and leave them to fend for themselves.
18. Song of Solomon, chapter 6.
19. Vol. 1: 53.
20. Heide W. Whelan. *Adapting to Modernity: Family, Caste and Capitalism among the Baltic German Nobility* (Cologne: Böhlau, 1999) 122.
21. Einleitung X.
22. Tallinn F1414 N3 51.
23. Visit with Barbara Streitberger in Hamburg, Germany in June 2001, during which she showed me family documents.
24. After the Prusso-Danish War, Denmark lost the duchies of Schleswig and Holstein at the Peace of Vienna on October 30, 1864.
25. *Deutsch-Baltisches Biographisches Lexikon* (Vienna: Böhlau, 1970) 710.
26. Baron Georges Wrangell. "Eduard von Löwenstern und die Dekabristen, Gebrüder Murawjew-Apostel" *Baltische Monatschrift* 72 (1911) 192.
27. Conversation with Sirje Aniist, archivist, Tallinn, June 1998.
28. Tartu F851 L1805-1909 S 1008.
29. *Studien zur volkstümlichen Aufklärung in Estland* ed. Johann Dietrich von Pezold (Göttingen: Uandenhoeck and Ruprecht, 1978) 43.
30. (Athens: Ohio U. Press, 1975) 7.
31. *The Harper Encyclopedia of Military History* ed. by R. Ernest Dupuy and Trevor N. Dupuey. 4th ed. (New York: Harper Collins, 1993) 672. John Masefield in *Sea Life in Nelson's Time* (United States Naval Institute, 1971) gives a lively account of the horrors of sea life in the 18th century.
32. Conversation with Sirje Aniist, archivist, Tallinn, June 1998.
33. J. Pawlowsky's *Russisch-Deutsches Wörterbuch* 3 ed. (Riga: Kymmel, 1900) 1749. Most of the information about naval officers and Baltic Germans is taken from the *Deutsch-Baltisches Biographisches Lexikon 1710–1960* and *Obshchii morskoi spisok* St. Petersburg, 1885–1894, vol. 2–8.

Chapter 1

1. Present day Tallinn, the capital of Estonia. From 1346–1561, Tallinn was ruled by the Livonian knights, from 1561–1710 by Sweden and then by Russia after 1721.
2. Cronstadt or Kronstadt, a naval base commanding the approach to St. Petersburg, was founded by Peter I (the Great) in 1703 and lies fourteen miles (22km) west of St. Petersburg.
3. George Tet (1745–1821) was Irish. He joined the Russian Navy under Rear Admiral D. Elphinstone in Portsmouth in 1770. Tet became an admiral in 1802 and a senator in 1816.
4. James (Iakov Ivanovich) Barret (?–1821) left the British Navy in 1789 at the rank of lieutenant and joined the Russian Navy where he rose to the rank of captain-lieutenant. After the American Revolutionary War, the British king halved the pay of naval officers and a good number of them joined the Russian naval service.
5. Dr. Karl Espenberg, a Baltic German from Estonia, was the doctor on the *Nadezhda*. He was the natural son of young Baron von Salza, whose father sent him to Germany to study medicine. Because the Russian government did not recognize Espenberg's German diploma, he had to pass a series of examinations before he could practice medicine in Estonia. He became the family doctor of the Krusensterns, which led to the invitation to join the voyage.
6. The dates are according to the Gregorian (New Style) and Julian (Old Style) calendars.

The New Style calendar was not adopted in Russia until February 14, 1918.

7. Makar Ivanovich Ratmanoff (1772–1833) was the eldest lieutenant on the *Nadezhda*. Before joining the expedition, he had participated in various campaigns in the Baltic, Mediterranean, and Black Seas. Later, he became a vice-admiral of the Russian Fleet.

8. Throughout his diary, Löwenstern uses Kaiser, i.e., he does not differentiate czar, emperor, or kaiser for the various rulers as English does. Here, the reference is to Emperor Alexander I (1777–1825), who became emperor on March 12, 1801, after the murder of his father Paul I through a court conspiracy. In 1793, he married Luise-Marie Auguste (Russian: Elisaveta Alekseevna) (1779–1826), the daughter of the Margrave of Baden.

9. Such an arende or leasehold would ensure that she would be cared for financially while her husband was away.

10. Iurii Fedorovich Lisianski (1773–1837) was born in St. Petersburg. He graduated from the Naval Cadet Corps in 1786 and served in the British Navy for the same period as Krusenstern. He was commander of the *Neva*, the *Nadezhda's* sister ship. The *Neva* separated from the *Nadezhda* in Kamchatka [Kamtschatka] and sailed to Alaska, where Lisianski spent more than a year. The ships then met in Canton before returning to St. Petersburg. The *Neva* was the first ship to sail non-stop from Canton to Portsmouth. Lisianski served in the Baltic Fleet until he retired in 1809.

11. He made demands that Krusenstern found impossible to accept and therefore caused him to reject Gamalei's participation in the Expedition.

12. Friedrich von Romberg (?–1811) was the second lieutenant on the *Nadezhda*. January 25, 1807, he married Elisabeth Julie Baronesse von Wrangell (1790–1873). From 1807 until 1810, he commanded Russian ships.

13. Fabian Gottlieb von Bellingshausen (1778–1852) was the fifth lieutenant on the *Nadezhda*. He was born in Estonia, entered the Naval Corps at Kronstadt at the age of ten, and served on frigates in the Baltic Fleet from 1797–1803. His abilities in nautical astronomy and in hydrography led Khanikov, his commanding officer, to recommend him to Krusenstern. He later became an admiral and in Russia is considered the discoverer of the Antarctic.

14. By a degree of June 8, 1799, Paul I established the Russian-American Company, which thus obtained a monopoly over trade in the Russian Far East and Alaska. Nikolai Petrovich Resanoff (1764–1807), here the Ambassador to Japan, working behind the scenes, was instrumental in convincing the emperor to issue the degree.

Nikolai Petrovich Rumianzoff (1754–1826) was well traveled in Europe and an important public figure who supported commercial and scholarly activities of the period. He was instrumental in planning this voyage.

Greek-born Evstratii Ivanovich Delarov (ca. 1740–1806), a pioneer in the Russian Pacific fur trade, relocated to St. Petersburg when the headquarters of the Russian-American Company, for which he was a director until his death, were moved from Irkutsk to St. Petersburg.

Mikhail Matfeevich Buldakov (1766–1827) was a merchant in northern Russia and a founder of the Russian-American Company. He became its first director and largest shareholder.

15. Unlike the other officers, Krusenstern did not know Peter (Piotr) Golovatscheff personally but hired him upon the recommendation of others.

16. *être de jour*—to be on duty.

17. Vasilii Nikolaevich Berg (Berkh) (1781–1834) was born in Moscow and entered the Cadet Corps in 1795, after which he was assigned to the Baltic Fleet. During this voyage, he was promoted to lieutenant on the *Neva*. He became important as a translator and historian.

18. *Schabasch* is always written in the Latin alphabet although it is a Russian word.

19. Otto von Kotzebue (1787–1846) and Moritz von Kotzebue (1789–1861) were the sons from the first marriage of August von Kotzebue, one of the most popular playwrights of the day. August von Kotzebue's three wives were Adam Johann von Krusenstern's cousins. Kotzebue was also

instrumental in helping Krusenstern publish his memoirs of this voyage. In 1818, Kotzebue was assassinated in Mannheim in front of his family by a religious fanatic. Moritz fought in the Napoleonic wars and spent 1812–14 as a French prisoner of war (*Der russische Kriegsgefangenen unter den Franzosen,* Leipzig: Kummer, 1815). In 1816, he became a member of Ermolov's embassy to Persia. In 1855, he was appointed senator for the Warsaw district. In 1815–1818 and again in 1823–1826, Otto von Kotzebue led Russian expeditions around the world. Kotzebue, Alaska, is named for him. He retired from the Russian Navy in 1829 and spent the rest of his life in Reval.

20. Councilor Fedor Fosse was a member of Ambassador Resanoff's Suite.

Hermann Karl von Friderici (1779–1869) was born in Estonia and entered Russian service in 1796. From 1797–1802, he was a topographer in Finland, after which he was sent to the Academy of Sciences in St. Petersburg to broaden his knowledge of astronomy. In 1826, he became the Commandant of Pavlovsk and in 1848 General of the Infantry.

Ahmed Salakhly (artacad@as4430.spb.edu) most kindly emailed me the following information. Stepan Semenovich Kurlandzoff [Kurliantsev] (1770–1822) was a student at the Imperial Academy of Art in the studio of Professor Ugrymov. In 1800, he won a second-place silver medal and in 1801 a first-place silver medal. In 1803, he was awarded the title of Academician (member of the Academy) for his painting "The Passion of Christ." President of the Academy of Art Stroganov recommended Kurlandzoff to Krusenstern. Kurlandzoff left the expedition in Kamchatka due to kidney disease. On his way overland, he had to stop in Kazan, where he taught drawing at the Russian Orthodox School for six years before finally returning to St. Petersburg. By 1818, he was so destitute that he wrote the Academy asking it to buy the paintings and drawings he had made on the expedition. He requested that the Academy petition the emperor to pay him the full pension promised before the expedition. The Academy answered that it did not need his work and could not support a petition to the emperor, because he had left the expedition earlier than agreed upon in his contract. (Ahmed Salakhly is of the opinion that Kurlandzoff's widow probably sold his works after his death in 1822. She, however, did receive a pension of 1,000 rubles after his death. He was survived by two sons, Konstantin and Vasily.) This information is from *Spisok' Russkih' Khudozhnikov'* (k' iubileinomy spravochniku imperatorskoi academii khudozhestv. Sostavil S. N. Kondakov) 1764–1914, published 1914–1916, p. 107.

21. Spanish dollars in additional sums.

22. Vasilii Iakovlevich Tschitschagoff (1726–1809) was educated in England and entered Russian service in 1742. He was in charge of secret expeditions in 1765 and 1766 that were commissioned to traverse the Arctic Ocean from Spitzbergen to the Bering Strait. His expedition sailed farther north than any ships had gone previously. He was promoted to admiral and made Commander of the Fleet upon the death of Admiral Samuel Greig in 1788.

Aleksei Samuilovich Greig (1775–1845), son of Samuel Karlovich Greig (1734–1788), like his father, became a Russian admiral. See: "Samuel Greig, Catherine the Great's Scottish Admiral" by A.G. Cross in *Mariner's Mirror* 60 (1974) 251–265.

23. Pavel Aleksandrovich Count Stroganoff (born 1772 in Paris, died 1817 in Copenhagen). During the French Revolution, he attended meetings of the Jacobin Club, which led Empress Catherine to recall him and exile him to one of his villages. In 1796, he was permitted to return to St. Petersburg, where he became a friend of the future Emperor Alexander. From 1802, he was first a senator and then from 1802–1807 deputy minister of the interior until he entered the military and participated in the wars against France, Sweden, and the Ottoman Empire.

24. Fedor Ivanovich Count Tolstoi (1782–1846) was known as "the American." After returning home from Kamchatka, he maintained he had been left on an Aleutian island. He liked to wear what he claimed was Aleutian-style clothing. *The Tolstoys: 24 Generations of Russian History: 1353–1983* by Nikolai Tolstoy (London: Hamilton, 1983).

25. Krusenstern's nephew, Otto von Bistram (1789–18??) was born in Estonia and rose to the rank of general lieutenant.

26. Since Russia at this time was involved in various wars in the Baltic, in Turkey, and in Europe, this requirement could easily be met, for example, in 1795 in the dismemberment of Poland, in 1796 in an unsuccessful war against Persia, and in 1799 together with the Austrians to check the French in Italy.

27. Hieromonk Gideon or Gedeon (1770–1843) or, according to Löwenstern, Edion, was assigned with the support of the emperor to inspect and report about the conditions of the churches in Kamchatka and Russia America. He wrote that Lisianski had a "hatred of religion and of clergy" and forbade Gideon to hold services on Sundays and church holidays during the long voyage. "Captain Lisianski and Midshipman Berkh were men with unruly natures and caused me much offence, against which my only cure was boundless patience." (*The Round the World Voyage of Hieromonk Gideon 1803–1809,* translated with an introduction and notes by Lydia Black, Limestone Press: Fairbanks, Alaska, 1989).

28. A translation of *Ken kai ibun*, these men's version of the voyage, edited by Stewart Culin can be found in *Asia*: vol. 20, 1920: May ("The Wreck of the Wakamiya Maru," 365–372), June ("Across Siberia in the Dragon Year of 1796," 505–512), July ("The Shogun's Subjects visit the Russian Court," 583–588), August ("Sightseeing in Petersburg a Century Ago," 704–711), and September ("The Return of the Shogun's Sailors," 807–814).

29. Fedor Schemelin was an agent in the Russian American Company. He published *Zhurnal pervogo puteshestviia Rossian vokrug zemnogo shara* (St. Petersburg, 1816), an account of this voyage that contains some detailed, lively descriptions of events that cannot be verified in other published and unpublished accounts and seem rather a figment of his imagination. He was partial to Rezanoff and ultranationalistic in his views.

30. Dr. Johann Caspar Horner (1774–1834) was born in Zürich. He studied astronomy and physics at the University of Göttingen. In 1798, he was planning to return to Zürich, but the French invaded Switzerland. He was offered employment and support for his scientific research in St. Petersburg and therefore entered the Russian service as an astronomer. In 1809, he returned to Zürich and continued working there.

Dr. Wilhelm Gottfried Tilesius (1769–1857), born at Mühlhausen in Thuringia, studied medicine in Leipzig. He is best known for the drawings done on this expedition. The czar raised him to the nobility as Tilesius von Tilenau as reward for his service to the expedition. Part of his unpublished diary still exists in the archives in Mühlhausen. In it, he complains of his treatment during the voyage, but he gives none of the details set down in this diary.

31. The offering of bread and salt, life's most basic necessities, as a greeting to a newcomer and as a blessing, is an old Russian tradition.

32. As one reads this diary, it becomes apparent that members of the expedition customarily took turns supplying the table for meals. The manner in which this was done led to discord and complaints. In an entry for October 6, Schemelin wrote: "Up to this date the supplying of the table was in the hands of one steward who, at everyone's request, took over the job on our departure from St. Petersburg, kept records of what was received and the daily expenditures for foodstuff. He has now been dismissed, and it was decided that two people from the group should be selected each week to take responsibility for food and drink and to give a report of expenditures. . . . Eight pairs were formed from the group. Bellingshausen and I were to be the first and we began to practice with success. The weekly stewards, in addition to taking care of meals, were obliged to make tea or coffee in the morning and evening, pour it into cups, and serve the company."

33. "In 1735, Duke Karl Frederick of Holstein-Gottorp instituted the Order of St. Anne in commemoration of his wife Anna Petrovna, the daughter of Peter the Great, who had died shortly before. . . . The Order of St. Anne was officially introduced into the Russian award system by

Paul I in 1789. . . . the star of the Order of St. Anne was worn on the right side of the chest. . . . Badges of the 2nd class were worn on a neck ribbon." V.A. Durov *Russian and Soviet Military Awards* (Lenin State History Museum, 1990) 11.

34. Order of St. Anne

35. Dr. Fedor Petrovich Brinkin was a physician and botanist in the ambassador's suite.

36. Georg Heinrich von Langsdorff (1774–1852) was born in Wöllstein, Rhinehesse. He studied medicine under Johann Friedrich Blumenbach in Göttingen. After completing his degree in 1797, he went to Lisbon as the personal physician of Prince Christian of Waldeck, who served as a general in the Portuguese Army until his death in 1798. While in Portugal, Langsdorff introduced vaccination against smallpox. He served from 1801 until the Peace of Amiens, March 27, 1802, in an English regiment and then returned to Göttingen by way of Paris and London. From 1812 to 1830, he was Russian consul in Rio de Janeiro. His first wife Wilhemine, who left him in 1819 and took their two daughters back to St. Petersburg, was the daughter of the astronomer Friedrich Theodor von Schubert. Due to a serious illness, he and his second wife and family returned from Brazil to Freiburg im Breisgau in 1830.

37. Paul I was emperor from 1796 until his assassination in 1801. Ivan Vladimirovich Lopukhin (1756–1816) had a printing company from 1783 to 1792, when it was dissolved by the government. He was a monarchist and apologist for serfdom who, as a senator and inspector, advocated humane judicial decisions and mitigated harsh sentences.

38. Lydia Black kindly provided a translation of the Russian. The poem is an example of an untranslated Russian crudity that was probably not erased because women reading the diary did not know Russian.

39. Aleksandr Yaroslavich Nevskii (1220?–1263), Prince of Novgorod, who won a series of victories against the Swedes, Germans, and Finns, is a Russian national hero.

40. In *Voyage Round the World in the Years 1803, 1804, 1805 and 1806*, Krusenstern writes: "On the 19th at four p.m., we perceived the southernmost point of Norway, Lindenö, which we call Derneus, the English call it the Nase" (vol. 1, 31).

41. Privateers or corsairs were privately armed vessels commissioned by governments in time of war to prey upon the commerce of their enemies. A prize was a captured vessel or property taken in a naval battle.

42. Krusenstern describes Berrisforth as "an old acquaintance with whom I had served nine years in America," 1: 33.

43. Undoubtedly, Löwenstern means that Resanoff could not disgrace his uniform and the Order of St. Anne as he had in Copenhagen.

44. He is describing Saint Elmo's fire, a reddish or bluish light, also called corposant. St. Elmo (303) was an Italian bishop and martyr who is the patron saint of sailors.

45. George III of England lived from 1738–1820 and reigned from 1760–1820.

46. Mikhail Semenovich Prince Vorenzoff (1782–1856) was born in Odessa. He was a member of an important, old, noble family, which owned extensive estates. He commanded the Russian occupation forces in France from 1815–1818.

Chapter 2

1. Krusenstern wrote "they saw a very extraordinary meteor, so bright that it lighted up the ship for half a minute and left a visible path for an hour afterwards" (1: 40).

2. Langsdorff wrote, "Captain von Krusenstern chose Tenerife instead of the Island of Madeira for our first port of call because on Madeira landing and provisions of all kinds are by far too expensive." *Remarks and Observations on a Voyage Around the World from 1803 to 1807* (Kingston, Ontario: Limestone, 1993) 1: 3.

Supercargo Schemelin wrote, "The [American] Company had instructed the Captain to go to Tenerife in the Canaries to rest the crew and supply them with fresh food, but the Captain for his own reasons did not obey and decided to go to Madeira Island to supply himself with Madeira wine and supplies before continuing on to Brazil. . . . Either contrary winds or an order from the leader of the expedition [Resanoff] forced the captain to abandon his intention of going to Madeira, since we were notified that he intended to sail to Tenerife" (*Zhurnal pervago puteshestviia Rossiian vokrug zimnago shara* . . . St. Petersburg: 1816).

3. Dr. Moritz Laband was the head physician on the *Neva*.

4. Schemelin imagined additional events not borne out by other accounts. Parallel to the Straits of Gibraltar, fear of Algerian privateers caused them to take precautions to repel "such barbarians." "This morning there was unusual activity on board. The captain ordered the sailors to prepare cartridges, clean rifles and pistols, and test the sharpness of swords, etc. At three o'clock in the afternoon, drum rolls on the quarterdeck signaled alarm. The staff officers as well as the chief officers and crew assembled immediately. Previously prepared orders were read assigning positions and duties, who was to give orders and which weapons were to be used and by whom. Then the drill began. Sailors were taught to man the cannon quickly, load, and fire them, then to leave them and rush for a rifle and prepare for boarding while at the same time preparing to set or repair the sails. Our sailors deserve great praise. It seemed they had long been prepared for this exercise. They rushed in good order with their swords bared to the spots where they thought the enemy might be gaining the upper hand and repelled them with fearless bravery. Our scholarly passengers were also assigned suitable positions behind the fighting men. Another gentleman, Mr. Kurliantsev [Kurlandzoff], and I were not assigned a position. Undoubtedly, the captain, on account of my age, considered Mr. Kurliantsev and me incapable of fighting and wished to excuse us from any obligations. Some of the naval officers however insisted, saying that in case of danger, no one onboard should be exempted and therefore requested that the captain assign us some kind of duties. The captain, forced by these arguments, came up to me, and, with a smile, said that he was assigning me to the doctor, whom I was to assist with bandaging the wounds of our heroes should the necessity arise. Kurliantsev was assigned to the powder room to issue gunpowder or to carry the powder bags for the cannon. A day and night passed without incident, and thank God I did not have the misfortune of witnessing the cutting out of Algerian bullets or of assisting in the binding up of wounds suffered by our brave sailors."

5. Horatio Viscount Nelson (1758–1805) lost his arm when a bullet shattered his right elbow during an abortive attack against Santa Cruz on July 24, 1797. In an earlier unpublished diary, Löwenstern describes his meeting with Nelson and Lady Hamilton in Palermo in August 1799: "We had been invited to the Russian Ambassador Count Musin Puschkin's for a ball and fireworks display. . . . Admiral Nelson and his inseparable companion Lady Hamilton were also present. He sat modestly in a nook and, smiling, watched the bustling throng. He nevertheless invited general interest more than all of the diamond-studded ministers for whom that idle stir had become second nature. The hat buckle which Nelson had been given by the Turkish Sultan is magnificent. The diamond-studded sword given by him by the City of London is even more beautiful."

6. Nikolai Mikhailovich Karamsin (1766–1826) was an influential writer, publicist, and historian who supported autocracy and serfdom. He traveled throughout Western Europe and was influenced by Russian literary developments.

7. The Guanches, the Berber inhabitants of the Canary Islands, were conquered by the Spanish in the fifteenth century.

8. Engelbert Kämpfer (1651–1716), a German physician and historian, had studied in Germany, the Netherlands, Poland, and Sweden before becoming the secretary of a Swedish embassy to Persia in 1683. After entering the service of the Dutch East India Company, he went to Batavia in 1689 and to Japan in 1690, where he was the physician at the Dutch factory for two years. His two volume *Geschichte Japans* [*History of Japan*] was the standard reference work about

Japan during the eighteenth century. *Kämpfer's Japan: Tokugawa Culture Observed* (Honolulu: University of Hawaii Press, 1999) is a new scholarly translation.

9. As Löwenstern notes in other places in his diary, the ship does not move in a straight line. Ernst von Rappard, Port Captain for Hapaglloyd in New York, agrees with his brother Achim in Hanover, Germany that Krusenstern probably ordered the ship to tack, even though the trade winds made it unnecessary, so that the sailors would be occupied during the day and not get into mischief from inactivity. (Letter dated October 11, 1998).

10. Punsch is a cold drink probably made from fruit or herbs, sugar and wine, possible with the addition of another alcoholic drink.

11. Nikolai Nikolaevich Novosilzoff (1768–1838) served in the military from 1783–1796. He was president of the St. Petersburg Academy of Sciences from 1803–1810, during which time (1804–1809) he was sent on a number of diplomatic missions to Western Europe.

12. Jettchen was Löwenstern's sister, Hedwig Henriette Elisabeth.

13. The cat-o'-nine-tails was so called because the person flogged with it had scratches on his body like those from a cat. It was a whip made of nine knotted cords attached to a handle.

14. Boston is a card game for four persons. It is played with two packs of 52 cards each.

15. Batavia was founded by the Dutch in 1619 and was an important center for the Dutch East India Company. With independence in 1949, the Indonesians renamed it Jakarta.

16. Étienne Marchand (1755–1793), a French seafarer, visited the Marquesas Islands in 1791 and named them "Revolution Islands." See Charles Claret de Fleurieu, *A Voyage Round the World by Étienne Marchand* (London: Longman and Rees, 1801) 2 vols.

17. Jupiter was the ancient Roman god of the heavens, father of the sky and light, who controlled and directed the weather and the future.

18. In other words, he was painting nonsense.

19. A dangerous act, usually a death-defying triple somersault done at a height.

20. Morpheus was the ancient Greek god of dreams.

21. Ratmanoff may well have had red hair, but the usage here is clearly pejorative. Judas, Christ's betrayer, was supposed to have had red hair. In Russia, this is a pejorative used against Jews, who have red hair more often than Russians.

22. Mitschmann comes from the Dutch mitsman and the English midshipman.

23. Ascençao—Ascension Island lies at 7° 57' S and 14° 22' W.

Jean-François de Galaup de la Pérouse (1741–1788) was a French explorer, who from 1778–1783 served on ships along the coasts of Canada and in Hudson's Bay. In 1785, he sailed as commander of a French expedition to explore the South Pacific as well as the coasts of North America and Asia in the hope of finding a Northwest Passage back to Europe. He disappeared in the South Pacific and only in 1826 were remains of his two ships found on the reefs of Vanikoro.

24. Löwenstern's sister, Hedwig Henriette Elisabeth.

25. Giuseppe Pinetti di Wildalle (1750–1800) was a well-known Italian magician and illusionist of the period.

Chapter 3

1. First Lord of the Admiralty George Anson (1697–1763) sailed around the world from 1740–1744. The account of his voyage was very popular and appeared in many editions and several translations. *A Voyage round the World in the years 1740–44* by George Anson, Esq., commander-in-chief of a squadron of His Majesty's ships, sent upon an expedition to the South Seas, compiled from papers and other materials of the Right Honorable George Lord Anson and published under his direction by Richard Walter (London: Printed for the author by J. and P. Knapton, 1748). The German translation appeared in 1749.

2. St. Nicolas is honored on the 6th of December. He is the patron saint of Russia and also

the special protector of children, scholars, seamen, and merchants.

3. Villa Nossa Senhora do Desterro was renamed Florianopolis after General Floriano Peixoto, the president of Brazil from November 1893 to November 1894.

4. Löwenstern uses "schwarze Wäsche" throughout the diary. Modern dictionaries I consulted do not have the term. Christian Friedrich Grieb *Englisch-Deutsches und Deutsch-Englisches Wörterbuch* (Philadelphia: Schäfer and Koradi, 1866, vol. 2) translates "schwarze Wäsche" by "foul linens." I therefore decided to translate the term literally, since schwarz/black evokes similar reactions in modern German and English speakers and dirty laundry seems so prosaic.

5. Surgeon John Sidham/Sydham was Espenberg's assistant.

6. Selli was one of the family's estates in Estonia.

7. Löwenstern is incorrect by about one hundred years. Maarten Gerritszoon Vries (de Vries, Fries or Uries) was a captain for the Dutch East India Company. He was best known for his voyage in 1643, which took him from Batavia to Hokkaido and the Kuril Islands, the Sea of Okhotsk, and Sakhalin, where he went on shore. He was looking for islands supposedly rich in precious metals. The cartographic information about the voyage was so vague that it confused voyagers into the nineteenth century. See Philipp Franz von Siebold *Geographical and ethnographical elucidations to the discoveries of Maerten Gerrits Vries, commander of the flute Castricum, A.D. 1643. In the east and north of Japan; to serve as a mariner's guide in the navigation of the east coast of Japan, and to Jezo, Krafto, and the Kurils* Tr. from the Dutch by F.M. Cowan . . . With a reduced chart of Vries' observations (Amsterdam, F. Muller, 1859).

8. Lydia Black provided the translation of the attest from Russian.

9. George Earl Macartney (1737–1806) had a brilliant career in the British service as a diplomat and administrator to Russia, India, Italy, and China. In 1793, in China, he avoided kowtowing to the emperor. His embassy collected much information about China but was refused permission to have a British minister reside in China. He is said to have left public office as few in his time did, "with pure hands."

10. Kaura is a magical little chestnut horse of Russian folk tales that grants wishes.

11. The emperor's brother.

12. Epiphany, January 6 (New Style) is the feast day of the Magi, the day on which Jesus' divine nature was revealed to the Gentiles.

13. Pierre Bouguer (1698–1757) was a French mathematician and hydrographer. He invented a heliometer and wrote extensively about the theory of navigation.

Chapter 4

1. René Antoine Ferchault de Réaumur (1683–1757) devised a thermometer containing alcohol. He took the freezing point of water as zero. The alcohol he used in his thermometer determined the boiling point of water to be 80 degrees.

2. Commander Nathaniel Portlock (1748?–1817) explored the northwest coast of North America up to Alaska in 1785–1788. In 1789 he published *A Voyage Round the World, but more particularly to the North-West Coast of America. . . .* (London: John Stockdale, 1789). He was also part of the 1791–1793 expedition, which transported breadfruit plants from the Pacific to the West Indies.

3. Resanoff, before his transfer to St. Petersburg in 1800, had been stationed in Irkutsk.

4. Captain James Cook (1728–1779) is best known for his voyages around the world, first on the *Endeavour* from 1769–1771 and the *Resolution* from 1772–1775 and 1776 until he was murdered on Hawaii in 1779. *A voyage to the Pacific Ocean. Undertaken, by the command of His Majesty, for making discoveries in the northern hemisphere. Performed under the direction of Captains Cook, Clerke, and Gore, in His Majesty's ships the Resolution and Discovery; in the Years 1776, 1777, 1778, 1779, and 1780.* Vol. I and II written by Captain James Cook. Vol. III by Captain James King. Pub. by order of the lords commissioner of the Admiralty (London: B. Nicol and T. Cadell, 1784).

5. Étienne Marchand (1755–1793), a French explorer and navigator, visited the Marquesas in 1791 and named them "Revolution Islands." See Charles Claret de Fleurieu, *A Voyage Round the World by Etienne Marchand* (London: Longman and Rees, 1801) 2 vols.

6. Captain, later First Lord of the Admiralty, George Anson (1697–1763) sailed around the world from 1740 to 1744. *A Voyage round the World in the years 1740–1744* by George Anson, Esq., commander-in-chief of a squadron of His Majesty's ships, sent upon an expedition to the South Seas, compiled from papers and other materials for the Right Honourable George Lord Anson and published under his direction by Richard Walter (London: Printed for the author by J. and P. Knapton, 1748) was translated into several languages, including German.

7. The Order of St. George was established in 1769 as an award for officers and generals who displayed valor in battle. It was divided into four classes.

8. The estate in Estonia belonging to Löwenstern's sister Amalie and her husband Baron von Tiesenhausen.

9. Spanish fly was made by crushing the dried bodies of the European blister beetle. It was a counterirritant for skin blisters and also an aphrodisiac.

10. Rear-admiral Joseph-Antoine Bruni D'Entrecasteaux (1739–1793), after completing a successful voyage to China in 1791, was selected to command an expedition sent to find information about La Pérouse, who had disappeared in 1788. He found nothing but did collect important geographical data in the South Pacific. After leaving Tasmania, he sailed toward the East Indies, and, while sailing along the coast of Java, he died of scurvy on July 20, 1793.

Chapter 5

1. Edward Roberts (Robarts) (ca. 1771–1832) deserted from a whaler in 1798 and stayed on Nukahiva until 1806, when he left because of an impending civil war. From Nukahiva, he went to India, where he lived in poverty until he died in 1832. His autobiography *The Marquesan Journal of Edward Robarts* ed. by Greg Dening (Canberra: Australian National University Press, 1974) is an important source of Marquesan history during the early period of Western contact.

2. Langsdorff reports that Tilesius felt he "had never seen proportions more beautifully united in a living body" than in a "certain Mau-ka-u or Mufau Taputakaya." Upon returning to Europe, Langsdorff turned his information over to Blumenbach in Göttingen, who, when comparing Apollo to Mufau, "discovered in the evidence given him something no one suspected—that this masterpiece of Greek creative art, uniting everything admired as the ideal of male beauty, has the same proportions and relationships as our Mufau" (1: 69–71).

3. Löwenstern probably drew the "modest" Katenuä. Judging by the hands and other details, Tilesius did the other watercolor and possibly sent it after the voyage ended.

4. Jean or Joseph Cabri or Cadiche, Kabrit, Cabrit died in France in either 1818 or 1822. After sailing on the *Nadezhda* to Kamtschatka, he went to St. Petersburg by way of Moscow. He earned a living by exhibiting his tattoos, performing Marquesan dances, and teaching marine cadets to swim at Kronstadt. Later, he earned his living at fairs in Brittany and Paris. After his death, there was some discussion of preserving and exhibiting his skin for posterity.

5. The Herrenhüter, also known as Pietists or Moravians, are so-called after Herrnhut, where, upon the invitation of Nicolas Count Zinzendorf, they established a settlement around 1722 upon his estate. Since then, they have an important missionary movement all over the world.

6. Undoubtedly because women would be reading his diary later, Löwenstern or someone else has rendered parts of this description in German illegible and left details to the readers' imagination.

7. In Langsdorff's account, he implies that only the sailors disappeared into "the inner parts of the ship, and the goddess of the night with her dark veil covered everything that might have happened" (1, 59).

8. Once again lines have been deleted. The . . . indicate he meant the girls who had stayed onboard and had been rewarded for their services.

Chapter 6

1. This might refer to the timetable Krusenstern established to avoid monsoons.

2. In his description of the voyage, Krusenstern wrote that he had been given particular instructions to look for the island that had been repeatedly sought in the preceding two hundred years by the Spanish and the Dutch because it was supposed to have had rich deposits of gold and silver. La Pérouse in 1787 was the most recent navigator to make a serious attempt to find it (1: 204).

3. Estonian and German.

4. In Greek mythology, Boreas was the god of the north wind.

Chapter 7

1. Charles Clerke (1743–1779) sailed under Captain James Cook on each of his three voyages and, as noted here, served as captain of the *Discovery* on the third voyage.

2. Delisle (also de l'Isle) de la Croyère was a French scientist and astronomer who was part of the Bering expedition. He died on shipboard just before the expedition arrived in Petropavlovsk in 1741. *The Journal of Jean-François de Galaup de la Pérouse 1785–1788* translated and edited by John Dunmore states that he was shown Croyère's grave. "We attached the following inscription to it, engraved on copper, written by Mr. D'agelet who, like him, is a member of the Academy of Sciences: 'Here lies Louis de l'isle de la Croyère, of the Royal Academy of Sciences of Paris, died 1741 on his return from an expedition carried out by order of the tsar to explore the coasts of America; astronomer and geographer, emulator of two brothers famous in the sciences, he deserved his fatherland's sorrow. In 1786, the Count de la Pérouse, commanding the king's frigates Boussole and Astrolabe, honoured his memory by giving his name to an island close to where this savant landed.' We also asked Mr. Coslof's permission to engrave on copper the inscription on Captain Klerck's tomb, which was only painted on a piece of wood, too fragile a material for the memory of such a worthy navigator" (2: 359).

3. Joseph Billings (1761–1806) was an able seaman on Cook's third voyage. Upon his return, he served on various merchant ships until 1783 when he went to St. Petersburg, where he joined the Russian Navy as a midshipman but quickly rose to lieutenant and then captain lieutenant. In 1785, he was appointed commander of an expedition to explore the coasts of eastern Siberia and America (*Russian America: A Biographical Dictionary* by Richard A. Pierce. Fairbanks, Alaska: Limestone Press, 1990, 57–59).

4. Christian August Vulpius (1762–1827), Goethe's brother-in-law, wrote *Rinaldo Rinaldini, der Räuber Hauptmann* [Rinaldo Rinaldini, the Bandit Captain] (Hildesheim: Olms Press, 1974. Reprint of the 1799 ed.) 3 vols.

5. Lydia Black kindly translated these letters from the Russian.

6. Peter Ludwig Constantin von Ungern-Sternberg (1779–1836) served in the Russian Navy from 1793 to 1801, when he retired to his estates in Estonia. He and Löwenstern served together on ships in the Baltic, North, and Mediterranean Seas.

7. Probably, Löwenstern means Vladimir Ivanovich Shteingel (Steinheil) (1783–1862) whose father emigrated from Saxony to Russia. His father was posted in Kamchatka and Irkutsk. At the age of ten, Steinheil joined the naval cadet corps in Kronstadt, where he finished first in his class. In 1802, he participated in expeditions along the coast of Holland, after which he served in Okhotsk and Irkutsk before retiring from the Navy in 1810. In 1812, he volunteered for service in the Army against Napoleon. In 1814, he published a book about this service. Later, he became part of the Decembrist movement. He was arrested and sentenced to a life at hard labor in 1826. Finally, in 1856, he was allowed to return to European Russia.

8. The following is an English translation of the transcription made by Renate von Rappard of Krusenstern's uncensored manuscript for his book:

"Less through mediation than through the presence of Governor General Koscheleff, an upright and honest noble man, was peace made between me and Resanoff on 17 August [1804]. The whole expedition was at an end. Everyone was making preparations for a return trip. The cause was an exceedingly coarse insult inflicted on me by Resanoff that took things so far, making it impossible for me to think of reconciliation. I demanded to be arrested and shackled and taken to Petersburg if Resanoff's charges were to be accepted. I demanded this in writing. I demanded that the least that could be done was to relieve me of my command, since a mutineer (that is what Resanoff called me) could not command a ship of war. Resanoff finally owned that he was wrong. He informed the governor that he desired to reconcile with me in order to be able to sail to Japan. I rejected this proposal with contempt. The suggestions of my friend Dr. Espenberg gave me the opportunity to consider the whole matter calmly. In my opinion, the final goal of our good emperor was abortive—at least his nation will be the laughing stock of Europe. This voyage, so boundlessly important for Russian trade, had now finished. The ship would suffer the same fate as the one from Billings' voyage that lies sunk here. A similar expedition will perhaps not be undertaken for several years. All of the prospects for the American Company, for her trade, which for all of Russia is so exceedingly important, would perhaps be destroyed without this reconciliation. All of Russia must suffer because Resanoff had insulted me. A sacrifice was my duty. Several conditions made this reconciliation difficult for me. All of the upright people who only from devotion to me had undertaken this voyage would end up buried for over an entire year in the wilderness of Kamtschatka, even though the admirable governor has offered everything available at least to ensure the stay would not be damaging to their health. The scholars would lose their pensions since the voyage has not been completed. Thus, they would have to undertake a journey of 12,000 versts to get to Petersburg, a journey that is not only difficult but also dangerous. The sons my friend Kotzebue entrusted to me would possibly not be able to endure that journey at their tender ages. In addition, their careers would be disrupted and the object of the voyage totally wasted. I answered the offer made me that I would be ready to continue the voyage if the governor, whose noble-mindedness had now convinced me, would act as mediator between us. It nevertheless was impossible to forget the insult I had suffered but, so that this important expedition, which until now had been so successful, should not end here to the detriment of Russia, I intended to forget everything for a period of time. I conferred with all of my officers about the offer. Several were of the opinion that I had been so deeply insulted, an insult that included all of the officers, that it made the thought of reconciliation impossible and I should press to be sent back to Petersburg immediately so that we would be tried. I was also of this opinion, and the one truth that it alone depended upon was the furtherance of the welfare of our fatherland, and even more importantly of our fatherland's honor. Thus, all private matters had to be put aside. I gave several examples from ancient history—also from the time of the French Revolution. Reconciliation took place on the 17th in the presence of the governor. I demanded nothing but that Mr. Resanoff leave the discipline of the ship absolutely to me, that it depended upon him only to sail where he asked but never without my authorization. Secondly, I demanded he should request pardon of the emperor for having insulted me and that he should do the same of me in the presence of all of the officers. That he did immediately. He confessed he had acted rashly, and he asked that everything be forgotten. He intended to let me read anything he wrote the 3mperor and I could seal his letter myself and give it to the governor. All of the officers witnessed the negotiations. A general reconciliation occurred." (Tartu Eesti Ajalooarhiiv F1414 N3 S7)

Chapter 8

1. Löwenstern noted after his return to Estonia, "Brinkin poisoned himself after his return to Petersburg. Nothing has been heard of Kurlandzoff. He is and will continue to be worthless."

2. This refers to Voltaire's satire *Candide,* which was popular in Russia.

3. The Portuguese presence lasted in Japan from 1543 to 1639, when they were expelled and Christianity eradicated.

4. This is a translation of Löwenstern's translation from the Russian. Langsdorff's version deviates slightly in *A Voyage Around the World 1803–1807* (Fairbanks, Alaska: Limestone Press, 1993) II, 151–152.

5. Krusenstern spells the name "Sikofk." Langsdorff has "Sikokf" with a footnote that Klaproth (Julius Heinrich von 1773–1835), a famous orientalist who traveled through Russia to China, writes that the promontory in Japanese is Scheissui-saki, i.e., the Cape of Clear Water (II, 153).

6. Aaron Arrowsmith (1750–1823) and his family were famous London mapmakers of the period.

7. Lydia Black kindly translated these instructions from the Russian. These instructions are based upon ones drawn up by Rumianzoff (Rumiantsev): "I cannot repeat to you enough how essential it will be for you to consider the dissimilarity of their customs with ours and not to degrade theirs. . . . In 1624, the envoy of the King of Spain, two cavaliers of the Golden Fleece, were not received and returned only because they did not wish to conform with Japanese customs." *The Russian Push toward Japan: Russo-Japanese Relations 1697–1875* by George Alexander Lensen (Princeton: Princeton University Press, 1959) 132.

Chapter 9

1. Lydia Black kindly translated these questions and answers from the Russian.

2. He is wrong by about ten years. Adam Laxmann (Adam Erikovich Laxman, 1766–1796?) led an expedition to Japan in 1792–93 organized by his father Eric Laxman, the Finnish naturalist.

3. Lydia Black kindly translated the copy of the translation from the Japanese, the edict, and the emperor's letter from the Russian. Lensen (133) gives a description: "The document was magnificently written in gold on vellum and beautifully decorated. Alexander I signed it himself as well as his chancellor. The documents with Manchu and Japanese translations were placed in gold brocade, which in turn was put in a box lined with green cloth. Rezanov also had smaller copies of the documents printed on Dutch paper to show the authorities in Nagasaki."

4. Hendrik Doeff (1777–1835) went to Japan in 1798 and was the director of the Dutch Factory from 1803 to 1817.

5. Modern Japanese Bugyo was the name given to the chief of an administrative area; e.g., Nagasaki-bugyo was the administrator in Nagasaki overseeing the Dutch and Chinese trade and the defenses along the neighboring coast.

6. Negotiations were conducted in Dutch. It remains unclear what language the Russians used, although it is highly probable that they used German or a mixture of German and Low German (Plattdeutsch), even French and English. Löwenstern adopted the Dutch words, mar, tolk, oberbanjos, etc., since he heard them so often. The spellings of Dutch are Löwenstern's. In his memoirs, written after his return to the Netherlands in 1819, Duff (Hendrik Doeff, Japanese Dofu 1777–1835) maintained he did not find his behavior degrading, since one should abide by the customs of a country in which one is and not by those of one's homeland. *Herinneringen uit Japan* [*Memoirs of Japan*] (Haarlem: Bijde erven D. Bohn, 1833) 91.

7. Langsdorff states that "grote Herrn or Opperbanjos" have the same meaning "high statesman" I: 162. Löwenstern does not distinguish the German singular Herr(n) from the plural Herren. Thus, it is sometimes unclear which he means.

8. Papenberg (Priests' Mountain) is the name that the Dutch gave a mountain near Nagasaki Harbor, from which Christians were said to have been thrown at the beginning of the 17th century, when Christianity was eradicated from Japan.

9. A knotted handkerchief. John Masefield in *Sea Life in Nelson's Time* (United States Naval

Institute, 1971) describes "able whackets" as "a pastime in which cards, blasphemy, and hard knocks were agreeably mingled" (37).

10. Adam Laxman took Kodei, Kaikokuya Kodayu (1751–1828), and two other Japanese back to Japan. In 1791, Kodei had been taken to St. Petersburg where he had had an audience with Catherine II. He then had returned to Siberia and joined the Laxman expedition. After his return to Japan, he was thoroughly cross-examined and then spent to rest of his life in mild confinement on the grounds of a garden for medicinal plants in Edo.

Chapter 10

1. The returning Japanese sailors related, "All of the gifts presented by the ambassador to the government were extraordinarily curious. Among them, the four great mirrors were largest in size. They were twenty-four feet long, ten feet wide, and more than four inches thick. They were backed with boards and framed with gold, on which something like *karakusa* (the ornamental figure of a vine) was carved. There were likewise some forty glass mirrors of various sizes and white stone called *muramura* (marble) cut in tablets and plates and made into stands for gifts, some of which were sculptured images of emperors. There were also several rolls of woven stuff and fifteen or sixteen walrus tusks, each three or four feet long." "The Return of the Shogun's Sailors" *Asia* 20 (September) 813.

Chapter 11

1. The returning Japanese later gave the Japanese authorities a quite different version of the events, "Our comrade Tajuro, who now grew very ill, was naturally an eccentric and gloomy man. It may be that he became melancholy through the delay in our landing, caused by the prolonged examination, and feared that we might not be received by the Japanese authorities. For that or some other reason, he lost his mind one day and, stealing a knife in the kitchen, thrust it into his mouth and turned it around. The blood flowed so copiously that it seemed it would be difficult to save his life. The Japanese and the Russians in the house made a great outcry and, announcing the matter to the authorities, called the inspectors, who came and examined Tajuro and clearly established the fact of his insanity. He required the services of two Japanese physicians and of a surgeon, who performed an operation and afterward visited him every day. He had cut his tongue so that he could neither eat nor speak and he suffered exceedingly. We three Japanese nursed him day and night and, since he had lost his reason, watched him sleeplessly with painstaking care. In time, the wound in his mouth healed but he could not eat or drink for thirty days. His case taxed the skill even of the foreign doctors. It was difficult to treat him but fortunately the doctors made a gargle that relieved him so that he was able to take food. Later, his appetite improved and, to our great distress, he so craved food that, upon the slightest negligence on our part, he would steal it. Afterwards, he did not want to eat at all, took only what was given him and lay silent in bed. In this condition, he remains at the present day." "The Return of the Shogun's Sailors" *Asia* 20 (September) 813.

2. Resanoff is like the hare with its long back legs that can suddenly change the direction it is running.

3. Langsdorff provides a quite detailed description of this gift and its symbolism, 2: 266.

4. These cities were famous for their manufacturing industries. Nankin(g) was famous for satin, nankeen, paper, pottery, and artificial flowers.

Chapter 12

1. Catherine II, the Great (1729–1796) (Russian: Ekaterina Alekseevna), was Empress of Russia from 1762 to 1796. She was born in Stettin as Sophie Auguste Friederike, Princess of Anhalt-Zerbst.

2. Löwenstern has Resanoff using the "du" (thou) forms in German instead of the polite, formal, respectful "Sie" forms one might expect. This would correspond to Russian usage and indicated Resanoff's arrogance and contempt for the Japanese, to which the Japanese interpreters reacted.

3. Moxa treatment, moxibustion was first described in Huang di nei jing (Huang ti nei ching's *The Yellow Emperor's Classic or the Canon of Medicine*), said to be about 2,000 years old. Moxa is prepared from the fine hairs from the undersurface of the leaves of the mugwort. When burned, as described here, they cause a sensation of intense but bearable heat.

4. The returning Japanese sailors' description: "Before the interview, an officer showed us the place of audience and told us the Emperor would soon arrive, but, since he was at supper we should have to wait for half an hour. When we were called to the audience room, we found that seats were arranged for us according to our ages and four or five officers were in attendance. They told us we should be questioned at the audience and should be allowed to express our preference as to whether we desired to stay in Russia or to go home.

"After a time the Emperor, accompanied by his mother, his wife, the Empress, and his brother, led by the Garafu, entered the room. The Emperor escorted his mother, holding her hand. It was her left hand, for it is the custom of this country to regard the left hand. His countenance was majestic and dignified, and we felt unworthy and awe-stricken. Bowing our heads, we were about to prostrate ourselves before him, but one of the attendants told us we must not do this as it was Russian etiquette to remain standing. Accordingly we stood, slightly bowing our heads. Then the mother of the Emperor approached and, looking at us all, pointed with her finger and showed us each of the imperial party, saying, 'This is the Emperor. This is his brother. This is the Empress.' The Emperor then approached us and asked us directly whether we wanted to return home. As we stood in a respectful manner the Garafu explained to us that the Emperor had no unreasonable desire to keep us in Russia and that we should answer just as we had in mind. Shigejiro and Minosuke, who hitherto had wanted to go home, suddenly replied they wished to stay in Russia. We do not know why they changed their minds. Tsudayu, Gihei, Sahei, and Tajuro answered that they had been about ten years in a strange land and that it was their earnest desire to return to Japan. Shinzo interpreted for each of us. The Emperor nodded his head, and, saying it was most reasonable that they should want to go back to Japan, laid his hand on the shoulders of each of the last four. He did not do this to any of the others or address them a word, why we did not know. Then the Emperor's brother spoke and evidently was about to ask us what gods we worshiped in Japan, but the emperor stopped him with a look which seemed to say that such a question was unnecessary.

"The Empress was dressed in beautiful attire and was attended by five or six women who seemed to be court ladies. She did not rise from her seat and soon retired with the modesty natural to young women. Both the mother and the wife of the Emperor had holes pierced in their ears from which beautiful objects were suspended, and they wore something like a rosary of gold around their necks. The hair of the Empress was bound with an exceedingly beautiful object resembling a winged knot and seemed to be fastened with pins. The heads of both the man and women were sprinkled with white powder so that their hair looked like silver. . . . The dress of the Emperor was of fine blue wool, with a star hanging by a silver cord from the left shoulder. He wore also another beautiful object hanging from his robe. The star worn by his brother had a golden cord. The Emperor wore nothing that resembled a crown. His name was said to be Orekisandara Paurowichi (Alexander Pavlovich), and we were told he was twenty-seven years of age. The Emperor's brother, who was called Konokino Paurowicki, seemed to be twenty-three or twenty-four years of age. There was no one in attendance on the Emperor except the Garafu, and there were no ornamental objects, even chairs, in the audience room." "The Shogun's Subjects Visit the Russian Court" *Asia* 20 (July) 588.

5. "In this theater, we were entertained at a play. The stage must have been sixty feet in width.

The interior of the building, which was closed, so that all light was excluded from without, was illuminated with innumerable candles. The audience on the day of our visit consisted only of the imperial family, the attendants and ourselves. The imperial seats directly faced the stage. Upon the entrance of the Emperor, the musicians struck up their music on flutes, drums, lutes, violins and other instruments, with which the imperial steps seemed to keep time. The musicians were seated in front of the stage. A man who looked like a joruri-dayu, or musical interpreter, sang the music, holding a book in his hand. A curtain painted with various figures was drawn across the stage. The performance appeared to be a representation of events in various countries, and the story did not seem to be continuous. Russian events were shown in the Russian manner. One of the actors wore waraji (straw sandals, which seemed to indicate that the people of Russia wore sandals in the old times. When the play was about a negro-land, the houses and men were painted black, and the costumes and accessories were in accordance with the customs of that land. The performers included both men and women, the former taking male parts and the latter female parts. The actors quickly reappeared after having changed their aspect from youth to age. Though we did not understand a word of the language, and could not follow the details of their acting, we thought it much the same as in our own theater. The dancing was done by some fifteen men and women, who were divided into two parties. Three of the women stood on a lofty rock, which sank and lowered when the dancers sprang from it and joined the others. Then five or six jumped up to a height of five or six feet and twirled round on one leg. On this, the audience applauded by clapping their hands. It seemed that they had to applaud when the Emperor did so.

"Subsequently, we visited a large theater in the city. This theater also seemed to have been founded by the Emperor, who occasionally visited it. The admission fee was five hundred pieces of copper, which, for some reason we do not know, was said to be paid to the government. The building was of stone, and both the roof and the ceiling below it were round. A special chair was reserved for the Emperor. The seats for the audience were located on the floor and in the balconies that may be described as *sajiki* (galleries) surrounding it. These triple balconies were constructed to hold 1,000 people. The people seated at a distance used a kind of far-seeing glass. The interior of this theater also was closed to darken it and was lighted with candles. From the middle of the house hung a large glass chandelier in which many candles were arranged. These made the room brighter than it would have been by daylight. The programme was not very different from that of the performance we saw at the villa. We returned from the theater at night, and we recall that it was the end of the 5th month and that, although we wrapped ourselves in something like a woolen *kappa* (rain-coat), we were very cold." "Sightseeing in Petersburg a Century ago" *Asia* 20 (August) 708.

Chapter 13

1. Lydia Black translated these cartoons from the Russian. She suggests that they are an oblique hint about Resanoff and someone in his suite being corrupt.
2. Daimo/daimyos were feudal lords whose fief exceeded 10,000 koku rice (about 51,000 bushels). They were direct vassals of the shogun but were practically autonomous rulers in their lands.
3. Kiakhta: a trading center on the Russian-Chinese border.
4. A reference to the samurai who had both sides of their heads shaved and carried two swords.

Chapter 14

1. The returning sailors said, "When talking about affairs from day to day, the Ambassador told us how much he appreciated the polite treatment that he received on this occasion. Others remarked that, although the embassy had not been received, they were treated with the courtesy they should have been accorded had they been invited guests. . . . And, when we too were notified that we would be received by our government, the Ambassador told us he wished to

give us something as a souvenir but was afraid that, under the circumstances, it might not be allowed. Still, he thought it might not do any harm for us to take some little things from him, and he asked us what we wanted. We replied that we were grateful for his favors during these three long years and that we wanted nothing; we felt just the same as if we actually had his presents, and we hoped he would not think about them. Then replying that if that was really our desire, he would like to give us at least a piece of cloth, he took out a roll of woolen cloth, saying that he would mention it to the authorities to save us trouble. Though we declined it, fearing our national law, he spoke about it to the inspectors, and we were told to receive it. It may be added that, on our arrival at Edo, we presented it to our Lord, asking him to accept it. Regretting to part with us, the Ambassador told us that, if his mission were successful, other Russian ships would come and there was a chance we should meet again, but that, if his embassy were not received and he had to sail back home, there would be no likelihood of our meeting again in this world. Then he trampled the earth with his feet and, saying that we should surely meet when we were under the ground, he shed a tear. . . . We let the house on the 10th of the 9th month, to be turned over to the Japanese authorities. At parting with us, the Russians wept, saying we should never meet again. Then we were called to the government office at Tateyama and, after a general examination, we retired. We were thereupon ordered to do *fumie* (treading, that is, on an image, to prove one is not a Christian) and were put in the *agariua* (jail) according to the law. We were allowed to go out from time to time and sometimes were taken to see the city. We were grateful for this cordial treatment. On the 18th of the same month, we heard that the Russian ship had set sail and that the order had been dispatched to the landowner of our district to send men to receive us. Glad to be so near the fulfillment of our heart's desire, we awaited the message from our country. Now we were impatient to begin again, after the wanderings of thirteen years, our journey home." "The Return of the Shogun's Sailors" *Asia* (20) 814.

2. A tray with the dishes necessary for an individual breakfast.

3. The last King of Lydia in the 6th century B.C. renowned for his vast wealth.

4. He means through suggestions getting him to do whatever they wanted him to.

5. The returning Japanese sailors related, "Before leaving the house, we brought out to the Ambassador all the things that we were taking home to be examined by the inspectors. They comprised chiefly garments of cotton, linen, silk, and wool, hats, bags, shoes, and other articles made of leather, gold, silver, and copper coins, silver watches, scissors, tobacco-pipes, mirrors, a pair of spectacles, and other ingenious contrivances; a book in the horizontal writing; maps of the world and pictures of the ship; and an oil painting on linen of the emperor and empress. Some of these things were bought with money saved from our earnings during our stay, and some were given us from time to time by our acquaintances. Lists of these things were made at the examination. We understood that all the gold, silver, and copper coins were confiscated when the sailors were taken over by the authorities and that, instead, Japanese silver money of equal value was given them. The other things were first taken to the government office and later given back. When the sailors were consigned to our (Sendai) authorities, all these things were delivered with them and, after being shown to our Lord, were returned to the sailors, who took them to their homes. The Japanese wished to present all the watches to the government, but all but one were returned to them." "The Return of the Shogun's Sailors" *Asia* (20) 814.

Chapter 16

1. Collinet (Colinet) was second lieutenant on the ship with La Pérouse.

2. R.H. Blyth states that "beginning in the 17th century Otsu-e, inexpensive pictures of Buddhas, demons, beautiful women, animals, and so on, sold at inns and such places . . . to travellers and pilgrims." They included pictures of "a courtesan sitting on a low bench playing a samisen. Her face is beautiful . . . , but her real character is shown by the fox's tail that peeps

from under her kimono." The verses on each side of her relate: "Her heart no one knows, / But, deceived by her face, / Somebody'll marry her. / This creature from the same hole / As a fox. If you don't find out, / You'll be made fool of / By this charming fox, / And be sorry / When it's too late." *Japanese Humour* (Tokyo: Japan Travel Bureau, 1963) xii.

3. Charles-Gabriel Morell d'Escures (1751–1786).

4. Johann Georg Adam Forster (1754–1794) and his father Johann Reinhold Forster (1729–1798) accompanied Captain James Cook on his second voyage. Georg Forster wrote what is considered among the best and most influential travel and scientific literature of the period.

5. Compte Charles Pierre Claret de Fleurieu (1738–1810). In the 1790s, he was Napoleon's Navy Minister. In "A New General Chart of the Atlantic or Western Ocean and Adjacent Seas (London: Sayer and Bennet, 1777), he emphasizes geographic accuracy based on astronomical calculations based on longitude and latitude.

Chapter 17

1. For a detailed description of Davidoff and Chvastoff, see Langsdorff, 11, 177–181.

2. Aleksandr Andreevich Baranov (1746–1818) was the first governor (1790–1818) of the Russian settlements in Alaska.

3. The Russo-Swedish War from 1788–1790 came as a result of Sweden's desire to regain territory lost in earlier wars. General F.F. Buksgeveden commanded the Russian forces which lost to the Swedes, though in the end the Russians defeated the Swedes.

4. The intimate "du" forms are used in this dialogue and not the formal "Sie " forms.

Chapter 18

1. William Robert Broughton (1762–1821), *A Voyage of Discovery to the North Pacific Ocean in which the coast of Asia from latitude 35° North to latitude 52° North, the Island of Insu (commonly known under the name of the land of Jesso), the north, south and east coasts of Japan, the Lieuchieux and the adjacent isles, as well as the coast of Corea, have been examined and surveyed; Performed in His Majesty's sloop Providence and her tender, in the years 1795, 1796, 1797, 1798* (London: Printed for T. Cadell and W. Davies, 1804). This work appeared in German in 1805 and in French in 1807.

2. Gavrila Saritscheff or Sarytscheff (Gavriil Andreevich Sarychev, 1763–1831) *Account of a voyage of discovery in the north-east Siberia, the frozen ocean and the north-east sea,* translated from Russian (London: Printed for R. Philips by J.G. Barnard, 1807–1808) 2 vols. in one.

3. *An Account of a Geographical and Astronomical Expedition to the Northern Parts of Russia . . . performed . . . by Commodore Joseph Billings in the years 1785–1794,* narrated from the original papers by Martin Sauer, Secretary to the Expedition, 1802, 4to.

4. These are Russian words written in the Latin alphabet with German endings: wide, billowing pants with a bib and jacket.

5. Pier Simon LaPlace (1749–1627) was a French mathematician and astronomer.

Chapter 19

1. James King (1750–1784) served as an astronomer aboard the *Resolution* on Captain James Cook's third voyage of discovery. After the death of Captain Charles Clerke, King took over the command of the *Discovery,* the second vessel of the expedition.

2. William Bligh (1754–1817) was the sailing master of the *Resolution* on Captain James Cook's second and third voyages of discovery. He is best known as the captain of the *Bounty*.

3. Löwenstern's older brother.

4. The Hittite captain whom David caused to be killed in battle so that he could have his wife Bathsheba.

Chapter 21

1. All foreign cargo passed through the Hong or Chinese security merchants, and they also furnished outgoing cargo. Their small group guaranteed the payment of customs duties. It was criminal for other merchants to trade with foreigners. Above them was the Hoppo or superintendent of maritime customs and above him was the viceroy of the province. The Europeans called the viceroy "John Tuck."

2. Löwenstern probably means Howqua, Houqua, or Wu Tunyuen (1769–1843), described as "great, good, and rich." He was the wealthiest and most famous of the Hong, known for his generosity to his friends and punctuality in delivering quality goods. James R. Gibson. *Otter Skins, Boston Ships and China Goods: The Maritime Fur Trade of the Northwest Coast, 1785–1841* (Montreal: McGill-Queen's University Press, 1992) 87. In an entry from 5/17 December, Löwenstern also mentions "Luqua, Auqua, etc." and his inappropriate laughter at the sound of Chinese.

3. Dr. Franz Joseph Gall (1758–1828) is called the father of phrenology. He studied medicine in Strasbourg and Vienna, where he began his first medical practice. His lectures made him known throughout Europe. In 1807, he moved to Paris and was naturalized in 1819. His theories were influential and yet controversial. The Vatican put his works on the Index. His skull, marked with the location of various "organs," as Gall called them, is preserved as part of a skull collection in a Paris Museum.

4. Maria I (1777–1816) became mentally ill in 1792. Her son João VI was regent until her death and then king until 1826.

5. Sir George Thomas Staunton (1781–1859) first traveled to China with his father. He learned to speak, read, and write Chinese. He translated George Pearson's treatise on vaccination into Chinese, thus introducing the practice to China.

6. Tiffin, originally a word from India, is a cold lunch, especially at midday.

7. Satrap was the governor of a province in ancient Persia.

Chapter 23

1. Probably William Wyndham Baron Grenville (1759–1834). William Pitt (1759–1806), second son of statesman William Pitt First Earl of Chatham (1708–1778), also became a well-known Chancellor of the Exchequer, prime minister, statesman, and reformer who lived only to serve his country.

2. Maureen R. Stevens, Custodian of Records for St. Helena, wrote 25 January 2000, that unfortunately "there is a piece of the records worn away from April 1806 to June 1806. Peter Golovatscheff could have been entered in that particular worn area. His gravestone no longer exists. In 1957, a children's playground was built on the old cemetery. The few remaining gravestones were placed in the garden of St. James' Church. The St. Helena Records, sometimes called The Consultations contains an entry stating that the Russian ship, *Nadeskola*, with the captain Krusenstern called on 4 May 1806."

Chapter 24

1. Friedrich Theodor von Schubert (1758–1825) *Lehrbuch der theoretischen Astronomie* [Manual of Theoretical Astronomy] was published in French in 1791 and then in St. Petersburg in German in 1798.

2. William Pitt and Charles James Fox (1749–1806), the foremost British statesmen of the period, were opponents but yet are buried next to each other in Westminister Abbey.

Bibliography

Allgemeine Deutsche Bibliographie. Berlin: Duncker and Humblot, 1967.

Allgemeine deutsche Real-Encyclopädie für gebildeten Stände. Leipzig: Brockhaus, 1822.

Andreyev, A.I. ed. *Russian Discoveries in the Pacific and in North America in the 18th and 19th Centuries,* trans. by Carl Ginsburg. Washington, D.C.: American Council of Learned Societies, 1952.

Anderson, M.S. "Great Britain and the Growth of the Russian Navy in the Eighteenth Century" in *Mariner's Mirror,* vol. 42, 1956, 132–147.

Anson, George. *A Voyage round the World in the years 1740–1744 by George Anson, Esq., commander-in-chief of a squadron of His Majesty's ships, sent upon an expedition to the south Seas, compiled from papers and other materials of the Right Honorable George Lord Anson and published under his direction by Richard Walter.* London: Printed for the author by J. and P. Knapton, 1748.

Barratt, Glynn. *Bellingshausen, A Visit to New Zealand, 1820.* Palmerston North, New Zealand: Dunmore Press, 1979.

———. *The Rebel on the Bridge: A Life of the Decembrist Baron Andrey Rozen* (1800–1884). Athens: Ohio University Press, 1975.

Blyth, R.H. *Japanese Humour.* Tokyo: Japan Travel Bureau, 1963.

Brosse, Jacques. *Great Voyages of Discovery: Circumnavigators and Scientists* 1764–1843. Trans. by Stanley Hochman. New York: Facts on File, 1983.

Broughton, William Robert. *A Voyage of Discovery to the North Pacific Ocean in which the coast of Asia from latitude 35° North to latitude 52° North, the Island of Insu (commonly known under the name of the land of Jesso), the north, south and east coasts of Japan, the Lieuchieux and the adjacent isles, as well as the coast of Corea, have been examined and surveyed; Performed in His Majesty's sloop Providence and her tender, in the years 1795, 1796, 1797, 1798.* London: Printed for T. Cadell and W. Davies, 1804.

Brown, Yu-Ying. *Engelbert Kaempfer: First Interpreter of Japan London: British Library Board,* 1994. Also: www.fathom.com/feature/122226.

Carroll, Paul. *The South Atlantic and Subantartic Islands.* www.btinternet.com/~sa_sa/sasa.html.

Chevigny, Hector. *Lost Empire: The Life of Nikolai Rezanov.* Portland: Binford & Morts, 1958.

Cook, Captain James. *A voyage to the Pacific Ocean. Undertaken, by the command of His Majesty, for making discoveries in the northern hemisphere. Performed under the direction of Captains Cook, Clerke, and Gore, in His Majesty's ships the Resolution and Discovery; in the Years 1776, 1777, 1778, 1779, and 1780.* Vols. I and II written by Captain James Cook. Vol. III by Captain James King. London: B. Nicol and T. Cadell, 1784.

Cross, A.G. "Samuel Greig, Catherine the Great's Scottish Admiral" in *Mariner's Mirror* 60 (1974) 251–265.

Dansk Biografisk Leksikon. Copenhagen: Schultz, 1933.

Dening, Greg (ed.). *The Marquesan Journal of Edward Robarts.* Canberra: Australian National University Press, 1974.

Deutsch-Baltisches Biographisches Lexikon 1710–1960. Vienna: Böhlau, 1970.

The Dictionary of National Biography from the Earliest Times to 1900. Oxford: Oxford University Press, 1967.

Dmytryshyn, Basil, Crownhart-Vaughan, E.A.P., and Vaughan, Thomas. *The Russian American Colonies,* 1798–1867. Oregon Historical Society, 1989.

Doeff, Henrik. *Herinneringen uit Japan.* Haarlem: Bijde erven D. Bohn, 1833.

Durov, V.A. *Russian and Soviet Military Awards.* Lenin State History Museum, 1990.

Ellis, Henry. *Journal of the Proceedings of the Late Embassy to China; Comprising a Correct Narrative of the Public Transactions of the Embassy, of the Voyage to and from China, and of the Journey from the Mouth of the Pei-ho to the Return to Canton.* Philadelphia: A. Small, 1818.

The Encyclopedia Britannica. 11 ed. New York: Britannica, 1910.

Fairbanks, John K. (ed.) *The Cambridge History of China: Volume 10, Late Ch'ing, 1800– 1911.* London: Cambridge University Press, 1978.

Falck. P. Th. "Woldemar Freiherr von Löwenstern und seine Memoiren" in *Baltische Monatsschrift* 71 (1911) 314–318.

Fleurieu, Charles Claret de. *A Voyage Round the World by Étienne Marchand.* London: Longman and Rees, 1801, 2 vols.

Forster, Georg. *Reise um die Welt.* Berlin: Rütten & Loening, 1960.

Gernot, Axel von. *Forschungen zur Geschichte des Baltischen Adels.* Reval: Kluge, 1893.

———. *Geschichte und System des bäurlichen Agrarrechts in Estland.* Reval: Kluge, 1901.

Gibson, James R. *Otter Skins, Boston Ships and China Goods: The Maritime fur trade of the Nortwest Coast, 1785–1841.* Montreal: McGill-Queen's University Press, 1992.

Gideon, Hieromonk. *The Round the World Voyage of Hieromonk Gideon 1803–1809, trans. with an intro. and notes by Lydia Black.* Fairbanks, Alaska: Limestone Press, 1989.

Great Soviet Encyclopedia. New York: Macmillan, 1970.

Griep, Wolfgang and Pelz, Annegret. *Frauen reisen: ein bibliographisches Verzeichnis deutschsprachiger Frauenreisen 1700 bis 1810.* Bremen: Ed. Temmen, 1995.

Höffken, Christoph. "Die Beschreibung der ersten von japanischen Augenzeugen beobachteten Ballonfahrten in Gentaku's [Kankai ibun] (eine kommentierte Übersetzung)." Hirosaki: Hirosaki University, 2001

Iwao, Seuchi (ed.) *Biographical Dictionary of Japanese History,* trans. by Burton Watson. New York: Harper & Rowe, 1978.

Jane, Fred. T. *The Imperial Russian Navy.* London: Conway Maritime Press, 1904.

Kaempfer, Engelbert. *Geschichte und Beschreibung von Japan* ed. by Christian Wilhelm Dohm. Stuttgart: Brockhaus, 1964.

———. *Kaempfer's Japan: Tokugawa Culture Observed* trans., ed. and ann. by Beatrice M. Bodart-Bailey. Honolulu: University of Hawaii Press, 1999.

Ken kai ibun in Asia, vol. 20, 1920: May "The Wreck of the Wakamiya Maru," 365–372; June "Across Siberia in the Dragon Year of 1796" 505–512; July "The Shogun's Subjects Visit the Russian Court" 583–588; August "Sightseeing in Petersburg a Century Ago" 704–711; and September "The Return of the Shogun's Sailors" 807–814.

Kind, Dean. *Harbors and High Seas.* New York: Holt, 1996.

Kodansha Encyclopedia of Japan. Tokyo: Kandansha, 1983.

Kotzebue, Moritz von. *Der russische Kriegsgefangenen unter den Franzosen.* Leipzig: Kummer, 1815.

Krusenstern, Adam Johann von. *Voyage round the world, in the years 1803, 1804, 1805, & 1806, by order of His Imperial Majesty Alexander the First, on board the ships Nadeshda and Neva, under the command of Adam Johann von Krusenstern.* London, Printed by C. Roworth for J. Murray, 1813.

———. *Reise um die Welt in den Jahren 1803, 1804, 1805 und 1806.* 3 vols. St. Petersburg, 1810–1812; Atlas. St. Petersburg, 1814.

Krusenstjern, Ewert von. *Weltumsegler und Wissenschaftler: Adam Johann von Krusenstern 1770–1846: Ein Lebensbericht.* Gernsbach: Casimir Katz, 1991.

Langsdorff, Georg Heinrich von. *Remarks and Observations on a Voyage Around the World 1803– 1806, 2 vols.* Trans. and ann. by Victoria J. Moessner. Kingston, Ontario: Limstone Press, 1993.

Lensen, George Alexander. *Report from Hokkaido: The Remains of Russian Culture in Northern Japan.* Hakodate, Japan: Municipal Library, 1954.

———. *The Russian Push toward Japan: Russo-Japanese Relations 1697–1875.* Princeton: Princeton University Press, 1959.

——— (ed.). *Russia's Eastward Expansion.* Englewood Cliffs, N.J.: Prentice Hall, 1964.

Löwenstern, Eduard von. *Mit Graf Pahlens Reiterei gegen Napoleon: Denkwürdigkeiten des russischen Generals Eduard von Löwenstern (1790–1837)* ed. and pub. by Baron Georges Wrangell. Berlin: Mittler, 1910.

Löwenstern, Woldemar von. *Denkwürdigkeiten eines Livländers aus den Jahren 1790–1815.* Leipzig: Winter 1854, 2 vols.

———. *Mémoires du general major Baron de Löwenstern, publiés original et annotés par M.H.Weil.* Paris 1903, 2 vols.

Lowood, Henry E. *Patriotism, Profit, and the Promotion of Science in the German Enlightenment.* New York: Garland, 1991.

Masefield, John. *Sea Life in Nelson's Time.* United States Naval Institute, 1971.

Mody, N.H.N. *A Collection of Nagasaki Colour Prints and Paintings Showing the Influence of Chinese and European Art on that of Japan.* Rutland, Vermont: Tuttle, 1969.

Meyers Konversations-Lexikon. Leipzig: Bibliographisches Institut 1894–1900.

Oba, Osamu. "Scroll Paintings of Chinese Junks which Sailed to Nagasaki in the 18th Century and their Equipment" in *Mariner's Mirror,* vol. 60, 1974, 351–362.

Obshchii morskoi spisok St. Petersburg, 1885–1894, vol. 2–8.

O'Grady, Alix. "The Baltic Connection in Russian America" in *Jahrbücher für Geschichte Osteuropas.* vol. 42, 1994. 321–339.

The Oxford Companion to Ships and the Sea ed. by Peter Kemp. Oxford: Oxford University Press, 1976.

Paasch, Heinrich. *From Keel to Truck: Marine Dictionary in English, French, and German.* London: David Nutt, 1901.

Papinot, Edmond. *Historical and Geographical Dictionary of Japan.* New York: Frederick Ungar, 1964.

Pawlowsky's Russisch-Deutsches Wörterbuch 3 ed. Riga: Kymmel, 1900.

Pezold, Johann Dietrich von (ed.) *Studien zur volkstümlichen Aufklärung in Estland.* Göttingen: Uandenhoeck and Ruprecht, 1978.

Pérouse, Jean-François. *The Journal of Jean-François de Galaup de la Pérouse 1785–1788,* trans. and ed. by John Dunmore.

Pierce, Richard A. *Russian America: A Biographical Dictionary.* Kingston, Ontario: Limstone Press, 1990.

Plischke, Hans. *Johann Friedrich Blumenbachs Einfluß auf die Entdeckungsreisen seiner Zeit.* Göttingen: Vandenhoeck & Ruprecht, 1937.

Plummer, Katherine. *The Shogun's Reluctant Ambassadors: Sea Drifters.* Tokyo: Lotus Press, 1984.

Portloc, Nathaniel. *A Voyage Round the World, but more particularly to the North-West Coast of America . . .* London: John Stockdale, 1798.

Ramming, Martin. *Reisen Schiffbrüchiger Japaner im XVIII.* Jahrhundert. Berlin: Würfel Verlag, 1931.

Raun, Toiva. *Estonia and the Estonians.* Stanford: Hoover Institution Press, 1991.

Reehorst, K.P. *New Dictionary of Technical Terms.* London: Clyde, 1841.

Robarts, Edward. *The Marquesan Journal of Edward Robarts,* ed. by Greg Dening. Canberra: Australian National University Press, 1974.

Röding, Johann Hinrich. *Allgemeines Wörterbuch der Marine in allen Europaeischen Seesprache nebst vollstaendigen Erklaerungen.* Hamburg: Gebauer, 1793–1798.

Russell, William Clark. *Sailors' Language.* London: Sampson Low, Marston, Searle, & Rivington, 1883.

Sakamaki, Shunzo. "Western Concepts of Japan and the Japanese, 1800–1854" in *The Pacific Historical Review,* vol. 6, 1937, 1–14.

Saritscheff or Sarytscheff, Gavrila (Gavriil Andreevich Sarychev) *Account of a voyage of discovery in the north-east Siberia, the frozen ocean and the north-east sea, trans. from Russian.* London: Printed for R. Philips by J.G. Barnard, 1807–1808. 2 vols. in one.

Sauer, Martin. *An Account of a Geographical and Astronomical Expedition to the Northern Parts of Russia . . . performed . . . by Commodore Joseph Billings in the years 1785–1794,* narrated from the original papers by Martin Sauer, Secretary to the Expedition, 1802, 4to.

Schemelin (Shemilin), *Fedor Zhurnal pervogo puteshestviia Rossia vokrug zemnogo shara.* St. Petersburg, 1816.

Schönborn, Sybille. *Das Buch der Seele: Tagebuchliteratur zwischen Aufklärung und Kunstperiode.* Tübingen: Niemeyer, 1999

Schubert, Friedrich Theodor von. *Lehrbuch der theoretischen Astronomie.* St. Petersburg: Academy of Sciences, 1798.

———. *Traité d'astronomie théorique.* St. Petersburg: Academy of Sciences, 1822.

———. *Unter dem Doppeladler.* Stuttgart: Koehler, 1962.

Semjonow, Juri. *Siberien: Schatzkammer des Ostens.* Wien: Econ, 1975.

Shelikhov, Grigorii. *A Voyage to America,* trans. by Marina Ramsay with an intro. by Richard A. Pierce. Kingston, Ontario: Limestone Press, 1981.

Siebold, Phillipp Franz von. *Geographical and ethnographical elucidations to the discoveries of Maerten Gerrits Vries, commander of the flute Castricum, A.D. 1643. In the east and north of Japan; to serve as a mariner's guide in the navigation fo the east coast of Japan, and to Jezo, Krafto, and the Kurils.* Trans. from the Dutch by G.M. Cowan. Amsterdam: F. Muller, 1859.

Singer, Aubrey. *The Lion and the Dragon: The Story of the First British Embassy to the Court of the Emperor Qianlong in Peking, 1792–94.* London: Barrie & Jenkins, 1992.

Spence, Jonathan D. *The Chan's Great Continent: China inWestern Minds.* NewYork: Norton, 1998.

Thomson, Erik. *Porträt einer Ostseestadt: Reval/Tallinn.* Köln: Liebig, 1979.

Tikhmenev. P.A. *A History of the Russian American Company,* trans. by Dmitri Krenov. Kingston, Ontario: Limestone Press, 1979.

Tolstoy, Nikolai. *The Tolstoys: 24 Generations of Russian History: 1353–1983.* London: Hamilton, 1983.

Vökl, Ekkehard. *Russland und Lateinamerika, 1741–1841.* Wiesbaden: Harrasowitz, 1968.

Vulpius, Christian. *Rinaldo Rinaldini, der Räuber Hauptmann.* Hildesheim: Olms Press, 1974. Reprint of the 1799 ed., 3 vols.

Wall, Richard, Robin, Jean, and Laslett, Peter. *Family Forms in historic Europe.* Cambridge: Cambridge University Press. 1983.

Whelan, Heide W. *Adapting to Modernity: Family, Caste and Capitolism among Baltic German Nobility.* Cologne: Böhlau, 1999.

Willams, Cas. *Outlines of Chinese Symbolism and Art Motives.* Tokyo: Tuttle, 1974.

Wittram, Reinhold. *Balltische Geschichte: Die Ostseelande Livland, Estland, Kurland 1180–1918.* München: Verlag R. Oldenbourg, 1954.

Wrangell Baron, Wilhelm von. *Die estländische Ritterschaft, ihre Ritterschaftshauptmänner und Landräte.* Limburg, Lahn: C.A.Starke, 1967.

Wrangell, Baron Georges von. "Eduard von Löwenstern und die Dekabristen, Gebrüder Murawjew-Apostol" in *Baltische Monatsschrift* 72 (1911) 192–205.

Index

References to drawings are printed in boldface type.